MUSSOLINI

MUSSOLINI

Denis Mack Smith

Alfred A. Knopf
New York
1982

THIS IS A BORZOI BOOK
PUBLISHED BY ALFRED A. KNOPF, INC.

Copyright © 1982 by Denis Mack Smith
All rights reserved under International
and Pan-American Copyright Conventions.

Published in the United States by
Alfred A. Knopf, Inc., New York.
Distributed by Random House, Inc.,
New York.
Originally published in Great Britain
by George Weidenfeld & Nicolson Ltd.,
London.

Library of Congress Cataloging in Publication Data
Mack Smith, Denis [date]
    Mussolini.
    Bibliography: p.
    Includes index.
    1. Mussolini, Benito, 1883-1945.   2. Italy—
Politics and government—1922-1945.   3. Fascism—
Italy—History.   4. Heads of state—Italy—
Biography.   I. Title.
DG575.M8M223   1982   945.091'092'4   [B]   81-48127
ISBN 0-394-50694-4   AACR2

Manufactured in the United States
of America

First American Edition

For
Catharine, Sophie, and Jacintha

ALSO BY DENIS MACK SMITH

Garibaldi *(editor)*
Italy, A Modern History
Making of Italy 1796 – 1870
Medieval Sicily
Mussolini's Roman Empire

Contents

Illustrations

*All of the photographs in this volume
are reproduced by kind permission
of Rizzoli Editore, Milan, and
belong to the Rizzoli Photographic
Archive.*

Preface

This is a political biography of Benito Mussolini, not a history of fascist Italy, and still less a general history of the years between 1920 and 1945 when fascism became a dominant theme in European politics. The focus is on the public life of one man, with only enough of the wider context and general background to make his career intelligible.

Mussolini was neither born great nor had greatness thrust on him but had to fight his way out of obscurity by his own ambition and talents. So well did he succeed that he ruled Italy as a dictator for over twenty years and attracted more popular admiration than anyone else had received in the whole course of Italian history. At a peak of success he then fell an easy victim to the flattery that he invited or ordered from his cronies, and was beguiled into playing for the yet higher stakes of world dominion. But he lacked the necessary resources, whether the material resources of a rich country, or the requisite personal qualities of mind and character. By the time of his death in 1945 he left to his successors an Italy destroyed by military defeat and civil war; he was, by his own admission, the most hated person in the country; and having once been praised to excess, was now being blamed for doing more harm to Italy than anyone had ever done before.

Many people outside Italy had to suffer because of Mussolini, yet it is also true that many foreigners liked and admired him so long as he kept his ambition under control. He was not only a person of shrewd political intelligence, but had the ability to fascinate and charm whenever he set his mind to it, and he led a movement that could be dressed up to look plausible. Fascism was an Italian word for an Italian invention which as a body of ideas and practices reached its classic form in Italy as perhaps nowhere else; but great numbers of people in other countries had their lives altered by it, and either looked hopefully towards what they took as a promising solution to the problems of the twentieth century, or were so repelled that they fought against it in a world war. Mussolini was able to claim that no one, friendly or hostile, could understand the modern world without taking fascism into account. It is equally true that the birth and development of fascism owe far more to this one man than to anyone else.

That is enough by itself to make him an interesting subject of study. Moreover his influence has been durable and not only inside Italy. Most people, but not all, would call his legacy disastrous. Though the fascist regime may be credited with some positive achievements especially in its early years, its crude belief in political violence and authoritarian repression had negative effects that lasted long after 1945, and its praise of war as something inherently beautiful and beneficial was a cruel absurdity that did untold harm and ultimately turned any positive achievements to dust and ashes.

Italian fascism was more than just Mussolini. But the quirks of character in this one man were a crucial factor in both its successes and failures. Anyone who could deserve such an extreme of popularity and then move so quickly to an opposite extreme of popular revulsion was clearly a very unusual person. One difficulty in understanding him is that, though he had a host of admirers, he was a very private person and at no moment in his life possessed a friend who could pass on to posterity a balanced and convincing assessment of his personality, nor was there any close associate to whom he revealed himself naturally and unambiguously. Always in his relations with other people he was, as it were, on stage, acting a part, or rather acting a continual and baffling series of parts that are not always easy to disentangle and reconcile. As well as being a gifted actor, he possessed superlative ability as a propagandist whose public statements and private comments were often intended to conceal the truth as much as to reveal it; and this facility, though it served well enough at first, was eventually his undoing.

With the passage of time since 1945, many of the obscurities about his life have become clearer and the controversies less charged with political passion, but there is still room for disagreement over individual episodes and differences of interpretation about someone who contradicted himself so freely. In a simple narrative biography there is not always room for a discussion of such differences, but in notes at the end of the book I have given summary references to substantiate my own interpretation of events and to indicate the source of more important or lesser-known facts. Anyone requiring a more detailed chronology of Mussolini's life will find it in the four-volume biography by Giorgio Pini and Duilio Susmel, or in the annotated forty-four-volume edition of the Duce's writings edited by Susmel and his father. More balanced in judgement and more critical of Mussolini – if not always critical enough – is the substantial study of fascism being written by Renzo De Felice who has done more than anyone to open up the subject to research in the archives. Other shorter biographies in English are by Ivone Kirkpatrick, Laura Fermi, Christopher Hibbert, and Richard Collier.

Denis Mack Smith

Youth

1

Boyhood, 1883–1901

Mussolini liked to recall that he was born very soon after the death of
Garibaldi, as if the hero of Italy's national unification had handed on the torch
to a successor destined to create an Italian empire. The date of birth was 29
July 1883, the place a small house outside the village of Predappio. This region
of the Romagna was an expanse of bare hillsides and dirt tracks, far from the
railway and other civilised amenities. The nearest town, Forlì, was fifteen
kilometres away.

The Romagna had a reputation of being an area prone to violent
revolution, and Mussolini was given the Christian names of three famous left-
wing revolutionaries – Benito Juarez, Andrea Costa, and Amilcare Cipriani.
His father and grandfather were both natural rebels who had been in prison
for their beliefs. They came from a family of smallholders who, finding it hard
to earn a good living, were at odds with what they saw as an oppressive society.
Benito Mussolini said it was a trump card in his life that he had been born into
the working class, and was annoyed when flatterers later tried to give him an
aristocratic pedigree.

His mother, Rosa, was a devout Catholic who had the children baptised and
took them to church each Sunday. She was the local schoolmistress and
provided the family's regular income. Alessandro, her husband, was a
blacksmith who worked only intermittently. He was a man of strong
character, but idle, often in debt, given to womanising and excessive drinking.
He never accompanied his wife and children to church. Though he had no
formal schooling, he taught himself to read the main revolutionary texts. He
believed in corporal punishment and a thick leather strap played a part in the
family's upbringing.[1]

Benito looked back on his father as a better person than himself – as
someone with more humanity and altruism, being feared but also widely
admired for his honesty, courage, and idealism. No one else had more
influence on his son's character and beliefs. Alessandro was one of the earliest
proclaimed socialists in Italy and was for a short time a socialist councillor in
the municipality of Predappio. He combined a fundamentally non-ideological
socialism with an instinctive belief in anarchism. Though he knew something
of Marx and used to read parts of *Das Kapital* to the family, he also took his

I

precepts from Mazzini and Machiavelli, and, like his son after him, nurtured a mixture of sometimes contradictory ideals without always being able to discriminate between them. He helped to start one of the first co-operative movements in the area as well as a local group of the Socialist International, and although he was remembered by his son as having been too much a republican and too little a revolutionary socialist, the children were sometimes taken to socialist meetings – despite their mother's objections – and grew up with the idea that their home was a haven for political refugees and those in trouble with the police.

Such a household provided no easy beginning in life, however stimulating it may have been to a precocious political consciousness. Benito recollected a lack of tenderness and affection and gave this as one reason why he developed a closed personality – embittered and 'almost savage', he called it.[2] He felt crushed and isolated for his first fifteen years which he accepted as being by far the most formative period of his life. The family lived in a tied two-room cottage that went with the job of schoolmistress. The second room was a smoky kitchen in which Benito shared a bed with his younger brother Arnaldo, and the building was entered through a third room that housed the village school. Alessandro's carelessness about money made it a struggle for Rosa to bring up her family; black bread and soup was their staple food, with meat on Sundays.

This, at least, was Benito's later recollection but, like Hitler, he exaggerated in retrospect the privations of his youth.[3] There were plenty of books in the house and his parents could afford domestic help. They had land from which they made their own wine, and the food – if simple – was abundant.[4] The boys were able to remain at school until they were eighteen, something that must have been quite exceptional in such a neighbourhood.

Benito had difficulty in learning to speak. For long months his parents feared he might be altogether dumb and only with much patient attention did they manage to extract his first articulate sounds. He eventually became a bright child, but was so uncontrollable that they sent him away to a boarding school at Faenza run by a religious order. He regarded this as a punishment and it contributed to his sense of rejection: by his own admission, his character was already flawed, but the Salesian fathers made it incorrigible.

He particularly remembered having to eat at a special table for those who could not afford the full school fees. There was no speaking at mealtimes and absolute silence was enforced throughout the week before Easter, during which lessons were replaced by spiritual exercises and meditation. Hot baths were provided only in winter and chilblains made him lame. The children were woken at five o'clock in summer, six in winter, and daily mass was compulsory. He imagined he was specially singled out for beatings because of his father's politics. In addition to these, he was sometimes punished by isolation for days at a time. He later recalled the reverend headmaster as a frightful 'walking skeleton' and his form master as someone who 'diabolically poisoned the best years of my life'.[5] Two years at this school helped to make him feel 'like a wild flower in an orderly plantation'[6] and fuelled his resentment against society. He occasionally thought of running away. Yet in the holidays, the cramped life at Predappio left him almost as depressed and miserable.[7] During one summer he helped his father with the first steam threshing-machine the area had ever seen; at other times he worked the bellows in the forge. But school had exacerbated a mischievous rebelliousness that made him 'the desperation of my parents and a pest to the neighbours'.[8] He was a boy who did not shed tears and rarely laughed, who spoke little and liked his own company, who preferred reading to playing with others.

A number of stories were told later which suggest that the young Mussolini had a bad-tempered wilfulness and a streak of brutality. A perhaps untrustworthy legend has it that he plucked live chickens and blinded captive birds.[9] He was remembered for pinching people in church to make them cry. As a gang leader he used to bully others into joining his escapades, and a close disciple confirmed that he was always the one to start a fight. As he had a pronounced sense of vendetta, no insult was allowed to pass without his exacting vengeance, but he also 'sought quarrels for their own sake and because he needed to dominate; if he won a bet he asked more than his due, if he lost he tried to avoid payment'.[10] In later years he used to smile with pleasure at the thought that his schoolfellows would still carry the scars of wounds he had inflicted.[11]

Back at boarding school for his second year in 1893, the ten-year-old Mussolini led a revolt against the quality of the food. He once refused to go to morning mass and had to be dragged there by force. Impatient of discipline, punished often and – as he thought – unjustly, this fiery-tempered boy exploded into violence. After he had drawn a knife on another boy and wounded him one evening at supper, the school decided that enough was enough. He was expelled and the Salesians had to sue his family for their fees. The facts about this stabbing and Mussolini's consequent expulsion were played down or altogether suppressed by later fascist historians.

Benito spent some months at home educating himself with his mother's help but she clearly could not cope and he was eventually sent to a school at Forlimpopoli. She wrote to the authorities asking for a scholarship but was turned down and the family decided they could afford the payments on their own. The new school was not run by priests, and church attendance was voluntary. Mussolini thought it was like moving from hell to heaven – the food was better, the discipline more humane, and he could go home at weekends. However, he soon found himself in much the same trouble as before. Brawling and bullying led to a fight after which he was again asked to leave. This crisis passed, but on two other occasions he was suspended and sent home for ten days – once for impertinence and once for stabbing another pupil.[12]

It says something for both Mussolini and the school that he was allowed back and completed six years at Forlimpopoli. He liked to describe himself as having been top of his class but the headmaster recollected him as a mediocre student displaying no promise of great things to come.[13] Mussolini in turn described his chief teacher as a second-rate pedant who made the children learn everything by rote. Evidence from other pupils suggests that the boy Mussolini inspired fear and not much liking.[14] But some, at least, of his gifts were recognised: he played the trombone in the school band; and at the age of seventeen was called upon to make a speech in the local theatre to commemorate Verdi.

His last years at school were spent studying for an educational diploma which he obtained in 1901. He enjoyed being a senior boy, though his boredom during the holidays in the dreary atmosphere of Predappio increased. He was temporarily expelled for a fourth time because of being absent for a night – he used to tell how some of the boarders used to climb down knotted sheets to go dancing in the town until daybreak.

Mussolini was not reticent about his love affairs except later in his life; he prided himself on being a Don Juan and chronicled a long list of casual encounters from the age of seventeen when he began to make the conventional visit each Sunday to the brothels of Forlì. He used the word fiancée for a number of girls, sometimes for more than one at the same time. One conquest he described thus in his autobiography:

I caught her on the stairs, throwing her into a corner behind a door, and made her mine. When she got up weeping and humiliated she insulted me by saying I had robbed her of her honour and it is not impossible she spoke the truth. But I ask you, what kind of honour can she have meant?[15]

Mussolini used to admit in later life that he never had any male friends: indeed he liked to consider this unwillingness or inability to make friends as a necessary and even admirable side of his character. But he always had followers and often mistresses or girl-friends though few of his affairs lasted long. By the time he left Forlimpopoli he had the reputation of being someone who rarely left his house except occasionally after dark; he was known as a hermit and misanthrope.

Exile, 1902–4

By 1901 there was already much of the intellectual bohemian about him. He was writing poems and trying, if unsuccessfully, to get them published. He knew long passages of Dante by heart and was a voracious reader of novels and political tracts. He once applied to become secretary of the village council at Predappio, but his family's anti-clericalism told against him. His appearance was also unattractive, with unbrushed hair, deliberately unconventional manners, and an uncouth shabbiness sometimes concealed under a romantic mantle. Lacking employment, and penniless (according to his own account), he nevertheless managed to spend part of the summer on holiday by the sea.

In 1902, at eighteen, he became a substitute teacher at an elementary school in Gualtieri. The village had a socialist administration and looked on his advanced opinions indulgently, but the arrival of this outsider caused something of a stir. His liking for alcohol and cards upset some parents; so did his liaison with a woman whose husband was away on military service – dreadful scenes of jealousy and violence soon became public knowledge. Mussolini described how 'I accustomed her to my exclusive and tyrannical love: she obeyed me blindly, and let me dispose of her just as I wished.'[16] To intimidate critics of his behaviour, he used to carry a metal knuckle-duster and once knifed his girl-friend: physical violence was instinctively his method of getting what he wanted.

Mussolini was often called an anarchist, and though he sometimes rejected the ascription, at other times he accepted it with pride. He used to say that inside every anarchist was a failed dictator – a saying that in his case can perhaps be as truthfully reversed. One genuine anarchist of his acquaintance, Errico Malatesta, noted how, like his father, he habitually and almost indiscriminately ranged from one belief to another, giving the impression that he was an instinctive revolutionary who was unsure what kind of revolution he wanted. By 1902, however, he was moving towards a vague international socialism. Even while at school he had called himself a socialist and at Gualtieri became secretary of a socialist group, writing articles for various left-wing magazines. He also practised public speaking and created an impression when, without notice, he improvised a ninety-minute speech in memory of Garibaldi – another man who had combined the temperament of an anarchist with belief in socialism.

When his job as a temporary teacher ended in June 1902, Mussolini escaped to Switzerland. As he told so many untruths in an attempt to dramatise his early life, we cannot be entirely sure why he went. One reason he gave was that he needed money, but – though it is true he was borrowing from three or four people – he can hardly have expected to earn much in Switzerland. More probably he was running away from his parents, from military service, unwelcome love affairs, and debts; in particular his rent at Gualtieri.[17] He felt an urge to escape, to travel and learn about a wider world. He pretended to his parents that he had a job already arranged in Switzerland and on the strength of this his mother sent him the price of his ticket: her month's salary. He left in a hurry without going home to say good-bye, and when at the frontier he heard that his father had been arrested, not even this news changed his mind. Alessandro remained in prison for six months, during which time Rosa had to run the family and send further remittances to keep her son from destitution. Although Mussolini always claimed to be deeply fond of his mother, he hardly acted towards her with much consideration.

In Switzerland, just before his nineteenth birthday, he began the two most desolate and desperate years of his life. He left his first post – as a manual labourer building a chocolate factory – almost at once and it was quickly apparent that, like Hitler in Vienna a few years later, he disliked hard work and lacked the will or capacity to hold down a regular job. Stories were told of him begging and seizing food with menaces. After a few days he was without any money; all he had in his pocket was a nickel medal bearing the image of Karl Marx. He turned to living in doss-houses but found contact with other tramps unbearable and spent at least one night in a packing case under the Grand Pont at Lausanne. Several weeks after leaving Italy he was arrested as a vagabond; the police reported that he was ill and showed little inclination for work.[18]

His poverty in Switzerland was not, however, as unmitigated as he later pretended. Photographs and letters show him well dressed and far from emaciated by hunger. Over the months he held a succession of short jobs in building construction, as a butcher's boy, and working for a wine merchant (where he was accused of taking too much wine).[19] But his instinct took him towards politics and agitation. A month after his arrival he was writing for a socialist newspaper and soon afterwards became secretary to a builders' union. Among a largely illiterate population of Italian expatriates he made good use of his gift for public speaking; his particular talent was more for exhorting and denouncing than for exposition and he found plenty to denounce in an environment where the local socialists were mostly moderate democrats and far from thoughts of revolution. One of his companions noted that beneath his tough appearance there lurked an obvious inferiority complex.[20] Another heard him say he would succeed either as a rebel or by dominating others but could see no alternative in between.[21] An ambitious and powerful personality was beginning to appear inside someone who was still unsure of himself.

6

By 1903 he was calling himself an 'authoritarian communist'.[22] From his father he had learnt to have little patience with sentimental, reformist socialism or with democratic and parliamentary methods; instead he preached revolution to expropriate a ruling class that would never voluntarily renounce power and possessions. Parliament should be abolished; class struggle must replace class collaboration; private property should disappear altogether. Socialists should never collaborate with bourgeois governments and never pursue a policy of strikes merely to get better wages, but should be ready to use terrorism and mob violence to effect a wholesale social revolution.[23]

Mussolini later told people that he met Lenin in Switzerland, and even that Lenin admired him. But on other occasions he could say that he had no recollection of any such meeting.[24] The one Russian of whom he saw a great deal was another revolutionary socialist, Angelica Balabanoff; she was the first intellectual he knew well and through her he became more familiar with the classics of European socialism. If one can judge by the references in Mussolini's writings, Marx had a very big influence on him and more than the French syndicalist, Georges Sorel or Nietzsche. In later years, fascists and communists were anxious to deny that he had ever been a marxist, but from 1904 to 1914 he was accepted by others as one, and although he admitted that some of Marx's dogmas had been superseded, he continued to say that most of them were still relevant.[25] According to Mussolini, 'Marx was the greatest of all theorists of socialism', the man who stressed the values of materialism, personal egoism, and economic determinism, the writer who first pointed out the fallacy of class co-operation, who rescued socialism from the Christian philanthropists and made it scientific.[26]

Mussolini's encouragement of industrial unrest among Italian casual labourers, particularly his advocacy of violence, was strongly disliked by the Swiss authorities who depended on immigrant workers for the hotel and tourist trade. He was arrested as an agitator in Berne and again in Lausanne. In July 1903, he was expelled from Switzerland and handed over to the Italian police; they had to release him but opened a dossier on this 'impulsive and violent' young man.[27]

As men of his age were due for military training in January 1904, he escaped back to Switzerland in time to avoid the draft. Since his passport had meanwhile expired, he fraudulently changed the date of its expiry to 1905. He was not running away out of cowardice but because – again like Hitler – he was not prepared to fight for a patriotic cause in which he did not believe. It was a carefully planned step and he openly encouraged soldiers to desert,[28] an offence for which later, as dictator, he had people shot. Fascist documents, his entry in the Italian *Who's Who* for example, concealed the fact that he tried to escape from conscription.

Early in 1904, he spent several months in France where he was arrested yet again.[29] He recalled that he walked all the way to Paris and for a time lived by telling fortunes.[30] Another short visit took him to Germany and Austria.[31] Back in Switzerland he again moved from job to job, including work in a distillery and a factory for agricultural machinery. Often out of work and living what he called a *vie de Bohème*, he was helped by some of the socialist companions whom he later bitterly persecuted: the socialist leader Serrati pawned his own possessions to help Mussolini and let him sleep in his bed during the daytime.

From his father he had learnt to be a thoroughgoing anti-clerical. He proclaimed himself to be an atheist and several times tried to shock an audience by calling on God to strike him dead. He forcibly denounced those socialists who thought religion a matter for individual conscience or had their children baptised. Science had proved that God did not exist and the Jesus of history was an ignorant Jew whose family thought him mad, and who was a pigmy compared to the Buddha. Religion, he said, was a disease of the psyche, an epidemic to be cured by psychiatrists, and Christianity in particular was vitiated by preaching the senseless virtues of resignation and cowardice, whereas the new socialist morality should celebrate violence and rebellion.[32]

By 1904 he was already publicly labelled an enemy of society and in his absence was tried and found guilty of desertion by an Italian court. In Switzerland he was expelled from several cantons, and there was much talk of wild and riotous behaviour. For a time he thought of emigrating further afield, either to the plantations of Madagascar or to join other socialist exiles in Vermont, and he once considered an offer to work in New York on a socialist weekly, *Il Proletario*, to which he was contributing occasional articles. Meanwhile he continued to study German as well as French, and practised translating books from both languages.

He was anxious to establish that he was no proletarian but an intellectual, and to improve his education he made good use of excellent public libraries that could not be found at home. He later tried to make others believe that, in his journeying from town to town in search of work, he invariably carried with him a volume of poems or philosophy. Legends were invented of his attending university at Zurich, and Sarfatti's official biography has a mythical chapter about him as a university student at Geneva. But he succeeded in spending two months, during the summer session, at Lausanne university. He used to say that at Lausanne he attended a series of lectures by the Italian sociologist, Vilfredo Pareto, and confirmation exists that he did attend at least one such lecture; but the main advantage was the opportunity of spending long hours in the university library on a somewhat rambling and random course of reading that later stood him in good stead.[33]

The socialist

2

Political apprenticeship, 1905–9

Doubts about his future in Switzerland, combined with homesickness, persuaded Mussolini, at the age of twenty-one, to take advantage of a general amnesty and return to Italy for eighteen months' military service. For a few weeks he helped his mother with her teaching duties until, in January 1905, he joined one of the best Italian regiments. His military dossier describes him as of less than medium height, with a long face, large nose, projecting chin, and dark eyes under a low forehead.[1] Because of his year of evasion he was older than the other conscripts. He arrived with a reputation as a revolutionary and was regarded with suspicion by the officers; but although he continued to believe in subverting the loyalty of soldiers, his outward conduct was exemplary – he realised that he must be patient until the message of revolutionary socialism had time to reach the common people. A private letter he wrote to one officer was subsequently published to prove his inner patriotic fervour, but Mussolini was ready to trim his sails to get on in the world and was no doubt trying to ingratiate himself with his superiors in a letter that his fellow socialists would not see.

In February his mother died and he tried to get an early release but was turned down and had to remain with the colours for his full term. His mother's death at the age of only forty-six caused him great grief and perhaps some feelings of guilt for having been so inattentive a son; his contradictory stories about her death suggest this. Once he said he arrived just in time for her to recognise him, once that he could not bear to enter the house but hid outside for hours until he knew she was dead. When writing for an Anglo-Saxon audience he invented a suitable story about his deep religious beliefs being unable to alleviate his sorrow.[2]

Alessandro was left with his wife's smallholding but also with many debts and was obliged to move out of the family house to make way for the new schoolmistress. Benito did not join him after being released from the army in September 1906, but was involved in another love affair until, in November, he took a teaching post in the mountain village of Tolmezzo near the Austrian frontier. During his nine months here the local police had orders to keep him under observation. His priest-baiting and bad language did not endear him to the local population: the local girls and the forty children to whom he taught

9

the alphabet nicknamed him 'the tyrant'. He was not a successful teacher and confessed himself unable to maintain order – he used to keep the children quiet by giving them sweets.[3] He appears to have led a life of dissipation at Tolmezzo, drinking too much and borrowing money – and it was probably here that he contracted venereal disease from a married woman who was 'fortunately older and less strong than I was' and who, as usual, 'loved me madly'.[4] There were stories of coarse practical jokes, of playing at ghosts in the ruins of the local castle and of nocturnal parties in the cemetery where he astonished his companions by declaiming speeches to the dead.[5]

At the end of the school year his post was not renewed because some of the parents were protesting at his behaviour and kept their children at home to avoid his bad influence. So he moved to his father's new house near Predappio, where for a few months he took lessons in Latin and French, and in November 1907 sat successfully for an examination in French that along with the coveted title of 'Professor' qualified him to teach in secondary school. Later he tried and failed to get the same qualification in German. He made an unsuccessful appeal to have his police record cancelled by promising that he had given up his advanced opinions and now wanted simply to better himself. He undertook to renounce politics and devote his time to further education.[6]

In March 1908 he took another teaching post at Oneglia on the Riviera, and here revived his interest in politics after several years of abstinence. He began writing again and edited a socialist periodical – the collection of *La Lima* in the local library disappeared mysteriously when, as fascist dictator, he needed to draw attention away from his left-wing, anti-clerical past.[7] He recollected this brief period at Oneglia as the calmest in his life and clearly was beginning to discover his true *métier* when, after four months, he again found himself unemployed. Possibly this was owing to nothing discreditable on his part, but it is noteworthy that three schools, as well as many other employers in Switzerland, failed to renew his appointment.

Within days of returning home after this experience, Mussolini had a practical lesson in political agitation: the agricultural labourers at Predappio went on strike against the landowners and share-croppers. He at once recognised the opportunity for an experiment in the dynamics of insurrectionary socialism. Threshing-machines using outside workers were pushed over and damaged; the prefect called in the troops and some people were injured. Benito himself was arrested for threatening physical violence and was taken to Forlì by a squadron of cavalry. As he commented, 'I suddenly found myself famous'.[8] Condemned to a prison sentence, he was released on appeal.

Despite his continuing allegiance to Marx, there was little precise doctrine in his eclectic brand of socialism. He sometimes called himself a syndicalist, but in private spoke unkindly about most other socialists and to some acquaintances seemed above all an anarchist.[9] Angelica Balabanoff thought his views were 'more the reflection of his early environment and his own rebellious egoism than the product of understanding and conviction; his hatred of oppression was not that impersonal hatred of a system shared by all revolutionaries; it sprang rather from his own sense of indignity and frustration, from a passion to assert his own ego and from a determination for personal revenge'.[10]

What had not changed was his belief in violent defiance of the law. He positively did not believe in legal sanctions, and advised other socialists never to resort to the law courts of a bourgeois society but rather to take an eye for an eye with their own hand.[11] The proletariat and the bourgeoisie had nothing in common: 'one of the two must disappear' and this could only be achieved by a major catastrophe that would lead to the dictatorship of the proletariat. A bloody social revolution was necessary. The middle classes had themselves won power a hundred years earlier through violence and their example should be copied. Just as the barbarian invasions had once injected new life into the Roman empire, so present day socialists must proclaim themselves 'barbarians': they might need the barbarism of a world war to demolish the existing European civilisation and produce something more vital.[12]

Some of his fierce talk was an affectation adopted by a person still trying to discover himself, but throughout his life much of the real Mussolini was hidden by a succession of poses, many or all of which reveal aspects of his character. The frequent changes of opinion do not necessarily mean that he was an intellectual light-weight, but rather that he placed little value on ideas. He appeared to adopt opinions merely because they fitted some new attitude or would help his career. He sometimes seemed to change his whole philosophical outlook overnight and would justify the fact as an example of an inner intuition that he came to consider as infallible.

Any discussion as to who chiefly influenced him must take account of the fact that he was to some extent an intellectual poseur and cultural exhibitionist. In a later phase he sometimes wanted to stress the originality of his fascist beliefs and would then claim that he had no precursors; but at other times he wanted to impress an audience with the fact that fascism was part of a long and respectable intellectual tradition, in which case he would drop every name that came to mind. He did not give the impression of possessing an original intelligence; his particular skill was to pick up ideas almost at random if they coincided with some prejudice or tactical need; and he would renounce them as easily once they ceased to serve his turn.

One of his few enduring beliefs was in violence as a political weapon, and though he sometimes found it politically useful to say that he had learnt this from Sorel, the resort to violence was a basic instinct already well developed in his mind. His sister used to say that there was more in him of their father, Alessandro, than of all the people with whom he sometimes claimed an intellectual affiliation. Perhaps he learnt from Pareto's anti-parliamentarianism and theory of elites, but more likely these ideas just reinforced an already half-formulated prejudice. Other ideas in time came from Marinetti's futurism, Hervé's pacifism, Malatesta's anarchism, Sorel's revolutionary syndicalism, and the exaggerated nationalism of Oriani and Corradini: each and all of these were, at different moments, grist to his intellectual mill. It depended on the occasion or the particular audience whether he claimed that anyone had influenced him, and inevitably he sometimes contradicted himself or was wildly implausible. He liked Americans to think that he had a veneration for William James and Mark Twain, just as he could say that *Robinson Crusoe* remained one of his favourite books when most likely he had never read it in his life.

However, there was one writer apart from Marx who especially impressed Mussolini: this was Nietzsche, who filled him with a 'spiritual eroticism' and who he felt had done more to move the world in a new direction than any other philosopher. In Nietzsche he found justification for his crusade against the Christian virtues of humility, resignation, charity, and goodness, and it was also in Nietzsche that he found some of his favourite phrases including 'live dangerously', and 'the will to power'. Here, too, was the splendid concept of the superman, the supreme egoist who defied both God and the masses, who despised egalitarianism and democracy, who believed in the weakest going to the wall and pushing them if they did not go fast enough.[13]

Editing a periodical at Oneglia opened up new vistas for Mussolini: he liked the work and the local renown it brought him. He began to dream of editing a daily paper and, with scant respect for union solidarity, announced that he would take a low salary if an offer were forthcoming.[14] When this failed he rejoined his father at Forlì where, near the railway station, Alessandro was now running a tavern, 'Il Bersagliere', in which the neighbouring hotheads congregated. Benito helped out there for a few months and would sometimes talk politics with his father until it was dawn or they fell asleep at the table.[15]

About this time he claimed to have written a history of philosophy that one of his lovers tore up after a quarrel; the story is improbable. He also claimed to have written an even longer treatise on the history of Christianity.[16] Both of these works were, perhaps, just the unfulfilled dreams of a would-be intellectual. At Forlì he found fewer possibilities for self-education, although an anarchist who ran a newspaper stall allowed him to read papers and periodicals without payment.[17] Here, too, he acquired the reputation of someone clearly eccentric, dissipated and misanthropic. He was usually unshaven and used to pull his heavy coat up to his ears and his hat over his eyes to avoid being recognised and having to talk to people. If he bought new clothes he would rumple them so as not to seem elegant. He preferred the company of artists and liked to shock people with his nonconformity and vulgar language.[18]

In this his native province of the Romagna, Mussolini found few fellow spirits, as republicans outnumbered socialists and he had no patron to further his career in journalism. So, early in 1909, he emigrated once more, this time to the Austrian province of Trentino, taking a post as secretary to the Chamber of Labour and editor of a weekly socialist paper, *L'Avvenire del Lavoratore*. As editor, he was expected to organise the local socialists, a task he evidently performed indifferently,[19] and to travel round giving weekly speeches in the local beerhouses. This was hard work, especially as he had almost no help on the paper. He did not like Trent and after a few days would have liked to resign, but other employment was hard to find. The Austrian libraries were much better than those in Italy, and he again read a great deal of French and German, practising the latter by translating Schopenhauer and Kant. He also read Edgar Allan Poe and tried his hand at writing a novella in the style of Poe, hoping that it was even more hair-raising and perverse; but was unable to find a publisher for it.[20]

After six months he changed his job, becoming sub-editor of the *Popolo*, which belonged to the famous Italian patriot and irredentist, Cesare Battisti. Possibly this association with Battisti began the process that would turn Mussolini into a patriot, but the report that the two became close friends was a later invention. Though it lasted only a month, his experience of working on a daily paper was excellent training. He remembered how it taught him many tricks of the trade, including how to invent a news story and how to write a whole article about some non-event without arousing disbelief.[21] Few other lessons in his life were to be more useful.

During the seven months spent in the Austrian empire he was put in prison more than once and was convicted on five other occasions for various offences. His paper was confiscated at least ten times because of his style which was characterised by ferocious libel and quite unrestrained language. Nor did he stop short of physical assault against his political enemies. In Trent his chief target was the clerical party and a rival editor he specially disliked was the Catholic, Alcide De Gasperi, who became prime minister of Italy in 1945 after fascism collapsed. Having experienced earlier arrests in Italy, Switzerland and France, Mussolini was able to confirm that the Austrian prisons were the most humane, just as the Austrian police and courts were the fairest and most generally respected. This conclusion was unacceptable to the Italian patriots for whom everything Austrian was bad, but he had not yet learnt to put patriotism high on his list of priorities. It is possible that he so disliked Trent

13

that he was deliberately seeking the notoriety of being expelled from yet another country, and when an expulsion order arrived, even the socialists of Trent were not sorry, though they helped to pay his numerous fines. Most of them did not share his marxist internationalism but rather adhered to the reformist socialism and patriotism of Battisti. Later he encouraged the myth that the Austrians expelled him because of his patriotic insistence that Trent rightly belonged to Italy.[22] Gaudens Megaro, the American author who disproved this, found that documents concerning Mussolini's views on Trentino had been concealed or forged to hide the truth. His real opinion at this time was that Italian annexation of the Trentino would be absurd; in any case, proletarians of the world should reject patriotic loyalty of any kind as a bourgeois fetish.[23]

The agitator, 1910–12

At the age of twenty-six, Mussolini returned to Italy to help once more in his father's *taverna*. But the uneventful existence bored him and he briefly thought again of becoming a journalist in America.[24] He had another short stay in prison for inability to pay a fine. Then the socialist clubs of Forlì chose him to be their political organiser and asked him to edit a four-page weekly magazine; its name, which he probably chose himself, was *La Lotta di Classe*, or *The Class Struggle*, and the title fitted his growing conviction that it was time to stop studying the world and begin trying to change it. This was one of a hundred socialist weeklies in Italy and had an initial circulation of only a thousand copies, but in two years he doubled its sales and, in the process, further developed his style of pugnacious and passionate invective. Copies of this paper disappeared from local libraries after 1922.[25]

During his two years as editor, it became obvious that his particular talents would lead him to make a career in journalism and political agitation. There was no money in the life, but money never meant much to him. Weeks went by in almost perpetual speech-making and he felt himself becoming a 'walking gramophone'; yet he took delight in frequent brushes with the police and in the applause of small socialist audiences. His chief message was that parliamentary politics were a waste of time, since the democratic system in Italy catered only for men on the make – for lawyers who wanted the prestige of being in parliament to increase their practice, professors who saw it as a path to academic promotion, journalists eager for the governmental hand-outs that were used for bribing the press.[26]

Mussolini was far from becoming an orthodox marxist and his natural bent was to reject all systems of belief. Nevertheless, he still hung a portrait of Marx in his office and pinned his faith on the central teachings of the *Communist Manifesto*. The first issue of *La Lotta di Classe* referred to Marx and Darwin as the greatest thinkers of the past century; Marx more than anyone, the paper claimed, had an acceptable answer to contemporary problems and in particular had taught the proletariat that only by violence could the *ancien régime* be destroyed. Nor was this just a casual allegiance on Mussolini's part: he had said all this five years earlier, and it remained his belief even in the fascist period that any student of political reality should pass through the school of Marx as well as of Machiavelli.[27]

Another continuing constituent of his creed was manifested in his vitriolic attacks against the Church, which he accompanied with provocative and blasphemous remarks about the consecrated host and about a love affair between Christ and Mary Magdalen. According to him, priests were 'black microbes', servants of capitalism, persecutors of Jews, and poisoners of young minds. Socialists who believed in Christianity or accepted religious marriage should be expelled from the party. The Church was reproached for its authoritarianism and refusal to allow freedom of thought[28] – strange accusations coming from a man who would one day himself preach authoritarianism and be praised by the Pope as someone sent by Providence to deliver Italy from liberalism and religious error.

As well as being anti-Christian, his new paper was strongly anti-militaristic; he called the army 'a criminal organisation designed to protect capitalism and bourgeois society' and broke the law by inviting soldiers to disobey their officers, for which he was again put in prison. Just as anti-fascists were to do later, he blamed Italy's poverty on the fact that taxes were used for buying battleships instead of teachers and agricultural machinery. He thought it ridiculous to fight to win Trent and Trieste from the Austrians so long as most Italians were illiterate. Proletarians had no fatherland and should refuse to fight for purely patriotic reasons: 'the national flag is for us a rag to plant on a dunghill', and if war broke out, he said, the common people in each country should rather launch a civil war against their own governments.[29]

If Mussolini later changed his mind on this point, one belief he retained was that the parliamentary system was a foreign importation which did not work in an Italian context. The parliament at Rome was, he thought, more corrupt than parliaments elsewhere, partly because Rome was a pernicious influence, a town of priests, prostitutes and bureaucrats, a 'centre of infection poisoning the whole of our national life'. He noted with disgust that some deputies were elected to parliament by employing private armies of hooligans to invade the voting booths[30] – an example that he himself later followed with notable success. Even if the impossible happened and the socialists won a parliamentary majority, he was sure that this in itself would never bring about socialism: only direct proletarian action battling in the streets and town squares could do that.[31] Even assassination might be legitimate if it brought the day of revolution nearer. Killing people was not to be recommended in normal times but it might be the only effective weapon against a tyrant. The assassination of Tsar Alexander in 1881 and the Italian King Umberto in 1900 were justifiable. If governments suppressed free speech and imprisoned militant revolutionaries, then even the throwing of a bomb into a crowded theatre might be acceptable, and good socialists must steel their minds against any sense of pity that Christianity might have taught them. A bomb could be more effective than a hundred speeches.[32]

In 1910, Mussolini set up house with his future wife, Rachele. As she was the daughter of his father's mistress, it was inevitable that the gossips sometimes referred to her as Benito's half-sister.[33] She had briefly been in his class when he was a teacher; then she became a housemaid. They became engaged just before he emigrated in 1909. For seven months while he was in Trent he never sent her so much as a postcard, but on his return he persuaded their parents to let them marry – by melodramatically drawing a pistol and threatening to kill himself. Probably she never knew that he had a child by a relationship he had made in Trent.[34]

Despite his lack of consideration and fierce outward behaviour he was generally kind to her, though jealous of her ever leaving the house, and her own fully justified jealousy was instrumental (according to their daughter) in driving him out of the house into the public life of politics.[35] Rachele lacked any interest in his journalism or in politics, and had no intellectual pursuits of her own. They started their family in a one-room apartment. There was often not enough food, since he cared little for material things and even tried on grounds of socialist principle to refuse an increase in his editor's salary. Life was so hard that when he received an offer to edit a newspaper in Brazil he was keen to go and only Rachele's pregnancy dissuaded him.

To help keep the family and his now partly paralysed father, he wrote a pulp novel for serialisation in Battisti's newspaper at Trent. *Claudia Particella* was a violently anti-clerical book and its villain was a lecherous cardinal – perhaps Mussolini was deliberately copying Garibaldi's equally jejune novel *Clelia*. The book earned him some notoriety, and though he himself called it trash, he obviously understood popular taste and knew how to cater for it. Eventually the book was translated into several languages, but for obvious reasons did not appear in Italy until after his death. He wrote another novelette on the tragedy of the Archduke Rudolph at Mayerling that remained unpublished, as well as a serious sociological study of the Trentino that deserved more success than it received.

So far he had shown evidence of only minor talent and was hardly maturing into an attractive personality. Essentially a loner who liked long solitary walks in the countryside, he was still understood by nobody, valued by very few and thought to have no real affection for anyone. He was naturally un-communicative except on the platform and was learning to manufacture a mask to conceal his real personality.[36] He rarely smiled or laughed at a joke and indeed never in his life showed more than a limited and wry sense of humour.[37] To others he seemed selfish, awkward and embarrassingly rude, and he would not look into people's eyes when he spoke to them.[38] As well as being thought a tyrant by pupils, he was accustomed to being nicknamed 'the madman' and to accusations of insincerity, delinquency and even paranoia.[39]

In October 1910, he visited Milan for the annual socialist party congress. The socialists were still only a small party and were not yet sure if they belonged on the extreme left or the centre-left of Italian politics. On this, his first appearance on a national stage, the unshaven, already slightly balding, ill-dressed young man from the provinces seemed a gauche peasant among the middle-class intellectuals who ran the party. The arguments he put forward in a fierce, disorganised speech were directed against those who accepted universal suffrage and social reform as the best means of advancing socialism, but they were greeted by laughter. After the revolutionary faction had been heavily voted down, he tried to persuade this small group that they would be better off outside the party because the need was not for reforms but for armed insurrection. The means of production were still in the hands of a small, closed oligarchy against whom any talk of trade unions and co-operatives and democracy was no use whatever.[40]

In the previous year he had threatened that he would secede if the party did not adopt a more intransigent stance – he feared that the main body of reformists was drawing closer to the parliamentary system and to the liberal coalition presided over by Giovanni Giolitti. In April 1911, he decided to act on this threat and go it alone. His was a coolly calculated step based on the hope of creating a new and more revolutionary party (in something of the same way as the bolsheviks subsequently broke away from the socialists in Russia). His secession found local support in Forlì, but his hope of winning nationwide support was unfulfilled.

He was saved from the consequences of this when, in September, the prime minister Giolitti decided to conquer Libya. Along with many moderate as well as revolutionary socialists, Mussolini condemned this colonial war against the Turks as an attempt by Giolitti to distract the country from pressing internal problems. He described the nationalists' rhetoric about the economic advantages of colonialism as sheer lies; he said that what they took to be an easy war would become a long and costly enterprise, and here he was right.

Once again he called the idea of patriotic loyalty 'a lying and outdated fiction' and hoped that the proletariat would exploit the emergency by paralysing society in open class war. Always, he added hopefully, 'war is the prelude to revolution', and just possibly the moment of reckoning against the bourgeoisie might have arrived.[41] Both his pacifism and his preaching of class war were to be denied or ignored by later fascist historiography.[42] For several days he tried to organise an insurrection against the war, and if other socialist groups had done the same he thought they might have succeeded. He was in his element haranguing the mob. Tram and railway lines were torn up to stop the transport of troops, many shops in Forlì were boarded up, and factories came to a standstill; but the movement was easily suppressed with a few casualties on both sides. He castigated the citizens of Forlì as cowards for refusing to continue the fight: sabotage was not enough – they should have turned the strike into a revolution.[43]

He was arrested and, at his trial, tried to diminish his own responsibility and put the blame on others. He denied the accusation of having stirred up the mob to vandalism and of having anything to do with acts of violence. He explained to the court that the people of Forlì did not even like him and few bought his newspaper. He tried to maintain that, far from being anti-patriotic, his arguments against the war were essentially patriotic.[44] But he was found guilty and spent the next five months in prison.

By his arrest and trial he had at last won a reputation that went beyond the confines of the Romagna. A complete man, he used to say, should have several years in prison as part of his education, especially if his imprisonment could be depicted as martyrdom.[45] Though he had to share a cell with seven or eight others, the enforced leisure gave him time to read, and it was in prison, at the age of only twenty-eight, that he self-importantly wrote his first autobiography. He also published a polemical booklet, *John Huss, the man of truth*, which was another attack on the Church and a passionate plea for religious freedom that ran completely counter to later fascist dogma. Pietro Nenni, the socialist leader who was in prison with him, remembered him as a model prisoner, cheerful, noisy, and indulgent to the other hardened criminals whose offences he was always ready to explain in terms of their social deprivation.[46]

Mussolini subsequently made his name as an ardent imperialist, and in the 1920s was responsible for great brutalities against the Libyan people, but in 1911 he utterly condemned this early war in Libya as a crime against humanity and an act of international brigandage. He said a thousand million lire were being wasted on the entirely false expectation that North Africa could become a home for Italian emigrants. Instead of increasing the wealth of the mother country as the nationalists argued, colonialism would in his view do the opposite, and he pointed to bankruptcies and closed factories as proof. He even boasted of being on the side of the Libyans and roundly condemned as an atrocity the way in which Arabs were (he said) massacred and sometimes dismembered by the invading force.[47] The Libyan war of 1911–12 thus accentuated his anti-patriotism and once again he contended that no socialist could be a patriot, because 'we socialists are not Italians but Europeans'. Patriotism was bound to develop into militarism and so bring disaster by enslaving the common people at home as well as abroad. The proletariat should realise that, by fighting in Africa, Italy was increasing the likelihood of a major European war, and to avert such a catastrophe there was no alternative but to rebel and hasten the decline of the warmongering bourgeoisie.[48]

After serving his prison sentence he found that he had become a local celebrity at Forlì but now had bigger things in mind. Isolated action had proved insufficient, so he persuaded his local socialist group to rejoin the socialist party and prepare for the next national congress due to meet in July 1912 at Reggio. He now accepted that the best tactic was to reassert the unity of the party and then try to capture it from the reformists. He announced his intention of trying to persuade the congress to expel the gradualists and all socialists who had supported Giolitti's colonial war or who advocated parliamentary rather than revolutionary methods.[49]

His proposal gained credit in March when Leonida Bissolati, a prominent reformist, ostentatiously congratulated the king on the failure of another assassination attempt. Quite apart from whether political assassination was right or wrong, for a socialist to visit the royal palace was going too far. It was proof that some socialists were still misguided enough to hope for a legal victory inside the bourgeois system; such moderates would only weaken the revolutionary momentum which socialism needed.[50]

Few of the delegates who assembled at Reggio Emilia had heard of Mussolini, and he himself had never met Bissolati or the other party leaders whom he now set about unseating. However, this emaciated, dishevelled young man won on this occasion an enthusiastic hearing. It was fortunate for him that the marxist faction in the party had few good speakers and his forceful, quick-fire style appealed to people who felt disorientated as they saw their leaders becoming more and more conformist and moderate. His speech was carefully rehearsed and gave the impression of sincerity and decisiveness. After the fiasco of his performance at a previous congress, the delegates witnessed something altogether different: his motion to expel Bissolati and Bonomi (a future prime minister) was accepted by a surprisingly large majority and Mussolini and Balabanoff were among the revolutionaries who became the dominant faction on the party directorate. He was only twenty-eight.

Avanti!, 1912–14

Four months later, when a vacancy occurred in the editorship of the socialist newspaper, *Avanti!*, Mussolini was appointed to the post by his colleagues on the party executive; this was an unusual stroke of luck for a young journalist who had never worked on a big national daily. During two years as editor he established his position as one of the leaders of the party and carefully cultivated the special relationship with a wider public that such a newspaper afforded him. *Avanti!* was not a particularly good paper; it had a disappointing circulation and paid its staff so little that the better correspondents tended to leave. Nevertheless, he ruthlessly got rid of some of the older, better-known writers, tearing up contracts if necessary; and told those who remained that he was going to be an authoritarian commander with no nonsense about industrial democracy. His policy was an outright rejection of the compromises of reformism, placing an intransigent emphasis on maximalism, in other words the maximum programme of undiluted socialism.[51] Aiming at a wider lower-class readership, he eventually more than doubled the circulation.

He also started another fortnightly magazine which he himself owned and which he called *Utopia*; the title was a tribute to Sir Thomas More whom he regarded as one of the first socialists. *Utopia* was directed at a more intelligent audience, but met with only moderate success. Mussolini's strong point was agitation and denunciation, not doctrine and reasoned criticism.

The assistant editor he chose for *Avanti!* was Angelica Balabanoff, a woman of strong character and great energy on whom he seems to have been still intellectually dependent. He flattered himself that others thought of her as his mistress but this was probably nothing more than sexual boasting. Another woman in his life at this period was Ida Dalser, with whom he lived on and off for several years after setting up a home for Rachele: indeed Ida claimed that he promised marriage to her and that he was living off her money. Hers was the one illegitimate child he acknowledged as his own, but in 1915 he abandoned mother and child to a miserable and finally tragic existence. In later years, to avoid scandal, he had her forcibly confined in a mental home, where she died in 1937.

A third woman who he said 'loved me madly' was Margherita Sarfatti, a rich Milanese who was art critic for *Avanti!*. Signora Sarfatti later moved with him from socialism to fascism and not only wrote his first 'official' biography but later became editor of his magazine, *Gerarchia*. Their affair lasted into the 1930s and she seems to have been Rachele's only serious rival until he lost his head over a much younger girl, Clara Petacci: eventually Margherita fell victim to Mussolini's anti-Jewish legislation. Interestingly enough, none of these women was particularly pretty, except possibly Clara Petacci: the others were sometimes called ugly and positively unattractive. His taste in such matters was something of a puzzle to his associates.

A more interesting person whom he pursued unsuccessfully in 1913–14 was Leda Rafanelli, an anarchist and convert to Islam. Well-educated and unconventional, she too seems to have possessed a stronger personality than his own. She was not, if she can be believed, sexually attracted to him but was fascinated by the strangeness of his character, until she discovered that his protestation of having no family or other ties was blatantly untrue. When she found him out, he explained that his wife was accustomed to his infidelities, and he was upset when the news failed to make her jealous. He informed her that, like other newspaper editors, he needed a talented woman to support him as his official mistress. She, however, came to think that he was not altogether serious as a person or a socialist and might even be a bit unbalanced. His clamorous defection from pacifism and from the socialist party ended their relationship in 1914. Mussolini was not accustomed to having his masculinity rebuffed, and when he later became dictator he had her harassed by the police and her letters from him confiscated.[52]

Leda Rafanelli's memories of Mussolini have the stamp of greater veracity than other contemporary descriptions and they pin-point characteristics later confirmed by others. She noted the comic way in which he affected an ill-dressed, dirty and unshaven appearance when on a public platform, as befitted a proletarian leader, and then quickly changed into absurd over-modish patent-leather shoes and a silk-lapelled coat for his private life. At some moments he seemed to her like a burlesque actor; he appeared to lack a well-defined inner personality – he told her that he did not understand his real self.[53] She found his views superficial; he seemed to know little about anything except politics and was without savoir faire or experience of the world. He had the disconcerting habit of changing his mind in the course of a single conversation in order to agree with what she said; other people in later years confirmed that he always tended to agree with the person to whom he had last spoken.[54] He admitted that he had once wanted to be a celebrated writer or musician until he found he lacked the ability, but was still determined to be a great man whose name would be on everyone's lips. 'I need glory and wealth, I am always looking for the tumultuous and the new.' He told Leda that he was going to be a 'man of destiny'. 'Like Napoleon?', she asked mischievously. 'No, greater than Napoleon,' he replied.[55] Above all he was set on becoming a great orator, a modern Demosthenes, and confessed he felt much more at home on a public rostrum than in private conversation.

At the beginning of 1913, a few weeks after his appointment to *Avanti!*, he found just the kind of issue he needed to help him make a name for himself.

This was after clashes with the police in backward areas of the country by people demonstrating against poor conditions. In a series of pungent editorials he pointed out that many Italians were living in an almost primitive society without adequate schools or even water supplies. In some parts of the south, life was still little better than in the troglodyte communities of North Africa, and Italian capitalists evidently found it more profitable to build 'prestige railways' in Tripoli than roads in Sardinia. A quarter of Italian villages still had no post office, and hundreds of them were cut off from the outside world except by mule track. For demonstrators to protest against such primitive conditions was an elementary human right, he wrote, and if Giolitti's government tried to stop this by police action, no one could deny the right to use violence in reply.[56] He argued that the Libyan war had begun a process leading towards a revolution from which the proletariat had nothing to lose and everything to gain:[57] he had in mind what he called 'a necessary blood-bath',[58] the 'physical extermination' of the bourgeoisie through which the proletariat would gain 'a totality of power'.[59]

He used the years 1912–14 at *Avanti!* to prepare people for the great day of social liberation, expecting that a revolution might be triggered off by the outbreak of a European war. Later he claimed that in these years he was already a convert to nationalism.[60] But at the time he wrote angrily against the nationalism of the 1890s associated with the name of Francesco Crispi, and against Giolitti's precipitating Italy into an arms race she could not afford. He was especially angry with the moderate socialists in parliament who voted military budgets that might be used in a war against workers in Germany or France. 'Let us have no more talk of battleships, barracks, cannon, at a time when thousands of villages have no schools, roads, electricity, or doctors, but still live tragically beyond the pale of civilised life.' If a European war broke out, soldiers should mutiny and ordinary citizens rise in civil war against the government.[61]

Despite his tirades against parliament and his insistence that a newspaper editor should never become an elected deputy, his views were adaptable enough to let his name be put forward for the general election of October 1913; though he campaigned very little, it is clear that he had come to recognise that the socialists needed the boost to morale afforded by an increasing parliamentary representation. He failed in his home constituency of Forlì where a republican candidate was chosen, but was successful a few months later in becoming a town councillor in Milan.

The socialists in the nationwide elections of 1913 won nearly a million votes and fifty-three parliamentary seats. This was a considerable success, and suggests that *Avanti!*'s uncompromising advocacy of revolution may well have won voters. The paper was also an inspiration to Antonio Gramsci and the younger generation of socialist activists. Addressing himself to a growing audience, Mussolini redoubled the urgency of his utopian propaganda: 'private property is theft' and should be abolished as Italy moved through the phase of collectivisation forwards to the ultimate goal of communism. Marx had shown how all history was the history of class struggle, and had explained how a wholesale expropriation of private wealth would be needed before the proletariat could assume its predetermined position as the dominant class in society.[62]

There was nothing specially democratic about such a programme, and indeed Mussolini had learnt from the syndicalists to have no illusions about democracy: there was 'an irreducible antithesis between democracy and socialism'. Politics were about force, not consent. The masses were passive and minorities alone could be dynamic. A small minority among the proletariat was destined to take over government from the existing bourgeois elite, while ordinary folk, whom he openly despised for their ignorance and pleasure-loving inertia, would have no alternative but to follow and submit. He repeatedly said – and it was an important message for his future career – that the masses needed not to understand but to *believe*; 'if only we can give them faith that mountains can be moved, they will accept the illusion that mountains are moveable, and thus an illusion may become reality'.[63]

After two years of revolutionary propaganda, he was caught surprisingly off guard when, during 'Red week' in June 1914, Italy came close to a real revolution with a million or more people taking to the streets. His immediate reaction was to hope that perhaps, if only a hundred demonstrators would be killed by the police, the great moment of catastrophe might have arrived. But the riots were disorganised and aimless – proof, as he himself soon realised, that his talk about universal insurrection had been naive. So instead of going to the centre of action, as did Nenni and Malatesta, he remained at his editor's desk and, though he took part in one demonstration, failed to give his readers an unequivocal lead.[64]

From the consequences of his half-heartedly provocative behaviour Mussolini was again saved by an outside event when, a few days later, the Archduke Ferdinand was murdered at Sarajevo and a world war soon afterwards began. Austria and Germany were on one side; France, Britain and Russia on the other. According to subsequent fascist legend, Mussolini at once realised the need for Italy to declare war on Austria, and it is true that he himself later blessed Ferdinand's murderers as benefactors of humankind for starting such a conflagration.[65] But at the time, as a leading representative of a party that was anti-militaristic and internationalist, he argued on principle and on grounds of *Realpolitik* for neutrality 'at all costs' and said that intervention would be an 'unpardonable crime': the war was a purely bourgeois concern and proletarians must not only refuse to fight but rise in rebellion against it.[66]

Though continuing for several months to demand that Italy stay neutral, he quickly began to see that anti-militarist dogma might split the party, and the defection of an increasing number of his companions belied his outward self-confidence. The workers of the world were not rising in revolt against their masters as he had hoped, and instead some socialists called his pacifism cowardly and hypocritical, not to say ingenuous and muddled. He continued to write as though, in Italy's state of weakness, entering another war might be fatal, but he gave up his earlier advocacy of desertion and began to admit that, in some circumstances, intervention in the war would be permissible. At all events he came to accept that, if Italy decided to fight, the proletariat should not start a civil war but remain passive and merely register disapproval. Until early October he nevertheless maintained in public an attitude of absolute and 'implacable' opposition to fighting in what was a purely capitalist war. He even threatened resignation if others disagreed[67] and no doubt feared that he might lose the editorship of *Avanti!* if he moved too strongly against the official socialist policy of neutrality. But beneath an outward certainty his doubts grew. After the battle of the Marne it began to look as though the Germans were going to lose the war, in which case neutrality made less sense than before. More importantly, neutralism was obviously not helping the cause of revolutionary socialism; on the contrary, the war itself might turn out to be that very 'blood-bath' he had been hoping for; it was, after all, 'only blood that makes the wheels of history turn'.[68]

His false position became apparent to those around him as his public and private remarks became less and less reconcilable. Challenged in public about the apparent contradiction, he first denied that there was any inconsistency, then admitted he had indeed been wavering and finally, on 18 October, without consulting the other socialist leaders or even his co-editors, he suddenly confessed in *Avanti!* that he had been wrong: it was now clear to him that socialists could not afford to be mere spectators of the tragedy overwhelming Europe and he hoped he could persuade the party to agree with him. This was a brave decision, but the change was too sudden, too inconsiderate of others, and it undermined confidence in his judgement and good faith. He made a very poor showing when the party executive was summoned to examine the question and, when he found himself in complete isolation, decided to resign his editorship.

War and peace

3

War, 1914–17

For a few days Mussolini may have been hoping that enough socialist leaders would accept his change of policy to make his personal domination of the party unassailable,[1] but by leaving his editorial post so dramatically he had given away his best card. The natural reaction was to doubt both the sincerity of his socialist ideas and his powers of political analysis.

Criticism of his 'betrayal' changed to anger when he immediately started a new paper in competition with *Avanti!* – he gave it the name of *Il Popolo d'Italia*. To launch a daily newspaper in just two weeks had the appearance of premeditation and even lack of integrity. It was well known that he wanted to own a daily newspaper,[2] and it looked as though, to fulfil this ambition, he was giving up neutrality just so that he could get French money. The *Popolo d'Italia* was subsidised at various times by other belligerent countries, including Britain and perhaps also Russia and the United States. This does not necessarily mean that he was bribed to change his views or that he was ready to let financial backers dictate his policy. Nevertheless the charge of bribery remained an embarrassment to him, as is demonstrated by his indignant and untruthful denial of ever having accepted foreign money for the paper.[3]

Still more embarrassing was the fact that, though he claimed to be founding a socialist paper, he was partially financed by rich Italian industrialists who stood to gain from Italy's entering the war: by Fiat and other arms manufacturers; also by agrarian interests – the very people he had hitherto labelled as the enemy. Further subsidies came indirectly from the Italian government itself.[4] None of this meant that he had at one stroke joined the political establishment, but the association with big business does mark a radical change in his political development. It also greatly changed his private life and he now began to frequent the more elegant Milan restaurants.[5] Not a man to alter his views for reasons of greed, he was certainly vulnerable to the temptations of power and often showed that to get power he would adapt his principles. Ownership of the *Popolo d'Italia*, even with its limited circulation, provided not only a livelihood but also a very useful launching pad into national politics.

The paper began publication on 15 November 1914. Though bitter against the socialist party, it still claimed to support socialism; its novelty was in being pro-war and in arguing that war would pave the way for social revolution. But his party did not accept this and formally expelled him. He himself had once urged the expulsion of all deviationists and, after his own treatment of Bissolati's pro-war group in 1912, he had little ground for complaint; nevertheless, he called his own expulsion unforgiveable. He had hoped to persuade the party to follow him, but had once again miscalculated and it was small satisfaction to tell the socialists that they would one day regret his departure.

By now he was an experienced journalist with a practised ability to sense public opinion and he instinctively set about discovering a readership on whom he could base the next stage in his career. In searching for readers, he was not primarily concerned with consistency or coherence of policy. Preferably he would have to address himself not only to dissident socialists but also to democratic idealists who had anticipated him in accepting the war. He also needed to appeal to patriots who wanted the 'redemption' of Trieste and Trentino from Austria, and in order to attract the imperialists he began to justify the Libyan war of 1911-12 which he had once condemned.[6] At the same time he reiterated that the new war he demanded should be for the liberation of subject peoples rather than for nationalism and imperialism: Italy should not dream of annexing Dalmatia, because the Jugoslavs were brothers in a common war of liberation.[7] Nor did Mussolini's initial war aims include the annexation of Fiume, or Trieste (which he was ready to see internationalised); nor did he demand for Italy a frontier as far north as the Alps.[8]

Early in 1915, however, he moved closer to the nationalists in believing that, if the government decided to enter the war, new and welcome vistas of Italian expansion might be opened up. A few months later he would be demanding Trieste, Fiume, an Alpine frontier, and 'immense booty' to be conquered in the Balkans and Middle East.[9] He now insisted that Italy had to show the world she was capable of a 'really great war'; national honour demanded that she obliterate the legend of Italians being pleasure-loving and unwarlike.[10] Here, at last, was the authentic voice of Mussolini the fascist.

Subsequently, he described how he had created the *fascisti* in December 1914, as a pressure-group to bring about military intervention. The first *fascio* had, in fact, already been formed several months earlier by another group (the word *fascio* means 'bundle') of left-wing interventionists, many of whom had preceded him in leaving the main body of socialism.[11] Although it was later maintained that no one had preceded him, it was actually these earlier *fascisti* who were joined and then virtually taken over by Mussolini in December. He wrote a manifesto for them which shows that he had put aside his marxist ideas of class war, for the moment at least. His new hero was not Marx but Mazzini, who dreamt of a patriotic war to secure Italy's 'natural frontiers' of language and race.[12]

A majority in parliament was against participating in the war; the deputies preferred the policy held in common by both Salandra, the new conservative prime minister, and Giolitti, his leading opponent: to bargain with both sides to obtain as much as possible, and perhaps without fighting. Outside parliament, almost certainly a large majority of Italians wished to remain neutral. Even the leading interventionists, including King Vittorio Emanuele and Mussolini himself, were sure that, since only a small minority wanted war, the country would have to be cajoled or bullied into fighting.

Mussolini began by threatening civil war and an anti-monarchist *coup* if the government refused to give up neutrality.[13] At the same time he tried to persuade his readers that the war would be a short one, possibly lasting no more than weeks, because the Italian army was ready to attack and would at once tip the scales against Germany and Austria; nor would the economy have any difficulty in coping with a major European war.[14] Events soon revealed these arguments to be rhetorical nonsense but they influenced readers because, as he well knew, they were what some people wanted to hear. He later claimed, with great exaggeration, that his propaganda was chiefly responsible for forcing Italy into war.[15] He certainly showed immense zeal. When parliament refused to act he demanded the abolition of 'that pestiferous plague-spot that poisons the blood of the nation' and called on people to prepare for civil war and be ready to take to the streets.[16] After widespread rioting in May, the politicians capitulated, led by Salandra, who realised this was a way to defeat Giolitti and the parliamentary majority. Without consulting the deputies, the king signed a declaration of war against Austria. In retrospect Mussolini called these riots the beginning of the fascist revolution and even thought that he might have used this moment to seize power.[17] But it was just a day-dream; his personal contribution was less than he imagined and he still represented only a tiny minority. The one incontrovertible fact was that Italy had been forced into war by non- or anti-parliamentary means. He himself hailed this as a glorious and decisive fact; it was 'Italy's baptism as a great power', 'a culminating point in world history'.[18] Wiser observers rather considered it to be an ill-considered and greatly damaging decision.[19] Not only by loss of lives, but also by injuring Italy's political institutions, weakening her economy, destabilising her society, the First World War was to create conditions favourable to the rise of fascism.

Most advocates of intervention at once volunteered for active service. Mussolini later claimed that he did so, even insisting falsely that he was accepted as a volunteer.[20] But the army was not keen to have such a dangerous revolutionary, and as he was expecting a very short war he probably preferred to remain at his editorial desk where he could direct public opinion. Whatever the truth or the motive, he waited for three months to be called up with the other conscripts of his class, trying to shrug off as best he could the accusations of shirking.

By the time he was conscripted, in September 1915, he was beginning to understand that his romantic idea of another 'Garibaldian' war of heroism and quick victory was unrealistic. The conditions of static trench fighting were something he had never imagined. It soon became apparent that he and the other interventionists had been acting under entirely false assumptions, because the army, despite what he had written, was badly armed and, as Giolitti knew well, quite unready for war. He reacted by blaming this lack of preparation on government inefficiency; he never admitted that either his years of pacifist propaganda or his rhetorical talk of easy victory gave him any share of responsibility.

His enemies called his record as a soldier in 1915–17 unimpressive. He himself told stories of courageously going over the top in frontal attacks on the Austrian positions and of picking up enemy grenades and throwing them back before they exploded. Probably he performed his unexciting duties more than satisfactorily. It must have been a miserable life – in waterlogged trenches, without protection from frost, infested by lice and in 'daily contact with soldiers of low intellect';[21] yet he remained resilient and cheerful. He was, like Hitler, promoted to the rank of corporal but received no equivalent of Hitler's Iron Cross. He resented this promotion because he took it to be due to seniority rather than merit and complained of not reaching higher rank.[22] He once began an officers' training course but was rejected, no doubt in part because of his political views,[23] and in the end only reached the rank of sergeant. His younger brother obtained a commission.

In February 1917, during a training exercise, he was operating a grenade thrower that became too hot and exploded, killing a number of people and leaving him with forty fragments in his body. Since none of his wounds was serious, he was able to recall the explosion as 'the most beautiful moment in my life'[24] and the episode became part of fascist hagiology. In one official biography it was said that from the moment Mussolini had to leave the front line, the war began going badly for Italy.[25] A thousand people later claimed credit for having carried the wounded man to hospital. He liked to recount how he bravely refused an anaesthetic as the splinters were removed and how the Austrians, hearing where their great enemy was stationed, tried to kill him by shelling the hospital:[26] narcissism and self-dramatisation were important elements in his character.

Invalided out of the army in June 1917, he again took over editorship of the

Popolo d'Italia. Without the presence of its owner and in the difficult circumstances of a war economy the paper had flagged, but it had recently found more financial backing and was moving further away from its socialist origins.[27] Mussolini once again demonstrated his combative nature. He chastised the ageing politicians who were failing to carry out the kind of attacking war he wanted and who were blind enough to be continuing with a system of parliamentary government that he hoped had been destroyed in 1915 by the riots of 'radiant May'. They lacked, he said, any sense of leadership. They were also imposing a ridiculous censorship to stop criticism of their obvious failures:[28] he was always able to see the dangers of censorship – except when imposed by himself.

In a difficult moment when the war was going none too well, he thought seriously about once again encouraging the mob to sweep away parliament and establish a dictatorship. With a number of other discontented politicians, as well as the commander-in-chief himself, General Cadorna, a plan was discussed for a *coup d'état*. But Cadorna backed down, possibly because he was unwilling to see political power pass into such hands.[29]

This tentative plotting of a revolution made the authorities wonder if Mussolini was planning to emulate the bolsheviks. From the very beginning he had seen the war as the first step towards revolution, and in particular had welcomed the possibility of revolution in Russia.[30] But the first news from Petrograd found him sceptical. Lenin, he wrote, was 'a man of straw', a coward, a betrayer of the real revolution; 'only a Tartar and Mongolian people could fall for such a programme as his'; he was another autocrat like the tsar, if not worse; he was simply appealing to terrorism and bestial instincts. As Marx had taught, the Russians were a primitive Asiatic people who should be forced back at bayonet-point beyond the Ural mountains.[31]

Part of this angry reaction was due to the fact that Russia's defection from the alliance allowed Austria to transfer more troops to her Alpine front where the Italians were already in difficulties. Mussolini's propaganda about popular enthusiasm for fighting had been exposed as false. Many Italian soldiers were unenthusiastic about and even actively opposed to the war, and not nearly enough men had volunteered to fight. In moments of pessimism he speculated that the government might have to impose martial law and shoot some of the rank and file in order to encourage the rest to greater efforts; ordinary people did not understand patriotism any more than they understood socialism, but must be forced into obedience.[32] His lofty and autocratic disdain for the masses was similar to Cadorna's attitude to his troops – an attitude that contributed to the crumbling of the Italian front at Caporetto.

The defeat at Caporetto was an immense and unexpected shock. Mussolini

29

wrote with typical exaggeration that this one day, 24 October 1917, witnessed the greatest defeat in world history, adding that nothing in his life caused him greater humiliation. To make matters worse, Cadorna unfairly blamed the defeat on his men's cowardice and thousands were executed. Mussolini thought such punishment wrong; he put the blame rather on the army leaders – who, he now argued, were almost all against the war. He blamed his former socialist companions for their defeatism, and also the new prime minister, Orlando. What Italy needed was a dictator who would discard parliament and militarise the nation. All independent newspapers should be forced to cease publication, since what the country now needed was not criticism but discipline.[33]

Victory, 1918–19

Mussolini did what he could to raise morale at this moment of crisis. He demanded a single allied command and a unified allied strategy – something he himself signally failed to supply in the Second World War – and asked for more French and British soldiers to be sent to reinforce the Italian front. He called somewhat vaguely for an offensive strategy rather than one relying on defensive trench warfare, and for terroristic bombing of German cities. The war should become one of hate, and Italians must realise that a victorious Germany would turn Italy into a desert peopled by slaves.[34]

Before Caporetto, the United States had declared war on Germany and this one fact convinced him – it was another judgement he failed to make in the Second World War – that victory would be ensured in the long term by America's economic potential. In expectation of this he began to prepare his peacetime strategy.

The main problem for his own political future was where to find a *point d'appui* – by choosing the correct lever and fulcrum, he used to say, one could move mountains.[35] A potential fulcrum already existed in those *fascisti* who had come together in May 1915 from many different parties to form the interventionist movement. He saw the possibility of manipulating them in order to upset the existing party structure. In 1916, he was already talking of a possible *trincerocrazia* or 'government by men in the trenches'. When the soldiers returned to peacetime Italy they would have grievances that he could exploit to cut across existing allegiances and create a radical new alignment of forces; they might become 'the aristocracy of tomorrow', the hard core of a new ruling class.[36]

No one else in Italy showed so much prescience or such instinctive political cunning. To appeal to the ex-servicemen he adopted an odd mixture of nationalist and revolutionary ideas overlaid with a populist appeal to both national grandeur and individual prosperity. While waiting to see if they would be predominantly on the right or the left of politics, he wanted to pre-empt their support either way. He thus took care to demand a new deal for the poor, a share in company profits for industrial workers, an eight-hour day for everyone, and smallholdings for landless peasants.[37] He guessed that the returning soldiers would be bitter against those who had taken their jobs and would be attracted to a leader who denounced the stay-at-homes and the anti-war socialist party. He also foresaw that those who, as officers, had become accustomed to good pay and positions of command might be open to subversion when confronted by the harsh economic realities of peacetime.[38]

Another force he could tap was the growing fervour for nationalism and irredentism. Here his views changed considerably in the course of 1918. Until then he sometimes continued to assume that Italians were fighting a war of liberation and idealism rather than of territorial conquests. Even early in 1918, recognising that Italy would need the Serbs to help defeat Austria, he agreed that Italians should support the 'suppressed nationalities' in the Austrian empire and look to a strong Jugoslavia as the best hope of winning influence in the Balkans.[39] But by the summer of 1918, Serbian help was less necessary; indeed the Serbs were showing reluctance to act as grateful and submissive protégés of Italy. Moreover the Austrian breakthrough at Caporetto had shown the desirability of a strong Alpine frontier disregarding ethnic and linguistic considerations. So although Mussolini at first welcomed President Wilson's famous 'fourteen points', with their insistence on national self-determination as the best basis for a peace settlement, he later denounced them when they seemed to impugn Italy's right to annex large German- and Slav-speaking areas inside Italy's 'natural frontiers'. He then demanded the annexation of not only Trieste, but the Italian Tyrol (Alto Adige), Fiume and most of Dalmatia. Jugoslavia should be regarded not as an ally but as an enemy, while the Adriatic and the Mediterranean must become Italian seas.[40] He was fully aware that this irredentist policy could be made to coincide with the frustrated sentiments of men from the trenches, who could be persuaded to fear that without these spoils of war they might have fought in vain.

Expectations for the future reached a pitch of enthusiasm in October, when the Italian victory at Vittorio Veneto brought the fighting to a triumphant end. Until the last moment Mussolini had been expecting hostilities to continue for another year or two,[41] but he quickly adjusted his sights. He even started claiming that Italy was responsible for the allied victory and described Vittorio Veneto as 'the greatest victory in world history'.[42] This dubious assertion, though momentarily good for morale, eventually caused bitter

31

disillusionment: designed as a basis for ambitious territorial claims at the peace table, the fictions and exaggerations about the Italian victory created hopes that could not be realised.

Since returning to run the *Popolo d'Italia*, Mussolini had increased its circulation to what was claimed to be 60,000 copies.[43] From the end of 1917, he received a good deal of advertising from some of the big arms manufacturers, and revenue from advertisements increased nearly eightfold in the first three months of 1918. Possibly this inflow of money from big business in no way affected the politics of his paper,[44] but it certainly coincided with a further shift away from the residual socialism of his youth, and his enemies suggested that he set less store by sincerely held beliefs than by the overriding need to keep his paper in existence for the next stage in his career. The question was inevitably asked, why these firms would support such a small newspaper unless it was for services rendered.[45]

The *Popolo d'Italia* had been originally launched as a socialist paper, but by 1918 the message had changed a good deal. It now condemned marxism as a 'heap of ruins' containing obsolete doctrines such as class war, economic determinism and the dictatorship of the proletariat. In March 1918, Mussolini dropped the quotation printed on the front page – 'revolution is an idea that has found bayonets'. In May, editorials proclaimed that capitalism, far from having been superseded, was in its early stages. In July, the subtitle of the paper was changed from 'a socialist newspaper' to 'the newspaper of combatants and producers'. The editor wrote that some months previously he had suddenly realised that he no longer believed in socialism but in the *trincerocrazia*: he explained that every intelligent man must change his views from time to time, adding that giving up the pretence of being a socialist afforded him a sense of genuine relief.[46]

He took pains to justify the part he had played in forcing an unenthusiastic Italy into the war, trying to establish that the war had been a huge success, winning almost all the nationalist gains he had ever hoped for. It had secured 'natural frontiers' in the north and north-east;[47] it had succeeded in being a 'war to end wars' by inaugurating a new era of liberty and justice. It had also helped to emancipate the working classes who now had the prospect of a more prosperous life and 'centuries of celestial felicity'; in this sense it had truly been a 'war for democracy', ending the reign of monarchic dynasties and enfranchising the masses.[48]

Almost at once, however, he sensed that it would be more expedient to go to the other extreme and foster dissatisfaction with the war. In place of the rosy myth of a triumphal victory he began to create an equally false myth of a 'mutilated peace'. For example, the League of Nations, for which he had once ardently worked,[49] he now saw as a hindrance to Italian ambitions and a mere instrument of Anglo-Saxon hegemony.[50] More than any other country, Italy should insist on her right to a 'great imperial destiny' and territorial expansion must be a primary aim, whether the rest of the world approved or not.[51] He sometimes tried to deny that this could be classified as imperialism: all imperialism was wrong, but Italians were being cheated out of the 'booty' in the Middle East that was their due and defrauded of their right to be the dominant power in the Mediterranean.[52] Therefore, without waiting for international consent, they should annex Fiume and Dalmatia,[53] while at the same time helping the patriotic forces in India, Egypt and Ireland to undermine that pillar of the status quo, the British Empire.[54]

Mussolini's journalistic style prompted him to take an extreme position whenever possible. Extremism was always dramatic and eye-catching. He was far more concerned with tactics than with ideas, and his violent changeability was bound to seem confused if measured by strict logic; but he had discovered that readers liked extreme views and rarely bothered much about inconsistency. If he appeared successively as champion of the League and then nationalist, as socialist and then conservative, as monarchist and then republican, this was less out of muddle-headedness than out of a search for striking headlines and a wish to become all things to all men. He carefully avoided alliance with any existing political group, because he did not want to help any one party into power except his own and he himself would be better served by perpetuating an unstable balance of forces that he could exploit. An eclectic policy cutting across party barriers would provide the best opportunity of entering politics on his own terms. Socialism, nationalism, internationalism and anti-clericalism had each been pre-empted by other parties, but he might be able to create a mixture of ideas drawn from all the others. He had to grasp opportunities as they offered themselves, to ride the crest of the wave produced by post-war instability. Inflation, demobilisation, the excessive expectations from peace, and a new upthrust from a growing middle class, put a premium on a populist policy that appealed to discontent and ambition wherever they might be found. He called himself a man for all seasons, 'an adventurer for all roads'.[55] As he said, 'I put my finger on the pulse of the masses and suddenly discovered in the general mood of disorientation that a public opinion was waiting for me, and I just had to make it recognise me through my newspaper'.[56]

In the early months of 1919, he was fairly sure that the parliamentary regime in Italy was drifting to an end and 'the succession was now open'.[57] As he felt his way towards a new public, he openly played up to the capitalist classes[58] but hinted privately to the socialists that he might be at their disposal if they were ready to support his brand of populist dictatorship.[59] The main difficulty was that he needed anti-capitalist slogans to capture a broad base among the masses and the demobilised soldiers, yet needed the reputation of being a potential anti-socialist in order to reassure the rich and win financial support for his newspaper. In riding these two horses at once he learnt the valuable lesson of how it is possible for a skilled politician to reconcile apparent opposites.

The fascist movement

4

1919

On 23 March 1919, Mussolini launched a movement that was to become, two years later, the fascist party. The word 'fascist' had already been appropriated by other groups, but through his newspaper he gradually established exclusive claim to it. The meeting of 23 March took place in a hall provided by Milanese businessmen in the Piazza San Sepolcro, and those present were eventually given the name of *sansepolcristi*. According to Mussolini only about fifty people were there; however, in later years, when the fact of being a *sansepolcrista* automatically entitled someone to a higher salary, hundreds of others managed to have their names added to the list.

Mussolini had hoped for a much more imposing assembly to inaugurate a movement that he hoped would aim at supplanting the parliamentary regime, but the meeting was barely noticed by the national press and it was hard to take seriously such a rag-bag of futurists, anarchists, communists, syndicalists, republicans, Catholics, nationalists and liberals of various kinds. Few of those present had much idea as to what the objectives of the movement should be.[1] The *Popolo d'Italia* pretended that a programme was agreed unanimously but Mussolini on the contrary stated that he had no programme. He was still feeling his way – anxious to make a composite movement and to leave various paths open for alternative developments as might become advisable.[2] Between March and June, however, certain items of policy gradually emerged which suggest that the futurists surrounding Marinetti were the predominant element in the Milanese *fascio*.[3] The ideas put forward by this group bear little relation to Mussolini's political philosophy of ten years later. These early fascists were strongly anti-clerical and wanted confiscation of ecclesiastical property;[4] they favoured ending the monarchy;[5] they opposed any kind of dictatorship or arbitrary power and demanded an independent judiciary.[6] 'We are libertarians above all,' wrote Mussolini, 'loving liberty for everyone, even for our enemies.' He said he would do everything possible to prevent censorship and preserve free thought and speech, because these were among the 'highest expressions of human civilisation'.[7]

These libertarian ideals were stressed by Mussolini as distinguishing fascism from socialism, yet this early fascist programme was in favour of almost as radical a change in society as that advocated by the socialists. It called for 'land to the peasants' and workers' representation in industrial management,[8] as well as a progressive tax on capital,[9] expropriation of land and factories,[10] greater inheritance taxes and confiscation of excessive war profits.[11] In addition, it demanded nationalisation of the armaments industry, a legally fixed minimum wage, abolition of the senate, votes for women and a large-scale decentralisation of government.[12] These proposals were almost all quietly discarded later, as soon as Mussolini decided that his best hope of winning power lay in an entirely different direction.

If the futurists were largely responsible for formulating this initial fascist programme, the first activist success was largely the handiwork of the *arditi*, a loose organisation of ex-servicemen that pre-dated the fascist movement by some months. Its freebooting activities were similar to those of the *Freikorps* in post-war Germany and its achievements taught Mussolini the invaluable lesson that squads of armed men could be very useful in intimidating opposition.

On 15 April 1919, the office and printing-works of the socialist newspaper *Avanti!*, including linotype machinery and list of subscribers, were attacked and destroyed. The futurist leader, Marinetti, and Ferruccio Vecchi the leader of the *arditi* – both of whom had attended the inaugural fascist meeting – were the directing force behind the attack. Mussolini himself held aloof,[13] judging that he lacked the strength to risk a street battle, but was quick to defend what had happened and was soon claiming this riot in Milan as the first material achievement of the fascist revolution.[14] He took good note that when the victims of street violence were on the extreme left the police would intervene very little if at all; also that the socialists, for all their talk of revolution, were essentially pacifists who could be easily overcome by a tiny group of men prepared to shoot and be shot. He at once proceeded to recruit a private army of several hundred *arditi*, and sackloads of military equipment were brought to the offices of the *Popolo d'Italia* in case of a counter-attack by other *arditi* who had joined the socialists.

When Francesco Saverio Nitti became prime minister in June 1919, the fascists announced their opposition to him as a man who had not wanted the war of 1914–18. They opposed him also as representing a parliamentary system which they intended to supersede. Parliament was, to them, a vulgar deception whose continued existence kept an ageing and useless ruling class in power.[15] As it contained no one party with anything like a majority of deputies, cabinets tended to be simply coalitions of factions, each one trying to thwart the rest. Mussolini argued that new constitutional forms were necessary – for example, small technical assemblies to deal with different aspects of national life. Though he was no longer so eager for violent revolution, he still talked of a possible 'bath of blood'[16] and during the summer his name was linked with more rumours of a planned *coup d'état*.[17]

In the area of foreign policy, he espoused a popular cause by asserting Italy's right to predominate in the Adriatic. Rejecting his earlier view, he now argued that the whole Dalmatian coast should become Italian, asserting that such an indisputable claim need not be brought before the peace conference at Paris. The new Jugoslav kingdom he condemned as an absurdity; the 'so-called Jugoslavs' should be split up into small Croat, Serb and Slovene states in order to facilitate Italy's penetration of the Balkans.[18] He let it be known that his fascists were ready to launch a piratical expedition to capture Fiume: seizing this port would be a fine example of rebellion against the 'Anglo-Saxon tyranny' being imposed on Europe at Paris. It would be a noble act of national self-assertion and a defiance of Nitti and parliament.[19]

In September 1919, not Mussolini but the poet Gabriele D'Annunzio led a raid on Fiume, supported by mutinous elements of the Italian army. Mussolini had already talked to D'Annunzio about such a raid, but his immediate reaction to the news was one of alarm at being upstaged by a more picturesque and daring personality. Nevertheless, once it had happened and when neither the Italian nor any other government intervened to stop it, with his sure political intuition he pledged his support for what looked like another episode in the anti-parliamentary movement that had begun with the declaration of war in May 1915. He had to operate another difficult balancing act, being anxious to accept some of the credit in the event of success, yet not wanting to risk being too closely associated with failure. D'Annunzio wrote to call him a coward for not coming to fight in person in Fiume. But these offensive words were removed before the letter was published in the *Popolo d'Italia*:[20] it was important for Mussolini not to let readers imagine D'Annunzio to be more revolutionary and courageous than himself.

The 'march on Rome' by which the fascists came to power in 1922 was developed as an idea at Fiume in 1919. D'Annunzio claimed that it was he who first thought of using Fiume as a base for the march.[21] The proposal was supported by the futurists and some nationalists, as well as by some socialists and anarchists. It also had the active support of dissident fascists who were impatient with their leader's indecision.[22]

Mussolini wrote guardedly in public on this delicate topic. Although he did not wish to appear to be hesitating, he wanted no one but himself to lead the revolution; he also felt sure, and probably correctly, that D'Annunzio would bungle it. In a private note, he outlined a plan for capturing various Italian cities and proclaiming D'Annunzio as honorary president of an Italian republic. In public, he referred to the possibility of an insurrection that would win support from the armed services before marching on Rome. But, again in private, he counselled D'Annunzio not to risk such a dangerous move and to pin his hopes instead on the parliamentary elections in November: these elections might register a defeat for the government and give the revolution a better chance of success.[23] In the meantime, some of the money collected by the *Popolo d'Italia* for the Fiume enterprise (much of it from the United States) was diverted by Mussolini for use in his own election campaign.

The elections of November 1919 took place under new rules with proportional representation and without single-member constituencies. Mussolini said these new rules were absolutely necessary, perhaps envisaging that they would make effective government more difficult by producing a parliament that was even more of a patchwork of small parties. However, the fascists approached the election in some disarray, with each local group deciding its own electoral programme, some moving sharply to the right. At Milan, Mussolini himself put forward a decidedly leftist and anti-clerical programme, asking once again for a capital levy, greater inheritance taxes, and a constituent assembly to oust the monarchy.[24] He also suggested forming electoral alliances with the socialists and other parties on the left, but they would not agree unless he himself stood down, since they thought he might be a liability with the voters.[25] The correctness of their analysis was proved when, despite his own confidence in success, Mussolini failed miserably against the socialists who obtained forty times as many votes. In Mussolini's home village of Predappio there was not a single supporter of fascism. Nor, indeed, did any other fascist candidate succeed – their first deputy was elected a year later and in very different circumstances. Mussolini employed his squads of paid and uniformed fighters to attend his own meetings, boasting that he preferred using bombs and guns rather than ballot papers against his opponents.[26]

The illegal possession of arms led the police to arrest him after the elections, along with Vecchi, Marinetti and a hundred other fascists. He was released the next day by government order. This was an ominous sign: it shows that the authorities, just as by their passive attitude towards D'Annunzio, were deliberately conniving at illegality, and their astonishing reluctance to punish illegal fascist activities during the next two years was to be a major factor in bringing Mussolini to power. Disappointed by their defeat, a group of fascists (including a petty criminal, Albino Volpi, who was especially close to Mussolini and was used later to assassinate the socialist leader Matteotti) threw a bomb into a celebration parade held by the socialists. Several small bombs were also sent in packages to the cardinal archbishop of Milan and the socialist mayor. Arnaldo Mussolini commented after these outrages that deep down in his brother's character there was a deplorable streak of delinquency.[27]

As a result of such an electoral catastrophe, many fascists abandoned the movement, and at the end of 1919, according to one member of the central committee, fewer than 4,000 committed adherents were left in the whole of Italy.[28] Their leader seemed finished. As his paper was moving into deficit and his family was short of money,[29] he briefly reconsidered emigrating. He said he was tired of journalism and as an alternative was planning the plots of several books – they were going to be distinctly sordid, treating of murder, venereal disease, incest and madness.[30] But within days he recovered his poise and in making the most of a few shreds of consolation he showed talent and resilience of an exceptional order. Fortunately for him the new parliament was more unmanageable than ever, with 300 out of 500 deputies elected for the first time and so many small groups that there could hardly be an effective governmental coalition of any kind. The socialist deputies were the largest group of all, and this also proved fortunate as it alarmed the conservatives in the country, encouraging some of them to purchase the support of the fascist squads. As Mussolini had failed to persuade the electorate by argument in free elections, he saw instead that he might be able to use brute force as D'Annunzio had done so successfully; the fascists had failed as a leftist movement but might have better luck on the right.

His one important asset was ownership of the *Popolo d'Italia*, insofar as this paper, like Hitler's *Völkischer Beobachter*, could be used to mobilise a personal following; in later years he took care not to let others have similar facility of contact with a mass audience. He was also lucky to find a new source of finance from moneyed interests which recognised that such a newspaper, if it adjusted its politics, might be worth their support. At this point several of his chief assistants resigned: they resented his continuing employment of desperadoes for purposes of intimidation and, even more, his adoption of a more conservative policy for the paper without consulting his staff.[31]

As an editor, Mussolini used to concentrate on his own leading articles which he wrote at speed in about twenty minutes with little need for corrections. He was less concerned with the other pages and regularly left his collaborators in the dark about general policy until they read his own article, often just before going to press.[32] He sometimes failed to recognise members of his staff when they had been working in his office for months.[33] As he paid them little, they were comparatively undistinguished, but his own contributions gave the paper a polemical and aggressive stance: he had developed a very effective style, energetic and incisive enough to cover up weaknesses of argument. The technique that he recommended was to be always 'electric' and 'explosive'.[34] He took pride in being able to write on either side of any subject and in adopting a simple but always forceful line; there was no point in rehearsing all the arguments on an issue, because the object was to sweep readers off their feet, not to provide them with the material for a continuing debate.

1920

The elections indicated that the prevailing sentiment in the country was to the left and Mussolini acknowledged this fact by still in 1920 calling himself a socialist, albeit a dissident. He continued to campaign for nationalisation of the land, workers' participation in the running of factories and partial expropriation of capital;[35] but he took care to confuse the issue by stressing that inside his movement there was room for all political beliefs or none at all.[36] Fascism, according to circumstance, could be either 'reactionary' or 'revolutionary' and could adapt as necessary to either class war or class co-operation.[37] Some observers were reminded of the magic mirror in which everyone, whether militaristic reactionary or extreme pacifist on the left, could see his heart's desire.[38]

To preside over such a varied collection of people and ideas was far from easy. In some areas, the local group or *fascio* knew little about Mussolini and tended to follow their own immediate leader. These local leaders were called *ras*, a catchword taken from the semi-independent chieftains of Abyssinia. Some of them were not only independent but powerful, with their own uniformed bodyguards of *squadristi*, or members of the fascist squads, that were employed to enforce local protection rackets and sometimes to poach on each other's territory. One *ras* could be on the political left, his neighbour on the right; one would be a republican, another a monarchist; some were anti-clerical, others the opposite; some were no better than gangsters, while some were idealists who sincerely wished to renew the political life of the country. Mussolini's great skill was to keep such a variegated coalition together and eventually to convince all its elements that he alone could gain some leverage for fascism in national politics. He sensed that the centre of gravity of the movement was gradually shifting away from the left and, though it would be wise to remain as long as possible an *omnium gatherum*, a leftist programme offered small chance of success in competition with the recently triumphant socialists; his best hope of acquiring readers and a good financial basis lay more to the right. During 1920 he therefore moved away from his earlier anti-clericalism and even came to admit that there could be some advantage in being labelled reactionary and imperialist.[39]

According to later mythology, Mussolini saved Italy not only from German militarism in 1915, but also from a bolshevist revolution in 1920–2. Both claims were false. Writing at the time, he agreed that the danger of bolshevism was no worse than in England or France and, although strikes and inflation were as serious a problem in Italy as elsewhere, they were less so in 1921 than in 1920.[40] He knew very well that Italian socialists lacked anyone capable of carrying out their own kind of revolution. The one leader who might have led a socialist revolution was – according to Lenin and Trotsky – Mussolini himself,[41] and he was now discovering that the best chance of revolution lay elsewhere.

Nevertheless, Lenin was the contemporary politician whom he most admired and he studied the Russian revolution closely to see what lessons it offered.[42] Lenin seemed to him 'the very negation of socialism' because he had not created a dictatorship of the proletariat or of the socialist party, but only of a few intellectuals who had found the secret of winning power.[43] Mussolini was, in truth, envious. He criticised the lack of free speech in Russia and the refusal to permit strikes or tolerate opposition newspapers; even more he condemned the barbarities he saw in Russia and claimed to be shocked at what he called a tyranny worse than that of the tsars;[44] but he was still prepared to learn from Lenin's successes and failures. At the same time, he carefully promoted the legend of a communist danger in Italy against which he would be in the front line of attack.

An event that fuelled this legend was the occupation of a number of factories by the workers in northern Italy during September 1920. Mussolini later presented this as a symptom and symbol of Italy's imminent slide towards communist barbarianism, but at the time his attitude was one of tolerant acceptance.[45] He even arranged a secret meeting with the workers' representatives and hinted to them that he was the man who might lead them to victory.[46] No doubt he was waiting to see how far they succeeded. But the movement soon fizzled out – further evidence that Italy's trade unionists and socialists were not of Lenin's ilk and would never seize control of the state: they were revolutionaries only in name and would be defenceless if the fascist armed squads went into action against them.[47]

By the autumn of 1920, Mussolini's qualified support of D'Annunzio's *coup* in Fiume gave him a useful following among those who wanted a stronger Italian presence in the Balkans. At Trieste, a frontier town where Italian and Slav met in awkward contiguity, a group of fascists proved that the squads would find enthusiastic local support when they beat up Slavs in the streets and he delightedly encouraged them to further acts of bloodshed and vandalism. On a short visit to Trieste, he was mobbed by an enthusiastic crowd and applauded by uniformed soldiers in what was his first real taste of popular acclaim.[48]

Further south in the Adriatic, he found another patriotic cause when the liberal-minded and pacific Giolitti, now prime minister again, withdrew Italian troops from Albania where they had been since 1914. Mussolini, in his typically rhetorical style, called this withdrawal a blow to Italian prestige worse even than Caporetto: it was 'a disgusting exhibition of national cowardice', especially as it might make the Jugoslavs think that Italy was now feeble and unwarlike; the people responsible should be shot. Italy on the contrary needed to wield a 'big stick' against the 'barbarian' Slavs and open a path for expansion to the Near East. Mussolini was beginning to envisage a time when Italy would dominate the whole Mediterranean and the axis of European power would move away from London and Paris to Rome – a natural bridgehead between east and west.[49]

Giolitti's refusal to use the big stick in Albania and Dalmatia was the kind of issue to arouse demobilised officers who found themselves without a job. Mussolini again contacted D'Annunzio about the possibility of marching on Rome and overthrowing such a spineless government. They might well get support from the conservatives and the Vatican, as well as among university students, schoolboys and the young unemployed; they might also be able to suborn elements of the armed forces to mutiny in such a patriotic cause. Mussolini feared that France and Britain would try to stop any revolution that threatened the existing equilibrium in the Mediterranean, in which case he would turn for help to the recently defeated Germans who would be glad to redress the balance of European power. His assumption was that, since the old regime in Italy was decrepit, a well-prepared push might eliminate it altogether. Apart from Giolitti, who was now too old, no parliamentary leader had the political skill and strength of character to resist a determined insurrection.[50]

1921

In January 1921 the socialist party was weakened in numbers when its more extreme wing defected to found a communist party. This posed a possible threat to fascism, because the socialists who remained – and they were still more numerous than any other group in parliament – were mostly moderates who might conceivably be persuaded to join Giolitti's coalition. Such an alliance between liberals and socialists would provide a parliamentary majority that might make effective government possible. To prevent it, Mussolini indicated to Giolitti that the fascists would be an alternative political alliance for him, and the offer was accepted. The government could easily have crushed the disorderly fascist squads in the same way as in

December 1920 they had already put paid to D'Annunzio's rebellion at Fiume, but Giolitti misread the situation. His intention was to tame the fascists by bringing them inside his coalition, using them in the general elections of May 1921 to weaken some of the other opposition parties. But he proved less skilful than they in the game of mutual deceit.

Mussolini annoyed many of his own followers when he agreed to join the liberals and nationalists in a common election campaign, because this was a distinctively conservative grouping. What was worse, his psychological urge to pose as an extremist led him to claim that he represented the extreme right wing of this conservative group. His argument was that only by becoming more conservative and respectable would he succeed in being a real force in the country,[51] but he also argued that it would be an immense tactical advantage for the fascists to fight the elections with the authority of the police and the prefects behind them. To appeal to the extreme right, he issued further demands for the British to be chased out of the Mediterranean and claimed that Italians alone, proud representatives of the Aryan race, had a right to domination over *mare nostrum*. Fascist foreign policy, he repeated, was summed up in the words 'imperialism' and 'national expansion'.[52]

The elections took place in conditions of unusual violence: perhaps as many as a hundred people were killed, and the atmosphere of officially permitted intimidation influenced the results significantly – some areas of Italy were virtually under fascist control and socialists could not even hold their election meetings.[53] The police sometimes lent their trucks to the fascist squads; some units of the army gave them weapons; magistrates tended to decide any prosecutions in their favour and thus assure them of impunity.[54] Giolotti said he regretted the extent of this unpunished violence, but made only half-hearted attempts to stop it, and his fascist allies felt strong enough to threaten that they would suppress any other parties that dared to put up resistance.[55] The result was that Mussolini, though in 1919 he had obtained no deputies and almost no votes at all, picked up 35 parliamentary seats in 1921 – about 7 per cent of the total. He had hoped for even more and was very disappointed that the 122 socialists were still the largest group of deputies, followed by the Catholic *popolari* with 107. Yet Giolitti and the liberals, by helping him into parliament, had given him a new authority, a new respectability and a valuable freedom from arrest: a judicial case against him was pending 'for intent to overthrow the government by violence', and he was now saved from this by his immunity as an elected deputy.[56]

The liberals saw their mistake too late when, despite Mussolini's name being included on the list of government-sponsored candidates, he suddenly announced that he would vote with the opposition as soon as parliament met. He had got all he wanted out of his electoral alliance with liberalism and once he realised that Giolitti did not have enough support to form a new government, preferred to make himself available for other developments.

As he had so little enthusiasm for parliament as an institution, he did not look forward to sitting through long, inconsequential debates, especially since he must have feared that his style of oratory would not suit a parliamentary audience. Judging that Italian politics were likely to move further towards the right,[57] he defied parliamentary custom and took his seat on the extreme right of the amphitheatre where few people before him had liked to be seen; but he rarely attended sessions and refused all familiarity with the other deputies.[58] The main advantage to him of being in parliament was to be the publicity given to debates. His first speech, appealing ostentatiously to the conservatives, took what he called a 'reactionary' stand against collectivisation and nationalisation: he even asked for the postal and railway services to be given to private enterprise.[59] Nor did he conceal his view that, before very long, Italy might decide to renounce the democratic system and turn to a dictator.[60]

The new parliament was hardly in session before the fascist deputies, under his personal direction,[61] physically attacked the communist deputy Misiano and threw him out of the building on the pretext of having been a deserter during the war; they brandished revolvers in the chamber and threatened other socialists with the same treatment.[62] Astonishing though it may seem, the government took no action against such behaviour: the various liberal factions surrounding Nitti, Giolitti, Salandra and Orlando were still more interested in quarrelling among themselves than in gratuitously offending the fascists.

Mussolini overreached himself, however, when he tried to compel the other fascist deputies to boycott the king's speech. This strange action suggests that perhaps he did not want to be identified too closely with the conservatives. He appears to have assumed that the other fascists would take their programme from him without discussion; when they refused he threatened them, too, with physical violence.[63] But, unlike others, they were not to be intimidated; they outvoted him over the tactics to adopt, and this damaging defeat led some observers to consider that he might lack the subtlety of other parliamentary leaders.[64]

But he was quickly learning about the deviousness that a policy of opportunism required. One of the valuable lessons he had learnt as a journalist was that the public was easily deceived and an editor could change his views without most readers worrying or even noticing. For example, a few months earlier he had condemned Christianity as 'detestable' and called on the Pope to leave Rome for good,[65] but at once changed when he realised that there would be advantages in an alliance with the Church. He began to advocate that the government should subsidise churches and religious schools,[66] hoping that in return the Vatican – which had already condemned liberalism and socialism – would take a further step of discountenancing the Catholic *popolari* as being too far to the left. This would weaken his opponents and assist him by further undermining the free operation of parliament.

Whether fascism had a generally accepted programme on this or other matters was hard for most observers to say. Mussolini still sometimes denied that he had any programme because he wanted to appeal simultaneously to 'aristocrats and democrats, revolutionaries and reactionaries, proletarians and anti-proletarians, pacifists and anti-pacifists'.[67] But he also feared that people would undervalue fascism if it appeared to believe in so little and changed its mind so blatantly. In August 1921 he announced the establishment of a school of 'fascist culture' in Milan to study and demonstrate fascist doctrine[68] and already he had made clear that the 'extreme leftist' programme of 1919 would be discarded.[69] This reflected a change that had been taking place in the composition of the movement. Only one of the fascists who entered parliament in 1921 had been a *sansepolcrista* in March 1919:[70] most of its original adherents – including Marinetti, Vecchi, and the conductor Toscanini – had left or lost interest on the grounds that fascism was becoming unprincipled, corrupt, authoritarian, and moving far away from its earlier left-wing idealism.[71]

In July, Mussolini, though still sitting on the extreme right of the Chamber, effected another radical shift in policy when he unexpectedly suggested a coalition between fascists, socialists and *popolari*.[72] This remarkable volte-face appears to have been a calculated and surreptitious bid for power; or perhaps he was hoping that the conservatives would be frightened into buying him off. Possibly it was just a tactic to divert people's minds away from an event that had occurred a few days previously. In the small town of Sarzana a dozen policemen had fired on and routed a large mob of rioting fascists. This had called the bluff of fascist violence – it was proof that, when they wanted to, the authorities could easily quell the terrifying excesses of *squadrismo* that were now taking place every weekend throughout Italy.

Mussolini himself, the representative of 'urban fascism' in Milan, did not altogether like the more violent 'agrarian fascism' of the *ras* that was backed by the rich landowners of Emilia and the Po valley; he feared agrarian fascism as a rival contender for the leadership of his movement and was especially worried that, after the catastrophe of Sarzana, a continuation of brutal squad violence might lead to a more general defeat at the hands of the police. Early in August, therefore, he challenged these potential rivals head-on by signing a formal pact of pacification with the socialists and undertaking to bring punitive raids to an end. The *ras* – in particular three of the leading provincial

45

bosses, Dino Grandi, Italo Balbo and Roberto Farinacci – refused to accept such an entirely unexpected agreement with the enemy, because they rightly feared that the end of *squadrismo* would mean the end of their local power. Their attempt at insubordination prompted Mussolini to retort that fascism was his child: it must obey him or he would destroy it.[73] Agrarian fascism, he wrote, represented 'the private interests of the most sinister and contemptible classes in Italy'. He was not entirely wrong in this judgement, but he had overestimated his own strength and a few days later, finding himself once again in a minority, he resigned his position as *Duce*, or leader of fascism, saying that it was a title he had never much liked.[74]

Resignation was an acknowledgement that his pact with the socialists was a tactical error, but he quickly shifted ground to regain his position of command; as he reminded people in private, fascism was not a system of immutable beliefs but a path to political power.[75] The change became public knowledge in November at the third national congress of fascism in Rome. During the first two days of the congress the 'urban fascists' seemed in a minority, with most of the applause going to Grandi, but later Mussolini won a great oratorical victory, confessing his mistake over the pact with socialism and convincing the rank and file that he was the one man who could lead them to victory. The congress, as well as accepting a thoroughly anti-socialist and pro-free-enterprise policy, also agreed to his request that the movement become a properly disciplined party, and a directorate was appointed in which his own Milanese faction was dominant. This was a personal success, but in order to heal the rift with the agrarians he had to confirm his adherence to Grandi's policy of squad violence. Thousands of armed fascists ran riot in Rome while the discussions were in progress and there was no effective intervention by the authorities. The suggestion was even made to Mussolini that this would be the right moment to use these armed squads to take over the government by force. But he judged it to be too risky and told the activists they should wait for another year.[76]

Looking back over 1921, Mussolini accepted that the most solid and promising achievement of his movement had been the quasi-military organisation of these fascist squads, and the best hope for the future lay in the fact that the police, if not directly provoked, acted only half-heartedly against them. If the party was divided over policies and personalities, it was at least united over the tactics of violence, which were proving a powerful aid to recruitment. Violence obviously attracted youth, and students in particular took pleasure in administering castor oil by the litre to their victims. In September, a band of fascist students killed the socialist deputy for Bari, Di Vagno. During the same month, in a 'march on Ravenna', Balbo's squads employed young men wearing the black shirts of the war-time *arditi* as a regular military uniform; they had learnt from D'Annunzio at Fiume to use the Roman salute with raised arm and sing Salvatore Gotta's song of youth, 'Giovinezza', that the *arditi* had made popular.

In November, all local fascist groups were enjoined by Mussolini to form their own squad; his assumption was that, if every fascist was a *squadrista*, the government would not dare to suppress these armed units without putting itself in the wrong by having to outlaw the whole fascist party.[77] An open threat was issued that if there was any attempt at suppression the fascists might move to the other extreme and join the communists in revolutionary action.[78] Meanwhile the squads were organised into something like a national militia, being grouped into cohorts which were in turn grouped into legions commanded by 'consuls'; these in turn were organised under zone commanders. Mussolini himself used to travel with his bodyguard of armed *squadristi* and by the end of 1921 was claiming, no doubt with great exaggeration, that he had 400,000 armed and disciplined men at his command.[79]

Even in his early days as a socialist he had advocated the formation of armed groups for violent action[80] and in 1921 he took it as axiomatic that terrorist tactics were a necessary weapon to achieve political victory. Fascism thrived in an environment of insecurity, so it was expedient to foment disorder. The main qualification was that terrorism should not be taken to the point where it would cause a revulsion of feeling in the country or appear as simply violence for its own sake. Used judiciously, it was highly effective. Fascism was in fact succeeding not because of ideology but much more because punitive expeditions intimidated the socialist opposition and attracted rich backers. Mussolini had, of course, to admit that not all fascists agreed with these tactics – some were horrified as they saw *squadrismo* and a doctrine of authoritarianism conferring almost dictatorial powers on a ruthless man who might lead Italy to its ruin.[81] But he knew that in compensation he would gain recruits from those who liked extremism, enjoyed violence, or found in squad action a means of acquiring power and wealth in their home towns.

Equally valuable were recruits from other parties who saw in fascism a way of replacing an anarchic parliamentary system by a more disciplined, centralised state. These included some of the conservative liberals who looked on Giolitti as dangerously easy-going and almost a socialist. It was these to whom Mussolini was appealing when he announced that capitalism would flourish best if Italy discarded democracy and accepted dictatorship as necessary in order to crush socialism and make government effective.[82] He attended parliament less and less: he saw it as increasingly irrelevant. He was still prepared to use legal or parliamentary means to win power if that were

47

possible but did not conceal the fact that he was also preparing to use the legions of his private army.[83]

1922

Following a succession of half a dozen short-lived governments after the war, Luigi Facta became prime minister in February 1922, the last liberal premier before Mussolini took over. Facta, a negligible politician, was chosen because the other liberal leaders were too jealous of each other to form a strong coalition against the anti-democratic forces on the left and right. His appointment suited the fascists admirably because it was a final demonstration that the parliamentary regime could not produce a stable government or defend law and order. A few days afterwards, they tested the government's resolution by instigating another insurrection at Fiume, dispossessing the urban authorities at gunpoint and appointing a new administration.

When the experiment proved successful, Mussolini ordered attacks on other strategically placed cities in Italy. Balbo, who, like Grandi, had joined the fascist movement late in the day, proved just the man to use terrorist tactics for intimidating local government authorities. Cynical, brave, ambitious, and a ruthless hatchet-man, Balbo was admired by Mussolini and other fascists who were more squeamish and less imaginative in their cruelties. This 25-year-old gang leader led his armed columns through the provinces of Ferrara and Ravenna, leaving a trail of destruction and death behind him. Since his chief targets were socialist administrations and property belonging to trade unions, some public authorities actively encouraged this terrifying breakdown of the law, and Balbo was supplied with plenty of money to acquire explosives and machine guns.

Such connivance is an indication that many people were delighted to see the socialist movement destroyed; but the general disorientation also reflects Mussolini's clever policy of adapting to widely differing local conditions and leading other political parties to believe that he was secretly working in their interests. Fascism, he reminded them, was a 'super-relativist movement' with no fixed principles, ready for almost any alliance.[84] In July 1922 he even hinted again at a possible association with the socialists and *popolari*, as an earnest of which he momentarily ordered his followers to stop their public brutalities.[85]

But his appeal continued to be mostly to the conservatives: the world, he repeated, was moving rapidly away from liberalism, even in England.[86] He dissembled with the monarchists by privately assuring them that his republican utterances were not intended seriously,[87] and he courted the right-wing liberals by suggesting to Salandra that since they agreed on foreign policy they should form a parliamentary alliance.[88] The eager search for allies indicates a fear of becoming isolated. This was especially true after three of his small group of deputies deserted to join the nationalists while Grandi and Balbo were less than enthusiastic over his leadership. To encourage support from the nationalists, he tried to deny that he had ever spoken of the national flag as a rag to plant on a dunghill: on the contrary, fascists believed in war and in empire – admittedly they were also revolutionary but revolutions did not come only from the left.[89]

At the beginning of August the socialists made the feeble gesture of calling a general strike in protest at the lack of law and order and this played into Mussolini's hands. The fascists at once concentrated on strike-breaking, thus greatly increasing their value to the conservatives while at the same time giving the squads more experience of working together. Suddenly he was able to pose as no longer an enemy of the law but its defender. Better still, he used the opportunity to smash the printing presses of other socialist newspapers. Most important of all, by helping to crush the strike he destroyed the morale of the socialists just when the government was demonstrating its own incompetence.

Without saying much even to his own colleagues, he continued the double policy he found so effective, saying that he was ready to seek power inside the parliamentary system but also hinting that he might be ready for a *coup d'état*.[90] Facta knew he was preparing for a *coup*, but the cabinet could never agree on the appropriate action to prevent it.[91] Nor were the socialists able to rouse their large following to counter the threat: some, after being demoralised by a failed strike, became simply passive spectators, while others welcomed the 'reactionary buffoonery' of fascism as a means of destroying what was left of social democracy and so preparing the way for communist revolution. It was most fortunate for Mussolini that his opponents did not take him entirely seriously, looking on him either as a mere journalist, a charlatan they could ignore, or someone they could possibly exploit.[92]

Throughout September and part of October, he pushed both aspects of his double policy. With one hand he held out the expectation that the fascists, if accepted inside a government coalition, would not only make parliament work but would renounce republicanism, reduce taxes, and balance the budget, while also annexing Dalmatia and making Italy a major power in the Mediterranean. With the other hand he allowed his fascist squads to launch an attack on the towns of Bolzano and Trent, this time not against socialist town councils but in direct challenge to the government itself. When it succeeded beyond his expectations, he realised that the cabinet was so divided that he could increase the pressure with little risk. So confused and partisan were the

Italian liberals that senator Luigi Albertini, one of the most sophisticated spokesmen and editor of the leading liberal newspaper, thought that the fascist occupation of Trent should persuade Facta to include Mussolini in the cabinet.[93]

For many people in Italy this was a time of depression, hopelessness and fear, similar to that which followed the defeat of Caporetto. Many were as frightened of socialist talk as of revolution and were ready to look on Mussolini as a lesser evil – someone who, if not providing the answer, would be better than nothing. The middle classes were not yet prepared to accept their social inferiors as a partner in government, and assumed that any concession to the left would be a step towards revolution. They were not able to imagine that the real danger of revolution came from a patriotic movement on the right. They were appalled by the lack of public order in what Mussolini himself referred to as a civil war.[94] The railway and postal services were breaking down; there was an alarming growth in robbery and assassination;[95] above all, no parliamentary leader could suggest what ought to be done about it and the parliamentary system itself seemed condemned by its own inactivity.

Though many things were playing into Mussolini's hands, his own political skill and sense of timing were remarkable. Hitler, by comparison, after spending several years planning a *Putsch* that failed in 1923, won power only ten years afterwards. Mussolini kept his own counsel and said little to the other fascist leaders, partly because he feared the disloyalty of the *ras* and the indiscipline of their squads. For a time he seems to have had no precise plan, except to keep open many possibilities of both advance and retreat. He was probably still anticipating a parliamentary and legal victory, though he was also intensifying preparations for a seizure of power – an armed *coup* would, no doubt, have been more to his liking.[96]

Meanwhile he worked out his tactics for dealing with possible opponents. He needed to sound out, and if possible neutralise, both the Vatican and the king.[97] He also needed the passive or active help of D'Annunzio, who as a more prestigious leader than himself, might be extremely dangerous as an enemy. His chief luck was that the liberal parliamentarians, unable to agree among themselves, were all seeking to promote their own careers by bringing him into a coalition and were as anxious to scuttle each other as to prevent a fascist revolution. Orlando and Amendola thought the best answer was a coalition that included fascism;[98] and Nitti, hoping for the premiership once more, now accepted that an alliance with Mussolini would be the best means of by-passing his enemy, Giolitti.[99] Even some ministers in Facta's government were in touch with the fascists and through them Mussolini had the advantage of knowing what was said about him in cabinet.[100]

One person who, according to Mussolini, might have prevented the march on Rome and who had already shown that he was ready to use the army to put down the rebellion in Fiume was Giolitti. But this grand old man of Italian politics, whose eightieth birthday fell on 27 October, did not want to travel all the way south to Rome until there was a genuine likelihood that the king would ask him to form a government. Facta asked him repeatedly to come but he waited until too late – a mistake he later regretted. The fascists flattered and partially neutralised Giolitti by sending privately to say that they wanted him as head of government again.[101] Unbeknown to him, they were saying much the same to Nitti, Salandra and Facta. Giolitti, like the others, therefore used his influence to try to bring the fascists into a coalition, encouraged by leading industrialists in Milan, including Pirelli and Olivetti, two of the most familiar names in Italian economic life. He saw this as the best way to avoid a government that included socialists or *popolari*: without knowing it, he was playing Mussolini's game.[102]

On 16 October, a private meeting of the fascist leadership agreed on a plan for insurrection. Balbo, who wrote the minutes, believed that Mussolini was pushed by others into this decision but the latter claimed the opposite, asserting that he threatened to proceed on his own if the others refused.[103] Probably he feared that the movement would collapse or at least escape from his direction if he did not act soon. The next day, he told selected journalists that the meeting had agreed to reject the idea of coalition government because it would leave fascism in a minority and thus ineffective;[104] but at the same time he said the precise opposite to all the politicians in order to keep them guessing and to weaken any potential opposition. Publicly, he spoke about not wanting the responsibilities of office;[105] privately, on the contrary, he repeated that fascism had been created as a means of acquiring power – he was still ready to destroy the movement if it deviated from this aim.[106]

On 24 October, at a mass meeting of fascists in Naples, the plan for an insurrection crystallised. Mussolini also made a public speech to the citizenry and municipal authorities of Naples. On the stage of the San Carlo theatre, against a back-drop from *Madame Butterfly*, he explained the advantages of a fascist policy of financial retrenchment and effective administration of the law. He made another speech to the fascist militiamen who had converged on Naples from all over southern Italy. To them his tone was different: 'either we are allowed to govern, or we will seize power by marching on Rome' to 'take by the throat the miserable political class that governs us'.[107] There was no concealment in these remarks and they were fully reported. Before they left the town, the fascists also devastated the offices of opposition newspapers.[108] Yet even now the government – no doubt because some of the ministers did not want to exclude themselves from a new coalition that included the fascists – failed to declare a state of emergency.

The conquest of power

5

The march on Rome

Mussolini knew he had no hope if the army was ever ordered into action against the gathering rebellion and he therefore took pains to canvass support among officers and ex-officers. As well as three or four retired generals who were consulted about insurrectionary tactics, it is certain that many other senior, and still more junior, officers were sympathetic to his movement; yet it is unthinkable that the vast majority would ever have supported an armed rebellion against the king. The powerful 'union of ex-combatants' was loyal and actively opposed to fascism. A former chief of staff of the army, General Badoglio, thought that fascism would crumble at the first shot after a bare dozen arrests, as did other ranking officers in a position to know.[1]

After returning to Milan from Naples, Mussolini tried not to give the appearance that anything unusual was afoot. While some of his colleagues were quietly mobilising the squads for the final move, he rarely went to his office; he used to take drives in the country by day and go to the theatre by night, letting very few people know what he intended. In private, however, he talked to leading opinion-makers in Milan and convinced some at least that the economy would gain from having fascists in the government: he repeated that he wanted a balanced budget, a smaller bureaucracy, a more stable currency and reduced inflation. He naturally gave no hint of anything unpleasant in store for anyone. On the contrary he undertook that his blackshirt army would be disbanded after victory.[2]

Meanwhile, other fascists kept in touch with the individual liberal leaders, giving each to understand severally and secretly that the fascists would be content with a modest representation in a coalition led by any one of them. Nor did former prime ministers think it improper to conduct such talks, though they knew Mussolini was building up a large private militia and using it for illegal purposes. Facta still refused to declare an emergency or recall army reservists, and on the evening of 27 October, when civil strife was obviously threatening, he rejected a request by the army commander in Rome, General Pugliese, to impose martial law.[3] As the hours went by, Mussolini became ever more confident that the governing classes were reconciled to accepting almost anything he asked for.

During the night of 27–28 October, fascist squads began to occupy telephone exchanges and government offices, and just after midnight Facta at last agreed to act. The ministers, hastily summoned, agreed with him unanimously to advise the king to use the army, and Pugliese again assured them that the threatened insurrection would be crushed in a few hours. It cannot have crossed the ministers' minds that the king would depart from constitutional practice and reject their advice.

Vittorio Emanuele was a timid, enigmatic person who had no desire to play the unconstitutional king but had to admit that the liberal leaders had no answer to anarchy and parliamentary stalemate. Temperamentally he was drawn to anyone who would take firm decisions and control domestic unrest, especially if they also favoured imperial expansion and would stand up for Italian interests better than Orlando had done in negotiating the treaty of Versailles.[4] Along with growing numbers of other responsible statesmen, he had come to accept that Mussolini's entry into the cabinet in a subordinate role might be the best way to resolve the political impasse. He saw his own chief duty as that of avoiding the outbreak of an armed revolution and he now threatened to abdicate in the event of civil war.

Early on 28 October, at about 2.00 a.m., the king was informed that insurrections had begun at Milan and elsewhere; he at once agreed with the cabinet's formal advice to declare a state of emergency and use the army to impose martial law. The necessary decree was hurriedly prepared. At breakfast time, the prime minister returned to secure the formality of the royal signature while the military went into action to crush the revolt. The fascists offered little resistance; buildings captured overnight were re-occupied and roads and railways blocked so that no march on Rome could take place.[5] Not only the right-wing nationalist party, but even some of the fascist hierarchy including Cesare De Vecchi, one of the four designated commanders of the 'march', declared that, faced by the choice, they would obey the king – there was talk of killing Mussolini if necessary.[6]

Meanwhile in Milan at about 6.00 a.m., the fascist leader arrived at his office, barricaded by his staff as if for a siege. The army was already assuming full powers in the town without waiting for the official decree to be promulgated, and an order was drawn up for his arrest.[7] However, in private discussions the fascists gave the prefect of Milan, Alfredo Lusignoli, to understand that he would be rewarded with a place in the cabinet if the order were ignored. Lusignoli's refusal to act was a crucial factor in the success of the rebellion. His motive was presumably ambition, or at least fear of losing his job if the fascists won[8], and no doubt some rich Milanese encouraged him.

Even more important was the king's change of mind – at some time before 9.00 a.m. he refused to sign the decree that he had accepted and indeed demanded a few hours previously. To refuse the recommendation of a cabinet, particularly a unanimous one, was an arbitrary breach of constitutional convention. But Vittorio Emanuele had no confidence in Facta's ability to control events; furthermore, he was privately advised not to sign by Salandra's friends who hoped that this would force Facta's resignation and give them the chance of forming a government. The king was also informed – privately, inaccurately, almost certainly with intent to deceive – that the army was outnumbered by fascist militiamen and could not defend Rome from attack.[9]

His decision converted the fascists from outlaws into indispensable members of the next government. When Facta resigned, Salandra was invited to become prime minister and he asked Mussolini to join the new administration; but the latter refused, on the assumption that he could now name his own price. Salandra thereupon withdrew and, fearing that the choice might otherwise be Giolitti, advised the king to appoint Mussolini[10] – a man who was leading an armed rebellion against the state and whose private army was responsible for countless atrocities throughout Italy. On 29 October, the king accepted this advice and Mussolini, at the age of only thirty-nine, became the twenty-seventh prime minister of Italy.

But the fascist leader was not satisfied with something so unspectacular as a royal appointment. He needed to develop the myth of a march on Rome by 300,000 armed fascists to enforce an 'ultimatum' he had given to the king, and eventually a legend was invented of Mussolini on horseback leading his legions across the Rubicon.[11] In reality there were fewer than 30,000 fascist militiamen ready to march, many of whom had no arms at all and would have been quite unable to stand up to the garrison troops in Rome with their machine guns and armoured cars: indeed 400 policemen proved sufficient to hold up the fascist trains long before they reached Rome.[12] Mussolini subsequently admitted this in private with amused satisfaction.[13] His fascist squads did not arrive in Rome until twenty-four hours after he had been asked to form a government and only after General Pugliese had orders to let them through. But the photographers were waiting to picture their arrival and the myth was launched of fascism winning power by an armed insurrection after a civil war and the loss of 3,000 men.[14] These fictitious 3,000 'fascist martyrs' soon took their place in the government-sponsored history books.

Mussolini did not hurry to leave Milan. He needed a few hours to organise a tumultuous send-off at the station and to give his counterfeit 'march' time to get under way. To create an atmosphere of emergency, he announced that he was ready to govern by force – by machine gun if need be – and to show that he meant business he ordered his *squadristi* once again to destroy the printing machinery of opposition newspapers:[15] it was important to prevent the general public from knowing anything except the fascist version of events. For a while he thought of leaving his sleeping car at a stop before Rome so that he could enter the city on horseback with a guard of blackshirts,[16] but there was a risk of looking ridiculous, so he went the whole way by train and arrived during the morning of 30 October. His list of ministers, only a minority of whom were fascists, was accepted by the king that same evening. Rarely had a premier shown such speed and decision or found colleagues so immediately ready to join his cabinet.

By this time, the blackshirts had begun to arrive in Rome and some of the familiar violent episodes were taking place. The editor of at least one liberal paper was forced to drink the 'fascist medicine', castor oil; socialist newspapers and bookstores were ransacked and heaps of books burnt in the street; shops were pillaged, houses belonging to political opponents broken into and foreign embassies compelled to fly the Italian flag. A number of private grievances were settled in the turmoil and a dozen people killed. Some fascists were disappointed that the casualties were not higher,[17] and Mussolini subsequently made the comment that, in those 'radiant days of October', he should have had more people put against a wall and shot.[18]

Italy had become too numbed by a succession of outrages to be alarmed by this excess of high spirits. Though the lira fell drastically on the foreign *bourses*, the Italian stock market registered satisfaction at Mussolini's appointment. Marconi wired his congratulations; Giolitti and Salandra, the two senior members of the liberal establishment, expressed approval. Not even the extreme left was willing to react strongly. Mussolini had feared that a general strike might be proclaimed, which would create serious difficulties for him, but the socialist leaders remained passive; for years they had been looking forward to the collapse of the liberal state as a necessary step towards their own triumph.[19] Whereas in Germany a strike checked the Kapp *Putsch*, in Italy the railwaymen made no difficulty about driving Mussolini's train to victory.

The absence of resistance implies that the public lacked confidence in the liberal leaders and was ready to accept the new government with resignation, if not pleasure. Fear of communism can have been only a minor motive as there was no communist threat. A much more realistic fear was felt by those among the wealthy who were concerned lest Giolitti return to power with a policy of high taxes and social reform. Still more widespread was the feeling that fascism was an alternative to anarchy – the last resort, as it were, after parliament had failed to function in defence of law and order; few were troubled by the fact that the anarchy had been deliberately fanned by fascism itself. There were popular demonstrations of joy as Rome was swept by a holiday mood. Happy crowds paraded through streets decked with flags and demonstrated in front of the royal palace, applauding the king's decision not to invoke martial law. Foreign journalists reported that florists ran out of flowers as the city was overtaken by 'a fever of delight' at the prospect of years of misgovernment coming to an end.[20] These pro-fascist demonstrations, unlike most later ones, must have been spontaneous.

First months in power

With now only thirty-two fascist deputies and urgently needing to persuade everyone to accept the situation, Mussolini had the immediate problem of winning a favourable vote in parliament. He therefore formed his government predominantly of non-fascists in a coalition that included the Catholic *popolari*, the nationalist party, and representatives of most of the liberal factions. No one seems to have refused his invitation to join; even a socialist was on the point of becoming a minister until the new prime minister had second thoughts. The more prominent fascists were all excluded from office, to their great annoyance; most of them had hoped for a purely fascist government, but Mussolini was much shrewder and already foresaw that his own comrades might be his biggest stumbling-block. He took the two most important posts for himself – those of foreign minister and minister of the interior.

To restore an appearance of normality he ordered the immediate demobilisation of his irregulars. First, however, those of the squads that had not yet reached Rome were brought into town by truck and train and on 31 October were allowed to parade past the royal palace: he needed to fabricate more evidence of a conquest of power by force. He did not watch the march-past himself; according to one story he spent most of the day with a lady friend. But as soon as the demonstration was over, the blackshirts were packed off to their homes in special trains. It was important that everyone, particularly the parliamentary deputies, should see that he could control his squads and that he alone could restore Italy to its former tranquillity.

Lacking as he did any experience of government, Mussolini was remarkably undaunted by the task confronting him, and the fact testifies to his ability and self-confidence. All his new ministers, except one taken over from Facta's cabinet, were equally inexperienced. At his first cabinet meeting he laid down his general policy – pacification, national discipline and budget economies.[21] Many fascists were expecting him to discard the constitution and establish armed rule,[22] but, whatever he said to the contrary, he knew that he was in power not as a result of revolution, but following a series of compromises with the king and representatives of the former liberal regime. He had no preconstituted solutions that he could impose; he needed to proceed gradually, with the consent, and preferably help, of others. He knew not only that the fascist party lacked capable men, but also that unless he broadened his appeal the habitual independence of the *ras* could prove dangerous to him – more dangerous than the liberals on whose support he was bound to rely until he was properly entrenched in office.

He took up residence in a luxury hotel in which his armed guard of ill-dressed blackshirts looked quite out of place. He gave generously of his time to journalists, going out of his way to show them that he treated other fascist leaders with condescension, even contempt.[23] To one foreign reporter he explained the secret of political success: 'keep your heart a desert'; because loyalties and friendships had to give way to the one important objective, power. He confessed to being obsessed with bending people to his will – he repeated the word 'bending' several times with an appropriate gesture. There was no right or wrong in politics, only force. He added that he planned to improve living standards for the poor, but had some ugly surprises in store for the bourgeoisie, and no one apart from himself would be allowed to play at politics. This particular journalist, Clare Sheridan, noted that the only pictures in his room were of himself. He put on a forceful act for her benefit, but she guessed that he was probably a weak man controlled by those around him – he was less impressive than Lenin, Kemal, and other leaders she had known.[24]

Among other casual remarks – and in general he kept very quiet about this – he let drop that fascism was ready to stay in power for twenty years because the old liberal order had been destroyed for ever.[25] He had no interest in fetish concepts such as 'liberty'; the word 'discipline' was better, and he intended to make Italians obey – something they had never done in the past.[26] If necessary he would proclaim himself 'the prince of reactionaries' and he already had plans to create a special ministry of police. He had once learnt from his father how to forge iron; now he had the tougher task of 'manipulating souls'.[27]

On 16 November he confronted parliament, where some of his own party now appeared in the uniform of the fascist militia, ominously booted and spurred.[28] Dropping his mask, with studied derision he treated the deputies to what he called 'the most anti-parliamentary speech that history records'. Though he was not going to abolish the constitution – not yet, at least – he taunted them by saying he 'might easily have turned this bleak assembly hall into a bivouac for my platoons'. Threatening that he might still decide to govern without their help, relying instead on the 'fascist revolutionaries', he asked to be given full powers to carry out any necessary changes in the law.[29]

The liberals were not, strangely, much offended by this speech; they liked to think that his contempt was aimed at the extreme left who, in their turn,

57

thought the opposite; and the socialists, though they alone voted against his bold request, cheered his remarks more than once as they saw liberal institutions disintegrating. One or two deputies dared to point out that a man could not be trusted who had once defended desertion from the army and regicide, or who in 1919 had propounded a programme differing little from bolshevism.[30] But Mussolini browbeat them with a barrage of interjections – eighty-five times in one day, without being called to order. The comment was made that Cromwell, who had once spoken to another parliament in similar vein, had at least run into severe opposition; by comparison, Mussolini met with acquiescence and resignation, and foreigners took good note of the fact.

The fascists were a tiny minority in the Chamber but at once the seats next to them on the extreme right, hitherto almost deserted, began to fill up[31] and a huge majority gave Mussolini a vote of confidence larger than anyone could remember. Only the socialists and communists opposed him. Nitti alone walked out during the debate. Amendola was one of only seven deputies who abstained. Five liberal ex–prime ministers voted with the majority – Giolitti, Salandra, Orlando, Bonomi and Facta. Salandra defended his vote by explaining that, although he was ashamed to see the deputies humiliated, they had brought it on themselves. Giolitti, who had learnt nothing from Mussolini's deceitful behaviour in June 1921, said that he approved the latter's speech in its entirety, as did De Gasperi and the Christian democrats of the *popolari*. Even the socialist leader Filippo Turati wrote that Mussolini's continuation in power might be the country's only hope.[32] Outside commentators noted that the non-fascist majority, by its vote of confidence after a speech 'without parallel in the annals of modern parliaments', had utterly discredited liberalism and parliament itself; and this proved that fascism might be a necessary, if illegal and dangerous, remedy for the collapse of the ruling class.[33]

The Senate, which contained almost no fascists at all, backed Mussolini by an even more convincing majority than the Chamber, in spite of the fact that he openly expressed his scorn for such turncoats and admitted to them that his actions had been illegal.[34] Only twenty-six senators voted against the concession of full powers and the few opposition speakers were howled down.[35] The liberal economist, Luigi Einaudi, was among those strongly in favour,[36] as was Luigi Albertini, the editor of the liberal-conservative *Corriere della Sera*, who voiced his delight that fascism 'had saved Italy from the danger of socialism';[37] other speakers begged Mussolini to go further and impose a dictatorship.[38] After the debate there was a competitive rush of senators to congratulate the new prime minister and shake his hand.[39] They had given him full power to govern and raise taxes without having to seek parliamentary approval.

Mussolini knew from the start that foreign policy was to be his primary concern.[40] If he talked of internal discipline, one reason was so that a strong foreign policy should be possible, and a forceful international position would enhance his prestige at home.[41] He prudently disclaimed any intention of being adventurous abroad[42] – although he had already expressed his view that peace was 'just a pause between wars' and substantial rearmament would be necessary.[43] He would not follow an ideological foreign policy: 'fascism was not for export'. Neither would he be guided by the principles of absolute morality.[44] Nor would he strive to be original; though he qualified these last remarks by an unrehearsed and slightly ominous interjection, warning people that in course of time a truly fascist foreign policy would emerge.[45]

One of his first acts was to move the foreign office away from the Palazzo della Consulta to the much smaller Palazzo Chigi. The former, being next to the royal palace, would not provide sufficient room for the crowd scenes he intended to stage-manage, whereas the Chigi palace had a balcony overlooking a busy square in the centre of Rome. He insisted that the move be carried out in a single week and it caused considerable disorganisation of the archives, as a result of which it was going to be hard to locate the documents needed for proper continuity of policy.[46] But he was helped by the fact that very few senior civil servants resigned and most of the existing ambassadors seem to have welcomed a more forceful style of diplomacy.[47]

After only a week in office, Mussolini decided to attend a congress at Lausanne to discuss the Turkish peace treaty. Though he had nothing to contribute to the discussion, he seized on the chance of cutting a figure and suddenly discerned how, by making minor difficulties, he could persuade other countries to take fascism more seriously. First he tried to get the congress moved to Capri, then to Territet, a Swiss town nearer the Italian frontier;[48] but it was too late to change. Next the French and British delegates arriving in Lausanne were surprised to find peremptory instructions that he would be waiting for them at Territet for preliminary talks. There they were even more surprised to find him surrounded by a phalanx of blackshirts and a band playing 'Giovinezza', now the fascist anthem. The only point of this preliminary discussion turned out to be his insistence that other delegates should make a public promise to treat Italy on an equal footing. His own officials thought this strange demand most undignified; it was, however, made out by the newspapers to be Italy's first diplomatic victory since 1860.[49]

Although the congress lasted for several months, Mussolini stayed for a mere two days during which he 'never stirred without his bodyguard of stalwart *fascisti*'. But in those two days he made at least eleven statements to the press and put on an act of carefully studied disdain to all the foreign journalists – except to one woman who had to be rescued from his attentions.

They were glad to have a chance of reporting on this little-known personality; they found him egocentric, self-conscious, revelling in the novelty of massive public attention.[50] One of these correspondents, Ernest Hemingway, noted that the young premier seemed always to be thinking of the next day's newspaper headlines and hence was more interested in the journalists than in the congress itself. Hemingway arrived at one press conference to discover Mussolini 'registering dictator' – frowning over a book and pretending not to notice that his audience was ready. Hemingway tip-toed over and found that the book was a French–English dictionary held upside down.[51] Another pressman was charmed by Mussolini off-stage but observed that, if ever private conversation developed into a more public occasion, there was a sudden switch to a hard and contemptuous demeanour that was extremely unattractive. The general verdict by the press was that he was ill-at-ease with foreigners, and he failed to leave much impression except of quirks of character that seemed contrived and theatrical.[52]

The assembled delegates at the conference were given much the same treatment as the journalists. First – to the embarrassment of Mussolini's Italian colleagues – everyone was kept waiting by him for the inaugural ceremony;[53] then, in the public sessions, he uttered nothing but the words 'I agree'.[54] By his own account he achieved a brilliant success in persuading the British to accept an increase in Italian colonial territory,[55] but the British delegates categorically denied having so much as discussed the subject. Indeed, the diplomats were so little impressed by his knowledge, ability and seriousness that they wrote him off somewhat cavalierly as an 'absurd little man', a second-rate cinema actor and someone who would not continue in power for long.[56] Eventually he himself came to see that the congress had not been an unqualified personal success. Nevertheless, in order to make up for this, he played up to the newspapers by staging one more noisy popular demonstration as he left Lausanne with his armed bodyguard.

Hardly had he returned home than he decided to attend another international assembly in London to discuss the question of German reparations, and London witnessed a repeat performance of his conduct at Lausanne. First he tried and failed to have the meeting moved to somewhere nearer Italy.[57] Then there was another trial of nerves at Claridges Hotel when he heard that the French delegation had a more luxurious set of rooms and tried to have them ejected.[58] Officials of the Italian embassy in London followed instructions to impress the British by laying on a military-style parade of blackshirts to salute his arrival and once again there was much ostentatious singing of 'Giovinezza'. But they managed to persuade him not to carry his *manganello*, the heavy wooden club which had become the symbol of *squadrismo*; in the end, he was content to wear only his fascist badge when he made his official courtesy call upon King George at Buckingham Palace.[59]

According to one Italian journalist, Mussolini managed to offend almost everyone during his three days in London. This time he gave only six statements to the press: on a seventh occasion the British journalists were sent away after being told that he might be in bed with a girl and could not be disturbed.[60] Once again he exaggerated his personal contribution to the political discussions, casting himself in the role of chief figure in a congress which was 'deciding the future of Europe'. Again the occasion was said to be the first time in modern history that an Italian statesman had played a primary role in world politics.[61] Privately, however, he was ready to admit that his gifts were not suited to the slow process of negotiation and compromise.[62] The other Italian delegates were disturbed to find that he did not know the basic techniques of diplomacy – in negotiating he was always seeking a *coup de théâtre* by giving away either nothing at all or too much. They recommended in private that he be dissuaded from exposing himself again at any conference abroad. According to one future ambassador, 'the man who when addressing a crowd was like a lion, became a real sheep in private conversation, especially with foreigners: he was ready to give away all the cards in his hand, and then would try to conceal this by posing as a great statesman who could not bother about tiny points'.[63] British politicians thought poorly of him after this first encounter, and he himself was afterwards reluctant to move away from home territory where he could dictate press comments and organise crowd scenes. England had not impressed him: 'it was just as in the novels of Galsworthy, since when nothing has changed'.[64]

One immediate difference of opinion with the British was over war reparations owed by Germany. They wanted to be lenient, while he was for severity, and in January 1923 he encouraged the French when they decided to move their troops into the Rhineland as security for German payments.[65] He talked excitedly of creating a 'continental bloc' against Britain and once again hoped that, by threatening the continued existence of the British empire, he could open new possibilities of extending Italian influence in the wider world.[66] When reports of his anti-British remarks leaked out, he denied them out of hand.[67] He also backed down over the Ruhr and pretended that he had opposed the French policy of military occupation.[68] By that time, however, the damage had been done. In France he began to be described as a *César de carnaval*, while the British saw his policy as 'one of pure opportunism ... "sacred egotism" carried to extreme limits'. They were ready to acknowledge his strength of character and his sincere wish to regenerate Italy, but he was 'a braggart and an actor', a dangerous 'rascal', and possibly slightly off his head.[69]

Dominating the opposition

Returning to Italy, Mussolini found several serious problems awaiting him. A group of legalistic fascists had apparently been working with some of the moderate socialists to dispose of him,[70] while, at the opposite extreme of the party, criminal elements were running riot in an attempt to crush all opposition and win a monopoly of power for fascism.[71] Many of the larger cities were witnessing terrible examples of lawlessness, whether arising out of personal vendettas or in defence of various corrupt practices, or resulting from conflicts between rival fascist gangs and the need to intimidate political opponents. Turin was the scene of one of the worst incidents: a fascist execution squad ran completely out of control and the police made no attempt to stop it, nor was there any serious move afterwards to investigate and punish those responsible for so many deaths. Since the police were Mussolini's direct responsibility, it was clear that he had no intention of acting with sufficient force against criminal factions inside his own party. He remarked privately that, whatever, he might say in public, he wished the squads had killed even more people.[72] He could not afford to let the extremists think he was going soft.

Several days later, an official amnesty was promulgated for thousands of fascists accused or suspected of 'political' illegalities and some magistrates promised to interpret it so as to pardon as many as possible.[73] Hardened criminals, for example Albino Volpi and Amerigo Dumini who were needed by Mussolini for the 'second wave' of violence, had to be freed from any pending prosecutions.[74] He also ordered that students wounded in the cause of fascism should obtain their degrees without examination and that fascist casualties of the 'civil war' should enjoy state pensions as though they had died fighting for their country.[75]

Mussolini continued to state for the public record that fascist illegalism must and would stop,[76] but in practice the squads were needed as a threat to the opposition and he could not deny all personal responsibility for their actions.[77] In December he gave them legal status, converting them into a 'national militia': this had the additional advantage of making the *squadristi* a charge on state funds, as well as bringing them under his direct authority, thus severing or at least weakening their allegiance to the individual *ras*. The militia was officially enjoined to act as a political police force and 'to defend the revolution of October 1922'. Incidentally the need to provide it with senior officers, glamorously entitled 'consuls' and 'centurions', gave him many extremely well-paid jobs to distribute to the strong-arm men of the revolution.

Although the squads were in theory absorbed into the regular militia, the need for their illegalities persisted and the prime minister continued to encourage acts of intimidation and assassination: some people thought he would hardly have lasted six months without them.[78] While claiming to restore law and order, he was privately subsidising Dumini, Volpi and Bonaccorsi to violate the law and was able to arrange that very few fascists were brought to trial for the many brutalities of the next two years. Any evidence implicating Mussolini in these acts was never allowed in court proceedings, but witnesses testified elsewhere that he ordered beatings and shootings. Local authorities and officers of the militia were regularly sent orders from his office that a certain person 'must be beaten without pity', 'must have his back broken', or indeed 'must be bumped off'.[79]

Mussolini knew instinctively that one way to consolidate his power was to create a reign of terror. Three opposition members of parliament were killed by fascists and some fifty others physically attacked, mostly in public and in broad daylight; some people were assassinated while in prison; castor oil, sometimes mixed with petrol, was administered in quantities that could prove fatal, and individual militiamen were able to cudgel and kill without fear of police intervention.[80] Few of the victims were courageous or foolhardy enough to attempt a private prosecution: few witnesses would support them and further amnesties would always annul any alleged offence. During the first twelve months of fascism, the newspapers reported an average of five acts of violence a day.[81] Most of these were against leftist politicians or were acts of private vengeance, but the most savage attacks were against any dissident fascists who revealed secrets of fascist corruption and terrorism or fled abroad and told foreigners what was really happening. Special punitive squads were paid by Mussolini to harass such dangerous men even in foreign countries.[82]

Corruption was closely connected with violence. Immediately after 28 October the party was flooded with new recruits, many of them undesirable characters who wanted to get their hands on the spoils of office and jobs in the militia and the bureaucracy available to the faithful. Most of the fascist leaders arrived in Rome poor, yet few escaped the imputation of using their immunity from the law to become corrupt and rich – to some outsiders it seemed that a primary aim in joining the party was to make money.[83] Mussolini made hesitant efforts to stop corruption, but preferred not to create public scandal by arresting anyone. Instead, he sometimes intervened to stop investigations or halt prosecutions before they became generally known. 'Revolutions', he explained, 'are not made by saints'. To stop all public references to corruption was easy – and quite as effective, so far as public opinion was concerned, as to stop corruption itself. He had to accept that most of the fascist elite were men of bad or violent character who were bound to become worse under cover of their new unaccountability. So he just exploited the fact that they were useful for purposes of intimidation, while his knowledge of their malpractices gave him a useful hold over them.[84]

He had an early trial of strength with those party leaders who did not like finding themselves swamped by newcomers and who feared that his obvious inclination towards a personal dictatorship would curtail their own freedom of action. Some people thought for a time that he had been forced to capitulate entirely to corrupt elements in the party,[85] but Mussolini was too cunning to capitulate to anyone. He sometimes toyed with the idea of getting rid of some of those who had helped to put him in power, possibly even dissolving the party and seeking the alternative of wider support from the nation as a whole.[86] He even referred angrily to fascists 'in spite of whom I carried out the revolution'.[87] But perhaps he feared that the party machine might be too strong for him, or at least he felt that ordinary citizens would be less trustworthy as allies. He therefore sensibly decided that his own interests were best served by utilising the party, fostering divisions inside it when necessary and striving to keep it under his own shadow.

It was becoming habitual with him to set individuals and cliques against each other in order to maximise his personal power. To limit the influence of the party directorate, he had an almost rival institution in the cabinet of ministers, and in December 1922 added yet another organisation to counterbalance the cabinet – the Grand Council of Fascism, which was designed to discuss general policy. As he appointed its members, and he alone decided if and when to summon it and what it should discuss, the Grand Council helped to establish his personal primacy, though he took care to give it consultative rather than executive functions. It was useful to him at first, but in course of time he set less and less store by discussion and increasingly disregarded the advice of its members, or, indeed, of anyone else.

Another move by which Mussolini weakened the old guard of the party was his fusion of the fascist and nationalist parties early in 1923. He himself called this 'a marriage of convenience and a purely tactical move for reasons of internal politics'.[88] The nationalists attracted him because they had more men of ability than the fascists; they had ideas and ideals and represented solid national interests; they shared his hostility to liberalism; they were conservative, monarchical, even clerical, and this was also advantageous. The fusion of the two parties meant a shift of policy for many of his colleagues. Some fascists warned him against it because the nationalists might prove cleverer than he, but Mussolini trusted in his own ability to balance the various elements in his grand coalition against one other. He welcomed the nationalists as people from whom fascism had already borrowed much of its policy and who could be used to make his new ruling class appear more respectable.[89]

Another and equally important marriage of convenience was made with the conservative wing of Catholicism. Mussolini saw it as vital to gratify and disarm the Vatican, firstly because Italians were overwhelmingly Catholic; secondly because with the Pope's help he could eliminate – or at least divide – the Catholic *popolari*, the second largest party in parliament. Renouncing, or pretending to renounce, the atheism of his youth and the stridently anti-clerical programme of early fascism, he tried to convince journalists that he was a 'profoundly religious man' and that fascism itself was an essentially religious phenomenon. He also tried to create the impression that he was himself 'deeply a Catholic'.[90] Cardinal Gasparri, the secretary of state of Pope Pius XI, may have doubted such statements, but thought that Catholics would find it easier to collaborate with fascism than with liberalism.[91] Mussolini encouraged this belief by making a generous grant to increase the stipends of priests and bishops, in sharp contrast to his undertaking in 1919 to confiscate ecclesiastical property; he ordered the introduction of religious instruction into schools and universities; he banned obscene publications and declared swearing in public and distribution of contraceptives to be crimes against the state. All this was well received by the Vatican, and it was a great help to fascism when the leading Catholic in active politics, the priest Don Sturzo, was ordered by the Pope to leave Italy. Without this courageous and irreconcilable enemy of the regime, the *popolari* languished and the 'clerical-fascists' rallied strongly behind fascism.

Despite the fact that he temporarily observed existing constitutional forms, Mussolini was intent on becoming a dictator. Individual fascists were told that they had only one duty, that of absolute obedience to himself; ordinary citizens, he insisted, were tired of liberty: what was required was the centralisation of power in a single hand, trampling 'on the more or less decomposing body of the Goddess Liberty'.[92] This remark came from the same man who, when in opposition, set freedom of thought higher than all religious teachings and political laws. When asked how to define the state, however, he now replied 'it is the police', and he felt justified in arresting opposition leaders for the new crime of 'defaming the fascist government'. He had established not just a new government, but a regime,[93] with a new fascist calendar dating events no longer from the birth of Christ, but from October 1922 which inaugurated *anno primo*; eventually the fascist symbol of the lictors became the official insignia, not just of a party, but of the state, and the Roman salute with outstretched arm became an almost compulsory official greeting.

From his first day in office, Mussolini personally took over the direction of the police. In the next few months he arrested several thousand political opponents and there was widespread replacement of elected local government authorities by fascist nominees.[94] His attitude to those who remained in opposition was to 'pluck them like a chicken, feather by feather'; he intended to eliminate them absolutely from public life but, changing the metaphor, only by taking out one tooth at a time, so that people would not notice the full scale of what was occurring.[95] He was determined to stay in power and anyone who challenged his right to do so would be crushed.[96]

Among previous prime ministers still in parliament, senators Luzzatti and Boselli showed not the slightest urge to oppose him; Nitti never returned to the Chamber; while Giolitti, Orlando, Salandra and Facta, though they cannot have greatly liked what was happening, continued to accept it fairly passively. Mussolini still needed their help, for most of the liberal parliamentarians would look to them for a lead. He also took careful note that chaos had been caused in Russia when representatives of the old order were defenestrated *en masse* during the revolution: fascism could hardly have survived if the police, the magistrates, the army leaders and the civil service had not continued to work just as before, and the complicity of these older politicians was eagerly sought and helped to preserve the important illusion that nothing had changed.

The liberals failed to use the leverage afforded by his need for their approbation. Most of them saw some good in fascism as a way of defending social order and thought Italians too intelligent and civilised to permit the establishment of a complete dictatorship. Above all, there was the very persuasive argument that the only alternative was to return to the anarchy and parliamentary stalemate they remembered under Facta. Mussolini had convincingly proved that he was the most effective politician of them all: he alone could have asked parliament for full powers and been given what he asked; he alone provided a defence against, and an alternative to, socialism. And of course the old parliamentarians still hoped to capture and absorb him into their own system in the long run; their optimism was encouraged by the fact that his fascist collaborators were so second-rate.

Fortunately for Mussolini, Giolitti and Salandra, the two most authoritative politicians outside fascism, had not been on speaking terms since Salandra's decision to enter the First World War in 1915. Moreover they both strongly disliked Nitti and neither could abide the *popolari*. They looked on socialism as something that threatened to change the structure of society, whereas the *popolari* implied clerical influence and hence the threat of religious war. Giolitti, still sure that Mussolini could not possibly last long, commented wryly that in fascism the Italians had the government they deserved, and not even the fact that Mussolini despised his liberalism and derided him as a 'walking corpse' made this veteran liberal change his mind.[97] One of Mussolini's first acts was to tap the telephones of the leading parliamentarians[98] – something of which they were almost certainly aware.

Nevertheless, Salandra went out of his way to offer his full co-operation in everything necessary 'to increase the prestige and the greatness of Italy.'[99] Here he spoke for what was already being called 'the silent majority',[100] in other words people who simply wanted a quiet life and a chance to earn a decent livelihood without having to worry about politics.

The new premier was exceptional in having made his name as a newspaper editor and journalism continued to be one of his great passions. He was probably the best popular journalist of his day, and his ability to simplify and vulgarise issues, to disregard consistency where necessary – in his own words, to over-dramatise or even invent facts[101] – all these early lessons greatly helped to make him effective in the kind of populist politics he was drawn to instinctively. They made him a successful politician, if a bad statesman.

He now decided to change the rules of journalism so that no one else could succeed as he had done. While in opposition, he had condemned censorship of newspapers as shameful and dangerous, and his pledge to maintain freedom of the press received unanimous support in the first fascist party congress;[102] but as a dictator he seized on the fact that anyone who could manipulate the press might be able to change public opinion overnight, and even before the march on Rome he had prepared measures to control the newspapers.[103] Here was the main novelty of Mussolini's revolution and one of the principal reasons for his success. His sort of fascism could never have appeared before the days of popular journalism; nor in all probability could it have happened later, once Italy became a more literate and politically more sophisticated society.

In October 1922 he was fortunate in that others had not tumbled to this truth or realised how far he was prepared to go in gagging criticism. Owners of newspapers, however, quickly discovered how vulnerable they were. At first he did not need to suppress papers because whole issues could be burnt by squads on the rampage or sequestered by the prefects, both of which methods were very damaging to profits. If this did not work, either editors were personally threatened, or the police were ordered to seize lists of subscribers who would then be intimidated individually. Financial difficulties led to the *Secolo* being taken over by fascists; the editor of the *Giornale d'Italia* was browbeaten until he resigned; other liberal editors were imprisoned on trumped-up charges; and subsidies were given to the *Resto del Carlino* to win its support. Huge sums, no doubt of taxpayers' money, were also spent to produce new fascist dailies that were read by practically no one; this was a convenient way of keeping *squadristi* on the payroll as so-called journalists.

Not even the *Popolo d'Italia* could win a quarter (some said a tenth) of the readership of the *Corriere della Sera*, and this suggests that the silent majority, while appreciative of what Mussolini was doing, hardly took fascism seriously as a body of ideas and did not expect it to last. In November 1922 the *Popolo d'Italia* was handed over to Mussolini's brother Arnaldo, who however failed to adapt its vulgar and blustering style to the more respectable audience they now would have liked to reach. Benito kept in close contact with his brother, sending regular comments on individual issues.

All the daily papers were closely monitored. Editors had orders to send a copy of each issue to the prime minister's private address, and a press-cutting service collected all references to himself in the world press. It was his frequent boast that he continued to read hundreds of newspapers a day; as many as 350, he once said.[104] He liked to impress journalists by telling them that he followed them all individually and was carefully watching out for their peccadilloes. It was his belief that by studying the newspapers each day he could keep his finger on the pulse of public opinion, but this was a dangerous piece of self-deceit – he forgot that the news and comments on the news were increasingly being manufactured in his own press office.

The Matteotti crisis

6

Preparation for the elections, 1923

Mussolini continued to express distaste for parliamentary government but did not yet judge himself strong enough to think of recasting the constitution. He had, in any case, the great advantage of having been given far larger votes of confidence than his liberal predecessors. Parliament could also be used to curb and counterbalance the hard-liners in his own party. There was some surprise that he did not at once hold new elections to increase the number of fascist deputies – he was not alone in thinking that he might have scored a landslide victory.[1] But he decided that serious preparation was needed before risking a popular vote: it would be catastrophic if elections gave him only a small majority, and almost as bad if fascism won so overwhelmingly that his field of manoeuvre was reduced.

The acquiescence and submissiveness of both houses of parliament is a tribute to what one member called the collective hypnosis engendered by this masterful man.[2] They gladly granted him a year with full emergency powers and, in July 1923, even agreed to his proposal that the electoral law be changed. Henceforth any party obtaining a quarter of the votes would automatically take two-thirds of the seats in the chamber; acceptance of this drastic measure effectively guaranteed the permanence of fascism in power. To win the votes needed for this bill – the fascists had only 47 members in the lower house after their fusion with the nationalists – he used not only guile but also the clear threat that parliament might otherwise be abolished.[3] Giolitti, Orlando and Salandra advised their followers to accept, and others among the liberal deputies prudently adjusted their views in the same direction when they realised that their best chance of re-election would be Mussolini's endorsement of their individual candidature. To make doubly sure of sufficient votes, armed fascists guarded the doors of parliament during the debate and militiamen in the public galleries ostentatiously fingered their daggers and revolvers.[4] The result was that an overwhelmingly non-fascist parliament passed, by a large majority, a law putting an end to parliamentary government as hitherto known.

As well as disciplining the deputies, Mussolini was trying to exert his authority over the fascist extremists in the provinces. He still needed these *ras* and their gangs to intimidate any opposition, and remained closer to them in temperament than to the moderates whom he sometimes pretended to favour. But he also feared them and was worried lest they alienate middle-of-the-road public opinion.

The most prominent and potentially dangerous of the *ras* was Roberto Farinacci, who was said to be more powerful in his fief of Cremona than Mussolini himself[5] and who for the next twenty years remained a nuisance and occasionally a mild threat to the central government. Farinacci had once been a revolutionary socialist; he was a dedicated believer in political violence, despite an undistinguished war record about which he kept very quiet. He was always to some extent a law to himself, and his highly remunerative legal career began with a doctoral thesis copied word for word from someone else's, though fascist legislation made this a crime punishable by imprisonment. Mussolini knew about Farinacci's malpractices and, where necessary, used his knowledge to neutralise a man he despised, feared, yet needed.

Farinacci and the extremists were useful counters for the game of 'divide and rule' in which Mussolini's political skill was most apparent, though for much of 1923 the prime minister preferred to encourage the moderate 'revisionists' in the party – the compromisers who distrusted the methods of *squadrismo*. But as soon as he had used these revisionists to obtain a more balanced directorate of the party, he moved back towards the intransigent fanatics and away from any ideas of compromise and discussion inside the party. Permission was given for the moderates to be physically assaulted, and though Mussolini continued to speak of restoring normality and 'reconciliation', privately he instructed his lieutenants to step up their acts of violence. Fascism might fail if it stopped relying on threats and terrorism, so fascists must be ready to kill and be killed if the revolution required it.[6]

This was especially true in the period preceding the general elections of 1924 when it was important to frighten and, if necessary, silence the opposition press.[7] A systematic campaign of coercion aimed at independent newspapers was conducted and their editors were marked down for assault. Among politicians, Nitti, who apart from the socialists and communists was the only parliamentary leader who consistently refused to vote for Mussolini, had his house ransacked as an indication that it would be safer to leave Rome. Subsequently, the police were told to have Nitti put away for good, but this order was then rescinded or else quietly disobeyed.[8] The socialist Matteotti was another to be repeatedly attacked by hired thugs; so was the liberal-conservative deputy, Giovanni Amendola – this was with the connivance of the police after the *Popolo d'Italia* marked him out as someone to be 'liquidated'. On one occasion Amendola discovered that proceedings were to begin against him for criminal assault of five fascist militiamen – after they had attacked him in the street, he had damaged their reputation by successfully beating them off with his umbrella.[9] Among his attackers were Albino Volpi and Amerigo Dumini who had led the fascist squad routed at Sarzana. Both these men were professional gangsters used by Mussolini to harass anti-fascist exiles in France, after which they were brought by him to Rome to overawe the deputies during the voting on electoral reform. Early in 1924, he chose them to head a special *ceka*, or squad set up for purposes of intimidation, and he was quoted as saying that he now 'needed illegal means to put the opposition in their place'.[10]

So effective was the mixture of intimidation and bribery that Mussolini no longer needed to ask parliament for renewal of his special statutory powers. The Chamber of Deputies, once it had changed the constitution by accepting his electoral bill, could be disregarded – in ten months it met only once. He referred scornfully to the next parliamentary election as a 'paper game' in which he had little interest, because fascism based its power on the legions of blackshirts. The election was the last he intended to hold, and he said he would not be particularly displeased if the results were unfavourable for he could then turn to the unabashed use of force.[11] As he said, 'fifty thousand guns are better than the support of five million voters', and he had no intention of resigning if the elections went against him.[12]

In practice he had little to worry about as his preparations were thorough. Various opposition journals were suspended by the police on the pretence of being a danger to public order; tens of thousands of copies of newspapers were destroyed by squad action against kiosks and delivery trucks; and the most widely read paper of all, the *Corriere della Sera*, was cowed into a defeatist decision to avoid all political comment at the very time when comment was most needed.[13] Meanwhile, almost half the elected provincial councils and over ten thousand town councils were dissolved and replaced by nominated officials, thus placing the administration of the elections in any doubtful area securely in fascist hands.[14] Mussolini guessed correctly that, if such things were done gradually over a period of months, the public outcry could be minimised.

At the same time he increased the electoral attractiveness of fascism to the former political elite by talk of 'national greatness' and of once more giving Italy an active role in international politics. He had already formulated the goal of an imperialist Italy whose right to expand at the expense of other 'declining peoples' was incontrovertible.[15] Ever since 1919, he had spoken of 'revisionism', in the other sense of revising the treaty of Versailles to commence a process of national expansion, and this kind of 'revisionism' was said to be fascist policy from the very moment he won power.[16] Though at first he had welcomed the peace settlement as giving Italy more than other victor countries, he soon changed and began complaining that she should have been allowed to occupy Vienna and Budapest.[17] She had also been cheated out of colonies in Asia Minor and the eastern Mediterranean.[18] Almost immediately after becoming prime minister, Mussolini was helping autonomist movements in Malta[19] and Corsica; he even thought of enrolling Corsican refugees in a foreign legion ready for the day when France would bite the dust.[20]

The suspicion was soon aroused that he was casting about for some striking act of international brigandage that would eclipse memories of D'Annunzio's invasion of Fiume. After failing to cut much of a figure at either Lausanne or London, he was fretting at the accusation that fascist foreign policy differed little from that of previous liberal governments. But in July 1923, he began preparations for the first venture that the world would come to recognise as bearing the authentic fascist stamp: he ordered plans to be prepared for a landing on the Greek island of Corfu, and a few weeks later, after he learned that there was no defensive artillery on the island, a naval force was placed on the alert to reply to the Greek 'provocations' that he intended to organise.[21]

A week later General Tellini, an Italian working with an international boundary commission, was murdered on Greek territory. No one ever discovered who the murderers were; almost certainly they came from Albania and some people have believed, unlikely though it may seem, that Mussolini arranged the killing.[22] At all events he acted with surprising speed and, although the Greek government could in no sense have been held responsible, he by-passed his own foreign office in sending an immediate ultimatum[23] which was followed by military occupation of the island three days later. This suspicious haste was one reason why the enterprise was badly bungled. The squadron arrived five hours later than scheduled, and landing operations had to be hurried on before nightfall without giving the Greek authorities time to reply to a demand for their surrender. Against orders, the admiral in charge quite unnecessarily began bombarding the town citadel where, as he knew, many hundreds of Armenian refugees were housed. A number of children were killed and world-wide public opinion turned strongly against the Italian action.

It surprised some people that Mussolini seemed pleased to find himself the object of almost universal indignation.[24] The naval authorities were equally surprised when, after international protests at his action, he ordered them to prepare for a possible war against Britain.[25] He threatened that if the London press did not become more favourable to fascist Italy he would find ways of making them regret it, adding that the British, by sympathising with the Greeks, were defying 'every principle of international morality'.[26] As an afterthought, he added that he would destroy the League of Nations if it tried to intervene: small states should never be allowed to criticise big states, and certainly not Italy.

A month after landing in Corfu, Mussolini was forced to withdraw. He tried to maintain that the expedition had been a great success and had increased Italian prestige: indeed the now familiar claim was made that it had been Italy's most important and successful initiative for the last hundred years, and the promise was given that it would be the first stage in a triumphant march of the fascist legions along the road to national greatness.[27] The Greeks paid Italy fifty million lire in partial compensation for the considerable expense to Italy of this ill-advised expedition, and Mussolini generously gave some of the money to help the refugees whose lives had been ruined.

In spite of his public utterances he knew it was a defeat and he never forgave the Greeks for it, nor the British for their refusal to support him.[28] He had been hoping to annex the island: Italian postage stamps overstamped 'Corfu' were already on sale and the issue had to be withdrawn abruptly.[29] He had failed to realise that, far from increasing his prestige, such an action would damage Italy by earning him the resentment of smaller countries and the reputation of a bully. He was now labelled as someone who would defy treaties and break the Covenant of the League of Nations whenever it served his interests. Already the fear was being expressed by foreigners that he was a 'megalomaniac' who, if cornered, might commit a 'mad dog act' and even push Europe into a major war.[30]

This was a reputation he savoured. And although individuals and minority groups in Italy learnt from this act of bravado to mistrust his ambition, the overwhelming majority strongly supported it; he was thus given the valuable lesson that an adventurous foreign policy would be enthusiastically received even by many non- and anti-fascists and would help to consolidate his authority. Salandra thought his action was bound to raise Italian prestige, and so did former members of the nationalist party. Not only the more conservative papers, but Amendola's *Il Mondo* and, with more qualifications, the socialist *Il Lavoro* were favourable. Foreign observers could not fail to be impressed by the breadth of this support and had to adjust their attitude accordingly.

The appearance of popular support for fascism was confirmed by the election in the spring of 1924. Three thousand people applied to be placed on the fascist list of candidates and so acquire a safe seat. Mussolini was disgusted to see this rush of would-be placemen to join an institution he despised, but being a deputy was much sought after even among fascists because it conferred a good salary, a highly profitable honorific title, free transport on the railways, and virtual immunity from arrest. Though he pretended that he had no interest in who was chosen, Mussolini in fact looked over each name individually, determined that a majority of deputies should be personally appointed by himself. He tried hard to include some liberals and conservative

Catholics on the list so as to give it a wider appeal, and in the end only 200 names were of fascists; 150 belonged to other parties and even some of the more amenable socialists were not entirely ruled out from consideration. Against this broad coalition there were twenty small lists representing a thoroughly divided opposition. Salandra admitted that he was proud to join Mussolini's *listone*; Orlando also joined, a capitulation that ensured a big swing towards fascism in his native Sicily; Giolitti, while remaining on a separate list, still made it clear that he was not campaigning against Mussolini but alongside him against socialism; and Benedetto Croce, the high priest of Italian liberalism, positively advised people to vote for the fascist candidates. To delude and confuse these leading liberals took skill of a high order; all of them later regretted their decision .

Murder incorporated

By March 1924, the election campaign was in full swing. Mussolini instructed the prefects to interfere with opposition meetings and to prevent or curtail any criticisms of the government.[31] The familiar practice of promising lavish grants to local authorities was employed – grants of which, as usual, little more was ever heard.[32] He said, or at least pretended, that he did not want violence, especially 'useless violence', yet there was a sudden increase in the number of public assaults; those familiar figures Dumini and Volpi were responsible for some of the worst. In many areas of Italy the elections took place in a climate of terror, indicating that the fascists knew violence was necessary for the overwhelming victory they required. Outside witnesses concluded from this that the salient feature of fascism was illegality: 'the fascists are, in their methods, as barbarous as the bolsheviks: for the moment, at any rate, foreigners cannot regard Italy as a civilised country'.[33] Amendola was prevented from holding meetings, and the socialist leader, Matteotti, was tortured in a manner too vulgar and horrific to be reported in the press.[34] There was less severity against communist candidates, probably because any communist success would further divide the opposition as well as fostering the useful illusion that a bolshevik danger still existed.[35] One socialist candidate was killed; many other candidates withdrew from the elections; hundreds of other people were killed and wounded; and individual *ras* saw to it that doubtful areas were systematically terrorised on election day itself.[36]

The cruelties were especially evident in the case of rebellious fascists who challenged party discipline and voiced their revulsion at what was happening. Several such dissidents were nearly killed by Dumini's gang when they were savagely beaten in broad daylight outside Milan station as a warning to others. Mussolini expressed his delight at such actions and ordered that Dumini be given a special bonus payment; he specified that 'traitors must be treated as traitors' and 'a good beating never does any harm'. Attacks on at least two prominent candidates – the socialist Gonzales and the dissident fascist Forni – appear to have been ordered personally by him.[37]

The police took little action against such barbarities and several foreign journalists who reported them were flogged or expelled from the country.[38] The official story was that no intimidation was ever employed,[39] because the secret of success lay in obtaining the effects of violence while maintaining the reputation of non-violence. Mussolini often played the innocent, pretending that he would not have wished to 'stain with blood the essentially spiritual movement that I led to victory'.[40]

Apart from the use of intimidation, these elections were gerrymandered more shamelessly than any election before them. Voting certificates were confiscated from opponents and then used many times over by fascists; the secrecy of the ballot was violated in a dozen ways; illiterates were illegally put on the voting roll, as were names of the dead; official circulars to local fascist parties gave detailed instructions about destroying opposition voting papers in the urns and otherwise manipulating results. It was evidently possible for the fascists to take away the ballot boxes before the count, and perhaps this explains why in some areas over 100 per cent of the registered voters appeared to have voted.[41] Such things had happened before, but never, it seems, on anything like this scale.

In the final result the fascists found themselves with 65 per cent of the votes – many more than the 25 per cent needed to win a majority of seats – and they plausibly claimed that in no previous election had any party done so well; the various opposition groups had only three million votes between them and some 180 seats against 374. Whether Mussolini would have obtained a majority in a free vote can never be known; the opposition said not, and the fact that he used force and fraud on such a scale suggests that he was far from confident. Intimidation was so necessary to his purpose that after the elections he again ordered his punitive squads into action wherever any opponent had done well, and the offices of the *Corriere della Sera* were attacked because its neutral attitude was blamed for the high opposition vote in Milan.[42]

Some fascists tried to check the orgy of violence but Mussolini told them to desist, explaining that people would only respect leaders of whom they were afraid.[43] To increase the climate of fear, Dumini was ordered to reconvene the *ceka* in Rome just as parliament was about to reassemble. There this gang of criminals found that rooms had been booked for them in a hotel next to the Chamber of Deputies where they were told to register under false names. The

75

rooms were paid for and each member of the gang received daily payments from Mussolini's personal press office. Their task was to employ against selected deputies the tactics of intimidation that had been so efficacious with the electorate.[44]

One man was specially released from prison by order of the chief of police for the purpose of joining Dumini's gang. He was asked by the latter if he had committed murder before and was then informed that their main job was to deal with Giacomo Matteotti – the most prominent opposition leader in parliament.[45] Dumini boasted that he himself had a dozen murders on his conscience and later confirmed that he had been working for some years on Mussolini's behalf.[46] Several weeks later, in what some people liked to consider an accident, the *ceka* killed Matteotti; the circumstances surrounding this crime brought the regime nearer to defeat than at any time until 1943.

Matteotti was killed because he tried to have the election declared invalid. This was in answer to a provocative speech by Mussolini who, on 30 May, astonished the opposition by asking parliament for the approval *en bloc* of several thousand laws. He further demanded that the many complaints against illegalities during the elections – about a million breaches of the law had been alleged[47] – be ruled out of order, again *en bloc*. In reply, Matteotti improvised a short but courageous speech that was noisily interrupted a hundred times in a concerted attempt to silence him. Mussolini could not contain his anger as the socialist leader spelt out in detail how the election had been won only by fraud and violence and how only a minority of electors had been able to vote freely; moreover Mussolini was provoked to admit in reply that he would have taken no account of the vote if it had gone against him. Matteotti had already been assaulted several times by fascist thugs and Mussolini's personally owned newspaper warned of worse to come if he did not keep quiet,[48] yet the socialist leader told English friends that, though he knew his life was in danger, he had a duty to tell the world that fascism continued to exist only through terrorism and financial corruption on a huge scale.[49] Such accusations made by a responsible parliamentary leader were bound to throw doubt on the legitimacy of the regime and challenge the impression of widespread popular support that the fascists were at such pains to manufacture. More dangerous still, Matteotti had prepared a large dossier of fascist crimes based on evidence taken only from fascist sources, and it was known that translations of this dossier were being prepared in Belgium and England.

Mussolini could never allow a single deputy to stand in his way and publicly called on his strong-arm men to take more tangible action.[50] His meaning could be inferred from other remarks he now made in private about his leading opponents: 'get rid of him',[51] 'teach him a lesson,'[52] 'he must be made to disappear secretly but finally', and 'with adversaries such as Matteotti one must fall back on the revolver'.[53] Past experience had taught Mussolini that, given such hints, his more zealous legionaries would leap to carry out a suitable act of punishment. It is sometimes said that, in anathematising Matteotti, Mussolini did not intend to be taken seriously. But he must have known the risk of talking in this vein to people who over the years had become habituated to using guns and bludgeons to intimidate socialist leaders. He cannot have been unaware of the likelihood that one of his hearers would act against an enemy whom he designated by name, because such enemies were invariably attacked. Nor was he in much danger of being held personally responsible because no one would dare to give evidence against him, and, if the worst happened, he could claim that they had exceeded his instructions and he had not meant what they thought he said.

At the beginning of June, some days before the assassination, several deputies were once again assaulted by blackshirts outside the parliament building as a warning that criticism was no longer permissible.[54] Debates in parliament had lost all pretence of seriousness and Mussolini personally engaged in his own kind of intimidation, interrupting dozens of times a day and threatening to use violence against the opposition – he talked more than once of shooting them in the back if necessary.[55] On 7 June, he controlled himself sufficiently to make a moderate speech appealing for support but, for perhaps the only time in his life, the words were spoken so softly that they could hardly be heard,[56] and were presumably intended only for the record. In private, he spoke of 'execution squads' and of stringing up the corpses of anti-fascist leaders in the square outside his office.[57] On 9 June, he was heard telling Dumini that the *ceka* must hurry up and do something to justify its existence.[58]

On 10 June, Dumini and Volpi killed Matteotti and took the body into the countryside to bury it and conceal all traces of the murder. Conceivably the intention was only to kidnap their victim, but – and again we have to guess from the few known facts – a corpse could be concealed, whereas a kidnapped person might return one day to tell his story, and Matteotti's previous history made it abundantly clear that no mere kidnapping or torture would ever have forced him into silence. The attack took place on orders from Filippo Marinelli and perhaps also from Cesare Rossi, the two leading figures in the fascist hierarchy immediately under the Duce, both of whom regularly met Mussolini each day to know his orders. Not one of these men would have attacked the leading figure of the parliamentary opposition unless they were sure of immunity and sure that it was Mussolini's wish. Everyone involved said later that they were certain he wanted it, and the fact that Marinelli (after a few months in prison) remained at the top of the fascist party for the next twenty years – unlike anyone else – is further confirmation that the *ceka* did what was expected of them on this occasion.

Late on 10 June, a few hours after the murder, Dumini came to Mussolini's office to report what had happened. He showed no anxiety or agitation,[59] which suggests that he was expecting approval. He brought with him a piece of bloodstained upholstery from the car in which Matteotti had been stabbed to death: not all the material, just a small piece, suggesting that the intention was not to destroy incriminating evidence but to prove to his employers that the deed was done.

The following day, 11 June, Mussolini publicly denied all knowledge that a crime had been committed and did not, of course, arrest those he now knew to be the culprits. He said very little even to his closest aides but cynically instructed them to spread the rumour that Matteotti had escaped abroad.[60] In public he showed no surprise or concern, but put on an act of gaiety and laughter that was unusual for him.[61] But he privately gave orders that any suspicious evidence be concealed, particularly the car that Dumini had used to transport the body;[62] he added that his execution squads might similarly dispose before long of the other leaders of the opposition, Albertini, Treves and Filippo Turati.[63] Meanwhile his staff were told to create 'as much confusion as possible' about what had happened: 'if I get away with this we all survive, otherwise we shall all sink together'.[64]

On 12 June he told parliament that, although he was now beginning to suspect foul play he was still in the dark. In fact, however, he already had a most unwelcome piece of information: an observant apartment caretaker had given the police the number of a car full of suspicious-looking people that had been seen for several days near Matteotti's home, and the car, with its incriminating bloodstains, was quickly traced to the murderers. Mussolini was shattered by this news;[65] what had nearly been a perfect crime was now almost bound to be solved and Dumini was dangerously close to his own person. For several days a sense of shock paralysed the government and Mussolini later confessed that a few resolute men could easily have alerted public opinion and started an insurrection that would have swept fascism away.[66]

Nothing happened. Even the main industrial towns – Milan, Turin, and Bologna – which, two years earlier, would have seen immense popular demonstrations at such an outrage, were quiet:[67] the squads had done their job of intimidation only too well. Mussolini after a few days recovered his poise. He prorogued parliament to prevent any further debates and mobilised the fascist militia – or as many as were not too frightened to obey. He also ordered the arrest of Dumini and his gang so as to have someone to blame.

The chief of police, General De Bono, took over the investigation personally, though according to Italian law this was the job of the magistrates and not the police. De Bono went at once to interrogate Dumini accompanied by two generals of the fascist militia: this again was quite illegal and was bound to suggest that they wanted to concoct with the accused a plausible story for the courts. De Bono refused to hand over the case to the correct authorities for a whole week, during which time most of the *ceka* and their accomplices were allowed to escape and some of the evidence disappeared altogether. He would hardly have acted so improperly and exposed himself to accusations of illegal procedure if he had not feared the revelation of some inexpedient truths.[68]

Dumini went to prison for murder but was released after two years and, on emerging, told other people that Mussolini had been primarily responsible for the crime; for which imputation he was imprisoned again and for a much longer period. Such an awkward accusation had to be hushed up, and over the next fifteen years large sums were paid to this convicted murderer by the police, as well as by the fascist party and Mussolini himself – Dumini's income from these sources seems to have been considerably higher than that of a cabinet minister.[69] Such payments can only have been hush-money, and no doubt there was fear of possible revelations from a dossier which Dumini said he had given into the custody of lawyers in Texas. Somehow it was arranged that Mussolini's name hardly appeared at all in the hundred volumes of evidence collected by the judiciary on the Matteotti case and he was never asked to testify, despite damaging accusations made against him by Cesare Rossi and others. He once confessed that the days after the murder were among the most terrible of his life. Practically never again did he mention the name of Matteotti, his most redoubtable opponent in twenty years.

Recovery, June – December 1924

How Mussolini recovered his position in the next six months is further evidence of his political ability. He started with public opinion apparently ranged against him and the likelihood that, if the opposition played their cards well, he could not survive. Fascist newspapers were almost without readers and the *Corriere della Sera* sold approximately twenty copies to every one sold by his own *Popolo d'Italia*.[70] Many fascists showed a willingness to abandon someone so suspect, and both the extremists and moderate 'normalisers' in the party had reason to lose faith in him. Fascism could now be seen to be almost bereft of talent except for himself; it was associated with a long string of violent outrages that could not be other than deliberate – though fascist historians now called them 'errors' rather than misdeeds – and which he as minister of the interior had shown no wish to prevent or bring to justice. Half a dozen of his collaborators were under arrest and implicated in a political murder. His original promise to restore law, order and efficient government was exposed as bunkum. Any of his predecessors would have felt bound to resign, but this was the one thing he never seriously contemplated, partly because it would certainly have meant being arrested for complicity in crime. Instead he forced other fascists to resign in the hope of allaying public clamour: De Bono had to go as head of the police and the militia; his two most trusted lieutenants, Marinelli and Rossi, were arrested, and incredibly he tried to pretend that neither had been close to him.[71] Four other cabinet ministers resigned in the hope that a new government of national reconciliation would be formed. He himself was determined to remain – he claimed to be backed by 300,000 bayonets of the fascist militia, a private army that was answerable to no one but himself.[72]

It is hard to point to any single person in politics who would have had the ability and political power to succeed him; nor was there anyone else with the authority and reckless physical courage of Matteotti to denounce him before Europe as an accomplice in murder. By preventing any meeting of the Chamber of Deputies he deprived the opposition of their main forum of protest, and in any case his opponents were radically divided about what action to take. He noted with some pleasurable irony that seventeen different political groups were now opposing fascism.[73]

The socialists and *popolari* chose this moment to withdraw altogether from parliament as a sign of protest; they were joined by Amendola's group of liberal-conservatives. But this 'Aventine secession' was condemned by Giolitti and his friends as a useless boycott of the legislature: rather than join such dangerous company, Giolitti preferred to give fascism another chance to justify itself in parliament. Mussolini once admitted that, if only the elder statesman of liberalism had joined the Aventine secession, it would have spelt the end of fascism,[74] whereas this split among the liberals helped to convince him that he could still win. The Vatican, too, dissociated itself from the Catholic *popolari* who joined the Aventine. The Pope was ready to admit that Mussolini must have been partly responsible for Matteotti's death, but the Church did not want to return to the agnostic liberal governments of the past and, above all, did not like seeing Catholics ranged in close alliance with socialists.[75]

What clinched Mussolini's victory was a debate in the Senate of 24 June. Only 29 people had been appointed to the Senate since fascism came to power, yet only 21 out of 398 possible votes could be mustered against him. Not only foreign countries but the king – whose intervention at this point would almost certainly have been decisive with the silent majority – took this overwhelming vote to mean that the more respectable elements in the country were still pro-fascist. Liberal senators were frightened that to pass a vote of censure would mean Mussolini's being replaced by either a socialist government or a more extreme cabal of fascists who might precipitate civil war. The philosopher Benedetto Croce went further in justification of his vote for Mussolini by insisting that fascism had done much good; it had foiled the socialists and should stay in power until there was no further danger. Since 'Mussolini is now our prisoner',[76] he could be discarded at leisure when his task was done. With Croce's full approval, three of Salandra's liberals agreed to join a reconstructed government as ministers under Mussolini. One of these three had said a few days previously that fascism was finished for ever;[77] his sudden change of mind shows that many in the old liberal establishment were lacking in either perception or courage.

This rallying behind Mussolini took place just when more of the surviving idealists inside fascism were leaving what D'Annunzio now described as a 'fetid ruin'.[78] Some fascists could not understand why a crime attributable to Mussolini's criminal temperament should be blamed on the party as a whole or even on a few scapegoats; others deserted the government for more opportunist reasons and began hinting to Giolitti that they were ready to change sides if he would offer them a ministry or undersecretaryship in a new government. For one reason or another, many fascists now deserted more or less openly.[79] The anteroom of Mussolini's office was no longer besieged by place-hunters and flatterers, and many members of the militia did not answer his call for mobilisation. It was rather the liberal senators and others outside his own party who, not understanding the kind of man they were dealing with, gave him the vital support he needed to survive.

He was also powerfully backed by the extremists, the local bosses of fascism, most of whom had violent crimes to answer for and had to conserve their local power in order to preserve an immunity from prosecution. These *ras* were aware that Mussolini, now he had strengthened his cabinet with old-style liberals, might turn against their brand of extremism just as he had ditched Marinelli and Rossi. Though Mussolini told outsiders that he was frightened of the *ras* and feared he was unable to control them, some believed that it was only with the brutal elements of fascism that he felt truly at home.[80] Whichever was true, he was now delighted to have their support and soon there were further assaults on editors of liberal papers to warn them against going too far in open criticism. There was even talk of a general massacre of non-fascists. Farinacci, the leading spokesman of the extremists, asked to be entrusted with the legal defence of Dumini against the charge of murder.

Farinacci was quoted as saying that 'by shooting a few thousand people we can put everything to rights'.[81]

Mussolini employed his usual double policy. At the same time as he posed as a liberal with his ministers, he had to appear an anti-liberal in the eyes of the men of violence who were proving to be the most stable element in his party. He could do this because, as he had learnt, people automatically seized on those parts of his speeches and actions that suited them, either ignoring any inconsistencies or explaining them away. But, of the two main groups, it was the *ras* he now needed more. In reply to their demand that the fascist revolution be protected from accountability in the courts, he stated that his regime was above the law and 'could not be prosecuted except at the bar of history'.[82] By an order in council he introduced press laws that gave him powers to bring all newspapers under the control of government officials. Since parliament was not in session, this decree was a violation of the written constitution, but he confused the liberals by pretending that it was designed to curb the extreme left.

When the national council of the fascist party met in August, Mussolini placed himself firmly alongside the men of violence who were the most applauded among the various speakers. 'Live dangerously' was the ominous watchword he gave the delegates, adding with a smile that people were asking him not for liberty but for strong government: liberty was all right for cavemen, but civilisation meant a progressive diminution in personal freedoms and, if the opposition ever tried to move from words to action, he would order the blackshirts to make mincemeat of them. In a speech he did not allow to be published he repeated that cruelty was necessary; it should be surgical cruelty and not continuously mentioned in public – ordinary citizens would accept violence as long as it was talked about only after it had been perpetrated.[83] Amendola said he had certain evidence that in September Mussolini had a plan to kill the other leaders of the opposition and abandoned it only when alternative measures were seen to be equally effective and less dangerous.[84]

In November, still pursuing his double policy, Mussolini made a public speech implying that he would now renounce extremism and dissociate himself from the *ras*; he promised that the leaders of the fascist party would henceforward be elected instead of appointed; the party would try to lessen the tensions in society by reducing its provocative public solemnities and not wearing the black shirt so often in public.[85] A few hours later, however, he unguardedly told an American journalist about more private plans to abolish parliament and set up a dictatorship to place Italy 'among the foremost nations of the world': he would soon let his squads loose and then the opposition would disappear '"like that" – here the premier blew on his palms as if blowing off dust'. As he spoke he looked like a lion about to attack.[86] When this incautious interview became public knowledge, the prime minister's press office denied that he could possibly have used such words. Nevertheless it helped to convince Giolitti at long last that Mussolini was no longer to be trusted. Giolitti said he would still vote for Mussolini on issues of foreign policy, but that at home fascism was depriving Italy of free speech; it had ended the system of elected local government laid down in the constitution; it was destroying Italian prestige abroad by insisting that Italians, unlike other peoples, were unfit to govern themselves. Fascism was rule by the bludgeon, and this had become more true since the elections.[87]

Only five deputies joined Giolitti against the massive vote of 315 'ayes' for the government after this debate: most of the opposition was still boycotting parliament. Orlando abstained and, for his benefit, Mussolini pretended once again that he would shortly be able to return to constitutional 'normality'.[88] Orlando still put the blame on socialism for having made parliament unworkable before October 1922, and accepted that a further period of dictatorship might be needed to undo this damage. Salandra, too, maintained that fascism should stay in power, since it had 'not yet completed its work'; and, despite all its illegalities, the attempt to achieve a balanced budget was still in its favour.[89]

Mussolini's main problem was not with these slightly ingenuous liberals, but rather with the disorderly men of violence upon whom he had increasingly to rely as moderate opinion began to desert him. Foreign newspapers described how the names of twenty *ras* were becoming household words for being quite outside the law, and hundreds of minor *rassini* were equally able in their own no-go areas to commit murder against their personal enemies with little or no control by the courts and the police.[90] Throughout November these men – most of them senior officers in the fascist militia – became increasingly reckless. De Bono had been suspended as commandant of the militia because of his involvement in the Matteotti murder, and his successor, Italo Balbo, was now publicly implicated in the murder of the priest Don Minzoni and in many other brutal crimes in and around Ferrara. Such was the public outcry that Balbo resigned, but Mussolini, who very possibly feared this man as his chief potential rival, gave him fulsome and public praise.

Early in December, Mussolini sent out a plea to the squads to refrain from their usual behaviour during the few days when foreign journalists were in Rome for the meeting of the council of the League of Nations; the moment for violence would come again, but later. This was not the first time he had called them to order when an international congress met in Rome: and it suggests that he could control the terrorists whenever he needed to.[91] In private, he was already contemplating a new *coup* against the relics of parliamentary government and the survivors of the old liberal ruling class,[92] but in public he preferred to show the velvet glove. He informed the Senate that he rejected any idea of dictatorship, for the simple reason that Italians would never stand for it and would always rebel against a dictator. He said he was prepared to resign if ever the king told him to, but he would warn any critics that by ending fascism they might be paving the way for communism.[93]

The largely non-fascist Senate still voted for him in December with another impressive majority – 208 votes to 54. But the very next day a public charge was preferred by an individual member of the opposition against Senator De Bono for involvement in Matteotti's murder. Meanwhile, Balbo and Dino Grandi were being attacked in the opposition press for serious alleged misdeeds. Even more alarming, another document came to light written by a deputy speaker of the Chamber of Deputies, Francesco Giunta, who had ordered the squads into action against a member of parliament on the grounds that this was the prime minister's personal wish. Mussolini at first intervened to defend Giunta, but then changed his mind and forced Giunta to submit his resignation in order to allay the mounting dismay in the country. Both decisions were unpopular with many fascists: some of his followers thought him too weak, others too authoritarian, while others accused him of changing his mind from one day to another. The government seemed close to disintegration and the *Corriere della Sera* predicted that, after these latest revelations, Mussolini would have to resign.[94]

In the last two weeks of the year, there was a concerted rebellion by some of the *ras* and consuls of the militia who feared that he might be so shaken that he would desert them and hand them over to due process of law. They called him a bungler, even a traitor and a turncoat, who had failed because he had been content to bludgeon his enemies instead of killing a few thousand.[95] Some of them began to suspect that he had sold out to the world of big business. Meanwhile, a parallel rebellion from the 'normalising' wing of the party was demanding a return to more 'constitutional' government. Some of the critics accused him of setting up a regime that was too much like bolshevism for comfort.[96] Three or four dozen fascist deputies met privately and condemned the *ras* and their squads: some wanted Mussolini's resignation, and most were in favour of asking the left-wing deputies on the 'Aventine' to return to parliament and co-operate in a new government of national reconciliation.[97]

Up till the end of December the non-fascist opposition continued to assume that, faced with these difficulties, Mussolini was bound to fall. Giolitti commented that in some provinces, notably Piedmont and Sicily, fascism no longer existed and elsewhere was rapidly losing ground; Amendola thought that a defection by fascist deputies might be sufficient to enable a vote against Mussolini to be carried in parliament, in which case even the squads of the fascist militia might desert him.[98] This seemed all the more likely after publication of the most damaging document of all – Cesare Rossi's memorandum which ascribed some of the worst crimes of the past two years directly to Mussolini. But in fact it was publication of this document which eventually pushed him into setting up a full dictatorship, because his only alternative was to challenge such accusations in the courts, and this would very likely have ended his career.

For a brief while he drifted without direction as he considered how to save himself.[99] Some of his colleagues advised him to resign, and at first he was almost ready to accept their advice against the obvious alternative which was to mobilise the militia and threaten civil war.[100] The remaining liberal ministers decided to abandon him at this point and were at first backed by Federzoni, the ex-nationalist in the cabinet; but a few hours later Federzoni changed his mind – either because he guessed which side would win or because he saw a chance of succeeding to the premiership.[101] At this critical moment, fifty or more senior officers in the militia hurried to Rome and burst into Mussolini's office to tell him that he must act forcefully or they would depose him. One account of this dramatic scene described how he tried to recall them to a sense of discipline; another how he burst into tears.[102] In the afternoon of the same day, a rumour began to circulate that he had resigned. In some parts of Italy everyone poured into the streets to celebrate the end of fascism and even the local authorities and many fascists themselves joined in a night of jubilation.[103] Nothing like this was to be seen again for twenty years.

On 2 January 1925, Amendola told the local correspondent of the London *Times* that Mussolini 'was finished',[104] but the Duce was in fact already planning his counter attack. He had to act quickly, because the militia might move against him if he faltered, or the opposition might produce further criminal revelations that would make his continuance in office impossible, or else the king might use the occasion to dismiss him as morally and politically unfit to rule. Salandra's group of conservative liberals was on the point of leaving his coalition and that would have had a dramatic effect on opinion at court as well as in the country at large.

His first reaction was to recall parliament – there he would have a clear majority because of the continuing boycott by the 'Aventine' deputies of the opposition. Then on 3 January he announced to the deputies that he took personal responsibility for all that had happened. He denied that any *ceka* had existed and said that the deeds of Dumini's friends were too stupid to be blamed on an intelligent person such as himself. Moreover he had admired Matteotti whose courage and obstinate determination 'sometimes equalled my own'. Nevertheless he would take responsibility for everything – and this was authoritatively stated to include Matteotti's murder. If fascism had

Mussolini

turned out to be not a great idealistic movement of national renewal but rather a vulgar riot of bludgeons and castor oil, he alone was to blame; he alone would take responsibility for putting the country to rights – something that could be done only through a personal dictatorship.[105]

Fascist government at work

7

Taming the opposition, 1925

Mussolini looked back on his speech of 3 January 1925 as one of the two or three most decisive events in the fascist revolution. Already before he spoke, squads all over Italy were already moving into action to sack property, beat up opponents and prevent opposition newspapers being sold; and they were supported by orders from Rome.[1] The two remaining liberals in the government resigned – one of them reluctantly, as he still feared that the socialists might win power if the government fell.[2] One fascist minister also resigned and another, De' Stefani, was sufficiently shaken to say that fascism should go into reverse and return to the free working of the constitution.[3] But Mussolini, once he had taken personal responsibility for so many illegalities, could never contemplate the possibility of losing power. He felt instinctively that as soon as public opinion saw he was firmly in charge, the lukewarm, the time-servers, the place-hunters and the silent majority would again range themselves behind him.

One vital fact in his favour was support from Federzoni and the former nationalists. Still more important was the fact that the fascist militia was put on stand-by while the police arrested the more dangerous members of the opposition. British newspapers described what followed as a campaign of intimidation on a scale almost impossible to conceive which 'in any self-respecting country' would have forced Mussolini's resignation.[4] The more extreme fascists, on the other hand, were amazed at his moderation; they correctly feared that he still wanted to keep the king and the conservatives on his side as a counterbalance to themselves. To retain a middle position, he sequestered occasional numbers of the fascist newspapers *Impero* and *Conquista dello Stato*, but the communist *Unità* was confiscated eleven times in thirteen days.[5] The liberal press, too, was effectively muzzled for a few critical weeks and police commissioners were attached to each paper to ensure that readers knew only such facts as Mussolini selected. At the beginning of January, it was estimated that all the fascist newspapers together sold about 300,000 copies daily, compared with four million sold by the main liberal journals; but a month later foreigners noted that in Rome, though people were still refusing to read the former, liberal newspapers could hardly be found at all.[6]

If the king had asked for the government's resignation or had abdicated as he had threatened to do several times, fascism would have been hard put to it to survive: almost certainly the army, as well as the aristocracy and the higher civil service, would have obeyed any orders from the crown. Croce and other liberals later criticised Vittorio Emanuele for remaining passive, but they themselves had until now been passive or active supporters of fascism. Failing a clear parliamentary decision, the king could not act against fascism without infringing the constitution once again, and he could be forgiven for thinking that the liberals merely looked upon him as a cat's-paw to do what they dared not do themselves. Yet he had already favoured the fascists more than he had ever favoured any other party. He told people that 'he had never had a premier with whom he found it so satisfactory to deal as with Signor Mussolini'.[7] He greatly appreciated the prime minister's outward deference to the monarchy and admired him for always knowing his own mind and expressing his views with clarity and brevity – without preaching or arrogance. Vittorio Emanuele, like so many others, misread the situation and may still have been expecting that fascism would eventually return to something like constitutional government.

On 3 January, Mussolini challenged his opponents to impeach him, as the constitution allowed, but this was for rhetorical effect only and when a motion of censure was tabled he at once proposed an adjournment, thus avoiding a vote.[8] Without newspapers and without parliament, the opposition was helpless. He knew that even some of the more prominent fascists criticised him for behaving with dangerous constitutional impropriety, and yet at this crucial moment, as he had foreseen, many of the more irresolute and time-serving liberals broke ranks to rejoin his camp when they saw that he was likely to succeed. Most members of Salandra's group, who in December had agreed to detach themselves from the government, changed their tune in January and refused to follow Salandra into opposition. Half a dozen liberal ex-ministers who had served under Giolitti and Nitti did the same and rallied behind the government. The philosopher Giovanni Gentile heaped praise on the 3 January speech and declared that Mussolini represented the true liberal tradition.[9] On 16 January, another vote of censure was moved by some of the braver liberals against what was called an attempt to take Italy back into the Middle Ages, but only thirty-seven deputies could be mustered to support it: these included the elder statesmen Giolitti, Salandra and Orlando, but they could barely make themselves heard as they were howled down with taunts that they alone had made fascist victory possible by their earlier complaisance.[10]

Meanwhile, the socialists still refused to attend parliament – a now fruitless boycott that merely hastened the process towards dictatorship. One critic commented that another Matteotti was needed brave enough to risk his life by openly challenging the regime instead of abstaining.[11] The small group of communists returned to the Chamber to accuse Mussolini of holding power by terrorism. They said that he lacked any consensus except that deriving from *manganello* and castor oil; and they added that he must realise this, as otherwise he would not have felt the need to suppress free speech. When one communist tried to follow Matteotti's example and read out in parliament some of the evidence of Mussolini's complicity in murder, he was assaulted and prevented from speaking.[12]

In reply to these few critics, Mussolini tried to throw ridicule on their merely vocal opposition. He pointed out that there was not the least sign of open rebellion, and he took this to mean that his was the only conceivable government, given the existing balance of forces. To show his disregard for the legislature he presented parliament with another bloc of 2,364 decrees which the deputies were expected to approve without discussion.[13]

In February another turn of the screw was the appointment of Farinacci as secretary of the fascist party. Farinacci was still the most powerful of the local *ras*; this ambitious, vindictive ex-socialist had not deserted the cause of fanatical extremism even in the difficult days after Matteotti's murder when other fascists had faltered. 'We have won a battle and now we must win the war': that was Mussolini's order to the man who now took over what had become the second most important post in politics. The new party secretary interpreted this order as meaning that intransigence, blind discipline and more violence were needed to intimidate the doubters and the faint-hearted. Any dissidents inside the party, whether moderates or extremists, had to accept discipline or be expelled. This applied to those consuls of the militia who had dared to threaten rebellion against Mussolini in December; equally, it applied to those among the ex-liberals and ex-nationalists who might be intending to turn the movement into a defence of conservative and bourgeois interests. Such 'normalisers', according to Farinacci, ought to have been shot in October 1922. The death penalty should be introduced to compensate for this omission as it was important to 'legalise the holy and healthy fascist illegalism' that had proved so successful in the past.[14]

A short time after Farinacci's appointment, Mussolini fell gravely ill and was virtually out of politics for a month. He always assiduously cultivated the myth of being in robust health but the truth was different. For fifteen years he had undergone regular treatment for a worrying venereal disease and some people continued to suspect that he was still suffering from it.[15] He himself was worried enough to send samples of blood for testing in England. The results of a Wassermann test proved negative and he had to be dissuaded from the odd idea of proclaiming the fact in a public communiqué to put an end to rumours.[16] More worrying were the stomach cramps from which he had suffered ever since his impoverished exile in Switzerland.[17] These recurred periodically, notably at the time of Matteotti's murder.[18] In February 1925 after the terrible tension of his successful counter-attack against the critics, he collapsed completely one day in his car; not for the first time, he vomited blood, and X-rays showed that he had a severe gastro-duodenal ulcer.[19]

Considerable public alarm and a lot of gossip were encouraged by the decision not to release a public bulletin about his month-long absence from work. There was even a moment when Farinacci and the extremists began once again to think that they might be able to displace him and take over the government.[20] Such was the danger that many non-fascists were greatly relieved when he reappeared in parliament; the whole assembly rose to its feet to greet him and chant 'Giovinezza' – except for seven communist deputies who remained seated and then tried to sing the 'Internationale' as an antiphon.[21] The story was circulated that he was completely cured and a severe recurrence shortly afterwards was kept quiet.[22] But from now onwards he was always something of an invalid; he was put on a strict diet and his dislike of eating in company was reinforced as he wanted to avoid revealing the full extent of his ill-health.

Shortly after his reappearance, another wave of fascist violence took place and once again many of the chosen victims were the newspaper editors and parliamentary leaders who still refused to submit. Farinacci told the fascist militia that Amendola, the socialist leader Filippo Turati, Albertini and De Gasperi should have suffered the same fate as Matteotti and he would not censure anyone who took it upon himself to punish them suitably. One result in July was a cowardly assault on Amendola by hundreds of fascists led by a member of parliament, Carlo Scorza, who later became one of Farinacci's successors as secretary of the fascist party. Amendola had already been attacked a number of times, but this was the worst and last: he suffered injuries that caused his death. After Matteotti's assassination, Amendola had been Mussolini's chief opponent in Italy. There had been no provocation from the victim except a refusal to submit – the attack was an act of pure vendetta and intimidation. Mussolini had just lectured the fascist party, saying that, while deprecating 'brutal and unintelligent violence', he welcomed 'surgical violence' and preferred 'the *squadrista* who acts' to the impotent intellectual who just talked; he added that he still needed the cudgel and cold steel. These words, greeted with the usual tumultuous applause, left little doubt as to his meaning.[23]

One by one the opposition leaders were picked off. The Rosselli family had to endure 'punitive action' three times; Filippo Turati, like that other embattled socialist, Professor Gaetano Salvemini, was driven to follow Nitti and Don Sturzo into exile, and attacks against minor figures throughout Italy continued to be reported each day. Particularly brutal treatment was given to the mild Piero Gobetti, most sensible and subtle of all Italian journalists: Mussolini sent instructions that life be made difficult for him[24] and he died in exile at the age of only twenty-four after being savagely beaten. His death was a tragic loss for the country.

Mussolini's personal involvement in these crimes was kept secret as far as possible and he may well not have always approved of what was done. Some fascist violence, as he well knew, arose out of personal rivalry and was a cover for actions of petty crime, or was intended to destroy the livelihood of a business competitor.[25] Naturally he deprecated the kind of casual hooliganism that caused unnecessary scandal. Although he employed known criminals for 'surgical' action, he was distressed when fascism acquired the reputation of being a criminal organisation, or when violence broke out at a moment when he was posing as a man of moderation and goodwill. He then had to lay the blame on unruly subordinates or claim that communists had infiltrated into the fascist party to give it a bad name.[26]

Fortunately for him, methods other than violent ones were often equally effective. Gentle pressure was enough to persuade the rich Crespi brothers of Milan, owners of the *Corriere della Sera*, to get rid of its editor, Albertini. The *Corriere* was the only Italian paper read abroad and had to be controlled if fascist atrocities were to be concealed from foreigners.[27] Likewise senator Frassati was forced to resign from *La Stampa*, Vettori from *Il Giornale d'Italia* and Giordana from *La Tribuna*; all four papers were then given hand-picked fascist editors. Mussolini was especially sensitive over humorous periodicals – perhaps because he felt more vulnerable to ridicule than to reasoned argument – and Giannini, who ran the very successful satirical *Il Becco Giallo*, was driven into exile. Some journalists were persecuted even after they had left the country, their relatives held as hostages or maltreated, their property confiscated, and lawyers who defended their interests assaulted. To ingratiate himself with the leader, one prominent fascist offered to follow these exiles abroad and assassinate them.[28]

Censorship was something Mussolini had once condemned outright and some of his associates still disliked it. But once he was in power he meant to control journalism. Newspaper readers were gullible and impotent; he owed them no respect but claimed he had a duty to protect them from irresponsible editors whose lies were discrediting Italy abroad.[29] Suddenly on 20 June 1925, late in the evening, he caught parliament unawares and proposed new press laws. All was over in half an hour with no debate and only five dissentient votes; parliament was then closed until the end of the year.

With the foreign press, different techniques were necessary. To allay the shock caused by his new censorship laws, he wrote a letter to the London *Times* insisting that he had abolished no liberties at all and had the enthusiastic backing of almost every Italian.[30] Nevertheless, a number of foreign correspondents were expelled for smuggling out undesirable stories about Amendola's murder and about the corruption and inefficiency of the regime. Just as foreign diplomats in Italy could be declared *persona non grata* if they kept in contact with the opposition, so the new undersecretary of state, Dino Grandi, operated an 'intimidation department' against foreign journalists and occasionally they were physically assaulted by fascist hooligans.[31] Foreign editors who wanted to keep correspondents in Italy were given stringent rules to obey; failure to comply with these would result in cables arriving so garbled as to be meaningless or held up on some pretext until a story was too cold for publication.[32] On the other hand, foreign correspondents who obeyed the unwritten rules were given privileged information and allowed to send their news without payment through the official telegraph services; some of them were bribed with a monthly cheque from the press office and the more amenable were exempted from paying taxes. On sensitive issues like the murder of Matteotti, they were strictly forbidden to send anything except the official press release.[33] Threats and bribes thus helped Mussolini not only to conceal from foreign readers the extent of his brutality, but also to convince many people abroad that he had saved Europe from bolshevism and that fascism had a social philosophy worthy of serious consideration.

This was a brilliant exercise in public relations and it was very helpful to him that so little unbiased news about Italy was reported in the world's press.[34] Mussolini demanded that foreign countries should not interfere with Italy's domestic affairs and threatened other governments with retaliation if they failed to stop propaganda against fascist Italy;[35] though he was quite ready to plant favourable stories in foreign newspapers, later to be reported in the Italian press, because it was important to give the impression that fascism was everywhere admired.[36] But if foreign governments complained about hostile comments on their countries in the Italian press, they were told that papers in Italy were free from government control.[37]

Being a skilled journalist himself, Mussolini saw most problems from the public relations angle and in terms of how much personal prestige their solution could offer him. On his very first day in office, he announced that the problem of the deep south, one of the most obdurate and insoluble in Italy, would soon be solved.[38] A few months later, he arrived in Sicily on a battleship escorted by planes and submarines and promised Sicilians that in the next ten years their poverty would be turned into riches. He said he knew all about their difficulties – about the *latifondi*, the terrible sulphur mines and the lack of security in the countryside; he was especially appalled to find that, fifteen years after the great Messina earthquake, many thousands were still living in makeshift huts and shanty towns. This was a fact 'that dishonoured the human race' – he said that he would not sleep till he had tackled it, adding that he would not make such a promise unless he knew he could keep his word.[39] But the shanty towns were still there at his death twenty years later and the 'southern problem', despite repeated claims that it no longer existed, was no nearer a solution.[40]

To some extent these harsh facts could be covered up cosmetically through his control of the press. Journalists were instructed not to refer to bandits in Sardinia; at most they might talk of 'fugitives from justice' and only when the police killed or captured one. The malaria that was epidemic in Sardinia had to be called 'intermittent fever', and the Sicilian Mafia and Neapolitan Camorra were best not referred to at all.[41]

The outward manifestations of the Mafia, however, were dealt with far more effectively by Mussolini than by any liberal government in modern times. This was done partly by accepting an alliance with certain criminal elements in Sicily. But a more important factor was his rejection of elections and the jury system, because the Mafia had flourished mainly by threatening witnesses and juries and by manipulating the electoral system. Two thousand people were quickly put in prison – many of them merely on suspicion, with little positive evidence – and the worst examples of Mafia disorderliness immediately ceased.[42] This proved that a government prepared to ignore constitutional guarantees could subdue, if not eliminate, a scourge that was more responsible than anything else for keeping Sicily poor and backward.

Some of his other problems were tackled by using the carrot rather than the stick. There was for instance the problem posed by Gabriele D'Annunzio, who had a great following in the country at large and who, being closely in touch with some of the leading anti-fascists, might have been a dangerous enemy in the critical months following Matteotti's death. D'Annunzio was far better known than Mussolini until 1922 and was envied by the fascists as someone whose rich fantasy invented the outward choreography of crowd scenes that they later borrowed with scant acknowledgement. Mussolini never liked to confess how much he profited from D'Annunzio's example and cannot have enjoyed begging the latter to desert the opposition and help fascism; nor can he have relished receiving in reply a complaint that fascism had invented nothing but had taken its best ideas from *dannunzianesimo*.[43] No other Italian was ever allowed to speak to Mussolini in this vein. But he was always skilful at knowing and using the weaknesses of others – in D'Annunzio's case, avarice and vanity. He gave him the title of prince, something never done previously in modern Italian history. The law was also manipulated to make it possible for the bankrupt poet to live out his days in a splendid palace on Lake Garda; in the garden was mounted the prow of a cruiser from which a sàlute of guns was fired periodically as the whim of this strange man dictated. A magnificent edition of his writings was publicly financed, on which he was paid a royalty of 30 per cent; his creditors were 'persuaded' to forgo payment and princely sums of up to a million lire a year were paid to him from 1924 till his death in 1938.[44] Mussolini, though not avaricious himself, knew how to corrupt others with the lure of money. D'Annunzio, for his part, knew how to blackmail the fascists into paying for his silent acquiescence. The result was that these two men, who at once despised and envied one another, maintained a strange association based on mutual flattery, from which both profited.

Early foreign policy

Despite his outward pretence that fascism was not for export, Mussolini set considerable store on spreading the message abroad, using Italian embassies as well as unofficial channels, for instance setting up bogus trade companies which used their profits for propaganda.[45] Soon he spoke openly of his mission to extend fascism 'everywhere' and his propagandists began to talk about sweeping away the 'Protestant civilisation' of northern Europe.[46] By April 1925 it was estimated that fascist parties existed in forty different countries, and a consignment of black shirts was sent as far away as Hyderabad. Already the possibility of forming an international anti-communist movement was being discussed.[47]

Mussolini's style abroad, as at home, was that of the bully rather than the negotiator and here too he firmly believed that in politics it was more advantageous to be feared than liked. In foreign policy he was concerned less to reduce international animosities than to foster them, challenging other countries one after another to create the impression of being a difficult person who had to be bought off with victories of prestige. 'Running about biting everybody' was how the South African leader, Smuts, described him at the end of 1923.[48]

Some of his immediate subordinates were sure he acted in foreign affairs with an eye on domestic policy. Either he was trying to distract attention from internal problems or he wanted to impress Italians with successes abroad, even if these successes were ephemeral or illusory and won him few foreign friends.[49] What he seemed to be searching for was the grand gesture, whether at the level of posing for the cameras brandishing a sword, or with the outward trappings of diplomacy, as at Territet and Corfu. At the same time as he told foreigners that his policy was one of peace and co-operation, he told Italians that his aim was national grandeur. Italy, which had once dominated the world, might again become 'the greatest and most powerful nation' and in five or ten years her position in the world would have changed profoundly.[50]

The League of Nations could not much appeal to someone bent on upsetting the world community. Sometimes he condemned it as 'a holy alliance of the plutocratic nations' against smaller and poorer countries such as Italy;[51] later, when many of those smaller countries expressed outrage at his bullying over Corfu, he used the almost opposite argument that too many small and 'semi-barbarian nations' claimed an equal voice in it, whereas they should learn to keep their place and not interfere with their more civilised neighbours.[52] Though he went on telling foreigners he would do all in his power to support the League,[53] his representative at Geneva was actively sabotaging its work, and Italy remained a member only because he realised that international conflicts would otherwise be resolved without an Italian voice being heard.[54]

The Balkans were the obvious area for an extension of Italy's influence; here were her weakest neighbours and their rivalry offered him the best chance of a striking success. One of his first actions in foreign affairs was to support the Bulgarians in their wish for a warm-water port in the Aegean.[55] As well as attacking Greece in 1923, he prepared to fight Turkey to establish an Italian colony in Asia Minor.[56] Much more successful was his agreement with Jugoslavia in January 1924 by which Fiume was finally annexed to the Italian state. Here he proved that he could use traditional methods of diplomacy when it was really necessary, and with great advantage to Italy, but he was angry over the criticism that his policy towards Jugoslavia was the same as that of previous Italian governments. He insisted that, on the contrary, fascism was entirely original in this as in everything else.[57]

To stress the difference from his predecessors he was especially anxious to win a predominant position in Albania across the Adriatic Sea. He tried to convince the Albanians that they could not stand alone and only by accepting an Italian protectorate could they keep some vestigial independence.[58] He was caught unawares when, at the end of 1924, Ahmed Zog came to power at Tirana with Jugoslav backing, but he at once lavished money and arms on Zog to turn him into an Italian puppet and tried to make it a condition that similar help be no longer accepted from other countries.[59] By 1925 it was being claimed, somewhat prematurely, that the annexation of Albania was virtually complete, though Italian newspapers had instructions to say nothing about economic or political penetration by Italy in the area.[60]

Another diplomatic success was his recognition of Soviet Russia in 1924. It occasionally crossed his mind that there was an approximation of communism to fascism in that both were opposed to liberalism, and others took note that the two regimes worked fairly harmoniously together, or even that fascism deliberately copied some aspects of communism.[61] Mussolini had once belonged to the bolshevik wing of the Italian socialist party and still, in 1924, confessed admiration for Lenin, while Trotsky was quoted as saying that Mussolini was his best pupil.[62] The Russians stood almost alone in not criticising the fascist occupation of Corfu, and despite the persecution of communists in Italy, the Russian ambassador in Rome had fewer scruples than other diplomatic representatives about entertaining Mussolini to a party soon after Matteotti's murder.[63] Mussolini was anxious to maintain that his was the first western government to give formal recognition to the Soviets. When the British preceded him by a few days he was angry and sent highly undiplomatic protests to both London and Moscow at the 'impudence of such a blow to Italian prestige'.[64] The fact that this small matter of precedence worried him so much would be hard to explain except in terms of the fact that for him foreign policy was often merely a question of prestige and outward appearance.

He also enjoyed its conspiratorial aspect and at once developed the habit of using private envoys behind the backs of his own ambassadors, sometimes pursuing quite a different policy from theirs. In 1924, he sent an army general to Germany with the offer of assistance for a right-wing *coup*. It appears that, by 1924, he was secretly sending arms to Germany in defiance of the peace treaty recently signed by Italy, and offering to send poison gas if required so that he could keep his chemical factories in operation.[65] Mussolini at first strongly favoured the union of Germany and Austria.[66] Then it occurred to him that the territorial expansion of a warlike Germany might be a danger and he suddenly changed his mind, threatening to fight to prevent this *Anschluss* – such a union would, he said, negate Italy's greatest gain from the peace settlement, which was the creation of a weak Austria on the other side of the Brenner Pass.[67]

The most northerly province of Italy was the largely German-speaking South Tyrol which Italy had taken from Austria in 1919 and absorbed into the region now renamed Alto Adige. Italy's acquisition of this region, together with the Slav-speaking areas of the north-east, meant that the peace settlement had added half a million aliens to the country. To these people repeated assurances were given, by – among others – Mussolini himself,[68] that their language, customs and local administrative autonomy would be protected and guaranteed. Meanwhile, he considered deporting them *en masse*;[69] then he decided instead to 'Italianise' the area – closing schools, forbidding German and Slovene as languages of education, abolishing local self-government, confiscating private property where necessary, and even forcing people to change their names to ones that sounded more Italian.[70] These methods were ruthless and were called barbaric by their victims, but when Austrians protested that they were a breach of promise, he retorted that no outside comment could be tolerated on what was a purely Italian problem.

In October 1925, delegates from the leading European powers met at Locarno to guarantee the Franco-German frontier on the Rhine. Mussolini at first wanted a supplementary guarantee for the Italian frontier with Austria but on second thoughts rejected this in case it was taken as a confession of weakness.[71] He made another of his habitual attempts to transfer the conference from Locarno to Italy since, after his experience at Territet, he wanted the press arrangements to be under his personal control.[72] When this failed he gave others the impression that he was trying to sabotage the conference as he was not being permitted to play the star role. But he could not afford to seem isolated in the councils of Europe and the signing of treaties was, anyway, chiefly a matter of the publicity he could extract from them. He was ready, as his staff knew, to sign a treaty just for its effect on the public and without bothering too much about Italian interests or the details of what it contained; treaties were pieces of paper with no binding force if circumstances changed.[73]

Mussolini finally decided he had better go to Locarno and arrived there in as dramatic a manner as possible – by speedboat and with his usual bodyguard of boisterous fascists.[74] The Italian press claimed that his arrival at the conference was the critical factor in its success. No mention was made of the fact that he attended only one session for just a few minutes; nor that a hundred journalists boycotted his appearance in protest against fascist brutality – only a few days earlier another of his murder squads had run amok in Florence, killing many innocent bystanders. He arrived at one press conference escorted by his usual stage crowd of blackshirts, but the journalists refused to attend and waited outside the room to greet him in silent contempt as he emerged into the hotel lobby.[75] This did not stop the *Popolo d'Italia* from describing how a large audience was deeply impressed by what he had to say.[76] But never again did he invite a similar rebuff; henceforth, he preferred to stay at home.

In his youth he had ridiculed the waste of national resources on colonial ventures, and in 1918–19 had been perceptive enough to approve the first steps towards decolonisation.[77] But his initial opposition to any form of imperialism was firmly denied as soon as he saw the political reason for changing tack.[78] He began pressing for the concession of a colonial mandate to Italy; if necessary, he would use force to get one, and no other country would have any right to stop him.[79] When his officials explained to him that

Italy lacked the economic and financial capability for colonial expansion, he dismissed this argument as irrelevant.

Meanwhile, his orders were to place every possible difficulty in the way of France and Britain, whatever their policy might be; they had to be opposed in the administration of their mandates and colonies, but also opposed if they made any move towards decolonisation and self-rule.[80] In public, he attacked the British and French for being too brutal and domineering towards their colonies. Fascist policy was defined as seeking 'a middle way between Franco-British brutality and the over-generous concessions made in pre-fascist days by the liberals in Italy'.[81]

What he intended to do with Italy's existing colonies was first revealed in his appointment of the governor of Somalia; he chose his militia commander, Cesare De Vecchi, who preferably had to be found some post outside Italy after being implicated in some particularly savage cruelties. De Vecchi, in typical fascist vein, sent an order to this impoverished colony to prepare lavish accommodation for himself and his accompanying militiamen and for crowds to be assembled to greet his arrival. He described himself to his new subjects as a severe man who wanted no criticism. His declared policy was to make Somalia into a base from which an Italian empire in East Africa could be developed and to crush 'indigenism'. To show his disrespect for local custom he used to ride into mosques on horseback. True to his habit as a *squadrista*, he ordered the burning and sacking of rebellious villages and, to increase fascist prestige, the shooting of captured prisoners, hundreds at a time.[82]

One objective in East Africa was to bring large numbers of Italian settlers to Somalia[83] and then to encroach gradually into Ethiopian territory; while fascism was publicly promising to respect Ethiopian independence, there was already in 1922–3 a plan to establish an Italian protectorate over this enormous landlocked empire.[84] At first, Mussolini tried to further this plan by blocking Ethiopia's entry into the League of Nations; only on second thoughts, when he saw he could not prevent it, did he champion Ethiopia's membership and try to convince other members that Ras Tafari was an enlightened ruler who had succeeded in abolishing slavery.[85] By 1925, however, he was making military preparations for the moment when events in Europe would make possible a full-scale military invasion – the word 'military' was underlined by him three times to prevent any misunderstanding.[86] His generals recommended that phosgene and mustard gas – use of which was prohibited by the Geneva protocol he had just signed – be ready on the spot for the day of conquest.[87]

In Libya, too, Mussolini ordered a 'hard-hitting' policy as soon as he came to power, and unilaterally denounced the treaties by which the liberal government of Italy had guaranteed free speech and parliaments to the Arab population of Tripoli and Cyrenaica.[88] The governor, Giuseppe Volpi, while not as severe as De Vecchi in Somalia, punished any tribal leaders who dared to criticise this flagrant breach of treaty. One local leader, El Hadi Coobar, who surrendered on what he took to be a promise of clemency, was executed after a summary trial (this kind of severity was said to have increased Italian prestige among the Moslem population but it was in fact a characteristic piece of fascist miscalculation).[89] Any fertile land that Volpi thought could be used by white settlers was expropriated by what was proudly called another typically fascist law.[90] Mussolini made a grand theatrical gesture in 1926 when he visited Libya in person, arriving with two battleships and fifteen other naval vessels to give a proper impression of force. The visit was said to have caught the imagination of the Arab population and to have been worth fifty years of peaceful penetration,[91] but in fact this attempt to inspire fear had a very different effect and indeed exacerbated what became a protracted and expensive war against Libyan 'rebels'. As officials in the foreign office occasionally pointed out, his obsession with acquiring prestige for fascism was sometimes self-defeating.[92]

Fascist administrators in Libya, Somalia and Eritrea did much that was good. They poured far more money into these colonies than they took out (though this was by no means what was intended); they did much to control slavery, epidemics, and inter-tribal fighting. But this must be balanced against cynical cruelties and racialist policies, which were common enough in all colonies but were as bad here as anywhere. The basic aim was domination and conquest, not economic growth or social improvement. A lesser aim in fascist colonial policy was simply to make trouble – for example, by sending arms to the Yemen for use against the British in the expectation that the Red Sea could be made into 'a zone of purely Italian influence'.[93] When this failed, Mussolini welcomed Russian intervention in the Arabian peninsula, on the grounds – very different from what he was claiming elsewhere – that Italy would gain from the unstabilising effect of communist penetration of the Arab world.[94]

The desire to cause trouble was one reason for his intervention in Tangier. Here and in Morocco his policy was 'to keep this region in a continuously precarious state' and to increase all 'potential conflicts' wherever possible, as this would weaken Spain and France and leave the way open for a stronger Italian presence: he wondered briefly whether he might one day be able to annex Morocco.[95] There was talk of setting up an Italian submarine and air base there, and for this purpose he got in touch with the rebel leader Abd-el-Krim – he would have been enraged if the French had similarly tried to negotiate with the rebel Senussi in Libya.[96]

Another part of the world where Mussolini demonstrated characteristic aspects of fascist foreign policy was Afghanistan; he guessed that this country was destined to play a preponderant part in the politics of central Asia and by 1925 was sending arms there.[97] Friendship quickly turned to enmity when, in another typical piece of Mussolinian bravado, he sent an ultimatum to Afghanistan after an Italian had been executed for murder; he did not question the man's guilt, but demanded £6,000 in compensation and a public apology for what he considered a blow to Italian prestige. As an afterthought he ordered the press to play down his demand in case it might be thought unnecessarily humiliating for the Afghans.[98]

By 1925, he had formulated the basic principles of fascist policy towards the outside world. The aim was 'to found an empire', to win 'glory and power', 'to create in the laboratory a new generation of warriors ready at any moment to lay down their lives'.[99] The essence of fascism was said to be a 'military style'.[100] 'It is a crime not to be strong', and all Italians should consider themselves mobilised even in peacetime, while he himself intended to raise their military efficiency 'to the very limit of what is possible'. 'Peacemongering' was folly. He was going to build an air force that would 'dominate the skies', and Italians must learn to feel themselves to be 'in a permanent state of war' as they moved towards making this 'the century of Italian power'.[101] One possibility in his mind was that the whole of Europe might become a powerful fascist bloc. Fascism was a creed that was bound to spread throughout the world, and he believed that even Britain and France were abandoning liberal ideals as they were forced to accept that parliamentary government no longer worked. Any contradictory evidence from foreign countries was rarely brought to his attention or mentioned in the Italian press; on the contrary, there was the daily and monotonous reiteration that fascism was everywhere either feared or admired.[102]

Organising the state

Mussolini knew that existing political institutions would have to be abolished or drastically altered if he was to avoid being voted out of power. He also knew that to succeed in amending the constitution he would need to keep the support of two very different groups, both internally divided and fearing one another, and both needing his help. The first was the fascist party, now led by Farinacci; the second consisted of the eleventh-hour converts to fascism from the old conservative ruling class and was represented in the cabinet by Federzoni. Mussolini demonstrated his skill by keeping both groups ranged behind him for twenty years, sometimes playing one against the other, giving out contradictory statements to please each in turn and never making changes so fast as to destroy the balance between them. His ultimate intention was to maximise power in his own hands, but he had to proceed gradually – 'plucking the chicken feather by feather' with the help of others.

The bureaucracy, for example, could not be changed in a hurry, nor could its old ways of behaviour. He once expressed regret that he had not drastically purged the civil service in November 1922[103] and in 1927 the party still complained that only some 15 per cent of civil servants were truly fascist;[104] but Mussolini accepted this fact as something that would alter with time. He won some initial support from the conservatives by proclaiming his intention of reducing the size of the bureaucracy and took powers to get rid of 'non-reliable' elements who refused to conform;[105] in practice, however, he realised that any purge should be on a small scale. Indeed he rather needed to increase jobs in the administration in order to gain support among intellectuals and the *petite bourgeoisie*; eventually, as part of the logic of increased state control, the number of bureaucrats was more than doubled.[106]

Another law enabled him to dismiss recalcitrant judges. Though he continued to claim that he never interfered with the judiciary,[107] in practice the judges like the legislature had to become subordinate to the executive – that is, to himself. Fascism, he said, had a perfect right to appoint judges who were fascists and to punish or dismiss those magistrates who failed to decide cases the way he wanted: scores of judges were in fact dismissed for their 'political incompatability'.[108] Soon he was intervening personally in particular cases: sometimes to order leniency, more often to specify that the accused be found guilty after a summary trial, and sometimes ordering that 'the maximum penalties' be imposed.[109]

In moving towards a personal dictatorship, Mussolini had as much difficulty with his own party as with the magistracy or the civil service. Four or five different groups existed inside fascism, despite his wish to weld them into a single manifestation of his personal will.[110] To deal with this lack of unity, he summoned the party in June 1925 for what was to be its last congress: his motive was not to debate policy but to put an end to internal controversy, since further discussion of objectives would be a 'waste of time' now that he was firmly in power.[111]

His message to the delegates was 'absolute intransigence' and renunciation of the outmoded 'phraseology and mentality' of liberal Italy; they should aim at the 'fascistisation' of every institution to the point where the words 'Italian' and 'fascist' would become synonymous. The party was told that he meant to 'legalise fascist illegalism' and to disregard any protest from 'so-called intellectuals'; faith, said the party secretary, Farinacci, was more useful than brains.[112] From now onwards there were to be no more criticisms, no more divisions or 'currents' in the party, but a rigid discipline imposed from above:

not just a formal discipline, but one of substance, even 'religious'.[113]

The general theme and procedure of this congress came as a surprise to many fascists. Some delegates were hoping that they would be allowed to discuss the issues on the agenda, but were shouted down; others soon realised what was expected of them and withdrew their applications to speak. Instead of lasting for three days as announced, all was over in a few hours, and in retrospect this can be seen as a decisive occasion when controversy was stifled and conformity imposed on everyone. For this reason Mussolini looked back on it as one of the great triumphs of the regime; it was certainly a personal triumph, for he dominated the proceedings – the several thousand delegates behaved 'as wax in his hands'.[114]

What applied to the party had then to be extended to the community at large. Mussolini had once tilted against 'statolatry' and demanded a reduction in the powers of the state (as he did again at the end of his career);[115] but for most of the fascist period he accepted that he would best increase his personal authority by bringing every aspect of life under central direction. At the end of 1925, he thought he had reached the point where fascism could no longer be removed by legal means, only by force.[116] The next objective was the conscription of every Italian into either military or non-military work,[117] which would in turn make it easier for him to play the strong part in world affairs that was his dearest wish.

He had taken these objectives from the ex-nationalists and it was upon them, especially Federzoni and Alfredo Rocco (the man whom, as minister of justice from 1925 to 1932, Mussolini called 'the legislator of the fascist revolution'), that he relied to carry them out. As another ex-nationalist put it, fascism had to be totalitarian – tyrannical, if necessary – as though it were a religious order with a monastic rule of life.[118] The Italian people, said Mussolini, must learn to obey and so come of age; they must then learn to believe and so be ready to fight whenever he gave the word.[119]

Local self-government was therefore abolished: district and town councils would no longer be elected, and a centrally-nominated *podestà* would replace every elected mayor. The prefect would continue to act as the chief agent of the government in each province, but alongside him would be the local party-secretary or *federale* who – since Mussolini liked to divide and rule – was given a parallel and independent authority.[120] By using party officials and the state bureaucracy to oversee each other, he created a system of checks and balances that deprived other people of effective responsibility, leaving himself with the substance of power.

He justified this progressive approximation to a dictatorship by arguing that the co-ordination of all the forces of the nation in the hands of a single man was in the interests of everyone. In earlier life, he had said the very opposite, and fascism had at first repudiated any idea of dictatorship;[121] but though as prime minister he continued to pretend that he condemned the cult of personality,[122] in practice he deliberately developed the myth of *mussolinismo* as the one essential dogma of his regime.[123] Even non-fascists were quickly caught up in this cult of the man who alone could be trusted, the benevolent ruler who was perhaps being deceived by subordinates and surrounded by inferior beings, but who would eventually put all to rights. Farinacci begged him to proclaim himself a dictator; he was called 'almost divine'; he was a miracle-worker who was said to have halted the lava on Mount Etna before it destroyed a village, and by a mere act of will; he was the man of the century, someone in whose epoch 'we are privileged to live'.[124] Sometimes he resisted, or pretended to resist, the more extravagant flattery and said he did not like the way some people were trying to turn him into a supernatural or sacred being. Nevertheless a dictator had to erect a barrier between himself and his followers, and a sure instinct taught him that the best way to appeal to popular fantasy was to propagate the notion that he could do no wrong. Increasingly he persuaded himself that he was governed by 'a mystic force' and would always reach the right answers as long as he refused to be deterred by criticism or advice.[125]

This delusion was encouraged not just by the radical fascists round Farinacci who saw the Duce as a heaven-sent saviour to improve Italy's and their own fortunes, but by the more level-headed Federzoni[126] – all the fascist leaders increasingly realised that their own survival was tied up in the myth of the great dictator. Nor was Mussolini's capacity for self-criticism strong enough to see through attempts to exploit his name. In Sicily, with great solemnity, he laid the foundation stone of a new town that was said to be the first of thousands, each with ten thousand or more inhabitants; this one was given the name of 'Mussolinia', but little was ever heard of it or them again.[127] A whole-page advertisement was placed in the newspapers by Perugina confectionery quoting a personal endorsement by the Duce himself: 'I tell you, and authorise you to repeat it, that your chocolate is truly exquisite'.[128] It was not easy for him to encourage others to let him know if or when he strayed into the ridiculous.

At the end of 1925, he assumed a new title: not just prime minister, but 'head of government'. A law defining the prerogatives of this office passed through the Chamber with no discussion at all and there was one lone dissentient voice in the Senate. Parliament declared it a crime to 'offend the honour or prestige of the head of government', incurring penalties of up to five years in prison. The new office was compared to Cromwell's lord protectorship and Bismarck's chancellorship, though the comparison irritated Mussolini who insisted that the idea was incomparable and original.[129]

One practical result was that the cabinet of ministers was demoted to a purely consultative position. The *capo del governo* was allowed to legislate without parliamentary consent, even to specify his own emoluments by decree. Nor could parliament discuss any matter at all unless he invited it to do so; and this meant that he could no longer be removed or so much as challenged by a vote of censure. He told a foreign correspondent that parliamentary government had proved 'totally unsuited to the character, education and mentality of the Italian people',[130] and if he let it remain nominally in existence, this was only because to suppress it might make foreigners doubt the purity of his intentions. From now onwards he expected parliament to show a sense of discipline; its role in the regime was, by voting unanimously, to impress outside opinion and make it appear that everyone in Italy was behind him.[131]

By the end of 1925, parliament, the bureaucracy and the judiciary had all been brought within the system, with the result that there was less need to rely on violence and the fascist party itself. Farinacci led some of the extremists in one more effort to assert themselves and prevent the Duce removing himself from party influence. Claiming as he did to be number two in the regime, the party secretary was deeply offended to find himself obliged to submit to orders from the prefect of Cremona, and tried to encourage local fascist groups to challenge and, if necessary, disobey the prefects. He also embarrassed the government by hinting at a revival of the anti-clerical programme of 1919 and followed this by resuscitating the squads in a new wave of sporadic terrorism.[132]

Mussolini did what he could to keep secret the fact that these were acts of defiance and insubordination, but in private severely censured such 'criminal' indiscipline and threatened to use the army to force the party to obey. Unfortunately, as he lamented, revolutionaries still remain after a revolution is over, and some of those revolutionaries were, he admitted, no better than common delinquents using fascism as a cover for crime.[133] Now that the opposition parties had been defeated, he could not permit his own party to challenge the authority of the leader if the regime was, as he planned, to become the dominant fact of the century's history.

Farinacci, on the other hand, in his fight for the 'autonomy of the party' and to defend its record of violence, took on himself the legal defence of Dumini in a case that awoke unwelcome memories of the Matteotti crisis. Mussolini would have liked Dumini and his accomplices to be acquitted at law, but knew that the evidence of guilt had been so publicised that it would be more prudent to settle for a light sentence. He did his best to play down the trial and sent explicit orders to Farinacci not to dramatise it, but to exclude photographers and, if possible, keep comment out of the papers.[134] Farinacci promised to obey but broke his promise in every particular because he wanted maximum coverage for his great moment in court. By his own confession, he was now the most hated man in Italy,[135] but he had the great strength of the party behind him and guessed that his best chance of keeping his position was to stay in the public eye. He was wrong – Mussolini dismissed him and even threatened to expel him from the party if he continued to play the 'anti-pope': there was room for only one Duce in Italy and the party could never be allowed to become a state within the state.[136]

Mussolini as leader

8

The private person

By his fortieth birthday in July 1923, Mussolini's features had become familiar throughout Europe and he was already a favourite subject for photographers and caricaturists. Much shorter than the official photographers made him out to be, he was also broad-shouldered and muscular, and a receding hair-line made him seem older than his years. When on display he liked to throw his chest forward and hold his large head tilted back – a mannerism that stressed the aggressive chin. He used to stand with legs astride, hands on hips, and with a slightly scowling face that some took to be self-consciously Napoleonic; or sometimes he would strike an attitude for the cameras with his hand inside his jacket – another Napoleonic affectation. Prominent features were the large protuberant eyes which he was learning to open wide and roll in a way that Londoners in December 1922 found alarming, but which the faithful saw as giving an air of eagerness and command to his expression.

As prime minister, he quickly adjusted to the manners of polite society and controlled his uncouth language in public; but he often omitted to shave and his dark hair made this very noticeable. Later, he decided to shave his whole head to conceal the process of ageing, and employed one of his police guards to act as a barber. His table manners caused some embarrassment and were possibly one reason why he disliked eating in public. A young foreign office functionary was given the task of teaching him the conventions of bourgeois dress and the rudiments of protocol and etiquette.[1]

For most of the 1920s, Mussolini continued to wear civilian clothes. On his first official visit to the king he borrowed an ill-fitting morning suit and top hat, and liked it so much that for a time he tried to impose this incongruous formality on his entourage.[2] Sometimes he would wear formal evening clothes when dining alone in a restaurant; sometimes he would wear tails together with canary-coloured shoes, and many photographs taken in 1922–4 show his new partiality for spats and a butterfly collar. He gave up these stagey mannerisms after a year or two, and also discarded his bowler hat when he noticed that in American comedy films (for which he had a passion and installed a projector at home) they were no longer worn except by his favourite stars, Laurel and Hardy.[3] Increasingly he turned to uniforms and at first these, too, could be exaggeratedly histrionic. Ministers were encouraged to wear their gold-edged blue tunic and cocked hat, sometimes with cere-monial sword and bedecked with ornate orders of chivalry.[4] After 1930, nearly all photographs show Mussolini in uniform, unless posing among bathers at Riccione or with bare torso among the peasants at harvest time – two affectations that Hitler, who lacked the physique, thought most undignified.

For some months after becoming prime minister he lived in hotels; later he found a modest bachelor apartment on the top floor of the Palazzo Tittoni where he had meals sent up to him. One of his few visitors commented on the tastelessness of its furniture and the huge painting of himself which dominated its main room.[5] After several years he moved to the much more magnificent Villa Torlonia which a complaisant aristocrat let him have for a peppercorn rent. Here, too, his existence was abstemious to the point of frugality. Few even among his own relatives were invited to his home, nor did he like accepting outside invitations because 'a dictator must never allow intrusions into the intimacies of his existence'.[6] Meals took preferably not more than three minutes and he used to say that ten minutes a day were as much as anyone should spend on eating, something that cannot have helped to improve his terrible digestion.[7] By 1923 he had almost entirely given up alcohol and tobacco.

Only one or two retainers were normally allowed into this seclusion and they were chosen for their unobtrusiveness and discretion. One was Cesira Carrocci, a vivacious and somewhat fierce lady who acted as cook and housekeeper. Another was Camillo Ridolfi, his fencing teacher and stable-man, with whom he used to ride most mornings in the extensive grounds of the villa. Horse riding was a new pleasure and soon became another passion. Ridolfi acted as major-domo whenever Mussolini travelled, and enjoyed a well-paid sinecure as a general in the fascist militia. Quinto Navarra – part usher, part private secretary – arrived each morning at eight o'clock (or at nine in winter) to take Mussolini to his office and saw more of him than anyone else for over twenty years. Mussolini had inherited Navarra from previous prime ministers and he was not a fascist. Alessandro Chiavolini, the official secretary, was an officer in the militia and had once been a journalist on the *Popolo d'Italia*: he required particular discretion, as he had to attend to delicate matters of personal finance. With Ercole Boratto, a faithful chauffeur for twenty years, Mussolini said he hardly ever exchanged a word.[8]

The Duce owned seventy acres of good agricultural land in the Romagna, which he turned into a model farm furnished with all the best equipment.[9] In 1925 he had the grandiose notion of rebuilding most of the nearby village where he had been born, and this personal monument was constructed at considerable expense.[10] A much larger country house not far away was given to him by public subscription: this was Rocca delle Caminate, an old castle lavishly restored for the purpose, which became the main holiday home of the family. Seaside vacations were regularly spent at Riccione on the Adriatic, and the king also let Mussolini use a small cottage by the sea on one of the royal estates near Rome, where his wife Rachele was apparently never allowed to go.

The family lived a comfortable life and had the use of a private yacht for the rare occasions when they needed one.[11] It was perhaps strange that someone so adept at corrupting others with money had so little interest in wealth; but he did have unlimited call on state funds for himself and his children, with no obligation to render a public account.[12] He also had a good income as a member of parliament and a landowner.[13] He took his salary as prime minister only until 1928[14] and again after 1943. His newspapers were not always very profitable and in the mid-1920s were apparently in deficit, but, as their owner, he was regularly paid a dividend and the *Popolo d'Italia* – which eventually employed over 700 people – represented a very substantial capital asset that ultimately he was able to realise.[15] In addition there were his author's royalties. Articles he wrote for American journals (or rather which were secretly written on his behalf by an American journalist in collaboration with his brother and Margherita Sarfatti) were at one point earning him $1,500 a week from the Hearst press alone.[16] Royalties were also paid on his speeches which were published as propaganda in several different languages. His second autobiography, written in 1927–8, earned him over a million lire in its first two years and an equal sum was made by another book he wrote in 1944[17] – figures that can be judged by comparing them to the prime minister's annual salary of 32,000 lire. Much of the money he earned may even have been given away and very large sums presented to him privately by Italians and foreigners went largely in unostentatious and often unrecorded works of charity.

Not until the encouragement of family life became an article of fascist faith did Mussolini bring his wife and children to live in Rome, and that was five years after becoming prime minister. Until then he would travel north three or four times a year for a few days, but sometimes this was to visit Signora Sarfatti rather than his wife.[18] Not even when he was desperately ill in 1925 did Rachele come to look after him: she disliked Roman society and still had no interest in sharing his political life, preferring to work on the farm. Even anniversary greetings were sent between them by telegram or telephone. She could refer to her husband as 'Duce' even in the family circle. There was respect and some affection between the two, if never much closeness, and some people thought him a little afraid of her. He did not seem to enjoy a family existence and at home seems to have lived largely apart, even preferring to take meals on his own.[19] But the official picture was different, especially after fascism laid down the duty of all Italians to produce more children. He then insisted on a religious marriage to set the correct example, and the general public was given a description of the dictator's family as an oasis of security and calm refreshment.[20] Rachele was made out to be the ideal fascist woman, a hard-working, dutiful stay-at-home. A questionnaire submitted to her by an American journalist was filled out by her husband who said her favourite occupations were sewing and watching films;[21] but for the most part her name and picture were kept out of the newspapers.

Their eldest child Edda, born in 1910, remained his favourite and, some thought, the only person really close to him. For a while she had an English governess but was later sent to an aristocratic finishing school from which she ran away. Vittorio was born in 1916 and recalled hardly ever seeing his father when young.[22] Bruno was born in 1918, Romano in 1927, Anna Maria in 1929. Mussolini admitted that he was not a very attentive father and others noted that he could talk to his children as though they were a public meeting.[23] They were sometimes described as precociously clever, and although he noted with some disapproval that their teachers always wanted to give them full marks for work in class, he tried to convince himself that their brilliant examination results were merited.[24] In the end, however, they were a disappointment to their father and they seem to have had a sad time trying to live up to such an exalted position.

Closer to Mussolini than any of them was his younger brother, and it was Arnaldo who concocted Benito's second 'autobiography' as well as ghost-writing some of his articles.[25] Arnaldo, like his brother, had been a schoolmaster. He was a much quieter person and acquired a public reputation for moderation and good sense, through he secretly sometimes encouraged Benito to acts of severity and aggression. As editor of the *Popolo d'Italia*, he contributed not a little to the exaggerated worship of the Duce, but was generally more humane, less quarrelsome and less vindictive, and his death in 1931 marked a stage in his brother's progressive loss of self-restraint. Arnaldo, too, was praised ecstatically by the fascist press as a brilliant writer and profoundly original thinker, but this reputation was undeserved.

No one else ever came as near to Mussolini as his brother; and even he was none too near. As well as distrusting almost everyone, the dictator respected very few of the other fascist leaders.[26] He was not simply a solitary, but a misanthrope with an abysmal view of human nature that discounted altruism and idealism. He assumed that everyone was utterly selfish and nearly everyone incompetent and untrustworthy: this was another point of agreement he found with Machiavelli – the supreme master of politics and 'perhaps the greatest of all Italian philosophers', although he thought

Machiavelli did not go far enough in his contempt for humankind.[27]

This contempt was reflected in Mussolini's instinctive dislike of social occasions and mixing with people. Sometimes he was apprehensive about his isolation and sense of superiority to everyone else, but more usually he justified this aloofness as necessary for his personal style of government.[28] He liked to think of himself as a man excluded from communion with others as if by some divine law, alone on his pedestal, open to no outside influence; and this is one reason why he took pride in always controlling his feelings, never letting his face show any strong emotion except for his two standard poses of fierceness and benevolence.[29] He used to talk of a protective wall being necessary to keep others away and even of a 'physical repulsion' at human contact. When he abolished the handshake and replaced it with what he called the 'more hygienic' Roman salute, this derived in part from an almost morbid dislike of physical touch.[30]

As Mussolini told one French interviewer, 'a leader can have no equals, no friends, and must give his confidence to no one'.[31] He used to remind himself that even at school he had never possessed a friend, since when he had deliberately chosen to live in solitude. Nor could he accept that this was a loss – friendship was a sentiment he had learnt to scorn.[32]   He went on to justify his solitude by claiming that he did not need advice and rarely felt the need even to discuss policy with anyone.[33] The claim was not entirely true, but his making it throws light on his personality. He liked people to think of his character as being not like that of other men since he was lacking in egoism or personal vanity:[34] this was equally untrue, and others close to him believed that, on the contrary, his vanity and vulnerability to flatterers knew no bounds.[35] He once confessed that 'often I would like to be wrong, but so far it has never happened and events have always turned out just as I foresaw';[36] but whether he was deluding himself or consciously creating a myth he knew to be false is hard to guess.

Mussolini had no inclination for drawing-room conversation: he tried occasionally but the result was unsuccessful and his natural preference in small talk was for gibes, wisecracks and bad language.[37] Though easily moved to sarcasm, he had little feeling for irony or humour, and increasingly lacked a sense of the ridiculous. In earlier days he appreciated the work of cartoonists and satirists but came to believe that 'fascism was too sacred a thing to be laughed at'. He would habitually freeze anyone who tried to make a joke, unless it was some foreign visitor he was trying to put in good humour; if a journalist described him as laughing, he might insist that the reference be removed, and for many years used to veto any photographs showing a smile, preferring instead the ponderous pout.[38] The impression he usually preferred to impart was one of fierceness and severity.

Despite misanthropy and lack of humour, Mussolini did have some attractive qualities. He could charm whenever he wished, and his critics acknowledged that he could be interesting and sometimes impressive to talk to. No doubt his personal magnetism worked best with those who saw him rarely; nevertheless he could always impress a visitor when he tried, and all the fascist leaders remembered how they had at times fallen under a real spell, especially in the early days before his faults became more obvious.[39] They were thrilled by his immense vitality, intelligence and quickness of mind, and everyone agreed that the practice of journalism had also given him an excellent memory for facts. These were the qualities he most prized in himself – great intelligence, memory, a will of iron, and a perfect sense of political timing.[40]

He was also anxious for the public to think of him as an immensely hard worker, whose working day might last eighteen or nineteen hours (and fourteen on Sundays), yet whose desk was always clear of paper and who could carry all the complex business of state in his head.[41] It was he who suggested to journalists that they might like to spread stories of his industriousness, and newspaper readers therefore learnt that he liked only five hours in bed and, in emergencies, could work night after night with no sleep at all.[42] This legend, like so many others, was false. His staff sometimes had orders to leave a light in his office at night to create the impression that he was working late. He was, in fact, a heavy sleeper who liked going to bed early and staying there for nine hours, not being disturbed even in emergencies. He did not take a regular siesta, but could sometimes fall asleep at his desk in the afternoon.[43] Mussolini was no idler but the stories of his extraordinary industry and efficiency were exaggerated. Statements were made that he took few days off, even none at all.[44] He tried to persuade people that he kept up an average of twenty-five meetings a day throughout the year and that in seven years he had transacted 1,887,112 items of business:[45] this last figure invites suspicion by its characteristic precision and works out at nearly 100 items each hour over a sixty-hour week. Moreover, he said that each day he found time for some sporting activity and, each evening, for playing his collection of precious violins,[46] quite apart from a careful daily reading of the national and international press. Foreign policy was said to take up most of his time, though according to one ambassador he was so 'completely swamped by the multiplicity of his duties and obligations' that he could hardly attend to foreign affairs at all.[47] On another occasion he said he spent most of each day supervising the three defence ministries. But in practice he seems to have skimped each of his many duties and was mainly interested in giving the mere appearance of superhuman activity.

These discrepancies are best explained if one sees Mussolini as an actor, a dissimulator, an exhibitionist who changed his role from hour to hour to suit the occasion. This was, of course, denied by the official propagandists[48] because it hinted at charlatanism or, at least, hypocrisy; nevertheless it is the aspect which many of those who knew him saw as the key to his personality.[49] Histrionics, wrote De Ambris, were not just second nature to him; they were his real nature.[50] As another disillusioned disciple later confessed with regret, the Duce turned out to be a mirage and the reality was closer to that arch-impostor of the eighteenth century, Cagliostro, than to Garibaldi.[51] The dramatist Pirandello was another student of human nature who interpreted Mussolini as being essentially an actor pretending to be the person Italians wanted him to be.[52] Cesare Rossi, too, who was for a time his closest collaborator, described the Duce as possessing 'a marvellous facility for playing the most diverse and contradictory parts one after the other. ... One day he says a certain thing is white, the next day he says it is black'; and, of course, expected to be believed each time. Rossi instanced the way he moved quickly from cynicism to idealism, from impulsiveness to caution, generosity to cruelty, resolution to indecision, moderation to intransigence. It was as though he never knew his genuine self and was always striving after some counterfeit impersonation.[53]

As Mussolini himself confessed, he set little store by coherence of ideas or opinions, though of course this did not stop the propaganda machine stressing that he was invariably consistent. He had learnt the effectiveness of alternating menace and conciliation, of being – in his own words – 'reactionary or revolutionary according to circumstances'. He knew the value of violent effects and contrasts and was enough of an illusionist to revel in the way they baffled the successive audiences he met each day.[54]

Mussolini the actor was, as he himself knew, living on his nerves, with a perpetual tension of muscle and mind that was only partly concealed by an outward appearance of imperturbability.[55] When he appeared relaxed and charming, that too was usually a mask; it was rarely adopted with Italians, except with D'Annunzio who was the one Italian apart from the king to be treated as almost an equal. Foreign visitors, on the other hand, were delighted to see him appear to drop his public affectations of expression and gait,[56] though they also observed how the kindly, easy-going behaviour might change abruptly if a third person appeared in the room.[57] The truculent posturing pose was no less artificial than the other, but he confessed that he needed to inculcate fear and it was deliberate policy to adopt a terrifying appearance.[58]

How far his health improved after his serious illness in 1925 it is hard to be sure, because no inkling of any indisposition was allowed into the press; foreign journalists were expelled if they hinted at anything wrong. In 1929 he had another threat of internal haemorrhage and was treated with antacids and antispasmodics as his ulcer gave periodic trouble. For years, as the symptoms persisted, he remained on a mainly liquid diet. He regularly used to drink three litres of milk a day, and eat fruit as often as six times or more a day. Occasionally, in the early 1930s, he was in pain and unable to concentrate.[59]

Yet he continued all the more to cultivate physical fitness and the appearance of youth. Attempts were made to stop even foreign newspapers referring to his age;[60] he also successfully concealed the fact that he wore spectacles and began to use a special typewriter with large characters so that he could read the notes for his speeches.[61] Another strange way of demonstrating his youthful vigour was by running down a line of soldiers when inspecting a military parade;[62] and this he continued to do in his late fifties.

Every kind of sport was said to be close to his heart, and especially those involving danger. His horse-riding became legendary, as did the speed at which he drove a car.[63] Every year he liked the public to know exactly how many hours he had flown as an aircraft pilot, and some biographers have accepted a total figure of 17,000 flying hours – as many as a full-time pilot in a lifetime.[64] Occasionally he invited foreign journalists to see him fence, play tennis or ride, and told them he hoped they would report how fit and expert he was; sometimes their honesty as reporters was sorely taxed.[65]

Another appearance he adopted was that of working to a precise plan. He would say that he had an exact calculation of what he would do for the next twelve months or even longer, and he once pronounced that no one who could not see at least fifty years ahead should govern a country.[66] Nor is it impossible that some decisions which seemed casual at the time were in fact carefully thought out in advance. On the other hand, he also took pride in acting by instinct and intuition, unlike ordinary mortals who needed to calculate pros and cons with care,[67] and this second pose was not easy to reconcile with the other.

Mussolini liked to be seen as incalculable, inscrutable, always taking others by surprise; he thought this a sign of creative genius, proof that he dominated events instead of being drawn along by them. If ever news of an appointment leaked out before a public announcement, he would instinctively look for another candidate in order to demonstrate his incalculability, and this was a habit that some people learnt to exploit by spreading rumours to foil a rival.[68] On one occasion he admitted that he was an improviser who 'invented his policy anew each day';[69] and many fascist leaders agreed that his impulsiveness was uncontrollable, that he lacked the patience and perseverance for any long-term strategy and acted mostly on the spur of the moment.[70]

Action, he used to say enigmatically, is desirable for its own sake 'even when it is wrong'.[71] He admitted that he instinctively resorted to action in moments when he did not know what to do; he had to show he was leading and not being led; he had to go against the current, to give an impression of being always on the move and never indecisive.[72] He was anxious to appear as the *volitivo*, the man of strong will and sudden decisions, who from his youth onwards wanted to 'put my stamp on institutions and people' by an act of will, to pass into history as a superior being, a superman. Margherita Sarfatti's 'official' biography ended by describing Mussolini, 'his eyes shining with an interior fire', saying he was consumed to the point of feeling physically ill with the desire to impose himself on the century like a lion with its claw: 'and, as with a claw, he scratched the covering of a chair-back from end to end'.[73]

Signora Sarfatti and Angelica Balabanoff both said that their first memory of Mussolini was of a *teppista* – a hooligan and brawler – and others confirmed that the schoolboy so free with his knife carried this love of violence and illegality into manhood.[74] He said he loved to watch boxing, which was almost as admirable as fighting in war, and he used to boast – perhaps fancifully – of having a boxing instructor with whom he liked to fight: punching, he once said, 'is an exquisitely fascist means of self-expression'.[75] The fascist bludgeon or *manganello* was still, in 1929, said to be a proper weapon in domestic politics, and when an American asked him if the pen or the sword was mightier, he at once replied, the sword, 'because it cuts. Cuts. Ends things. Finish.' This last word he emphasised, translating it into his oddly pronounced English.[76]

As a young man he had been a notorious dueller. He had an extremely vehement style with the sabre and here, too, he was remembered as an exhibitionist, always seeking spectacular effects and being careless about the accepted rules of chivalrous encounter. To all outward appearance he was a brave man, but it is interesting that some people questioned this. Others associated his duelling with an inferiority complex, and many who knew him best thought that his violence of speech and urge to domineer were attempts to overcome an inner timidity. He once asked his great admirer Pini to remove the word 'timid' from his biography, but so many others used the same word of him that timidity must have been a manifest constituent of his character.[77] Some went so far as to use the word 'feminine' and saw him as much less virile than his legend.[78] According to his wife, he only 'seemed like a lion, but really was a *pover'uomo*, a poor chap',[79] and Alfred Adler, the psychoanalyst, was sure that his early childhood must have left him with pronounced feelings of inadequacy.[80] Really brave men, commented Hemingway, did not have to fight duels; nor did they have to pose for photographers with a tame lioness; nor, especially if they were bad drivers and accident-prone, would they drive a car at dangerous speeds along bad roads and boast of it.[81]

'Live dangerously' was, nevertheless, the motto he gave to fascist youth, and he reminded them that even before fascism he had preached the therapeutic properties of a 'bath of blood'.[82] Just as he was proud to have used violence to capture power inside Italy, so he was not displeased at acquiring a reputation abroad for possessing an 'incalculable personality and violent temper', 'capable of a rush of blood to the head ... a surge of demonic wilfulness that may end in smoke, lava, destruction'.[83] Such words as 'battle', 'conflict' and 'struggle' were revealingly frequent in his speeches. He successively launched what he called a battle for the lira, a battle for wheat, a battle for births, a battle over the southern problem, and battles against sparrows, mice and houseflies.[84]

Another ingredient in his public reputation was that of a forgiving person, generous to those in need, whose violence was more in word than deed. On the other hand some acquaintances considered his occasional philanthropy to be compounded more of personal pride than good nature, demonstrated usually when the cost to him was less than the potential benefit. Though he subsidised the families of those who had suffered fascist persecution – the Matteotti family, for example – this was only when they had submitted and begged for clemency, or as an inducement to make others submit.[85]

Mussolini was less cruel than many, perhaps than most, dictators, but behind minor acts of inexpensive leniency he was, as he himself acknowledged, a vindictive man who enjoyed hating and being hated. There was a manifest element of sadism in his treatment of Clara Petacci and his many other mistresses.[86] The families of some exiles were treated with quite unnecessary cruelty, and some among his old acquaintances who were too proud to confess their errors were left mercilessly to rot in the penal settlements, even when they were no danger to him.[87] One of his least likeable qualities was the lack of generosity to former associates, though this may well have been an ingredient in his political success. As he himself sometimes admitted, a rancorous vindictiveness against some of his enemies – and even some who considered themselves his friends – lasted all his life.[88] He took pleasure in commuting some severe punishments, but he could also intervene with judges to instruct them to apply the death penalty – as long as his intervention did not become generally known.[89]

Death is a subject about which he was always squeamish, and it is hard to imagine him killing anyone with his own hands or enjoying the sight of an execution as Hitler did. Nevertheless he did order killings in cold blood. He specifically disclaimed the morality of humanitarianism and, as time went by, it became harder to discern any morality or idealism in his actions. The fact that he made little distinction between good and bad or justice and injustice was regarded even by some of his close colleagues as a grave weakness.[90] His relations with Dumini and Albino Volpi make clear that he did not disdain the company of common delinquents and was prepared to use them with no compunction so long as his name was not publicly involved. His own brother, who greatly admired him, thought him close to being a criminal,[91] and many other people had few doubts about calling him a murderer.

Mussolini and the economy

Mussolini invented a story that he had studied economics in his youth as a pupil of that 'prince of economists', Vilfredo Pareto,[92] and was evidently anxious to establish his own credentials as those of someone whose economic policy was sound – indeed, as he told one of the richest men in Italy, his economic intuition 'was almost infallible'.[93] Here as elsewhere he knew it was psychologically right to give an impression of confidence and certainty, though the truth was that, like Hitler, he had little understanding of the subject and not much interest in it. All the experts knew this[94] and his lack of knowledge obviously placed Italy in some danger.

He arrived in government with debts owing to many rich people who had helped his movement and whose help he still needed. They had preferred fascism to the liberal governments of 1919–22, especially to Giolitti who had threatened not only to confiscate surplus war profits but to make tax evasion more difficult and break up the large estates. Fascism had therefore renounced its earlier demand for the wholesale expropriation of capital and appealed to its rich backers by making strikes difficult and ejecting the socialists from local government. Mussolini attracted many among the richer classes by his praise of free enterprise, his talk of reducing the bureaucracy and abolishing unemployment relief, and by his occasional admission that the inequalities in society, far from needing removal, should be increased still further;[95] the fact that he could say the very opposite on other occasions could usually be suppressed or disregarded.

Naturally he did not want to appear too obviously pro-capitalist because he wished to appeal to all classes. He therefore tried to explain that he was neither against the workers nor intent on giving privileges to the rich. In any case he knew that fascism still had a left wing that hoped for a return to the radical programme of 1919, and he sometimes encouraged these leftists to maintain that the party was in essence a proletarian movement whose chief enemy was the bourgeoisie.[96]

Although it was always possible to deceive the man in the street about his true intention, there were bound to be doubts among his wealthier supporters as they saw that he was unreliable and unpredictable and his promises to help were a matter of expediency, not conviction. Some of them soon began to vote against him in parliament and subsidise the opposition press.[97] The majority, however, were apparently motivated by self-interest to continue backing fascism even after Matteotti's murder because, compared with what had gone before, the years 1922–5 were from their point of view an 'absolute paradise', with few strikes, plenty of tax concessions for the well-to-do, an end to rent controls and generally high profits for business. Nor were they ungrateful when the threat of clawing back hundreds of millions of illicit war profits was removed.[98] The support of bankers, industrialists and landowners was invaluable, not least because it helped to delude opinion abroad into thinking that the vulgar bestialities of the regime were accidental and could be disregarded. He also needed their help to finance his party and give Italy the economic backing for a strong foreign policy. Determined to revive the economy and improve the balance of payments, he was obliged to favour the exporting industries; he knew that, for a time at least, it would be wise to bolster private property and 'create exceptionally favourable conditions for the capitalist economy'.[99]

It is sometimes assumed that Mussolini was little more than an instrument in the hands of Italian capitalists, but his support for them was never unqualified, and neither was theirs for him. He needed the formal submission of the Confederation of Industry so that he could publicise through his embassies abroad that all the economic forces of the nation had been brought inside the fascist system; but in practice he never succeeded completely in imposing fascist policies on the wealthy classes and he eventually admitted that they gave only 'a purely formal adherence to the regime'.[100] Nor did he ever abandon an instinctive dislike of them, stemming from his impoverished and revolutionary youth. He confessed to a secret wish 'that ultimately no Italian would be able to own a large estate or live in a *palazzo*'.[101] The rich, for their part, sometimes disliked and feared what he was doing, but they also received many tangible compensations and in any case they found in practice that it was 'easier to evoke the devil than to exorcise him'.[102]

The first fascist minister of finance was the former squad leader, Professor De' Stefani, whose views as a free-trader and whose belief in liberalising the economy appealed to some industrialists, though not all. Mussolini supported this liberalising policy and continued for a time to assert that the state should keep out of the economic life of the nation; indeed, that government intervention in general was 'absolutely ruinous to the development of the economy'.[103] Other fascists, on the contrary, preached state intervention on a very big scale. At first there was a move to let private capitalists own a share in life insurance and the telephone system, both hitherto government monopolies; but in other fields the opposite tendency prevailed almost from the beginning.[104]

De' Stefani succeeded in more or less balancing the budget after three years of a relatively liberal economic regime and his policy gave impetus to an economic revival that had begun before fascism took over. The first motorway in Europe was built in 1923, from Milan to the lakes. The railway system, which had been badly run down during the First World War, was much improved, and the claim was advanced that Italian trains were the envy of all Europe. This was an exaggeration, but Mussolini did his best to make the train service into a symbol of fascist efficiency and managed to conceal that much had been done before 1922 in repairing railway beds and rolling stock. His propaganda was very successful, yet some travellers reported that the celebrated trains running invariably on time were, to some extent at least, a convenient myth.[105]

It was always his habit to get rid of ministers if ever they became either too unpopular or too popular. De' Stefani's economy drive was bound to invite unpopularity by clashing with the corruption and extravagance of a fascist regime that, while claiming to reduce an inflated bureaucracy, needed to do precisely the opposite in order to reward personal 'clients' and followers. The minister was compelled to revive Giolitti's policy of curbing tax evasion and this was strongly resented, as were his refusal to increase hand-outs to the militia and to fascist newspapers and his attempt to limit stock exchange speculation; moreover, his free-trade policies were far from helpful to a heavy industry accustomed to government subsidies and high tariff protection.[106] Here was one of the few ministers, in twenty-three years of fascism, who was of above average competence and matched most of his predecessors in intelligence and honesty; but these were not qualities greatly prized by Mussolini, who soon allowed rivals to discredit a useful scapegoat.

One of fascism's least uninteresting contributions to economic history was the corporative system by which it was intended to replace or transcend the out-of-date ideas of liberalism and socialism. The corporations, originally envisaged by the nationalists and by D'Annunzio at Fiume, were trade unions that included both employers and employees. The expectation was that each corporation, as well as regulating its individual trade, would minimise industrial strife and mobilise productive potential in the interests of the whole community. Mussolini also had a vague idea that corporative assemblies – in which each member would represent a specialised interest – might take over from parliament the task of legislating on economic matters.[107] This was an attractive suggestion, because a prolonged period of social peace would in theory enable Italy to maximise production and compete more favourably in international markets. He showed 'almost a boyish enthusiasm' in demonstrating to his own satisfaction that, since capital and labour would both be represented in each corporation by convinced fascists, they would always reach agreement without wasting time in strikes and lock-outs. Such a harmony of interest could, in his view, survive only in a fascist system where 'the individual has no existence at all except insofar as he is subordinated to the needs of the state',[108] where it would be for the state to prescribe a 'just wage' instead of relying on the laws of supply and demand.

These principles were developed very gradually. At first, a limited number of 'fascist strikes' were permitted to pressurise the captains of industry into accepting state control. Then in July 1926 Mussolini created a special ministry of corporations and explained that a new corporative machinery, as well as fixing wages and conditions of work, would eventually regulate the whole economy. He thought it possible that one day the corporations would effect what would amount to compulsory recruitment of all Italian citizens for civilian work.[109] In 1929, he announced optimistically that the former antagonism between capital and labour was at an end: both sides of industry were working together with complete parity of rights and duties – something to be seen nowhere else in the world.[110]

By this time, the unions had been brought within the fascist system and their leaders were no longer elected by members but appointed from above, just as fascist dogma prescribed. Employers, on the other hand, while grateful for the forcible submission of labour, were always strong enough to avoid being centrally organised by official appointees. Strictly speaking, there were thus no real corporations in existence, and though the 'corporative system' was said to be an established fact – indeed it was called the 'corner stone of the fascist state', the directing force for the whole economy and the most original creation of the regime[111] – it was, in practice, little more than an unrealised idea. As such, it was useful in the propaganda war against liberalism and socialism but unable to produce the new economic order that had been promised.[112]

On the contrary, a plethoric corporative bureaucracy – with higher salaries than the civil service and often duplicating work done elsewhere – was already by 1930 becoming a grave burden on the national economy.[113] Mussolini knew this, but explained that there were political reasons why he had to find employment for the potentially dangerous intellectual proletariat, especially in southern Italy.[114] One of the graver weaknesses of fascism was thus accentuated and even was a source of pride to its creator.

Though lacking much substance, corporativism became a happy hunting-ground for hundreds of place-seeking academics who endlessly discussed its theory and practice. They were helped when fascist economic theory was codified by Mussolini in the 'Charter of Labour' of April 1927, which the propagandists hailed as the Magna Carta of the fascist revolution and even 'the greatest document in the whole of history'.[115] This charter made work 'a social duty' and voluntary withdrawal of labour a punishable offence. It agreed that private enterprise was needed for running large sections of the economy and that governments should intervene only where the higher interests of the nation were involved, yet every business and factory would be obliged – in theory – to hire labour from lists provided for them by the government, and preference had to be given to fascists, especially those who had been party members for the longest time.[116] The provisions of the charter were no more than a statement of general principles, though Mussolini tried to pretend that they were legally enforceable from the moment of promulgation. They were, of course, said to have been greeted with general enthusiasm, and though this was far from the truth, the claim – as usual – mattered more than the reality.

Another often-repeated claim was that he did more for ordinary workers than any other ruler in the world,[117] but he reiterated this so frequently as to suggest that he knew it was a debatable point. Speaking to factory workers, he listed his achievements in labour legislation – the eight-hour day, sickness compensation, old age pensions, maternity pay. There were also the organised holidays by the *dopolavoro*, which was a government organisation dedicated to popular leisure-time activities. But on this occasion the audience, very unusually, greeted his words in silent disbelief and disapproval. Even judging by the official figures, which were often entirely unreliable, it can be seen that the reality was less spectacular than the claims. Legislation could look good on paper but be ineffective in operation.[118]

Sometimes he said that his primary duty was to close the gap between rich and poor and sometimes he boasted that fascism greatly improved the basic standard of living.[119] But those who had time to study the facts did not always believe him and some reported that standards remained among the lowest in Europe.[120] He once made a promise that in the space of ten years he would make Italy unrecognisably rich,[121] but he can hardly have meant this seriously, and when the ten years were over he began to say something very different – that living standards were almost bound to fall. Once, when off his guard, he admitted knowing towns in southern Italy and Sardinia where the inhabitants existed for months on nothing but wild plants; but luckily, he explained, Italians were a frugal people who noticed hardship less than others.[122] Fortunately, too, he could instruct the press not to mention hard times or the world economic crisis; instead, they had to drum into their readers the fact that fascist Italy could stand comparison with any country in the world.[123]

Prosperity, as he had to confess, was not very high on his list of priorities[124] except for its propaganda value; national strength was far more important. He was expecting a war at any time after 1934 and wanted the country to become self-sufficient in food before then. This was one reason why he hoped Italy would remain mainly agricultural: urbanisation was threatening to endanger the food supply of a rapidly growing community. Another hazard was that as people moved to the towns they began to think and talk too much. Peasants, he asserted, were more necessary to fascism than intellectuals or town artisans, both of which latter categories were, as he had to admit, unenthusiastic about his regime if not strongly hostile.[125]

Several years went by before he learnt the necessity for 'ruralisation'. At first he encouraged the growth of the big cities,[126] but then suddenly went into reverse and declared that 'fascism is a predominantly rural phenomenon'; the healthiest nations were those based on a population of small proprietors who worked 'obediently, and preferably in silence'. On the other hand, urban conditions encouraged not only disobedience but a wish for higher wages and greater comfort which, in turn, would result in smaller families, all of which would be profoundly unfascist.[127] To 'ruralise Italy' would, he knew, be immensely costly and might take half a century, but it would have to be effected. Less should be spent on improving conditions in towns because 'cities are pernicious and parasitic'; even in the countryside, he thought it necessary to restrict improvements in popular housing because better conditions might lead to fewer children being born.[128] Such beliefs became an obsession with him. He ordered the prefects to stop any move away from the land and to use force if necessary; Rome should not become an industrial city but remain the centre of an agricultural region, and many other important towns should be forcibly reduced in size. But he had chosen a hopelessly unequal battle and the towns went on expanding as before. At first he falsified the census returns to conceal this untoward fact, but eventually went into reverse and decided to spend a great deal of money to make Rome into a great centre of industry.[129]

More successful was the 'battle for wheat' launched in June 1925, when high import taxes were imposed with the long-term purpose of making Italy self-sufficient in cereals. This was based on the assumption that the country could and should grow her basic food requirements with something left over for export.[130] Many economists, on the contrary, thought that Italy had too much land under wheat already: many other cash crops could be produced far more profitably, given the Italian climate, and would earn foreign credits with which to buy cereals on the world market at less than half the price that now had to be paid by Italian consumers.[131]

But the battle for wheat was very close to Mussolini's heart – he even wrote and published a poem on it.[132] It was also very successful in increasing production, but only at the cost of decreasing the profitability of agriculture, since import duties on cereals kept high-cost producers and inefficient methods in existence. It caused great hardship by placing a high domestic price on an essential foodstuff, and it led to a loss of export markets for other more valuable agricultural products no longer produced on land that was converted to cereal growing. Those who gained were the owners of *latifundia* and the propertied classes in general:[133] he had been hoping to increase peasant proprietorship,[134] but in effect his policy conferred a heavy subsidy on the *latifondisti*.

Success in this battle was thus another illusory propaganda victory won at the expense of the Italian economy in general and consumers in particular. Italy appeared superficially to be almost self-sufficient in cereals when war began in 1940 but little had been done to make her self-sufficient in fertilisers, and production plummeted when outside supplies of natural and chemical fertilisers were cut in wartime.

A more genuine victory was the battle for land reclamation. A great deal of money was allocated by the fascist government to drainage, irrigation, reafforestation and farm buildings. It is hard to discover exactly how much, though it was less than claimed and the objectives of the battle were only partially attained. Nevertheless, Italy was bound to gain from the draining of marshland and the results were quite properly made into a success story for fascism.

De' Stefani's successor as minister of finance was Count Giuseppe Volpi, one of the leading Italian financiers and an industrialist with many international connections. His major achievement was to persuade the Americans and British to forgo a large part of the war debts owed them by Italy: Volpi wisely ascribed this success to Mussolini rather than himself.[135] Debt settlement opened the way to investment in Italy by the United States and this was of great benefit to the regime.

Not so obviously beneficial was Mussolini's revaluation of the currency in 1926–7. Within days of taking office in 1922, he had decided on a modest revaluation and decided to make this into a symbol of fascist strength.[136] But for the next three years the lira continued to fall in value from about 100 to the pound sterling to as much as 150, and this was altogether too public a challenge to his authority and credibility. He insisted that, cost what it might, the earlier figure must be regained or bettered; he explained that this was for political rather than economic reasons – in other words, his personal prestige and that of fascism demanded a severely deflationary policy, irrespective of its economic effects.[137]

Stabilisation of the currency and a return to the gold standard did have some good results and the newspapers were encouraged to stress them, but most expert opinion agreed with De' Stefani and Volpi that the figure of 90 lire to the pound went much too far and this prestige success proved to be a far heavier burden on the Italian economy than Mussolini could have foreseen. Exporters were affected very badly indeed by the new rate, share prices fell sharply, unemployment rose, costs of production increased, as did the cost of living. But Mussolini stuck to his guns because his reputation was at stake and he could not admit to having been wrong. Some years later he did reluctantly agree to a very substantial devaluation that corrected some of the harmful effects of this earlier decision, but the newspapers were told to play it down and no one was ever allowed to say in public that 'quota ninety' had been ill-advised.

The manipulation of economic facts was an essential part of Mussolini's system. He gained much credit by promising that his annual budget would be of a 'crystalline simplicity' so that every citizen could know how his money was being spent;[138] but in practice the figures became more obscure than ever. By the end of the 1920s, even the experts were baffled when they tried to find out about the balance of payments or how much was being spent on public works or the militia.[139] The *corte dei conti*, whose job was to supervise expenditure, was artfully removed from parliamentary scrutiny and placed directly under the head of government. So was the Institute of Statistics, whose director was instructed to publish no figures without higher approval. Mussolini recognised the publicity value of statistics and thought it no sin to 'attenuate' those he objected to in the monthly statistical bulletin.[140] Foreigners, as a result, learnt to pay little attention to official publications.

The Duce

The years after 1926 saw an ever-increasing propagation of the legend of an omniscient, all-wise Duce, and this cult of *ducismo* was revealing itself to be the most novel and effective feature of Italian fascism. Mussolini fostered it not just out of vanity but as an instrument of power. The ministers of the faith were the other leading fascists who all – even when jealous or rebellious – realised that their own future depended on his. Without him they were nothing: the greater he was, the greater would they be. Augusto Turati, who succeeded Farinacci as party secretary in 1926, institutionalised the worship of the leader.[141] Another who helped to make the cult intellectually respectable was the well-known journalist-politician Giuseppe Bottai, one of the more intelligent fascists, who proclaimed his belief that no figure in history could compare with this exceptional person, without whom fascism would be meaningless.[142] But the high priest of the new religion was Arnaldo Mussolini who, day after day in the *Popolo d'Italia*, described his brother as a demi-god whose eye was on everyone and who knew everything that happened in Italy; who, as well as being the leading statesman in Europe, had placed his wisdom, heroism and vast intellect at the service of his own people, and whose person should therefore be deemed sacred and inviolable.[143]

The Duce himself came to believe, or pretended to believe, that he was almost infallible and needed servants rather than associates. Even as a relatively obscure newspaper editor he had been temperamentally inclined to behave as a dictator, simply giving orders to his staff and inviting no advice. As prime minister, if he asked others for information he habitually gave the impression that the answers only confirmed what he had already intuited. 'Mussolini is always right' very soon became one of the catch-phrases of the regime and, with his eye for a good headline, he deliberately disseminated it. He admitted to the German publicist Emil Ludwig that he sometimes did stupid things, but this was one of the remarks that had to be deleted from the Italian translation of his interview.[144]

Another catch-phrase stencilled on walls everywhere told Italians that their duty was to believe, fight and obey. Mussolini was sure that Italians thirsted for discipline and that obedience must become 'absolute and religious' if Italy and fascism were to dominate the twentieth century: one person alone should command, and even in insignificant matters his fiat must not be questioned. Fascism should be seen as his personal creation, as something that, without submission to him, would cease to exist.[145]

By 1926–7, the religion of *ducismo* was in full swing. Schoolteachers were ordered to magnify this solitary figure, to stress his disinterestedness, his wonderful courage and brilliant mind, and to teach that obedience to such a man was the highest virtue.[146] His picture – often in one of his Napoleonic poses – was already displayed on all public buildings and would sometimes be carried in procession through the streets like the image of a patron saint. Devout fascists might have his photograph printed at the head of their writing-paper, together with one of his short apodictic pronouncements.[147] He was compared to Aristotle, Kant and Aquinas; he was the greatest genius in Italian history, greater than Dante or Michelangelo, greater than Washington, Lincoln or Napoleon; he was, in fact, a god, and the other fascist leaders should consider themselves his priests and acolytes.[148]

This legendary figure became more humanly familiar through the biography written by Signora Sarfatti which was published first in an English version in 1925, followed (much altered for a different audience) by an Italian edition in 1926. Mussolini corrected the proofs,[149] and his preface to the English edition includes one of his pretentious lapses comparing the eventfulness of his life with that of 'the late Mr Savage Landor, the great traveller'. Only much later, after Sarfatti had been displaced in his life by other mistresses, did he confess that the book was ridiculous rubbish published just because he knew that 'invention was more useful than the truth';[150] by this time it had been translated into numerous other languages including Danish and Lettish, and had acquired semi-oracular status inside Italy.

He himself preferred the 'official' biography by another journalist, Giorgio Pini, which – as it was yet more uncritical and flattering – was better suited to Italian readers and not widely translated into other languages until 1939. In 1926, Pini was already able to inform Italians that 'when the Duce makes a speech, the whole world listens in fear and admiration'.[151] His volume, like Sarfatti's, was subsidized for circulation in schools and ran easily into fifteen editions.[152]

A third, still more official, book was an 'autobiography' that was in fact a compilation put together by Mussolini's brother with help from Luigi Barzini and a former United States ambassador in Rome. It was commissioned by a London agent who paid the unusually large advance of £10,000, and in England, where it was published in 1928, it sold 4,000 copies – a cheap sixpenny edition published in 1939 sold 50,000 after Mussolini had become a favourite bogeyman. At the last moment the Duce tried, albeit too late, to cancel the contract; but he did succeed in preventing the appearance of an Italian edition. Evidently it contained material which he either did not want people to know or feared they might disbelieve.[153]

Though he said he did not care what was said about him abroad, he scrutinised the work of his press-cutting service with great attention in order to make sure that the right image was being projected, and sometimes the foreign office was treated as though it were primarily a ministry of propaganda. He had once ridiculed the 'immoral exhibitionism' of democratic politicians who granted interviews, but as Duce he became a great practitioner of the art so as to make foreign correspondents write flattering comments about him; in return he sometimes gave them privileged information that not even ambassadors were told.[154]

Mussolini always retained his special relationship with pressmen, not just because he was himself a journalist by instinct and profession, but because he needed their help. Where ministers were expected to remain standing in his presence, foreign journalists were allowed to sit if they came from an important country that he was trying to impress. Occasionally they were given the extremely rare privilege of being invited home to the Villa Torlonia. The degree of affability and condescension was carefully graded to suit each individual. Mussolini was sometimes gracious enough to meet them at the door of his huge office, instead of submitting them to the ordeal of walking the twenty yards to his desk alone or, worse still, having to run this distance, as his own ministers and generals were encouraged to do in later years. Only friends of fascism or potential friends were, of course, allowed an interview; even so, not all of them were impressed by his histrionics and attitudinising. Occasionally he had to doctor reports of interviews in the foreign press before they were seen in Italy, as it was important to convince Italians that he was universally admired abroad. His autobiography states bluntly that after seeing him everyone thought him 'the greatest personality in Europe'. Any issue of a foreign newspaper that contradicted this legend ran the risk of confiscation. And the result was that Italians were ill-informed about foreign criticisms of fascism and its leader.[155]

He took equal trouble with public appearances and his speeches were usually carefully prepared, though he sometimes pretended otherwise. He also liked to pretend that he disapproved of making speeches as something essentially unfascist, yet in practice they were one of his chief preoccupations. Italy, he used to say, was a land of theatre and its leaders must orchestrate their public contacts. Part of the secret of his success was that he disdainfully regarded the masses as easy to deceive and dominate; he thought them, as in his early socialist days, to be like children, to be helped but also corrected and punished – 'they are stupid, dirty, do not work hard enough and are content with their little cinema shows'.[156] At the same time, he was glad to find that the herd – this was the word he liked to use – would gratefully accept inequality and discipline in place of equality and liberty. If given bread and circuses they could dispense with ideals except those chosen for them. 'The crowd doesn't have to know, it must believe; it must submit to being shaped.' Since the masses felt that they were unable to judge for themselves, they did not want discussion or debate; they preferred to be commanded, and he admitted that his attitude here was the same as Stalin's.[157]

Despite the fact that Mussolini affected a disregard for public opinion and the applause of the multitude,[158] he carefully nurtured what he thought of as one of his greatest gifts, 'a tactile and even visual sense of what ordinary citizens want and think'. Even those who thought him ineffective in committee acknowledged his skill at managing a crowd. As he explained, 'one must always know how to strike the imagination of the public: that is the real secret of how to govern'. The art of politics is to avoid wearying or disillusioning your public and never to lose your hold over them, but to maintain a spectacle, 'to keep people at their windows' for year after year in the anxious expectation of some great and apocalyptic event.[159]

Mussolini's speeches are not interesting to read but his declamatory style was very effective *viva voce* with an audience he understood. One sceptical listener said it was like the periodic liquefaction of St Januarius's blood at Naples: you could not explain how, but it worked.[160] His speeches sometimes sound like a succession of newspaper headlines – simple, oft-repeated statements, with little obvious artifice and employing a small vocabulary. The general tone is usually aggressive and strident. He used to refer to the balcony outside his office as his 'stage': standing on this stage, he would invite the crowd to answer his rhetorical questions in chorus so as to involve them in active participation. He confessed that this gave him the pleasure of feeling like a sculptor wrestling with his material, 'violating' it, moulding it into shape.[161]

In this important area of his political life he, like Hitler, acknowledged his debt to Gustave Le Bon, whose book on the psychology of the crowd he said he read times without number.[162] Le Bon explained how crowds are moved, not by reason, but by delusions, often quite simple delusions, by irrational and involuntary beliefs that could spread by contagion if an orator knew how to arouse emotion. Here Mussolini found confirmation of his belief that the essential art of government was the use of words. Words well used – whether in speeches or mass journalism, and especially when no one was permitted to reply except in a chorus of approbation – allowed a politician to dispense with argument and stir people up to acts of heroism or mock heroism that could, if need be, verge on the absurd.

He was less happy dealing with colleagues and usually tried to depreciate their collaboration. He was by instinct and calculation a centraliser of authority and continually increased his own responsibilities. As well as running the prime minister's office, he had by 1926 taken into his own hands six ministerial departments out of a total of thirteen, and by 1929 had acquired two more. In addition he presided over the fascist party, the Grand Council and the national council of corporations, as well as cabinet meetings. He was also commandant general of the militia and, later, of all the armed services. Among other important bodies of which he was chairman there were the Supreme Commission for Defence, the Council of State, the Court of Accounts, the Army Council, the Supreme Council of Statistics, the Permanent Committee on Cereal Production, and the Committee on Civilian Mobilisation, as well as each of the twenty-two corporations established after 1934. In later years the list grew yet longer. To someone who asked him if this was not excessive, he replied, 'It is really simpler to give orders myself instead of having to send for the minister concerned and convince him about what I want done'.[163]

As the main work naturally fell to underlings and under-secretaries in each department, who rarely felt able to act on their own[164] and who had a mere few minutes of his time each day, this centralisation of power was too much. Previous prime ministers had found coping with just two ministries simultaneously an intolerable burden, let alone eight.[165] Mussolini sometimes assumed temporary control of the few ministries not officially his own or made decisions in others without bothering to consult the titular ministers.[166] He took pleasure in by-passing the cabinet and suddenly announcing a major change of policy, since he was anxious for Italians to think himself personally responsible for everything. Of course this meant that his ministers were often left with no real feeling of responsibility and became timid about acting on their own initiative.[167] However good this may have been for Mussolini's ego, it was to prove disastrous for the country.

If a leader can be judged by his chosen subordinates, Mussolini ranks very poorly indeed. He despised his colleagues and used to admit that 'they are all rotten to the core'.[168] One or two ministers were of more than moderate ability, but most were less than competent and some would have been in prison in any other country. When choosing ministers, he admitted that he might well prefer an imbecile to a person of merit and might even choose a real crook: with a villain, you knew where you were and would not be deceived by hypocrisy.[169] So sure was he of his own abilities, so anxious to appear superior, so convinced of the stupidity and dishonesty of others, that he cheerfully appointed the unintelligent and the second-rate, the result being that he surrounded himself with sycophants, dissemblers and place-hunters. He was described as having a positive gift for putting people in the wrong jobs and disregarding all who were honest or told him the truth. He liked to be encircled by courtiers who would laugh at his attempts at wit. Equally, he disliked people of character and culture who were brave enough to disagree with him, few of whom survived long in office.[170]

It appears that he sometimes selected ministers by simply running his eye down a list of deputies until he recalled a face or a name that sounded well – better still if they were less tall than himself.[171] When De Vecchi, one of the more brutal and foolish fascists, was made minister of education, this seemed deliberately designed to humiliate the teaching profession. Some thought that De Vecchi was chosen merely because he had the reputation of bringing good luck; and the same was said of some appointments in the army. Mussolini was superstitious and did not become less so with the years: he was frightened of anyone with the 'evil eye' and anxious not to give them offence.[172]

When complaint was made that the *gerarchi*, as he called the hierarchs of fascism, were dishonest, he preferred to ignore the accusation whenever possible as he could not afford to let the public know that he had made a bad choice. With his low view of human nature he assumed that everyone had his price, though in public he made great play with the claim that fascism was dedicated to clean politics.[173] From police investigations he knew that many of the *gerarchi* were hardly models of honesty, yet he rarely took action against them. He even used to joke about this, saying he could not sack those who had made their fortune in office because that would leave the way open for others with their fortune still to make. One of his acquaintances who dared to warn him that the dishonesty of the regime was becoming a public scandal was met with the answer that every revolution had a right to let its leaders make money on the side, and this was, with little doubt, his genuine conviction.[174]

The selection of the fascist hierarchy was, as he eventually came to accept, a weak point of his regime, but he fell back on the excuse that he could trust no one, least of all those he knew to be able. Whatever the reason, no one with genuine talent lasted long in authority or was allowed much scope, and all the ministers and *gerarchi*, good and bad, were kept at arm's length, and preferably never allowed more than a short innings in positions of responsibility. All of them quickly learnt to recognise his need for solitude and his dislike of any familiarity; they knew that no one could be allowed near enough to see behind his mask. His frequent change of ministers was sometimes attributed to his wish for a scapegoat whenever things went wrong, sometimes to his need to prevent potential rivals learning the ropes and building an independent power base. In part he was simply encouraging subservience by giving as many people as possible the hope of preferment. Fascist officials did not resign; at least that was the illusion he tried very successfully to maintain. Nor did he like telling them to their face that they were dismissed; they frequently learnt this fact from the newspapers or the radio, and he took a strange delight in the embarrassment this caused.[175]

Another idiosyncrasy was his pleasure in encouraging squabbles between ministers and generals, almost as though his job was not one of co-ordination but of division.[176] He liked them to tell tales against each other and would regularly pass on any spiteful stories to the offended party so as to exacerbate tension and jealousy between them.[177] A vast amount of such gossip was filed away in his private archives along with miscellaneous tittle-tattle collected for him by spies and telephone taps. He rarely fired anyone as a result of hearing malicious gossip, but used it to reinforce the impression that he knew what individuals were saying in private, and by playing the voyeur he also indulged his desire to feel superior to those around him.

Such was the extreme centralisation of power that almost everything depended on him; if he was away from Rome, much of the administration simply came to a halt. Cabinet meetings could approve a multiplicity of laws at a single session, sometimes all of them proposed by Mussolini personally in his different ministerial capacities.[178] Not infrequently, he made contradictory decisions in different departments on the same day.[179] He personally might feel obliged to decree the number of buttons on a uniform, decide which day the band could start playing on the Venetian Lido, whether trees along a road at Piacenza should be pollarded, or whether to appoint an assistant bugle instructor at the police college; and he demanded to be continuously informed of the names of all civil servants not at their desks by nine in the morning. This astonishing expenditure of energy on trivialities was something he positively enjoyed as a way of deluding people – and possibly himself – into believing that he had the whole life of the nation under constant scrutiny.[180]

Administration and legislation were thus another field in which Mussolini could display his great sense of showmanship and theatre. Under the tremendous weight of his responsibilities, he rarely had time to ensure that his commands were actually enforced,[181] and in a sense this did not matter all that much because there was more drama in their promulgation than their application. And drama in his hands could be an extremely cost-effective instrument of authority. He told English newspapermen that in a single cabinet meeting he had done more for the economy than the British government had done in a year because, while the latter had to go through long debates in a parliament of amateurs, he was a professional who ran the whole life of the nation from a battery of eighty different buttons on his desk.[182] This claim was, of course, an illusion, however much it may have had its own limited effectiveness as theatre. In fact he never knew, as Giolitti had done, how to control his lieutenants and hence often failed to translate his wishes into practical action. Despite appearances he was in many respects a weak person who changed his mind continually and seemed to lack the capacity to control any really difficult situation: among senior officials it used to be said that his was a 'dictatorship of soft cheese'.[183]

Spectacular gestures did something to cloak his inefficiency and impracticality. They covered his incapacity to confront difficulties or to take decisions at critical moments, and to conceal the fact that he usually preferred to have policy imposed on him by events. One not unfriendly senator described him as 'a lion of cardboard' who was easily led.[184] If he continued to earn the strange reputation of always agreeing with the last person he spoke to,[185] this was also because he thought it undignified to be worsted or influenced in argument and so tried to avoid discussion whenever possible.[186]

Close acquaintances, as well as his own family, found that even in private conversation he preferred to hector them as if addressing a large crowd.[187] He was ready, especially in the early days, to listen to experts, but to allow a frank exchange of views or discussion of alternatives might have damaged the legend of his omniscience and infallibility; so, perhaps sometimes unintentionally, he discouraged criticism and as a general rule made advice seem unwelcome. He sometimes adopted the pose of wanting to hear the truth even if it was unpleasant, but the type of person he selected for office belied this: his chosen subordinates, as he must have known, were mostly people who waited to know what he wanted to believe and then reinforced his self-esteem by agreeing with him.[188]

The man of culture

When asked which of the arts he liked best, Mussolini would sometimes say the theatre,[189] sometimes music,[190] or films,[191] or architecture;[192] but he was always eager to show that he was actively involved in every aspect of culture and he liked to be praised as having few equals in knowledge stretching over a wide field of intellectual and artistic interests.[193] He thought he might have made a career as a university professor but cut out of Ludwig's interviews a reference to his didactic mannerisms[194] – which were a legacy of his time as a teacher in elementary school. Stories were circulated about how he could skim the most difficult books without missing anything,[195] though some people who did not need to flatter him wondered whether his knowledge on any subject was more than superficial.[196] He let people think he had read all thirty-five volumes of the new 'Italian Encyclopedia' and habitually looked up individual articles in it so as to appear in interviews as a polymath with a prodigious memory.[197]

As an author, he was said by some famous writers and professors of literature to produce prose that would rank among the Italian classics and there were few quicker ways to his heart than to call him the finest stylist of the age.[198] Scores of citations from his works were employed in grammars and dictionaries as examples to be copied,[199] and many of the neologisms he enjoyed coining were given general, almost compulsory, currency. One of his special affectations was to impose on Italians a single method of address: for most of his life he had used the familiar *lei* and was not too happy with the formal *voi*; then early in 1938 he unexpectedly went into reverse and a bevy of intellectuals was mobilised to justify an absolute ban on what had hitherto been one of the commonest words in the language.[200] He claimed co-authorship in three plays, though his own contribution, apart from the general themes, was nil. The three subjects he chose were Napoleon, Julius Caesar and Cavour, and it is interesting that all dealt with much the same topic: a great man betrayed by his friends. All three plays were given a fantastic reception by the critics and compared to Shakespearian and Wagnerian drama at their best,[201] though in private there was less enthusiasm.[202] Two of them were turned into films about which a great fuss was made, without much box-office success.[203]

Though he used to say that he was sceptical about the influence of books and boasted of learning only from 'the book of life lived',[204] he thought it important to be considered a man of culture and wide reading. He claimed to have read all of Shakespeare and almost all of Molière and Corneille, and to know long passages of Goethe by heart, while he read Dante every day and repeatedly kept the dialogues of Plato open on his desk for visitors to see. Fiction, he once declared, could be mostly disregarded,[205] and one of his characteristic quips was that good novelists were as rare as honest women; secretly, though, he liked cheap romances and he sometimes liked lecturing novelists on their art.[206] He estimated that he read about seventy books a year.[207]

His cultural pretentiousness was harmless enough and indicates that he meant well, but cannot be taken too seriously. Its main interest is in showing his wish to be considered a superman set apart from other mortals, and to that extent it had a political use. Sometimes he was caught out – for example when to the British he compared himself to Savage Landor or when he pretended he read Greek authors in the original.[208] He sometimes made a condescending mock apology after citing some erudite reference, but no court jester was at hand to point out when the reference was obviously wrong.[209] There is little confirmation that he knew more of Shakespeare and Molière than he could have learnt from the encyclopedia or indeed from the mere titles of their plays; nor can we accept the assertion that Defoe was one of his favourite writers, or that he was a devotee of Whitman, Longfellow, Emerson, William James and Mark Twain.[210] These were just names to drop, not authors to be read.

His disciples went even further in eulogy. Some of them called him a creative thinker whose writings compelled all other Italian philosophers to rethink their ideas.[211] In knowledge of Roman archaeology he was said to have few equals,[212] and even if his tall talk about studying Herodotus and Livy was a fabrication, a lecture to university students on Roman history earned him sycophantic praise from the leading professor of the subject.[213] Other short pieces he wrote on Machiavelli and Goethe were equally magnified by the propagandists who perhaps did not know that he had researchers and speechwriters to help him.[214]

Eventually he insisted on changing the school curriculum in order to provide fascism with correct antecedents and a context of historical inevitability. Ancient Rome, 'the greatest empire in all history', had to take pride of place; less attention need be given to the 'centuries of Italian decadence' – in other words the Middle Ages, the Renaissance, or later periods characterised by military defeats and foreign occupation. Mainstream history began again with the Italian *Risorgimento* in the nineteenth century, but this period of patriotic revival had to be purged of falsities introduced by foreign writers and entirely rewritten from a fascist point of view. The liberals were now said to have had little, if any, part in the unification of Italy which was the handiwork of Garibaldi and Mazzini, from whom fascism was directly descended.[215]

Mussolini was genuinely fond of music, and the composers he claimed to prefer ranged from Palestrina and Vivaldi to Wagner and Verdi. As well as playing the violin, he enjoyed the gramophone and pianola, his favourite pieces being triumphal marches and tunes from the great symphonies.[216] His violin technique was much praised by aspiring music critics, less so by others, and long after he had given up playing he encouraged foreign journalists to think that this continued to be the daily solace of an overworked politician.[217] By the time he reached fifty, his musical taste had moved further in the direction of big orchestral works which better suggested 'collective mass discipline',[218] and above all he liked grand opera – though he preferred cut versions as he found it hard to stay awake through an entire work.[219]

His favourite conductor was Toscanini – 'a great artist but a contemptible man'.[220] Toscanini had been a fascist in 1919 but quickly defected and, as early as December 1922, made a scene at the Scala theatre by refusing to play 'Giovinezza'.[221] In 1926, Mussolini had arranged to be present in the Scala for the first night of Puccini's *Turandot* until he realised that Toscanini would persist in his refusal. So plans were abruptly changed and, at the very moment the opera was starting, the Duce began an extempore address to a huge crowd hurriedly assembled just outside the theatre in the pouring rain.[222] Toscanini was one of those creative artists who categorically refused to compromise; he suffered a public beating from fascist hooligans and then departed to work in the more congenial atmosphere of the United States. Just possibly it says something for fascism that he was allowed to go.

In 1926, Mussolini decided to copy Napoleon and set up an Italian academy, with the task of 'co-ordinating and directing' Italian culture and extending its influence in the outside world. The first batch of academicians – all personally selected by himself – included the futurist poet Marinetti, the composer Mascagni, Pirandello the dramatist, and the brilliant 28-year-old physicist Enrico Fermi, though the general level was well below this plane of distinction. They begged him to accept election himself but he protested that he was unworthy, adding that he might reconsider their offer later.[223] To the annoyance of loyal supporters, he was particularly eager to elect non-fascists or lukewarm fascists because he intended the academy to be a bribe to attract intellectuals and artists into at least outward conformity.[224] Academicians received a very large salary for doing nothing, but had to swear an oath of loyalty to fascism and open their meetings with a formal 'salute to the Duce'. Almost no one refused his invitation to join what he called this assemblage of 'immortals'.

By some oversight, the name of Guglielmo Marconi appeared only in the third list of those elected to the academy but he at once became its president. He had joined the fascist party some years earlier and Mussolini was anxious that, through him, fascist science should be properly disciplined. Science had to be directed to meet the exigencies of national policy.

Free scientific investigation was said to have been typical of liberal Italy and had not worked; it was characterised by Einstein, whom Mussolini condemned as a Jewish fraud lacking in originality;[225] free science could, by definition, produce only contradictory solutions, whereas central direction under fascism would bring quick results. Science could no longer afford to be 'politically neutral'; nor must Italian scientists be allowed to attend congresses abroad unless personally selected by the Duce.[226] Italian inventors, he maintained, were as good as others and had the great advantage of working 'in the moral climate created by fascism'.[227]

What he required of them and other intellectuals was to demonstrate the primacy of Italy in all fields of human achievement. They duly obliged and much effort went into proving that Pasteur, Harvey, Faraday, Ampère, Daguerre, Koch and other great names in scientific history had all merely developed discoveries originally made in Italy. The telephone, the typewriter, the dynamo and the internal combustion engine were Italian inventions; even Shakespeare was proved by one scholar to have been the pseudonym of an Italian poet, and the discovery was said to have caused great alarm in England. This kind of cultural nationalism was considered important and was characteristic of fascism as it was of Stalinism.

In the visual arts, Mussolini had a less easy task. He liked to stress the great importance of art[228] and he himself, inevitably, was claimed to be a seminal influence upon contemporary artists;[229] but in private he was ready to confess that he did not understand pictures[230] and inwardly he resented that Italy had been held back from political greatness by the illusory and corrupting pursuit of aesthetic values.[231] Foreigners were sometimes told of his delight in visiting picture galleries,[232] but he informed others that he had never been inside one unless compelled – as for example when Hitler bored him to desperation by insisting on a visit to the Uffizi Palace.[233] Nevertheless, since he also feared that fascism might not be taken sufficiently seriously if it failed to produce a characteristic art form, he promised that as soon as he had solved Italy's political problems he would start an artistic revolution.[234] Some ideas for this revolution were contributed by the futurists, from whom he learnt that fascist art should owe nothing to foreign exemplars and should repudiate all that was charming, pretty and feminine. But futurism, being pre-fascist, was to some extent suspect. Fascist art had to be novel, universal, not sectarian; somehow it had to be traditional as well as modern; it also had to be aggressive and warlike.[235] For a time he thought he had found the answer in the *novecentisti* favoured by his mistress Sarfatti, but a few years later he was calling their work ridiculous and horrible, and his own instinctive preference seems to have been for something similar to the socialist realism found in Russia.[236]

Mussolini sometimes talked of artists being free under fascism to follow their own bent, but his words carried more conviction when he also spoke of art being controlled and politically attuned. With its 'totalitarian concept of culture', fascism in his view did more for the arts than any government had done before. He appointed committees to end the squabbling between rival artistic cliques whose continued existence, he thought, would only confuse people and suggest that fascism did not know its own mind.[237] Artists and intellectuals must be content with a subordinate role in the state; there was to be no more 'neutral intellectual speculation'. Italy was said to help artists more than any other country did, but in return they must see themselves as an instrument of government and must express in their creations a pride at living in what he now confidently termed 'the century of fascism and of Mussolini'.[238] IIis minister in charge of the arts, Bottai, later spelt out in greater detail fascism's 'artistic policy': it eschewed surrealism, dadaism, abstractionism, and other 'nostalgias' as well as anything that was 'politically useless'; fascist artists were not expected to adopt any one style, but their work had to be straightforward, and it had to be 'useful'.[239]

As so often under fascism, fierce words were not matched by effective action and many fine artists continued to work productively. Some of them, and not always the least distinguished, profited from the very large sums allocated to official patronage, especially in the 1930s. Lavish prizes were offered. One of the most important annual prizes was for a painting that would be vigorous, epic, Roman, imperial and on a subject chosen by Mussolini himself: in successive years his prescribed themes were – 'listening to a speech by the Duce on the radio', 'states of mind created by fascism', 'the battle for wheat', and 'the new Europe emerging out of bloodshed'. He was upset that established artists were reluctant to compete.[240]

When a truly fascist art was slow in appearing, his enthusiasm waned and he again began to inveigh against the love of pictures that, over the centuries, 'had turned Italians into cowards'; he talked of exporting some of the national treasures to earn more foreign currency for rearmament; he 'would prefer to have fewer statues and pictures in Italian museums and more flags captured from the enemy'.[241]

He was less disappointed in architecture and saw the very monumentality of big buildings as being essentially fascist. His one recorded comment on seeing the Parthenon was that the Capitol in Rome was much bigger.[242] He expressed a delight in skyscrapers – the taller the better – and one day suddenly ordered the building of an immense gothic campanile, 164 metres high, next to Milan cathedral: no one wanted to tell him that it would be an aesthetic absurdity.[243] Above all, he set his heart on building 'the Rome of Mussolini', changing the whole character of the city in a way that would challenge and surpass the work of emperors and popes in the last two thousand years. Rome, in blatant contradiction to his campaign against 'urbanisation', was to become a vast metropolis as in the time of the Emperor Augustus; it would more than double its population and expand across twenty kilometres of countryside until it reached the sea. He ordered that, in the space of five years, everything built during the 'centuries of decadence' since Augustus should be pulled down, to be replaced by new constructions worthy of a great imperial centre. He was going to be remembered as the greatest builder Rome had ever known and also 'the greatest destroyer'; he would pull down all the 'filthy picturesque' houses of the 'centuries of decadence' (which in his book included the baroque and the Counter-Reformation) so that the Colosseum, the Pantheon, the Capitol and the tomb of Augustus would stand alone in imperial majesty.[244]

Almost at once he learnt that his grandiloquent ideas were far too ambitious. Twenty years went by and only a few individual areas of Rome were cleared. One undoubted achievement, however, was the acres of asphalt poured over the remains of the great Roman forums to make a new 'Avenue of the Empire' connecting the Colosseum and the Capitol, and he was proud to announce that eleven existing streets were demolished to make this triumphal way suitable for the gigantic military parades he had in mind. Fifteen ancient churches in various parts of old Rome disappeared, as did many inconveniently sited palaces, and many thousands of people had to be rehoused.[245]

Among his projects was a plan to erect on the site of the ancient forums a great palace of fascism that would be one of the largest buildings in the world, destined to outlast all other Roman monuments as an emblem of fascist force and virility; he promised that it would be ready by 1939 but fortunately, as with his gothic campanile, the architects could not agree among themselves and it was never begun:[246] once again, it was the announcement itself that mattered and achievement was less necessary.

Italy had her full share of good architects and some new buildings were greatly admired. But in general the 'fascist style' was grandiose and sometimes brutal. In the 1930s, the Duce ordered a new 'Mussolini forum' to be constructed between Monte Mario and the Tiber, covering an area as large as the whole of fifteenth-century Rome. He specified that it should be grander than St Peter's and the Colosseum and was to contain the 'largest monolith in the world' – a marble obelisk 36 metres tall, weighing 770 tons.[247] But this was not enough, and eventually the idea was conceived that this *foro Mussolini* should be dominated by a great bronze colossus symbolising fascism: a half-naked figure of Hercules, one hand holding a truncheon, the other raised in a Roman salute, the face bearing Mussolini's features. It would stand 80 metres high looking down on the cupola of St Peter's across the river. A number of foundries were set to work on this project but, after using 100 tons of metal, they had completed only part of the face and a foot that was several times the height of a man: Mussolini was delighted, but money and metal ran out and this extravagant folly was quietly abandoned.[248]

Consolidation and achievement

9

The doctrine of fascism

Italian fascism originated not as doctrine but as method, as a technique for winning power, and at first its principles were unclear even to its own members. Some thought and continued to think it on the left of politics, others on the right, others that it was both left and right simultaneously. Perhaps this ambiguity was needed in order to weld together a coalition broad enough to take over government, a coalition that contained revolutionaries and conservatives, monarchists and republicans, clericals and anti-clericals, socialists and reactionaries, anarchists and nationalists; and inside Mussolini's own personality most of these contradictory elements co-existed.[1] As Dino Grandi once wrote, there was something in fascism for everyone,[2] and this was a vital element in its success. It enabled local fascist groups to adapt their political colour to suit the tactics dictated by the nature of the power struggle in their neighbourhood. To some extent, internal differences were mitigated by the fact that open discussion in the party became so difficult. They were also partially concealed by the compulsory belief in the Duce and his genius; but they never entirely disappeared.

Mussolini himself shared the confusion or at least did little to resolve it. On one occasion in 1921, he had given the intellectuals in the party two months to resolve all doubts and produce a satisfactory 'philosophy of fascism',[3] but when they failed he fell back on the comfortable belief that deeds, not words, justified the holding of power: ideologies, he used to say, were a luxury and for intellectuals only. Though he felt instinctively that fascism should represent some great universal idea, he also saw the advantage in not being too precise too soon,[4] and it was an awkward fact that there is not a single belief or idea in all his voluminous writings that he did not directly contradict somewhere else.

He tried, therefore, to make people believe that fascism was neither on the left nor the right:[5] it was not so much a dogmatic party as a religion and an essentially spiritual movement; it was a 'synthesis of every negation and every affirmation'; it should be thought of as an embodiment of beauty and courage, with a love of risk, a hatred of 'peacemongers', and above all a burning desire to obey Mussolini's personal authority.[6] Any foreigner who presumed to think this definition suspect or feeble could be told that fascism was too subtle to be easily understood by the layman. Alternatively, the more plausible excuse was given that fascists were too busy winning power to bother with defining their political beliefs. 'I have a horror of dogma', he explained, 'and fascist dogma is an impossibility'. He added that what might seem necessary today was bound to look much less important tomorrow, and to seek coherence of thought in his views was therefore an irrelevance.[7]

However, with his usual ability to face two ways at once, he continued to insist that fascism had a doctrine; on every contemporary problem it had views that were 'intellectually precise' and clearer than those of any other party.[8] Furthermore, his own opinions were said not to have changed since his early days as a revolutionary socialist.[9] Such statements may have satisfied some people, but many of the intellectuals on whom he relied to expound doctrine had to admit that they were left with only a vague idea of what the movement stood for. Outsiders could even see it as 'a chaos of contradictions' held together by the need to retain power – fascism was a force to be reckoned with in politics, but not a body of beliefs to be taken seriously.[10]

Similar doubts were expressed on the question as to whether the replacement of liberalism by fascism could properly be called a revolution. Some of its opponents claimed that fascism won power on the prospectus of carrying out the necessary process of renovating Italy and then, in order to keep power, went into reverse and became a reactionary movement blocking all substantial change. While some fascists were ready to admit the regime was 'essentially conservative and reactionary', Mussolini, on the contrary, maintained that *anno primo* of the fascist epoch marked the inauguration of something altogether new in Italian history, and the word 'revolution' had a magic that he did not want to forgo.[11] At the same time he wanted to call it a 'restoration', a revival of order, a continuation and not a violation of past Italian traditions.[12] But eventually, with some occasional doubts, he settled on its being a revolution: 'a profound political, moral, social revolution that in all probability will leave nothing or almost nothing of the past still in existence'.[13]

The contradiction arose quite logically because he at first needed to appear both conservative and innovatory. But his conservatism was, for the most part, tactical and temporary. Inwardly he was hoping that, as in Soviet Russia, fascism would replace one political class with another and supersede existing political institutions; it would then reveal itself to be an intellectual, as well as a political, revolution.[14] When the facts were slow to bear out his hopes he at first explained that the real revolution was still to come,[15] and then began talking of fascism as a 'permanent revolution', perpetually changing, without a final objective or point of rest.

This 'permanent revolution' was a happy phrase that concealed an inward uncertainty – a phrase which, to his great satisfaction, seemed to 'exert a mystical influence on the masses'[16] but which left some fascists more confused than ever. To impress everyone still more he began saying that the fascist revolution of 1922 was incomparably bigger, more complex and bloodier than the Russian revolution of 1917:[17] anything Lenin could do, he could do better.

The fascist revolution also had to be seen as far more substantial than the French revolution of 1789 that had launched the principles of free speech, liberty of conscience and equality before the law. Those 'immortal principles' had, a few years earlier, been championed by Mussolini himself[18] but his new movement had got to be the 'clear, categoric, final antithesis' of such out-of-date beliefs.[19] Equality and democracy were wrong because they would 'stamp out all beauty and interest and individuality from life'. Neither liberalism nor democracy was suited to the Italian temperament and against both he now promised war to the death.[20]

On second thoughts, he did not want to lose the appeal of the word 'democratic': indeed, in one sense fascist Italy was, he claimed, the most democratic country of all, since an ordinary Italian now had 'a greater influence on the conduct of those affairs which affected him than the citizen of any so-called democratic country'. This paradox was not properly explained, nor was the fact that some fascists were allowed to go on pretending that they were the sole champions of genuine liberty or indeed that liberalism and fascism were almost identical.[21]

Liberalism was merely an idea and hence not very important, but one thing Mussolini could not permit was practical liberty. Only intellectuals, he said, asked him for liberty and they could be disregarded. Ordinary people did not want it; they had too much of it and pined rather for order and discipline. Liberty was a 'decomposing corpse' and he now described civilisation as the antithesis of personal freedom: 'the individual exists only insofar as he is subordinated to the interests of the state, and as civilisation becomes more complex, so the liberty of the individual must be increasingly restricted'.[22] A bold interviewer once put it to Mussolini that his own career would have been blighted had he been subjected to the discipline and obedience he now forced on others; he thought for a moment and replied simply that 'new epochs call for new behaviour'.[23]

In 1925 it was arranged that fascist intellectuals should make a collective pronouncement to the outside world to demonstrate that there was no truth in 'the absurd legend of an incompatibility between fascism and intelligence'; on the contrary, a 'close and necessary link existed between the two'.[24] Some difficulty was encountered in producing enough suitable intellectuals, but eventually two hundred were assembled at Bologna.[25] They were told in advance that no serious discussion would be allowed before they made their decision, but some were adventurous enough to propose setting up a commission to lay down the credo of fascism once and for all: this was perilous ground and in the end they were persuaded to agree that Mussolini alone, 'the one theorist of fascism', was competent to decide the matter. They contented themselves with accepting that fascism was something spiritual and in time it would put paid to the 'traditional culture of Italy', whatever that might mean.[26]

A congress of philosophers held the following year was less successful because one of the participants triggered off an outburst of anti-fascist enthusiasm by pointing out that, since fascism did not allow the free debate that was indispensable to a vigorous cultural life, it was bound to prove sterile and could not possibly be compared to the French revolution. When the huge applause indicated that the congress was out of control, the proceedings were at once terminated.[27]

Mussolini was greatly embarrassed, since there were foreign participants at the congress; he ordered that two of the country's leading philosophers should lose their university posts for countenancing such a shaming episode and that henceforth such assemblies should be forbidden or strictly controlled. Other fascist intellectuals – some no doubt seeking to create vacancies for themselves – went further and demanded that all professors and teachers should be dismissed if they were not active believers in the new religion.[28] Mussolini reassured them that his movement would soon produce great philosophy, great poetry and great art, but meanwhile they should not push events too fast.[29]

In the early years of fascism, the official philosopher of the regime was Giovanni Gentile, who became minister of education in 1922 and whose educational reform of 1923 was much praised. Mussolini was determined to change the educational system and so produce a new fascist ruling class. His idea was to 'take hold of the citizen when he is six years old and return him to his family at sixteen'.[30] The education of every age group had to be imbued with fascist ideas, and a new series of compulsory textbooks was issued to popularise the myth of the Duce as well as to preach national greatness and the necessity of imperial expansion.

Mussolini affected a contempt for intellectuals in general, though some of those close to him thought he had a subconscious feeling of inferiority towards anyone who had been to university.[31] He used to say, and other fascists copied him, that intellectuals were less useful than peasants or *squadristi*. Too many of them seemed unwilling to accept fascism.[32] Those who did accept it were instructed by him to become propagandists for the regime, to export 'fascist culture' and prove that in intellectual productivity Italy was the equal of any other nation. This is what he termed 'spiritual imperialism'.[33] It was a sorrow to him that Benedetto Croce, the Italian intellectual best known in the outside world and who had at first been claimed as a precursor and supporter of fascism, utterly repudiated the movement in 1925. Mussolini once invited Croce to be minister of education and later offered him the first position in the Italian Academy, but was turned down on both occasions.

Giovanni Gentile, on the other hand, was eager to support the regime. In the opinion of this distinguished professor of philosophy, the worst defect of Italians was their tendency to intellectualise, so it was easy for him to accept Mussolini's statement that fascism was action rather than theory and to demand that teachers – especially in history and philosophy – be convinced fascists.[34] He was ready to accept censorship and, if necessary, the burning of heretical books; he believed in a single-party system and was also ready to denounce freedom of thought and the rights of the individual as outmoded foolishness.[35] But, more important, Gentile gave powerful encouragement to the legend of Mussolini as the great philosopher and teacher, a man of genius whose views were beyond criticism.[36] He was also prepared, if without much enthusiasm, to justify the brutalities of *squadrismo* and to echo fascist ideas about the revivifying effects of war and a bath of blood: brutality was something in the Italian character and an inescapable part of the fascist process of redemption.[37]

Mussolini was grateful for such powerful support, but, in the late 1920s, was still anxious to avoid a more precise formulation of fascist dogma. He pointed out again that one of the secrets of his success had been the lack of a programme, and that fascism was method rather than theory – or, at least, anyone searching for the philosophy of fascism must look for it in the anti-intellectual world of *squadrismo*.[38] The official apologists for the regime were thus glad to admit that, since no two fascists would agree on basic principles,[39] they had no doctrine but simply derived their motive force from Mussolini's genius.[40] Foreign critics could, on the contrary, interpret this as meaning that fascism was illogical, nonsensical, contradictory, a mere expedient to rivet the domination of one man onto Italian society.

Inside Italy, criticism or even doubt was not so easy. By commanding all public means of communication, Mussolini could persuade public opinion that the outside world admired fascism as 'a new type of civilisation' more original than bolshevism. Its originality was something he stressed in public, even though in private he admitted that it was not original at all. The important point was to convince Italians that foreigners saw it as the one truly revolutionary doctrine of the twentieth century;[41] and everyone could rest assured that the details of that doctrine were being worked out in serious centres of study such as the faculty of fascist studies at Perugia university, the school of fascist mysticism at Milan and the international centre of fascist studies at Lausanne.

Eventually, in 1932, when the fourteenth volume of the *Enciclopedia Italiana* was scheduled to appear and an entry on fascist 'doctrine' had to be written, Mussolini could no longer put off assembling the main principles of the movement as he then saw them. He put his name to the article even though much of it was written by Gentile, with corrections by other fascist leaders: it was the only signed article in the whole encyclopedia. Some points of doctrine were still, not surprisingly, doubtful at the moment of writing and the volume had to be withdrawn from circulation almost at once after publication so that this one article could be amended.[42]

Since fascism was now a 'permanent revolution', it had to continue changing after 1932. There is for example no reference in this article to the racialism that soon afterwards became a fundamental fascist doctrine. Much of the quasi-socialist programme that Mussolini had formulated in 1919 was contradicted by him in 1932, then later reinstated as fascist orthodoxy, which left the would-be theorists in a state of some confusion.[43] But contradictions did not matter much to someone who had learnt how easily yesterday's headlines were forgotten: indeed he continued to speak of contradictions as a strength rather than a weakness and made cynical comments in private about those fascists who still bothered about intellectual consistency.

Totalitarianism

Attempts to assassinate previous Italian prime ministers had been kept secret or made light of, but an attack on Mussolini in 1925 was given great publicity and used very effectively to attract sympathy and support. Several other attempts on his life followed in the next year, all of them much publicised. After 1926 little was heard of any incident of this kind; indeed the newspapers were instructed to keep reporting of all crime to a minimum in order to convince people of the moral effects of fascism. As a former advocate of tyrannicide, Mussolini knew he was in danger. Sometimes he was accused of using *agents provocateurs* to exploit the publicity and sympathy attending attempts to kill him.[44] Certainly when they happened his very first thought was of exploiting them: an attempt by a demented Irishwoman to shoot him was thus at once magnified into an international anti-fascist plot and became another excuse to harass opposition newspapers.[45]

Another attempted shooting by the socialist deputy Zaniboni was certainly encouraged by an *agent provocateur* and, again, the occasion was used to attack imaginary foreign instigators. As part of the campaign against the freemasons, an almost certainly innocent man, General Capello, was convicted of complicity in this shooting and, again, the pretext was taken to persecute or shut down some of the major independent newspapers. A third attempt was made by an anarchist who had been living in France and this was useful to fuel a campaign against France and the many Italian anti-fascist exiles who had gone for refuge to Paris.

The fourth attempt, which took place at Bologna in October 1926, was used as the final justification for setting up a totalitarian dictatorship. The presumed marksman, a boy of sixteen, was lynched on the spot by fascist guards and his body torn to pieces and carried round the town in a horrifyingly macabre ceremony. The boy was almost certainly an innocent bystander, and there were no very convincing eye-witnesses except Mussolini himself who gave two contradictory descriptions of his assailant, neither of which fitted the youth.[46] There was a suspicion that leading fascists had been intending to kill him and, when the shot missed, needed an innocent victim they could blame; though this seems unlikely, there were some awkward doubts that had to be suppressed. Reasons of state persuaded Mussolini to instruct the judge to sentence two of the boy's family to long terms in prison as accomplices, despite the fact that the police were entirely unconvinced of their involvement.[47]

This incident in Bologna provided a useful excuse for whipping up an artificial panic and Mussolini's reaction was immediate, just as though he was all ready for it. He hastily jotted down the emergency measures to be taken, including the final abolition of all parties other than the fascist party, the suspension of any remaining independent papers, the creation of a new 'political' police force and, in a further blatant defiance of Italy's written constitution, a special revolutionary tribunal. During four days, in which he took care to remain out of reach in his country house, local fascist groups ran riot in what appeared to be organised attacks on foreign consulates and the houses of anti-fascist parliamentarians. He later ascribed this rioting to common criminals and ordered the courts to give them maximum penalties.[48]

After the briefest of debates, 124 members of parliament – including socialists, communists and *popolari* – were then declared to have forfeited their seats in parliament and thereby also their parliamentary immunity from prosecution. The communist deputy, Antonio Gramsci, was at once arrested. Only 12 deputies were brave and independent enough to vote against this package of emergency regulations; in the Senate there were as many as 49 dissenting votes but foreign governments were told that the approval was unanimous.[49]

The new revolutionary tribunal to judge 'political offences' was needed because the ordinary courts were thought to be too slow and insufficiently subservient. Mussolini had once rejected the very idea of such a tribunal as entirely improper and he privately expressed some contempt for those who agreed to serve on it as judges;[50] nevertheless, he wanted a judicial body that was summary, secret and intimidating, which could disregard witnesses and against which there was no appeal. The judges would be personally chosen by him, most of them officers in the fascist militia, and the law they enforced would be martial law.

Capital punishment was another fascist novelty, another measure that Mussolini himself had recently condemned as uncivilised, but for which extremists and moderates in his party were clamouring.[51] This one-time champion of political assassination was now on the other side of the barricades and demanded the execution of anyone who tried to kill the head of government or so much as conceived the idea of doing so. He told the Grand Council that he needed the death penalty in order 'to make Italians more virile, to habituate them to the sight of blood and to the idea of death', and at these spirited words a murmur of approval went round the listening *gerarchi*. Parliamentarians who wanted to vote against it on grounds of conscience were beaten up or threatened with physical violence.[52]

Not many executions took place as a result of this emergency legislation because the main intention was simply to inspire terror. Some other dictatorships were, in fact, far more savage; nevertheless, there were many examples of unnecessary brutality; there was something especially ugly about the eagerness with which people competed for appointment as judges on the special tribunal and the way defence counsel would beg the judges to impose sentence of death on a client – before sending a bill to the dead man's family.[53]

The written constitution of Italy, as inherited by Mussolini, prescribed a representative system, a free press and equality before the law. But the constitution had been virtually superseded by the end of 1926 after King Vittorio Emanuele, who had sworn an oath to maintain it, had signed every one of the derogations of this fundamental law that were brought to him. Against those who thought he should have made a stand, the king could argue that as long as the Senate with its many non-fascists did nothing, he could not act against what was clearly a parliamentary majority. Owing to his 'unconstitutional' acceptance of fascism in October 1922, he well knew that he stood to lose his throne if there was any return to constitutional government.

The king's relations with his prime minister remained good, if never very friendly. Vittorio Emanuele had always thought it his duty to conceal nothing from his ministers and presumably told Mussolini of any private approaches made to the palace by the opposition. He remained head of state and, in theory, kept the legal right to dismiss the government if he thought fit, but in fact accepted the fascist revolution and made clear that there was no going back.[54] He referred to the surviving liberals as *revenants*, and in 1928 neither he nor Mussolini bothered to turn up at the funeral of Giolitti – the prime minister who had served Italy and the royal house so well.

A key figure in the regime was Arturo Bocchini, the chief of the security police from 1926 to 1940, who, though his name hardly ever appeared in the newspapers, was the third most powerful man in Italy – sometimes, when the party secretary was weak, he was second only to Mussolini himself. There were said to be some twenty different police organisations under fascism[55] and they did not always work in harmony. They were never either excessively efficient or particularly cruel and the Duce wisely took care after 1926 that the police remained independent of the fascist party.

Though he paid close attention to the information given him each day by the prefects, the *carabinieri*, the secret police and the security services of the militia, it was to the cynical, unscrupulous, but moderately good-natured Bocchini that he listened most closely of all. Bocchini's network of spies told him what was happening in every department of national life – and not least about the peccadilloes of the fascist *gerarchi*. Apart from reading newspapers, it was skimming through these often petty and mendacious trivia that appears to have taken up more of Mussolini's time than almost anything. Nor did he appreciate how tainted was such a source of information as – like so many others – these faceless men learnt to tell him what he liked to hear.[56]

This very fact makes it hard for us – as no doubt it sometimes was for him – to gauge the strength of the remaining opposition. Foreign observers disagreed, some thinking that fascism was secretly detested by the vast majority of Italians,[57] others believing almost the opposite;[58] one guess was that 80 per cent of Italians would back him in a free vote.[59] Mussolini asserted that no government in history had had so much support,[60] and told one British journalist that the opposition consisted of some two thousand men, only a hundred of whom were against him personally. The same journalist, on the other hand, thought that a small pretorian guard of armed men was holding down a country which was mainly neutral or hostile to the regime.[61]

Mussolini had no illusions about the industrial proletariat, knowing that it had still not been won for fascism by 1927.[62] But if any of his speeches was greeted with hostility by such people,[63] the official accounts cheerfully said the very opposite, and usually any lack of enthusiasm at public meetings could be effectively swamped by the official claque. Wall slogans continued to appear against his regime though of course these were never mentioned in public or in the newspapers, and information sometimes leaked across the Swiss frontier about sporadic violent demonstrations.[64] But in the absence of a free press the degree of criticism or hostility is impossible to assess.

Individual examples of discontent are easy enough to find. Former fascist

The young Mussolini

Mussolini arrested in 1915 for socialist agitation

The prime minister at his desk

Brandishing the sword of Islam in Libya

The man of the people

Clara Petacci

Mussolini and his family

At the time of the Vatican treaty

The Grand Council of fascism

With Carnera, the boxer

supporters – the leading nationalist, Corradini, for example – were privately outspoken in their denunciation of the corruption and megalomania overtaking the regime, and occasionally in the Senate there was guarded criticism of the waste, the useless extravagance, the bureaucratisation and 'creeping socialism' that appeared to be government policy.[65] Many intellectuals, many lawyers, and others among the upper classes who had access to sources of information outside fascist control, were evidently disgusted with the all too obvious peculation and inefficiency.[66] But there was no apparent and practical alternative to fascism, so most people saw little point in refusing to conform. On the rare occasions when an alternative presented itself – as in June 1924 after Matteotti's murder and in July 1943, or in some individual areas in December 1924 – the whole machinery of totalitarian consent disintegrated in a moment. This suggests that the consensus behind fascism must have been largely cynical, depending on a continuation of outward successes and, if necessary, the invention of successes by means of propaganda.

The same conclusion is suggested by the fact that Mussolini could never risk allowing any free speech or disbandment of the militia. He was accused of spending twice as much as France on public security and over a quarter of a million lire on the surveillance of a single innocuous person, Benedetto Croce; in reply he tried to make people believe that Italy was less of a police state than any country in Europe[67] – and privately ordered the watch on Croce to stop. When he discovered that another harmless individual, Dr Guido Bergamo who had early abandoned fascism because of republican scruples, had thirty policemen on duty at his house, he ordered this surveillance also to be halved. The guard on the historian of ancient Rome, Guglielmo Ferrero, was reduced to a single person until the censorship intercepted some of Ferrero's letters which criticised the regime.[68] The intention behind these surveillances was merely petty harassment and intimidation but the cost must have been large. Exactly how much was wasted in this way will never be known.

For political prisoners, Mussolini set up penal settlements on Lipari and other islands, a procedure which he said he deeply regretted and which he had once condemned as quite unworthy of a civilised country; but he now called it a necessary process of 'social hygiene'.[69] A lesser punishment was *confino* or banishment to some specified and usually remote village. Newspapers were instructed that these political punishments were to be kept as secret as possible,[70] but some members of the legal profession applauded the fact that anyone sent to *confino* was not allowed a defence lawyer or to produce witnesses and could not appeal to the ordinary courts.[71] Even those found not guilty by the special tribunal could languish in *confino* for years, merely because Mussolini said he wished it, and he used to joke that many wives would beg him to give their husbands an even longer sentence.[72]

Conditions on the islands were generally humane but far from easy and torture was used on some occasions.[73] Mussolini was annoyed when he found that, because of the lack of publicity and control by the ordinary magistrates, the fascist *gerarchi* were sometimes able to send their own personal enemies to *confino*.[74] But he did not want to change a practice that got rid of opponents with so little fuss or publicity, and perhaps never understood how profoundly corrupting was a system that produced an enormous number of anonymous delations by individuals with private grudges to work off.[75]

Mussolini once said sardonically that governing Italians is not hard; it is merely useless.[76] 'To govern them,' he remarked, 'you need only two things, policemen, and bands playing in the streets,'[77] though he also liked to say that he based his regime on spontaneous consent and in no sense depended on police action. Experience of politics had taught him early in life that you could usually get away with 'ninety-seven cents-worth of mere public clamour and three cents-worth of solid achievement'.[78] The difficulty was to find the correct mixture of 'carrot and stick' – it is interesting that he used this phrase for the title of a book – and he spent much more time juggling the various methods of inducement and compulsion than on ordinary administration or formulation of policy.

Everywhere he went, especially after the assassination attempts, he was surrounded by policemen: the cost to the exchequer is unrecorded. Though he boasted that he was the first Italian prime minister who could move freely among the people,[79] he could never, in fact, walk through the streets of Rome like some of his predecessors and successors. These plain-clothes officers were the peasants he posed with for photographs, the swimmers round him in the sea at Riccione, the clapping bystanders as he drove through the streets, and everywhere they formed what one of his own police chiefs called a *cordon sanitaire* shutting him off from contact with the ordinary world. He joked about this when, at one meeting, he asked the real farmers to step forward so that he could see who they were.[80]

In 1927, Bocchini set up a secret force of political police, and Mussolini coined for it the name *ovra*, a meaningless word that he hoped would arouse fear and curiosity.[81] The *ovra* does not seem to have been particularly efficient; its members, who were paid more than ordinary policemen, were said to include some non-fascists and Mussolini sometimes used it to supervise the lives and work of his own fascist colleagues. Farinacci was appalled to find himself spied upon and was sad to discover that Mussolini in this and other ways was intent on undermining and neutralising the party as well as every other organisation in the country.[82]

From 1926 to 1930 the party secretary was Augusto Turati, a journalist who, like all the other leading fascists, had made his reputation as a squad leader. Alongside him as administrative secretary and in control of party finances was the grey eminence Marinelli: after being in prison for his involvement in the Matteotti killing, Marinelli was freed by an amnesty and was back in high office several months later.[83] Turati ordered that the party must consist of 'the most honest and intelligent' people in Italy but they also had to be ready to die for fascism or, if need be, to kill: they now had to take an oath to obey Mussolini in everything without discussion and be ready to shed their blood in his defence.

Farinacci, the previous party secretary, had not entirely banned discussions in the party despite his authoritarianism, and Mussolini had agreed for a time that some *gerarchi* could still be elected by other fascists, not appointed from above. This had to be changed and the very idea of elections was now said to be thoroughly un-fascist: Mussolini announced that henceforth he alone would select the top *gerarchi*. Since he was the man who had prepared and carried out the revolution, he could not admit discussion or contradiction of his actions and, as for his own position as supreme leader, 'supermen elect themselves'. Discussion was superfluous and the only opposition he needed was within himself.[84] The intellectuals of the party had to accept this decision, if perhaps with reluctance, and write articles proving how wise it was.[85]

With the abolition of all other political parties and the expulsion of the opposition deputies from parliament in November 1926, the fascist party was, in outward appearance, alone and all-powerful. An order was put out by Turati that all passers-by had to salute when the party flags were carried in procession,[86] and in December 1926 a decree incorporated the *fasces* into the state insignia. But the party, like everything else, was in fact being deprived of independence and initiative: its job was to conform, applaud, and obey. When someone made a disparaging reference to Italy becoming a 'Prussian barracks', the reply came that this was just what the country needed, and Mussolini expressed himself as delighted that he need spend no more time in sterile debate with his colleagues.[87]

Some of the more independent fascists were now expelled from the party, mainly those who found it hard to think that the old rebellious ways of *squadrismo* were over, or who did not realise that Mussolini – once he had succeeded in seizing power and getting rid of all opponents – had little further use for the *ras* and their petty criminal ways. Once his purge was effective, he set the party to discipline itself and then 'fascistise' the nation from top to bottom by gradually seizing all the levers of command, displacing all non-fascist job holders, and infiltrating all cultural, social and economic institutions and the entire educational system.[88]

From the very beginning he had the idea of producing a completely new ruling class. The fascist elite in 1922 had numbered little more than a thousand dedicated followers, but he believed that, with forty or fifty thousand men taking all positions of command and trained 'to work with the absolute precision of clockwork', he could lead the country to greatness.[89] He had hoped this new class would be in existence by 1927 but soon began to see that it would take ten or fifteen years longer.[90] He must also have realised at some point that, instead of recruiting an elite that others would admire, fascism was continuing to promote the undesirables, the unprincipled, the time-servers, the cheats and the bullies; possibly this was precisely what he needed and wanted. The oath that was imposed on virtually the whole of Italian youth at the age of eighteen to obey Mussolini in everything could only encourage the brainless and the insincere. Before long, some of his more idealistic followers perceived that his veto on discussion and his insistence on appointments being made from above would inevitably obstruct the discovery of new creative talent.[91] But any such doubts were officially discouraged and silenced.

He happily admitted that he was now a dictator:[92] his regime was totalitarian in theory and would become more so in practice as individual freedoms were progressively restricted. 'The individual has no existence except insofar as he is part of the state and subordinate to its requirements', and the rights of the state were something sacred that had to be clearly differentiated from the profane – in other words, from the rights of the individual.[93] Foreign visitors sometimes saw the Italy of 1927 as being like a prison or a cemetery; no one dared talk politics and ordinary human rights were effectively abolished. Totalitarianism was becoming, as the constitutional lawyers defined it, the absolute rule of a single man.[94]

When one brave and loyal fascist hinted to Mussolini that it was undignified and even dangerous to treat Italians like helpless children, his answer was that on this point he could admit no contradiction: 'I am making superhuman efforts to educate this people and I know I shall succeed. They must realise that they can come of age only by accepting obedience. When they have learnt to obey, they must and they will believe what I tell them and then they will march in compact ranks at my command.' He wanted to reach the point where he could march them past a military cap stuck on a pole and have them salute it.[95]

The idea of changing the character of Italians was quite fundamental. In ten years' time, he claimed, the transformation would have taken place and Italians would be reshaped after his own image and bear no resemblance to what they had been before. He liked to think of fascism as a laboratory from which a new culture, a new way of thinking and a new kind of person would emerge, warriors 'who are always ready to sacrifice their lives' and prepare the country for its imperial destiny.[96] Italians must learn that even their clothes, their habits of eating, working and sleeping must be changed to show that fascism was not just a new method of government but a fundamental and totalitarian change in their way of life. Just as four centuries earlier there had been a typical Renaissance Italian, so there must now be a typical fascist Italian, and a prize was offered for a book describing the characteristics required in this 'Italian of Mussolini'.[97]

The formula gradually emerged that, first of all, the ideal fascist would be physically different: precise descriptions were sometimes given of his physique that made him look just like Mussolini himself, and the Duce's personal mannerisms were soon being copied everywhere.[98] The new Italian would also be far less individualistic than his predecessors, more heroic, less disorganised, less optimistic, less critical. He would be more serious, more hard-working, less talkative, less rhetorical, less corrupt: the true fascist would be known by his disinterestedness, his courage, tenacity and frankness.[99] Among his other characteristics the new Italian would reject altruism[100] and abjure 'comfort', that terrible word invented by the British.[101] He would sleep less and spend less time on pleasure and entertainment.[102] He would also despise the cynicism and materialism typified by the American way of life that was threatening to engulf the more idealistic and intelligent world of Europe.[103]

Already, by 1929, Mussolini tried to make out that these changes had largely taken place as his new society was being moulded into shape. Already, he insisted, any outside observer could see that Italians were unrecognisable: they spoke less, gesticulated less, were less picturesque, less amusing, less prepossessing. Already they were being trained to accept the philosophy of the superman and to know the joy of obedience to a single will.[104]

Foreign policy, 1926–30

It was entirely in character that Mussolini should continue to act in foreign politics with the same lack of consideration for the rights of others as he did at home. Italians had to be not just respected abroad but feared, and he meant to win for them a 'power without limit' so that Italy would have an acknowledged primacy over other nations: such was the destiny that had been carved out for them 'by the infallible hand of God'.[105] One of his senior ambassadors, when early in 1926 he watched the Duce thump the table and roll his eyes at the prospect of future greatness, began to speculate about possible mental disturbance and incipient paranoia.[106] He was not mad but simply trying to impress people as a man of power, and the impression was reinforced by the official spokesmen of the regime. If only their Duce could be acknowledged abroad as the foremost personality in the world and the leader of the universal retreat from liberalism and democracy, fascist Italy would be well on its way to what was sometimes spoken of as the ultimate goal of world domination.[107] They knew now that he expected them to demonstrate that fascism had a general application and might well be adopted in other countries, even those with quite different historical traditions. Since parliamentary regimes were on the decline in every country of Europe, the general acceptance of fascism would eventually mean the acceptance of an Italian primacy.[108] His earlier phrase about fascism being 'not for export' was repudiated as too foolish a remark for him ever to have uttered,[109] and though he still sometimes repeated it in order to allay foreign suspicions, loyal intellectuals tried hard to demonstrate that there was no real contradiction between these various assertions.[110]

Of course he continued to need foreign friends and foreign capital, so other countries were asked not to take too seriously his bellicose outbursts, which, it was explained, were designed for internal consumption only: the reality behind the occasional bluster was said to be that 'we shall all make ugly faces at each other, but nobody means to fight'.[111] Other countries should realise that he was, on the contrary, the great peacemaker. He even thought it 'inadmissible' that he should fail to be given the Nobel peace prize for his contribution to the Locarno settlement, and his ambassador in Oslo had a difficult time when this could not be arranged.[112]

Other European statesmen were left with the problem of how to reconcile the proclaimed man of peace with the man who spoke of Italy as being in 'a permanent state of war' and already possessing armed services stronger than those 'of any other country in the world'.[113] He announced that he wanted an army of five million men with a forest of bayonets, an air force so large that it would blot out the sun over Italy, and a navy that other countries would see as a real threat to their security.[114] Such remarks led the journalists, whose job was to divine and expound his inner thoughts, to speak of another world war not just as inevitable, but as positively welcome and assuredly victorious for Italy.[115] Italians had to adopt a militarist mentality and to learn to despise neighbouring countries as pacifist and decadent.[116]

This two-faced posture of aggression and pacifism was too much for one or two of the senior civil servants, who were already under attack for insufficient fascist zeal. The permanent secretary at the foreign office, Salvatore Contarini, decided to retire in March 1926, unable to stand the confusion and disgusted by what he saw of the financial corruption of the regime. The last straw was an unguarded speech by Mussolini hinting at a possible invasion of Germany. Contarini, though himself a good nationalist, felt helpless against the tide of violence being brought into foreign affairs, and his own policy of trying to conciliate France and Germany was not popular with a man dreaming of world domination and forests of bayonets.

Mussolini took this opportunity to dismiss other officials and replace them with convinced fascists. He had already, in a welcome and overdue reform, ended the restrictions that confined the diplomatic service to men of wealth. Now, after specifying that the foreign office must become the most fascist of all government departments, more than a hundred party stalwarts were given diplomatic posts so as to increase respect for Italy abroad: a formal examination was no longer required for the job and preference was given to those with party membership dating back to before October 1922.[117] This was called one of the most significant changes brought by fascism, but the result was that the quality of Italian representatives abroad fell drastically, and the fact brought considerable discredit on the regime and on Italy. It also resulted in the government's henceforth lacking enough accurate information from foreign capitals.[118]

One country Mussolini tried not to offend was Great Britain, and here he was fortunate that the British foreign minister, Austen Chamberlain, found him easier to deal with than the old school of professional diplomats. The British were anxious to obtain Italian support for their policy in the Middle East and Mussolini was more than ready to oblige. He also tried to convince them that the authoritarianism and violence in fascism were purely temporary.[119] Only in the course of 1927 did this friendliness begin to wear thin as it became clearer to British politicians that the basic principle in fascist foreign policy was to make trouble and thus threaten world peace; the assumption seemed to be that the greater the friction the greater the fear and hence the more prestige.[120]

This became particularly obvious in the eastern Mediterranean where encouragement was given by Mussolini to anti-democratic forces in Egypt and anti-French rebels in Syria and the Lebanon.[121] Moreover, he was still hoping to establish an Italian settlement on the mainland of Asia Minor.[122] He admired the Turkish ruler Kemal Pasha – an admiration not reciprocated[123] – but was ready to stake a claim if Kemal fell from power[124] and, in the meantime, proceeded to fortify the islands of Rhodes and Leros off the Turkish coast.[125]

These islands of the Dodecanese had been governed by the Turks until their conquest by Italy in 1912 and, under the Turks, their Greek-speaking inhabitants had enjoyed considerable autonomy and almost no taxation. In 1912 the Italians promised to respect local rights of autonomy but Mussolini could not permit colonial dependencies to enjoy human rights that he was suppressing at home.[126] Italian was therefore imposed as the only language of education in the schools, Greek newspapers were stopped and Greek lettering had even to be removed from tombstones. All the familiar methods of castor oil, beating and torture were used to coerce the population,[127] and Roman Catholicism was forcibly imposed on a Greek Orthodox community. Some of the best land, despite a formal undertaking, was confiscated from private owners and given to Italian settlers; the hope was expressed that, by inducing the native Greek population to emigrate, the islands would be latinised and stand 'as an Italian sentinel in the Levant'.[128] Here was another example of what fascist colonisation was to mean in practice.

In the Balkans, where Italy had one of her most substantial markets, Mussolini's policy was to supplant the influence of Britain in Albania and of France in Jugoslavia. Instead he meant to create a group of client states that looked exclusively to Rome; these would act as bridgeheads, making the whole Balkan peninsula and the Danube basin into a field for Italy's political and economic expansion.[129] Politicians from the area were summoned peremptorily to Rome and sometimes treated with a discourtesy that was presumably meant to intimidate: when the prime minister of Greece, Venizelos, was invited to a formal dinner, Mussolini said not a single word to him, carrying on a long conversation with the waiters instead.[130]

His policy in the Balkans was said, of course, to be one of peace, but in October 1926 he ordered twenty divisions to be ready for a sudden attack on Jugoslavia, telling his chiefs of staff that there was not a moment to lose.[131] Then, just as suddenly, he backed down; Jugoslavia had, if possible, to be split up, so he supported a number of secessionist movements and paid considerable sums to several groups of Croat rebels. Ante Pavelic, the leading Croat terrorist, came to Italy in 1927 and had secret talks at the foreign office; he was given money to start a fascist-style movement among Jugoslav dissidents and a school was set up near Parma to teach them terrorist tactics.[132]

During 1927 Mussolini also got in touch with groups of Macedonian terrorists, with the same aim of stirring up trouble against existing governments. His under-secretary, Grandi, was instructed to meet their leaders and keep them secretly supplied with money and arms,[133] though some of these men – as Grandi quickly discovered – were little better than common murderers and the fact that they were at odds with each other and with the Croat separatists made them less than useless to Italy.[134] Foreign politicians soon learnt that the Duce was subsidising assassination squads and it did not help his reputation as a responsible statesman when his name was linked publicly with killing. In 1928, hurried orders were given for certain compromising documents in the Italian embassy in Belgrade to be destroyed.[135]

In Albania he continued to subsidise the plausible but unscrupulous King

Zog, as well as supporting other rival groups of Albanians belonging to an anti-monarchist opposition. There was a hope that large numbers of Italians would one day settle in Albania, but he also wanted to build up an army of Albanians that could be used at the right moment in a war against Jugoslavia.[136]

Naturally there was much bad feeling – especially at Geneva – against the stirring up of hatreds in such a delicately-poised area, and this was another reason why Mussolini was unsympathetic towards the League of Nations. In 1926 he was hoping to provoke an international crisis that would hasten the League's demise. When this failed, he tried to get the League's offices removed from Switzerland to somewhere more authoritarian. But eventually he allowed himself to be persuaded that Geneva could be useful as a radiating point for fascist propaganda[137] and he successfully promoted the appointment of one of his trusted assistants as under-secretary-general of the League. This official was then sent secret and regular orders from Rome and at once set about arranging for other Italian fascists to be employed by the international secretariat. These Italians at Geneva had to act in the way Mussolini required or face the threat of imprisonment and he was therefore able to intervene unobtrusively in some administrative decisions. He used these men to block the giving of help to political refugees and to stop an international move to mediate between Jugoslavia and Albania. One Italian who was high commissioner for the League in Danzig was instructed to hold himself ready to create a crisis and to favour German annexation of that city whenever Mussolini thought fit.[138]

Though the League had powers to supervise the treatment of most national minorities in Europe, it was allowed no such authority in Italy. Apart from 100,000 Greeks in the Dodecanese, there were almost as many French-speakers in the Val d'Aosta, quite apart from the much bigger Slav and German minorities in Istria and the Alto Adige. But Mussolini continued to pretend, in defiance of all the evidence, that Italy was the most homogeneous state in Europe and that her minorities were statistically insignificant.[139] He did not hesitate to protest against the French for trying to denationalise the Italian-speaking community in Tunisia, against the Swiss for seeming to do the same in Canton Ticino, and against the British for encouraging Maltese instead of the Italian language in Malta; inside Italy, on the other hand, all 'ethnic survivals' had to be removed – by force, if necessary.[140]

It was also in defiance of the League and of the demilitarisation clauses in the treaties of 1919–20 that Mussolini secretly continued to rearm Germany, Bulgaria and Austria, hoping thereby to create dissensions and increase Italy's leverage in Europe.[141] Arms were also sent to Hungary and, in direct contravention of treaties, he brought Hungarian soldiers and airmen to Italy for military training.[142] In January 1928, what was thought to be an eighth consignment of arms was uncovered at the Austrian frontier and some 'agricultural machinery' turned out to be machine guns. The Italian representatives in Geneva tried, with partial success, to prevent a major international scandal about this illicit gun-running; but other consignments were soon being prepared.[143] Obviously he thought he was getting something in return, though quite what this was is difficult to see. Some of the weapons were designed to help a putsch in Vienna by the *Heimwehren*, a para-military right-wing organisation, despite the fact that the extreme conservatives in Austria were far from friendly towards Italy. The Italian taxpayer had to foot the bill for something that had little chance of success; and at the same time money was being sent to nazi groups in Austria that were, as his foreign office well knew, opposed to the *Heimwehren*.[144] Evidently, Mussolini was just trying to make as many difficulties for other governments as possible.

In 1928 he signed the Kellogg Pact outlawing war as an instrument of national policy. At first he was not keen to accept such an absurd proposal; then he said he would agree to it, but only if delegates came to Italy for the signature and so let him organise the publicity. But in the end he gave way on both points, saying in private that he did not believe in the Pact and hoped it would fail, but could not afford to be left out.[145] He added jocularly that he had already agreed to 134 different international conventions in two years and could hardly baulk at one more. His sarcastic remarks in parliament about pacifism and the Kellogg Pact caused much mirth among the deputies, but when he went on to say that, notwithstanding this pact, he was increasing expenditure on rearmament, the whole parliament rose to its feet and applauded.[146] He referred several times to a war that was bound to break out in or after 1935 and for which Italy must be prepared. Most serious of all, he deliberately began to encourage the highly dangerous belief among his followers that no other country would ever be able to resist the might of fascist Italy.[147]

Except during 1929–32, Mussolini was always in personal charge of the three service ministries, despite the fact that he lacked the time or knowledge to cope with this additional responsibility. To improve Italy's capacity for war was said to be one of his primary objectives and, to allay any doubts, he announced after five years as minister that a profound revolution had already taken place which had prepared the army for whatever might happen. The three services, he said, had all been given a new fighting spirit and been welded into a single co-ordinated force that obviated the need to create a unified ministry of defence. In fact, however, almost nothing had been done that could remotely justify his claim: the generals sometimes tried to pretend that they were ahead of the rest of the world in their capacity for an emergency mobilisation, but they were deceiving him, just as he was deceiving the rest of Italy.[148]

In 1929 he decided that his own position was so unassailable that he could afford to give up some of his many offices. For the post of foreign minister he chose the former under-secretary Grandi, who had the correct fascist credentials as a man of violence but also had more intelligence and sophistication than the other squad leaders. Grandi had already shown that he favoured a strong, not to say warlike, foreign policy;[149] he now confirmed that, behind public talk about good-neighbourliness and international morality, he was still a *squadrista* who preferred the big stick; he wanted Italy to become more Machiavellian, more isolated, less anglophile, and militarily so strong that she would tip the scales in Europe when the great day of war came. Grandi agreed that Italy, whatever had to be said in public, should be distrustful of disarmament and against the League, and must prepare in silence for the moment when the Duce decided that the time was ripe for war.[150]

Mussolini, of course, still directed general policy. He agreed that his new foreign minister should attend the disarmament conference in 1930 and there maintain the right to naval parity with France in the Mediterranean; anything less than parity would reduce the stature of Italy in the world, so Grandi was authorised to sabotage the conference if it was not confirmed.[151] This committed Italy to a vastly expensive programme of naval construction; to mitigate which, Grandi sought to persuade other countries to abolish the more expensive weapons such as tanks, aircraft carriers and heavy artillery, in which area Italy was finding it ever harder to compete.[152] This was no doubt a forlorn hope but was worth a try: Italy would stand to gain if she could concentrate on cheaper weapons – the midget submarines, for instance, that were to be so successful in the Second World War, or poison gas which, in the late 1920s, Mussolini was using secretly against rebellious tribesmen in Libya.

The subject of peace was never very congenial to him, and while he continued to speak to the outside world of disarmament, inside Italy he preferred to talk of his 'adorable' machine guns, of bomber aircraft that were more beautiful and far more efficacious than words. He stressed that there was something 'divine' about Italy's inevitable march towards greatness, and when the right moment arrived he would be ready to mobilise every Italian – even children – 'to constitute a single mass, or rather to make a thunderbolt that I can hurl against anyone anywhere'.[153] Grandi congratulated him on these fighting words and said he hoped foreigners would be suitably daunted at the prospect, though privately he apologised to the British ambassador. This particular speech had been long premeditated, but was intended to impress Italians rather than to alarm other countries,[154] and the record shows that its more bellicose passages were greeted by the audience with 'delirious applause'.

It is always hard to know when Mussolini was in real earnest and when he was merely striking an attitude or else being carried away by excitement. He explained that it was his deliberate policy to confuse and soften up opponents by alternating suddenly between tension and détente, between fierceness and sweet reasonableness.[155] He also confessed that he sometimes tried to arouse his audience simply in order to discover how far he could count upon them in an emergency.[156] But perhaps some of these belligerent outbursts were instinctive and uncalculated. Later in 1930 he repeated that Italy would soon be a militarist nation, indeed the only truly military nation in Europe, the only one with the courage to risk a major war and seek military glory. Italians had to learn to hate; meanwhile, they should be disciplined and keep silent.[157]

It is not surprising that, even among his own close associates, he was earning the reputation of understanding little about diplomacy or even about what others called Italian national interests. He had small patience with slow negotiations or the search for compromise. He seemed ready to sign almost any international agreement without bothering too much about its content so long as it would help to show him as being a strong man of decisive action.[158]

Foreign diplomats knew and took advantage of the fact that he was mostly concerned with prestige, personal and national, for which he could sometimes be persuaded to sacrifice more practical assets.[159] Nevertheless, they must have been alarmed at his lack of interest in learning about points of view other than his own. One foreign ambassador – and perhaps this was not untypical – without being allowed to say a single word was given an hour-long lecture about the ambassador's own country ranging from its past history to its current economic statistics, which could have had no purpose at all except as a vain display of second-hand erudition.[160] One British ambassador at Rome, who liked Mussolini well enough, found him an amateur and an opportunist as far as foreign politics were concerned, interested mainly in any repercussions on domestic policy, and 'impatient in his desire to secure spectacular diplomatic successes';[161] his continual threatening and bluster, therefore, did not need to be taken too seriously. An American commented that 'he aims chiefly at maintaining a "nuisance value" so that sometimes the people who want peace will beg that he can be given something somewhere to keep him quiet. In fine, he probably is playing for prestige, keeping the Balkan pot and every other possible pot boiling in Mr Micawber's hope that something would turn up.' The main worry was that he might not be able to go on threatening for ever without one day having to back threats by force.[162]

Settlement with the Church

Mussolini needed to call himself a Christian but since boyhood had never been a churchgoer[163] and his earlier anti-clericalism was never far beneath the surface. Some of his followers were self-proclaimed atheists or pagans,[164] and he himself in private scorned the rites and dogmas of the Church.[165] But, though fascism in its talk of 'everything in the state nothing outside the state' contained an explicit challenge to Christianity, Italy was nevertheless a Catholic country and history taught him that he would hardly emerge unscathed from a head-on struggle with the papacy.[166] On the contrary, the Church and fascism could both help each other. Friendly words from the Church would help to convince foreigners that he could be trusted,[167] and inside Italy the clergy could be of incalculable advantage to fascism in mobilising popular approval.

These were sufficient reasons for him to give out publicly that he had been once more converted to Christianity and was now a good Catholic.[168] Stories and pictures were published to show him as a pious man of religion and some of the *dévots* went so far as to note his close resemblance to St Ignatius of Loyola;[169] as a start, he had his children baptised in 1923 and then regularised his family status by a religious marriage with Rachele. His early pamphlet *God does not exist* and his heretical booklet on John Huss were either out of print or withdrawn from circulation and did not therefore have to be placed on the Church's 'Index of Prohibited Books'. It greatly pleased the Vatican when he outlawed freemasonry, exempted the clergy from taxation, and used public funds to save Catholic banks from collapse. As well as promoting the holy year which the Pope proclaimed in 1925, much was gained at little cost when he restricted the work of Protestant missions in Italy and forbad the construction of a mosque in Rome.[170]

Outside Italy, the interests of fascism and of the Church were sometimes very close. Mussolini did what he could to champion the Catholic cause in Palestine against the Orthodox Patriarch and against the British who, to his great regret, held the mandate.[171] In Albania, he forced the Orthodox Church to renounce its allegiance to the Patriarch of Constantinople and acknowledge the headship of the Vatican.[172] He did the same at Rhodes, using considerable violence in a provocative affront to the local population that for some reason was thought beneficial to Italian prestige.[173]

Inside Italy, the bishops not only gave substantial support to fascism in its fight against liberalism and socialism, but strongly sympathised with Mussolini's attitude towards women and the family. He no doubt went much too far for them when he called women incorrigibly frivolous, uncreative and unintellectual,[174] but he was sound on birth control. During his anti-

Christian youth he had been a convinced believer in artificial contraception as a positive duty for each family,[175] but in 1924 he introduced penal sanctions against anyone who advocated it, and in 1926 mounted a nationwide campaign to increase the birth rate.[176] He set an example by bringing his family to live with him and begetting two more children, but he specified twelve children as the ideal number. In a moment of optimism, he told parliament that the birth rate must be doubled, giving the strange but to his mind conclusive argument that only in this way could Italians stand up to the 90 million Germans and 200 million Slavs; in 1927 a precise target was specified of raising the Italian population from 40 to 60 million in the next 25 years, and he rashly said that, since Italy needed large families so as to have more soldiers, this would be the real test of the vitality of his fascist revolution.[177] The ineffectiveness of legislation and propaganda to bring about such a drastic change caused him some perplexity as the years went by and the birth rate, far from doubling, continued to fall, but his objectives had the secondary advantage of being close to those of the Church.

Although, until 1925, he was in favour of increasing the number of jobs for women, [178] he soon afterwards made an about-turn and encouraged them to stay at home to produce children. He imposed a tax on 'unjustified celibacy' and proposed one on childless marriages, while private firms and the civil service were ordered to discriminate in favour of employing family men. Severe punishments were meanwhile prescribed for adultery, harsher for women than for men, and in general the new fascist legal codes increased the authority of the husband as head of the family. There was no question of divorce being permitted and penalties for abortion were increased – in 1929 abortions were thought to be running as high as 30 per cent of all conceptions. Infection with syphilis was, by Mussolini's personal wish, made a crime.[179]

Many fascists were extremely dissolute men, as Mussolini knew and accepted, but in public he affected an admiration for the puritanism of Cromwell and said he would turn Rome into the most moral town in the world.[180] As well as making swearing into an indictable offence an attempt was made to stop gambling, though this was too contrary to the taste of many fascist leaders to succeed.[181] He tried to regulate dancing on the grounds that modern dances were 'immoral and improper, evil germs that will breed immorality in the minds of my people'.[182] Night life was severely restricted, a fact for which the Pope was particularly thankful, though he complained that nude shows still continued in defiance of the law.[183] A press campaign was also launched against alcoholism, and 25,000 wine shops were said to have been shut in the first years of the regime.[184]

The effectiveness of these measures was less than hoped, but fascism continued to assume an austere and strait-laced appearance for the outside world. Foreign visitors noticed that people in fascist Italy smiled less readily than before, and even young children used to adopt 'a fierce and gladiatorial pose . . . as though all their sense of humour had been lost'.[185] Mussolini went through periods when he vetoed publication of any photographs showing him in lighter mood. As the philosopher Gentile explained, fascism was something deadly serious, 'even religious'; 'laughter is of the devil, and true believers do not smile except in bitter sarcasm'.[186]

The same puritanical strictness revealed itself in an attempt to regulate women's fashion and behaviour. Prudish rules were prescribed for the shape of bathing costumes and the length of skirts, and fierce remarks were sometimes made about cosmetics and high heels, while the general movement towards female emancipation was said to be decidedly unfascist.[187] Attempts were made to encourage women to give up 'negro dances' imported from America and instead to take up running or some other more decorous sport. Here the Vatican intervened and objected to women participating publicly in sporting activities: 'if woman's hand must be lifted, we hope and pray that it may be lifted only in prayer or for acts of beneficence'.[188] Mussolini tended to agree; he was strongly impressed by the evidence suggesting that 'masculine sports' such as riding, skiing or cycling were a cause of infertility in women and would distract them from 'their natural and fundamental mission in life'; likewise it was thought that the current vogue of renouncing breast feeding, by making women more masculine, would develop other 'egoistic, authoritarian and aggressive characteristics' that were appropriate to masculinity.[189]

Although Church and State had been politically at loggerheads since Italian troops captured Rome in 1870, both sides accepted in theory the need for agreement. While the Vatican criticised the fascist use of violence and knew Mussolini to be partly responsible for it, he was accepted as preferable to all conceivable alternatives.[190] For his part he rejected the Pope's plea that Catholic organisations should remain free from control by the totalitarian state, yet was prepared to compromise in return for being able to say that his was the first Italian government in modern history to be officially recognised by the Vatican. In reaching a formal settlement of their differences, it was advisable to conceal that several previous governments had been close to making an agreement with the Church and had thus paved the way for fascism to take the credit.[191]

Negotiations continued in secret for some years, helped by telephone taps on the Vatican to keep Mussolini informed as to how far the other side was ready to go on each point at issue. The Church thus claimed 4,000 million lire as compensation for what had been confiscated in 1870, but by the time the agreement was signed in February 1929, this claim had been reduced by more than half. Fascism, too, gave way on some substantial matters, including the right of the clergy to have jurisdiction over marriage and the family;[192] though in later years it became clear that this was a merely theoretical concession that Mussolini could and would disregard at will.

In his concordat and treaty with the Roman Church, some people thought that Mussolini gave away more than he needed to,[193] but most of the opposition to the settlement could be easily suppressed, even to the point of expunging criticism from the official parliamentary record.[194] Most people were delighted with it. He himself looked back on his conciliation with the Church as his masterpiece and it was undoubtedly an immense political success that won him the enthusiastic acclamation of the great bulk of Catholics.

However, once he had used the concordat to win popular support, he immediately proceeded to push his victory much further than Pius XI had ever intended. In a wounding speech he claimed that the Church, as a result of their treaty, was no longer free but subordinate to the State: he heretically referred to Catholicism as, in origin, a minor sect that had spread beyond Palestine only because grafted onto the organisation of the Roman empire.[195] At no time was tension with the Vatican so bitter as in the years after the concordat, and he confiscated more issues of Catholic newspapers in the next three months than in the previous seven years.[196] It was now – presumably with his permission – that his catchpenny novel, *The Cardinal's Mistress*, began to appear in various translations. Against claims by the Church for the right to have its own say in education he was absolutely intractable and, by his own confession, came close to being excommunicated; but he kept up the pressure and, in effect, won the totalitarian control of youth that he required.[197]

In reply, the Pope contented himself with a verbal protest against 'the pagan worship of the state' and against the exclusive oath of obedience imposed by fascism, but did his utmost to avoid a direct confrontation. After explaining in private that he was not afraid of Mussolini, he added that unfortunately the Duce had received no real religious education 'or indeed any education at all', and he sent to warn Mussolini against making himself a demi-god half-way between heaven and earth – a warning that was, apparently, accepted with good humour.[198]

Eventually the two men agreed on an uneasy truce from which both gained considerably and which each tried to interpret in his own favour. When, in February 1932, Mussolini went to visit the Pope, he pretended to take the latter's remarks as meaning that there was nothing in fascism contrary to Catholic teaching,[199] whereas Pius got the quite different impression that his visitor had come in repentance as an act of reparation.[200]

Mussolini was interested mainly in appearances: he wanted the appearance of being greatly favoured by the Pope but, at the same time, the appearance of being subordinate to no one. He wanted to convince the Americans that he believed in absolute freedom of conscience and was actively helping Jews and Protestants,[201] though in practice he pleased the Pope by showing he was ready to persecute the Waldensians, the Pentecostalists, and the Salvation Army;[202] before long, also the Jews. He needed to persuade Catholics that fascism was Catholic and he himself a believer who spent some of each day in prayer,[203] while he said something very different to other people and took care to exclude from the newspapers any photographs of himself kneeling or showing deference to the Pope.[204]

The apotheosis

By referring to 'a man sent by Providence' to deliver Italy from the heresies of liberalism, Pope Pius gave much more assistance to fascism than he had probably intended; he was authenticating the motif of 'the man sent by God to Italy' that was by now a cliché of the regime.[205] The high priests of fascism were calling Mussolini 'divine Caesar',[206] another St Francis,[207] our 'spiritual father' and 'sublime redeemer in the Roman heavens'.[208] By order of the party, pronouns referring to him had to be capitalised like those referring to God, and though he himself modestly disclaimed such extravagant eulogies and said they left him unmoved, everyone knew that the chief passport to a successful career was to outdo the next man in obsequious adulation.

The orchestration of flattery in the fascist press remained under the direction of Mussolini's brother until his death in 1931. Arnaldo Mussolini had found that newspapers, even after 1925, continued to sell almost in inverse ratio to their fascist commitment.[209] To change this it was decided to restrict the profession of journalism to fascists and to give them salaries and fringe benefits well above what was found elsewhere in Europe.[210] Since the press was the best medium through which to shape public attitudes, a purge of newspapermen was of first importance,[211] and expulsion from the profession would henceforth be decided by a committee under Arnaldo that would meet in secret without the presence of anyone accused.[212] Those who survived were told by Arnaldo to concern themselves with information and not criticism, with reporting rather than comment, while editors were left in no doubt that any political infraction would be punished.[213]

The fascist press took its tone from Mussolini's own *Popolo d'Italia* for which the preposterous claim was made that it had more influence than any other paper in the world.[214] Despite hidden subsidies and, in some places, an enforced sale because of its semi-official status, the *Popolo d'Italia* had been taking a sometimes large annual loss.[215] It continued to sell only a quarter of the number of copies sold by the now pro-fascist *Corriere della Sera* and sales seem actually to have fallen in the years 1927–31,[216] no doubt because fascist journalism was so wearisomely monotonous; there could be no great popular appeal in newspapers when a column of repetitive and jejune editorial comment was the obligatory daily accompaniment to the prime minister's every chance remark.

The Duce himself used to spend a good deal of time looking critically at yesterday's newspapers and planning the presentation of the next day's news; he regularly telephoned editors and newspaper proprietors to instruct them about this and even about the layout of their front page.[217] The proper manipulation of opinion, as he well knew, depended on pride of place being given to whatever he happened to have done each day. The head of his personal press office, who saw him frequently and was sometimes present at cabinet meetings, would send round the appropriate orders – if necessary, several times a day and sometimes much more often. As far as possible, this basic machinery of propaganda was kept secret from the general public; indeed Mussolini denied that any such instructions were given and he cut out of Ludwig's book a phrase about the press being 'muzzled'.[218]

It continued to be true that many *gerarchi* came from the profession of journalism since management of the news was their most important function. Half of the ministers in 1930 and half of the Grand Council were journalists; twenty other newspapermen had become senior diplomats and sixty-eight were in parliament.[219] Mussolini commented that they were among the best in each field of public life.[220] In the early years, he once told an assembly of newsmen that they perhaps carried a marshal's baton in their knapsack,[221] and the reference was apt because they were the nearest equivalent to Napoleon's marshals. Most leading fascists had their own subsidised newspaper or periodical – read by almost no one, but a convenient way of attracting official funds and building up for each *gerarca* a following or clientele of paid courtiers and personal propagandists.

Another symptom of Mussolini's personal aggrandisement was the increasing loss of independence by the fascist party, one sign of which came when, at the end of 1928, the Grand Council of the party was formally converted into an institution of government. Much fuss was made about this, but it was in reality another cosmetic exercise and in fact was intended to diminish the council's importance. He summoned it less and less – only once in the whole of 1934. At some of its meetings, no one spoke except himself, and in practice it did little else but rubber-stamp his decisions. Some leading fascists were disappointed and even disturbed by this,[222] but most were content with the outward vestiges of power, celebrity, and the immunity from arrest that membership of the Grand Council conferred. They therefore, as many of them later regretted, took no action to curb the growth of an irresponsible dictatorship and did not turn against him until their final dramatic meeting in July 1943. Other organs of the fascist party were similarly deprived of initiative. The fact that the party secretary was henceforth appointed by royal decree indicated that this office had been turned into yet another organ of state without independent existence.

Augusto Turati, who held the post of secretary from 1926 to 1930, eventually became restive and put up some slight resistance; he made one last attempt to preserve the practice of elections in the party, but committed the mistake of advocating this in newspaper articles that failed to contain the conventional pinch of incense to the Duce.[223] The fact that Turati was reputedly an honest man sufficed to win him the enmity of many other *gerarchi*, and his denunciation of profiteering by other fascists – in particular by the family of Costanzo Ciano, the minister for communications – probably brought about his dismissal.[224] Mussolini appreciated Turati's loyal service but thought him too independent-minded and too popular. In the end, Farinacci and Starace toppled this rival *gerarca* after collecting accusations against him that ranged from sado-masochism, incest and pederasty to drug addiction and insanity.[225] When reports of these accusations leaked out, many people must have been shocked to learn that a man so flawed had been Mussolini's right-hand man for five years; or perhaps they had learnt not to believe all they read. In any case, the most effective party secretary of the whole fascist period was exiled in disgrace to the island of Rhodes.

To some foreign observers able to speak their minds, fascism was becoming notorious for the corruption and licentiousness that flourished because of the lack of public criticism and the great amount of public money spent with no effective audit.[226] A contributory factor in this corruption was the fact that local fascist bosses had influence over the courts and police in each region, failing which they had free use of armed gangsters to defend their privileged positions. When Mussolini discovered that some fascist leaders (including Farinacci who had been financially embarrassed in 1922) were said to be living like millionaires,[227] he was troubled not by the corruption itself so much as by the fear that the public would think the worse of him if it became known that he was appointing scoundrels to high office. Hence he continued to bury scandals whenever possible and keep the culprits in positions of power. Anyone who tried to tell him about examples of impropriety could well be forced into resignation or even beaten up and savagely mutilated.[228]

One particularly serious case concerned dishonest profits made out of loans and contracts in the administration of Milan. The main villains were fascists who, as so often happened, had risen to the top by the most outrageous flattery of Mussolini and then used their position to exclude themselves from the ordinary workings of the law.[229] This time, however, there was an additional problem: his own brother, Arnaldo, a smooth-tongued preacher of morality,[230] was himself implicated. The Duce tried as usual to hush this up and, when the scandal broke, tried to keep the details as secret as possible.[231]

In 1929 the twenty-seventh legislature of Italy was due to expire. Mussolini would no doubt have abolished parliament had he not wanted to perpetuate the illusion – especially abroad – that his was only a partial dictatorship. But he did decide to change the method of election for the twenty-eighth legislature: the country would be presented with a single, carefully-chosen list of 400 names and could accept or reject them only *en bloc*. There was no need, he said, for parliament to debate the law enacting this fundamental change, since discussion was no longer part of the 'fascist style' and in fact only 45 out of 5,553 laws had been discussed in parliament during the past five years. He was proud to impose on the country what would be 'an entirely original system of representation ... without parallel in the history of the world'.[232] The 86-year-old Giolitti made his final speech in opposition to this law but his few words were drowned in uproar.[233] The elections were fixed for May 1929, though Mussolini again made it clear in advance that, even if they went against him, he had no intention of surrendering power.[234]

They took place just after his treaty with the Church. The Pope made representations for a contingent of convinced Catholics to be among the 400 designated candidates and issued a threat that otherwise he might not allow his flock to co-operate;[235] but his wishes were met in part and Catholics were therefore advised by their pastors to vote for the official list. Mussolini promised that no pressure would be used on electors, but eyewitnesses reported abundant threats and physical violence being used, and in private he admitted that such plebiscites were easily and always rigged. There was little pretence of secrecy in the voting and it may be assumed that there was falsification of figures if threats proved insufficient. The overwhelmingly favourable vote recorded in the German-speaking areas of the Alto Adige was enough to expose it as an obvious imposture.[236]

The result of the election showed 98.4 per cent in favour of the fascist list. Though a million electors disobeyed instructions and refused to turn up at the voting urns, only 135,773 people were officially recorded as registering a negative vote. Another similar plebiscite in 1934 registered only 15,215 voting 'no' and in some areas no negative votes at all,[237] but the fact that only 1,219 out of ten million voters were said to have, whether accidentally or deliberately, spoilt their voting papers was another sure sign that the results were in part invented.

These two plebiscites tell us little about public attitudes: everyone knew that opposition was of no use. Parliament continued to exist, voting often unanimously or by acclamation; every member would rise to his feet in the Chamber to greet Mussolini's arrival or departure, and sometimes they would accompany their proceedings by chanting the songs of the revolution. Each time he opened his mouth in parliament there was immense applause and every deputy competed with his neighbours to applaud louder and longer. Visitors in the galleries noted that he habitually paid no attention to other speakers but sat fidgeting in boredom, 'heavy-jawed and scowling, with folded arms, pursing his lips into a pout as he stared ahead, solitary and meditating amid the assembly of his adulators'. Parliamentary debates henceforth contained little of interest except as publicity for the regime – even the reports of debates and the voting lists were sometimes doctored according to the requirements of publicity.[238]

With both party and parliament deprived of any independence, Mussolini had reached a pinnacle of personal authority. Until the summer of 1929, he personally held two-thirds of the departmental ministries but in September felt strong enough to give up some of these ministerial posts. Other ministers were fully content to consider themselves as soldiers who had to obey orders,[239] and hence constituted no threat to his personal autocracy. He preferred a frequent rotation among office holders, explaining that for anyone to hold a ministry for more than three years would be too much for their strength,[240] he alone being an exception: and of course these frequent 'changes of guard', as he called them, helped prevent anyone but himself from becoming too powerful.

In September 1929 he signalised his more elevated status by transferring his personal headquarters to the austere Palazzo Venezia, still in the centre of Rome but away from the other offices of state. Here, legend said, he would regularly work until nearly midnight, after which he would return home to read reports and mature his decisions in the night hours 'which he finds the most creative'. In the daytime, as well as practising every kind of sport, he still found time to read just about everything; 'no books published in Italy or abroad escape his eye', and no item of news, no newspaper article, but was read and weighed.[241] His powers of judgement were equally accorded every superlative in the book. The infallibility of his intuition and his genius for seeing into the future were described as the secret that now made him the dominant figure in world politics. To some foreign visitors it seemed that fascism no longer existed in Italy, only *mussolinismo*. Another convenient legend explained that 'everything bad is the fault of the fascists, but all that is good is due to Mussolini'.[242] His picture was in shops, in offices and in the streets, conveying a sensation of omnipresence that was consoling or menacing according to one's taste, and when newsreels were shown in cinemas the audience might stand up if his face appeared.[243] Even during meetings of the Grand Council, members would rise to their feet at suitable moments to cry 'long live the Duce',[244] while the ordinary man in the street was said to find an infectious joy in an uncritical obedience to his slightest whim.[245]

The various fascist leaders had learnt that to continue sharing in power they had no option but to collaborate in perpetuating the myth of this genius, whose judgements were final, who never erred, who was said to need no sleep at all, and whom everyone must learn to imitate.[246] His own newspapers set an example by writing the whole of the word 'Duce' in capital letters and failure to do so could be met by an angry telephone call from Rome.[247] His monthly periodical, *Gerarchia*, described him as a person whose ideas derived from no one, 'whose creative force has no limit in time or space', and who – this was now a familiar incantation – could be considered only alongside or above Socrates, Plato, Machiavelli and Napoleon.[248]

In particular, he was revered as a great jurist, as the main inspiration behind the new fascist law codes that were intended also for adoption by other countries and would become to the twentieth century what Napoleon's code had been to the nineteenth. The penal code came into force in 1931 and represented a sharp move away from individual rights to those of the state: fascism wanted juries abolished, strikes and lock-outs made illegal; and merely to injure the prestige of the Duce became a crime. Mussolini was almost alone among the long line of Italian prime ministers in having no legal training, not even a university degree; yet he was revered for laying down the general principles of this code by the 'divine power' of intuition and for having made substantial changes on his own initiative. Unlike Napoleon, he did not preside over the drafting commission, as he was increasingly averse to submitting himself to even the appearance of discussion by committee; but in the final stages he read through all 734 clauses in a single night, making any alterations he thought fit.[249]

He was delighted to have this kind of story known by the general public[250] because his style of government depended more and more on such illusions of omnicompetence. Although he still hinted occasionally that he knew the danger of being surrounded by yes-men, in practice he increasingly shut himself away in his palace; demanding only applause and obedience, appreciating only servility. He no longer liked to be addressed with the familiar *tu*, because he was no longer to be treated as on the same level as other men.[251]

Until 1929 he had been fairly readily available for talks with journalists and sometimes saw them without formality if they arrived with no prior arrangement, but gradually this contact with the outside world was supplanted by a formal audience at which he was merely on show.[252] Instead of listening to visitors, far more reliance was placed by him on the vast amounts of information that poured into his office through the various surveillance agencies, but there was too much of it to be more than glanced at and a lot of it was highly inaccurate. Nor did he ever realise how much he thereby cut himself off from much that it was important to understand.

Likewise, for his information about foreign countries he continued to use private agents, the local correspondents of the *Popolo d'Italia*, for instance, who sometimes had orders from him to work at cross purposes against the official policy of the Italian ambassador.[253] Everyone from prefects and ambassadors to party officials and captains of industry – even sometimes his own foreign minister – might be left on their own to guess at his policy; often they dared not ask him and, if they were wise, took no action on their own initiative.[254]

Occasionally he was asked who he would like as his successor: it was a question he shrank from.[255] He told several people that he had already chosen someone whose name would eventually be found in his testament; if there ever existed such a name, it was probably that of Costanzo Ciano, one of the older fascists, a hero of the First World War, whose son married Mussolini's daughter Edda.[256] The Grand Council should, by law, have kept a list of possible successors from which the king would be able to choose, and on one occasion Mussolini embarrassed the Grand Council by asking them to consider the matter: subsequently he said that they had agreed on certain names, but it is unlikely.[257] His unwillingness to confront this vital question confirms the suspicion that fascism meant little to him except as a vehicle for his own power, and he admitted or hinted more than once (egged on by his flattering courtiers) that it would die with him.[258] To Ludwig he added that the Italians would never endure a second Duce, but this is one of the phrases found in the German and English editions of Ludwig's book but not in the Italian.[259] He once explained that he would prefer to let the strongest contender succeed him.[260] More to the point, he also said that he had too great a contempt for the *gerarchi* to consider any of them seriously;[261] moreover, unlike Hitler, he feared that the nomination of a successor or vice-duce might weaken his own position. Whatever his reasons, the refusal to consider what might happen at his death was a sign of weakness as well as an indication that he put his own interests above those of his regime or his country.

In search of strife

10

Increasingly belligerent, 1929–32

Imperial expansion became more and more a favourite theme of Mussolini's speeches. He argued that colonial settlements were a physical necessity for Italy because of her surplus population, and other countries must therefore, in their own interests, help to make such expansion possible.[1] But since on other occasions – especially when arguing for an increased birth rate – he used to talk of there being ample room for another twenty million people in Italy, his real reasons must be sought elsewhere. Italy had, in his view, to become the dominant power in the Mediterranean, able to challenge France or Britain. Sometimes a phrase was used about winning free access to the Atlantic, and this apparently meant a vast programme of colonial expansion towards Nigeria, the Cameroons and the Guinea coast of West Africa. Only when he had managed to acquire a continuous stretch of colonies all the way from the Indian to the Atlantic oceans, and when ten million Italians had gone to settle in them, would Italy be able to breathe easily.[2]

All through the 1920s, fascist Italy was tied down in a colonial war to 'pacify' her enormous colony of Libya, a war about which the government kept very quiet because the fighting was so slow and frustrating. The 'rebel' force in Libya was seldom larger than 1,000 men, but against it a much bigger army had to be employed: the bulk of this colonial army was made up of what were called Eritreans but were mostly men from Ethiopia, Aden and British Somaliland – 10,000 mercenaries were recruited from these countries each year.[3] Even this small operation cost more than could be afforded or than Mussolini expected,[4] yet the generals pointed out that a far bigger effort would be needed if his glib talk about imperial expansion was to be taken seriously.[5]

In 1929, Marshal Badoglio obeyed an order from Mussolini to economise by arranging a truce with the local patriotic leader, Omar el Mukhtar, but tried to pretend in Italy that the rebels were submitting to the superior might of fascism.[6] Omar categorically denied this interpretation and the war broke out all over again; but this time Badoglio threatened that, since the prestige of fascism had been challenged, any of the Arab leaders who did not surrender would be executed at once if caught and their families held responsible; he also threatened that the population of Cyrenaica would be starved into submission and even exterminated if any of them continued to fight.[7]

Here, as some observers predicted, the search for the illusory goal of prestige led to a savage war of reprisal from which there was little if anything to be gained but hatred and destruction. The religious order of the Senussi forfeited half a million acres of property – confiscated for the use of Italian settlers[8] – and almost everyone in the area was moved into specially constructed concentration camps surrounded by barbed wire. Gas bombs were used on some of the surviving rebels, though the fact was kept rigorously secret.[9] Omar was captured and publicly hanged on orders from Rome. Italians were told that this heroic and noble man was a cruel, cowardly and corrupt barbarian whose death brought joy to the whole Arab population. Stories about fascist cruelties were said to be pure invention and there was much arrogant talk about how Mussolini was bringing the benefits of civilisation to a primitive people.[10]

Fascism was now very much for export and was said to be advancing rapidly in Britain and the United States, indeed it was Italy's main article of exportation.[11] There was even a fair chance that Stalin was abandoning communism and might align himself with fascist Italy.[12] It made economic sense to build ships and planes for Russia, and in return Russia provided Italy with a third of her oil supplies;[13] but the more interesting possibility was that Stalin was turning out to be a true heir of the tsars and an imperialist with whom fascism could see eye to eye. Mussolini tried to convince himself that Russian communism was proving less revolutionary than fascism,[14] and some of his followers wondered if the two movements were coming so close as to be no longer easily distinguishable; he himself considered such an approximation to be at least a possibility.[15]

From 1930 onwards, official propaganda increasingly stressed the theme that foreigners feared and admired him and looked to him as 'the redeemer of Europe', the 'creator of a new civilisation'. In India, in Australia, in the Congo, among the gangsters of Detroit, indeed all over the world, he was said to be recognised as a potential world leader and someone who guaranteed Italy's primacy among the nations. The masses in Great Britain were deeply envious of his dictatorial methods, and 'even in North America, whites and blacks, farmers and industrial workers, are all exclaiming in chorus, "if only we had a Mussolini here!"'[16] This was pure invention. It is true that some foreigners were charmed by Mussolini and some admired him, especially those who continued to think of fascism as less of a danger than communism. Winston Churchill, for example, though in private he referred to Mussolini as a 'swine' for his cruelties, was ready in public to pay fulsome tribute to his achievements as a bulwark against red revolution;[17] whereas Mussolini, on the contrary, praised Churchill in private but was not quite so keen for his approbation to be made public.[18] The Italian press was mobilised to spread the conviction inside Italy that public opinion in the outside world was solidly behind him (this conviction long outlasted fascism itself).[19] Journalists travelling abroad were instructed to invent stories demonstrating it; they could even be told to write from the Far East that everyone in China admired him, at a time when his name would have been known in China by almost no one.[20]

By 1930, many fascists were insisting that creating international dissension and disseminating fear were necessary in order to make Italy the 'axis of Europe', and some foreign diplomats were learning to see Mussolini as 'one of the chief existing dangers to European peace'.[21] His bullying tactics in the Balkans were further revealed in 1930 when the Jugoslavs exposed another spy ring operating from the Italian embassy in Belgrade,[22] and indeed he was making preparations for a possible invasion of both Jugoslavia and southern France. The chief of army staff, who pointed out that a bellicose foreign policy would require more arms production, was made to resign for his impertinence and his successors learnt to be less outspoken.[23] Mussolini and Grandi both believed'that a war against France would be feasible before long[24] and further plans were discussed for the possible annexation of Tunisia, Corsica and French Somaliland.[25]

In view of these plans, it was obvious that Mussolini would want to play off the Germans against the French. A pro-fascist government in Berlin would suit him best and he was therefore secretly helping to rearm Germany, hinting that she might want to help him upset the peace-settlement of 1919.[26] His eyes used to glisten with admiration and envy as he thought of the discipline of the German army,[27] and this was long before Hitler came to power.

Until 1933 his contact with nazism was not particularly close. He had been briefly in touch in 1922 before the march on Rome. Then, in November 1922, Hitler sought Mussolini's advice about the possibility of a fascist-style revolution in Germany and the next year tried to acquire Italian help for a 'march on Berlin'.[28] Help was probably not forthcoming on this occasion but not long afterwards money was being sent to the nazis from Italy.[29] As Hitler's proclaimed policy was to incorporate Austria into a greater Germany, it seems strange that Mussolini was not more worried – especially as he knew that, if ever German forces reached the Alps, the Italian city of Trieste would be in serious danger.[30] But the Duce underestimated 'the German Mussolini' and even thought him a bit crazy; Hitler's *Mein Kampf* was brushed off as 'a boring tome that I have never been able to read' and his ideas as 'little more than commonplace clichés'.[31]

Mussolini sometimes thought of setting up an international fascist movement led by himself, in which the Germans would agree to take a subordinate role.[32] He was flattered on hearing that he was the object of Hitler's admiration and by the fact that another of the great powers was turning away from democracy to fascism.[33] Naturally, Hitler took care to let Rome know of his pride at being advised and encouraged by such a great man as Mussolini and the nazis promised that an alliance with Italy would be the basis of their foreign policy,[34] while a bronze bust of Mussolini was prominently on display at nazi headquarters in Munich.[35] Flattery invariably paid off with the Duce but he had other reasons for eventually deciding that, allied with Germany, he could be a major force in Europe whereas, allied with the western democracies, he could never be more than subsidiary;[36] quite apart from ideological similarities, it was only alongside Germany that he could challenge the dominant powers in the Mediterranean and break out of what he called 'imprisonment' in what must become *mare nostrum*, 'our sea'. Already, before Hitler came to power, Mussolini – as well as sending money to help the nazis in elections – allowed them to send para-military groups for training to Italy, despite the warning by his own foreign office that this was extremely dangerous. Later, he allowed German pilots to have secret combat training with the Italian air force.[37]

In 1931 he reminded his generals that they had to be ready for war by 1935,[38] though he still did remarkably little to re-equip the army and did not tell them who the likely enemies were or what strategic plans should have priority. He began to refer more frequently to war as one of the few truly ennobling and energising facts of human experience and to imperialism as the supreme test of a nation's vitality. To the fascist youth movement he gave the watchword 'believe, obey, fight'; to army conscripts it was 'better one day as a lion than a hundred years as a sheep'; to the party it was 'the more enemies, the greater the honour'.[39] The endless repetition of these ominous or comical phrases provided the core of fascist political education.

In 1932 he took back the foreign office from Grandi, possibly because he was worried that fascist Italy, despite all his verbal fireworks, was not cutting a bigger figure in the world; also because he wanted to maintain a more warlike and pro-German stance. Possibly he was jealous of a younger man getting too much of the international limelight and was certainly embarrassed when this junior minister had to cover up some of his more irresponsible gaffes.[40] More specifically, he referred to Grandi as having been too pro-League, too pacifist, too democratic, yet also too right-wing.[41] Perhaps he also knew that Grandi had been telling foreign diplomats that fascism was bound to evolve into something less extremist and totalitarian;[42] his own idea of the future was very different.

What he foresaw was that the inevitable war could be used by him to impose fascist ideas on Europe because the democracies were too corrupted by individualism to fight when the hour of destiny struck; and Italy could then resume her natural position as the 'pioneer nation in the van of contemporary culture'.[43] The propagandists were instructed to proclaim that Italy had nothing to learn from anyone else – was she not the envy of every foreigner?[44] Fascist ideas, wrote the sycophants, were ahead in every field of human achievement; all the other nations of the world put together had not produced a fraction of the number of men of genius that Italy had produced and, under fascism, this would become yet more obviously true because genius flourished best under authoritarianism.[45] Italy's railways were faster and more on time than those of other nations and her ships faster and bigger.[46] Mussolini would be able to crown her technical achievements by using his position of world leadership in defence of western civilisation against the coloured races: this was the 'universal mission of Rome'.[47]

Africans were, by fascist definition, inferior beings, and Ethiopians in particular were the enemy he had secretly chosen to fight. This had been his objective as early as 1925 and, despite signing a treaty of friendship with Ethiopia in 1928, he continued to build up arms in Eritrea and Somalia. Nor was this just for defensive purposes – his troops were unobtrusively pushed inside Ethiopian territory in many places, taking advantage of the fact that the frontier had never been properly fixed. Protests by the Ethiopian emperor, Haile Selassie, were rejected as was an Ethiopian request that an agreed frontier be found by mutual consent. Mussolini's intention was surreptitiously to obtain as much of Ogaden as possible and the fact that this was bound to lead to war in the long run was accepted and welcomed.[48]

The matter of timing was crucial: the proposed African war had to be over and won before Germany was strong enough to upset the balance of power in Europe, but the experts assumed that Ethiopia could be beaten without much difficulty provided that a large enough army could be put into the field.[49] Early in 1932 it was agreed that General De Bono should plan an offensive; the documentary evidence about this plan was later doctored to give the impression that Italy would merely be fighting a defensive war against Ethiopian aggression.[50] The regular army was not pleased that the chosen commander was a fascist officer, especially as he was to be De Bono, an elderly general who had taken part in the African campaign of 1887. Nor did the ministry of finance like having to find the money for these preparations at a time when all departments were being ordered to reduce expenditure. But by the end of 1932, Mussolini had approved an outline plan and agreed that the war ought probably to begin after the rainy season in the autumn of 1935.[51] He assumed that he would be able to get Britain and France to accept this, if only because they had built up their colonial empires by equally dubious means, and he took note that the League of Nations had imposed no sanctions on the Japanese for their aggressive war in Manchuria. Meanwhile he ordered preparations to be kept as secret as possible.[52]

Starace and the fascist party

The secretary of the fascist party from September 1930 to December 1931 was Giovanni Giuriati, a man whom Mussolini described as one of the few fascist leaders uncorrupted by power.[53] His honesty was perhaps one reason for the shortness of his duration in office. Another of his offences was to beg Mussolini not to monopolise so many offices of state. Giuriati repeatedly threatened to resign unless he was allowed to clean up the party, particularly to dispose of the arch-corruptors Marinelli and Starace;[54] but in December 1931, he read in the newspapers that Starace had been appointed to replace him. His kind of independence was rare under fascism and would become rarer.

Achille Starace never made such a mistake: he was just the man for Mussolini, if a disaster for Italy and for fascism. Unintelligent, humourless, utterly obedient, an unctuous flatterer, he was someone the Duce could despise yet depend on, someone who would never contradict or try to steal the headlines. In public he was praised as the ideal fascist and morally irreproachable, although Mussolini knew that his police dossier contained accusations of involvement in prostitution, drugs, peculation, rape and pederasty.[55] On the other hand Starace was a brave man, a good organiser and severe disciplinarian, adept at the choreography of the mass meetings that were more and more in demand. When Mussolini spoke to him on the telephone he would stand to attention and he told others to do the same.[56] If the regime wanted to create a new type of Italian, Starace was to all outward appearances the model of what a thorough fascist should be: this was why he lasted in office until 1939, much longer than any other secretary of the party.

Mussolini used to say that he had no great enthusiasm for Starace's proliferation of uniforms, parades and 'oceanic' assemblies, but he said this only when he realised they had not been an unqualified success. At the time he liked them as a means of arousing the masses[57] and they exemplified his own belief in ritual and ceremony as a means of accentuating his own superiority. One of Starace's first acts – and it would not have been without first consulting his master – was to introduce the elaborate 'salute to the Duce' at the start of fascist meetings.[58] He also ordered that the orchestrated cries on public occasions be directed towards Mussolini alone and to none of the other *gerarchi*; nor were other names and photographs to be published besides his:

'one man and one man alone must be allowed to dominate the news every day, and others must take pride in serving him in silence'. Good fascists were encouraged for a time to end their private correspondence with 'Viva il Duce', an analogue of 'Heil Hitler'.[59]

The 'Roman salute' with raised arm was now prescribed rigorously instead of the less aesthetic and less hygienic handshake. Foreign visitors arriving at their hotel had to be greeted only with this 'superbly aesthetic gesture', 'an exquisitely fascist greeting, envied and imitated throughout the world',[60] and Italians were told to use it freely when they travelled abroad. Some fanatics even liked to raise their arm whenever the Duce's name was mentioned.[61] Mussolini forgetfully went on shaking hands in private and occasionally making the conventional military salute, but photographs showing this were banned, and newspapers had orders to retouch photographs that showed unfascist methods of greeting.[62]

Another order to Starace was to put Italians into uniform,[63] and eventually the Duce's craze for uniforms became almost a mania as the regime was given the outward semblance of being martial and disciplined. He assumed that Italians would despise the British for their umbrellas and always refused to carry one himself, whereas military-style uniforms would appeal to their 'sense of the picturesque' and differentiate them handsomely from the pacifists and plutocrats of western Europe. He was convinced that the possibility of earning a more glamorous uniform by promotion was a truly effective means of encouraging obedience.[64]

One journalist noted that at times Mussolini himself became so overdressed that he 'looked like a circus performer in off hours'.[65] Cabinet ministers could possess at least ten uniforms to be used on different specified occasions, and might indeed have over twenty;[66] children had one, since they could with difficulty avoid membership of the *balilla* or youth organisation; even babies a few months old might have their picture taken in a black shirt.[67] Sometimes there were private protests that the simulated militarisation of civilians was becoming unseemly,[68] but another more serious objection, namely that it was a ridiculous extravagance, went by default. When these changes in outward behaviour turned out to be unpopular, they were attributed to Starace, although Mussolini himself was chiefly responsible.

Grand ceremonies meanwhile became more and more elaborate, beginning with the funeral of Arnaldo Mussolini in December 1931; some observers were shocked to find this second-rate journalist being given a treatment accorded to heads of state, with kneeling crowds lining the railway line as the coffin travelled across north Italy and the newspapers vying with each other in obsequious adulation of a great writer who was also 'the greatest thinker of the revolution'.[69] On another occasion three dozen 'fascist martyrs' were ceremonially buried in the national sacrarium of Santa Croce, in Florence, alongside the tombs of Michelangelo, Galileo and Machiavelli.[70]

In 1932 a great exhibition was mounted in Rome to commemorate the victories of the fascist revolution and a visit to it became almost obligatory. Outside the exhibition hall, a ceremonial guard of honour was regularly on duty and the various categories of fascists took it in turns: *gerarchi*, artists, writers, judges, professors, architects, scientists, industrialists, senators and journalists – everyone had to play his part in a set piece that Mussolini found impressive but others thought ludicrous or grotesque. Foreign dignitaries were regularly taken to see the exhibition, but much of it – the cudgels, the bottles of castor oil, the clothes stained with Mussolini's blood – revealed a lack of taste that gave some foreigners a very different impression from the one intended.[71]

Mussolini used to say that public opinion was a harlot and that he had no interest in what other people thought of him.[72] Nevertheless he took pains in organising mass demonstrations, perhaps hoping that they would appear to be spontaneous. By merely pressing a bell, he boasted, he could produce an applauding crowd.[73] Children were summoned out of school, workers from factories, and could sometimes waste several days rehearsing a major event.[74] A well-organised claque followed him round to be present at his speeches – the 'applause squad', it was sometimes called[75] – and a system of bells and prompt cards helped to produce the appropriate reaction at the correct moments.[76] But foreign diplomats who watched the rehearsals had ironic remarks to make and the assembled populace must have been perplexed to see that such artifice was thought necessary.[77]

Starace was the person charged with bringing greater uniformity into national life, but testified that he did nothing off his own bat and followed Mussolini's instructions to the letter.[78] One decision was the introduction of a law making membership of the party requisite for anyone with a job in the state administration. Like so many other laws under fascism, this proved impossible to enforce and perhaps its enforcement cannot have been seriously intended; but on paper, only a paid-up fascist could enjoy the full rights of an Italian citizen.[79]

Soon it was not enough just to be a fascist: it was preferable to have been one before October 1922 or, better still, a *sansepolcrista* dating from March 1919, so a lucrative practice started of backdating membership cards. Eventually, the number of those claiming to have taken part in the revolution of 1922 had multiplied by ten and included some who had been young children at the time.[80] Mussolini arranged that the first official certificate authenticating the select group of *sansepolcristi* was given to his brother Arnaldo, who had no right to the title. Others went one better and tried to win a useful degree of seniority by claiming membership from 1918, before the official foundation date.[81] This eagerness arose from the fact that seniority conferred not only a colourful ornament of badges and braid, but preference in jobs and generous increments in pensions and pay.[82] Occasionally, strong ministers could hold out against the attempt to force them into over-manning their departments with not particularly reputable fascists. But Mussolini assumed that the 80–90,000 old-time *squadristi* were the kernel of his regime, the most dependable of all, who therefore deserved some financial reward.[83]

Any intellectual who wished to make a career inside the fascist movement obeyed instructions and bestowed lavish praise on Starace for creating such a superb, disciplined party,[84] and Mussolini claimed that Italy had thereby been made into the most totalitarian and efficient of all countries:[85] he may have had in mind a favourable comparison with Russia, Stalin's policy being much admired by Starace.[86] Some fascists, on the other hand, saw these as the years when fascism finally renounced anything that remained of its earlier ideals and became a vast, lazy, oppressive bureaucracy which, by its sheer deadweight, prevented development and turned Italy into a corrupt and repressive police state.[87]

The *gerarchi* appointed by Starace were, with some exceptions, incompetents who were not only often corrupt but 'a real offence to the good sense and intelligence of the Italian people' – all the more so in that their office gave them an immunity from arrest unless by his permission.[88] They were told by Mussolini to set an example of seriousness, by which he meant avoiding theatres and expensive restaurants, preferring to walk instead of drive and, in any case, not following his bad example by driving dangerously.[89] The outer manifestations were what mattered, more than inner virtues of character and intellect.

Mussolini continued to say that his main task was to create a new and better ruling class, but his idea of an elite was the *squadristi*, in other words men whose chief virtues were not intelligence or imagination or even bureaucratic efficiency. He used to say that the way to supplant the old order was to choose younger fascists for jobs whenever possible: he reminded people that one of the best prime ministers in English history had been appointed at the age of twenty-four, and he thought Italians should learn to be 'ashamed of old age'. He therefore decided to stop recruiting to the party any but young men, who would now be admitted *en masse* and, in practice, compulsorily.[90] He based this policy on several false assumptions. These included the belief that the young were conditioned by their education to be 100 per cent fascist, also that they were competent enough to take over positions of authority, and that the first generation of fascists was ready to stand down without a fight. Nevertheless the fact that so many party members were eager to backdate their membership is an indication that in practice seniority still often took precedence over the much vaunted 'move towards youth'.[91]

In October 1932 he announced that the time had come for a further turn of the screw 'to fascistise still further what I could call the dead corners of our national life', because there was no room for anything outside the control of the state.[92] Many Italians had been hoping the opposite – that controls could be slackened once fascism was thoroughly in command: their counter-argument was that only by allowing more freedom to discuss and criticise would the regime reinvigorate itself and produce a ruling class with intelligence and a sense of personal responsibility.[93] Mussolini himself sometimes accepted in theory that a certain amount of discussion and nonconformity might be helpful, but in practice knew that these were the greatest threats to the system.

This is shown in his careful attention to the censorship of plays and films to ensure that entertainment carried the right fascist message. As many as 1,500 plays a year were regularly vetted and, if there was any doubt, each problem was referred for his personal consideration. He might insist that a play was altered to give it a happy ending, or he would cut out a scene where an Italian was shown to be drunk or criminal. He forbade altogether the showing of *Cyrano de Bergerac* and *La Mandragola* – despite his professed admiration for Machiavelli – and stopped a Pirandello play because the audience interpreted it as tilting against authority.[94] The least hint of satire affecting himself brought an immediate veto. He thus refused Shaw's *Caesar and Cleopatra* because it showed a bald dictator, and the censors had strict orders to be careful about any representation of Napoleon; they assumed that this was lest an audience should see some oblique reference to himself, or because he did not like great men to be shown in their shirt-sleeves and with an irregular private life.[95]

Some of the 'dead corners' of national life were not dangerous and hence no problem. There may, for instance, have been many other Italians who, like one peasant encountered by a foreign newspaperman fifty kilometres from Rome, had only a vague idea who Mussolini was.[96] Much more dangerous were the intellectuals and professional classes who, even when belonging to the fascist party, were sometimes unenthusiastic or even secretly hostile.[97] One by one each profession was therefore made into a closed organisation, to join which people would have to show proof of 'good moral and political conduct'; without such proof no one would be allowed to practise. These closed shops had already been created for journalists, doctors and lawyers, and new schemes were being drawn up to include architects, artists, inventors, chemists, engineers and most other professions. In no other country, boasted Mussolini, were intellectuals organised so efficiently and no other government had ever done so much for the educated classes. Two thousand intellectuals and representatives of the professions were summoned in October 1932 to be told this by him personally. There was no room for ivory towers, he told them, nor for criticism by people who deluded themselves that they knew better than he. 'Only one person in Italy is infallible' – and he did not mean the Pope. Italian intellectuals were expected to show the rest of the world the vitality of fascism by actively participating in and propagating the new values of the regime.[98]

Schoolteachers had already been forced to take an oath of loyalty to the fascist regime and in 1931, on the advice of the philosopher Gentile,[99] the same was required of university professors, failing which they would be dismissed. The minister of education privately reassured some doubters that they could regard the oath as a mere formality and no undue conformity would be imposed on them,[100] because what was required was simply to give the impression to the outside world that fascism had the unanimous backing of the universities; fewer than one per cent of the professors refused to swear.

Mussolini was surprised when this politicisation of the universities aroused indignation outside Italy and his ambassadors abroad were told to make public that the oath had been taken quite spontaneously.[101] Once they had made this first concession, the professors were soon afterwards and with less publicity invited to join the party and, like other fascists, swear a second oath to live and die for him.[102] Teaching could no longer be neutral; it had to be fascist and justify the new ethic of violence, obedience, and intellectual uniformity. The Duce was delighted to see many distinguished and venerable professors don their black shirts for graduation day and march in formation to the commemorative fascist exhibition to mount guard with the rest.

It is clear that many of the surviving professors, men such as Luigi Einaudi, Enrico Fermi and Federico Chabod, cannot have liked what they saw of fascism, and complaints continued to be made that the universities were still 'dead corners' partly outside the regime. But there were compensations for subservience: few intellectuals in positions of authority found it necessary to resign from their jobs as Italy moved further and further towards militarisation. In the early 1930s there seems to have been very little anti-fascist activity anywhere and Mussolini flattered himself that he had the 'spontaneous and totalitarian' support of almost everyone. Subsequently he recalled that he had hardly been a real dictator because his own will to command 'coincided perfectly with the will of Italians to obey'.[103]

He continued to hope that fascism would eventually succeed in making them entirely different in character.[104] He wanted them more disciplined, more 'prussianised', more like the Piedmontese and less like southern Italians. Schoolchildren were told to model themselves on him and only him. To arouse them from what he called centuries of torpor he would 'keep them lined up in uniform from morning to night, and give them stick, stick, stick'. They must learn to hate more and rejoice in being hated; he wanted them to be feared, not liked; they must become a 'master race, hard, implacable, odious'. They needed more character, less brain, and sometimes he spoke wildly of their needing less education since illiterates had more courage than the educated.[105]

In the years after 1934, Mussolini revived all his old enmity against the bourgeoisie and the bourgeois mentality, which he defined as unheroic, sceptical and humanitarian. Theirs was an un-fascist love of compromise and the quiet life,[106] and to fight them he would make Italians less comfortable because comfort was the great enemy of militarism. This was one reason for not mass-producing a cheap popular car like the Volkswagen, because popular motoring signified pleasure, comfort, and hence pacifism. He needed rather a succession of wars to inure people to hardship and keep them on their toes.[107] Against this bourgeois enemy he eventually planned to let loose a 'third wave' of violence and concentration camps.[108] His outbursts of anger against the rich became more common and were reminiscent of his early socialist writings. Foreigners confirmed that he was moving 'steadily leftwards' and that this was far from welcome to the world of commerce and banking.[109] A good 80 per cent of the bourgeoisie, he once remarked in a moment of anger, might have to be 'physically destroyed'; if only he had known them before 1920 as he knew them now, he would 'have carried out a pitiless revolution that made Lenin's look like an innocent joke'.[110]

Relations with Hitler, 1933–4

After the nazis won power in January 1933, Mussolini had ideological as well as pragmatic reasons for closer ties with Germany. 'The victory of Hitler is also our victory', was his immediate comment: a victory he had helped with arms and money and which raised the possibility of creating a new Rome–Berlin axis.[111] Hitler sent him messages of homage and admiration, and other Germans were ready with positive encouragement for Italy to replace France as the dominant power in North Africa and the Mediterranean.[112] If this encouragement was sincere, here was a basis for agreement. Tentative feelers were therefore put out to see whether the Germans would agree to confine their ambitions to Poland and the Baltic, leaving Italy free in the Mediterranean and the Balkans.[113]

But the idea was greatly over-optimistic. One obstacle to such an axis was

Hitler's ideas about racial inequality; because although Mussolini could accept that there might possibly be a Jewish danger and was already developing a racialist policy in his three African colonies,[114] he thought it ill-advised to provoke international Jewry by a head-on collision,[115] and particularly questioned the scientific validity of a dogma of racial superiority that left out Italians, giving pride of place to blue-eyed, blond northerners.[116] The nazi idea of sterilising the unfit was also unacceptable to a Catholic society, even though the fascists had quietly been practising it on a small scale in North Africa.[117]

A more serious obstacle to an entente with Germany was the nazi ambition to annex Austria, whereas Mussolini had confidently promised to defend this country against 'Prussian barbarism'.[118] Arms continued to be sent from Italy to encourage Engelbert Dollfuss, the chancellor of Austria, to set up a dictatorial government along fascist lines but excluding German influence. Three times in 1933, Dollfuss was brought to Italy and given a clear promise that, if both the nazi and socialist parties in Austria were suppressed, Italian military support could be relied on to prevent a German invasion.[119]

To show that Rome, rather than Geneva or Paris, was becoming the centre of European affairs, Mussolini no longer travelled abroad after 1925 but invariably insisted that foreign statesmen come to Italy, and it was his practice to use photographs of their arrival to suggest that their presence was in deference to fascism.[120] In June 1933, when representatives of the four great European powers met in Rome, a pact was signed that was said to be an acknowledgement of his leadership and a guarantee of peace for the next ten years.[121] As the pact was not ratified it never came into effect, but this fact was not much publicised inside Italy.

Another pact signed in 1933 committed him to friendship with Soviet Russia. This was one of those moments when it was hoped that Stalin might be moving towards corporativism and 'state capitalism' and possibly might be becoming something akin to a fascist.[122] In any case, Mussolini was ready to ignore differences over internal policy and made a formal promise that he would never join any international alliance hostile to Russia – promises in politics, he said on other occasions, were not binding. To seal this entente, a Soviet naval squadron visited Naples in October 1933 and an Italian military delegation went to Moscow.

In the second half of 1933, as his plan for a colonial war took shape, Mussolini once again transferred the three military ministries into his own hands and arranged for his son-in-law, Galeazzo Ciano, to take over the propaganda office and give it a more assertive tone. Fascist totalitarianism, he maintained, was ten years ahead on the road along which all other countries would be obliged to move. He alone had a political doctrine that was universally applicable and, now that Italy's domestic problems were on the way to being solved, he was ready to accept a wider mission as an arbiter between nations. This could be by force if need be, because on land, sea, and in the air his intention was to ensure that Italy excelled over everyone else.[123]

Nazi Germany was one country over which he meant to excel. He was put out at finding that Berlin, not Rome, was sometimes taken as the centre of the new fascist civilisation.[124] Germany's population, he scoffed, was declining even more than the French, so she was doomed.[125] Instead of nazism being the daughter or sister of fascism, the two movements were turning out to have little in common.[126] Hitler, he suggested once again, was 'an ideologue who talks more than he governs', and probably a prisoner of the army generals; he was 'simply a muddle-headed fellow; his brain is stuffed with philosophical and political tags that are utterly incoherent'; and the authenticity of his revolution was in any case vitiated by having won power through parliament instead of through violence as the fascists were now said to have done.[127]

Mussolini remained confident that he could effectively veto an *Anschluss* between Germany and Austria, and troop movements in the Alto Adige during September were intended as a warning.[128] He was annoyed when, in October, Germany unexpectedly withdrew from the League of Nations, because he had himself been threatening to do this for years and now could not follow suit without losing his title to precedence and originality. As a counter-move, he again suggested redesigning the League, perhaps confining it to Europe or to the great powers alone: the exclusion of smaller nations would suit the hierarchic and authoritarian ideas of fascism.[129] But the proposal was quickly buried before Italians could see how little note was taken of it elsewhere.

In 1933 there were indications that Mussolini's powers of judgement were becoming less sure, which may in part be ascribed to the recurrence of severe stomach pains,[130] but were more probably due to his growing remoteness from those who could give him information and advice. Among these misjudgements were an overconfident belief in fascist strength and foreign admiration. A lack of realism was also displayed in frequent changes of mind. At one moment he spoke as though Poland could beat Germany if it came to war;[131] at another moment he turned down a request from France and Britain to join them in guaranteeing Austria from attack; then went into reverse on this same point.[132]

In a meeting with Goering, whom he privately referred to as that 'ex-inmate of a lunatic asylum',[133] there was a foretaste of future linguistic misunderstandings; Goering came away thinking that the fascists accepted an *Anschluss* as inescapable, while Mussolini thought he had persuaded Goering to renounce any claim on Austria.[134] The Italians, in fact, now repeated their undertaking to fight in defence of Austrian independence, and further troop movements near the frontier early in 1934 were intended to give the impression that they were ready to act.[135]

In February 1934, at Italy's insistence, Dollfuss set up a one-party state on fascist lines and suppressed socialist opposition in Vienna by brute force. Here was another miscalculation by Mussolini, since he knew that Dollfuss had little backing and the bloody scenes in Vienna made Austrian socialists turn towards nazi Germany as a lesser evil.[136] To the British and French this act seemed to be gratuitously bringing an *Anschluss* one step nearer and suggested that fascist Italy was an unreliable, even dangerous, collaborator.[137]

At this point, Mussolini made a public declaration that fascist ambitions were directed towards Africa and Asia.[138] In April he installed four large marble maps in Rome along the grandiose, newly built Avenue of the Empire to illustrate the extent of the Roman empire in ancient history; the fourth map showed the empire in Trajan's time stretching from Britain to Asia Minor, Syria, and Egypt. Here, in front of these glorious symbols of the past and the possible future, he had the photographers take his picture wearing a newly-designed steel helmet – with the statues of the Caesars in the background.[139]

Then in May, a broadcasting service in Arabic was begun from a transmitter at Bari in southern Italy, and a bigger arms programme was announced accompanied by the warning that it would mean a lowering of living standards in Italy. Fascism, as Mussolini reminded everyone once again, was essentially warlike: war was to men what maternity was to women and nothing else would reveal the fundamental virtues of the Italian race.[140]

As the time came nearer for his planned invasion of Ethiopia, he needed to patch up any differences with Germany so as to have no trouble on his back doorstep while the Italian army was concentrating in Africa. He therefore agreed that it was time to end the restrictions on German rearmament that had been imposed by treaty in 1919. He repeated his promise to defend Austrian independence but was ready to accept that Austria was in a German rather than an Italian sphere of influence. Hitler was delighted: the more Italy could be persuaded to seek expansion in Africa and Asia, the harder it would be for her to avoid a conflict of interests with France, and the more Mussolini would have to realise that an alliance with Germany was his best bet.[141]

In June 1934, Hitler decided to come to Venice for their first meeting, hoping to find common ground in a fascist policy for Europe and to create a common front against the coloured and Semitic races.[142] He had asked for an informal meeting but arrived in Venice to find that Mussolini, determined to upstage his visitor, had invited the world's press; Hitler – in his raincoat, soft hat and patent-leather shoes – looked like a commercial traveller alongside the grandly uniformed Duce.[143] But the public *mise en scène* went badly wrong.

The military parades were embarrassingly untidy and a ceremonial concert became a farce as the music was punctuated by organised shouts of 'Duce, Duce'.[144] The Germans were able to see that organisation and discipline were not Mussolini's strong suit.

The talks between the two leaders were not an outstanding success either, mainly because Hitler monopolised the conversation and Mussolini, refusing to have an interpreter, seems to have lagged behind and misunderstood some crucial points.[145] Hitler talked of his plans to start a European war by attacking France suddenly and reaching Paris before the French had time to mobilise. He pointed out that the British had no politician of his calibre, and he was also understood to say that other races, including presumably the Italian race in which it was hinted there might be some taint of Negro blood, would be no match for an aggressive Germany.[146] Hitler repeated that he would not force a complete *Anschluss* but would be content with getting rid of Dollfuss and installing a pro-nazi government in Vienna. The Germans recorded that Mussolini apparently agreed to this compromise and did not seem greatly alarmed;[147] perhaps he was assuming that the Italian frontier at the Brenner Pass was strong enough, and this may have given the mistaken impression that he was no longer so much concerned as to whether Austria survived as an independent state.[148]

Hitler told people that their meeting went quite well, perhaps because he had met with no contradiction: he was especially impressed by the popular enthusiasm for the Duce and the spectacle of people bowing to him as to a religious leader.[149] Mussolini, on the contrary, commented that it had been no meeting but rather a 'collision'.[150] Once again he spoke of Hitler with contempt as a buffoon, as possibly slightly mad, without intelligence or dynamism: 'he was a gramophone with just seven tunes and once he had finished playing them he started all over again'.[151]

When, a few days after returning to Germany, Hitler murdered several hundred of his closest followers, Mussolini was astounded; and though he continued an outward display of friendliness, urgent advice was sent from Rome to Dollfuss to carry out a purge of the nazis in Austria.[152] Dollfuss was planning to do this when, towards the end of July, he was himself assassinated by those he was about to purge. As the victim was Mussolini's protégé, this was a direct personal affront. The Duce angrily referred to Hitler as a 'horrible sexual degenerate'; another promise was made that Austria would be defended against any German attack,[153] and Italian troops again took up threatening positions near the northern frontier. The violence of the reaction came as a surprise to Hitler who may have interpreted the Duce's passivity at Venice as meaning that a pro-nazi coup would be unopposed.[154]

Though for a time Mussolini continued to reassure the Austrians of his continued support,[155] he seems to have accepted that there was little hope of avoiding an eventual *Anschluss* and was simply anxious to delay it as long as possible.[156] He admitted that it might have been unwise to encourage Germany's rearmament and he cancelled a contract to sell military planes to her.[157] Secret talks were also begun with the French,[158] even though he was reluctant to accept an agreement with Britain and France about the defence of Austria.[159] His main concern was to keep a balance of power in central Europe without committing himself to either side: this would leave his hands free for Africa.

To cover up his public discomfiture over Dollfuss' death, he indulged in rhetorical sabre-rattling and the stirring up of artificial animosities against almost every country in turn; in the course of a few months the press, under Galeazzo Ciano's direction, was ordered to attack thirty different countries and warn them of the dire results of incurring the Duce's displeasure.[160] He again insisted that Italians must be taught to hate other countries. He repeated that Italy had to be made a military and indeed militarist state in which the whole of national life was directed towards war, because war alone was 'the court of appeal among the nations', and only by becoming militarist could Italy prepare for the 'punitive expeditions' beyond her frontiers which might become necessary.[161]

One immediate step in this direction was a new law making military instruction compulsory from the age of eight to thirty-two. The duty of ordinary citizens was to 'work and obey', not to enjoy themselves: people who wanted amusements would become soft. He explained that children must be taken at an early age into the system if their thoughts and souls were to be 'forged'. Saturday afternoons and some Sundays must therefore be spent in training.[162] He set great store by this 'military education of the people' and perhaps never realised a fact that his generals quickly realised:[163] it was a piece of absurd and dangerous self-deception. He thus cheated himself into thinking that he had eight or ten million men fully trained to fight, when he was merely diverting money and public attention away from more serious programmes of rearmament.

Warlike talk late in 1934 included some of his bitterest condemnations of German barbarism. Nazism was described as a product of paganism and the dark ages, 'a racialist lunatic asylum'; it might have some resemblance to fascism, but he preferred to think that his own movement allowed more rights to the individual, to religious sentiment, and to the family, while in many respects the two movements were at opposite poles.[164] German representatives were pointedly not present when, in December 1934, Mussolini tried to start a 'fascist international' in an attempt to rival the 'communist international'. A congress with 'representatives' of sixteen states met at

Montreux and agreed to accept him as their guiding genius; they also agreed that good fascists would not copy Germany's hate campaign against the Jews. But the movement, which was hopelessly disorganised and represented only tiny minorities, fizzled out almost at once.[165]

Mussolini was still hoping for the break-up of Jugoslavia and vaguely envisaged a separate Croatia under Italian patronage acting as a barrier to the advance of German influence into the Balkans. In the early thirties there were several training camps in Italy under the control of the Italian foreign office where Croat terrorists were secretly instructed in the use of arms and explosives against the Serb majority,[166] and Mussolini paid for these camps despite (or because of) his knowledge that the terrorists contemplated the assassination of King Alexander of Jugoslavia.[167] Ante Pavelic, their leader, was a man who ten years later massacred over half a million Serbs; from Italy, where he had fled to escape a murder charge, Pavelic organised a bomb outrage at Zagreb in 1931, and the next year tried to start a revolution in Jugoslavia. The attempt failed, but Alexander was murdered in October 1934, and some of the murderers turned out to have money and passports provided in Italy. Pavelic was condemned to death in France for this assassination but Mussolini refused his extradition and this Croat terrorist continued to live in Italy at Italian expense. The fascists chose instead to blame the murder on other countries and the 'Jewish international';[168] but evidently there had been a vague hope in Rome that the murder would be followed by the disintegration of Jugoslavia.[169]

Perhaps Mussolini had been hoping that a useful crime could be committed without personal blame attaching to himself, just as with Matteotti's death and the smuggling of arms to half a dozen terrorist organisations abroad. Possibly he had not wanted this particular outrage, but he was certainly an accessory after the fact if not before it, and it was a typical example of *squadrismo* transferred to foreign policy; he continued to pay these terrorists from secret service funds and admitted that he had plans to use them in the future.[170]

War policy

11

Preparations for war

That Mussolini carefully manufactured a personal cult was strenuously denied by his staff,[1] but occasionally he would admit it and, in justification, argue that a dictator needed fanatical believers in his infallibility.[2] If the newspapers continued sometimes to refer to him as 'our divine Duce' and to his regime as an 'incarnation of God', if he was made out to be a thaumaturge, someone whose name could be used in hospitals as an anaesthetic before operations,[3] this could not have been done without his tacit approval.

In 1933 he decided to publish what was called a 'definitive' edition of his writings and speeches, but took care to omit all he had written while socialist editor of *Avanti!*. At least sixty articles of 1919 were also left out; so were passages whose vulgarity or anti-clericalism might contradict his new image. Much of the real Mussolini had to remain concealed. The 'definitive' edition was a misnomer.

By this time he again held seven out of the fourteen posts in the cabinet and was seen to resent even the limited degree of authority possessed by other ministers.[4] He warned them never to disagree with him, 'because contradiction only raises doubts in my mind and diverts me from what I know to be the right path, whereas my own animal instincts are always right'.[5] He sometimes confessed that he was easily influenced by others and, for this reason, preferred to take all major decisions without consultation. Even quite junior officials were instructed to issue no executive orders without at least pretending that they emanated from himself.[6] Ministers and officials were therefore less and less willing to take decisions even on small matters,[7] while his own unwillingness to listen to advice or other opinions left him in a vacuum where his information about the outside world was partial and sometimes disastrously inaccurate.[8]

Subsequently some fascists were able to admit that this process of idolisation was one of the major mistakes of the regime and that his attempt to create an 'oriental despotism' was bound to produce an irremediable inefficiency,[9] but he personally thought the precise opposite. He now put himself on the level of Napoleon[10] and Julius Caesar, whom he said he admired more than anyone in history and about whom he read everything he could lay his hands on.[11] He thought he had already done as much for Italy as

Napoleon had done for France, and would occasionally point out in which respects he was Napoleon's superior:[12] this superiority to Napoleon became a common theme of the fascist propagandists who claimed that the Duce had greater vision and originality, better knowledge of men, more courage and less personal vanity.[13]

The flatterers also encouraged him to think that, like Napoleon, he had the innate qualities of a war leader and was fully capable of directing a military campaign:[14] they knew this was the kind of praise he preferred. Whereas to a wider international audience he continued to insist that all his energies were directed towards keeping the peace,[15] inwardly he was becoming fascinated and almost obsessed with the prospect of leading his country in a victorious war.[16] He repeated earlier statements that 1935 was the year when he would be ready for war, and fascism must seize its chance to capture another colony as proof that Italy under his leadership had become a great power.[17]

A first and necessary step was to increase his command over the economy. Speaking to foreigners in the early 1930s, Mussolini had been saying that he was against tariff barriers and in favour of as little state intervention in the economy as possible,[18] but he was soon talking in a very different vein. As the logic of fascism took him further towards controls and protection, he used to explain that he went unwillingly and only after other countries had forced him to act in self-defence. In fact, however, it was the world economic crisis of 1929 together with his warlike posture in foreign affairs that compelled him to change his policy and come to the aid of ailing sectors of the economy.[19] First it was simply a question of intervening to save important industries in temporary difficulties; then the success of this operation showed him that intervention could be used on a bigger scale to produce a more centralised control of economic life. By 1933 he was accustomed to repeating that the capitalist organisation of production was no longer acceptable.[20] The state, he now said, must intervene in every section of the economy, and one maverick senator accused him of becoming almost a communist because three-quarters of Italian industry was in the process of becoming controlled if not actually owned by the state.[21]

In 1934 Mussolini at last felt able to declare that the corporations were in existence, and he convinced himself that England and other countries were following his lead in introducing a corporative system of their own.[22] His hope was that the corporations would shortly be controlling the whole Italian economy;[23] nevertheless, he had to admit that there was still confusion in people's minds as to what they were or what they did, and other students of the subject had the greatest difficulty in discovering if they had any serious importance at all.[24] An expensive and cumbersome corporative bureaucracy had 'become a powerful vested interest that was determined to perpetuate itself', but its functions were not clear except that it cost a lot of money and sometimes acted to clog the wheels of industry.[25]

Of course, Mussolini could not admit in public that the corporations were a failure. He merely supplemented them with alternative agencies that often cut across each other in a constricting administrative tangle. Soon the vogue word was no longer corporativism, but rather autarky or self-sufficiency, as he recognised the need to prepare Italy for wartime conditions when importing would be difficult. In February 1935 he laid down an objective that the country must be freed as far as possible from dependence on outside supplies. He explained that ten years of the 'battle for wheat' had made Italy self-sufficient in basic foodstuffs so that she now had enough to feed a nation almost twice her size[26] – few of his hearers were to know that this was wildly untrue. He said he wished he had realised ten years earlier that he would equally need to be as self-sufficient as possible in industrial products.[27] What he apparently did not fully appreciate was that a major programme of arms production would inevitably increase, not diminish, Italy's dependence on imports; for him the word autarky – like corporativism – became, as it were, a magic incantation that would by itself solve the main problems of a war economy.[28] The word was attractive, but it was to prove no less of an illusion.

The war he had in mind was intended as another contribution to the solving of Italy's economic problems. The conquest of Ethiopia would link the two existing colonies of Eritrea and Somalia, and he had visions of sending millions – a figure of ten million was once mentioned – of Italian settlers to a unified East Africa.[29] Mussolini could not afford to listen to those realists who knew, as he had once known, that colonial enterprises usually cost much more than they were worth; he preferred the advice of others who guessed or pretended that Italian settlers could turn Ethiopia into a rich economic asset in a few years.[30] There was loose talk of abundant gold deposits, diamonds, copper, iron, coal and oil,[31] while quite as attractive to him was the prospect of conscripting one or two million Ethiopians into an army which, when once the new colony had been properly industrialised, would become a force dominating the whole African continent.[32]

After a preliminary plan of operations against Ethiopia had been prepared in 1932, Mussolini was ready to admit by August 1934 that war was not far off. Considerable quantities of war material were being sent in the late summer of 1934[33] and the French were approached in October with a request to allow Italy a free hand for the 'economic penetration' of the area.[34] Early in December, one of many minor skirmishes took place at Wal Wal, where the Italians had set up a garrison some eighty miles inside what was marked as Ethiopian territory even on Italian military maps.[35] Mussolini took this as a convenient pretext for further warlike preparations; he refused to submit the incident at Wal Wal to arbitration but – as at Corfu in 1923 – demanded monetary compensation and the punishment of those guilty of 'aggression' against Italy.

At the end of December he issued a secret order to prepare for the 'total conquest of Ethiopia'. There was now some urgency – not merely because German rearmament would soon force him to keep the bulk of his army at home, but also because Ethiopia was becoming Europeanised and he had to strike before she acquired enough modern weapons and military training.[36] He at first thought that 160,000 troops would be sufficient as long as they were mechanised and ready to use poison gas. He would make no formal declaration of war because surprise was important, and because he meant to claim that he was acting in self-defence;[37] that way he might avoid the matter's coming before the League of Nations. He thought he could first make a deal with France, and the British would then be bribed into inactivity by letting them take one region of Ethiopia for themselves.[38]

In January 1935 a formal treaty was signed with France. Its main intention was to set up a common front against nazi Germany, but the story was also circulated that the French premier, Pierre Laval, gave a secret verbal assurance that France would connive at an Italian invasion of Ethiopia. Laval always denied this and said he had been told only of Italian economic penetration.[39] Mussolini later admitted that he said nothing to Laval about a possible war.[40] But almost certainly he hinted to the French that economic penetration would imply some degree of political control and both parties were content to leave this point imprecise. Mussolini, however, was taking a considerable risk by relying on vague hints when he badly needed French help for a war that he was determined to fight.

Throughout February and March, he continued to reassure other countries that he had no aggressive intentions. By now, foreign diplomats were deeply suspicious but nevertheless found it hard to believe that he so underestimated the German threat as to contemplate a major war in Africa. Inside Italy he ordered absolute silence about military preparations, but in private let drop the remark that Italy would keep healthy only by fighting a war every twenty-five years.[41] Arrangements were made to distribute gas masks and to repatriate some of the ten million Italians thought to be living abroad.

He knew, of course, that the British would not much like his intended war against Ethiopia, but relied on their being so worried by Hitler that they would turn a blind eye;[42] in any case, their own colonial past should make them at least accept a *fait accompli* if he gave them a suitable bribe. On 29 January he sent word to London that he would like talks about spheres of influence in East Africa, but no urgency was expressed; indeed Ambassador Grandi told the British that the matter was relatively unimportant and again the promise was made that Italy had absolutely no aggressive intentions.[43] Perhaps Mussolini merely wanted another equivocal arrangement like that with France which, without tying his hands, would give him the excuse to say later that the government in London had no reason to be surprised when war broke out. In reply, the British welcomed his undertakings to avoid war and informed him unambiguously and more than once that he would put himself hopelessly in the wrong if he resorted to force.[44] Unfortunately, now as later, Grandi was chiefly anxious to flatter Mussolini into thinking that the British admired him excessively and were sufficiently hypocritical to support him in a war: if it came to the worst, they were a decadent race who could never stand up against the might of fascist Italy.[45]

Mussolini did not need to consult anyone except the king before deciding on war, certainly not his ministers, nor the Grand Council: he despised his civilian colleagues too much and, as he confessed, was afraid they might argue against what his instinct and 'better judgement' had already decided. Consultation, he explained, was the resort only of men without will-power.[46] He informed the chief of police that there would be a war some time in the next few months, but would not say against whom.[47] Only in February 1935 was he more explicit when he spelt out to his ministers that a major military operation was being prepared: he told them that the armed services were ready, basic food supplies were assured and even supplies of coal and oil were no longer a problem.[48]

The Duce intended to reserve for himself the general direction of the campaign, and the field commander, De Bono, was at one point instructed to have no direct dealings with the army staff. By March, plans had been revised to envisage a force of 300,000 made up of an equal number of fascist militiamen and regular soldiers, but De Bono found that the militia had little, if any, military training and were almost no use.[49] When pressed, Mussolini said he was ready to send many more men: the prestige of fascism demanded that the war be won quickly and decisively at whatever cost.

In the end, over half a million soldiers and civilian workers were sent to East Africa – an immense army, far larger than had ever been used before in a colonial war. Several million tons of equipment had to be transported 2,000 or more miles: one senior officer thought this was nearly ten times as much as was needed,[50] but Mussolini insisted that to send one army corps too many would be an error on the right side, especially as 'afterwards we may need them to conquer Egypt and the Sudan'.[51] De Bono was dismayed to find his specified requirements multiplied in this casual and haphazard way and, as harbour facilities at Massawa could deal with only 3,000 tons a day, some ships had to wait weeks or months before they could unload.[52]

Hitler waited until these preparations were well advanced and then startled the world by formally announcing that the Germans would rearm in defiance of treaty restrictions. Mussolini, who had secretly been helping their rearmament, suddenly realised that he was very vulnerable with almost all his army commited to Africa.[53] An article in his own monthly magazine reflected his anxiety when it accused Germany and Japan of trying to dominate the world, but also claimed that the Germans were terrified of Mussolini and knew he was strong enough to prevent their expansion in central Europe.[54] He was shameless enough to warn the British government that Hitler was sending arms to Africa and might be intending to excite 'the Negro race generally against Europeans': perhaps British politicians 'could not realise the German mentality', but they would be well advised to take his advice and build a strong air force as soon as they could.[55]

To meet this potential challenge from the nazis, a discussion was held with the French and British prime ministers in April: the chosen venue was Stresa, so that Mussolini would not have to leave Italy.[56] As he was the host, it was for him to preside and draw up the agenda: his foreign office suggested that he take this opportunity to bring up the matter of Ethiopia, but as he knew that Britain was hostile to his African ambitions, he did not want to risk either a veto on them or the loss of face if a conference under his chairmanship should fail in its main work.

His chief interest was to win agreement to set up what became known as the 'Stresa front' against Germany, because without security on his northern frontier he could not risk a war in Africa. He therefore asked the British delegates not to discuss Ethiopia except informally outside the conference room.[57] They agreed, though some of their officials – like his own – thought this might be a bad mistake.[58] Their silence later gave him the excuse to claim that, as no formal protest had been registered at Stresa, the British – like the French – would let him have his way.

This was Mussolini at his cleverest and most brazen. But his achievement was formal, not substantial: he already knew that the British were strongly opposed to his war, and their opposition was unequivocally repeated at Stresa behind the scenes. Ethiopia, they pointed out, was a member of the League and any attack on her territorial integrity was bound to involve the outside world.[59] No doubt they hoped that the Italians were no more than trying to browbeat Ethiopia into making concessions. Mussolini did not enlighten them. He subsequently invented a story that, at the last session of the conference, he wrote the words 'in Europe' into the final agreement and this bound the others to accept that outside Europe he had a free hand. But the story was untrue:[60] he had himself been anxious to persuade the others to keep Ethiopia out of the main conference on the grounds that it was a secondary matter, and then afterwards used their silence as a justification for his colonial war.

The ambiguity that resulted was deliberately engineered by him, as he knew that otherwise he would have to heed a repeated, and this time public, warning against war made by the British the very next day after the Stresa meeting.[61] As his military preparations became more obvious, further private messages were sent from London to warn him that, since Ethiopia was willing to accept arbitration, Italy's bullying of a much weaker country would alienate potential friends, and hostilities would ruin the system of collective security from which Italy as well as others had a great deal to gain.[62]

Mussolini was not the man to be moved by such arguments and made clear that, if thwarted, he would leave the League never to return; he hoped, from what Grandi said and from the right-wing press in London, that in the last resort most English people except 'pacifists and old ladies' would accept if not actively support Italian imperialism.[63] In any case, he added, the hostility of world opinion meant nothing to him.[64] He had already spent vast sums in preparation for his colonial war and 'intended to give Italy a return for his investment'.[65] In Grandi's opinion, this new prospect of challenging the League gave Mussolini even more pleasure than annexing Ethiopia.[66]

As late as May 1935, he had not abandoned his anti-German stance and still talked of 'destroying' Hitler if necessary.[67] A secret military agreement was also signed with France for the joint defence of Austrian independence, and the strategy of a war against Germany was discussed with the French general staff.[68] But in fact he was on the point of moving in the opposite direction: already at the end of May, even before his military pact with France, he informed the Germans that he was ready for a basic reorientation of policy away from the 'Stresa front' and against the western democracies.[69]

For several years he had been intercepting communications through the French and British embassies in Rome,[70] and must have had confirmation from this source that in London and Paris, despite what others tried to make him believe, there was a firm determination not to risk war against Italy at almost any cost. When, in June, the British proposed a negotiated settlement over Ethiopia he therefore did not think it need be taken seriously: British rearmament had barely started and he would have known that there was a secret commitment in London to giving priority to the Japanese threat in the Far East.

He also believed dogmatically that Britain was a declining power that had lost the will to defend her empire,[71] and Grandi sent advice from London that, just as the British had refused to stand up to Japan and Germany, so they would give way to Italy if she remained firm.[72] An earlier debate in the Oxford Union Society rejecting the idea of fighting for king and country reinforced this view, and the vote of one small undergraduate society was gradually magnified by fascist propaganda into the unanimous opinion of students at

Oxford and Cambridge, and then into a pacifist vote by all British youth; and Mussolini refused to listen to anyone who questioned this reasoning.[73]

As the weeks went by with no more than verbal protests from other members of the League, he felt that his plan was going well and became the more belligerent. In public he listed ninety-one examples of Ethiopian 'aggression' and claimed that he was just exercising the right to self-defence;[74] but in private he said that, even if he could acquire the whole of this vast empire by negotiation, he would prefer war – because military victory alone would avenge Italy's defeat by Ethiopia in 1896. He wanted 'war for war's sake, since fascism needs the glory of a victory',[75] and this despite the fact that some people were again suggesting his name for a Nobel peace prize.[76] For a time he toyed with the idea of going in person to East Africa to supervise the attack.[77] In unpublished speeches he said he meant to make the whole world bend to his will and, if the Ethiopians resisted, put their country 'to pillage and fire'.[78]

By August he began to talk of fighting against Britain as well if she stood in his way.[79] His generals and admirals were greatly alarmed and tried to convince him that there was no possibility of fighting such a war, but he himself, as minister for air, boldly stated that he could attack and sink the British fleet in Alexandria in a matter of hours. Perhaps he did not know, as the general staff surely knew, that only about half a dozen planes had the requisite range and that they lacked armour-piercing bombs to damage enemy ships.[80]

At such moments of euphoria he had no interest in listening to reasoned argument. He was ready, if necessary, for a European war and fancifully announced that he could in a single day mobilise ten million men or even more – though in all the four years of the Second World War he could mobilise barely one-third of this number. He was ready to see Europe 'going up in a blaze'.[81] 'If I fail', he added, 'it will be the gallows for me'; but if he won, he would take Ethiopia and then the Sudan, thus linking up his East African empire with Libya. Orders went out on 19 September to plan for a possible attack on the Sudan, as well as on Kenya and British Somaliland,[82] while his propaganda services accused the British of opposing him only because they intended to capture Ethiopia for themselves.[83]

British policy in September, as Mussolini knew from intercepts, continued to be one of appeasement towards Italy; with their limited capacity and multiple commitments especially in the Far East, there could be no serious possibility of the British intervening on their own to defend Ethiopian independence. But as articles began to appear in the Italian press about possible attacks on Suez, Gibraltar and Malta, it was thought wise in London to strengthen the fleet in the Mediterranean. Mussolini privately told the

British that he would have done just the same in their position,[84] but in public made out that this was an intolerable threat and cunningly used the fact to excite patriotic feeling at home. There was talk of sinking the British fleet in one surprise attack and of a suicide squad of pilots led by the senior air-force commander in person – also of an imaginary bomber that could fly from Italy to London at such a height that it would entirely escape detection.[85]

The service chiefs were amazed at his confidence because they knew that his story about the relative weakness of the British fleet was pure fantasy. The fact that Italy obtained over three-quarters of her imports by sea and had even to send drinking water by sea to her forces in East Africa, made her extremely vulnerable, and the senior admirals reported that they could not even defend the Italian coast from bombardment if it came to war.[86] But Mussolini correctly judged that the British would never fire the first shot against Italy as long as they believed that the major danger was either Germany or Japan, and the service commanders, as well as the rest of Italy, were full of admiration when he was proved right.

There was something impressively defiant about him in these final weeks before war began. He had few friends in the League of Nations; in the Vatican it was thought that he might be slightly demented and the Pope, despite the widespread sympathy for this 'Catholic crusade', was meditating a public censure against 'a civilised nation setting out to grab another country';[87] according to the US ambassador, Mussolini was not mad but 'deliberate, determined, obdurate, ruthless, and almost vicious'; the British ambassador saw him as 'astonishingly untroubled by the remorse of conscience' but giving the 'constant impression of a man who is the victim, not the master of his destiny'.[88]

Public opinion in the world at large was building up against someone who, by challenging the League and destroying the idea of collective security, was demolishing the illusions of a whole generation. Without collective security, the nations would have to fall back on an expensive armaments race. But Mussolini repeated that he cared nothing for public opinion, which in every country was simply manufactured by newspaper owners, as he knew only too well from personal experience.

War in East Africa, 1935–6

Mussolini's strategic plans depended on the assumption that the Ethiopians were poorly equipped: they may have possessed several hundred machine guns and perhaps ten unarmed planes (though in public he pretended that they were well-armed with the most modern weapons). With unchallenged air superiority, he knew that his air force could carry out its long-prepared strategy of terrorising civilian populations into surrender, and he planned to destroy the main Ethiopian towns by bombing where necessary.[89] He also relied on offering substantial bribes to undermine the loyalty of enemy commanders,[90] as he subsequently did with other countries he intended to attack.

On 2 October, the people of Italy were summoned into the town squares by bells and sirens to hear over loudspeakers his announcement that war had begun. This summons was a procedure that Starace had carefully rehearsed during the previous month, and twenty-seven million people were said to have taken part in what was the largest staged function in human history. There was no declaration of war so as to avoid an admission that Ethiopia was in any sense an equal. Meanwhile, as a fleet of planes set off to bomb the town of Adowa, Mussolini informed the League of Nations that Italy was the victim of barbarous and unprovoked aggression. In the planes were his two eldest sons and Galeazzo Ciano, his son-in-law. The younger son, Bruno, was taken out of school to share in this glorious moment and, at the age of just seventeen, after less than the required period of training, was given a pilot's licence.

Italians greeted the commencement of war with surprisingly little enthusiasm, as Mussolini himself had to agree,[91] and his claim that it was a war of defence against a barbaric aggressor lacked credibility; nor did many of them answer his call for volunteers.[92] What eventually roused popular excitement, as he may have expected, was the unanimous condemnation by fifty members of the League of Nations. This was all he needed to convince Italians that their country was in danger and at once all good patriots rallied to the cause.

Under the terms of the Covenant of the League, any member state that attacked another was deemed to have committed an act of war against all other members, who were thereby required to sever trade with her. Mussolini admitted violating the Covenant,[93] but argued that censure of Italy would be an unwarranted attempt to humiliate her: she ought not to be treated as though on the same plane as uncivilised Ethiopia. Nevertheless he was condemned and this public denunciation at Geneva, while it had the disadvantage of cutting him off from the western democracies, won him support at home which, as he admitted, might otherwise have been lacking.

The imposition of economic sanctions was not only mandatory under the Covenant, but made a good deal of political sense for countries who still saw collective security as their only system of defence. In practice, however, sanctions proved worse than useless: as there were no precedents, it was a slow job devising the mechanism for their application by so many different countries. While effective enough to make the war popular in Italy, they were not nearly sufficient to halt the fighting. In particular, there was no agreement over closing the Suez Canal to military traffic or to ban oil supplies, let alone to take military action against Italy. Mussolini said, as also have others, that oil sanctions would have stopped the war inside a week,[94] though on another occasion he claimed he had ample reserves and evidently the Russians and the Americans were ready to make up any deficiency:[95] as usual, such contradictory remarks were made to impress whoever was listening and bore no necessary relation to fact.

So much had been said about fascist military proficiency, and so important was it to gain as much territory as possible before international reactions made themselves felt, that Mussolini overrode the advice of his military commanders and formally ordered them to disregard their supply lines and advance at once into the heartland of Ethiopia. De Bono grumbled at Mussolini's incompetence as an organiser and a strategist;[96] others reported back that the real incompetent was De Bono himself who was counting on a long war and not the quick spectacular victory that the political situation required. The choice of such a commander had evidently been a bad mistake and, within a few hours of the first attack, Mussolini was looking for a replacement.[97]

Meanwhile, in London and Paris there was the greatest alarm at this breach in the 'Stresa front' formed by the three anti-German powers. Grandi in London was kept so little informed of policy decisions in Rome that he sometimes had to ask the British government what was happening and privately tried to convince the British that Mussolini's bellicose public statements, since they were intended for Italian ears, need not be taken seriously abroad.[98]

Without informing his ambassador, Mussolini sent private envoys to London who only added to the confusion, and one of them put forward proposals for a compromise settlement.[99] But when the Ethiopians sent an envoy to Rome to discuss possible terms, Mussolini refused to see him on the pretence that he might be a hired assassin.[100] Instead, the Duce made a strange agreement with a charming rogue named Jacir Bey who undertook either to kidnap Haile Selassie and bring him to Italy, or else to secure the latter's collusion in staging a mock battle which the Italians would be allowed to win; following which, the Ethiopians would, by a face-saving agreement, accept a compromise peace. For two months the fascist government continued to play along with this incredible scheme, after which Jacir Bey was bought off handsomely to keep quiet about what came to be recognised as a somewhat discreditable episode, and some of the documents referring to it were removed from the archives.[101]

In December, the French and British presented further suggestions for a compromise that would give Italy much of what she wanted, and Mussolini was ready to accept this 'Hoare-Laval' plan as a basis for discussion and as a divisive influence among other League members.[102] But an outburst of popular indignation in Britain against such a betrayal of Ethiopia forced Samuel Hoare's resignation as foreign secretary and this enabled Mussolini to reject the whole idea, while claiming that the refusal was forced on him against his will.

December was a difficult month for the Duce. His colleagues thought he might be drifting without any clear policy; some wondered whether he could survive the almost unanimous condemnation by the western world. A number of ministers and *gerarchi* were sent off to fight in Ethiopia to demonstrate that they were still good *squadristi* at heart and, incidentally, to let everyone see that he could easily govern without their help. Balbo commented that their leader had forced the war on them without any prior discussion or consultation, and 'rarely had an enterprise of such scope been staged with such lack of skill, or with such frivolous *naïveté*. The political, diplomatic, financial and, indeed, even military preparations had been completely inadequate.' Mussolini 'was living in isolation, within four walls, seeing and hearing nothing of reality . . . surrounded only by flatterers who told him merely what he wanted to hear. If a man is told a hundred times a day that he is a genius, he will eventually believe in his own infallibility'.[103]

But victory is its own justification and what Mussolini was waiting for was a military victory from Marshal Badoglio, De Bono's replacement. Badoglio was authorised to employ terrorist methods at his discretion, including the destruction of villages and the use of poison gas on a large scale.[104] Though Mussolini had himself agreed to an international law banning the use of poison gas,[105] he had continued to regard it as a normal weapon of war as long as the fact of its use could be kept quiet; indeed, he was also prepared if necessary to use bacteria for spreading infectious diseases.[106] Since Jacir Bey and other intermediaries were failing to win Ethiopia by stealth, the decision was taken to use every possible military means, and there was no point in having spent ten years building up hundreds of tons of gas in East Africa without employing it to terrorise and demoralise the enemy. Some Italians protested when they discovered that such methods of warfare were being used, but the facts were successfully concealed from the general public. Any rumours were denied firmly[107] or else stories were invented that it was the Ethiopians who were using gas bombs against the Italians.[108] Long after the collapse of fascism, Badoglio finally admitted, after previous denials, that he had used gas but on one occasion only, as an experiment, and the minister in charge of African affairs eventually confessed that three small gas bombs were dropped,[109] but these admissions were made years after scores of documents had been published testifying to a quite different story.

The use of gas is perhaps less noteworthy than the great effort put into concealing the fact of its use. Mussolini needed the world to believe that Italy was a civilised country engaged in fighting a barbarous one, so the record had to be carefully doctored. Nor did he want people to think – as, in fact, some of them came to suspect[110] – that the Italians won only by resorting to illegal barbarities. Above all, he knew that much damage would be done to fascist prestige if the facts became known and potential sympathisers were alienated.[111] Mustard gas was Mussolini's secret weapon and he wanted to keep the secret so that it could be used again.

Early in 1936, Badoglio's immense army began to move from the north while Graziani's advanced from Somalia in the south, and Mussolini realised that a compromise peace might be avoided altogether. A new danger arose when the British decided at last to propose a ban on oil supplies, but in reply he threatened that oil sanctions would be the signal for him to abandon the League of Nations and possibly to attack the Sudan. He also encouraged the appeasers by persevering with separate discussions in Rome, Geneva and Jibuti to maintain the impression that he might still be open to an offer.

Grandi meanwhile tried to recapture Mussolini's confidence. He reported from London the slightly improbable story that King Edward wanted Italians to know that he was secretly on their side, and the king allegedly told this foreign ambassador that the British government was engaged in a 'grotesque and criminal' attempt to support the League.[112] Grandi's orders were to create panic in London by threatening war: articles were to be planted in English newspapers to say that Italy had an army of eight million men as well as the strongest air force in Europe, and any resistance to her just demands would not only fail but might lead to the hegemony of Germany in Europe.[113]

Early in May, Badoglio occupied Addis Ababa and to all appearance the war came to a triumphant end. The fact that most of Ethiopia remained independent, and that fighting continued fiercely for the next three years, were other details concealed from the Italian public. Vittorio Emanuele was proclaimed emperor in place of 'Signor Tafari', and Mussolini announced that any Ethiopian prisoners would now be executed as 'rebels': his generals were authorised to continue using poison gas and to carry out a 'systematic policy of terrorism and extermination' so long as it could be kept secret. In particular, they were instructed to eliminate the small class of intellectuals who might lead a resistance movement, and to do this by executing ten Ethiopians for every Italian casualty.[114]

By creating an Italian empire, Mussolini reached the goal he had set himself many years earlier. The Italian public was delighted at being told that

Ethiopians were unanimously hailing the conquerors for bringing civilisation, justice and the virtues of western civilisation, while the rest of Europe was reassured by being informed that Italy was now a 'satisfied power' without further territorial ambitions. Fascism would now be conservative, against violence, against the revolutionaries, and 'on the other side of the barricades'; he further promised the British that there was no substance in the rumour that he meant to recruit a large army of Ethiopians – none of these remarks was true, but he hoped they would be believed.[115]

Mussolini privately confessed that bringing about such a war had perhaps been immoral but it was also his belief that success was the only acceptable morality in politics.[116] 'The greatest colonial war in all history' had been planned and won by him personally, as he hoped everyone realised, and he ordered that the achievements of his field commanders – De Bono, Badoglio and Graziani – should not be allowed to obscure the glory that belonged to himself.[117] The victory was described as 'a masterpiece' that had astonished the world, since the military experts of Europe were said to have been convinced that Ethiopia was unbeatable, and foreigners were hired to write books that were then quoted in Italy as evidence of unanimous admiration abroad.[118] The fact that some foreign experts thought the campaign could have been won in half the time[119] was not mentioned.

The cost of the war is hard to estimate; Ethiopians, by their own probably exaggerated account, lost anything up to half a million lives, while Italy gave her own losses as about 5,000 soldiers, mostly coloured colonial troops. Mussolini commented unkindly that he wished more Italians had been killed so as to make the war seem more serious.[120] In terms of money, he had spent nearly an entire year's national revenue.[121] The necessary replacements of war material expended in Africa were thought to be equivalent to the strength of seventy-five divisions or, in financial terms, to the whole military budget for the next three years.[122] Mussolini, however, thought he could make people believe that the army emerged from the war stronger in weapons and material than ever before.[123] With equal exaggeration he spoke of the new colony as a 'promised land', the solution to Italy's economic problems,[124] whereas in fact it was to prove an enormous drain on her limited resources.[125]

The needs of propaganda demanded the perpetuation of many such delusions, and yet it was easy for observers out of range of his propaganda to see that this vast effort left Italy much weaker than before. Her long supply route to the Red Sea was costly and extremely vulnerable, especially now that Mussolini's bullying threats encouraged an unwilling Britain to rearm even faster. Economic sanctions, though ineffectively applied, had still been damaging. By alienating the western democracies, Mussolini was pushed closer to a German alliance and so began to lose Italy's one great advantage of being able to play off both major power groups against one another. His options in foreign policy were rapidly disappearing: he was now a marked man – the United States was encouraged to think of the fascists as a pack of unscrupulous gangsters, and a number of people were beginning to suggest once again that he was, if not mentally deranged, at least capable of another 'mad dog act' somewhere else.[126]

The negative aspects of his African victory were fully understood only later. In the short run he had successfully challenged fifty nations in the League; he had briefly become the central figure in world politics and made the British accept that he had defied them and won. Inside Italy he had convinced many doubters of his genius and reached what may have been his moment of greatest popularity.

But though he spoke of being satisfied and without further ambitions, Mussolini convinced himself that if he could win the greatest colonial war in human history he had the capacity to do something still bigger. 'Whoever stops is lost', he said to an old acquaintance, and would not have admitted that this was a dangerous slogan. Somehow he was going to set up a large metallurgical industry in Ethiopia capable of producing all the arms needed for the million soldiers he was going to recruit there, and he let it be known that he was busy learning Amharic as befitted an imperial ruler.[127] Already in March 1936 he spoke of the inevitability of another war and of the need to direct the whole of the nation's economy to this one end: a large part of industry would have to stop working for private consumers and concentrate solely on arms production.[128] Some of his ministers eventually recognised that this over-confidence, resulting from a too easy triumph over the poorly equipped and disorganised Ethiopian armies, was a trick of fate luring him along the road to final defeat.[129]

The months following the Ethiopian war registered a new peak in the religion of *ducismo* and it would have taken a stronger personality than Mussolini's to resist the flattery now lavished upon him: peasants knelt to him in the fields, women held up their children for him to bless,[130] and cabinet ministers were expected to stand in his presence for hours at a time. Now was the time when Starace laid down the general rule for interviews that people should run all the way to the Duce's desk and then run out at the double, stopping to salute at the door.[131]

Some people must have realised that this was excessive and dangerous, but he himself did not. A bevy of semi-official, over-paid journalists ingratiated themselves by promulgating the by now familiar clichés that he was a minor divinity, an agent of God working in history, ruler of a race destined to dominate the centuries.[132] His mother became a cult figure to whose memory schoolchildren intoned the *Felix Mater*, while his own birthplace and the tomb of his parents were made into shrines where visitors would come to kneel in thanksgiving.[133] A new edition of Pini's – officially inspired – biography claimed (in a passage prudently deleted from the English translation) that he was regarded throughout the world as a superman, even as the greatest genius alive; those who thought this were said to include Gandhi, Douglas Fairbanks, Kipling, De Valera, Stravinsky, Lehar, Pierpont Morgan, Franklin Roosevelt and 'an infinity of others'.[134]

War in Spain, 1936–7

Mussolini once criticised Napoleon for a flaw in his character by which dreams of empire and military victories eventually overwhelmed him and led to his fall,[135] but by 1936 others perceived this very flaw in the Duce.[136] Less and less could he bear to hear his wisdom called into question or even appreciate praise unless it was excessive. Yvon De Begnac, a journalist who got to know him well at this period, was struck by his terrifying solitude and loss of contact with ordinary humankind, while he even disliked receiving helpful suggestions lest they should seem an implied criticism of something he had omitted to do. He preferred to be surrounded by applauding crowds and admiring courtiers so as to be quite sure that his authority was unchallenged.[137]

One of his old and trusted colleagues on the *Popolo d'Italia*, Ottavio Dinale, was brave enough to warn him to leave well enough alone in foreign policy now that he had reached such a pinnacle of success, and at home to avoid cutting himself off from others or trusting simply in his interior voices. He replied that, unlike other dictators, he was immune to the dangers of vainglory and self-deceit. Eschewing false modesty, he compared himself to Garibaldi and Cesare Borgia; he was 'the invincible Duce' – an appellation he had once found tiresome but which now gave him an almost voluptuous pleasure. He told Dinale that 'the conquest of Ethiopia is not a goal in itself but one step towards other goals that I already have clearly in mind'. Meanwhile he was 'on the alert, studying history, waiting to choose the right timing', governed not by caprice but by a directing providence and an overwhelming sense of mission.[138]

Another old acquaintance who had been away for three years was the fascist diplomat, Roberto Cantalupo, who observed on returning to Italy in 1936 that the Duce had put on a lot of weight, and that his eyes were vitreous and abstracted as though he no longer saw those to whom he was talking. More than ever he spoke in private as though lecturing to a large crowd, as if trying to show what an immense distance separated him from ordinary mortals. He radiated the same personal fascination that Cantalupo remembered from earlier days and gave the same impression of immense controlled force, but now seemed to dwell in a world apart where he no longer wanted or needed to be informed about what was happening outside.[139]

Another of Mussolini's great admirers, the former *squadrista* Giuseppe Bottai, who was the second longest holder of ministerial office under fascism, noted this change in his diary and was discouraged as he saw the growing difficulty of penetrating such a closed personality. According to Bottai, the old disputatious Mussolini had given way to someone who cut every subject short with a simple order *ex cathedra*. He might listen to objections but no longer took them in, because he could not afford to let others imagine that he ever had doubts or second thoughts. Bottai had his own reasons for pandering to this sense of infallibility, as did so many others who could not bear to resign from their positions of profit and power, but many of them felt something was wrong; they knew Mussolini was being taken over by his own myth and becoming obsessed by it.[140]

A similar story was told by one of the more successful fascist ambassadors, Giuseppe Bastianini, who in 1936 found himself in close proximity to Mussolini after a decade away from him. Bastianini now described him as seeking to conceal a timid personality by consciously trying to make himself feared, as a result of which he was unable to speak freely to those around him. It was as though an invisible partition separated him from others and anyone who came too close was humiliated or punished. Surrounding himself with nobodies, he less and less saw politics as the art of finding agreement or composing differences, but liked to hit out, to stop others taking any initiative, to act as though he could 'take the world by assault' on his own. Any minister who dared to suggest that Britain was still a power to be reckoned with might be angrily told to hold his tongue. The other fascists, said Bastianini, had given up trying to speak honestly and openly to someone who had such an imperative need to believe he was always in the right. Luckily, he changed his mind so often that if they wanted anything they could often just wait for the wind to change; hence they connived at a defective system because they had learnt how to profit from it.[141]

The habit of double-talk, like his quick changes of opinion, was something the Duce tried to justify by claiming that it reflected the complication and subtlety of his inner thoughts. According to one devotedly loyal minister, Alfredo Rocco, his mind habitually moved 'not in a straight line, but zig-zag, giving different people holding different opinions the idea that he agreed with them, when really he was merely trying to make up his own mind for himself'.[142] Another slightly more critical and less committed ministerial colleague, Baron Pompeo Aloisi, observed the extraordinary fact that it was his customary method in foreign affairs to follow two different and sometimes opposing policies simultaneously, 'trusting that the complications which might develop would eventually liberate him from any contradictory engagements'.[143]

He now seemed bored with domestic matters: his time, he said, was more than ever taken up with foreign affairs – that is, with devising means of imposing his own views on other countries.[144] Italy's foreign policy hitherto, both before and during fascism, had tended towards trying to preserve an equilibrium of power in Europe that would let her act as a makeweight and so give an illusion of strength, but he was now confident enough to think of upsetting that equilibrium so as to exploit a more destabilised European system. By challenging the League of Nations, he had forced the rest of the world to bend to his will,[145] and he did not intend to let Italians enjoy the easy pleasures of peace. They had somehow to be given a 'warlike mentality', and in 1936 he was already looking forward to a larger European war that would be a test of his own skill and the strength of the fascist revolution.[146]

Other people could now recognise, as Contarini had observed ten years earlier, that he was not interested in negotiation as a way of resolving international differences so much as in manufacturing additional tensions in order to frighten other countries into buying his goodwill.[147] He knew that France and Britain were not ready for war and were prepared to pay a high price for peace, and he could exploit this fact at home by creating the exciting sensation that Italy was feared abroad. In particular he was hoping that the British might give way to some of his demands if he threatened to ally himself with Hitler.[148]

His suggestion to the Germans in May 1935 that the two countries should come closer together[149] had met with little initial enthusiasm from Hitler, because the latter, though he liked Mussolini and badly needed a friend in Europe, regarded fascist Italy with some disparagement and would have preferred a British to an Italian alliance.[150] Later in the year, Italian representatives attended the nazi rally at Nuremberg which greatly impressed them and, in September, talks took place between the heads of German and Italian military intelligence.[151] By the end of 1935, Mussolini was assuming that a return by Germany to a position of strength in Europe would help Italy, and was still confident that he could stop this readjustment of the balance of power from going too far.[152] After war broke out in Ethiopia he dropped another hint about arranging a closer alliance with Germany and argued that fascist ideology was creating a common link between the two countries: he flatteringly called Hitler a genius and told him that there was a bond between them 'dictated by destiny and which was bound to become stronger and stronger'.[153] Hitler still did not take the hint – perhaps he knew that the fascists were making entirely contradictory proposals to the French.[154] While he did not want the Italians to be beaten in Ethiopia, he did not want them to be too successful either, so at the same time as he helped by selling them weapons and coal, he secretly assisted the Ethiopians and was glad that prolongation of the war gave him a chance to conquer Italy's markets in the Balkans.[155]

Hitler also took the opportunity of the Ethiopian crisis to march German troops into the demilitarised Rhineland. Though the success of this bold challenge to democratic Europe surprised and indeed alarmed Mussolini, it also reinforced his interest in a German alliance. A few days later, on 1 April 1936, he ordered the Italian press to do an about-turn and become pro-German. At the same time his police chief, Bocchini, signed an agreement with Himmler and agreed to collaborate closely with the Gestapo; this was followed by talks between the general staffs of the two armies.[156]

Mussolini nevertheless continued to give formal assurances to France and Britain that he was really on their side, not on that of Germany;[157] and when the Germans discovered this and complained about his double policy, he begged them not to be too offended if he had to tell lies in London.[158] With equal dissimulation he sometimes went on saying that he would never allow a union between Germany and Austria,[159] at the same time as he was already beginning to admit, against the advice of his own foreign office, that Austrian independence might have to be sacrificed as the price of an entente with Germany.[160]

In June 1936 he appointed as foreign minister the 33-year-old Galeazzo Ciano, whose chief – some said only – qualifications for the post were that he was the Duce's son-in-law, admirer and flatterer. Ciano belonged to a faction in the fascist party which was coming round to the view that Italy, instead of aiming to be the makeweight in the balance of power or a pendulum swinging between one power group and another, should opt frankly for a German alliance. This faction agreed with Mussolini that the western democracies were decadent and corrupted by the Jews, whereas Germans, Italians and Japanese would be the dominant races of tomorrow: Italians were surely clever enough to be able to exploit German power without being exploited and, in alliance with Germany, would eventually reach a position where they could dominate Europe for a century.[161]

Ciano's first task was to arrange Italy's intervention in the Spanish Civil War. Mussolini had a poor opinion of Spaniards because of what he took to be an Arab element in their racial composition,[162] but was concerned to ensure that Spain, while not being allowed to become too powerful, was brought into the fascist orbit as 'a card to play against the British'.[163] He had already sent arms to right-wing movements there and given military training in Italy to Spanish groups aiming to overthrow the government in Madrid.[164] After backing one *coup* that failed, he was at first reluctant to help General Franco's mutiny, but agreed to send a few transport planes after convincing himself that these would be enough to bring about a quick and complete victory.[165]

The calculation was badly wrong and, once the prestige of Italian fascism was involved, he had to send ever-increasing help, despite his formal protestation that he was observing a strict neutrality and had no dealings at all with Franco.[166] The military leaders in Italy, who knew the real weakness of their forces, were far from happy about this military intervention, especially when dreams of a quick victory evaporated.[167] But Mussolini kept the operation out of their hands and in those of Ciano.

When troops had to be sent to Spain, the Duce was hoping to rely less on regular soldiers than on the blackshirt militia, and this proved to be another mistake. He gave orders to select 'volunteers' who were tall enough to be a good advertisement for fascism when seen alongside Spanish soldiers,[168] but some were drafted against their will and many arrived without even elementary training in the weapons they were expected to use:[169] once more, as in Ethiopia, the regular army was forced to take over. At one point, an attempt was made to persuade the Germans to co-ordinate a joint intervention in Spain and bring the war to a quick end, but they were not keen and, indeed, realised the advantages of Italy's being tied down in another debilitating war that would further antagonise the western democracies.[170]

One immediate success was the Italian occupation of the Balearic Islands where Mussolini had the idea of setting up a permanent military base for future use against France.[171] One of the more brutal militia leaders, Arconovaldo Bonaccorsi, was sent to act as proconsul in Majorca and, within weeks, a fascist reign of terror, including an indiscriminate massacre of prisoners, was reviving memories of the worst excesses of *squadrismo*.[172] Exactly the same was happening simultaneously in East Africa where Marshal Graziani, applauded by Mussolini for his fascist zeal, continued to carry out mass daily executions.[173]

In September 1936, Mussolini was invited to Germany. He accepted but asked to be allowed to wait until the groundwork had been properly prepared for the meeting, because any visit would have to be a tumultuous success in terms of propaganda for the Duce.[174] One preliminary request he made without avail was that the nazis should play down their 'hatred against Catholicism'; he was not so worried by their anti-semitism, but rightly predicted that nazi religious policy would make it hard for the Italian public to welcome a full alliance.[175] Other political differences were less important, especially when Hitler promised to leave Italy a free hand in the Mediterranean.[176] Mussolini tried to convince the Germans that Italy had complete air supremacy in *mare nostrum* and that the British Mediterranean fleet was at his mercy. He agreed to back any German demand for colonies, but warned the nazis against making any agreement behind his back with Britain and still less with France, both of which were nations in decline.[177] The German entente was something he wanted exclusively for Italy.

In October he sent Ciano to Berlin to confirm the existence of what he publicly referred to as the Italo-German axis.[178] To erect a more substantial barrier between Germany and Britain he also sent copies of intercepted British documents to suggest, quite falsely, that the British were preparing for war against the two fascist states: fortunately – so Ciano now told people – Italy was now superior in military strength to either Britain or France, so there was nothing to fear from any British action.[179]

In reply, Hitler again confirmed that Germany looked to eastern Europe and the Baltic for her expansion so that Italy could have the Mediterranean to herself, adding with well-calculated flattery that 'Mussolini is the leading statesman in the world, to whom no one else can be remotely compared'.[180] Ciano came back from Berlin confident that he 'had the Germans in my pocket' and Hitler was a scatterbrained lightweight who entirely lacked Mussolini's gifts and could be easily manipulated to serve Italian interests.[181]

The formation of this axis gave Mussolini a frisson of excitement and once again he spoke of his eagerness to show his prowess as a military leader. By October 1936 he already had a clear idea as to how he would make a surprise attack on the British fleet in Malta: the war, he calculated, would be over in seven weeks. The chief journals of the regime took up this theme and repeated how the fascists had developed a new style of attack based on the *squadrismo* technique; this so-called 'lightning attack' could defeat any other country; the democracies should have learnt by now that their idea of collective security was an illusion – fascism preferred to rely on its own armed might to obtain a fairer share of the world's riches.[182]

Mussolini knew from the foreign press and from intercepts that he was increasingly disliked and mocked in London. Unaccustomed to criticism and derision, he sometimes reacted to this by an uncontrolled anger.[183] It was insulting to have fascism compared to a Latin American dictatorship, especially when the comparison was made by 'inferior races' in northern Europe who had been deceived by mendacious historians such as Hume and Gibbon to look on Italy with disrespect;[184] Britain was perhaps jealous of Italy's new strength under fascism, or possibly just unable to realise that the British Empire was doomed and a new Italian empire had inherited the task of defending western civilisation and the white races.[185]

Mussolini's contempt for the British had been increased by the fact that he thought they were afraid to fight to stop the Ethiopian war in September 1935. In fact he went much further and propagated the story that they, as well as the Ethiopians, had been beaten in that war.[186] Theirs, he claimed, was a decadent and impoverished society that had not changed since Dickens' time;[187] articles in his monthly magazine pointed out that the British had no literature, no art, no scholarship; they knew nothing of other countries and were preoccupied only with their immediate material interests.[188] The average Englishman was stupid and took a week to puzzle out what an Italian understood in no time at all.[189] The spread of communism, he said, was a very real threat in Britain;[190] her fleet was no longer effective, which meant that London was indefensible. Moreover, the Italian air force was so strong that war against Britain would hold no terrors.[191]

He added that both the British and the French, as well as lacking brains and material power, had a declining population, which fact alone meant that Italy could challenge them without risk.[192] To Mussolini's mind – and the office of statistics under his personal supervision carefully monitored the falling birth rate in each major country – this fall in population was fundamental, 'the problem above all other problems': population growth was much more important than increased arms production in deciding which country would win the next war.[193] For this very odd reason he claimed that the United States would soon cease to exist as a serious nation, and in twenty years' time the population of France and Britain would be reduced by almost half and be composed only of the old. 'No one over the age of forty likes to fight', he believed. Already there were in Britain four million more women than men – sexually unsatisfied and hence pacifist by nature, afraid of the pain of childbirth and hence unworthy of empire; when he spoke on this topic he became agitated and vehement to a degree that his hearers sometimes found astonishing.[194]

Even stranger was his continuing conviction that by an act of will he could reverse the decline of the birth rate in Italy; if he failed, he said, Italy would have no future,[195] but he was confident that if he directed Italians to feel a proper sense of mission they would increase the size of their families to between eight and twenty children.[196] For this purpose, female emancipation had to be reversed and male supremacy entrenched more firmly into the legal system. He gave special praise to those who called intellectual women a monstrosity, for which reason higher education for women should preferably be reduced to those subjects where the 'feminine brain' could adequately operate – for example, household management. In this way they could be returned from the employment market to their natural function of child-bearing.[197]

Mussolini put his whole heart into this 'battle for births'. Each year he honoured the ninety-five most prolific Italian mothers at an elaborate ceremony in the Palazzo Venezia, giving each a monetary prize and a free insurance policy; in 1939 he added a special medal with a silver bar for each child in the family.[198] To his chagrin, the nazis seemed to succeed better in increasing the birth rate, but he tried to persuade himself that Italians, with their greater sense of discipline, would eventually surpass the more individualistic Germans and before long the population of the two nations would be almost identical.[199]

Unfortunately, however, he eventually had to admit that he was wrong. In the thirteen years after 1924, Italy 'lost' the equivalent of fifteen army divisions because of births that had not taken place.[200] This was due to the 'bourgeois egoism' of those who wanted comfort and convenience rather than produce soldiers for the fatherland.[201] Moreover, the number of women in work was inexplicably growing, despite law after law, and this was true even inside the state administration: which was immoral as well as unfair to men without jobs.[202] When he drew up a list of the top *gerarchi* to examine their performance, he was appalled to find some of them actually unmarried and the rest with an average of only two children each: it was a disgraceful case of 'unfecundity all down the line.'[203]

Possibly this sense of disillusionment, together with the unexpected continuance of the Spanish Civil War, were factors in his decision not to burn his boats too finally with the declining populations of the west. In November 1936 he asked the British to make what he called a 'gentleman's agreement' in which both sides would renounce any change in the territorial status quo in the Mediterranean, the very place where he was secretly determined to make such a change. The agreement was signed in January 1937, although Anthony Eden, the British foreign secretary, disliked the reference to gentlemen because 'Mussolini has the mentality of a gangster'. While Grandi heroically continued to deny that Italian soldiers were drafted to Spain, the Duce was in fact using these negotiations with the British to confuse them or distract their attention from the fact of Italian intervention – throughout January he continued to send a shipload of men and munitions to Spain each day, and the British secret service knew of this immediately and in detail.[204]

Some Italian experts, notably the then ambassador in Spain, Cantalupo, almost at once perceived that intervention in the Civil War was an expensive mistake founded on the naïve miscalculation that Franco could win in a matter of weeks. Early in 1937 Cantalupo advised disengagement, but Mussolini convinced himself that Madrid was about to fall and had no notion that the war could last for two more years. He also had the far-fetched idea of persuading Franco to accept an Italian king of Spain.[205] Best of all would be a purely Italian military victory there, and, in the hope of winning the race for Madrid, he went against Franco's wishes by encouraging his Italian expeditionary force to push ahead too fast;[206] the result was a military defeat at Guadalajara. So much had been written about fascist martial qualities and superiority in battle that this minor reverse came as a stunning blow to morale, all the more depressing in that the victors were anti-fascists – many of them Italian anti-fascists. They were not even trained soldiers but simply an improvised multinational army of amateurs.[207]

Many of the fascist soldiery in Spain had been so patronising that there was a good deal of secret pleasure among their Spanish colleagues over this setback, and Franco dropped hints that he would not be sorry to see the Italians go home altogether.[208] Mussolini, on the other hand, had no alternative but to stay until fascism was victorious[209] – to such an extent had ideological considerations swamped those of national interest. He was in Tripoli when he heard the news from Guadalajara, but, without waiting for details, issued a story blaming the defeat on Franco[210] and promised that the reverse would be fully avenged in two weeks' time.[211] When nothing happened, he turned his skilled hand to persuading public opinion that Guadalajara had not been a defeat but a victory,[212] and perhaps some people believed him.

To help maintain this illusion he banned the entry into Italy of English newspapers containing articles about weaknesses in the Italian army or which referred to atrocities committed in Ethiopia; any such criticism was unforgiveable and had to be kept out of the hands of Italian readers. He had just ordered the Italian press to stop its anti-British campaign,[213] but the very next day ordered the exact opposite. When the British government refused his request to censor hostile articles,[214] he told Italian journalists in London to retaliate by 'stressing any unfortunate incident that may happen' during the coronation of George VI: their job was to slant the news in general so that Italians learnt to despise and hate the western democracies.[215] He claimed that he was 'imperturbably calm' despite all the 'hysterical oratory from Anglican pulpits', but Ciano observed that he was more angry over these imputations of military inadequacy than he had been at the imposition of sanctions in 1935.[216] This was an ominous and dangerous symptom.

A more serious retaliation was the murder of Carlo Rosselli, a military leader on the opposite side in Spain, and thought to be the most dangerous of Italian anti-fascists. In June 1937, Rosselli and his brother were assassinated in France after an earlier attempt had failed,[217] and it became known subsequently that the killing was organised by the Italian military intelligence organisation which was responsible to Ciano and to the minister of war, Mussolini.[218] No documentary evidence exists to show that the Duce was directly involved and later he accepted that the murder – like those of Matteotti and Amendola – had been greatly damaging to him, but this carefully planned crime, like the other two, could not have been committed had it not been thought to be his wish.

There is no doubt that his own personal orders were responsible in the summer of 1937 for Italian submarines torpedoing neutral ships which were suspected of carrying supplies for the Spanish republicans. Mussolini was secretly proud of these acts of piracy, though Italian responsibility was insistently denied.[219] In no case was warning given, nor were the submarines allowed to surface and save survivors – a fact that, though it was understandable enough, caused enormous indignation.[220] When his naval commanders raised moral and practical objections, Mussolini told them to redouble the number of attacks,[221] and forty submarines were eventually employed until he discovered from the Germans that the British were intercepting their radio messages and knew who was responsible.[222] This realisation, together with the French and British announcement that they would sink any suspected submarines, made a change of policy advisable.

The axis with Germany

12

The first year of the axis, 1937

The experience of two wars in Ethiopia and Spain stimulated rather than reduced Mussolini's instinctive delight in 'punitive action'. He had to hurry because he now knew that the decadent, pacifist British were engaged on a programme of rearmament that would easily outstrip his own if he waited too long before provoking a European war. In a private address to senior army officers, in March 1937, he spoke of his plan to destroy England and stated casually that he was preparing to start a war against the British in North Africa; this came as another shock to the generals, who had not seriously considered fighting Britain and had concentrated on the traditional hypothesis of an Alpine war.[1] In the Duce's view, however, France no longer counted – he was now going to concentrate on defeating the British and was already building up a locally recruited army in Africa for the purpose. Once again he spoke threateningly of his intention to sweep away the lingering remains of democratic ideals in Europe.[2]

Just possibly this belligerent attitude may not have been meant altogether seriously, but, whether genuine or artificial, his warlike rhetoric was developing a new intensity. He again professed his pleasure at being hated by foreigners and sharply corrected those who assumed that Italy could not afford an armaments race. The Italian armed services were said to be at the peak of perfection, able to outdo those of Britain, especially now that preparation for war had been placed at the very centre of Italian national life.[3]

Mussolini was constructing a naval base at Pantelleria, a rock-bound island in the straits of Sicily whose military importance he claimed to have discovered entirely by himself. He insisted that the Mediterranean could, as a result, be blocked to all hostile shipping whenever he wished, and in January 1937 his own newspaper was ordered to delete any non-Italian flag from photographs of this 'Roman sea'.[4] He confirmed to his cabinet that his black army would eventually control the whole of Africa and, meanwhile, he was sending more troops to Spain in order to give more Italians a personal experience of war.[5]

In earlier years he had frankly acknowledged his own incompetence in military questions,[6] but as minister for the three armed services he now insisted on personally deciding the smallest details.[7] Saluted by the

213

propagandists as a military genius deeply versed in matters of war, he pretended he spent the greater part of his time on nothing else.[8] As for the chiefs of staff, they were permitted little initiative and rarely consulted, while the Supreme Commission for Defence met once a year and was allowed to consider only technical or industrial matters, never strategy, never what kind of war to prepare for or against what enemy.[9] The upshot was that when the war Mussolini had been predicting for years actually came about in 1940, Italy was without the right weapons or even any effective plan of operations.[10]

Here his experience as a newspaper editor failed him because he was nearing the outer limit of what mere propaganda could achieve. His very excellence as a phrase-maker and coiner of headlines gave a false idea of the extent of military preparations. One of his catchwords had referred to the 'lightning war' that Italy was now ready to undertake: any expert who so much as hinted that this was fantasy was sacked,[11] and the army leaders who survived in office tended to be those who reinforced his conviction that planning for a long war, or even for a greater degree of mechanisation, was unnecessary.

Another journalistic phrase of his referred to Italy's 'eight million bayonets'; it was first heard in October 1936, and frequent usage thereafter reinforced the impression that an army of eight million soldiers could be mobilised in a matter of hours. This faulty assumption was easily exposed by knowledgeable elements of the foreign press, but not in Italy.[12] By doctoring the statistics, Mussolini first arrived at a figure which sounded impressive, after which his only option was to increase it, until eventually the authoritative announcement was made that twelve million soldiers were available and all splendidly equipped with modern weapons.[13] The true figure was less than one million and, despite much talk about tanks, the Italian army, whether in actuality or on the drawing-board, had nothing heavier than a three-ton armoured car.

This boasting about a quick victory and vastly superior numbers was no doubt intended to deter enemies and impress Italians, but many foreigners did not believe it,[14] whereas many Italians were thereby given quite unrealistic expectations that made war more likely. General Pariani, the chief of army staff and under-secretary for war, pretended that by early 1939 the army would be fully equipped for what he called an inevitable war against France and Britain: he was certain that such a war could be won, and talked of having plans ready for a surprise attack on Egypt, as well as on France and Switzerland.[15]

As other countries were beginning to suspect, Mussolini was intending to use poison gas on a big scale,[16] and it is just possible that he had persuaded himself he could thus obviate the necessity for a serious rearmament programme. But a more plausible explanation of his over-confidence was that he had promoted fascists to top military posts – men such as Pariani, who realised that to keep their place they had to reinforce the Duce's wishful thinking and cover any traces of their own inefficiency or corrupt practices. Mussolini had once promised he would never bring politics into the armed services, but had, in fact, done just that.[17] Pariani was much worse than incompetent: he helped to persuade Mussolini that he could fight and win a 'lightning war'.

By the autumn of 1937 a good deal was already known about the immense German rearmament programme,[18] and Mussolini had half made up his mind, despite occasional second thoughts, to convert the informal axis into a formal alliance with Germany in preparation for war.[19] He did all he could to persuade Hitler that Italy would be a strong and reliable ally. Exchanges of visits took place between fascist and nazi leaders, and a tentative – if unfruitful – move was made to exchange military information and harmonise plans.[20] General von Blomberg, the German minister of war, attended the Italian military manoeuvres in August and it was announced that he had been greatly impressed. But the truth was that, since he was seriously disturbed by the backwardness of Italian weapons and training, special representations had to be made in Berlin for him to comment favourably in public.[21] Italians were being told that these manoeuvres proved the Italian army to be the best in the world and to have the future of Europe in its hands;[22] no doubts on this point could be allowed to percolate through to the general public.

At the end of September it was thought in Rome that the two regimes were sufficiently close for Mussolini to accept the invitation to visit Germany. The message he now took to Berlin was a pledge of solidarity with nazism in hastening the process by which Europe was to become fascist; the two countries might differ on minor points, but they had the same enemies; together, Italy and Germany could confront the world with a solid mass of 115 million people united in a single unshakeable objective, and an incautious promise was now made by the Duce that 'we shall march together to the very end'.[23]

His large entourage for this visit was specially fitted out with gaudy uniforms in order to look impressive. They were greeted on their arrival by the nazi leaders drawn up in formation, and for hour after hour had to watch a march-past of disciplined storm-troopers; the welcome by the public was, to Hitler's chagrin, less effusive. Mussolini was taken to see blast furnaces, rolling mills, arms factories, and the tomb of Frederick the Great, as well as watching Goering play with his toy electric railway. The army manoeuvres laid on for him were the largest ever staged in Germany, but he claimed to be only moderately impressed and Marshal Badoglio assured him that Italy was ahead in such matters.[24] The high point was an address he made to a conscripted audience at a mass open-air meeting in Berlin during a drenching thunderstorm.

There was little time in four days for serious political discussion, but he gave the Germans a clear impression that he was prepared to concede an *Anschluss* with Austria in return for a strengthening of the axis.[25] He told them that he had begun to follow their example with an increasingly rigorous policy of anti-semitism.[26] Hitler afterwards regaled his cronies with a mocking impersonation of Mussolini's oratory, but hoped nevertheless that the Italians were so impressed with what they had seen that they would now accept German leadership.[27]

The Duce was greatly flattered by his reception and Italian newspapers called it an 'apotheosis'.[28] He did not immediately agree to a formal alliance, but his foreign office spoke as though only the formalities were wanting and it would have been hard to back down after his public commitment to march together to the end. He accepted and welcomed that the long-term result would be war, and said that the Germans could direct the actual fighting as long as they left political questions to him, he having more experience in such matters.[29] While he kept up the pretence that he had nothing to learn from what he had found in Germany – to his delight, some of the nazi parades had gone badly wrong – he was full of admiration and came home with the conviction that such people must be truly invincible.[30] He continued to speak in public of his commitment to peace, but in unsigned articles repeated that fascists believed in fighting and, as the democracies were pacifist, the fascist states would have no trouble in starting the war at the precise moment that suited them best.[31]

Ciano wondered if the time had not already come for 'the supreme game' to begin.[32] Mussolini repeated to him that Italians 'needed to have their character forged in battle' and had to be kept alert by being 'kicked in the shins', but better wait until the Spanish conflict was over before 'inventing' another war – that would be the time to finish England once and for all.[33] He was continuing to gather an army in North Africa because someone had convinced him that British troops could not fight in the tropical heat,[34] and it was known that quantities of gas bombs were kept in depots close to the Egyptian frontier. Stores of arms were also being assembled near the French frontier in case a right-wing revolt broke out in France that would give him an excuse to intervene.[35]

Despite the fact that the Spanish war was unpopular in Italy,[36] Mussolini continued, strangely, to view it as a means of toughening up Italians and making them more warlike.[37] Just as he had done in Ethiopia, he ordered the terrorist bombing of civilian targets in an attempt to break the enemy's morale and was delighted when this increased foreign dislike of Italy; he described such bombing as an essentially fascist method of warfare and was secretly proud of it. Nevertheless he instructed the Italian press to conceal some of the facts in view of his public assurances that he would never allow an attack on civilian populations.[38] Franco was indignant when this terroristic bombing took place without his knowledge or approval. Mussolini, however, was ready to go even further and use germ warfare if necessary. Some of the less attractive aspects of his character were again emerging as they had in 1921–4 and, indeed, as they did at any moment when the ordinary conventions of civilised behaviour seemed unrewarding. He ordered that anti-fascist Italians captured in Spain as prisoners of war should be executed, since 'dead men tell no tales'.[39]

In December 1937 he summoned the Grand Council for a meeting at which it was decided to leave the League of Nations. The meeting lasted only two minutes and, outside the Palazzo Venezia, the crowds had been assembling to salute the decision; evidently the consent of the supreme directing body of fascism was taken for granted, and some of its members claimed to be frightened as well as humiliated by this new evidence that the regime was becoming more obviously the uncontrolled dictatorship of a single man.[40]

The Council was not even consulted formally when Italy signed a tripartite pact with Germany and Japan against communism. Hitherto fascists had been strongly against the Japanese and in favour of the Chinese leader, Chiang Kai-shek, who was at war with Japan. But at the end of 1937, Mussolini unexpectedly changed sides in order to conform with German policy, and various military and financial missions were suddenly withdrawn from China. By encouraging Japan, just as by encouraging the Arab revolt in Palestine, he hoped to weaken the position of Britain in the Middle and Far East.

Ciano noted that he had rarely seen Mussolini so happy because, alongside Germany and Japan, he felt at the centre of the 'most formidable political and military combination that has ever existed'.[41] The order was given that a cargo of Italian arms on its way to China (which had already been paid for) should be deliberately wrecked in the South China Sea so as not to offend his new Japanese friends.[42] The newspapers were told to bring their editorial policy into line, and earlier articles against the 'yellow peril' had to give way to praise of the Japanese as a master race with undoubted Aryan credentials.[43]

The *Anschluss* and the racial laws, 1938

In February 1938, Mussolini confirmed to the Germans that preparations to fight Britain were continuing and he still felt that Italy was sufficiently strong on her own not to need active German help.[44] At the same time, he tried to allay any British apprehension by offering them another 'pact of friendship'. He privately accepted that the nazification of Austria was inescapable, though he mistakenly assumed that Hitler would warn Italy in time to prepare the Italian public for this *volte-face*.[45]

Meanwhile he was determined to introduce a further element of 'prussianisation' to give Italians more backbone,[46] and his soldiers were ordered to adopt the German goose step as a symbol of their new aggressive spirit. At its first public appearance, Mussolini surprised everyone by jumping down from his podium and leading the parade to show how it should be done.[47] To those who murmured against such a patent imitation of Germany, he indignantly replied that this was something quite different – it was the marching step of the ancient Roman legions – and anyway 'the goose was a Roman bird' that had once saved ancient Rome from attack by its cackling on the Capitol.[48] It was a sign of his poor judgement that this new parade step was said to be 'immensely important' for national morale and 'a serious warning to Italy's enemies': whereas in fact it provoked much secret derision and, as one fascist wrote, mockery is highly dangerous for a dictatorship.[49]

In March 1938, Hitler marched into Austria after notifying Rome only at the very last moment. Italy thus lost the immense advantage of having only a weak buffer state on her northern frontier. Having often promised in the past that he would fight to defend Austrian independence,[50] Mussolini in late February privately repeated his assurances of help to the Austrians, but now in March lamely protested that he had never said anything so foolish.[51] When he told parliament that the two totalitarian regimes shared common goals and would continue to march in step, his words were greeted with the usual ecstatic applause. Indeed, few days passed without the deputies rising to their feet to salute him in disciplined chorus and it sometimes happened many times in a single day; on this occasion, as a bonus, he ended his speech by chanting 'Giovinezza', quickly joined by all the deputies and the occupants of the public galleries.[52]

Hitler had been careful not to tell Mussolini of his plans to extend Germany's 'living space' and calculated that, as Italy had her hands full in Spain, he could meanwhile take Austria and Czechoslovakia, possibly without offering his partner anything in return.[53] He had gradually been displacing Italy in the commerce of south-eastern Europe and, after annexing Austria, brought the Italian port of Trieste almost to a standstill by severing its former trade routes.[54] Mussolini must have recognised that, despite the organised cheering in parliament, a groundswell of public opinion was emerging convinced that he had made a terrible mistake. There was little he could do about it but he was seriously worried; occasionally he spoke of changing sides in Europe, in which case he would ensure that 'Germany was crushed for at least two centuries', and secretly he decided to embark on an expensive programme of fortification along their new common frontier.[55]

Such behaviour was irresponsible and unrealistic and hardly that of a potential ally, but he still hoped to ride several horses at once – hinting to the Germans about a possible alliance, but also using the threat of such an alliance to force concessions out of the western democracies. Sometimes he continued to toy with the idea of starting a quick war before the democracies were ready; sometimes he preferred simply to use the rhetoric of war to frighten other countries and boost Italian morale, while privately determined to wait another four or five years until rearmament by the axis powers had progressed sufficiently. Parliament was told in March that, with at least eight million soldiers as well as the largest submarine fleet in the world and one of the largest air forces, he was ready for any emergency, and the Italians were given an additional reassurance that he personally would command their armed forces in the event of war. He was greatly envious of Hitler for taking effective command of the army and determined to persuade the king – who, by the terms of Italy's written constitution, was commander-in-chief – to let himself do likewise.[56]

A first step was to give himself military rank and for this purpose a new title was created, that of first marshal of the empire, which would be held only by the king and himself. He pretended a reluctance at accepting this appointment but actually took it with delight. Some of the generals were offended that a civilian possessing only a smattering of knowledge on military matters was being given the most senior rank in the Italian army. But when the news broke in parliament the disciplined deputies once more broke into 'Giovinezza'.[57]

In April 1938 the Duce signed his new pact of friendship with Britain – not wishing, as he put it, to burn all his boats with the other side.[58] But this agreement was purely for show and had no practical effect: the British made its ratification conditional on the withdrawal of Italian troops from Spain, and this was something Mussolini had no intention of permitting until he had avenged his defeat at Guadalajara.

In May, Hitler came to Italy to repay the visit of the previous year. Mussolini took personal charge of the preparations and went over every inch of the route to ensure that houses were painted (or, if necessary, pulled down), false trees erected and artificial façades constructed, to create an illusion of opulence and power. He himself was sure he was laying on a more magnificent display than he had witnessed in Germany[59] and Italian newspapers proudly wrote of the new types of weapons on show. The army leaders were among those who realised that this was simply another façade, and Marshal Graziani noted with dismay that some of the armoured cars carried wooden guns.[60]

Hitler returned home in a sober mood.[61] He had come to Italy in the hope of turning the axis into a formal Italo-German alliance in order to facilitate his next act of aggression – against Czechoslovakia.[62] The Italians, however, were in no hurry and did their best to avoid any serious political discussions:[63] they gave a general assurance of support against the Czechs, but the suggestion of an alliance was left in the air.

Mussolini was determined to use any further German advance as an opportunity to gain something for himself, and this posed a delicate question of timing and synchronisation. In public speeches he continued to proclaim that he was ready for war to assert Italy's domination over other countries, but sometimes realised that he was in danger of going too far and ordered the newspapers to suppress his more bellicose statements.[64] Nevertheless he was infuriated to discover that many Italians wanted a less adventurous foreign policy and were not happy at his remarks about upsetting the international order against the 'so-called demoplutocracies'. He therefore increased the tension, declaring that Italy was in a permanent state of mobilisation for war, and ordered his managers of public opinion to whip up a hate campaign against the French. Italians must be made to believe that the democracies were irremediably behind the times and sufficiently terrorised by the mere thought of war to constitute no danger at all to fascism with its greatly superior military strength.[65]

He was deceiving himself and his people, because other countries had good sources of military information inside Italy and knew as well as the Germans that Italian arms were obsolescent and the eight million soldiers non-existent. He and they were both aware that Italy depended on sea-borne imports; in 1939 an average of forty-four ships docked each day, of which thirty-five had passed through the Straits of Gibraltar – hence, with her lack of foreign currency and few stockpiles of material, Italy was extremely vulnerable to the French and British navies.[66] Possibly he was trying to impress people by the usual rodomontade; just possibly he believed those among his own generals who pretended that they were well ahead of Germany in the technical aspects of rearmament.[67] In fact the Italian army manoeuvres in August again reinforced the Germans in their conviction that his preparations for war were hopelessly backward, but how far he himself knew the full extent of the deficiencies is hard to know.[68]

At this moment he startled everyone by announcing that he was introducing racial laws on the German model as another way of consolidating his new entente. In the past, he and other leading fascists had sometimes categorically denied that any Jewish problem existed in Italy[69] and ridiculed the idea that pure races could exist.[70] Many Jews had been close colleagues of his in the fascist movement and for a time he had encouraged Zionism in the hope of exploiting it for anti-British purposes,[71] while as late as September 1934 he had still been talking of his 'sovereign contempt' for nazi racial doctrines.[72] Nevertheless from early days he had occasionally toyed with the notion that Italians belonged to an Aryan race that was ethnically homogeneous and superior to others — he had been particularly anxious to stress their superiority to Spaniards, Romanians, Greeks and 'Levantines'.[73] He was seriously worried that 'Levantine' qualities might have entered Italy with the slaves imported by the Roman empire and so given foreigners a false impression of the national character: that impression he meant to correct, and it was a pity such elements in the population could not be exterminated.[74] The same inner sensitivity to racial differences explains occasional early remarks against the Jews and the 'Jewish International'.[75] Other fascists had taken anti-semitism to much more extreme lengths;[76] but with Mussolini it was not until he needed to stress the domination of Italians over the Africans of Libya and Ethiopia that he developed his formal doctrine of racial superiority,[77] a doctrine which led him to call the racial question and the need to impose respect on native populations a fundamental fascist concern.[78]

Even in September 1937, he was still insisting that the 40–70,000 Jews in Italy constituted no problem that could be remotely compared to that of Italian coloured subjects in Africa,[79] but for some time before then he had been moving towards a more extreme anti-semitism; he talked early in 1936 of starting an anti-Jewish campaign[80] and by the end of 1936 was already discriminating against Jews by discouraging their employment.[81] Soon afterwards he began to call himself a full-blooded racialist and looked forward to the day when the Italian and German master races, which alone would be free from corruption by the Jews, would be generally recognised for their superior qualities.[82] Possibly it was during his four days in Germany in 1937 that he saw the political usefulness of anti-semitism, and his views developed rapidly in 1938 as he moved closer to a German alliance. Subsequently he tried to excuse himself by accusing the Germans of exerting pressure to push him into a racialist policy,[83] but it is hard to discover evidence of any such pressure; the motive was rather his own spontaneous decision to show solidarity with nazism and provide a convenient scapegoat for the years of austerity that he meant to impose on Italy.

He was, however, fairly cynical about what was a merely tactical move and occasionally continued to state that there was no real Jewish problem in Italy.[84] Then, by the beginning of 1938, the press was encouraged to inform the public that the Jews had wormed their way into strategic positions in Italian life.[85] Already he was thinking out the principles of the 'Charter of Race' which was published in July 1938 and which he claimed was largely drafted by himself.[86] He continued to assert that possession of an East African empire was what forced him to bring these racial questions into the open, yet the charter made it abundantly clear that not just Arabs and Ethiopians, but Jews too were an inferior race. As with the goose step, he was again anxious to insist that he was not copying anyone else; on the contrary he said he had himself been a consistent racialist for the last fifteen years.[87]

It had to be admitted, however, that despite the usual unanimous vote of approval in parliament, the new racial policy was not well received by the public.[88] Italians were therefore told that they must learn to feel like a master race and suppress any sense of pity for the persecuted. Every newspaper was obliged to carry articles justifying persecution and forbidden to print the protest which arrived from the Pope.[89]

Mussolini was especially delighted at the shocked reactions from the democracies.[90] When news arrived of some quite exceptionally savage persecutions by the Germans, he simply noted that in their place he would have been even more brutal.[91] He was going to teach Italians to behave with severity until there were no more Jews left in Europe. This exodus, he pretended, was essential and urgent in order to preserve the purity of the Italian race:[92] though he personally thought the idea of racial purity was nonsense,[93] it was politically expedient that others should think differently.

He used to boast, and justifiably, that the cruelties of fascism were on a small scale compared to what was happening elsewhere. Nevertheless he gloried in fascist deeds of bloodshed and, in the late 1930s, described himself as the same man of violence he had been in 1921–2; he talked of unleashing the squads again and said he was not averse to breaking a few heads to show that fascism was the same as ever.[94] The man who ordered prisoners of war to be executed,[95] and the gassing of whole villages in Libya and Ethiopia, who was sorry that so few Italians had been killed in East Africa[96] and who, according to Ciano, would not think twice before firing on a crowd of hunger demonstrators,[97] was not a man to stop short if he thought Hitler wished him to expel the Jews from Italy.

When the Vatican remonstrated strongly, Mussolini warned that racialism was by now a basic fascist dogma that left no room for compromise. To spite the Pope – whose death, he said, he was hoping for soon – he tried to persuade himself that religion, and indeed any belief in God, was on the decline: if Italians still went to church, 'that was merely because they knew that the Duce wanted them to'; they were anti-clerical at heart, and if he gave the word, were ready to get rid of the Pope for good.[98]

Mussolini's anti-clericalism was thus reasserting itself. Sometimes he now acknowledged that he was an outright disbeliever,[99] and once told a startled cabinet that Islam was perhaps a more effective religion than Christianity.[100] The papacy was a malignant tumour in the body of Italy and must 'be rooted out once and for all', because there was no room in Rome for both the Pope and himself.[101] When some of the younger fascists took him at his word and launched a furious campaign against religion, he backed down and repudiated them; but privately continued to talk in the same vein.[102]

Munich, 1938

Just as a feeling of racial superiority helped to mould Mussolini's attitude to Spaniards, he also wrote off the Czechs as inferior Slavs by race as well as out-of-date democrats by political allegiance. Czechoslovakia – like Switzerland, Belgium and Austria – was an artificial nation that should be 'removed from the map',[103] and the Germans were informed in May 1938 that he would, if necessary, back them with arms in this good cause.[104] Encouraged by such welcome news, Hitler proceeded with his plan of invasion to 'smash' what was the last obstacle to German expansion into eastern Europe. In September, when the attack was almost about to begin, Neville Chamberlain urgently asked the Italian government to intervene with Hitler, at which Mussolini commented triumphantly that the British must be suffering from a menopausal disorder and that their prestige in Europe was at an end if they had to come begging for his help. Again he assured Hitler that Italy was prepared to fight, and the army command confirmed that they were ready to use poison gas in a 'lightning war'.[105]

This casual incitement to start a world war was all the more remarkable coming from someone who was not obliged by any treaty to fight over Czechoslovakia and had little idea what precise objectives the Germans had in mind. Probably his assurance to Hitler was not meant seriously: at all events he made no attempt to support this dangerous talk by mobilising the army.[106] When he spoke of being sure that France and Britain could now be 'liquidated for ever',[107] he probably based this on his view that the democracies were too cowardly to fight; if this calculation proved wrong, he could wait until Germany was already beating them before he needed to intervene.

At the end of September, when he discovered that the British might be ready to accept a partial German annexation of Czechoslovakia.[108] Mussolini suddenly decided that there was more to be gained by a change of direction and it was his plea to Hitler that now prevented war. A conference was hurriedly summoned at Munich where he intervened dramatically with a solution that everyone accepted and which gave the Germans most of what they wanted: he called his proposals the work of an honest broker, though they had been drawn up in the German foreign office and handed to him just before the conference began.[109] He was embarrassed by having to go through the motions of public discussion with the two democratic prime ministers, Edouard Daladier and Neville Chamberlain, but his reputation gained enormously as he was looked upon as the peacemaker of Europe.

He returned home to a hero's welcome, with people kneeling as his train went by and the king waiting at Florence station to greet him. 'I have saved Europe', he announced; Chamberlain 'had licked his boots'; he said he felt himself an instrument of God in destroying bolshevism and giving Italy a preponderant role in world politics for the first time.[110] The British ambassador in Rome found him 'in a highly sensitive condition' and was pointedly told that favourable publicity in London over his personal triumph at Munich would be appreciated – so that it could be quoted in the Italian press as evidence of British admiration.[111] Mussolini later remembered this as his moment of greatest popularity in twenty years and was upset only at the thought that Italians were applauding him not as a victor in war, but in the unaccustomed role of peacemaker.[112] The popular welcome no doubt reflects a sense of relief in Italy, because his warlike pronouncements, together with the racial laws, the unpopular Spanish war and his flirtation with the pagan nazis, had been creating a great deal of subdued discontent. Whatever the reasons, his success at Munich was undeniable and he made the most of it. Even those who later saw this crisis as one of his great moments of irresponsibility – encouraging Hitler to the very brink of war and risking Italy's vital interests for Germany's benefit alone – felt obliged at the time to praise his triumph as a masterpiece of wisdom and political skill.

By letting Germany take Austria and make what was left of Czechoslovakia into a virtual German protectorate, Mussolini gratuitously helped the German drive into the Balkans and along the Danube, two areas that he had once marked out for himself: and all without receiving anything in exchange. The nazis had offered him a formal alliance in May, and again in September at Munich, but while agreeable in principle he was in no immediate hurry to commit himself finally. He enjoyed the sensation at Munich of feeling himself to be the arbiter of Europe, in credit with everyone, and hoped that this might be a card still worth playing. There was a good chance that mere threats would force the decadent democracies to yield some colonial territory without his having to fight for it.

In any case he would need time to prepare Italians to accept the idea of a German alliance. He reassured Hitler that the 'dynamism of history' would inevitably bring war against the western democracies within a few years, but he wanted at least to wait until his instinct told him that the time was ripe: even though he knew that the rearmament race was already proving too costly. He therefore spoke as though an 'affinity of destiny' obviated the need for any written pact with the nazis, and was content when they repeated their promise to help him make the Mediterranean into an Italian sea.[113]

In October he was applauded by the Grand Council on telling them that, as soon as the Spanish war was out of the way, he had other military adventures in store for them because he was determined 'never to leave the Italians in peace'.[114] The French might possibly have a stronger army on paper, but they were ruined by alcoholism and syphilis and lacked the will to fight, so an Italian victory would be guaranteed. 'Everything in Italy must be militarised', he announced to prolonged applause from the *gerarchi*, and he informed them that atlases were no longer being published in bound editions because everyone knew that further conquests were imminent – he meant to 'change the map of the world'. The totalitarian countries had no fear that others would assault them; they therefore had the great advantage of being able to choose the time and place for an attack.[115]

The French were probably unaware of his attempt to incite the Turks to start a war against them in the eastern Mediterranean, but they had no doubt that Mussolini needed a succession of *coups de théâtre* to maintain a state of continual international turbulence, and they knew he always needed an external enemy for reasons of internal politics. In any case, a variety of resentments against France now came to a crisis point. The Duce was indignant that French newspapers did not give him enough credit for the Munich settlement, and was especially annoyed to read intercepted despatches from the French embassy in Rome describing Italian public opinion as overwhelmingly against the idea of war.[116]

By November 1938 he had decided to create 'an untraversable abyss' between Italy and France. Raffaele Guariglia, his new ambassador to Paris, asked for a briefing on fascist foreign policy but was told absolutely nothing and, when the French asked him to explain what was happening, could not reply. During four critical months in Paris, Guariglia received only one telegram from Rome which dealt with the political situation.[117]

Mussolini's secret hope was that France could be bullied into giving up Corsica and Nice and establishing an Italo-French condominium in Tunisia and French Somalia. He also had plans to annex Albania and possibly the Swiss canton of Ticino; and the British were privately informed of these objectives, presumably on the odd assumption that it would frighten them into a mood of surrender.[118] Meanwhile the army was instructed to prepare to attack Jibuti,[119] and journalists dutifully wrote articles describing the unquenchable determination of everyone in Corsica to become Italian, even though the same journalists privately acknowledged that not a dozen Corsicans had any such wish.[120]

On 30 November, parliament was recalled after over six months in recess, and the French ambassador in Rome was requested to attend so that he could hear an important speech by Ciano. A theatrical scene was staged for his benefit: on eleven occasions the disciplined deputies rose to their feet in acclamation and, at a given signal, shouted in chorus for the annexation of Nice, Corsica and Tunis. Mussolini pretended that this demonstration was spontaneous,[121] but foreign ambassadors[122] and journalists[123] in Rome knew in advance exactly what was to happen. Students and civil servants had been given time off to demonstrate simultaneously in the streets but were warned not to shout for Malta as well – that claim was being postponed to the following year.[124]

Mussolini was delighted 'as always when he begins a battle', said Ciano, until he heard from Guariglia that no one in France took this strange episode seriously. He had gambled on the French being in mortal fear of him and giving way, whereas the effect was the opposite: pro-fascists and anti-fascists in France were driven by his action to make common cause in a determination to rearm. Equally unexpected was that the reputation for wisdom and moderation he had acquired at Munich disappeared overnight. As several Italian diplomats commented, it was an elementary mistake that gained absolutely nothing for Italy, and helped only Hitler by its final destruction of the 'Stresa front'.[125]

For several months, the fascist press was ordered to continue the campaign of insults against everything French. Mussolini was very sensitive lest Italians might note and resent the fact that only Germany had gained any material conquests from the axis, and France was a convenient scapegoat for this failure. He would try to copy Hitler who had already shown that mere intimidation could achieve a great deal. By manufacturing another war scare he hoped to demonstrate the readiness and determination of the Italians to fight. A new law prescribed that at the start of hostilities all the parliamentary deputies, even the old, the blind and the infirm, would be immediately conscripted and sent into the front line: it was passed by secret ballot with not a single dissident voice, and all the deputies once more broke into the strains of 'Giovinezza'.[126] Like many other laws, it was never applied and can hardly have been seriously meant, except as a means of striking terror into the hearts of the enemy.

In January 1939, Neville Chamberlain came to Rome in a last futile attempt to prise Italy loose from the axis. The visit was specially asked for by Mussolini who in turn was hoping to persuade the British to use their influence to make the French yield to at least some of his demands. However he also asked that the formal request for the meeting should come from London to make it appear as yet another visit of 'homage to the founder of the empire': he stressed that this was the eleventh visit of a British minister to fascist Rome, whereas he had not been to London since 1922.[127]

Despite orders that the British prime minister should not receive too enthusiastic a popular welcome,[128] the applause in the streets was very warm indeed; this was especially noteworthy in view of the fact that, unlike the applause for Hitler, it had not been officially organised. For the first time in years, dignitaries were told to wear civilian dress at an official reception as a mark of respect and condescension for their visitors, and Mussolini for the last time put on white tie and tails. Chamberlain was taken to see plenty of goose stepping and parades of children with miniature rifles, and Mussolini's personal guard of black-uniformed musketeers with drawn daggers was also much in evidence. A good deal of this struck the foreign visitors as both revolting and ridiculous.[129]

One negative result was that on his return home, Chamberlain accepted the need to hold secret staff conversations with the French.[130] Another result was to increase Mussolini's contempt for the British as a possible enemy. Chamberlain was seen as thoroughly unmartial and his umbrella as one more proof of bourgeois decadence: 'people who carry an umbrella can never found an empire' and 'could never understand the moral significance of war, because they cannot love that supreme, inexorable violence which is the chief motor force of world history'.[131] The fascist leader was reinforced in his opinion that he could ignore Britain and prepare for a war against France alone.

On reflection he admitted that the scene in parliament on 30 November had perhaps been unwise because it earned him no friends, only more enemies. The one advantage – or so he considered it – was that it brought him closer to Germany and deepened the unbridgeable gulf he was seeking to drive between Italy and France. Now that public claims had been made for Italy's annexation of Corsica, Somalia and Tunis, he could not back down from them without losing face. He was therefore committed to a possible war against France and, as he said, 'the French respect only those who have defeated them'.[132]

By the beginning of 1939 there was something increasingly frenzied and irrational about Mussolini. The threat of using force was again made explicitly and in public.[133] Then he explained that, though he was of course ready to fight, it might be better to wait another three years. However, when French newspapers began running stories about his irregular private life and, above all, when they spoke of his failing intelligence, 'these are insults that can be met only by cannon shot'. He claimed to possess a secret weapon that might be decisive in such a war, though he would not tell Ciano what it was; and he added that Frenchmen, after being conquered, would be treated to a physical devastation of their country from which it would never recover.[134]

Alliance with Germany

13

Victory in Spain and Albania

At the end of December 1938, as conflict with France drew nearer, Mussolini came closer to accepting a formal treaty with the nazis, because it crossed his mind that otherwise Germany might choose France rather than Italy as a favoured partner.[1] Although he wanted it to appear a merely defensive alliance, he actually intended it to be something much more forceful[2] – it did not occur to him that, as one of his colleagues put it, this objective made him into a fish being played on a hook from which there was no easy escape.[3] He did not even question the greatly exaggerated figures given to him about the strength of the German army. He preferred not to specify any precise war aims in the treaty because he wanted to keep his plans secret from the Germans, and did not stop to think that he would thereby be committing himself to an open-ended agreement that might prove disadvantageous.

What he did not know was that, without consulting him, his future ally was already planning to annex even more of Czechoslovakia than had been agreed at Munich. On the strength of what Hitler had promised him, Mussolini confidently told his ministers that no such annexation would happen. And when the news broke that the invasion of Czechoslovakia had begun, he was naturally perturbed by the thought that he would be laughed at for being so gullible.[4]

Confronted with a *fait accompli*, he had to pretend that he entirely approved of what Hitler was doing, while in private he knew it was a blow to his personal prestige, as it was also a further alteration to the balance of power inside the axis.[5] For a few days he gave up any idea of a treaty, denouncing Hitler as 'disloyal and untrustworthy'. The thought even entered his mind – not for the first or last time – that it might be more prudent to change sides so that he could resist any further German thrust into the Balkans. It was particularly bitter to hear himself referred to as the *Gauleiter* for Italy.[6]

But his loss of nerve was momentary. Several days later he told the Grand Council that there was no alternative to an alliance with Germany and his statement was, of course, welcomed unanimously. Grandi, who sometimes tried to pass for an Anglophile, now copied his master by referring to a German alliance as something 'dictated to Italy by history' and voiced his opinion that the British public would accept it meekly.[7] Mussolini rashly repeated that he was confident of being able to beat the French without

German help.[8] He added that he meant to start the war fairly soon because, in two years' time, the British might be strong enough to fight back. He thought that the fascist *squadristi* were eager to do battle to win Italy her 'living space' in the Mediterranean and, in pursuit of that aim, 'my will knows no obstacles' – the democracies would soon bend before his whip. He was determined on war, even if it meant a holocaust and 'the destruction of everything that passes for civilised life.'[9]

One consolation for his loss of face over Czechoslovakia was Franco's victory at Madrid at the end of March, in which Italian military help played a major part. In retrospect, Mussolini tried to convince himself that the war in Spain had been worth all the loss of life.[10] Ciano on the other hand sometimes admitted, like Hitler, that it might have been a stupid mistake.[11] As well as involving great and unnecessary risks, it had made the breach with the western democracies so wide that Italy was left with little freedom of action in foreign policy. By its cruelties, by its arrogant boasting and inefficiency, by its waste of scarce resources, the Spanish war had engendered a more critical attitude towards the regime among fascist sympathisers both inside and outside Italy.[12] Mussolini naïvely expected that Spain, in gratitude for his help, would side with him in a more extensive European war,[13] but Franco made it abundantly clear that Spanish national interests overrode ideology and demanded a long period of recuperative peace.[14]

One of the more effective members of the Italian cabinet, the financier Felice Guarneri, thought that, far from increasing fascist prestige, the Spanish war had diminished it, showing the outside world that the Italian army was not to be feared and thus making Mussolini's bluff easier to disregard. According to Guarneri, Mussolini had been induced to enter the Civil War without any careful calculation as to possible gains, but merely out of a desire for adventure and a vague hope that destabilising Europe would be to his advantage. Franco had played on the Duce's chief weakness: by flattering him he had obtained something for nothing, while Italy lost half her not very large foreign currency reserves and gained only unpopularity and distrust.[15]

The cost to Italy was between three and six thousand soldiers dead and missing – the published figures are contradictory and unreliable, possibly because of unaccountable desertions. The financial cost, mainly in un-requited 'loans', was over half a year's tax income, and vast stores of military equipment had to be left in Spain at a time when they were needed for Italy's rearmament programme.[16] The Germans had much more to show for their intervention, and at less than a quarter of the expense.[17] The cost to Italy of the Spanish war was something best kept secret, but the fact that Mussolini was compelled by the needs of propaganda to claim it as a huge success had the incidental effect of pushing him towards yet another military adventure;

together with the wish to get even with Hitler over the German occupation of Prague, it helped to trigger off the conquest of Albania in April 1939.

Mussolini had been contemplating this aggressive move for the past year. He was determined on it even if it meant precipitating a major European war.[18] But the odd fact was that Albania – though he had to pretend in public that it was completely independent – was already in effect an Italian province, with her economy and army largely under Italian control.[19] The war was, for this reason, quite unnecessary; it was also based on erroneous calculations by would-be profiteers in Ciano's entourage and journalists who called Albania a potentially rich country with room for several million Italian settlers.[20] Moreover it was assumed that, if Albanian leaders were bribed, the Italian invasion would encounter no effective resistance. Plans were laid for the assassination of King Zog, one of Zog's close associates being suborned for the purpose.[21] Help from the Jugoslavs was also solicited, with a promise that Italy would subsequently back them in conquering an outlet on the Aegean at Salonica.

One of the reasons Mussolini gave for his verbal attacks on France had been his wish to 'darken the waters' like an octopus and distract attention from this more immediate goal, Albania. By February 1939 a great deal of money had been spent on bribery.[22] Then, after the German invasion of Czechoslovakia, Hitler repeated his assurance that Mussolini had a free hand to seek territorial compensation. But other ministers were not to be told until the invasion was all over, and the military commanders were given only a week's notice.[23]

Mussolini was overjoyed at the prospect of another war, especially against such a minuscule opponent. He had an anxious moment when the Albanian government showed signs of giving in without a fight, because his mind was dominated by the need to copy Hitler in effective military action.[24] When other countries expressed their concern at his aggressive intentions against yet another member of the League of Nations, he claimed that his troops were going there merely to 'restore order and justice' and that he had no idea of remaining or injuring Albanian independence.[25]

So rushed were the last-minute preparations that the commander of the expedition was insufficiently briefed and Mussolini's plan to overwhelm the tiny Albanian army went badly wrong. The responsibility for this rested on himself and his son-in-law, but he refused to accept any blame and therefore failed to learn the important lesson that aggressive war was a complex operation and needed very careful study.[26] The official accounts stated, of course, that the whole operation had been faultless and had greatly raised Italy's prestige in the world. But by that time a great deal of harm had been done by alienating other countries who now had further evidence that the Duce had no regard for international treaties or for the independence of weaker nations. Mussolini, not untypically, said that he positively rejoiced in again becoming an object of fear and antipathy. Italians had now proved that their destiny was to dominate other countries, so he at once started planning to use his new Albanian base for an attack at some future date on Greece and Jugoslavia.[27]

The annexation of Albania proved a disappointment to all except Ciano and the profiteers, for it cost a lot of money and the economic potential of the country was negligible. Nor were the Germans very happy, even though they sent their formal congratulations. Pleased though they were to see him break more bridges with the democracies, they feared that Mussolini was trying to redress the internal balance of the axis by winning quick military successes for which he was not nearly strong enough; they knew he was planning a colonial campaign against the French which would be likely to trigger off a major European war before they themselves were ready for it. They were secretly planning their own next coup against Poland and did not want anyone else to spoil its timing, so they begged him to put off any further aggression for a year or two.[28]

His belligerent attitude was in part another pose. Early in 1939 he boasted once again to the Germans that he was strong enough to fight against the French on his own,[29] but he told other people that he had no intention of fighting anyone, and he could hardly ignore altogether the opinion of those generals who said that Italy was in no position to embark on any major war.[30] As he had not been able on his own to frighten the French into giving way, the next best thing was to impress the Germans so that they might underwrite Italian territorial ambitions. When the western powers reacted to his Albanian adventure by giving guarantees of military support to Greece and Turkey, his determination to accept the German offer of a formal alliance was reinforced.

The pact of steel, 1939

In May 1939 a treaty was at last signed. Mussolini, the great phrase-maker who had coined the word 'axis', called it the 'pact of steel' after prudently discarding his first choice, the 'pact of blood'. His final decision to sign was taken in a moment of pique after foreign journalists reported strong feelings against Germany among the Italian people. He described these reports as lies and perhaps had been deceived by the artificial demonstrations in favour of Germany that he himself had organised.[31]

At his instance, the alliance was drawn up not just for defence: since war against the democracies was unavoidable, it had for preference to be offensive so that the optimum moment and occasion could be carefully selected.[32] Whatever he later pretended, Mussolini signed in full knowledge that the Germans saw their next move as an invasion of Poland[33] and, despite this, he was quite content to leave them to draft the treaty; moreover he saw no reason to seek any advice from his own ministers and military advisers. Though the Germans had already deceived him more than once, he never bothered to ask them to spell out their intentions over Poland, but let them dictate the wording of an alliance that committed Italy to supporting them automatically. The simple fact of an alliance – not its terms – was what mattered to him, as is shown by the fact that he announced its existence before the terms had been decided.[34] A few hours after the pact was signed, Hitler secretly ordered his generals to prepare for an attack on Poland, and another order specified that this intention be kept strictly secret from Germany's new ally.[35]

Mussolini hardly doubted at all – and Ciano was certain – that skilful Italian diplomacy had completely out-manoeuvred Hitler.[36] He accepted that the Germans might possibly take Poland, but in return they would give him a free hand in the Balkans; the Italians could attack Greece, Turkey, Switzerland or even Romania, and do so with full German backing.[37] Mussolini boasted to Hitler – but it was an empty boast – that in the very first hours of war his intention was to occupy the Balkans and the Danube basin so as to have access to ample raw materials for his armaments programme. Meanwhile, he was planning to stir up anti-semitism and revolution in the French and British colonies, and was also intending to support autonomist movements in Alsace, Brittany, Corsica and Ireland.[38] He said he had no fear that intervention by the United States could save Britain or France, and it would be useless for the Soviet Union to intervene; on the contrary, it might even help if the Russians sided with the democracies as that would assist the disintegration brought by the spread of communism throughout the west.[39]

Mussolini derived enormous pleasure from such speculations and he slanted his public statements to show the world that he meant business. Nevertheless he spoke in private as though the war might be three years away, and the fact that in three years' time the much richer western countries would have overtaken Italy in rearmament does not seem to have worried him; or perhaps it was a fact better forgotten; or perhaps he did not believe it. At the end of May, he sent a belated message to Hitler to say that he would prefer to postpone their war until 1943. He then pretended, quite inaccurately, to his ministers that this delay was clearly specified in a secret clause of the pact of steel.[40] Hitler sent no written confirmation about any delay and secretly had other intentions.

Whatever his true wishes may have been about the timing of war, Mussolini did very little to restrain his partner and the presumption must be that he was mainly interested in exploiting Hitler's next act of aggression. No doubt he also hoped that Poland would give way without a struggle, but he made it abundantly clear to the Germans that, if the Polish question led to a general war, he would join them, just as he had told them earlier that he would help to crush Czechoslovakia.[41] War, he repeated, was a natural instinct for real men. Any Italian was worth three Frenchmen when it came to fighting, and the armed services – under his personal direction – were now equipped with all the latest weapons and ready for anything.[42] He thought once again of taking Tunisia or Algeria, and the chiefs of staff were told to have plans ready for an attack on Jugoslavia and Greece.[43] These were hardly the actions of someone dedicated to the cause of peace, as he later claimed, nor did they have much contact with reality.

In these critical days he could easily have tried to prevent the impending tragedy of war, but did nothing. His ambassadors abroad were, as usual, given little indication of his wishes and sometimes had no idea at all whether he wanted them to be conciliatory or aggressive;[44] nor could he bear to admit that he needed their advice, so their reports usually went unread and their letters unanswered.[45] Even the Italian ambassadors in Moscow[46] and Berlin[47] were often left entirely in the dark. The United States ambassador had spent five years in Rome before any official of the foreign office was allowed to engage him in frank discussion, and Roosevelt's offer of a personal meeting with the Duce was rejected as an irrelevance.[48] Diplomacy was, in Mussolini's view, mainly a cover operation, and the reality of foreign policy was better kept out of the hands of the professionals.

Early in June 1939, an urgent request came from Berlin for a meeting with Hitler to discuss their objectives in the light of the pact of steel, but the Duce did not comply and, in the next few weeks, allowed several more requests to go unanswered, even when warned that war was imminent.[49] Perhaps this fatal omission was due to the wish not to reveal his own plans to the Germans; perhaps he was anxious to keep on the sidelines and avoid being tied down by any commitment; or possibly this was another of those increasingly frequent moments when he was overcome by indecisiveness or loss of will-power. It is clear that he had temporarily lost his instinct for orienting the news, and for two months stopped making his hitherto almost daily telephone calls to the editor of the *Popolo d'Italia*.[50]

Fearing to meet the Germans on his own, he asked Hitler to call an international conference. He remembered the meeting at Munich where his own influence had seemed decisive and no doubt was hoping that the democracies would give way once more after another mere war of nerves. But he could not say this openly: on the contrary, he had to pretend to Hitler that he was irremovably behind Germany and was quite ready for war if necessary[51] – and, of course, this was the message the latter wished to hear. In a secret communication intercepted by the British, Mussolini went even further: he told Hitler 'clearly and unmistakably' that, though he would prefer to postpone the war envisaged in the pact of steel, 'if the Führer really thinks that today is the proper moment, then Italy is one hundred per cent ready', adding that he would back this undertaking with all the means at his disposal.[52]

Nothing can have been more calculated than this remarkable message to embolden Hitler to provoke a world war. Yet Mussolini had probably not meant to give this impression and realised his mistake a few days later when he found that he was not going to gain another easy victory of prestige. A German attack on Poland was imminent; this would, in turn, force France and Britain to join battle and so might involve Italy in a war she was unequipped to fight. He urgently sent Ciano to Germany to explain that such a war would be complete folly – they had better wait at least four years, if not seven or eight.[53] He seems to have been confident that, being the senior and more experienced of the two dictators, he would carry the day on this vital point, and in advance drew up a communiqué for publication stating that his ally agreed with him.[54]

He was wrong, for the nazis now had no intention of letting him stop them exploding the powder barrel. A dumbfounded Ciano first tried to explain to the Germans that Italy lacked the necessary arms, but then gave way, mesmerised by the self-confidence of Hitler and Ribbentrop. They positively assured him that the British and Russians would not intervene, so that the axis powers would be able to 'liquidate the pseudo-neutral states one after the other' and Italy could have Greece and Jugoslavia as her part of the deal; nor would active Italian help be required in the main fighting.[55] At this wonderful news, Ciano's doubts disappeared and he accepted that the German analysis of the situation must be right. He therefore failed to make the point that Hitler, by refusing to consult or inform Rome, had broken the terms of their alliance; and this was to prove a damaging omission. Mussolini's pacific communiqué was discarded and, instead, the Germans – without warning Ciano – issued a very different one saying that the Italians were in complete agreement with nazi policy; nor could Ciano publicly dissociate himself from this pronouncement – though tactless and almost insultingly presumptuous, it was close enough to the truth.[56]

Some of the wiser and better informed *gerarchi* now had further evidence that fascist policy had been entirely wrong, because Hitler had managed to deceive Italy into becoming his accomplice in a highly dangerous adventure. Some began to think that their only hope would be to denounce the alliance, but the few brave enough to hint as much to Mussolini were silenced by shouted obscenities or dismissed from their posts; and yet the Duce confessed more than once that they might be correct. He was galled to discover that, far from being the foremost dictator, he was held in so little account that his views were ignored in Berlin and his expressed wishes overridden, yet he did not dare to stand up to Hitler and, as day after day went by without any formal protest, his silence can only have encouraged the Germans to go ahead in the confidence that Italy would maintain her pledge to fight.

As conflicting emotions succeeded one another in the next ten days, Mussolini changed his mind again and again, sometimes more than once in a single day. If Germany was going to win a war, he wanted his share of the booty and he also began to fear a German invasion of Italy if he tried to back down.[57] On the other hand, he was equally afraid to fight and risk exposing his multiple bluff about the readiness of the Italian armed forces.[58] As always, he was obsessed by the idea of war as something glorious. He particularly feared the accusation of cowardice, and yet was desperately hoping either that the democracies would give way without fighting, or that German successes would win him the glory of victory without his having to engage in major hostilities. In the meantime, he once again ordered the army to prepare a limited war against Greece and Jugoslavia in order to make a few easy territorial acquisitions while the rest of Europe was distracted elsewhere.[59]

At one point, on 21 August, he decided to tell Hitler that he would prefer to withdraw his offer of 100 per cent military support,[60] but, just in time, heard that the Germans had signed an agreement with Russia and his whole outlook changed. This agreement was, strictly speaking, another violation of the pact of steel and made nonsense of the anti-bolshevist policy for which Mussolini had sent so many Italians to die in Spain; but instinctively he realised that a combination of Germany, Russia and Italy would be invincible, and he therefore hailed it as a masterstroke that completely altered the picture.[61]

On 22 August, Hitler informed the German generals that in the next few weeks he intended to 'annihilate' Poland, if necessary using the 'utmost brutality'. The reason he gave to them was that he could at last count on the backing of both Mussolini and Stalin. Germany and Russia would first dismember Poland and then agree on 'a new distribution of the world'; but it was made quite clear that Mussolini's support, though less important than Stalin's, was one reason why they could risk another world war.[62]

Hitler was not quite correct because Mussolini, though for a few hours he veered over once more to an emphatic enthusiasm for war,[63] quickly swung back to the other extreme of alarm. Not for the first or last time, an emergency found him incapable of taking a firm and rational decision, yet he still did not want to share the responsibility with the cabinet or the Grand Council so long as there existed some possibility of a great propaganda success. Nor did he act when secret messages arrived from several of Hitler's close associates begging him to refuse to fight and rather to use his influence to prevent the European conflagration that now threatened.[64] Meanwhile the Italian military experts tried to keep up with his varying moods – at one moment calculating that the French had a superiority of five to one against Italy, at another insisting that the Italian army was fully able to win any war he cared to fight.[65]

When, on 25 August, the British renewed their guarantee to support Poland if it came to war, Hitler realised that one of his calculations – namely, that he could fight a localised war in eastern Europe – might be wrong; and he blamed the Italians for secretly encouraging the British to be firm.[66] Several days earlier, the British had indeed been informed by an informer – she was a girl-friend of Ciano and may have been regularly passing on his views – that the state of the Italian army entirely ruled out any Italian intervention; the fact that this information was accepted in London as completely reliable and top secret suggests that Ciano may possibly have sent it on purpose in a desperate attempt to avoid war,[67] and the further fact that a few days later Mussolini agreed to reassure the British that he would not fight suggests that he may just possibly have authorised the indiscretion.

On 26 August, Hitler tried to insist that the Italians must decide one way or the other, and Mussolini pretended he was ready to join Germany but only on the condition that 17,000 train loads of materials were sent to help his rearmament. This was, as he well knew and intended, an impossible demand: the amount had been calculated in just a few minutes and some of the requirement figures had been doubled or trebled to make them quite impossible to meet.[68] The request was designed to be an excuse not to fight, but this was so obvious that Hitler was able to reproach him with cowardice and bad faith; after so many promises in the previous two years about fighting alongside Germany 'at once', 'to the end', and with 'one hundred per cent support', he was backing down at the very first sign that war was something more than bluff.

Hitler was apprehensive that 'some swine', in other words Mussolini, might deprive him of his war at this last moment by offering himself as a mediator;[69] and this is just what the Duce now tried to do, seeing it as his best and perhaps only chance of scoring a political success.[70] It was very upsetting to Mussolini when both Germans and British denied him the opportunity of presiding over another peace conference.[71] When Hitler begged him at least to keep his neutrality secret so that their opponents would be kept guessing,[72] he did the very opposite and sent word to London to confirm that he would in no circumstances initiate a war against either France or Britain.[73] It was prudent to curry favour with both sides until he had a clearer idea of the likely victor.

On 1 September, Mussolini told the cabinet that he had decided not to fight and Hitler's 'treachery' exonerated Italy from any treaty obligation.[74] Since the word 'neutral' was un-fascist, he expertly coined the term 'non-belligerent' to disguise the stark truth. The cabinet approved unanimously and gave him another of their customary rounds of applause, which seems to have disconcerted him – he would have preferred a more virile attitude of regret.[75] The newspapers were instructed not to talk of being 'neutral', and when people whom he labelled scathingly as 'the usual peacemongers' tried to stage a popular demonstration of joy outside the Palazzo Venezia, he told them to desist.[76] Most Italians must have realised with relief that he had made the right decision, even if they did not know how unwillingly and unintentionally he had stumbled into it. Some of them must have wondered whether Hitler, without Mussolini's repeated promises of support, would have invaded Poland on 1 September.

Non-belligerence

Mussolini was unhappy that, after so much preaching about the glories of war and Italy's readiness to fight, he had to appear in such an undignified light. After claiming that he had over 150 divisions, some of which were 'armoured divisions', with the most up-to-date weapons and backed by reserves of twelve million soldiers,[77] the prosaic truth turned out to be that only ten divisions were ready to fight and these were under strength, with antiquated and insufficient equipment, and none of them armoured in any accepted sense.[78] The air force, for which he had made such extravagant claims, was 'irremediably out of date' and he himself, though minister for aviation, seems to have had no idea how few planes were available.[79]

To extenuate any possible weaknesses, he continued to argue as though the war he intended to fight was still years away or, at worst, would be won without serious fighting because the Germans would do the main work and the democracies would cave in without a struggle.[80] But he cannot have liked such an unheroic excuse and he may have feared it to be untrue.

An attempt was made to blame others for not telling him the real facts of Italy's military potential and this, too, was a grave confession of personal inadequacy because he had boasted time and again that the whole military machine was organised down to the last detail under his personal direction.[81] For over ten years he had been immediately in charge of all three armed services and presided over all the committees responsible for rearmament, as well as personally holding a rank senior to that of any serving officer. Yet his choice of commanders had gone for preference to those who would give least trouble and who, therefore, were most lacking in initiative.[82] Those few officers brave enough to disagree with decisions of policy risked being humiliated and silenced.[83] Nor had parliament ever been allowed any serious discussion of either foreign policy or the military budget, and any public reference to possible weaknesses had always been stamped on at once,[84] while the chief of police – who was his main contact with public opinion – had learnt to keep him away from items of news that might be particularly unwelcome.[85]

All this was part of the pattern of fascist authoritarianism. Mussolini was, of course, far from being alone to blame but the ultimate responsibility was his. He had encouraged over-centralisation to such an extent that essential decisions were not taken because no one else dared act on his own. His own indecisiveness aggravated this deficiency, and the fact that he could change his views from day to day left the whole machinery of government in what sometimes appeared a state of suspension.[86] Fascist centralisation had once been called a sign of strength and said to compare favourably with Hitler's practice of delegating responsibility,[87] but when, unlike Hitler, he insisted on giving the appearance of controlling every detail of the administration,[88] the result was that other controls were defective and sometimes entirely lacking. Several close associates thought that there might be some psychological vagary that made him almost want to be disobeyed.[89]

It is an impressive fact that a person who, as all the professionals agreed, was perilously ignorant of military matters,[90] could get away with so much bluff for so long. Despite all he said about being ready to fight, he can hardly have avoided knowing at least the basic facts about the lack of military preparations – even though some foreign observers apparently knew more than he did.[91] He must also have realised the danger that his warlike talk would persuade Italians that they were invincible, with the result that, while foreigners were unimpressed, his own people would expect more and more of him.

It is almost certain, however, that as well as deceiving others he was in part deceiving himself, because the imperative needs of propaganda – the need to cover up what had happened in Albania, for example – prevented his permitting any analysis of the various deficiencies or revealing, even to senior colleagues, that he knew something was wrong. When he told the Germans that he was strong enough to fight Britain or France single-handed, he must have expected to be believed, as otherwise he would never have risked looking foolish by saying it. He must have expected to be believed when he spoke of mobilising ten million men in a single day or raising a coloured army of two million soldiers to dominate Africa, or when he talked as though Italy possessed armoured divisions and was self-sufficient in aviation fuel. All these claims were unrealistic, but he would not have dared make them if he had not thought them sufficiently plausible to be accepted. It may seem impossible that he believed them himself; yet he was a gullible person heavily protected from criticism and the colleagues he chose were second-rate men who knew they would keep their posts only by reinforcing his own prejudices. Ciano noted in his diary that his father-in-law 'must not be contradicted, because it only makes things worse', and he feared the truth so much that perhaps he preferred not to know it.[92]

Only in September 1939, after a partial mobilisation showed a great number of Italians that there were simply not enough uniforms and equipment and barracks, can doubts have become widespread. Mussolini knew that many people in Italy had been unhappy over the racial laws, the goose step, the compulsory use of *voi*, and the growing lack of things to buy in the shops.[93] He knew that the consensus behind fascism was often merely superficial and depended on his use of coercion and being able to show a continued run of apparent political successes. Even before September 1939, there were ominous signs of a growth in underground newspapers and some communist literature was being secretly printed on the presses of the *Popolo d'Italia* itself.[94] Starace continued to pretend that war would be universally popular, but Mussolini knew from the prefects that this was quite untrue, and it is unlikely that he did not know of the irreverent laughter and cat-calls sometimes heard under cover of darkness as newsreels were shown in the cinemas.[95]

The declaration of non-belligerence produced an immediate sense of shock; it no doubt came as a great relief, but also brought a realisation that fascist newspapers and the leader himself were lacking in credibility. One fascist intellectual wrote that he felt as though he was living once again through the aftermath of Matteotti's murder, because even prominent fascists spoke of turning against the system. One of them said that the regime was now represented by 30,000 people at most, who were all doing well out of it, but everyone else was suffering in their pockets and weakening in their allegiance.[96] A businessman who had served fascism in the past thought that it had never sunk so low in the general consideration of the man in the street.[97] Almost everyone, noted a British diplomat in Rome, had learnt to see through the 'spontaneous parades' and the 'lorry-loads of howling hooligans' who poured through the streets whenever the government wished.[98] And sales of the Vatican's *Osservatore Romano* were soaring.

Mussolini tried to cover his own responsibility by dismissing senior staff officers. The new chief of staff of the army, Marshal Gràziani, heard of his appointment on the radio and, on taking up his post, discovered that Mussolini's belligerent pronouncements had been empty *blague* because the bulk of the available weapons were almost prehistoric.[99] Graziani nevertheless obeyed orders by keeping up the pretence that Italy was ready to fight.[100] So did the chief of general staff, Badoglio, who had been allowed to hold this post since 1925 precisely because he was ready to go on underwriting fascist policy even though he knew it was bluff.[101]

Mussolini also got rid of several ministers and of Starace, the secretary of the fascist party, whose unimaginative regimentation of the country since 1931 had done a great deal to cause popular disaffection. Starace was another useful scapegoat for the increasingly obvious failures of the regime. He had recently taken the final decision to put all government employees and teachers into uniform and no one had been able to point out that, since the armed services would have to go short as a result, this seriously limited the number of people who could be conscripted in the event of war. Once again – and it was typical of fascist policy – the outward signs of militarisation were more useful than the reality, and had the additional advantage of being cheaper.

At the beginning of September 1939, Mussolini tried to persuade the Germans that his non-belligerency was not neutrality but designed to help Germany by constituting a gap in the British blockade. Mortified to think that Hitler might regard him as having betrayed earlier undertakings,[102] he promised not only to threaten France and hold down a French army on Italy's Alpine frontier, but to send to Berlin all the intelligence he could obtain from western sources.[103] One possibility was that the Germans would win quickly in Poland, in which case he could all the sooner recover a leading role as mediator.[104]

Just occasionally he hinted in private that, if Germany ever seemed to be losing, he might change sides and intervene against Hitler;[105] and Ciano, when for a time the western powers seemed to be winning, privately informed the French that they could rely on Italian help.[106] Mussolini was more cautious but sometimes confessed that he was jealous of Hitler's successes and far from enthusiastic about the prospect of a German victory:[107] the barbarities committed in Poland disturbed him and confirmed his opinion that the nazis would be very dangerous to have as an enemy.[108]

Hitler's attitude to Italy was more complicated. He did not think a great deal of Italians or even of fascism, and now knew that they could never be trusted with foreknowledge of his military plans[109] – Mussolini's indiscretion was almost as notorious as Ciano's. The Führer joked about the comic side of Mussolini's play-acting,[110] but though sometimes ridiculing him in private, saw him as the only man to whom he could talk on something like equal terms and, perhaps for that reason, as one of the few people whom he genuinely liked.[111]

Hitler was also fairly confident that Italy would join him as soon as the democracies looked like losing; 'so long as the Duce lives,' he said in November, 'so long can it be calculated that Italy will seize every opportunity to reach her imperialistic goals'.[112] Even if she did nothing else, she could help Germany by occupying Corsica and the Balearics, diverting the British air and naval forces and attacking in North Africa.[113] That had been his calculation since 1938, and now what he had to do was to convince his ally that victory was in sight. He added the inducement that, unless Italy decided to enter the war, she would lose her only chance of imperial expansion in the Mediterranean. Jugoslavia and Greece were hers for the asking as soon as she made up her mind to fight.

Mussolini's feelings became more mixed than ever as hostilities continued. A clear and quick victory for either side might leave him empty-handed and so should be prevented if possible. Preferably, the countries at war would so savage each other that his own hopes for a profitable mediation would be the greater, and he therefore did what little he could to pour oil on the flames.[114] He continued telling the Germans that he hoped to be ready to help them more actively in a few months' time; but privately he had no thought of the full-dress war against France for which they were hoping, only of a separate offensive to pick up easy conquests in the Balkans.[115] Meanwhile, the outside world was informed that he was the best hope of a return to peace.[116]

One sign of an inner uncertainty was his summoning of the Grand Council on 7 December. It had not met for a long time – although it was still called the controlling organ of the regime – and its members turned out to be strongly in favour of remaining neutral.[117] This, no doubt, was why he summoned them; any decision to fight a victorious war would have had to be seen to come from himself alone, but any decision for peace had to be covered by a collegiate responsibility. He obviously hankered for war and wanted his colleagues to think that he was still in the German camp, yet continued sometimes to confess a secret desire for the Germans to be defeated and even allowed his planning staff to prepare for a possible war against Germany; note was taken that when he congratulated Hitler on surviving an attempt at assassination, he gave the impression of insincerity.[118] Yet more obvious was his insincerity when, at the same time as he encouraged his ally to attack neutral Belgium, he secretly warned the Belgians of what was going to happen so that they could put up a better resistance.[119] Hitler learnt of this extraordinary action almost at once and had one more reason never to give Mussolini his full confidence.

Equally suspicious was the decision to continue fortifying Italy's northern frontier with Germany. It seems that another chance newspaper article convinced Mussolini that it was possible to make the Alpine passes quite inaccessible to an invader,[120] and the elaborate defences now erected, which in the end proved to be quite useless for the purpose, were lauded as one of the greatest engineering achievements in history. They were probably one of the most expensive operations conducted by fascism and – whether out of forgetfulness or prudence – were still being built two years after Italy entered the war on the German side.[121]

A further source of conflict was a plebiscite held in the Italian South Tyrol to see if anyone of the German-speaking population would prefer to emigrate to Germany. Mussolini was under the illusion that his policy of forcible 'italianisation' had created a new loyalty to Italy among these people, and was astounded when a large majority of them opted to leave Italy.[122] Since he had light-heartedly agreed to purchase the property of anyone leaving, this posed an intolerable economic burden on Italy. But far worse was the public confirmation of a complete failure in one major area of policy; an 80 per cent vote against fascism was something quite unheard of and unforeseen, and it made nonsense of the conventional myth about unanimous popular consent.

Yet another potential point of difference with Hitler was the latter's entente in August 1939 with Soviet Russia. Although Mussolini's reaction was to welcome this, and though once again the fascists began to speak about the resemblance between his own regime and Stalin's 'Slav fascism',[123] he changed his mind when the Russians took the opportunity to move into Poland and towards the Balkans, because he intended south-eastern Europe to be Italy's *Lebensraum*.[124] Early in January 1940, he wrote to Hitler with a strange request that Germany should make peace with the west so that they could both join in fighting against Russia, pointing out that the nazis and fascists could find all the booty and raw materials they needed in eastern Europe.[125] Hitler did not bother to reply.

At the end of 1939, it appeared to some people as though Mussolini was going through another of those periods of depression or perplexity in which he could not make up his mind about anything. One symptom was that for another six months he almost entirely gave up his regular telephone calls to the editor of his newspaper in Milan about how to slant each day's news. He seemed more averse than ever to discussion and to any possibility of being contradicted.[126] The head of military intelligence noted his incapacity to dominate any truly difficult situation, and his incoherence reached a point where Ciano and the chief of police talked about persuading him to undertake further treatment for what they took to be the results of his old venereal disease. Others confirmed that he was almost unrecognisable and hardly seemed sane, changing his mind from day to day, taking any excuse to avoid the really important questions, fearing that Germany might lose, or else fearing that she might win too easily.[127]

This changeableness continued through January 1940. Sometimes he was ready to announce that Italy would be strong enough to intervene with decisive effect in a few months' time; sometimes he remembered the defeat at Guadalajara and confessed that to fight was out of the question for years. He was occasionally prepared to admit that he could not enter the war except against the democracies, yet the Germans knew they could not trust him. They knew he had not only warned the Belgians but was selling arms to France and Russia. They felt sure he would prefer not to fight at all if he could get what he wanted otherwise and, in any case, would never intervene unless in the wake of some great German military success.[128]

At the end of January he became more convinced that Germany would win, in which case he would be forced 'by considerations of honour and morality' to join them. Italians might not like this because they were, so he said, a race of sheep; they must be beaten into positive action and, for their own good, kept in uniform from morning to night.[129] But he was still not intending to fight a joint war with the Germans; his thoughts turned rather to a less dangerous 'parallel war' for purely Italian objectives; he would not attack France or Britain, but would seize Jugoslavia and possibly Greece as counters to be used in future peace negotiations with the west.

In February, he put on a splendidly self-confident act for the defence committee, claiming personal responsibility for having prepared Italy to fight and promising that no eventuality would find him unready.[130] He accepted that the military possibilities were limited but thought the French might be frightened into giving way. Apart from a large Italian army that would soon be ready, he hoped to recruit another mercenary force in Albania, and sufficient arms were already available for the kind of war he had in mind.[131] Admittedly, raw materials were lacking, and he now blamed his officials for not realising that, since war was bound to come sooner or later, they had not built up adequate stocks: perhaps he forgot that he had told them nothing of his warlike plans, or perhaps he had omitted to read the detailed statements about stockpiles and deficiencies that had been regularly placed on his desk. He knew that Italy still had to import most of her coal requirements but tried to convince himself and others that, in an emergency, they could make a 'colossal effort' and repair the deficiency from domestic mines.[132]

The supply of coal was, in fact, a vital point he had not properly assessed and, since he left everyone else in the dark about possible requirements, no one else had either. He relied on the false supposition that Italy's deposits of low-grade brown coal could be quickly brought into production, economically transported, and easily adapted to industrial use. In fact, however, Italy's need for imported coal began to rise even further: before many months went by, the armaments industry was almost paralysed for want of fuel and was working to less than half its capacity.[133]

This should not have come as a surprise. Nearly all the ten million tons of coal imported each year had been brought by sea, but in any war against the west it would have to come overland. Yet only two of the nine railroads through the Alps had been provided with double tracks and their capacity was estimated as equal to little more than a quarter of Italy's peacetime needs.[134] Moreover, only in 1940 was it accepted that 10,000 new goods trucks would be needed at once when the war came, and this proved a massive under-estimate.[135] As the trains running on time had become one of the accepted myths of fascism, and as Mussolini had never charged anyone with the task of planning communications in the event of war, the matter had gone by default.

Another difficult problem, that of foreign currency reserves, was treated with more seriousness because, although he had not discussed the possibility of war with the officials in charge, he had been amply warned by them of imminent bankruptcy. But he was not the man to let lack of gold and foreign currency prevent his entering a war in which the map of Europe was being redrawn.[136] To obtain more hard currency, he encouraged the export of arms and, at a time when he might have been expected to concentrate on domestic rearmament, this export trade in weapons continued to grow quite substantially into 1940, much of it with countries against which he would soon be fighting.[137] He had once ordered one of his academicians to investigate a claim by an Indian quack about the transmutation of base metals into gold; more seriously, it was assumed that the gold reserves could be easily replaced once he had his hands on the deposits held in the Bank of France.[138]

Meanwhile, he was content to have his propagandists claim that industry was mobilising faster in Italy than in Russia or Germany.[139] They must have known this to be false, but he was relying on the war being so short that all industrial workers could be sent at once. to the front line,[140] and with a 'lightning war', there would be no need to convert factories to the large-scale production of armaments.[141] The idea of mass production, as he saw it in other countries, he disparaged as typical of a decadent bourgeois or soviet society.[142] Fascist Italy was geared rather to quality – to making one-off racing engines, for example, rather than aero-engines for general use in fighting aircraft. Factories, like so many other things in fascist Italy, were sometimes merely part of the *mise en scène* and might be built to make nothing at all.[143]

Mussolini took personal command of the campaign for autarky to free Italy from dependence on imports. Much was achieved, yet many necessary imports continued to increase. The new 'autarkic fibre' *lanital*, for instance, was intended to reduce textile imports, but could be made only from large quantities of imported milk. Two big steel complexes were nearing completion in 1939, as a result of which it was announced that Italy would soon be almost self-sufficient in the main requirements of wartime industrial production.[144] But this calculation would have been correct only with increased imports of coal and scrap metal – two other commodities that in wartime would be in short supply – and in fact, already before war began, production of steel was declining for this very reason.[145]

There were other miscalculations over food supplies. Mussolini still assumed that fundamental economic facts could be changed by an act of will: for example, in 1939 he ordered that the impoverished *latifondi* of Sicily should be turned into 'one of the most fertile regions on earth'.[146] The propagandists reassured people that basic supplies of cereals were guaranteed by the Duce's wise policies,[147] but were not encouraged to add that this would depend on continued imports of fertilisers by sea – already before the war it was clear that the target was hopelessly unrealistic.[148] Again, meat production was said to be sufficient, which was very far from the truth: consumption of meat had decreased sharply in the 1930s, in part a consequence of the conversion of land to cereal production. Mussolini, who was himself inclined to vegetarianism, expressed pleasure that twenty million Italians were now having to follow his example.[149]

The Second World War

14

The decision for war

Even before Hitler began his offensive in Norway, Mussolini's growing confidence in a German victory reinforced his underlying conviction that a war would be the answer to Italy's problems. The British were his natural enemy; they lacked fighting spirit, and the fact of his entering the combat against them would be the signal for their defeat.[1] He began to fear that the Germans wanted all the booty for themselves and might well get it unless he decided to take the plunge.[2]

On 10–11 March 1940, the German foreign minister came to Rome for talks, and Ribbentrop's deliberately exaggerated claims reinforced the Duce's expectation that the war would be soon over. Boasting in his turn, Mussolini again informed the German minister that the Italian navy outclassed the British and would force them to leave the Mediterranean as soon as Italy entered the war; the Italian air force, he added, was more efficient than ever, and he could guarantee this since it was directly under his personal control from general policy down to minor technical matters.[3]

A few days later, Hitler arranged another personal meeting at which he noted that Mussolini, when confronted with German facts and figures, was like a schoolboy who had not done his homework. The Duce was as usual spellbound, fascinated by Hitler's self-confidence, but also made to feel guilty over Italy's non-belligerence. Hitler did not directly ask the Italians to intervene, but repeated his covert threat that they must make up their minds fairly soon whether or not they wanted supremacy in the Mediterranean.[4]

In reply, Mussolini confirmed his determination to fight as soon as he was sure that the war would be a quick one. Unfortunately, he once again chose to talk in German without an interpreter and so failed to make clear some points which, being the 'doyen of all the dictators', he thought he had a right to put forward.[5] He would have liked to dissuade his ally from a major frontal attack against France, on the supposition that the Germans had already achieved their main objective and it might therefore be better for both of them if they now worked towards a compromise peace. He wondered afterwards whether he had succeeded in putting this view forcefully enough. He also feared he might have gone too far and too irretrievably in committing himself to fight. But he equally feared being left out if Germany won easily – a resounding

German victory without Italian participation would not suit him at all.[6] This was a subtle position to defend with all the right nuances in a foreign language, especially when talking to someone who spoke so fast and so continuously.

Some of his difficulties can be deduced from what he was saying to his entourage. He explained that the first requirement was to manoeuvre in such a way that he could always join Hitler in time to claim his share of the booty, and yet, as he would also prefer to avoid an all-out war, he still wanted to make soundings to see how much the British would concede in a negotiated peace.[7] Meanwhile he would delay any active intervention *as long as possible* – he underlined these last words in a minute dated 31 March.[8] He would also try to keep up the illusion that industry was fully mobilised for war and that the armed services were strong enough to make a decisive contribution; it was therefore reiterated that eight or possibly ten million soldiers could be mobilised almost at once,[9] though he ought to have known that there were enough arms and uniforms for only one tenth of this number – some of the conscripts were already having to make do with a single shirt and only civilian trousers.[10]

So sure of himself was he on the surface, and so little ready to let others have their share in the glory of victory, that he still did not fully consult his army or naval staff on strategy and sometimes omitted even to inform them of his general intentions.[11] Not until early April, two months before he entered the war, did he at last tell them in very general terms that, sooner or later, he intended to fight; but the army commanders were surprised to hear that he would expect them to remain on the defensive – and this made it obscure why he wanted to fight at all. The navy, on the other hand, was told that it would be expected to attack at once all over the Mediterranean 'and beyond it'. The admirals pointed out that, by itself, this was an impossible, even meaningless, command; never did the Duce clarify it; nor did he order detailed plans to be drawn up for an invasion of Malta, Corsica, Bizerta or Egypt.[12]

Though he had privately known for some years that he meant to fight a war in Africa,[13] he had neglected to prepare the strategic plans that would have been necessary. Great numbers of troops were concentrated in Libya, but without enough trucks to make them mobile, without proper plans to keep an attacking force supplied with water, and without investigation into the adaptability of tanks to desert conditions. Nor did he accept a recommendation to modernise the ports of Tripoli and Bengasi, though this was obviously a primary prerequisite.[14] If he had created a proper planning staff, or had taken senior officers more into his confidence, he could have informed himself about these deficiencies and certainly would have realised that an immediate attack on Malta could have been followed by an invasion of Egypt with good prospects of success.[15]

Malta and Egypt, according to the Germans, were the obvious targets for Italy and Hitler therefore offered 250 heavy tanks for a North African campaign.[16] But Mussolini refused, on the grounds that to accept help from Germany would be undignified and would upset his plans for a parallel war.[17] When Hitler also invited him to send twenty Italian divisions to Germany for a joint attack on France, he did not dare refuse outright and the Führer laid his plans accordingly; but six weeks passed without any action and the German army eventually realised with annoyance that they had better give up any idea of active Italian collaboration.[18] The failure to devise in broad outline a joint axis strategy was hardly Hitler's fault; Mussolini simply assumed that he would get more booty from a parallel war, and because of this faulty assumption was to end up with very little booty at all.

Though disappointed that Hitler gave him no warning, Mussolini was glad to hear of the invasion of Norway early in April and, after the British defeat in Scandinavia, announced that he could no longer bear to remain passive or to delay his 'appointment with history'.[19] He also reiterated his conviction that, if he did not fight, the Germans might invade Italy to compel him[20] – as though they had nothing more important to do. More seriously, he was impelled to action by an apprehension that the survival of fascism might by now be bound up with contributing to a German victory.[21] He tried to disguise his passivity by asserting that he thought of Italy as already at war, though still hoped to delay any actual fighting until after the harvest; he said he saw himself as a cat watching its prey and choosing precisely the right moment to jump, waiting until he had 'an almost mathematical certainty of success'.[22]

Throughout April, since there was little obvious enthusiasm for war among the Italian public, he again criticised his fellow-countrymen for being stupidly unwarlike; they would have to be kicked in the backside to make them understand that war alone determined the hierarchy of nations.[23] The message put across each day by the propaganda ministry was that war was glorious, heroic and profitable. People were told that fascism had perfected the art of 'total war', and the Duce had been years ahead of Germany and other countries in identifying the weapons and tactics needed in modern warfare; moreover the British were too cowardly to fight seriously, so an easy victory was assured.[24] As the German army advanced into Belgium and France, there was a growing awareness that Mussolini might, after all, be right. Some of the fascist leaders later pretended that they had done their best to prevent him fighting, but, at the time, were carried away by the excitement; as soon as they saw what the Duce required of them, Grandi and Federzoni obediently joined the others in clamouring for war.[25]

Mussolini's most cherished ambition was on the point of being realised:

that of being a victorious commander-in-chief. In his opinion, the secret of German success was that Hitler, not the generals, dictated strategy. So he relished the dramatic impact of telling his colleagues that as soon as war was declared he would 'mount his horse and take over command'.[26] Balbo and De Bono, two of the longest-serving fascist leaders, were not alone in wondering whether he was off his head if he could use such language.[27] But some of his civilian colleagues continued to flatter him that he was a military genius and he himself felt sure that, in addition to his many other responsibilities, he could personally do the work of supreme commander with only a single assistant.[28] The result was that Italy not only lacked an efficient command structure but lacked any awareness that one might be needed: most of the mistakes made in the next few months stemmed from this deficiency.

According to the Duce, there was no point in warning or consulting the civilian ministers and fascist *gerarchi*, and when someone suggested that the Grand Council should meet to discuss policy, he replied that he would not summon it until after the war was won.[29] It cannot have crossed his mind that this determination to take all the glory for himself might be a recipe for disaster, landing him with full responsibility for defeat. A final meeting of the cabinet took place a week before the date he had chosen for his declaration of war, but, in a piece of theatre that he must have relished, the possibility of war was not mentioned.[30]

One thing he took particular care not to reveal to others was that France and Britain had by now hinted that they were ready to negotiate and to guarantee that, even without fighting, he would have a full say in the peace settlement: they had also mentioned three or four possible concessions in Africa.[31] But to accept such an immense and inexpensive prize would be altogether too unheroic; even if he stood to gain twice as much without fighting, he was determined to refuse because only military victory would satisfy him. He had said the same when the Ethiopian and Albanian wars were about to begin: military success was far more desirable than territorial acquisition by peaceful means, and to back down now would mean 'relegation to the second division of nations.'[32]

At the end of May, after Calais had fallen, when Belgium had surrendered and as the evacuation of Dunkirk was beginning, Mussolini finally informed military leaders that he had decided to declare war the following week. He explained that he could wait no longer since in two weeks' time France would probably have been beaten and fascism 'did not believe in hitting a man when he is down'.[33] An essential part of the public legend was to be that the French were far from being on the point of collapse when he declared war.[34] In private, however, he took pride in the perfect timing of having waited until there were no further doubts about a German victory, and he was in fact already making preparations for the peace conference.[35]

The timing was nearly correct and, despite Roosevelt's angry talk of a 'stab in the back', it would have been extremely foolish for him to have entered the war earlier than at the very last moment. Mussolini was hoping that the Germans might still receive a few hard knocks before their final victory and did not forget that they were possibly a future enemy.[36] But above all he hoped – and said as much to many people – for one or two thousand Italians to be killed, so that he could claim his share of what he kept referring to as the booty.[37] He had been handed a splendid opportunity and thought he would never be forgiven if he missed it. With luck, he would not need to inconvenience the Italian people too much; he would not need a full mobilisation and would try to minimise any disruption in the ordinary life of society.[38]

The German generals had been anxious for Italian intervention in September 1939, but were now much less interested and saw Italy as probably more useful to them neutral than belligerent.[39] Their doubts were confirmed by Mussolini's confused strategic objectives. At the end of April, his intention had been to 'bring Jugoslavia to her knees', but when the Germans tried to divert him away from this valuable source of raw materials, he suddenly turned his attention to an invasion of Greece, causing considerable difficulty to the staff officers who were given only a few days to draw up the necessary plans.[40] At the end of May, when Hitler advised against any Balkan involvement at all, Mussolini again fell into line, making the comment that an invasion of the Balkans would be a waste of effort since Italy would receive this area as a free gift at the peace conference; and a new order went out to transfer his 'tanks' to Libya.[41]

On the Alpine frontier he ordered that, though he would be declaring war on France, there should be no offensive action at all, not even air sorties; he intended to keep his forces intact and not risk the ignominy of failure; his actual words were that he would declare war but not make war.[42] Nevertheless, as he was confident that the fighting was nearly over, he at last offered to send some of his soldiers to Germany so that he could claim to have been instrumental in the final victory, and a few days later made this sound better by offering a whole army corps which was, he said, superbly equipped with the finest weapons. He hinted that this might be used for the invasion of England, adding that it would include an armoured division[43] – Hitler must have known that there was no such unit in the Italian army. The Germans were also told that eight and a half million soldiers were ready, and this, too, Hitler would have known to be almost ten times higher than the true figure.

First months of war

Mussolini's declaration of war on 10 June 1940 seems to have met with more perplexity than enthusiasm among Italians, though he tried hard to convince himself that public opinion was behind him. On the assumption that the war would last only a few weeks, he confirmed his order that civilian life should continue much as usual and people should be protected from being incommoded by a full-scale mobilisation.[44] On the other hand, cabinet ministers and the *gerarchi* were told to leave their offices and at once take up military duties in the front line. This was not the last time he gave such an order. He had also sent them to fight in earlier wars and clearly liked to give the impression that fascist ministers, even when without serious military training, were instinctive fighters who could move at once to the command of a field battalion; he also liked people to think that he could govern the country without their help. But, in fact, their absence left the civil service in disarray. One example of the administrative confusion was that ships at sea and in foreign ports were not warned in time to return home, and a third of Italy's merchant marine was thus lost before any fighting took place at all: no other country made this mistake and its effects were grave. But for Mussolini such details did not matter: he expected to get these ships back soon in the peace settlement, as well as others belonging to Britain and France that would be due to him by way of reparation.

He still categorically refused to discuss common strategy or long-term war aims with the Germans, but since they had now been told that he was intending to fight with the utmost energy,[45] it came as a surprise to them that the expected attacks on Malta, Egypt and Corsica did not take place. They were equally surprised that his army on the French frontier remained strictly on the defensive, and German newspapers had to be instructed to make no ironic comments on what Hitler privately ridiculed as sheer cowardice.[46] Not until after the French asked for an armistice, on 17 June, did Mussolini order his generals to launch an offensive in the Alps. He suddenly realised that it might be important to occupy some enemy territory before the war came to an end and, although his staff hinted that it was an absurd decision because weeks would be needed to change from the defensive positions he had ordered previously, he overruled them and ordered an attack to begin at once without waiting to bring up the heavy artillery they needed.[47] Meanwhile, he asked the Germans to delay signing an armistice for as long as possible so that his offensive would have time to get under way.[48]

Before the attack could begin he gave Hitler a list of his territorial claims for an armistice: they included southern France, Corsica, Tunisia and French Somalia. But a few hours later he suddenly changed his mind and said he would not ask for any French colonies at all. His surprised staff officers were well aware that omitting to occupy Tunisia and the naval base of Bizerta might be very serious if the war continued, because only with Bizerta could they fully control the supply lines to Libya and block the straits of Sicily to enemy shipping. Unfortunately, he felt that, having given the Germans his list of demands and then almost at once having changed it, he could not reverse this second decision without looking ridiculous.[49] Only much later, after this one casual omission could be seen as a major reason for Italy's defeat, did he try to pretend that Hitler had asked him not to claim Bizerta. In fact the Germans regretted that he was asking for so little; the real explanation lay in the Duce's excessive trust in his own intuition, as well as his dislike of asking others for advice; his fear of looking foolish if he changed his mind a second time, and his assumption that the war was over.

The armistice was signed a week later, on 25 June, but in the interim the Italian attack on France made very little progress and outsiders could see that the Italian staff work and army equipment were totally inadequate.[50] The story was put about by Mussolini that they had scored a tremendous victory and occupied vast zones of French territory,[51] because he could never admit that his decision to attack had been too hurried, nor that he was at fault in not consulting his general staff, nor that the lack of preparation for this Alpine offensive had been his own personal responsibility. He had encouraged Italians to believe that they had the best air force in the world and could win a 'lightning war'; the consequent disillusionment was bound to come as a severe shock and reflect on the myth of his infallibility – several hundred thousand soldiers could now judge from what they had personally experienced, whatever his propaganda stories might claim.

Mussolini himself preferred to lay the blame on his troops and on Italians in general for not being worthy of his leadership. He remarked that the lack of success must chiefly be the fault of the bourgeoisie with their illusions about comfort and material prosperity; despite all he had done for them, they were thoroughly disobedient and anti-fascist. He said he would one day tell Italians the real truth about themselves and try harder to breed a tougher race; but in the meantime, he hoped the war would last a little longer so as to bring them serious hardship – even if it ended soon, he added menacingly, he already had plans for another war that would help to strengthen their character.[52]

One possibility still at the back of his mind was that any future war might have to be against his German ally. He did not at all like playing second fiddle to Hitler and, since he rightly feared that Italy was in danger of becoming another vassal state, was all the more determined to pursue his own separate war.[53] Many years earlier he had denounced those who could not see that a German hegemony would be especially dangerous for Italy,[54] but such a hegemony was precisely what he himself now risked creating, and he cannot have enjoyed the fact. He was already worried that Hitler might prefer to ally with defeated France, and this was one reason why the fascists now advocated that no pity be shown to their defeated enemy, especially as the French were trying to pretend that they had been beaten only by the Germans; theirs must become a subject state, reimbursing Italy for the cost and inconvenience of the war – even giving back Italian pictures from French art galleries – and certainly losing enough territory for them to be crushed for centuries so as never again to be able to speak on equal terms with fascist Italy.[55]

Once the French armistice was signed, Mussolini thought that the war was almost over, though on reconsideration he hoped the British would not give in before he had a chance to do some serious fighting against them;[56] he also thought and perhaps hoped that the Germans, in their invasion of England, might be weakened by up to a million casualties.[57] Characteristically, he was hoping for a military victory rather than a compromise peace so long as there was cheap glory to be won and German soldiers to do the fighting.[58] From Grandi and other Italian diplomats back from London he learnt that Britain was on the point of collapse,[59] and this confirmed his poor opinion of the 'Anglo-Saxon race' and what the propagandists referred to as the cowardice of British troops.[60] He was therefore encouraged to demand once again that Italian soldiers be allowed the privilege of taking part in the invasion of England[61] and was much put out when the Germans refused. The excuse given – that Italians would be better employed in the Mediterranean theatre of war – was unwelcome; he first assumed that his allies must be intending to keep all the booty in England for themselves, and then it crossed his mind that they were putting off the invasion just because they did not wish to humiliate Britain. In his view, this would be a major error of policy and one that could be avoided if only they would listen to someone with his own experience. The British must learn to humble their pride under the heel of an Italian occupying force.[62]

Confidence in a quick victory led him to make a number of incautious decisions. One was to order a partial demobilisation to provide labour for the harvest; another was to prepare for an attack on Jugoslavia, but to weaken that attack by simultaneously strengthening his African army for an invasion of Egypt. Marshal Graziani, chief of staff of the army, was apparently not consulted about the possibility of either offensive; Mussolini simply took it for granted that he had won full naval and air command over the whole Mediterranean, and also that 100,000 men could march on foot across 600 kilometres of desert in full summer without difficulty or risk.[63]

The main point was now to seize as much enemy territory as possible before the invasion of Britain brought the war to an end. He felt that in the Europe of tomorrow there would be no room for small nations and hence a small but immediate military effort might reap an immense reward for Italy at the peace conference. But his sudden decision to launch these two offensives caused some consternation among his generals. He worried them by repeated changes of plan from week to week and by his assumption that an attack could be laid on from one moment to the next with a minimum of thought and preparation. However, the Duce expressed a candid contempt for the generals and their worries.[64]

First, at the end of June, an order was sent for the army to change from defensive to offensive dispositions in Libya; then early in July, it was once again decided to concentrate rather on Jugoslavia, until Hitler, who had his own very different ideas, sent a reminder that after the war the axis powers would get all they wanted in the Balkans without having to fight for it. The advice from Germany was that Italian forces should put their whole effort into North Africa for a march on Suez, and Mussolini, in reply, said he would be in Egypt by the end of the month.[65]

On 9 July he came near to scoring a major naval victory off the coast of Calabria. A hazardous manoeuvre by the British fleet was known five days in advance through the skilful interception and deciphering of a message from Alexandria; if the information had been properly acted upon, the Italian navy could easily have concentrated in greatly superior strength under protection of shore-based planes. But the opportunity was lost, never to be repeated.[66] Mussolini, who always insisted on drawing up the daily war bulletin himself, compensated for this failure by inventing the story that half the British forces in the Mediterranean had been put out of action on this one day. Any discussion of what might have gone wrong was forbidden lest these claims (and his own judgement and leadership) be called in question.[67]

This engagement at Punta Stilo was, however, a costly mistake and a direct result of his unwillingness to delegate any responsibility or to organise a command structure that could take quick decisions and co-ordinate the actions of navy, army and air force. It also resulted from his decision that the heavy naval ships should preferably not be risked in a major action: though he later pretended otherwise, he was over-anxious to reach the end of the war with his fleet intact. The German naval experts, like many of his own, found this hard to accept and thought that, by taking greater risks, he could have closed the central Mediterranean to all British shipping at no great cost.[68]

One of the strangest facts of all is that Mussolini still omitted – perhaps simply forgot until too late – to prepare an attack on Malta, though he knew that the British had given up the idea of defending it. Later he confessed this was a major error, but he liked to put the blame on Hitler for not recognising the Mediterranean as a major theatre of war and not providing Italy with more assistance there.[69] This criticism was less than fair. In these early months, Hitler was quite ready to help exclude the British from the Mediterranean;[70] it was rather Mussolini who rejected repeated offers of German assistance because he had political reasons for wanting to win a 'parallel war' on his own and feared German influence extending into southern Europe.[71] If Hitler would not accept Italian troops to help invade Britain, Italy would lose her equality of status if she accepted German forces in the Mediterranean. And another strange excuse given for refusing their help was that Germans, like the British, would necessarily fight less well than Italians in the heat of North Africa.[72]

In May, Hitler had in fact offered tanks to aid the attack on Egypt and renewed the offer in July; again, early in September, he ordered two German armoured divisions to be trained for desert war in Libya,[73] and it is a fair assumption that, had these been accepted, Graziani's large army in North Africa could easily have reached Suez.[74] Though Mussolini's generals on the spot knew that they needed something larger than the three-ton Italian armoured car with its two machine guns, he obstinately refused to listen to them.

The Duce was adamant that the Italians had to invade Egypt by themselves and assumed that the British would have to concentrate all their forces at home to resist a German invasion. He ordered an attack in June, and repeated his order in July, but on both occasions his generals felt unable to move because they lacked enough equipment. A third time, in August, when he heard again that the German invasion of England might be imminent, he repeated his order to Marshal Graziani; but the latter, to Mussolini's disgust, called his senior officers to a council of war which unanimously agreed that they were not nearly strong enough to attack across the desert.[75]

Such a consultation with subordinates was denounced in Rome as thoroughly un-fascist. Graziani, however, was able to point out that all the claims about Italian air domination over the Mediterranean – claims which Mussolini did his best to encourage though he knew them to be false[76] – had been mere morale-raising propaganda. Graziani also pointed out that much of the motorised equipment they needed was waiting unused on the Jugoslav frontier, simply because Mussolini allowed very little initiative to his chiefs of staff and could not make up his own mind to concentrate his forces on a single front. But the reply from Rome was another peremptory command to advance and, in September, Graziani at last moved across the Egyptian frontier as far as Sidi el Barrani.

Mussolini was delighted because he had taken personal responsibility for rejecting the advice of the experts and so won for Italy the 'glory she had been vainly seeking for three centuries'. He assumed that the war was now as good

255

as won, not knowing that the invasion of England had been postponed indefinitely. He even tempted fortune by saying that he was sorry peace might come before he had the chance of further victories: war, he told the crown princess in September, was the one truly beautiful action that made life worth living.[77]

In the excitement of the moment, instead of correcting his mistake and mobilising his main forces in North Africa, he dreamed of further expeditions to seize Corsica and Tunisia in time for the peace settlement,[78] and adamantly insisted that a quarter of Italy's effective air force be allowed to help in the Battle of Britain. His staff officers, when they heard belatedly of this offer, vainly suggested that to weaken his air strength in the Mediterranean would be ill-advised and perhaps ruinous.[79] But only after the arrival of these planes in Belgium did Mussolini learn that their range and equipment made them quite unsuitable for the bombing of London to which he had been looking forward; after several months of wasted effort they had to be brought home, and by that time his forces in North Africa, lacking sufficient air cover, had suffered a major defeat.

These few months revealed his deficiencies as a war leader. He never learnt, even after this experience, to avoid diffusion of effort over a number of different fronts, but invariably left each sector with insufficient capacity to score a real success. He disliked taking advice on such a point from anyone: and whereas Hitler saw no indignity in bringing General Keitel to summit meetings, the Duce used to leave his generals at home lest Italians should suspect he could not make strategic decisions on his own.

Another weakness was his penchant for startling his chiefs of staff with sudden changes of plan as though this were a sign of decisive and imaginative generalship – without the least idea of the complexities involved. He could happily order subordinate officers to act against official instructions and, furthermore, without informing their commanders of what he had done. In war, as in peace, he made the mistake of sacrificing substance for effect, preoccupied above all with demonstrating that he alone was in command. He would not have been pleased to learn that the impression he gave was not that of a commander-in-chief or a minister of war, so much as of a journalist thinking mainly of tomorrow's headlines.[80]

The attack on Greece

Another insufficiently considered project was his continuing plan to bring Greece and Jugoslavia into the war, and this is further proof that he greatly overestimated the strength of his armed forces. He was repeatedly warned by the Germans against making new enemies unnecessarily, but ascribed their warning to a jealousy of his parallel war and a wish to take over the Balkans for themselves. Between July and September, three or four different plans for an attack into the Balkans were prepared, adopted and discarded, according to his changing whims. Ciano, who was particularly anxious to provoke a war against Greece, thought up a project to assassinate the Greek king and innocently imagined that a single bombing of Athens might be sufficient to force a capitulation.[81] Mussolini, too, assumed that the 'liquidation' of Greece would be profitable and easy. He forgot that, in order to make his army seem larger, he had almost halved the size of Italian divisions, and on the strength of what was therefore an entirely erroneous calculation he boasted that he had half a million men waiting on the Jugoslav frontier and 200,000 more ready to attack Greece.[82]

Yet he also thought it wise to pretend to Hitler that he had no serious intention of attacking Greece or Jugoslavia,[83] but was concentrating on an invasion of Egypt as the overall strategy of the axis required. Accordingly, early in October, the Germans offered once again to send tanks to Africa but were again turned down because Mussolini was determined that Italian forces should win the first battle on their own.[84] He went so far as to boast to Hitler that, despite the fact that his advisers thought it unwise, he had given Graziani a precise order for a further advance to begin on 15 October and a hundred heavy Italian tanks were already in position.[85]

This was pure armchair strategy and, in any case, the hundred heavy tanks simply did not exist. He must also have forgotten here was an even stranger fact – that a few days previously he had ordered a further substantial demobilisation: over half the total strength of the Italian army was now under orders to return to civilian life because he had decided that he could not afford to remain at full strength throughout the winter. The order to demobilise was taken without much consultation; the general staff merely added the very important rider that, in that case, no further military operations be considered until May 1941, at the earliest.[86]

Possibly the Duce read their comments too hurriedly to take in this warning, for he persisted in his order to attack Egypt and threatened to dismiss his commanders for suggesting that any further advance would need months of preparation. On second thoughts he agreed to put off an advance until December, only to revive his earlier project to attack Greece instead – again apparently without consulting his planning staff. They were told to be ready to start in two weeks' time and he added that 'if anyone makes any difficulties about beating the Greeks I shall resign from being an Italian'.[87]

Graziani, despite his exalted position as chief of army staff, heard of the invasion of Greece after it had begun, through listening to the radio news.[88] The chiefs of staff of the navy and air force knew a few days in advance and protested, but Mussolini ignored them and they were too cowed to persist. He told Hitler that he had no confidence in any of his senior officers and preferred to take these decisions on his own – a fact that made him all the more vulnerable to the deliberately deceitful figures with which Hitler duped him.[89]

As a result, certain elementary hazards were left out of account. The navy could have told him that there were no ports on the far coast of the Adriatic suitable for disembarking a large army; staff officers were also aware that the rainy season was due to start a few days before the invasion was planned to begin, and there were bound to be difficulties in mountain territory for which no maps had been prepared and where roads were non-existent. But since he expected a complete victory in a matter of days, such details appeared unimportant. Nor did anyone have time to think of issuing the attacking force with winter clothing, though the temperature would be below zero.

Mussolini later issued falsified evidence to conceal his responsibility for these mistakes.[90] Before publishing one document, he deleted the fact that a formal request was made by the chiefs of staff for twice as many troops and three more months of preparation. Although the generals can be censured for not persisting in their objections, the real responsibility rests with Mussolini because he had himself chosen pliant officers of little character who, in true fascist style, had learnt not to argue or answer back. He believed that anyone who made difficulties about fighting the racially inferior Greeks ought to be shot,[91] and to allay any remaining doubts he said that confidential information in his possession made any 'technical objections' unimportant.[92]

Unfortunately this confidential information was spurious. For example, he was assuming that he could count on receiving active help from Bulgaria, help which never materialised and which – inexplicably – he had done nothing to obtain.[93] False intelligence reports also convinced him that the invasion would be a 'military promenade' in which the invaders would have a two-to-one superiority in numbers: other authoritative reports said almost the exact opposite, but he refused to consider them.[94]

His trump card was the secret knowledge that Greek generals had been bribed not to fight – this was the same technique that the fascists had used earlier in Ethiopia and Albania. Many millions of lire had indeed been allocated to the corruption of Greek politicians and generals, but this had no practical effect whatever – if, indeed, the money was not purloined by fascist agents before it left Italy. Instead of a revolt breaking out behind the Greek lines as he had expected, it was his own Albanian mercenaries who deserted and went over *en masse* to the enemy.[95]

Preparations were hurriedly made for 'incidents' to take place in Greece that would provide a pretext for claiming that he was compelled to defend Italy against 'aggression'.[96] It was, he told his doubting colleagues, going to be a *Blitzkrieg* like that of the Germans in Poland: a savage bombing of major cities would bring victory 'in a few hours'.[97] He said he might go to the front line to command in person. On second thoughts, he set up his headquarters in southern Italy, ready to make his ceremonial entry into Athens at the moment of success. He apparently thought it unnecessary to stop the demobilisation of the army, or perhaps feared that to reverse this decision would have demonstrated the incoherence of fascist policy to too many Italian soldiers; or just possibly he forgot.

The war was timed to begin early on 28 October. The intention was to take the Greeks by surprise, but Ciano had been talking indiscreetly for days and a valuable advantage was lost. The Germans heard about these indiscretions a week in advance, though Ciano explicitly denied the rumour when they questioned him – Mussolini had been hoping to prevent their knowing in case they tried to stop this parallel war.[98] Hitler rushed to Italy for an urgent conference but arrived just too late; he brought his chief of general staff with him and was clearly hoping for serious military talks, but Marshal Badoglio, Keitel's opposite number, did not know about the conference until it had taken place.[99] Mussolini wanted no one else to share the glory of command as long as he thought the war would soon be over.

Hitler tried hard not to wound his fellow-dictator's feelings but in private was beside himself with anger. He simply could not understand the decision to fight such a profitless war after the rains had begun, and rightly feared that any military reverse would gravely damage the axis in the eyes of neutral states such as Bulgaria, Turkey, Spain and Jugoslavia. It would also give British planes a base in Greece from which they could bomb the Ploesti oilfields and, by barring the sea route from Romania along which Italy obtained much of her oil, would result in further overloading of the transalpine railways. From now onwards, Hitler had little confidence in Italian military co-operation.[100]

But the major disaster was that, despite fascist talk of a lightning war and despite unchallenged Italian air superiority, the Greeks pushed the invading army back into Albania within a week and for the next three months Mussolini had to fight a sometimes desperate defensive war. Another blow came on 11 November when half the Italian battle fleet was put out of action at Taranto by a British carrier-based attack; he had always dogmatically denied the utility of aircraft-carriers and, as he was planning for a short war, had not even used his nine months of non-belligerence to safeguard the vital Taranto anchorage. He could not bear to reveal the full damage in his daily bulletin, though he continued claiming that he was the only war leader to tell his people the whole truth; from now onwards, many Italians turned to British radio to learn what was happening,[101] and this was a major defeat in the field of propaganda where hitherto he had been almost invulnerable.

Worst of all, however, was the fact of being beaten by the much despised 'Levantine' Greeks. Repeatedly, but unavailingly, he demanded that the army renew its offensive as he was humiliated that the outside world should see such a shaming reverse, and he tried to insist that every one of the larger towns in Greece with over 10,000 inhabitants be systematically 'razed to the ground' so as to create panic among civilians.[102] His commanders were able to point out that this would be quite impossible, and though some of them were sufficiently anxious for promotion to reinforce his illusion that victory was just round the corner, Marshal Badoglio found the courage to point out that this campaign had been imposed on the general staff for purely political reasons and they had known from the first it was a military absurdity. The Duce was at last told outright that his own amateurishness and megalomania were leading Italy to defeat.[103]

For saying such things, especially in front of others, Badoglio lost his job as chief of general staff. Mussolini saw his own personal prestige as the one necessary factor in fascist policy; as had recently been said of him by the last British ambassador in Rome, 'his first consideration is Mussolini, his second is the fascist regime, his third Italy'.[104] Anything that went wrong had to be blamed on others.

As the army continued to fall back into Albania, many other people besides Hitler and Badoglio could perceive that an elementary error had been made in opening this front in the Balkans when the obvious area for attack was North Africa. A tank expert sent to Libya confirmed that, if only German help had been accepted, the small British force in Egypt could have been beaten by now without much difficulty; but Mussolini, who unlike the Germans had omitted to study this vital point, deluded himself that tanks would not be of much use in the desert sand, and still hoped to succeed in Egypt on his own.[105] Hitler, however, realised that there was little chance of Italians winning by themselves; and yet, though he knew it was vital to reach the Suez Canal, he also realised that the personal prestige of the Duce was at stake, so did not dare to press his criticisms too hard.

From now onwards, the relations between the two national leaders took on a new character. Mussolini had been trying to cling to his early conviction that he was the first of the dictators, the cleverer of the two, the leader of the more interesting movement and with a right to equal consultation, if not actually to take the lead.[106] A number of people who knew them both, including some Germans, have testified that they thought Mussolini the more interesting personality – the more intelligent, even – and certainly less unattractive; so his conceit was not entirely unfounded.[107] But under the stress of war even such a vain man must have begun to doubt his claim to superiority.

While Hitler continued to show friendship towards Mussolini that not even defeats could change, the feeling was hardly reciprocated. The Duce, as well as making sarcastic remarks about Hitler's rouged cheeks and presumed sexual tastes,[108] could not conceal his envy of a younger, taller, more obviously successful man; some people noticed a positive dislike, even a sense of puzzlement in Mussolini as to how the Germans could be taken in by such a person,[109] and this resentment became more obvious as Italy was forced into increasing dependence on German help. He used to say that the Führer had none of the decisive gestures or soldierlike demeanour that a dictator should possess; and while enjoying the residual sense of superiority that this gave him, he thought that Hitler's poor appearance reflected badly on other dictators by detracting from the qualities that this select band of supermen should be seen to possess.[110]

This, at any rate, was what he told his colleagues, but no doubt it masked a displeasure at being outshone and a growing feeling of helplessness and humiliation as the rickety structure of fascism was increasingly laid bare to the light of day. This dangerous state of mind must have encouraged Mussolini to abandon caution in one final attempt to win the glory he thought was his due.

Defeat, 1940–3

15

Setbacks in Libya and Greece

In October, after four months of talking about a decisive attack in North Africa, Mussolini threatened to dismiss Marshal Graziani if he did not advance at least one stage further into Egypt.[1] The latter boasted of commanding what he called 'the finest colonial army in the world,' but was reluctant to move because he thought the British had eighteen divisions in Egypt, or about 300,000 men, as many as he had himself. The numbers of the enemy were, in fact, less than 35,000, but his information services had been effectively deceived,[2] just as a few months earlier they had been deceived into overestimating the French Middle Eastern forces by a similar ratio.[3] In December, this smaller but more mobile and better trained British and Indian force caught him unawares by a surprise attack and within days his poor generalship turned a minor reverse into catastrophic defeat.

The fascist government had an easier task this time in blaming the incompetence of its own generals, but Graziani was emboldened by defeat to defend himself by protesting that the fault lay less with the army than with a fascist leadership that had repeatedly tried to force him into action against his better judgement.[4] Some of the fascist *gerarchi* were thus at last learning that the system itself was at fault in its exaggerated emphasis on centralised discipline; they now commented, if only in private, that no one had ever been allowed to point out weaknesses or faulty decisions because that would have meant criticising the system and hence the supreme leader himself, who was tabu.[5]

The defeats in Greece and North Africa were so unexpected that they caused panic among the top commanders. Graziani's first thought was a precipitate retreat to Tripoli – 1,500 kilometres away – 'rather than expose my person needlessly at the front'.[6] The commander in Albania, General Soddu, advised the supreme humiliation of asking the Greeks for an armistice.[7] But Mussolini, with admirable self-control, pretended that he was not particularly worried. He ordered the troops to die at their posts and never retreat.[8] He was able to blame not only second-rate commanders but Albanian and Arab units which had given way under fire, as well as soldiers from southern Italy where, in his opinion, the Italian race was proving defective. He said that deserters should be shot out of hand and any gaps filled by drafting prisoners from Italian gaols.[9]

General Cavallero was called out of retirement to succeed General Badoglio as chief of general staff, only to be sent at once to Albania to take a simultaneous field command. Mussolini had behaved in this way before. He liked being in sole charge at Rome without *comando supremo* being permitted any independent existence, and this even though he was unable on his own to achieve a proper co-ordination between the three services.[10] So determined was he to appear as the *generalissimo* who had everything under precise control that he proceeded to intervene more and more in the day-to-day running of operations, even down to the most minor details: in this attempt to impress other people he could sometimes give contradictory orders, which led only to confusion.[11]

Behind his calm façade, he was puzzled as to what had gone wrong.[12] He had carefully and deliberately singled out Greece as a much weaker country, choosing what he considered the best moment to attack her by surprise: not only was defeat therefore incomprehensible, but the rest of the world might thereby be tempted to think that fascism was empty blather. He could sack Badoglio, Graziani and other generals, but had to admit that even ordinary soldiers had fought without enthusiasm, almost as if the fascist revolution, far from improving the 'Italian race', had produced the reverse effect. It was incredible but true that Italians had fought better in the First World War before fascism was heard of,[13] and some people were bound to draw the conclusion that the flaw was at the very top – a failure of leadership and of fascist doctrine and practice.[14]

The Germans felt this strongly. If the Italian generals were bad, said Hitler, a true leader would not simply dismiss them; they should be shot and troops who retreated ought to be decimated.[15] The main blame should be placed on Mussolini himself, all the more so for dispersing Italy's forces and starting a quite unnecessary war against Greece. Although his armoured divisions had by now been shown up as pure invention, he continued to refuse offers of help and advice from the Germans and went on pretending that the Greeks were on the point of defeat.[16] Mussolini also refused German requests to encourage Arab independence movements in North Africa because this ran counter to his imperialist ambitions, and his determination to annex Tunisia led him to block any agreement with the defeated French, thus depriving himself of the short supply route to North Africa that ran through the Tunisian ports.[17]

In December, however, two major military defeats made him swallow his pride and beg the Germans urgently for material assistance; some people thought he should have gone further and asked them to impose a unified direction on their joint war.[18] Hitler knew that he would have to take over in

North Africa to restore morale and prevent Italy making a separate peace, but feared to do anything that might undermine the Duce's prestige. Though he agreed to send German troops and planes to Italy, the illusion of independence was preserved by pretending that they were under Italian command.[19]

Mussolini could, if with difficulty, accept that he needed help against the British in Africa, but not so easily against one of the 'Balkan agglomerations' he despised. The most he would do was ask Hitler to make a diversionary feint in the Balkans to distract Greek troops away from the Italian front. In reply, Hitler asked for another summit meeting and suggested that this time the Duce should come, not by himself, but with military experts who could talk seriously.[20] Mussolini put off accepting in the hope that the tide of battle would turn and make such an encounter less humiliating, but eventually they met on 19 January 1941; it was a protracted torture of embarrassment, as others could now see that the parallel war was over and only the support of Germany kept the tragi-comedy of fascism in being.[21]

Once again the Duce decided to send the ministers and party leaders to fight as 'volunteers', this time on the Albanian front. As well as demonstrating that he could run the country single-handed, it would force his colleagues to give up the comforts of bourgeois existence and return to a proper fascist combativeness. Public opinion, however, must have regarded the decision as absurd at such a time of national emergency: not only were ministers taking up senior command posts for which they were quite unfitted – physically, as well as through lack of military training – but the work of their departments was drastically slowed down for the next three months. Official documents had sometimes to be sent under fire into the Albanian mountains for signature.[22]

All through January 1941, as the army continued (though more slowly) to lose ground in Albania, Mussolini plied his generals with orders to counterattack and went on building up an enormous but unwieldy force there of half a million men. He now hoped that the German command would postpone any active intervention until he had retrieved his reputation by scoring some success,[23] and he promised himself that he would go in person to Albania to show himself as supreme commander at the final moment of victory. When Cavallero rashly assured him that the moment had come, he arrived on 2 March. He remained in Albania for three weeks, hoping each day that an advance would begin, carrying out his self-appointed role by giving detailed orders to the various commanders.

Quite inexplicably, the Greeks still refused to give way and he returned home angry with his generals for not protecting him from exposure to another public humiliation.[24] He tried to cover up by issuing the story that in Albania he had been commanding the 'greatest and most bloody battle in modern history', and the military bulletins pretended that there had been a huge success as a result of which the Greek army had virtually ceased to exist.[25] Those who, on the other hand, knew the sad tale of failure were given the explanation that he had never intended a real offensive, only 'a reconnaissance in force'; his visit to Albania was said to have been simply a well-merited reward for the troops[26] – an unfortunate phrase that came in for some ridicule as the truth leaked out.

At the end of March 1941, the Italian navy suffered a defeat off Cape Matapan in southern Greece. This was a victory for radar and 'ultra', the code-breaking mechanism by which the details of Italian naval plans were known in London – sometimes ahead even of *comando supremo* in Rome. Mussolini issued one of his usual bulletins calling the engagement a brilliant Italian success, but losses were the worst in Italy's naval history, and at the cost to the British of one plane and its crew.[27] From now onwards the bigger Italian ships, which ranked among the best in the world, were instructed to adopt a more passive strategy than ever and stay within 100 miles of coastal airports.[28] The much-vaunted aerial supremacy over the whole Mediterranean was no longer mentioned in the newspapers.

To repair these failures, the Germans decided to attack Greece and informed Rome that they expected to win this minor war in a matter of days.[29] Mussolini was therefore moved to make one final call to his troops in Albania to attack 'at whatever cost': the honour of the army demanded that history should not show Italy failing to beat a country one sixth its size, and only a quick Italian victory would prevent the Balkans falling under German influence.[30] He again raised the possibility of mass bombing raids on Athens,[31] but was warned that this might bring British retaliation against Rome where, relying on the immunity conferred by the presence of the Vatican, he continued to keep his military command.[32]

In April, the Germans attacked and the campaign lasted two weeks. They asked Mussolini to advance simultaneously but he now preferred caution and gave orders to remain on the defensive until the enemy's resistance had begun to crumble.[33] Hitler was not pleased and spoke of his ally in terms of some derision. He wrote to tell Rome that in the future it must be the Germans who took the decisions; this arrangement would be kept secret so as to be less humiliating but, in reality, Mussolini must now merely pretend that the orders he issued were his own.[34]

The Duce was hoping until the last moment to be able to go to Greece in time to take the surrender personally,[35] but the Greeks forestalled him by surrendering to the Germans rather than to an army which they claimed to have beaten and which, after six months, had still not crossed their frontier.[36]

He was outraged and demanded that due respect be paid to the honour of the Italian forces who had fought so hard for so long. Hitler half sympathised with the Greeks and momentarily thought of leaving the Italians to fight it out on their own; he would have preferred to make an honourable peace with an enemy who had fought bravely and whose help might now be useful. But Mussolini vindictively demanded a complete capitulation so that history would record that fascism had triumphed.[37]

The German generals had no respect at all for this clumsy attempt to falsify the record. Mussolini, however, went further and set about manufacturing a legend that the Greek army, as the rest of the world must surely know, had been in ignominious flight before the German attack had even begun.[38] But too many Italians had witnessed the failure with their own eyes, and many of them would have understood by now that none of his pronouncements could be believed without corroboration. The prestige of the regime never recovered from this setback.

In order to regain some of his lost reputation, and despite the opinions of some who saw the dangers in being too greedy,[39] Mussolini was anxious to occupy as much of the Balkans as possible. He then encouraged his proconsuls in the area to indulge in a typically fascist policy of savagery and repression that was meant to intimidate but merely provoked an equally savage opposition.[40] Though he spoke of acting liberally so as to win friends there against Germany, in practice he was determined upon the forcible Italianisation of Dalmatia and other parts of Jugoslavia.[41] And in Greece – which, for reasons of national pride, had to come under Italian, not German, administration – he knew in advance that there was no possibility of his providing enough food for the population; hundreds of thousands died of hunger and, though he sent what supplies he could, he had to admit his inability to help them survive a tragedy gratuitously inflicted on them by his own malign ambition.[42].

After a few months of fascist administration, the Balkan states were in full rebellion. Half a million Italian soldiers were tied down fighting a guerrilla war which they had little hope of winning and in which they suffered more casualties than in North Africa.[43] It was a brutalising war in which the fascist squads were given a free hand. Mussolini said that starvation in Greece need not bother them too much, since the population had brought it on themselves. He ordered the wholesale destruction of villages if necessary and that twenty hostages be executed for each Italian soldier killed.[44] And all to no purpose, because by now he was left with no definable strategic objective; what had begun as a misjudged attempt to annex part of Greece ended in a humiliating and exhausting war of attrition where no glory and no victories could be won.

The war in 1941

Once he had seized his booty in Greece and Dalmatia, Mussolini again very briefly contemplated offering the British a compromise peace[45] but then decided instead to bank on what he hoped would be a certain German victory.[46] In February 1941, General Rommel was allowed to take over command in North Africa and a few weeks later, without even waiting for his two German armoured divisions to assemble, this complete outsider scored a remarkable victory that pushed the British all the way back to the Egyptian frontier. The Duce of course claimed that it was an Italian success 'assisted by the Germans',[47] though in fact the Italian authorities in Libya had opposed the attack as being bound to fail.[48]

Mussolini was delighted by the success if understandably displeased at the comparison that would be made with fascist inefficiency. In an angry moment, he talked of executing Graziani for not having managed to win before the Germans arrived.[49] He now would have preferred to prevent more German troops arriving because, since Rommel had taught him what could be done, he wanted Italians to have the credit for conquering Egypt.[50] When the Germans requested the setting up of a joint field command and a combined chiefs of staff committee, he refused.[51] Nominally, at least, this German armoured force in Africa had to remain subordinate to *comando supremo* and himself. Under pressure, however, he agreed to make some concessions. He promised not to give any more orders except through Cavallero, who could therefore at last act with some degree of independence as a commander, in theory at least.[52] Nor, in practice, did the Duce dare protest at the arrival of more German reinforcements, nor at the fact that Rommel continued to act independently without much regard for orders from Rome.

In April 1941, the surrender of Addis Ababa to a mixed allied force was followed by the loss of Italy's East African empire, exactly five years after its creation; what Mussolini liked to call 'the pearl of the fascist regime'[53] regained its independence as his large army was defeated in much less time than taken by the victorious campaign of 1935–6. One reflection on his brand of imperialism was that almost all the coloured troops in the fascist army defected.[54] He was particularly annoyed when an Italian general in Ethiopia surrendered to a Belgian unit, since the Belgians were in his view another people who did not deserve to be called a nation and had no right to place themselves on a par with Italy.[55] Too many Italians had surrendered in East Africa and too few had been killed – a fact which he strangely interpreted as demonstrating another 'deficiency in the Italian race'.[56]

His ministers did not like hearing such ungenerous judgements, nor can they have been anything but appalled at his talk of a long war ahead that might give him time to recover lost prestige.[57] He spoke of recruiting a much larger army, forgetting that he already had more soldiers than could be provided with weapons and uniforms.[58] Sometimes he tried to convince the cabinet that there was no lack of munitions, though most of the ministers had been in the front line long enough to know he was wrong; but on one occasion he said the very opposite and, when asked to reconcile these contradictory remarks, refused to reply and abruptly closed the meeting.[59] Neither did he stop to listen to field officers who tried to tell him that the new light tank could not stand up to battle conditions.[60] Some truths were too unpleasant to be heard.

The presence on the Egyptian frontier of German troops with their far heavier equipment created an unforeseen problem of supplies. One answer would have been to revive the project for using the French port of Bizerta in Tunisia which, unlike Tripoli, was equipped with large cranes for unloading ships and was only ten hours' sailing time from Sicily: the usual route to Tripoli took thirty-two hours and was much more exposed to attack by Malta-based planes.[61] Mussolini had failed to take Bizerta when he had the chance in June 1940 – a mistake he belatedly admitted.[62] But now, in 1941, the Germans had good reason not to push France too hard in case Tunisia defected to De Gaulle. The fascists were humiliated and angry that the French still possessed an empire while their own was lost, yet were determined that Tunisia would become Italian at the peace settlement and for this reason still opposed Hitler's wish to reach an agreement with France that might have provided unloading facilities in Bizerta harbour. The result was that vital supply ships continued to rely on the perilous crossing to Tripoli and Rommel's advance troops could be supplied only with difficulty.

At the beginning of June, Hitler called a meeting at the Brenner Pass. Mussolini liked these encounters less and less, as he was usually so overwhelmed by the occasion that he could rarely say much and was merely reminded of his own inferiority.[63] He never found the courage to stand up to Hitler when they were face to face, although Molotov and General Franco had shown how it could be done by anyone brave enough. The Duce used to speak contemptuously of Franco as someone without brains or political flair,[64] but Franco's obstinate defiance of Hitler was completely successful; it saved Spain and earned Hitler's grudging respect, whereas Mussolini's irresolute compliance led Italy further and further towards disaster.

A few weeks later, the Germans unexpectedly attacked Russia. Mussolini had occasionally hoped that he might possibly be able one day to make a common front with Stalin against the democracies, and some fascists had welcomed the prospect.[65] But in June 1941 he had not a moment's hesitation in offering troops to invade Russia, even though the Germans were reluctant to accept and would have much preferred him to fix his complete attention on North Africa.[66] He had a poor opinion of the Russian army, which fascist propaganda had criticised for being too politicised and even too mechanised; and he realised that the booty would be greater if Italians were in force on the Russian front before the war came to an end.[67] This was the same mistake he had made in the previous year. Determined to show that he was in charge of the war as well as Hitler,[68] and convinced that the Russians were so racially inferior that they could put up no great resistance,[69] he persuaded himself that this new war would perhaps last only a few weeks or months. Hence there was no time for second thoughts and no need to hear the opinion of ministers and generals, his own political intuition being a safer guide.[70] He simply assumed that Italians would be enthusiastic at hearing they had one more enemy to fight.[71] Strange though it may seem, he also spoke of having better troops and arms for such a war than the Germans.[72] Even when, after a few days, he discovered that the Russians were far stronger than he had suspected, he did not change his mind but demanded the privilege of increasing the strength of the Italian contingent. At all costs, Italians had to outnumber Romanians and Spaniards on the Russian front in order to stake out their own claims to a dual partnership with Germany in the new order of Europe.[73]

In August he once more visited Hitler to discuss the eventual peace settlement.[74] At their meeting in East Prussia, he again took pleasure in observing that Hitler cut a less martial and dictatorial figure than he did himself.[75] And when German generals offered to shake hands with him, he thought that dignity required him to refuse and give the Roman salute, until it was pointed out that this might be taken as uncouth and bad-mannered:[76] such behaviour, as well as suggesting a sense of inferiority, shows his lack of *savoir faire* on the rare occasions when he had to step off his pedestal. Travelling in a German plane, he insisted on taking the controls alongside Hitler's personal pilot and demanded that this fact be recorded in the published communiqué.[77]

From what he observed of the eastern front he must have realised that there was to be nothing like the lightning war he had been expecting; but when his field commanders told him they had insufficient equipment, he appeared not to be listening;[78] instead he asked Hitler to let him send a further ten divisions.[79] No doubt he was once again encouraged by some of the false claims and concocted maps and statistics that Hitler used on such occasions.

In October 1941, after the latter had reassured him once more that the war was as good as won, he reacted by asking to be allowed to double the Italian strength on the Russian front.[80] His own army staff thought this quite absurd: the trucks and guns for such a force simply did not exist and the 'motorised divisions' he talked of were far from being motorised. But such a fact was unimportant if, as his propaganda services persisted in claiming, the war was virtually over:[81] 'two hundred thousand soldiers in Russia will weigh more than sixty thousand when finally we come to the peace conference', was his explanation.[82] It was important that a batch of Italian journalists should reach the front line in time to report on the capture of Moscow.

Relations between Italy and Germany were not becoming much closer as the result of fighting a war together. The Germans were irate that Mussolini gave away military secrets so carelessly, and hence told him of their plans only at the last moment or when they actually wanted to hoax the enemy.[83] Some of the nazis were looking forward to the time when they could openly treat Italy as a puppet state and no longer an independent ally.

Mussolini, for his part, found it unbearable that others should see him treated as a subordinate and, above all, became disillusioned with his allies as his initial confidence in their speedy victory ebbed away. He criticised them many times in private for being unintelligent, uncultured and untrustworthy; he positively looked forward to their suffering reverses in Russia and being bombed by the British; he even let the thought cross his mind again that Italy might gain more if the democracies won the war, or at least if the Germans had to endure some very serious setbacks.[84] He was aware that some of these anti-German remarks were known in Berlin, as was his equally perplexing order to continue building fortifications on Italy's frontier with Germany.[85]

Another sign of his subordinate position was the number of Italian civilians drafted to work in Germany to replace men conscripted into the army. At one moment, as many as 350,000 of these migrant Italian labourers were in Germany and he had difficulty in accepting the implication that, while the Germans were a race of soldiers, Italians were treated almost as camp followers. It was not easy to explain why these men were not in the Italian army or why there were so many unemployed in Italy in the middle of a major war. Still harder to explain was the fact that Italian workers in Germany were treated less well than British prisoners, sometimes far worse. Half the time of the Italian ambassador in Berlin was taken up with difficulties created by these civilian workers and the resentment shown to them in Germany.[86]

In October 1941, Hitler decided to send a powerful air force to Sicily under Field-Marshal Kesselring for an attack on Malta. He again asked for the setting up of a combined Italo-German military staff and wanted Kesselring to be given the title of 'supreme commander in the south'.[87] But Mussolini would not allow any German to command in Italy, even though he knew that German forces alone stood between him and defeat. This continued refusal to establish a combined command had unfortunate results: though he eventually allowed Kesselring to take the title of supreme commander, he refused to give the title much effective substance and so created unnecessary obstacles in the way of winning the two most important battles of all – the elimination of Malta, and the organisation of supplies to North Africa.[88]

Another battle that was proving hard to win was control of the economy. In his certainty about a quick war, Mussolini had begun by hoping it would not be necessary to alarm people by introducing serious food rationing, and had boasted of this as demonstrating the resilience and strength of fascist Italy while shortages were building up in every other European country.[89] Food stocks were said to be ample as late as the beginning of 1941,[90] though he was secretly having to beg Germany for supplies of cereals.[91] Eventually and reluctantly he was obliged to introduce a bread ration and, because this was so late, it subsequently fell to as low as 150 grams per person per day. He had to admit that he was at fault here but derived a curious satisfaction from the fact that Italians were having to make serious sacrifices and their rations were perhaps the lowest in Europe. In some areas of Italy, despite strict laws and controls, he had to accept that three-quarters of the agricultural produce was finding its way onto the black market.[92]

The war taught Mussolini some lessons in economics. Early in 1940, he hazarded a chance remark that galloping inflation might even have some advantages,[93] but early in 1942 he changed his mind and announced his 'unalterable determination' to hold down all prices and wages.[94] He personally took charge of a new committee to fix prices, only to find that, whatever price he fixed, the goods in question inexplicably disappeared from the shops for the next few weeks and prices continued to rise.[95] Rents, too, continued rising,[96] though they were blocked by law. And several million forged ration cards made complete nonsense of food distribution, which was organised – or disorganised – by forty or more overlapping and conflicting official bodies.[97]

All this he called a challenge to his regime and a touchstone by which its success would be judged.[98] But legislation proved to be no remedy at all. By the end of the year, there was a general run on savings banks and a rush to buy land and valuables, yet money was disappearing from circulation, making it impossible for employers to pay out wages. The black market, which he condemned as incompatible with the fascist ethic, was always resorted to by anyone rich enough, including the fascist leaders and even his own family.[99] Gaols were bursting and there was no room for more prisoners; he had to admit that if he had more police and prisons available, there would be no traders and shopkeepers left in the country.[100]

Mussolini had once said that the corporations were 'the fascist institution *par excellence*' and 'the fascist state is corporative or it is nothing'; but where, he now asked in dismay, were these corporations of which so much had been heard and so little seen for twenty years?[101] Until this moment it had hardly been possible to raise serious doubts about them, let alone to suggest that they were not only useless but harmful, expensive and a restriction on economic life. Now it could be seen, and actually said, that something had gone radically wrong with this central fascist institution. The corporations were intended to run the economic life of the country, but failed to do so. As they were unable even to control prices, this function was handed over to the fascist party; but the party, too, failed entirely, as did Mussolini himself when he personally took over the job.[102]

His favourite whipping-boy when things went wrong was, as usual, the bourgeoisie and he slated them as thoroughgoing egoists who had given only a formal adherence to fascism. Landowners and industrialists could now be identified as enemies of the fascist state. He began to talk of socialisation of the land and nationalisation of electricity, until other fascist leaders – including Grandi, Ciano and Volpi – were afraid that he was relapsing into the bolshevism of his youth.[103] Other more radical fascists, on the contrary, were delighted to see that the leftist programme of 1919 had not been forgotten, and issued statements claiming that their movement had always been socialist at heart.[104]

At one extreme, Count Giuseppe Volpi, Italy's leading industrialist and director of the fascist confederation of industry, brazenly assured Mussolini that Italy's industries were more efficient than those of Britain and the United States and fully able to cope with another three or four years of war.[105] Other industrialists contradicted this in private and said that productive capacity was seriously under-utilised, but it was Volpi's views that were adopted by the propagandists. Such optimism was, of course, dangerous nonsense, and Mussolini knew that the economy was in sad disarray. The older generation, he said, was secretly treacherous and heads would have to roll before things were put to rights. The rich were still liberals at heart despite so many years of fascist education; they were still looking to their profits and refusing to convert their factories to the mass production of arms.[106] The fact that he had not encouraged this mass production, and had done almost nothing to indicate that he thought it necessary, was left on one side. So was the fact that, to the astonishment of the Germans, he still feared to alarm the public by a full-scale mobilisation of resources and a policy of austerity. While some parts of Italy were on short rations, many luxury restaurants in Rome were virtually unrestricted and many stockpiles of material lay unused. But Mussolini preferred to blame others. He complained that only about 300,000 Italians were seriously supporting the war effort; the other forty million were dragging their feet or even helping the enemy.[107] After maintaining for so long that war would show the true mettle of his people, he now had to confess that too many of them were cowards, 'fearing to die and clinging to the ten years or so of miserable life left to them as though they wanted to live for ever'.[108] This belied one of the central doctrines of fascism.

Turn of the tide, 1942

In December 1941, the whole war changed its character when Japan attacked the United States. Mussolini was oddly delighted. He had tended to think of Americans as a basically stupid and uncultured people living in 'a country of Negroes and Jews' which, while pretending to be a democracy, in reality denied freedom of opinion.[109] Roosevelt he regarded as a butt for scatological jokes about paralysis that were neither funny nor in good taste.[110]

One fundamental fact he had known with his usual 'mathematical certainty' was that the United States would never enter the war – something he considered obvious to anyone reading the American press.[111] With equal certainty, he dismissed the stories of her industrial potential as a journalistic stunt that could be disregarded.[112] Her military importance was negligible;[113] even if she entered the war, it would be of no consequence, and long before the attack on Pearl Harbor he contemplated severing diplomatic relations with her.[114]

The Japanese notified Mussolini a few days before they were about to attack and immediately received his full support.[115] Although the Germans were not quite so sure, his own feeling was one of euphoric pleasure at a grand battle between the continents that he now said he had always foreseen. For some unexplained reason he said he was pleased that it was likely to mean a prolongation of the war for perhaps another five years.[116]

The Italian public could not follow him so easily in such pleasure. When he announced from the balcony of the Palazzo Venezia that they were at war with the United States, the reaction – except from the organised claque – was dispirited: many of his hearers had been expecting an announcement that hostilities were almost over, not that they were spreading. In response to popular disappointment he quickly changed tack and tried to start a rumour that the Germans had forced him into this new war against his will.[117]

Another British success in Libya in December 1941 pitched him suddenly from euphoria to gloom. At one point he even suggested that his army should give up Cyrenaica and retreat to a new line 500 kilometres back.[118] But Rommel chose this very moment to do the opposite and attack. Appalled by what he took to be the defeatism and lack of co-operation of the Italian generals, Rommel did this without so much as informing *comando supremo* in case Mussolini, his nominal commander-in-chief, tried to stop him.[119] When the news reached Rome, an order was sent to halt the German attack and, since Rommel refused to obey, the Italian troops under his command were at first instructed to break free and cease collaborating with him.[120] But this did not stop Rommel winning another striking victory, nor Mussolini, when all was over, once again claiming much of the credit.[121]

In the following months, encouraged by this success, the Duce was more confident that he had 'bet on the right horse'. Victory would soon place Italy at the very top of the hierarchy of nations where she would be able to 'direct the whole life of Europe', and the bigger the war became, the greater the reward of booty and reparation. He said it was just the kind of renovating bath of blood that fascism had been seeking, and anyone who disagreed with him on this point should be expelled from the party.[122] The Americans, he repeated, would pose no serious military problem; they were interested in making money, not in fighting, and rumours of their huge production of armaments were mere propaganda.[123] He himself was once again beginning to prepare for the peace settlement and could promise people that there would be no post-war problems – he already knew all the answers.[124]

In private he was not always so confident. An exhausted Italy might well have difficulty in a German-dominated Europe, and he therefore explained that he would maintain fifteen efficient divisions near the fortifications still being built along the German frontier.[125] Sometimes he continued to express pleasure at defeats sustained by his ally on the Russian front;[126] he said he far preferred the Japanese as people and would like to annoy Hitler by writing an article saying so.[127] He also grumbled that the Germans had broken their undertaking to send coal and steel and, in fact, had given him 'nothing or almost nothing of what they promised'. These were the words he used of a country that sent him forty million tons of coal in three years.[128]

At the end of April 1942, the two leaders met in another of those encounters that the outside world took to be important but which were said by one of his chiefs of staff to be of a 'desolating banality'.[129] Mussolini, as usual, let Hitler's torrent of words roll over his head, not daring to argue and hardly venturing to interject a few remarks; thus he gave the impression that he agreed with what was said when perhaps he simply failed to understand.[130] Hitler used to refer to these occasions as his 'hypnotic treatments' and Mussolini had every appearance of being hypnotised, as the Führer talked for hours without a pause, rambling from one subject to another in a manner that made it hard for others to keep awake.[131] Some Italians – the young party secretary Vidussoni, for example – tried to stand up to Hitler and did not fear to interrupt him,[132] but Mussolini could not, and arguments from the Italian side were therefore presented feebly or not at all.

In these Italo-German talks he still refused to be accompanied by one of his

With Starace

Jogging

With the Bersaglieri

The 'battle for grain'

The Duce with *gerarchi* on the
balcony of the Palazzo Venezia

In front of crowds

With Hitler

Neville Chamberlain, Mussolini, Halifax and Galeazzo Ciano at the opera in January 1939

With Vittorio Emanuele

At the front

After the Liberation

own interpreters. No doubt this was because he did not like his knowledge of languages to be called in question, but perhaps also because he did not want others to know how little he himself contributed to the discussion. The result was that the Italian foreign office failed to know everything that had been discussed and agreed, if indeed he knew himself.[133] From Germans who were present we learn that the two dictators spoke a lot about their early lives and discussed other trivia that had nothing to do with the war. Despite his claim to possess a perfect knowledge of German, Mussolini could not always make himself understood correctly and did not understand all that was said to him; yet he never liked to confess as much, and the fact not only placed Italy at a serious disadvantage *vis à vis* Hitler, but must have caused grave misunderstandings in the development of a common axis strategy. He also had to rely on the written report of their discussions, but this was always drawn up by the Germans and sent to him only after Hitler had made any necessary alterations.[134]

Back home in May, Mussolini had to decide whether to back Rommel in pushing on once again into Egypt or whether to concentrate first on the elimination of Malta. It was not an easy choice, but eventually he supported the advance into Egypt after being told that they might well reach Cairo by the end of the month – he added acidly that the British were no problem and his only doubt was whether the Italian generals were good enough. He took full responsibility for this decision to postpone the invasion of Malta and said afterwards that he did not regret it,[135] but it was a mistake. The attackers reached El Alamein and there ground to a halt in a position to which it was hard to bring sufficient munitions, while Malta retained its independence and soon became once more a vital element in the battle of supplies.

At the end of June, before the mistake was realised, Mussolini went to Africa with a large retinue of journalists and party leaders to prepare for a triumphal entry into Cairo and Alexandria. Mindful of a similar visit he had paid to Albania, he delayed his departure until Cavallero was doubly sure of victory,[136] but the timing again proved wrong. For three weeks he waited some 800 kilometres behind the front line – the very thing he blamed his own generals for doing – and he was very offended that Rommel, who always liked being with his foremost units, did not have the time or inclination to return for a meeting. The Germans, for their part, made sarcastic comments on the Duce's unwillingness to go nearer the scene of action.[137]

In his absence from Rome, the administration almost came to a halt because no one else would take responsibility for decisions and he never dared to appoint any 'vice-Duce' to act on his behalf. So after three weeks of anxiety and disconsolate boredom he decided to go home, leaving his personal baggage in the expectation of returning to Africa soon.[138] When at last the newspapers were permitted to reveal that he had been there, they omitted any mention of his true motives, describing his visit as one of inspection and another 'reward for the troops' who had fought so well. Mussolini was bitter towards the generals for making him look a fool once again.[139]

He should also have blamed himself for his credulity, for his inability to devise a system within which the truth could be told and individual responsibility encouraged. Just as he had deceived himself by his own propaganda into forgetting that his army divisions in Albania were only half-strength, so he forgot that the motorised and armoured divisions in Africa about which he boasted were still more myth than reality.[140]

Later, it became more apparent that the official war bulletins that he liked to draft painstakingly each day – and which had to be heard standing when given out over the radio – invented quite implausible victories as a means of raising morale.[141] One notorious example was when, in May 1942, a submarine commander reported having sunk an un-named American battleship, to the disbelief of the naval staff: Mussolini went over their heads and reported it as fact, awarding the commander the highest decoration of all. When the same commander announced a few months later that he had sunk yet another nameless battleship, Mussolini proclaimed him a national hero for an achievement without parallel in history – though both sinkings turned out to be complete invention.[142]

Deceived by his own and Hitler's optimism, and against the advice of Cavallero and other staff officers who again warned him about insufficient and defective equipment,[143] Mussolini was determined not to withdraw troops from Russia but to send more, and the whole of Italy's production of vehicles was pledged for months ahead to this eastern front. Yet he also asked Hitler to consider the possibility of making peace with Russia so as to be able to concentrate their efforts against Britain and America.[144]

His real views are hard to discover because he contradicted himself in trying both to justify the war in Russia and to exculpate himself from the failure to win it. Sometimes he pretended that he had always known how strong Russia was,[145] sometimes he admitted he had been completely surprised by her strength;[146] to some people he repeated that the war against Russia was inevitable and perfectly timed,[147] while to others he pretended that the Germans had attacked Russia despite his advice and the correct policy would have been a Russian alliance;[148] at one moment he ordered that twice as many troops be sent to Russia, at another he said that, if only these soldiers had been sent instead to North Africa, the whole war would by now have been won.[149]

In Libya, the Italian army suffered from one overwhelming disadvantage: messages from Rome were being read simultaneously in London and Italian supply ships could be precisely located in advance by the British planes and submarines.[150] Mussolini did not know this but realised that the problem of supplies was becoming desperate; he put on a brave front, talking as though the British could no longer hold Malta and had no possibility of offensive action.[151] As late as October 1942 it was stated that Italy held the initiative and was far stronger than she had ever been before. Mussolini pronounced that the enemy knew time was against them, whereas the Italians had sufficient strength to hold the Balkans and open other fronts in Corsica and southern France.[152] He said there was no disaffection inside Italy, though some Italians were admittedly beginning to feel the pinch of hunger.[153] He encouraged Hitler to think that there was no need to worry because their enemies were finally on the run.[154]

As he wrote these optimistic words, the battle of El Alamein had already begun. He later blamed the Germans for not having moved their troops back earlier from this dangerous salient,[155] but Rommel had already suggested that it would be wiser to be more flexible or even to draw back, and Mussolini had refused.[156] At the beginning of November, after Rommel at last felt compelled to order a retreat, Mussolini and Hitler – though more than a thousand miles away and both of them quite out of touch with a running battle – reversed the order and instructed the troops to hold their ground at whatever cost. This countermanding instruction, which was known to the British before Rommel even received it, was based on completely false information; it held up the retreat for only a few days but prevented a planned withdrawal that would have saved many lives.[157]

A few days later, an Anglo-American force landed in Morocco and Algeria, catching *comando supremo* unawares, though Mussolini was soon claiming that he had foreseen it and thought it nothing to worry about.[158] He desperately tried to convince people that the war was already won by the axis powers.[159] Ciano, on the other hand, thought it irretrievably lost and said that, if they failed to ask for an armistice now, they would make themselves responsible for useless slaughter.[160] Against all reason, however, Mussolini said that he wanted Libya held to the last man even though he accepted that there was little hope of keeping it. After constantly interfering to hinder Rommel's arduous withdrawal, he then blamed the Germans for not rescuing more of the Italian soldiers whom he himself had left almost entirely without adequate means of transport.[161]

Mussolini in defeat

If fascism was turning out to be unexpectedly feeble and without resilience, the main reason was Mussolini himself and the fact that, though a sick man and often unable to cope, he was compelled to go on pretending to be a superman controlling all aspects of national life. His ability to fascinate was, if anything, greater with the passage of time – at all events, on the fewer occasions he now wished to exert himself.[162] People continued to comment on his acute intelligence, even though they sometimes had to admit that it was mixed with a large dose of ingenuousness.[163] Up to the beginning of 1942 he still showed a quick grasp of complex issues and a gift for synthesis that could arouse the admiration of his cabinet, though his energies were so diffused that he sometimes gave the impression of an enormous power station generating a single tiny lamp.[164] His powers of memory, so he said, were elephantine, and he liked people to think he forgot absolutely nothing – but it is also true that he sometimes appeared weighed down by statistical information, unable to make proper sense of it or to single out what was truly important.[165]

One fatal flaw in the regime was an assumption – now repeated more explicitly – which formed the basis of the whole fascist movement, namely that the Duce had never once made a serious mistake and his pronouncements must be beyond criticism or discussion.[166] Just as his war bulletins had to be heard standing up, loyal fascists would stand during his filmed speeches in cinemas, and in some universities the professors would rise to their feet at the mere mention of his name.[167] His personal dictatorship was something he excused by saying it was positively desired by the Italian people who had never asked him for liberty, and in any case, since 'they lacked the capacity to make up their minds properly', ordinary citizens could not be trusted with liberty even in small amounts.[168]

Up to the middle of 1942, he succeeded by a great effort of will in preserving the outward appearance of self-confidence. He repeatedly told Italians that the whole world had accepted his ideas and that anyone reading his speeches could see for themselves that all the problems of modern society had been resolved: 'there is nothing left to discover, no question still unanswered'.[169] His own speeches had for some years been studied and read out loud in public on ceremonial occasions as though they were sacred texts.[170] Sometimes a million copies of a single speech were printed.[171] His writings were translated into thirty or more languages, mostly published in Rome and paid for by his own propaganda services; a Japanese edition in ten volumes was printed in 1941;[172] even the 'Mussolini law codes', more than 30,000 pages long, were being translated in Rome into the main languages to serve as an essential textbook for the post-war world.[173]

Personal vanity and desire for admiration were singled out by some of his collaborators as the dominant and perhaps most negative elements in his personality.[174] And the flattery which he thus invited was to be a main factor in his undoing; it led him to assume that the machinery of government was running well and effectively under his omnicompetent direction. One *gerarca* described him as being like the conductor of an orchestra who tried to play all the instruments simultaneously.[175] In 1942, as well as being *generalissimo*, he again held five separate ministerial posts, and early in 1943 he sacked Ciano and took over a sixth.

Despite the exigencies of the moment, his temperament was such that he could not concentrate his attention on general policy or on his duties as supreme commander, but continued to indulge his passion for petty administrative details in order to give the superficial appearance of being in charge at every level. It was still as true as ever that minor points of detail appeared to interest him more than major matters of policy;[176] he liked, for instance, to choose the announcers for the radio, to decide whether the Rome opera repertoire should include *Tannhaüser* or *Parsifal*, or at what precise date the city police should change into their summer uniforms; each day in 1942 a hundred articles from the foreign press were sent to him for perusal, and he still demanded a weekly report on every civil servant who arrived late for work in the morning.[177] The bulky files he collected on the private lives of his collaborators are another indication of the minor details that he considered politically important.

Even Ciano had been kept at a distance and often had little idea as to general policy while still holding the ministry of foreign affairs.[178] Since the whole system worked only by having Mussolini on a pedestal, any familiarity was more and more discouraged. Sometimes he recognised the danger of the isolation in which he forced himself to live and speculated that the strength of his personality might have a paralysing effect on others, but in fact it was an isolation which, either deliberately or instinctively, he cultivated as an instrument of government.[179]

The fact that he could not afford to let others think he needed their help or even their opinions was turning out to be one of the great weaknesses of the system. When selecting officials, his choice still fell so consistently on mediocrities and yes-men that it must have been deliberate, and he himself was ready to admit that the *gerarchi* he had chosen and kept in power for so long were all thoroughly second-rate.[180] No doubt his intention was to eliminate possible rivals and reinforce his self-esteem, but it is also true that few men of real worth and integrity would have continued serving such a regime.

Some of the German generals who had to make regular visits to him tried to avoid doing so when Italian generals were present, as the servility that he demanded from the latter was so excessive as to be embarrassing.[181] Civilian ministers, however, could be treated even worse, and only infrequently in these later years did he engage them in conversation or encourage them to make comments. He had an almost physical revulsion towards sharing power or allowing his mask of inscrutability to slip[182] – almost as though he knew that it was only the illusions about his self-sufficiency and the universality of his genius that kept fascism afloat.

This placed an intolerable burden on one man and was a perfect recipe for disaster. Just occasionally he told the *gerarchi* that he wanted to know from them if things were going wrong, but in practice they prudently acted as though his real wishes were very different, and not even Ciano, who as his son-in-law was nearer to him than the others, dared speak out.[183] Cabinet meetings were called sometimes at only two- or three-monthly intervals and might then be addressed by himself alone and closed without discussion.[184] His secrecy, his constant changing of orders, his failure to notify people when orders were changed, his refusal to unwind or relax or admit that he might need their help, all these idiosyncrasies were a constant source of discouragement to those near him.[185]

One of his foibles had always been to let others imagine that he knew everything that was going on in the country – or, when talking to his ambassadors, what was going on in other countries. To obtain his information he continued to spend much time each day studying police reports and telephone intercepts. But others could see that, as a result, his knowledge was often of trivialities and quite inaccurate. One inevitable consequence of this refusal to listen, coming on top of the centralisation of power and the absence of checks and balances, was that in these later years disobedience became much easier. It was said by his chief of police that he was deceived and disobeyed by almost everyone.[186] By trying to control everything, he ended by controlling very little.

The appearance – but only the appearance – was different. A never-ending stream of officials passed through his office each day to receive his instructions, though he had no means of checking that these myriad orders were carried out; moreover as officials knew this, they often merely pretended to obey and took no action at all.[187] His own chief preoccupation was to ensure that the newspapers reported each day that he had given directions on every conceivable topic, ranging from art and education to public works and sport; what eventually resulted was less important than the fact that the orders were a matter of public knowledge.

Equally unfortunate was the fact that any party official could issue an order purporting to come from the Duce, as its authenticity was hard to check. A jungle of overlapping bureaucracies, not only of the civil service but of the fascist party and corporations, created an administrative tangle through which few people could find their way and where Mussolini's own expressed wishes were constantly being lost or purposely mislaid; so much so that one courageous party secretary described him as 'the most disobeyed man in history'. He smiled on hearing this and admitted it was probably true, yet did little to correct it because effective action was much less important than the outward appearance of being the all-knowing, all-wise dictator.[188]

In August 1941, at a critical moment in the war, he suddenly announced that all Sicilian employees of the government, from janitors up to and including prefects and judges of appeal, had to leave Sicily as soon as possible.[189] This order is partly to be explained by his general distrust of southerners and the prevalent conviction in some fascist circles that they were insufficiently warlike and racially inferior.[190] Naturally it caused much offence, not only as a slight on Sicilian patriotism, but because it would mean grave economic hardship and family disruption. There were protests but he overrode them and took full responsibility for the decision. He had not bothered to mention it first to the departments most affected, or he would have realised that to carry it out would have caused administrative chaos; but fortunately his ministers, apparently without telling him, decided not to enforce it.[191]

Another strange decision in December 1941 was the appointment of Aldo Vidussoni as party secretary – an inexperienced, incompetent young man of twenty-six who had not yet completed his final examinations and had not the slightest experience of administration. The other ministers, far from being consulted, had some of them never heard of Vidussoni, and the appointment met with widespread misgiving. Few things can have done more to discredit the regime, yet, though Mussolini soon realised his mistake,[192] he had to pretend to be proud of his choice. The post was, as he acknowledged, the second most important in the country; it carried automatic membership of the cabinet and the Grand Council, as well as control of many senior appointments and, in practice, a veto over much legislation. He could hardly have found anyone less suitable.

In endless propaganda, fascism had been claimed to be more efficient than democracy simply because it was authoritarian, and Mussolini repeated in public his conviction that war would be a fair test of this claim; yet the sheer inefficiency of his preparations for war was the most obvious example of failure. Later, he grudgingly admitted that he had made his soldiers fight the Second World War with weapons left over from the First, though he tried to make out that this had no connection with their defeat.[193] He also had eventually to confess that the new thirteen-ton tank first introduced during the war was a failure and there was no heavy tank at all.[194] On paper, the army had a hundred or more divisions but the effective figure was less than half this number.[195] Authoritative stories continued to repeat the figure of twelve million soldiers ready to fight, four times as many as were ever in fact called up, and it must have surprised Mussolini that fewer soldiers were mobilised than in the previous world war when Italy had a much smaller population – there was insufficient equipment for any more.[196]

Productive capacity was also less directed to war purposes than in the First World War; he did not set up a ministry of war production until February 1943, too late to come into effective operation. By that time, some units of the army were without boots and the call-up of those born in 1924 had to be postponed for the same reason; but the shops were still selling luxury goods in leather and, quite clearly, the rationing of footwear had been introduced much too late.[197] Another awkward realisation was that many years of fascist talk about a 'lightning war' had been based on false premises which Mussolini had reached by mere intuition and never allowed the general staff to debate adequately, with the result that the wrong weapons and the wrong strategy had been adopted from the very beginning.[198]

By the beginning of 1943, many people must have been aware that few possibilities of resistance remained. Only 400 modern and effective fighter planes were in service and the aircraft industry could nowhere near keep pace with losses.[199] Three-quarters of the country's merchant marine had been lost and six ships were being sunk for every one built, while the general disorganisation was such that it was sometimes taking a month to unload a single ship and a year to carry out minor repairs that ought to have taken a few days.[200]

Mussolini could occasionally accept that the armaments industry was insufficiently organised, as he now acknowledged that the wrong moment might have been chosen to enter the war and that it had been wrong to disperse energies over so many fronts. But publicly he had to argue that all was well and try to maintain the pretence that, in a few months' time, Italy would be militarily stronger than ever, with a more formidable air force even than Britain or Germany. Such claims enabled him to repudiate any personal responsibility and blame others for incompetence, cowardice, or lack of patriotism.[201] Just as Badoglio was blamed for the defeat in Greece, so Cavallero eventually became a scapegoat for the defeat in North Africa.

Mussolini said in the last months of his life that he had always given his generals and admirals a completely free hand and had overruled them only once, in a naval battle of June 1942 which had been a great success – he was only sorry that they had too often refused his advice.[202] This was most unfair; it also avoided the criticism that the generals and admirals he promoted were usually the more politically reliable and least independent. Nor did he accept that, in his wish to show that he himself was personally taking the main decisions, he never permitted *comando supremo* to work effectively.

As well as blaming the generals, he always came back to blaming the failure of fascism on Italians in general; one of the files in his private archives was labelled 'immaturity and blameworthiness of the Italian people' and it was filled with any relevant information he could find.[203] He had set himself the task of changing their character and looked upon this as more important than anything else. Just like Stalin, therefore, it suited him to encourage those scientists who believed in the inheritance of acquired characteristics: by making life harder and less comfortable for Italians, he could turn their children into an altogether superior breed.[204] Up until 1942, he sometimes thought he had succeeded in producing a race that was more serious, more warlike, less individualistic, and that they now surpassed the Germans or the British at organisation. They were turning out to be perhaps the most intelligent people on earth and he wanted them to be accepted as at least the 'first people in Europe'. If he failed, theirs would remain merely a tourist country, a large Switzerland; but he was determined to succeed.[205]

Other fascists were not so sure, nor even sure that it was desirable to try, and Mussolini eventually had to accept that he failed. Italians were turning against him, and the fact could sometimes be acknowledged in private, while independent foreign witnesses estimated that, after the reverses in Greece, he had only a small minority of support and was rapidly becoming the most hated man in Italy.[206] Successive police chiefs and other Italians well placed to know said much the same.[207] One senior general suggested improbably that 99 per cent of Italians had reached the point where they hoped Italy would lose the war.[208]

How far the more unwelcome facts were concealed from Mussolini is hard to say, but he was well aware that he could no longer trust older people who had known better days and so had a standard of comparison.[209] He was also beginning to understand that many of the younger generation, despite their moulding by an authoritarian fascist education, were little more enthusiastic than their elders.[210] He clung to the hope that public opinion would change as soon as he looked like winning, but, in the meantime, his judgements on the Italian people became increasingly harsh.

Italians, he now said, were the same as they always had been: unwilling to stand up and fight.[211] They were a superficial people, immature and without character, too unheroic and bourgeois, too sentimental and artistic, too good-humoured and trivial. He had also made the mistake of overestimating their intelligence.[212] Too few of them were real descendants of the ancient Romans; too many had their ancestry in the slave populations absorbed by ancient Rome; too many were fascists only on the surface and hence unworthy of him.[213] His conclusion was that their individualism and readiness to criticise made them into bad citizens: 'governing Italians is not difficult, it is just futile', he was quoted as saying.[214] The intellectuals were the worst element of all; they were a useless burden on society and had always been opposed to him, though that was a matter of small consequence.[215] More important was that Italians in general were a race of sheep. They should be made to eat less and live a less self-indulgent existence, but even so it would take centuries for them to grow up. They failed to understand that only by the 'sublime holocaust' of war could they be made great or become respected and feared; that is why he would never give them a moment's peace until he died. He was ready to be pitiless against them, because only by being bludgeoned into it would they ever adopt a more serious attitude to life.[216]

These acidulous comments were in part the product of dyspepsia and failing health. Having always set great store by physical fitness he still tried hard to conceal his illnesses, but in 1940, as in previous years of political crisis, his stomach pains returned and he sometimes looked a wreck of a man;[217] his leg wound from 1917 reopened, too, and made it necessary for him to wear special boots.[218] Nevertheless, it was a point of honour to prevent others suspecting that he might be too unfit to be in sole charge of a nation at war.

Some observers, however, were able to notice a distinct decline in his intellectual powers and before long were again hinting at actual mental derangement.[219] His own personal fear was that he might be thought too old and he therefore went out of his way to show that he could do the goose step better and run faster than others. He once summoned several bus-loads of journalists to watch a carefully staged tennis match in which the minister for propaganda, acting as umpire, astonished them by unexpectedly announcing that Mussolini had won.[220] Any foreign journalist who so much as hinted at rumours of his ill-health (even to deny them) was expelled from the country within hours.[221]

The determination to show off his youthful vigour did not diminish with the years. He always detested old age and the process of growing old. Inside Italy there had for some time been a veto on any public reference to his age, but he had to make a special request that German newspapers should never give too much publicity to his birthday,[222] though Italian papers were positively instructed to record Hitler's;[223] Hitler was growing older while the Duce was perpetually young. In fact Mussolini was nearing his sixtieth year – an age when, he had once gone on record as saying, members of the fascist party should be made to resign.[224]

In the course of 1941, his ill-health was accentuated by the set-back in Greece and the death of his son Bruno in an air accident. He needed constant nursing and looked old, sometimes even emaciated.[225] Other people would find his behaviour inexplicable as he moved quickly from optimism to black depression. An inability to make up his mind became more marked, and he would spend long periods away from Rome on his country estate where he could be only remotely in touch.

During his frustrating visit to Africa, in July 1942, he experienced very severe internal pains and on his return home a consultant physician diagnosed worms and amoebic dysentery, though the prescribed treatment did him no good and the diagnosis was clearly inadequate. Such was his general disorientation that people again speculated about syphilis, until further tests proved negative.[226] Judging by the unrevealing post-mortem findings of 1945, it is hard to say positively that he was again suffering from a peptic ulcer; the abdominal pains that sometimes crippled him could have been produced by a combination of nervous strain and an eccentric diet.[227] Whatever the cause, there is little doubt that at this crucial moment in the war he was quite unfit to carry out his job.

In the autumn of 1942, more people began to be aware that he was in a pitiful state, though, to deceive the public, untrue stories were put about that he often piloted his own plane to the front line where he could share the hardship of life under fire. His face was ravaged by pain, his memory was failing and in three months he lost twenty kilogrammes in weight; when he turned up at meetings he looked almost moribund. His frequent absence through illness brought the government close to a standstill and other ministers wondered how such an invalid could continue to carry such a burden.[228] There was secret talk of Ciano or Farinacci replacing him.[229] New doctors were called in who gave new diagnoses: cancer was suspected but ruled out after extensive tests,[230] and it was rather accepted that the symptoms were of psychological origin, brought on by the enormous tension of keeping his worries to himself without being able to delegate responsibility or talk freely to others.[231]

Ciano, who had been sure for some time that his father-in-law was not only physically incapacitated but mentally below par,[232] was much too frightened to speak out openly, but was secretly trying to prepare the ground for his own succession to the leadership.[233] He began talking to others about getting rid of Mussolini and seems to have put out vague feelers to discover whether the western allies would be ready to discuss terms with a new government.[234] More than once he spoke of wanting to procure a deadly poison that left no trace.[235]

Towards the end of 1942, Mussolini's liaison with Clara Petacci, which in spite of many other infidelities had lasted for almost ten years without being generally known, became a subject of popular gossip.[236] His sexual prowess subsequently became legendary and some of the stories may well have been true. He used to say that women never influenced his political activity, yet although he knew that Clara's family was involved in a number of unsavoury financial scandals, he accorded them virtual immunity from police action.[237] She was a woman less than half his age and far more loyal and devoted to him

285

than he to her. Mussolini sent her husband to exile in Japan so as to minimise any scandal, but her visits to the Palazzo Venezia were so frequent and regular that the gossip eventually made her out to be the centre of many political intrigues. This was one more sign that he was losing his touch, and by all accounts the affair did his reputation a good deal of harm.[238] Dishonesty and immorality in high places were, as the police knew, alienating people from fascism, as the *gerarchi* could be seen pursuing their private pleasures and avoiding many of the hardships brought on by the war. Rumours – both true and false – spread fast, until 'public opinion came to equate the word *gerarca* with thief or worse'.[239]

The fall from power

16

The vice tightens

At the end of January 1943, as the last foothold in Libya was lost and Italian troops retreated into Tunisia, Cavallero was dismissed from his post as chief of staff. Apart from his doubtful loyalty and responsibility for military defeat, Cavallero had not been forgiven for exposing the Duce to irreverent comments following those two premature visits to assist at victories that never took place in Albania and Libya. Mussolini also asked for the removal of Rommel, whose harsh criticisms of the Duce's military leadership were becoming known and whom it was now fashionable in Italy to disparage as inferior to the Italian generals.[1]

During this month, one of the most critical in the whole war, Mussolini could barely get out of bed and his wife had never known him to suffer so much. He was on sedatives and taking only liquid food. Some of those near him expressed further doubts about his mental capacity and loss of will-power, and he was certainly in no condition to take the decisions that no one else was allowed to take.[2]

To some people it seemed as though the government had almost ceased to exist; and the leader on whom everything depended was too numbed to react. The new chief of general staff, Ambrosio, seeing no hope of victory, thought as Ciano did that the only sensible objective was to seek a separate peace.[3] The country at large was pervaded by a sense of unease that sometimes looked like submerged rebellion. Even loyal fascist writers could report publicly that practically no one seemed to feel that there was any reason for continuing to fight.[4] Mussolini's appearance in newsreels was sometimes greeted in complete silence, whereas a performance of *The Beggars' Opera*, which was seen as a parody of him, received an ovation.[5] In some factories there were damaging strikes on a scale not seen for twenty years; to which he reacted by protesting that he had done more for the working class than any other ruler anywhere. He was ready to compel obedience by using terrorist tactics and shooting any other workers who went on strike.[6] So he said, but probably he did not mean it.

To his *gerarchi* he tried to pretend that the loss of Libya was unimportant because it was still 'mathematically certain' that the axis was winning.[7] He was talking in clichés as he often did when under strain. The fighting would go on because 'war is the most important thing in any man's life': it had consistently been his view that war was the norm, peace the exception, and winning was basically a matter of will-power.[8] Fortunately, he said, the Anglo-American forces had over-stretched themselves; he also spoke of a mysterious terroristic weapon that he would soon launch against the enemy.[9]

He seemed to some of his listeners like a sleep-walker who no longer knew his own mind and did not understand the immense disaster he was bringing on the country. Ciano noted that his father-in-law had never allowed his sleep to be disturbed by the tragedy he had inflicted on so many people. Churchill at least went to visit bombed towns to raise popular morale, whereas Mussolini 'has never once seen anyone killed in the three wars he has commanded': on his visit to Libya he had carefully remained hundreds of miles behind the front line.[10]

To relieve any feelings of personal guilt, the Duce preferred, as usual, to blame Italians in general. He was annoyed that they did not seem to mind much about the loss of Tripoli and equally annoyed and surprised to find that many Italians in Ethiopia were readily accepting employment under the British occupying force.[11] Blame was placed on the Vatican as 'the centre of all the opposition to fascism',[12] and also on the Jews. He expressed approval of the Germans for shooting Jewish women and children. When, however, he discovered that certain Jewish engineers had knowledge that was indispensable to the war effort, he begged them to return to the jobs from which he had lately dismissed them,[13] while continuing to reassure Hitler that, as a race, the Jews were a disease to be cured by fire and the sword.[14]

Much of the blame was still reserved for his own generals – at the same time as he ordered them to fight every inch of the way and at whatever cost in order to delay an attack on mainland Italy. General Messe in Tunisia obeyed this order but thought it a cruel and senseless blunder when there was still time to bring his large army home. Although Mussolini authorised the sending of war material to Africa in hospital ships so as to escape enemy submarines,[15] this could not possibly have been sufficient. The generals had to reconcile themselves to fighting hopelessly to the end. Mussolini could have helped them by agreeing to support a rebellion by Arab nationalists in North Africa, as the Germans again wished, but he could not afford to let his ally dictate policy in the Mediterranean and still saw the Arabs of Tunisia and Libya as belonging to a post-war Italian empire.[16] His bad health probably prevented his comprehending the full tragedy of this military disaster. He was having to spend much of the time at his country retreat, trying half-heartedly to run the war by telephone; his doctor found him very unwell, distractedly playing cards and solitaire.[17]

In these early months of 1943, he appointed a new secretary of the fascist party, Carlo Scorza, a former *squadrista* whose gang had been responsible for the death of Amendola in 1926. Mussolini was no doubt hoping that such a man would revive the fighting spirit of those early years: the kernel of his regime, he said, consisted of the 90,000 ex-*squadristi* on whom alone he could really count.[18] New cabinet ministers were also appointed, and they were a poor choice as he soon had to admit.[19] As usual, he selected them in what seems a purely random manner. One turned out to have been for some time in a mental hospital and some of the others, though he probably did not know it, were inclined towards making peace.[20]

By his own admission, he himself thought of trying to back out of the war, with or without German agreement.[21] He again considered making a separate armistice with the Russians[22] and the Germans thought that he was trying to get in touch with the British in Switzerland.[23] Other fascists subsequently confirmed that he put out feelers to discover what terms he could expect from the western powers,[24] though he denied this allegation publicly and privately. As soon as he knew that the enemy would negotiate only with whoever succeeded him, he lost interest in making peace. Probably he was also frightened of Hitler and in any case was too much lacking in will-power to take the necessary decisions. In April, the Hungarian premier, Kallay, begged him to lead a group of smaller nations in breaking free from the Germans: to which request he made his standard reply that war alone would make Italy a great nation and no one had shown him how to withdraw with honour. Kallay noted, however, that he was greatly preoccupied by the prospect of defeat and a consequent internal revolution.[25]

The possibility of making a separate peace with the Russians was a point he intended to raise again when on a visit to Hitler later in April. A number of highly placed Germans encouraged him in this, though with little hope of success. They had never seen him stand up to Hitler on any serious matter and knew that without any interpreter he was always at a disadvantage; even if he promised to use these meetings to urge a change of policy, his resolution would invariably crumble the moment he entered Hitler's presence.[26]

This was more true than ever when the two now met in the castle of Klessheim near Munich, since the Duce was close to physical collapse, in great pain, barely able to speak, and in fear of being poisoned; someone again described him as looking like a corpse.[27] Hitler tried, not for the first time, to persuade him to see German specialists who might have more success in diagnosing and treating his illness, but the suggestion was turned down because of its implication that Italian doctors were not good enough.[28]

As usual, the meeting turned out to be a series of monologues – 'the usual gramophone record', as Mussolini called it – in a language which on some vital points he misunderstood.[29] He was in no state to reply or even to take an independent stance on any point. Only after his return to Rome did he raise enough spirit to rail against Hitler and say he would never go again to be lectured like a schoolboy by that 'tragic clown'.[30]

One revealing remark he made to the Germans was that fascism was nearing its end because no other Italian had enough ability to continue the revolution after his death.[31] His hosts suspected from this, and from his general demeanour, that he was losing his nerve and no longer was in command of the country. Hitler thereupon made the grave decision to withdraw some troops from Russia to be ready to occupy Italy if fascism should collapse:[32] the Germans had already considered the possibility of such an occupation, and when at Klessheim Mussolini refused an offer of five more German divisions for use in Italy, Hitler was confirmed in the suspicion that the Italians might be trying to break free.[33] In May, a special staff was set up in Germany to plan a take-over of the Italian government. Enough equipment was also sent to fit out what would have been the first Italian division possessing heavy tanks: these tanks were given, not to the army, but to the fascist militia, creating the impression that they were primarily intended for use against a possible revolution or coup.

There was, in fact, to be no open rebellion against Mussolini and nothing resembling the many attempts planned in Germany against Hitler's life. But many of the *gerarchi* were losing faith in fascism and none of the myths about the infallibility of a single man could survive such a series of defeats. There was another setback early in May when Mussolini authorised Messe to surrender with his army in Tunisia, only to fabricate the legend that this brave and dutiful officer had been a traitor who, by surrendering, had unnecessarily lost Italy's last foothold in Africa.[34]

As an invasion of Italy seemed imminent, the Vatican was quick to espy a danger of communist revolution and put up a proposal for mediation,[35] but in vain. Another half-hearted attempt was made by the fascist government to get in touch with the British in Lisbon.[36] But the allies would accept only a capitulation, which Mussolini said was out of the question as it would mean the end of Italy as a 'great power'.[37] Any of those brave enough to ask for more positive action to achieve peace were told by the Duce to wait until later in the summer;[38] alternatively, he would seem not to hear what they were saying – it was almost as though he were drugged or half-asleep. He was in bed for much of May and June, keeping in contact mainly by telephone.[39]

Despite his illness, Mussolini tried bravely by an almost automatic reflex to inspire others with confidence. He talked of being able to fight for three years or more, if necessary using 'execution platoons' to prevent a revolution.[40] Even in May, he still assumed or pretended that an allied invasion of Italy was out of the question and that the fortunes of battle would soon turn in his favour: when asked how, he did not reply.[41] In one speech he repeated that the allies 'had no further cards to play'. So remote was he from reality that he also spoke of food supplies being still abundant, at a time when most Italians were hungry, some even dying of hunger.[42]

Another strange and callous remark was that he was determined to fight to the last Italian: when asked what would be the purpose of such a war of extermination and what arms he would use, there was again no reply.[43] He sometimes hinted at being saved by a bolshevik or black revolution in America;[44] or perhaps the British would turn against American imperialism;[45] or just possibly the conservatives in Britain would be so upset by the 'Beveridge plan' of social reform that they would revolt and might discover someone – oddly, he named Leo Amery, the ardent imperialist and Churchill's friend – who might put an end to the war.[46]

As bombing raids on Italy became more common, he increasingly turned his anger against the Anglo-Saxons whom he called his primary enemy, much more his enemy than Russia. They were stupid and cruel and had the effrontery to despise the Italian race which was superior to theirs.[47] In reprisal for their bombing – which, forgetful of his own raids on Ethiopia, Spain and England, he condemned as barbarously inhuman – he agreed to send British internees to live in the worst-bombed Italian cities.[48] He had already protested to the Vatican when the *Osservatore Romano* described Italian war-prisoners as being well-treated by the British – even if true, such things must not be said because they would encourage surrender and lessen the combative spirit he needed to arouse.[49] British war-prisoners in Italy should, for the same reason, be treated harshly and Italians must be taught to hate such a brutal enemy.[50]

Propaganda stories about the British had by now changed. Instead of being decadent pacifists at the mercy of warlike Italy, they were callous warmongers who dragged an innocent and unwilling Italy into hostilities.[51] They were not only inhumane and unintelligent, but uncivilised.[52] Sometimes Churchill was described by Mussolini as a former friend and 'an adversary worthy of me',[53] but usually was treated to vulgar abuse as reeking of liquor and tobacco, without political ability and hated by his fellow-countrymen.[54] Italians were warned that, if they lost the war, they would be forced by Churchill and Roosevelt into slavery, their factories dismantled, their art treasures confiscated, their universities closed, their young men slaughtered or sterilised, and their children deported *en masse*. A headline in the *Popolo d'Italia* said that, if Britain won the war, Italians would simply be exterminated.[55]

As the prospect of an allied invasion drew nearer, Mussolini purported to be spending most of his time putting the country's defences in order,[56] but in fact did almost nothing.[57] The first piece of Italian territory to fall, on 11 June, was the island of Pantelleria which he had deluded himself into thinking he had made absolutely impregnable:[58] in fact, its defences were entirely inadequate and it could put up only a few days' resistance against a well-calculated attack.[59] He personally authorised its surrender, but when the Germans expressed astonishment he denied any responsibility, preferring to blame the admiral in command for treachery and cowardice.[60]

The news came as a tremendous blow to everyone, even to ministers who had accepted in good faith Mussolini's propaganda statements as to Pantelleria's impregnability. Several of them were at last moved to ask him at a cabinet meeting to bring them more into his confidence, but in reply he simply made the oracular statement that they must now burn their boats, and abruptly closed the meeting.[61] One member of the cabinet, the industrialist Count Cini, who had served fascism well but was also a man of courage and integrity, resigned in protest at such a terrifyingly defeatist remark. Cini said that almost all the other fascist leaders agreed with this protest but were unwilling or fearful to say so openly.[62] No one else joined him in resigning: to resign was something they had been taught that a good fascist never did; had it been otherwise, fascism might not have lasted for twenty years, nor would Italy have reached such a depth of disaster.

When the suggestion was again put to Mussolini that he should seek to negotiate with the Anglo-American enemy, he said he would think about it but only in several months' time: he was ready to break free from Hitler but only when he had scored some military success.[63] After this enigmatic remark he added, even more mysteriously, that he had certain cards up his sleeve that would surprise everyone.[64] On 4 July, the newspapers were told to give special prominence to his promise that plans were prepared for any enemy force landing in Sicily to be annihilated on the beaches. A week later, after the allies had landed and were rapidly moving inland, he said he was still not particularly worried:[65] he blamed the Germans and Sicilians for not fighting well but repeated that he had everything planned to throw the invaders into the sea, and all fascists were reminded of their oath to die for him if necessary.[66]

There was no such plan of defence and it soon became obvious that the government was drifting rudderless. Ministers again found that he would refuse to answer questions and he was sometimes so abstracted as to seem beside himself.[67] Behind the scenes, the hitherto unmentionable subject was raised of his somehow being replaced, or at least persuaded to relinquish the military departments and allow the general staff to function without constant intrusion.[68] Possibly the Grand Council, which he had not summoned since 1939, could meet and resume its lapsed duties as the supreme assembly of the regime. This was a point put to him on 16 July by a group of *gerarchi* led by

Farinacci, De Bono, and the party secretary, Scorza. Though he was uncommunicative, he agreed that this directing council of fascism should again be consulted the following week.

Several days later, the two dictators met again at Feltre in northern Italy. Hitler, too, had been casting around to find a replacement for Mussolini,[69] but could see no obvious candidate, so agreed to try once more to reinvigorate the Duce and at all costs prevent Italy making a separate peace. Best of all would be an agreement by the Italians to let their forces be reorganised under a German commander.[70] Hitler took up the whole meeting with a two-hour speech mainly concerned with listing the deficiencies of the Italian war effort, and Mussolini by remaining silent appeared to be tacitly accepting the accusations as true:[71] he obviously could not follow what Hitler was saying and as usual had to ask the Germans for a précis to be sent to him afterwards. He made the revealing comment that he had felt his own will-power ebbing away as Hitler spoke and was beginning to wonder whether they might not both be slightly mad.[72]

During a pause in the meeting, General Ambrosio and the under-secretary Bastianini reproached him for his passivity and told him it might be their last chance to convince the Germans that Italy could not continue to fight.[73] He agreed, but then in Hitler's presence his courage failed once more and he let himself be persuaded into believing that the British could not hold out much longer.[74] In private he repeated that one day he would break free from the Germans, but not now, especially not if it would mean surrender or the end of fascism.[75] His chief of staff was so disgusted by this feeble performance that he followed Cini's example and submitted his resignation: he could now see that Mussolini put his own survival in power above the good of his country and the lives of his fellow-countrymen.

While Hitler was still speaking at Feltre, the news arrived that Rome had been bombed for the first time. All through the war Mussolini had kept his headquarters at Rome, confident that the allies would never attack the holy city, and for the same reason the population had multiplied out of all knowledge: this raid on 19 July therefore came as a terrible shock. He briefly thought it might win him the sympathy of Catholics in the outside world, which in turn might help to bring about an Italian victory,[76] but in fact it caused a general panic among the population and a widespread awareness that fascism must be close to collapse.[77] The king at long last told him he ought to think of resignation – but commented that using such words to the Duce was like talking to the wind.[78]

Others were equally worried as they found Mussolini still speaking about victory being round the corner, yet unable to explain what he meant or to take any practical measures. Until now, few people had been allowed to know how ill he had been for the past year. But by his own account, his illness deprived him of all energy, leaving him indolent, indifferent, with a strange mental detachment that resulted in a lack of reaction to any outside stimulus.[79] One of his police chiefs, as well as noting that he now had difficulties in speech, observed that he sometimes showed not the slightest interest in what was said to him or indeed anything outside himself. He gave the impression of 'groping in a chaos of uncertainty', exhausted, increasingly out of touch with reality.[80] This helps to explain the mental paralysis he displayed at Feltre.

Dismissal and imprisonment

The Grand Council met on 24–5 July, and voted by nineteen votes to seven to ask the king if he could look for a more successful policy that would save Italy from further destruction; it asked that not only the king, but also parliament, ministers and the Grand Council itself should all be given back the powers that the law and the constitution gave them and which Mussolini had taken away. The vote was not explicitly directed by name against Mussolini and so fell short of looking like a palace revolution, but was a clear indication that the more intelligent among his senior colleagues had lost confidence in his dictatorship.

Why he let this vote take place without more of a fight can be explained only by his ill-health and his own inability to find an alternative policy that offered hope. Very rarely had the Grand Council been allowed a vote at the end of its deliberations and possibly his judgement was so impaired that he failed to appreciate that such a vote might go against him. He knew that there was dissatisfaction with his conduct of the war: he even knew that he might have become 'the most detested man in Italy':[81] but so spineless had his colleagues been over the years that he could hardly have expected such a vote of no confidence. These were people he used to talk of as cowardly and lacking in brains. Since they knew they depended entirely on his reflected light, he must presumably have assumed that they would vote whichever way would suit him.[82] In fascism, as he had recently asserted, there existed none of the factions, cliques and powerful personalities that were creating difficulties for Hitler in Germany;[83] in Italy he could rely on unquestioning obedience.

One possibility is that, consciously or unconsciously, he was indirectly seeking a pretext to disengage honourably from Berlin, or even perhaps to abdicate and leave someone else to take the decisions he did not know how to, or dared not, take. He had once speculated that Julius Caesar knew all about the conspiracy to murder him and subconsciously sought in it a way out of an impasse;[84] something similar may have been true of himself.

He certainly knew in advance that some members of the Grand Council wanted him to relinquish some of his powers and hand over military matters to the professionals, and he was ready to accept this partial degree of abdication. He can hardly have expected them to go further, and in any case felt sure that the king would never dare to turn altogether against fascism. Most unusually, he had only a very reduced police guard present at the Palazzo Venezia on the night of 24–5 July, and this was not through inadvertence. Possibly, as he himself explained, he wanted members to feel that they could speak freely so that he could at last discover what criticisms were made of him and who the critics were.[85] Several of these would-be critics, fearing the worst, had hand grenades in their pockets, but there was no need to use them, nor was any move made to arrest anyone or limit their freedom of speech.

His introductory remarks were rambling, ineffective, and so lacking in spirit that one member thought he was about to resign.[86] They were concerned very little with the tragedy of the moment and how to meet it, but mainly with accusing other people – as usual this meant the army first of all. There was no hint that the war had been politically mistimed or that general strategy had been at fault, let alone that it might have been the wrong war altogether or that the pact of steel had been a misjudgement.

One after the other, Ciano, Bottai, Grandi, Federzoni and De' Stefani spoke reaffirming their loyalty to the Duce and to fascism, even expressing readiness to continue the war if only it could be done successfully.[87] But in both moderates and extremists there was an undercurrent of resentment at having been left uninformed and powerless. The extremist Farinacci was the most explicit in his criticism, arguing that Mussolini had perverted or deserted the fine ideals of early fascism.[88] But what shook everyone was to learn at last that further resistance was hardly possible and that their idolised leader had led them into a trap from which he could see no escape; hence, that fascism itself was on the verge of collapse, its only hope of survival being to agree quickly on a change of direction. So the simple but vital question was put to him whether he saw any chance at all of victory or, if not, whether and how peace could be made.[89]

No answer was forthcoming. But nor was there any angry reaction from him at such presumption. So Bottai, from a point of view remote from Farinacci's, was emboldened to say outright that the war was being lost because Mussolini was isolating himself from other fascist leaders and showing 'that he could neither command nor make himself obeyed'.[90] Grandi, who was emerging as leader of the more moderate critics, followed this by putting much of the blame on the fascist party which – especially in the years of Starace's secretaryship – had turned Italy into something between a barracks and a prison. While outwardly respectful, Grandi argued that dictatorial methods had failed since, in the absence of public criticism, incompetents and worse had taken positions of power; by denying individual liberty, Mussolini had not merely alienated public opinion but brought Italy to the edge of catastrophe; hence Vittorio Emanuele should be asked to resume some of the powers of which fascism had deprived him.[91]

These were criticisms that had never come into the open until now; the Duce tried hard to look unperturbed as he listened. Scorza, the party secretary, began to think that some members of the Council were going much too far; he expected that at any moment Mussolini would show his hand and, as usual, impose his will on the critics; but gradually, to Scorza's amazement, it became apparent that there might be no hand to show and no considered policy to enunciate.[92] These doubts were reinforced when Grandi proposed that the discussion should not stop at midnight but ought to continue until morning if necessary, and the Duce, who some could now see was in great pain, could not rouse himself to object. It was almost as if he were drugged with sedatives.

Scorza, in a brief interval for refreshment, was hoping to be given private instructions as to what resolution should eventually be put to the meeting and was told – again to his bewilderment – that there would probably be no vote and no formal decision. Mussolini added, surprisingly, that the discussion had gone well so far and he agreed with 90 per cent of what had been said; he was quite ready for the monarch to be reinstated as effective commander-in-chief, although the palace revolution must stop there.[93]

Such a passive reaction was most unlike his usual self and neither Scorza nor anyone else was able to fathom his motives. As the discussion continued through the small hours, he seemed indifferent, almost apathetic.[94] At one point, he repeated that he had a plan to solve the crisis of the war but, when pressed, said he must keep it secret.[95] He then hinted, somewhat feebly, that among those present were some who had antagonised the country by corruptly enriching themselves, a fact of which he said he had proof.[96] But he was ready to consider making some changes: for example, to give up the practice of 'appointments from above', and to restore some element of democratic procedures, as well as bringing the king and parliament back to something like their former status in the constitution.[97]

At any moment in this ten-hour meeting, he could have asked Scorza to propose a motion of confidence, in which case it would easily have been carried, quite possibly with few if indeed any votes against him.[98] But instead, he puzzled the loyalists by eventually putting Grandi's much more critical motion to a vote and, just possibly by inadvertence, allowed many of those present to think that he was content to have it approved. At least one of them concluded that he must have lost control over the war and over himself and wanted to free himself from a responsibility that was more than he could bear.[99] Looking back later, not even Mussolini understood why he acted as he did, but again talked of a paralysis of will that left him powerless as events had to be allowed to take their own course.[100]

After the meeting was over, he at last showed some sign of irritation but still seemed fairly apathetic. The hard-liners advised him to arrest the nineteen who had voted in favour of Grandi's motion and later he said he regretted not having done so;[101] but at the time he looked almost indifferent to the result and shut himself up in a 'hermetic silence'.[102] For a brief moment, he thought he might retrospectively adopt Grandi's proposals so as to pretend that they came from himself and thus avoid the appearance of being outvoted – a further indication that he did not foresee much danger in handing over some power to the monarchy. Once again it crossed his mind that Churchill might agree to make peace and let him stay in office to save Europe from bolshevism. Presumably he was assuming that nothing had been irreparably lost by this vote.[103]

After he had returned home early on 25 July there can have been little if any time for sleep, since he was back at his desk punctually for the usual daily routine.[104] Even at this critical moment he was seen studying the daily consignment of telephone intercepts and reports by informers – one of his regular time-wasting occupations. Towards midday he had a cordial meeting with Hidaka, the Japanese ambassador, to whom he said that he was now determined to seek peace unless the Germans sent him more arms.[105] This remark would fit with the hypothesis that he intended to use the Grand Council's decision as a pretext for backing down honourably from his alliance with nazism. To others that morning he spoke of plans for a radical reform of the fascist party.[106]

He was now informed that some of the recalcitrant nineteen would like to alter their vote since they recognised belatedly its anti-fascist implications, but he said it was too late; he would go to report to the king and then 'resolve everything in the most energetic manner' by punishing the 'traitors',[107] which suggests that he was intending to treat them as scapegoats for what had gone wrong. He already had a list of new ministers to propose, and had secured the consent of Marshal Graziani to succeed Ambrosio as chief of staff 'with an emergency plan to resolve the situation'.[108]

The one person about whom he had no doubts was the king, who hitherto had been so closely implicated in the fascist revolution that it was assumed he could hardly survive its collapse. In all innocence, Mussolini went to Villa Savoia that afternoon to tell Vittorio Emanuele that the Grand Council had voted for a partial resumption of monarchical authority. Although the police had for some weeks been preparing secret plans for his arrest, he apparently had no idea of what was in store for him[109] but he was somewhat distracted and had, it seems, forgotten to shave after his brief night's rest.[110]

He began his twenty-minute talk with the king, as he always did, by summarising current political and military events, until Vittorio Emanuele broke in to say that, as the war seemed irremediably lost and the morale of the army was collapsing, Marshal Badoglio would take over as prime minister. On leaving the king's presence, a dumbfounded and unprotesting Mussolini was arrested, after first being reassured as to his personal safety – apparently his chief immediate worry.[111]

By midnight, the news had spread through Rome and the whole complex fabric of fascism, which people had taken to be so strong and durable, disintegrated in minutes. Even the leader's own newspaper, the *Popolo d'Italia*, far from calling on Italians to oppose his relegation, meekly accepted the change of regime as entirely logical and, on its front page, simply took out Mussolini's name and replaced the usual photograph of him with that of Badoglio.[112] Of the four million members of the party and an even larger number in the party's youth organisations, not one tried to organise any serious resistance,[113] despite their solemn oath to defend the Duce and the party's recent pronouncement that they were all prepared to die for him: possibly most of them were pleased that he had been ousted.

One minor *gerarca* committed suicide at the news and one or two others, including Farinacci, fled in disguise to hide in the German embassy: but dozens of leading fascists, headed by Grandi and Starace, at once wrote to ingratiate themselves with the new regime and congratulate Badoglio on his accession to power.[114] So overwhelming was the feeling of relief that there was some puzzlement as to how fascism could possibly have lasted so long; to which the obvious answer was Mussolini's very considerable skill in keeping such a flimsy structure together. Ultimately, however, he had failed to inspire more than a superficial loyalty. Not even the vast fascist militia, the heavily armed 'guard of the revolution' with its new German tanks, stirred a finger to rescue him, though some observers thought it would not have been difficult for them to reverse what had happened had they so wished.[115]

In Mussolini himself there was no fight left. Just as he had caved in before Hitler on 19 July, and again before the Grand Council and the king a few days later, so he now wrote a submissive letter to Badoglio offering 'every possible collaboration'[116] – a letter he preferred to forget when subsequently he condemned to death other *gerarchi* who accepted the change in regime with similar nonchalance.

A view held by some of his captors was that he should be at once handed over to the Anglo-American forces as proof of Italy's intention to withdraw from the German alliance.[117] But the king refused because, while secretly determined to end the war, he was too frightened of the Germans to say so openly, and instead deviously allowed the fighting to continue while privately seeking some means of contact with the allied forces.

Mussolini for a short time seemed almost relieved to be a prisoner and without further responsibility. He was first sent to a penal settlement on the island of Ponza where he lived under a very mild form of house arrest alongside Nenni and other anti-fascists whom he had incarcerated. A week later he was moved for better security to another island, La Maddalena, but still given privileged treatment. His diet still consisted of fruit and up to four litres of milk a day, at a time when it was almost impossible to obtain milk in such a remote area;[118] and it was noted that he again seemed to fear being poisoned.[119] His sixtieth birthday was spent as a prisoner. He read a life of Christ with great attention and, after talking to a local priest, expressed the wish to take part in the mass,[120] perhaps something he had never done since childhood.

In these few weeks of enforced leisure, he looked back over his life and found 'astonishing analogies' between his own betrayal and that of Christ.[121] Some of his other written *pensées* of this period are equally revealing. He wrote that it was a law of life that the populace would tear down yesterday's idol, only to regret it later.[122] He admitted that he had never possessed a true friend and that, on balance, this had been beneficial.[123] He believed that his defeat had been in some way predetermined, but wanted others to remember that he had in his time done great deeds, having been hailed by a Pope as 'the man sent by providence' and having shown the whole world a new way of life in fascism.[124] All the more inexplicable, therefore, was the fact that the *squadristi* had not risen in his defence. The probable answer, he said, was that Italians in general were deficient in character. Before long they would be sorry for his fall from power.[125]

His first instinct – confirming what had already gone through his mind more than once – was that Italy should now withdraw from the war. But a few days later he changed his mind,[126] perhaps when he realised that the Germans were trying to discover where he was and release him. To Hitler, as Mussolini must have guessed, the captivity of such a close ally was a nightmare as it threatened the concept of the intangible and sacred leader. Every effort was made in Germany to locate him, with a lavish use of forged banknotes to purchase information, and even astrologers and clairvoyants were mobilised for the purpose.[127]

To foil the search, Badoglio had him moved once again. By plane and ambulance, under protection of Red Cross markings, he was taken to an isolated skiing resort high in the Apennine mountains. Badoglio must have known that there could be little secrecy about his presence as an entire hotel had to be cleared to make room for him and a large guard of armed military police. Here he spent a few weeks gossiping and playing cards. His meals he took alone as he always preferred. The hotel manageress was surprised to find him eating three kilogrammes of grapes each day, and his internal pains became worse. He wearied the hotel staff with stories of his ill-health and explained to them that this was why he could do no serious work.[128] He also said that he was resolved to commit suicide rather than be handed over to the allies and, on one occasion, tried to cut his wrists, though he seems to have been less than entirely serious about it.[129]

His guards had orders to kill him if there was any attempt at rescue but, on 8 September, a confusing and presumably countermanding order came from Badoglio's chief of police that they should act 'with the utmost prudence'; this order was in turn cancelled, then repeated on the twelfth – Badoglio later excused this very strange behaviour by saying that he thought Mussolini had terminal cancer and only two months to live, in which case his security would have been a minor matter. Amid all the confusion there was a not very serious plot by air force officers to capture him and fly to the Argentine. Some of his guards had another idea of ingratiating themselves with Hitler by handing him over to the Germans.[130]

Finally on 12 September, in a brilliant commando operation, a German unit landed from the air on this difficult mountain peak: its commander, Colonel Skorzeny, was expecting armed resistance but not a shot was fired during the five minutes it took to overrun the hotel. Mussolini helped to clear boulders from the primitive runway from which they then took off, the *carabinieri* waving them goodbye.[131]

The return

In September 1943, after Badoglio had at last arranged an armistice with the Anglo-Americans, the nazis reacted by taking control of central and northern Italy. Mussolini cannot have liked this much except that it was his only hope of being reinstated. They then persuaded him to set up a puppet government under German protection, thus dividing Italy in two and initiating eighteen months of terrible civil war.

First he went to Hitler's headquarters on the Russian front, from which he announced over the radio his resumption of power; in this broadcast he appealed to Italians to help him eliminate the traitors who had voted him out of office, since only bloodshed could cancel such a shameful page in the book of Italian history.[132] There was no hint in this appeal that he himself carried any responsibility for the tragedy of defeat. If Italy was no longer an independent state, being occupied by Germans in the north and a mixed army of allied forces in the south, this grim fact was said to be due, not to fascism, but to the nineteen fascist leaders who had betrayed him.

At the end of September he set up his new fascist republic in northern Italy. According to a German doctor who was sent to help him he was a ruin of a man, sometimes in such pain that he hardly seemed responsible for his actions.[133] So embarrassed was the Duce by his haggard appearance that the newspapers were told not to publish his photograph.[134] His secretary found that, though devastated by recent experiences, he was still the same elusive character who hid behind contradictory views, who put up barriers against the outside world, and who, underneath a brave front, was essentially timid in personal relations. Often he seemed a dreamer out of touch with reality or someone who confused dreams with reality.[135]

Almost by instinct, he set himself to catch up lost time by reading all the newspapers he had missed while he was a prisoner. Through them and the telephone intercepts of the previous summer, he hoped to discover how fascism could have collapsed so abjectly and how the forty-five days of his imprisonment could have ruined the hard work of twenty years.[136] He learnt from these newspapers how much he was hated by most Italians for leading them to defeat, just as they had once loved him for being successful. His judgement on his fellow-countrymen became harsher than ever.[137] The king and, even more, Badoglio, the man who more than any other he had loaded with honours and wealth, aroused his scathing contempt, as did the military commanders who had defected to the western allies in obedience to the king's command.

His own wish would have been to return to Rome, but the Germans had no intention of letting him govern in reality as well as in name. They allowed him to live in a small town, Gargnano, on Lake Garda; and here, as well as being surrounded by German soldiers, he was cut off from even his own governmental departments which had been established at Salò and other north-Italian towns. There was little he could ever do without the permission of Rudolf Rahn, the German plenipotentiary.[138]

Of course he strongly resented the fact that the outside world would see him as merely another Quisling and Italy as just another German-occupied territory. Occasionally he tried to delude himself that, if only Hitler would allow him more freedom, he could again arouse the nation and reconquer southern Italy from the Anglo-American invaders; but at heart he must have known that this was an illusion. The Germans gave him back an outward semblance of power, but their presence aroused in him as much resentment as gratitude, and sometimes, in moments of annoyance, he was unrealistic enough to hope once again that they would lose the war.[139]

Some of the small minority of Mussolini's colleagues who remained loyal to him hoped that he would give up the word 'fascism', since it was by now associated with defeat, repression, and reaction.[140] Others, on the contrary, wanted to restore fascist authoritarianism in a more extremist form than ever. He himself had learnt to discard some of his former illusions. He sometimes admitted that fascism, far from being the dominant theme of the century, had been a mere expedient adopted by him as a means of winning personal power: it had been just an extension of himself, and would finish at his death.[141] But he would not give up the name, for the old myths still exerted some power, and by continuing to assert that the war was ideological, he would be able to capitalise on the growing fear that the likely alternative to his government would be a communist revolution.[142]

The 'Verona manifesto', a policy statement published by the party in November, recognised that fascism had hitherto been defective in some respects. Power, it could now be admitted, had corrupted the fascist leaders, as had lack of criticism.[143] He therefore agreed to return to a more genuinely elective system for choosing parliament and selecting the head of state. He also agreed to restore the independence of the judiciary and give guarantees against arbitrary arrest; there would be greater freedom for trade unions; the press would henceforward be free, and party members would cease to have preference in getting jobs.[114] Fascism, he confessed, had in the past permitted or even encouraged a good deal of peculation and bribery, so he agreed to investigate and confiscate any illicit fortunes made since 1919. Furthermore a constituent assembly would be convened to devise a new constitution.[145]

This radical new deal was an explicit condemnation of many of the central teaching of fascism in the previous twenty years. However, like those earlier doctrines, the 'Verona manifesto' was mainly window-dressing. The constituent assembly never met, nor were elections held, and the *Repubblica di Salò* became quite as much a police state as the pre-1943 regime. Despite talk of a free press, Mussolini could not in practice endure to have his views discussed and criticised, let alone his liaison with Clara Petacci mentioned in print. So, once it had served its purpose as propaganda, this new-style liberal fascism was quietly put aside. As he said, the Russians were winning a war despite – or, more likely, because of – the fact that they had just a single newspaper and a single radio programme;[146] Italian journalists were told once again that their job was not to criticise but to create public confidence in government policy.[147]

Some of the less attractive aspects of Mussolini's character became general knowledge when the public learnt of the execution of five top fascists who had voted against him in the Grand Council on 25 July, because this showed him as lacking any sense of justice. He called this execution the most dramatic fact in his whole life.[148] Those who died included his son-in-law, Ciano, and his old companions Marinelli and Marshal De Bono – the latter was almost eighty years old. The fascist leaders he would have preferred to kill were Grandi, Federzoni and Bottai but they managed to escape in time. The men he executed were less guilty – indeed, he sometimes acknowledged quite candidly that they were not guilty at all.[149] However, one of his first thoughts after his release had been the 'elimination' of the traitors of 25 July, and he felt instinctively that other would-be rebels must be deterred by a savage example.[150] Even though the minister of justice advised that there was no evidence of treason – since the vote on 25 July had been perfectly legal and had been accepted as such by Mussolini himself because he had asked the Grand Councillors for their frank advice – he now tried to pretend that these dissident fascists were responsible for the worst act of treason in all history. Despite the fact that his personal letter to Badoglio offering to co-operate with the king's government put him in the same boat, he was adamant that others who acted similarly must be condemned.[151] To sanction this decision, he set up a special military tribunal and issued a retrospective law permitting the death penalty for all who had 'betrayed the fascist idea', while anyone who had broken his oath to 'defend fascism to the death' could be imprisoned for up to thirty years. The judges he appointed to this tribunal had to be men of 'proven fascist faith' chosen by the party, and it was made clear that their job was to find the accused guilty and have them executed.[152]

The nazis wanted him to punish Ciano in particular, though they were careful to exert no active pressure and some wanted less severity than he did himself.[153] The demand for the death sentence came rather from the fascist *gerarchi* – especially those who had a guilty conscience for having fled in panic after 25 July.[154] The hard-core militiamen threatened not only the defence lawyers but the judges, as well as threatening to lynch the accused if they should escape execution.[155] They also openly warned Mussolini that any favour shown to Ciano would bring upon him their contempt.[156] And his wife, Rachele, was especially pitiless in demanding the execution of her son-in-law.[157]

Mussolini later claimed, to assuage his conscience, that he had not wanted a trial, let alone an execution.[158] In fact, however, he not only ordered in advance that the accused be condemned even when he knew that condemnation meant death, but refused a last-minute request from the Germans that this mock trial be put off. As he commented to several people, Ciano in his eyes was already dead.[159] His overriding preoccupation was that others must not think him weak or guilty of nepotism, and he explicitly said that 'reasons of state' must, on this occasion, take precedence over legality.[160] A final insult was that those accused had to pay the costs of their own trial.

The result was that the rump fascist regime condemned to death a large number of leading fascists, though only five could be executed as the others had absconded. One of the judges later confirmed in a detailed account of the proceedings that there was never any intention to have more than a show trial, and that judges as well as prisoners would have been shot by the fascist guards in the courtroom if there had not been a verdict of guilty.[161] Apparently, a majority of judges nevertheless decided to show mercy to the elderly De Bono, but they were forced to take a second vote to rectify this lapse.[162] Only the flimsiest indirect evidence was produced to suggest that there had ever been any plot against the regime, and such evidence implicated only Farinacci who was not among the accused but a witness for the prosecution. Witnesses for the defence were not heard, and defence lawyers were told not to protract the proceedings: two days were spent in and around Verona trying to find a lawyer brave enough to appear in Ciano's defence, but all made their excuses.[163]

After being sentenced to death, the five men sent a formal plea for mercy, though their intimate knowledge of Mussolini over so many years convinced them that this was futile.[164] He later pretended that he would have liked to commute the penalty because he knew they were not guilty,[165] though the truth is that he could easily have saved them and chose not to do so. He pretended that their plea for mercy never reached him, but this was at his own instigation so as to make believe that the responsibility lay elsewhere.[166]

The execution took place at Verona the next morning, 11 January 1944. Like the trial itself, it was filmed by the fascist propaganda services. Mussolini's private secretary was present to see that justice was done. The shooting was badly bungled and three rounds of firing were needed.

Although Mussolini, speaking to individual Italians, expressed horror when he learnt of this gruesome scene, the Germans on the same day found him entirely relaxed and sure of himself.[167] He summoned the prison officers to tell him every detail of Ciano's last hours and read his final letters before sending them on to the dead man's wife and mother; whether he also watched the film is not known, but not improbably he did, so great was his morbid curiosity. He reprimanded (but did not punish) those who had not let him exercise his right of commuting the sentence, perhaps because, to his surprise, this judicial murder was badly received by the public. His daughter never forgave him until after his death for his cruelty and his cowardly refusal to stand up to the fascist extremists: she had not even been permitted to visit her husband during his last days.

A few hours after the execution, he commented that his vendetta against the traitors was only beginning and he hoped that Grandi in particular, whom he thought the main architect of his misfortunes, would be found and shot.[168] He said that other generals and industrialists were almost equally guilty, so many other heads would also have to roll, and he drew up a list of two hundred *gerarchi* to be tried for treachery.[169] Thousands of other delations, mainly anonymous, poured into his office, some no doubt from fascists who wanted to dispose of private enemies; this was a practice he always encouraged, though some Germans found it nauseating.[170] Two former party secretaries, Starace and Scorza, were arrested; four generals were given long prison sentences (he would have liked them executed);[171] several of Italy's most successful admirals were shot on his personal instructions for having obeyed the king's orders (which they were bound to do by oath) rather than his own. The lawyers again warned him that there was no legal basis for such vindictive savagery, but he was relentless.[172]

The republic of Salò

17

Anarchy at Salò

One indication of Mussolini's state of mind at Gargnano was the choice of the journalist, Alessandro Pavolini, to be his second in command as secretary of the fascist party. Pavolini had formerly enjoyed a reputation for intelligence and sensitivity, but fascism had turned him into a fanatic, pitiless and revengeful, who believed in terrorism as a policy and liked to repeat conventional fascist remarks about the purifying effects of a blood-bath. Next in the hierarchy came Guido Buffarini-Guidi, the minister of the interior; he was more effective than other surviving fascists as a manager and administrator, but was a flawed personality disliked by almost everyone and known for his corruption and ready acceptance of violence. The third most important appointment was that of Tullio Tamburini as chief of police, an ex-*squadrista* with a reputation as a gunman and racketeer.

Such men, as Mussolini must have known, had little interest in a moderate policy of general pacification, nor would they do much to mitigate the horrors of civil war. Pavolini believed in fierce retaliation against the anti-fascist partisan guerrillas; sometimes the order was given to kill ten anti-fascists for every fascist killed. And, though Mussolini said he would have preferred his lieutenants to keep within the law, he himself set a personal example of lawlessness.[1] Nor did he ever replace Pavolini. The party secretary created his own independent militia, the 'republican guard', which was often in conflict with the regular police and was one among a number of separate forces that grew up either spontaneously or protected and subsidised by individual ministers in Mussolini's government. Such forces acted by their own rules and were not answerable to the courts.

The fascist tradition of semi-autonomous hooligan squads was thus reasserting itself to exploit and perhaps compensate for the continued feebleness of the central administration. A dozen squads were operating in Milan, some of them in receipt of government funds, some composed of criminals running various kinds of protection racket, some with their own private prisons and torture chambers. Mussolini knew about their killings and tortures and deplored the fact that Italians were revealing themselves to be one of 'the cruellest peoples in the world';[2] but he said he was powerless to stop it, and was so frightened of seeming too weak that he not only turned a blind eye but sometimes encouraged these fanatics.[3]

The notorious gang run by Dr Pietro Koch, for example, was set up with Mussolini's permission and paid and armed by the ministry of the interior.[4] It was eventually dissolved after it was found to be working for the Germans and disobeying governmental orders; to assist the police in its suppression, Buffarini had to employ the rival Muti gang which was equally autonomous and equally cruel and corrupt. Koch's headquarters was found to contain a number of prisoners and a variety of torture instruments; his organisation turned out to be involved in hard drug traffic and had become immensely rich.[5] The Muti gang was later raised by Mussolini to the honorific status of a fascist 'legion' because of its usefulness in suppressing strikes in a number of factories.[6]

The German occupying forces found these armed squads useful for gathering information and terrorising the subject population. But Mussolini's administration was looked on by the Germans as of little importance and was tolerated only on sufferance for as long as a simulacrum of fascism could be of use[7] – while he himself was considered by them to be something of a simpleton, perhaps not always in his right mind.[8] At their insistence he had no option but to recognise a virtual annexation by Germany of Trieste and the Alto Adige – two regions that had been won at huge cost by pre-fascist Italy. As he had originally sought a German alliance as a means of extending Italy's frontiers, it was a cruel irony to have to watch his ally seizing provinces conquered by the liberal predecessors he so despised.

Unaccustomed to taking orders, he of course resented the fact that his own authority counted for so little, but he had to admit that the German proconsul, Rahn, and the military commander, General Wolff, were in practice the real governors of northern Italy.[9] Sometimes he talked, not very seriously, of resigning in protest;[10] just occasionally he was able to resist German wishes in minor matters; but mostly he did what he was told. German officers were assigned to live in his house where, as he may not have known, they tapped and transcribed his telephone calls.[11] His personal guard included German SS troops who kept a list of all visitors and even photocopied some of his personal correspondence.

He visited Germany several times in the course of 1944, but encounters between the two dictators had less importance now than ever. He went in April determined to have his way as an equal partner in the alliance[12] but, on arrival, collapsed into silence as though numbed by embarrassment and timidity. Hitler lectured him as usual and criticised fascism for having proved to be so shallow and insubstantial, pointing out that Italian soldiers on the Russian front were singing communist songs and blaming Mussolini for defeat.[13]

In July, Mussolini went to visit his troops in Russia and their enthusiastic welcome partially compensated for these stories. As his journey was held up several times by air raids, he escaped by a few hours being present when Hitler was nearly killed by a bomb. Hitler made an emotional speech of greeting to say that the Italians were Germany's best, and perhaps only, friends in the world, but one observer thought these ingratiating words were spoken without much sincerity.[14] The usual inaccurate statistics were then produced to show the Italians that the war was as good as won. Some of the Germans had been hoping that Mussolini would take this chance to advocate making peace, but instead he returned home full of confidence in victory, convinced that Germany was building far more planes than the British and would shortly be able to destroy London.[15] He nevertheless was not altogether displeased by the bomb attack on Hitler, as it was proof that treachery was not confined to Italy.[16]

The bulk of the Italian army had been interned in September 1943 and sent to Germany, where, at the end of 1944, a million Italians were still living.[17] Mussolini wanted to use some of these men to build a new army that would give his regime more credibility, but the Germans, who alone could have provided arms and equipment, were convinced that an Italian army would be thoroughly unreliable. Hitler's requirement was rather for a million labourers to work in Germany – tens of thousands of Italians continued to be shanghaied into forced labour as though their country was no different from other German-occupied territories, and Mussolini had little option but to connive at this.[18]

The widespread fear of being drafted to Germany was another reason why he found it impossible to recruit a new army inside Italy itself. Convicts in Italian prisons were offered their freedom if they joined and the death penalty was decreed for anyone trying to escape the draft,[19] but inducements and numerous executions were equally ineffective. Other decrees made whole families liable to prison and loss of property if their menfolk refused to register; others ordered the execution of anyone helping fugitives, and the destruction of whole villages if necessary.[20] But the results were meagre, save that many younger men and women were left with little alternative but to join the partisan movement in the mountains.

The most feared units of the Italian armed forces were semi-autonomous groups over which Mussolini had little or no control. He tried to explain this by arguing that such volunteer corps were part of an Italian tradition dating back to the Middle Ages.[21] The most notorious and ferocious was the *Decima Mas* under Prince Valerio Borghese, who claimed to be virtually independent of the fascist government and who once even threatened to take Mussolini prisoner.[22] Another called itself the 'Italian SS' and wore a German uniform; and they, too, sometimes had political ambitions of their own.[23]

In June 1944 the slow allied advance up the peninsula reached Rome. Mussolini was not pleased to hear that the Germans intended to withdraw from this city without a fight and begged Hitler to reverse the decision.[24] He had not forgiven the Romans for the scenes of delight at his fall the previous July and, unlike the German commander, had no desire to spare them the horrors of a street-by-street defense.[25]

In August he was also hoping for a rearguard battle in Florence, where once again the Germans mercifully decided to destroy only the bridges, leaving the rest of the town relatively unscathed.[26] His own view was that the retreat northwards must be delayed as long as possible until Hitler's secret rocket weapons were ready: the whole country had to be defended 'inch by inch' and without any false sentimentality over its artistic heritage.[27] He was still hoping that the Germans would bring troops back from Russia in order to make Italy the main battleground of the axis, in which case he was optimistic that they could drive the allies back: fascism at least would survive, even if Italy itself had a rough time.[28]

As the fighting moved northwards and the partisan movement grew in strength, the war became more savage, with retaliation on both sides. Mussolini allowed the fascist party to raise a new group of armed squads calling themselves the 'black brigades'.[29] His ministers of war and of the interior resented the multiplication of para-military units outside the army command and thought it typical of what Marshal Graziani now saw to be Mussolini's greatest defect – the preference for 'divide and rule' and the refusal to allow his generals or ministers any real power. Graziani admitted that these black brigades committed the worst atrocities of the civil war;[30] the Germans found them unreliable and condemned their terrorist tactics as self-defeating.[31] But, as the fighting became more of a guerrilla war, the German army resorted equally to terrorist methods, ordering the killing of hostages and often refusing to treat the irregular partisans as prisoners of war. Mussolini confirmed that execution of hostages was a proper reprisal against guerrilla attacks.[32] As he had done earlier in Ethiopia and Spain, he gave permission for prisoners – even women and children – to be shot.[33]

Mussolini in decline

On his return from captivity, Mussolini had been so physically and psychologically ill that he had seemed almost moribund, but after a few weeks of quite different treatment and an altered diet – milk, his staple food for many years, was eliminated – he became dramatically better and was almost his old self again. Perhaps his health improved through knowing that he no longer had to take major decisions, but most of all it must have been owing to the skill of Dr Zachariae, his German doctor, who obtained far better results than previous consultants. Apparently there was nothing organically wrong and after a few weeks his constitution was declared to be that of a man twenty years his junior.[34] Zachariae was a good psychologist and realised that his patient needed someone to talk to, a confidant with whom pretences and posing would no longer be so necessary. A special request was sent to Berlin for this German doctor to stay in Italy, and his two daily visits continued after Mussolini ceased to be in urgent need of medical advice.[35]

There was little real companionship to be found inside the Duce's own family. His favourite child, Edda, could not bear to live near someone she denounced as cowardly and unjust.[36] Vittorio had been interested mainly in films, Romano in jazz, and it caused their father much grief that they took after their mother and lacked serious intellectual interests.[37] Vittorio was now egged on by various friends and relations to play a part in politics, and his father, by encouraging the ambition of these 'princes of the blood', showed poor judgement.[38] A numerous tribe of distant relatives continued to pester Mussolini for small gifts and privileges or for his intervention with the police to cover up their minor misdeeds. Over two thousand relatives had been docketed for this purpose by his personal secretariat; he despised them, but rarely refused them help.[39]

Rachele Mussolini had by now learnt, very belatedly, of her husband's affair with Clara Petacci, and her fierce jealousy made life almost intolerable for him. There were continual scenes and some days the two could not speak to each other.[40] He reached the point of hinting to the Germans that it would give him some peace of mind if they found somewhere else for Rachele to live.[41] Perhaps, underneath, he was still fond of her: indeed he briefly tried to give Clara up,[42] but his good resolution did not last. The Germans, realising that the presence of his mistress might suit their own purposes, brought her to Lake Garda and established her with a personal SS guard in a nearby house, in return for which she gave them secret information and copies of the Duce's private letters.[43] Nor did be break off the liaison after discovering this fact.

Mussolini continued at Gargnano to live modestly, with few luxuries except an occasional manicure, and made difficulties even about accepting more than a fraction of his salary.[44] He liked to work long office hours that his secretary found taxing, but occasionally played tennis or rode a bicycle for exercise. He revived the habit of taking a daily German lesson and began to translate Wagner's *Ring* into Italian. He also made careful notes on Plato's *Republic*, and still liked to show off a sometimes impressive, but not always genuine, erudition by discoursing to other people on history and literature.[45]

The pompous strutting of earlier days was much less in evidence now that there was a smaller audience and less point in pretending to infallibility. The peremptory and frowning mannerisms had gone; so had the gaudy uniforms. Not everyone could give up the practice of running to his desk and running out after the interview was over, but people were now invited to sit down when they talked to him[46] – a privilege formerly granted to few except foreigners. He was kinder, more courteous, more open in his talk, more anxious to be liked and readier to invite companionship. Despite the cruelties and executions, he contrived to give some observers the impression of being at heart a humane man anxious to help as much as he could.[47]

Possibly this was another pose – he could hardly be expected to renounce overnight his love of posing and striking an attitude. He was, for instance, hardly truthful when he talked of having returned to the Catholic faith.[48] Admittedly, he now spoke more about God and the obligations of conscience, but he still had little use for the priests and sacraments of the Church,[49] and for a time (though he tried to deny the fact) encouraged a group of excommunicated priests who were threatening schism with Rome.[50] He said he had made up his mind to revise the concordat of 1929 in order to reduce the power of the Church in society: his original hope in 1929 had been to secure the full endorsement of fascism by the Vatican but he had since learnt the need for greater governmental control over religion.[51]

On reviewing the past he was occasionally ready to recognise that he must have been deluded by flatterers into an excessive conceit; every day for years he had heard himself called a genius whose views on politics and economics – even on science and art – were infallible; a Pope had helped to persuade him into thinking himself sent by God to redeem society.[52] Such flattery, as he now admitted, might have been aimed at deceiving him. Nevertheless, he remained confident that he would one day be generally accepted as among the great men of history,[53] and in casual speech still habitually compared the vicissitudes of his career with those of Napoleon[54] – and of Jesus Christ.[55]

The Mussolini of 1944 reasserted the socialist beliefs of his youth because he now felt that he had been cheated by the world of finance and industry: after having gained immensely from fascism, the capitalists had secretly sabotaged his movement.[56] To maintain some intellectual coherence he tried to pretend that, notwithstanding appearances, he had never deserted the socialist programme he had put forward for fascism in 1919; he had allowed certain tactical deviations in the interim[57] but, for the most part, his basic views had never changed.[58] In anonymous articles he now confirmed that he had been right when, in 1910, he called on the proletariat to capture power from the capitalists by a bloody revolution.[59] It was claimed that he had been intending in 1939–40 to carry out a wide-ranging nationalisation of private property, and only the war had led to its postponement.[60] He now decreed that all industrial firms employing more than 100 workers would be nationalised.[61]

This reassertion of socialism explains why the person closest to him in 1944–5 – to the point of being called the '*éminence grise* of Salò' – was Nicola Bombacci, one of the leaders of the Italian communist party when it was founded in 1921.[62] Bombacci had once been a friend and disciple of Lenin and revived the story that, according to Lenin, Mussolini had been the one serious socialist in Italy.[63] No doubt the Duce was influenced by Bombacci when he called the fascism of Salò the only truly socialist government in existence – with the possible exception of Soviet Russia.[64]

In practice, however, all the leaders of fascism continued to have widely different and often incompatible ideas about fascist beliefs and policy. Even those charged to apply the new doctrine of nationalisation were not sure whether Mussolini meant it seriously or whether it was one more piece of bluffing propaganda,[65] and it clearly failed to arouse much enthusiasm among the workers. But his desire for revenge against the bourgeoisie was genuine enough; his intention was to inject the germs of social revolution into Italian society in order to ensure that, if Italy should lose the war, whoever won would have a difficult time of it.[66] In this way, fascism, which had once invented the myth of having saved Italy from bolshevism, ended up deliberately (and more successfully) doing the exact opposite. This was partly out of conviction, partly as a punishment of the rich, partly to leave behind him what he called a 'social minefield' to paralyse the work of his successors.

Mussolini's racialist prejudices were hardly modified very much by the horrors of nazi persecution. Sometimes he half admitted that his anti-semitism had been purely opportunist and might even have been a mistake.[67] Nevertheless, his inner convictions or calculations are reflected in the fact that, of all people, the man he chose to take charge of administering the racial laws was Giovanni Preziosi, another well-known journalist who was the most genuinely anti-semitic fanatic in Italy. The Duce agreed with Preziosi and Hitler that all Jews should be expelled from Europe, and repeated his strange instruction that Italians must become a pure race, free from contamination and cross-breeding.[68] There was some cynicism in this attitude because he could still ridicule those who talked of racial purity as something practical. There was also great cruelty in his racialism because the fascists knew by now that the Jews in Germany, even women and children, were being systematically exterminated.[69] Many subordinate officials reacted to this news with shock and compassion, but Mussolini, although he was far more humane than Hitler and sometimes showed that he disapproved of what was happening, was too afraid of his ally to prevent thousands of Jews being deported to their deaths in Germany; indeed he sometimes gave orders that they should be handed over.[70] Other satellite countries put up more resistance to the 'final solution' and, despite official denials, there were a number of concentration camps in Italy; indeed, Italian fascists joined the Germans in operating an extermination camp at San Sabba, near Trieste.[71]

Mussolini's weaknesses as an administrator persisted in these last years, and severe laws continued to be mitigated by inefficiency and casualness. At Gargnano, as previously in Rome, he was continually changing his mind and leaving officials unaware of his real intentions.[72] The Germans noted his unwillingness to discuss any serious matter and wondered if this meant that he lacked the ability to decide or simply that he had no coherent views of any kind.[73] In the old days he had enjoyed trying to impose his will, but now seemed to have learnt that this no longer worked or no longer mattered. Different departments continued to operate on their own without co-ordination; laws were continually made but often unenforced, and it was sometimes hard to be sure that a central government existed.[74]

Though he liked people to think of him as above all else a patriot, in private he claimed to be Duce of fascism first, national leader second,[75] and there were some who still thought that he continued to look on Italy as merely a vehicle for his own personal power, to be sacrificed in 'the sublime holocaust' of war if the country no longer served this purpose.[76] Yet he never tired of telling Italians that he had worked selflessly for them; he had tried to give them backbone and make them into a great power that would inspire fear and admiration; under his guidance they had for the first time in history given the rest of humanity a doctrine and a style of life, for which Italians would one day be grateful. If the next generation in Italy wanted to be important in the world they would have to return to his teaching. History would prove him correct, because one day a new leader would follow his example and once more make their country strong and feared.[77]

Such statements were part of the evidence he was painstakingly putting together for a justification of his career that he hoped historians would accept.[78] Fascism would be regretted. It would still prove to have been the dominant ideology of the century. Italians ought to be glad that he had taken from them some liberties that were self-destructive; he had never deprived them of real liberty, only of licence, and indeed had never been a real dictator. Rather he had been their servant, and had not imposed fascism on them but simply developed pre-existing tendencies that he had found in the collective unconscious: only by accepting this fact, he thought, could anyone explain how such an individualistic and insubordinate nation could have followed him so blindly for twenty years.[79]

Sometimes he speculated that fascism in the future might become quite different, possibly even more liberal. Instead of everything being brought under state control as the fascist theorists had once advocated, possibly 'the best way to govern a country is to ensure that the state is as little in evidence as possible'.[80] But the mutability of his views suggests that he was merely searching for a popular cause with which to recapture the sensation of being admired and wanted. In November 1943, the 'manifesto of Verona' appealed to the sacred rights of free criticism and private property; three months later he reverted to imposing rigid censorship and advocating the wholesale nationalisation of private industry; then, after another six months, he was agreeing that authoritarianism might work better for Russians than Italians, as a result of which he was ready to permit a plurality of parties with a limited right of criticism.[81] He even encouraged one 'independent' newspaper to start publication, though the experiment lasted only a few days.[82]

In his anxiety to straighten the record, he found time for fifty meetings with Carlo Silvestri, a socialist journalist whom he chose to chronicle his thoughts much as Emil Ludwig had done a dozen years before. Almost certainly, as with Ludwig, this was largely a publicity stunt. Silvestri was allowed to see his private archives as well as a long memorandum Mussolini had drawn up in justification of his political career, and the general tenor of Silvestri's conclusion as a result of these talks was that the old-style fascism was dead: it had been a temporary phenomenon which was now developing into a quite different regime based on socialism, perhaps also on Christian democracy.[83]

Mussolini's determination to get his own side of the story into print was also demonstrated by a series of nineteen articles in the *Corriere della Sera* concerning the events of 1940–3. No secret was made of the fact that Mussolini was their anonymous author, and a million copies of the paper were printed, after which another 300,000 copies were issued as a pamphlet. He was humiliated by the fact that the German censors insisted on first deleting some passages.[84]

The judgements made in these articles, though sometimes confused, were nonetheless revealing. He accepted that, had it not been for his decision to join Hitler in 1940, fascism might have survived intact in Italy as Franco's regime had in Spain, but his conscience was clear because he had done everything possible to stop the war breaking out.[85] Yet he simultaneously managed to convince himself that he had been right to seek a world war because there was no other way to make Italy powerful and rich.[86] Only through military glory could a country become great, 'only battle makes a man complete', only victory for the axis would bring peace with justice to the world.[87] In any case, he believed that the war would have been won with better generals, or if the king had not prevented Italy entering the war in September 1939 (this was a complete legend), or if the Germans had paid more attention to his good advice, or even if he had employed the inhumane methods of fighting adopted by others.[88] He was desperately looking for someone else to blame.

With so many good intentions on his part it was bitter to find Italians so ungrateful. He was reluctant to confront the crowd again as he feared its reactions. Only once – reluctantly and after pressure from the Germans[89] – did he agree to appear in public and indulge his former passion for oratory, on which occasion the public response in Milan showed that he had not forgotten how to arouse enthusiasm.[90] However, after the events of July 1943 he knew the fickleness of the mob. He suspected that, under the surface, Italians were united in their hatred of all he stood for and in blaming him personally for so many useless deaths.[91]

In self-justification he responded by throwing their reproaches back at them. Once again he concluded that they were not a serious nation, only an aggregate of individuals, and he had been wrong to think he could make much of them. They were despised by other peoples and rightly so; their boasted intelligence was turning out to be a fiction;[92] the applause they had poured out to him was no more than 'collective hysteria'.[93] All Italians, whether believers or non-believers, had in his view profited from fascism, only to turn against him the very moment he ceased to be successful, and whichever side won the war would automatically receive their servile adulation.[94] Their egoism and cowardice, not the country's enemies, had defeated fascism and brought his fine dreams to naught.[95]

Mussolini also, more than ever, blamed the Germans. He was perhaps not fully aware how much they regarded the Italian alliance as a factor in their own defeat. He preferred to reproach the German generals for being hopeless strategists and for their folly in not listening to him more.[96] They had gone wrong in failing to occupy Egypt,[97] and then in their decision to take the war into the Balkans,[98] and worst of all in their absurd insistence on fighting Russia.[99] The fact that he had started the Balkan war and advised Hitler to attack Russia was forgotten, and so was his refusal to accept German plans to attack Egypt. Instead he continued to say that, if only Hitler had let him run the war, the axis powers would have won it.[100] The Germans, he added, understood nothing about politics.[101] They were potentially a great people but deserved a better leader than Hitler who, despite great energy and drive, lacked experience of life or a proper sense of realism. Hitler was a fanatic, a 'thoroughgoing authoritarian', whereas Mussolini now saw himself as authoritarian 'only on the surface'; and unfortunately the Führer had proved incapable of recognising the 'superior spiritual gifts' of the Duce.[102]

The end

By the beginning of 1945 it was clear, as Mussolini occasionally confessed, that the Italians were likely to lose whichever side won the war.[103] A German victory would reduce them to a condition of slavery. The main question still open was who would be their new master, Germany, Britain or Russia; and his own view, which he thought 95 per cent of Italians would accept, was that Russia would be their best hope.[104]

Not that he had weakened his opposition to bolshevism; on the contrary, he was proud to think of himself as having been for twenty years Stalin's most consistent opponent.[105] But in private his admiration for the Russians grew as he witnessed their military success. Evidently they had discovered, where he had failed, how to impose a single disciplined system of belief and to invoke an apparently unanimous enthusiasm. More impressive still, indeed almost incredible to him, was to see the message of communism taking hold inside fascist Italy itself. Secretly he sometimes wondered again whether it might be possible to bring Russia into a bloc of 'proletarian' and dictatorial powers against the capitalist democracies of the west.[106]

This did not stop such an erratic politician from simultaneously wondering whether the western allies might be persuaded at this late hour that only by allying with fascism could they avoid the 'bolshevisation of Europe'.[107] Alternatively, Roosevelt might find Britain an untrustworthy ally;[108] or Churchill might realise that Italy could help the British to stand up to an over-powerful United States.[109] Mussolini sometimes liked people to think that he could easily reach an agreement with his 'intimate' friend Churchill if only Hitler would let him,[110] and indeed let others believe that negotiations were actually taking place.[111] At other times he repeated that, on the contrary, his worst enemies of all were the British, who would never forgive him for being the chief agent in destroying their empire, an achievement that he called his greatest pride.[112] He told Hitler in April 1944 that the axis would get its booty only by defeating Britain. But her defeat was now an accomplished fact.[113] Since Britain was mainly responsible for the war breaking out,[114] losing her empire would be her just punishment for a pertinacious policy against European peace.[115] Only Roosevelt was more guilty – he was a delinquent who ought to be brought to trial with Churchill, and both would have to be condemned as war criminals.[116]

As the allies gradually pushed the front line closer to northern Italy, such matters became increasingly academic and, though Mussolini sometimes managed to maintain his outward confidence that victory was just round the corner,[117] those close to him knew his inner pessimism.[118] He mentioned with regret a 'death ray' that Marconi had invented but kept secret[119] – and

Marconi was now dead. There was also talk of ten different 'V' bombs about to come into operation against the British and of an atomic device that the Germans were perfecting.[120] He said he had detailed information about secret weapons in Germany that were a guarantee of victory.[121]

His statement that 'he would fight to the last Italian'[122] suggests that, like Hitler, he was ready to destroy his country rather than accept a fascist defeat. Not only had be wanted to fight in the streets of Rome and Florence, but he now said he intended to defend every town, village and house in the countryside;[123] there was talk of 'another Thermopylae' and of Milan being turned into the 'Stalingrad of Italy', so that fascism could go down in a blaze of glory.[124] Possibly this was just an attempt to sound defiant. In September 1944, he ordered preparations to be made for a last-ditch stand in the Valtelline near the Swiss frontier, and he persuaded himself, quite falsely, that his instructions to assemble immense stores of food and arms there were being carried out.[125] His military experts told him the idea was an absurdity, but he was moving more and more into a world of make-believe.

At one point, secret arrangements were made to send the families of the leading fascist *gerarchi* to Switzerland, but this was vetoed by the Germans who instead allocated for the purpose a number of hotels in the Austrian Alps. One hotel at Zürs was cleared of guests to be ready for Mussolini and his relatives,[126] and no doubt he had some thought of a possible escape abroad for his family, perhaps also for himself. This might explain why he now sold the building and plant of the *Popolo d'Italia* for a large sum to be paid in Swiss francs.[127]

As the prospect of defeat drew nearer, he suffered another grave 'nervous collapse', being hardly able to eat or sleep, and his doctor reported 'an absolute loss of energy and intelligence'.[128] He feared an allied victory would mean 'the end of civilisation as we know it', but, as his own conscience was clear, he would not recriminate.[129] He accepted that even people of exceptional ability such as himself could become the plaything of circumstance – 'I challenged the world and it proved too strong for me; I despised other men and they are taking their revenge.'[130] One day Italians would listen to him again, but for the moment he felt helpless and drifting.

He wondered in retrospect if at some earlier stage he should not have been content with less and drawn back before it was too late; but he commented that no dictator could ever calculate with prudence, because all dictators in the end 'lose any sense of balance as they pursue their obsessive ambitions into a world of unreality'.[131]

Despite defiant talk of a last-ditch fight, both fascists and the German soldiers in Italy were ready to seek talks with the enemy – without telling each other.[132] Mussolini knew that the nazis were in contact with the Anglo-

American forces,[133] though he pretended otherwise in order to give himself the excuse for a dramatic scene of injured innocence. Individual fascist leaders were meanwhile investigating possible surrender terms, even suggesting that they might hand over Mussolini if the price was right, and he himself was indirectly in touch with the partisans' liberation committee as well as seeking contact with the western allies.[134] At the same time he used Silvestri as an intermediary to discover whether the underground socialist party would accept his surrender.

As usual, there was a lack of co-ordination and very little consultation with ministers and *gerarchi*, but merely the hope that something might turn up if sufficient escape routes were kept open. Sometimes he still talked of withdrawing into his non-existent Valtelline redoubt where he would either go down fighting or make an honourable peace settlement,[135] but he can hardly have meant this seriously, as he did nothing to check whether preparations were being made there for resistance. His main objective was to gain time and he talked mysteriously of a bundle of documents with which, if given enough time, he could 'win the peace'.[136]

On 18 April 1945, as the allies were about to enter Bologna and the Russians moved on Berlin, he left Lake Garda for Milan. This was against the wishes of his German guards and it seems as though he was trying to detach himself from them, but no one was sure what he had in mind. One suggestion put to him was that he should escape to Japan by submarine; another, more realistic, that he should fly to Spain or Argentina; but he refused to consider such ignominious flight.[137] Further enquiries were also made in Switzerland to see if he and the other fascist leaders would be accepted as refugees, but there was no enthusiasm on the part of the Swiss and he himself feared that they would hand him over to the allies.[138]

In all probability he could not make up his mind what to do as he lived through another of those periods when he lacked energy or will-power; though he remained calm, it seemed the calmness of helplessness and nervous exhaustion, and a person who saw him for the first time in months described him as a broken man.[139] Eventually on 25 April, he agreed – though without much enthusiasm – to go to the house of the archbishop of Milan to talk to leaders of the partisan movement, presumably in the hope that they would modify the earlier demand for his unconditional surrender. The archbishop counselled him to repent of his sins and was upset to find him far removed from feelings of penitence.[140] The partisans told him that if he accepted defeat he could rely on a fair trial, but no preconditions could be made, on hearing which he at first seemed reconciled to surrender.[141]

Then suddenly he decided to break off the discussions. His excuse – though the logic is hard to appreciate – was the shock of learning that the Germans had agreed to make terms without telling him. Perhaps the true explanation was his realisation that he had no chance of what he called an honourable surrender, since the partisan commanders had ordered that he be executed at once if captured, or at best he would be treated as a war criminal, the fate he had been reserving for Churchill and Roosevelt. It is said, perhaps correctly, that he was determined whatever else happened to avoid falling into Anglo-American hands. But he knew and said that the allies were likely to be more generous than the liberation committee.[142] Members of this committee, as it seems he heard later on 25 April, confirmed a final order for his summary execution.[143]

With the faithful Bombacci by his side, he left Milan by car saying that he meant to proceed to the Valtelline where 30,000 fascists were ready for a last battle. This was the final delusion, as he discovered on arrival at Como. His loyal supporters were in fact a rapidly dwindling band, and those who still remained faithful, shocked by what they now heard him say, realised that he had no serious idea of what to do. Staying with him any longer would only add to what would become a useless tragedy.[144]

As soon as he discovered how few were ready to make a fight of it, he changed his plans and, instead of moving up the east side of Lake Como towards the Valtelline, drove up the west side to a point near the Swiss border. He knew that the Swiss would refuse him entry but may have thought of crossing the frontier surreptitiously or by force.[145] A few hours earlier, such a plan might have succeeded, but during 26 April the frontier guards deserted to join the partisans and blocked this escape route. An alternative was to hide out until the allied forces arrived; but he was unable to make up his mind and wasted many hours doing absolutely nothing at all. This indecisiveness further depressed those few fascists who were still looking to him for a lead, and soon only a handful were left.[146]

After wasting the best part of a day he agreed, as a last despairing bid for freedom, to join a passing group of German soldiers who were hoping to be allowed through the partisan lines into Austria. As he knew that no Italian would be permitted to pass with them, he disguised himself in a Luftwaffe greatcoat and helmet, while the other remaining *gerarchi* were left to save themselves as best they could. A few minutes later, at Dongo near the head of the lake, the column was stopped by the fifty-second Garibaldi brigade of partisans and his presence discovered.

Many different stories have been told by presumed eyewitnesses of what happened next. The one certain fact is that, on 28 April, the 61-year-old Mussolini was executed by communist irregulars before he could be reached by the Americans who were only a few hours away. Time was too short for even the pretence of a trial. Clara Petacci stood by him to the last and insisted on dying with him. Bombacci was also shot, and so were Pavolini, Buffarini, Farinacci and Starace, all of them captured soon afterwards by the lake or in Milan. The bodies were piled into a truck and taken to be strung up by the heels in the Piazzale Loreto at Milan, mocked and vilified by the mob.

Notes

Note: An oblique stroke had been used throughout to distinguish the volume number of a work from the page number. Thus, for example, 34/143 indicates volume 34, page 143.

Chapter 1 Youth

1 Fiori, *Il grande nocchiero*, 41; Alessi, *Il giovane Mussolini*, 18–19
2 Sarfatti, *Dux*, 37–8
3 De Begnac, *Vita di Benito Mussolini*, 1/327
4 *Opera Omnia di Benito Mussolini* (OO), 34/143
5 Mussolini, *La mia vita*, 36
6 De Begnac, *Palazzo Venezia*, 134
7 Beltramelli, *L'uomo nuovo*, 119–20
8 Mussolini, *La mia vita*, 39
9 Iuvenalis, *Mussolini alla luce infrarossa*, 18–20
10 De Begnac, *Vita di Benito Mussolini*, 1/131, 136
11 Mussolini, *Il mio diario*, 224–5
12 Pini, *Benito Mussolini* (1926), 117; *ibid.* (1939), 28–9; De Begnac, *Vita di Benito Mussolini*, 1/317
13 De Begnac, *Trent'anni di Mussolini*, 44
14 Bedeschi and Alessi, *Anni giovanili di Mussolini*, 58
15 Mussolini, *La mia vita*, 69–70
16 Mussolini, *La mia vita*, 71
17 Sarfatti, *Dux*, 53
18 OO 1/245; Sarfatti, 85
19 Delcroix, *Un uomo e un popolo*, 66
20 Balabanoff, *My Life as a Rebel*, 57
21 Dinale, *Quàrant'anni di colloqui con lui*, 38
22 OO 1/47 (25 Oct. 1903)
23 OO 1/52–3, 60, 92, 251 (26 Mar. 1904); Dinale, 36
24 Ludwig, *Colloqui con Mussolini* (1932), 151; Benjamin, *Mussolini et son peuple*, 249; Agricola, *Mussolini in prigionia*, 11; Zachariae, *Mussolini si confessa*, 140; Moellhausen, *La carta perdente*, 295–6
25 OO 1/92 (10 Dec. 1904), 143, 263–4
26 OO 1/102–3 (14 Mar. 1908), 135, 142
27 Megaro, *Mussolini in the Making*, 62
28 OO 35/8 (6 Feb. 1904); OO 38/2 (8 Mar. 1903)
29 OO 2/239
30 Phayre, 'Mussolini', 80; Delcroix, 73
31 Sarfatti, *The Life of Benito Mussolini*, 92; Pini–Susmel, *Mussolini*, 1/115
32 OO 1/23–5, 32–6, 263
33 Dinale, 50; Bezençon, *La vie âpre*, 14; Megaro, 112; *Daily News*, 11 Jan. 1927

Chapter 2 The socialist

1 St A. 166/048913 (documents in St Antony's College, Oxford)
2 Mussolini, *My Autobiography*, 29
3 Mussolini, *La mia vita*, 136; Ward Price, *Extra-special Correspondent*, 205
4 Mussolini, *La mia vita*, 136–7; OO 1/221; Pini–Susmel, *Mussolini*, 1/427; De Felice, *Mussolini*, 1/49
5 Delcroix, *Un uomo e un popolo*, 83; De Begnac, *Vita di Benito Mussolini*, 2/34
6 De Begnac, *Vita di Benito Mussolini*, 2/266
7 Parenti, *Bibliografia Mussoliniana*, 9
8 OO 1/162
9 Borghi, *Mussolini in camicia*, 45; OO 3/286
10 Balabanoff, *My Life*, 60
11 OO 1/188; OO 2/63
12 OO 1/103, 128; OO 2/165, 247; Beltramelli, *L'uomo nuovo*, 175
13 Uhlig, *Mussolinis Deutsche Studien*, 96; Dinale, *Quarant'anni di colloqui con lui*, 192–3; Zachariae, *Mussolini si confessa*, 42; OO 1/174–84; Seldes, *The Truth*, 74
14 OO 38/4 (23 June 1908)
15 Nenni, *Sei anni*, 28; Sarfatti, *Dux*, 92
16 Carlini, *Filosofia ... di Mussolini*, 13; De Begnac, *Palazzo Venezia*, 132; Sarfatti, *Dux*, 110
17 Borghi *Mezzo secolo*, 111
18 Beltramelli, 217, 229–30; Pini, *Benito Mussolini* (1939), 45, 57
19 OO 3/409
20 Nanni, *Bolscevismo e fascismo*, 153, 159; Balabanoff, *My Life*, 118
21 OO 20/52–3 (24 Oct. 1923)
22 Mussolini, *My Autobiography*, 30; Pini, *Benito Mussolini* (1939), 53–4; Sarfatti, *Dux*, 114, 120
23 OO 2/64 (8 Apr. 1909), 170 (25 June 1909); OO 33/198; Megaro, *Mussolini in the Making*, 11–12
24 OO 2/268; OO 33/267
25 *Panorami di realizzazioni del fascismo*, 1/228
26 OO 2/84–5
27 Niekisch, *Gewagtes Leben*, 263; OO 2/8, 127, 165–6; OO 3/6, 199; OO 4/153; OO 6/74 (8 Feb. 1914)
28 OO 1/111, 131; OO 2/99, 188–9, 224; OO 3/9, 35, 74
29 OO 2/7; OO 3/137, 281, 325, 374–5; OO 35/11–13 (15 Aug. 1910); Bonavita, *Mussolini svelato*, 92
30 OO 3/43, 190; OO 4/18
31 OO 3/34, 324
32 OO 1/41; OO 3/135–40, 148, 286; OO 35/15; Nenni, *Sei anni*, 31; Riboldi, *Vicende socialiste*, 43
33 Monelli, *Mussolini piccolo borghese*, 5
34 Rachele Mussolini, *La mia vita*, 26–9; Pini–Susmel, *Mussolini*, 1/134
35 Edda Ciano, *My Truth*, 50
36 OO 38/23, 53 (5 Apr. 1914), 70 (25 Sept. 1914); Beltramelli, 130–1
37 Aniante, *Mussolini*, 41; Terzaghi, *Fascismo e massoneria*, 79; Rachele Mussolini, 26
38 Balabanoff, *My Life*, 64, 119
39 Beltramelli, 192; C. Rossi, *Mussolini com'era*, 41; Edvige Mussolini, *Mio fratello*, 44; Nenni, *Sei anni*, 31; OO 3/101

40 OO 3/208–10, 256–8, 260, 307, 406; Sarfatti, *Dux*, 147

41 OO 4/52–3, 59, 66, 74, 203

42 Bortolotto, *Storia del fascismo*, 15

43 Bonavita, 107; Beltramelli, 137

44 De Begnac, *Vita di Benito Mussolini*, 3/519; Megaro, 265–71; OO 4/104–6, 262

45 OO 6/142 (31 March 1914)

46 Nenni, *Sei anni*, 27

47 OO 4/129, 213–4, 234, 243–4; OO 5/41, 57–8, 286, 310; OO 7/66 (5 Dec. 1914)

48 OO 4/155, 199, 234–5; OO 35/18 (30 Nov. 1912)

49 OO 4/125–8

50 OO 4/113, 147; Nenni, *Sei annhi*, 31

51 OO 5/6; Mussolini, *Corrispondenza*, 30; Bonavita, 82; Nanni, *Bolscevismo e fascismo*, 174

52 Rafanelli, *Una donna e Mussolini*, 6, 42–6, 126, 132

53 OO 38/60 (June 1914)

54 Rafanelli, 250

55 Rafanelli, 67–9

56 OO 5/55, 68; OO 6/131 (26 Mar. 1914)

57 OO 5/85, 234

58 Sarfatti, *Dux*, 147; OO 13/252; OO 21/309

59 *Corriere della Sera*, 9 Apr. 1944 ('Il giramondo'); Ciano (3), 129

60 OO 21/311; Seldes, *The Truth*, 75; D'Andrea, *Mussolini motore del secolo*, 68–9

61 OO 5/39, 42, 285; OO 6/45

62 OO 6/47, 60, 74–5, 80, 181; Romano, *Gramsci*, 108–12; Riboldi, 30

63 OO 4/114, 174; OO 5/331; OO 6/51, 80–1; Pini–Susmel, *Mussolini*, 1/175; Rocca, *Come il fascismo divenne una dittatura*, 104

64 Gramsci, *Sul fascismo*, 211; Nenni, *Sei anni*, 42; Nanni, *Bolscevismo e fascismo*, 177; Lotti, *La settimana rossa*, 256–8

65 OO 8/69 (10 July 1915); Settimelli, *Benito*, 9

66 OO 6/214, 287–8, 298, 300, 318–9 (13 Aug. 1914)

67 OO 6/442

68 Marvasi, *Echi del terrore*, 51; Ludwig, *Colloqui con Mussolini* (1932), 87; OO 6/413; OO 7/81; OO 13/252; OO 41/297; *Utopia*, 15 Dec. 1914, 401

Chapter 3 War and peace

1 C. Rossi, *Trentatre vicende*, 444

2 Nanni, *Bolscevismo e fascismo*, 193; OO 7/476

3 OO 6/99; OO 7/432 (21 Nov. 1914)

4 De Felice (1), 277; Vivarelli, *Il dopoguerra*, 238; C. Rossi, *Mussolini com'era*, 70

5 C. Rossi, *Trentatre vicende*, 29

6 OO 7/233 (4 Mar. 1915), 349

7 OO 6/429; OO 35/36–7 (12 Dec. 1914)

8 OO 6/337 (23 Aug. 1914); OO 7/148 (24 Jan. 1915), 156

9 OO 7/233–4; OO 8/169, 179 (22 Aug. 1915)

10 OO 7/197, 236, 369

11 Rocca, *Come il fascismo*, 42–3; Bergamo, *Novissimo annuncio*, 90

12 Dorso, *Mussolini alla conquista*, 101

13 OO 7/140, 249, 285, 316, 386; Mussolini, *Corrispondenza*, 33 (16 May 1915)

14 OO 6/410; OO 7/77, 79, 172, 204, 292, 417

15 Mussolini, *My Autobiography*, 49; OO 9/92; Vigezzi, 'Le radiose giornate', 322–4

16 OO 7/376–7 (11 May 1915)

17 OO 8/237; OO 10/344; De Begnac, *Palazzo Venezia*, 161; Ludwig, *Colloqui con Mussolini*
    (1932), 145

18 OO 9/219 (27 Sept. 1917); OO 11/155, 200 (14 July 1918)

19 Flora, *Ritratto di un ventennio*, 10 (Nitti)

20 OO 13/353; *Chi è?* (1928), 344

21 OO 38/94

22 Mussolini, *Corrispondenza*, 35

23 De Felice (I), 320

24 Mussolini, *Scritti e discorsi*, 4/18

25 Pini, *Benito Mussolini* (1926), 54

26 Ludwig, *Colloqui con Mussolini* (1932), 52; Sarfatti, *Dux*, 185; Pini, *Benito Mussolini* (1939),
    80–1; De Begnac, *Palazzo Venezia*, 128

27 De Felice (I), 353–6

28 OO 8/283; OO 9/157–8

29 Dinale, *Quarant' anni di colloqui con lui*, 83–5; OO 8/285 (16 June 1917); *Vita Italiana*, Nov.
    1928, 72

30 OO 7/140 (24 Jan. 1915); OO 10/99; Malagodi, *Conversazioni*, 1/140–1

31 OO 8/184 (28 Aug. 1915), 277; OO 9/75–6 (25 July 1917); OO 11/8; OO 12/29

32 OO 8/301; OO 11/83; OO 34/70

33 OO 9/251, 266 (16 Oct.1917); OO 10/87, 144, 317 (11 Feb. 1918); OO 38/109

34 OO 10/25 (4 Nov. 1917); OO 11/84, 285–7 (19 Aug. 1918)

35 OO 11/121 (13 June 1918)

36 OO 8/272 (27 Dec. 1916), 297; OO 10/140–1 (15 Dec. 1917); Grandi, *Le origini*, 52

37 OO 10/57; OO 11/283, 349, 469, 471; Prezzolini, *Fascism*, 49

38 *Popolo d'Italia*, 27 Nov. 1918; OO 11/465; OO 12/79

39 OO 9/10, 178; OO 10/269, 328–9, 434; OO 35/63–4

40 OO 12/18, 26, 76–7 (20 Dec. 1918), 82

41 OO 11/455 (3 Nov. 1918)

42 OO 11/454; OO 13/84, 307; OO 20/50; OO 26/129

43 Cross, *Sir Samuel Hoare*, 55–6; Templewood, *Nine Troubled Years*, 154

44 OO 11/224; De Felice (I), 418

45 OO 11/506–7, 510–11; Berselli, *L'opinione pubblica inglese*, 22–3 (Rennell Rodd)

46 OO 11/35, 46–7, 241, 270–1 (11 Aug. 1918), 411; OO 12/93

47 OO 12/322 (23 Mar. 1919); OO 13/22 (1 Apr. 1919); *Nation*, 5 Mar. 1927, 749

48 OO 12/266–8; OO 13/171; OO 14/80, 106

49 De Begnac, *Palazzo Venezia*, 157; OO 11/429–31

50 OO 12/122, 230; OO 15/75

51 OO 12/310 (18 Mar. 1919); OO 13/145–6 (22 May 1919), 239

52 OO 12/280 (9 Mar. 1919); OO 13/142–3

53 OO 13/98 (3 May 1919)

54 OO 12/312; OO 13/71, 89 (28 Apr. 1919)

55 OO 12/291 (14 Mar. 1919)

56 De Begnac, *Palazzo Venezia*, 158 (Oct. 1939)

57 OO 12/326 (23 Mar. 1919)

58 OO 12/222; OO 13/79 (24 Apr. 1919)

59 De Felice (1), 497–8; Mecheri, *Chi ha tradito?*, 216; Dinale, 124; Rocca, *Come il fascismo*, 84; C. Rossi, *Trentatre vicende*, 17

Chapter 4 The fascist movement

1 Nanni, *Bolscevismo e fascismo*, 253
2 OO 12/327; OO 13/63; OO 14/43; Mussolini, *Dottrina* (1941), 9
3 Chiurco, *Storia della rivoluzione*, 1/22; Marinetti, *Futurismo e fascismo*, 19, 165–6
4 OO 13/113 (10 May 1919)
5 OO 12/326; OO 13/265; OO 14/52 (9 Oct. 1919)
6 OO 12/317 (21 Mar. 1919); OO 13/65, 255, 269; OO 14/47, 124, 133, 184 (7 Dec. 1919)
7 OO 14/88 (28 Oct. 1919), 102 (2 Nov. 1919), 133
8 *Popolo d'Italia*, 2 June 1919
9 OO 13/53 (13 Apr. 1919)
10 Pan, *Il fascismo*, 15
11 OO 13/209 (25 June 1919)
12 De Felice (1), 742–5 (June 1919); OO 13/33
13 Vecchi, *L'arditismo*, 4; Beltramelli *L'uomo nuovo* (1926), viii–ix (Marinetti); Rocca, *Come il fascismo*, 77; OO 13/62–5; *Ardito d'Italia*, Sept. 1932, 7 (Marinetti)
14 OO 18/201; OO 20/206
15 OO 13/231; OO 14/23–4 (25 Sept. 1919)
16 OO 13/26, 252 (19 July 1919)
17 De Felice (1), 727 (4 June 1919); OO 13/382 (13 June 1919)
18 OO 12/215 (11 Feb. 1919), 227, 235; OO 13/59 (15 Apr. 1919)
19 OO 13/114 (10 May 1919); OO 14/28
20 *Carteggio Arnaldo*, 223–4 (16 Sept. 1919)
21 Scaroni, *Con Vittorio Emanuele*, 29
22 Ojetti, *I taccuini*, 552–3
23 OO 14/35–8, 475–9
24 OO 13/281, 304; OO 14/47, 111 (6 Nov. 1919)
25 Tasca, *Nascita e avvento del fascismo*, 57
26 OO 14/478; OO 35/69; Daffinà, *Mussolini e il fascismo*, 68 (Balbo); De Begnac, *Trent'anni di Mussolini*, vii; Rossato, *Mussolini*, 37
27 C. Rossi, *Mussolini com'era*, 37; Mecheri, *Chi ha tradito?*, 127–9; Rossini, *Il delitto Matteotti*, 994–5; De Begnac, *Palazzo Venezia*, 191
28 Mecheri, 109
29 *Popolo d'Italia*, 1 Nov. 1923 (Binda)
30 Sarfatti, *Dux*, 232
31 OO 14/184, 505–8; Vigezzi, *Dopoguerra*, 447–8, 459 (Rumi); Castronovo, *La stampa*, 267–8
32 Dinale, *Quarant'anni di colloqui con lui*, 74; *Popolo nell'abisso*, 84–5; Bojano, *In the wake*, 35; Daffinà, 30 (Capasso-Torre)
33 Rossato, 30
34 Rossato, 31
35 OO 14/287 (5 Feb. 1920), 342, 381 (26 Mar. 1920)
36 OO 14/60 (13 Oct. 1919), 231 (1 Jan. 1920); OO 15/183 (5 Sept. 1920)
37 OO 14/262 (21 Jan. 1920); *Popolo d'Italia*, 3 July 1920

38 *Fortnightly Review*, Nov. 1924, 679 (Lina Waterfield); *ibid.*, Dec. 1925, 769–70 (J. Murphy); Lanzillo, *Le rivoluzioni*, 225

39 OO 14/416, 469–71 (24 May 1920)

40 OO 15/171 (27 Aug.1920), 188; OO 16/44 (7 Dec. 1920); OO 17/21 (2 July 1921); OO 35/68 (21 Sept. 1920); OO 44/3; Pomba, *La civiltà fascista*, 13 (Volpe)

41 *Corriere della Sera*, 27 Apr. 1924; Sarfatti, *Dux*, 235; Valeri, *D'Annunzio*, 51

42 Slocombe, *The Tumult*, 150; Navarra, *Memorie*, 49; C. Rossi, *Mussolini com'era*, 237; C. Rossi, *Trentatre vicende*, 340; Sarfatti, *The Life of Benito Mussolini*, 261

43 OO 13/168 (4 June 1919); OO 15/220 (20 Sept. 1920)

44 OO 14/455–6 (20 May 1920); OO 15/274, 300

45 OO 15/206, 219, 231

46 *Corriere della Sera*, 21 March 1944; Tuninetti, *Squadrismo*, 304–8; De Begnac, *Palazzo Venezia*, 210; Silvestri, *Mussolini*, 349

47 OO 20/321

48 OO 15/197–8 (12 Sept. 1920), 228, 323–5

49 OO 15/33, 69–70, 95; OO 16/63 (18 Dec. 1920); Chiurco, *Storia*, 2/270–1 (20 Sept. 1920)

50 OO 15/311–17 (June–Sept. 1920)

51 OO 16/212, 257 (9 Apr. 1921)

52 OO 16/105–6 (8 Jan. 1921), 159, 239, 300–1 (3 May 1921)

53 De Felice (2), 35: Grandi, *Le origini*, 56; Colarizi, *Dopoguerra*, 156; OO 16/261

54 *Camera: discussioni* (11 Mar. 1925), 2438; Nitti, *Rivelazioni*, 467; Nitti, *La democrazia*, 1/319; OO 38/143

55 OO 16/243 (3 Apr. 1921)

56 *Corriere della Sera*, 1 Jan. 1922

57 OO 17/18; Dinale, 116

58 Federzoni. *Italia di'ieri*, 67; Misuri, *Rivolta*, 31; *Daily News*, 12 Jan. 1927

59 OO 16/101, 441–5 (21 June 1921)

60 OO 16/348 (14 May 1921); OO 17/87, 268 (22 Nov. 1921)

61 Gorgolini, *Il fascismo*, 235

62 Chiurco, 3/352–3; OO 16/418

63 OO 16/380 (27 May 1921)

64 *Vita Italiana*, 15 July 1921, 2–3 (Pantaleoni)

65 OO 14/193 (12 Dec. 1919), 223; Margiotta Broglio, *Italia e Santa Sede*, 80

66 OO 16/444 (21 June 1921); OO 18/17

67 OO 16/212, 335; OO 17/268–9 (22 Nov. 1921)

68 OO 16/241, 297; OO 17/414–15

69 OO 16/364–5 (24 May 1921)

70 De Magistris, *I sansepolcristi*, 27

71 Pan, *Il fascismo*, 16–17; Mecheri, *Chi ha tradito?* 86–7; Misuri, *'Ad bestias'*, 357; Sachs, *Toscanini*, 154

72 OO 17/66 (23 July 1921)

73 OO 17/80 (3 Aug. 1921), 94–5

74 OO 17/89–91; Misuri, *Rivolta*, 197

75 Rocca, *Come il fascismo*, 97; C. Rossi, *Mussolini com'era*, 103

76 Chiurco, 5/6; OO 17/220

77 OO 17/262, 343–4; Chiurco, 3/613

78 OO 17/295 (1 Dec. 1921); Bonomi, *Dal socialismo*, 117

79 Slocombe, *The Tumult*, 150

80 OO 6/217 (11 Jan. 1914)

81 Rocca, *Come il fascismo*, 107; Rusinow, *Italy's Austrian Heritage*, 99; Bocca, *La repubblica di Mussolini*, 140 (Pisenti); OO 18/86
82 OO 18/56, 71, 261 (25 June 1922)
83 OO 18/51, 138 (4 Apr. 1922), 261–2, 292 (19 July 1922)
84 OO 17/267; Dorso, *Mussolini*, 217; Tasca, *Nascita e avvento del fascismo*, 279–81
85 OO 18/141, 321, 326 (30 July 1922)
86 OO 18/68–9, 278, 359–60 (19 Aug. 1922)
87 Tamaro, *Venti anni*, 1/224–5; C. Rossi, *Mussolini com'era*, 188–9
88 *Revue des Deux Mondes*, 1 Oct. 1922, 637 (Hazard); OO 17/300; OO 18/331 (2 Aug. 1922), 499
89 OO 18/258, 323 (29 July 1922), 410; OO 37/280 (24 June 1922)
90 A. Albertini, *Vita*, 209; De Begnac, *Palazzo Venezia*, 173; Rocca, *Come il fascismo*, 107; OO 18/349 (11 Aug. 1922)
91 Salandra, *Memorie*, 13; Alessio, *La crisi*, 27–8, 36–9
92 Filareti, *In margine*, 339; Slocombe, 152–3; Serge, *Memoirs*, 163; Tasca, *Nascita e avvento del fascismo* 540
93 *Senato: discussioni* (26 Nov. 1922), 4213
94 *The Times*, 23 May 1924
95 Ciccotti, *Il fascismo*, 244–8
96 *Popolo d'Italia*, 27 Oct. 1923 (Chiavolini), *Stampa*, 26 Oct. 1923 (Bianchi); Répaci, *La marchia su Roma*, 2/387 (Dottai), Bustianini, *Uomini, cose, fatti*, 17, 21; *Vita Italiana*, Nov. 1931, 591 (Preziosi)
97 Chiurco, *Storia*, 5/208; Binchy, *Church and State*, 137; Valeri, *D'Annunzio*, 86; C. Rossi, *Trentatre vicende*, 127
98 Répaci, 2/140 (Lusignoli); Amendola, *Una battaglia*, 186
99 Nitti, *Rivelazioni*, 346–7; Tasca, 413–15, 483; C. Senise, *Quando ero capo*, 9–10
100 Soleri, *Memorie*, 146; Alessio, *La crisi dello stato parlamentare*, 10; De Begnac, *Palazzo Venezia*, 357; *Popolo d'Italia*, 27 Oct.1923
101 Répaci, 2/125, 132
102 Répaci, 2/140; Vaina, *La monarchia*, 215–16; E. Conti, *Dal taccuino*, 297 (12 Oct. 1922); Labriola, *Spiegazioni*, 200; Melograni, *Gli industriali*, 28, 31
103 Monelli, *Mussolini*, 125; OO 18/582; De Begnac, *Palazzo Venezia*, 173–5
104 *Rivista Illustrata del 'Popolo d'Italia'*, Nov. 1942, 17 (Amicucci); Répaci, 2/143
105 OO 18/452 (20 Oct. 1922)
106 Tasca, 428
107 OO 18/459–60
108 Minergi, *Dal manganello alla feluca*, 94

Chapter 5 The conquest of power

1 Rochat, *L'esercito italiano*, 404; St A. 132/036813 (Anon. 15 Oct. 1922); *ibid.*, 251/068486 (De Vecchi, 19 Dec. 1922); Mecheri, *Chi ha tradito?* 102; Pugliese, *Io difendo l'esercito*, 23, 126; OO 18/443; Vaina, *La grande tragedia*, 21; Vailati, *Badoglio racconta*, 254–5; Vailati, *Badoglio risponde*, 257; Canevari, *La guerra italiana*, 1/145; Bolla, *Il segreto di due re*, 76
2 *Corriere della Sera*, 26 Oct. 1922 (Einaudi); *Rivista di Politica Economica*, 30 Nov. 1932, 1171 (Pirelli); De' Stefani, *La restaurazione*, 2–3; *Manchester Guardian*, 19 Oct. 1922
3 Ferraris, *La marcia su Roma*, 94; Pugliese, 54

The conquest of power

4 Scaroni, *Con Vittorio Emanuele*, 52
5 Pugliese, 139; Missiroli, *Il fascismo* (1969), 37
6 Paolucci, *Il mio piccolo mondo*, 240; Federzoni, *Italia di ieri*, 77–8; Ciano (2), 115; C. Rossi, *Mussolini com'era*, 115
7 C. Senise, *Quando ero capo*, 13; Salvemini, *Scritti*, 2/59–60; C. Rossi, *Mussolini com'era*, 123–6; St A., 261/072740
8 A. Albertini, *Vita*, 215; Salandra, *Memorie*, 25; Missiroli, *Il fascismo*, 37; *Critica Fascista*, 1 Apr. 1925, 133; C. Rossi, *Mussolini com'era*, 123; C. Rossi, *Trentatre vicende*, 155–7
9 Puntoni, *Parla Vittorio Emanuele*, 288; *Il Ponte*, Sept. 1951, 1072–4 (Cocco–Ortu)
10 Salandra, *Memorie*, 25–6
11 Tasca, *Nascita e avvento del fascismo*, 461; OO 19/17; OO 39/536
12 Répaci, *La marcia su Roma*, 2/415 (Pugliese); Pugliese, 66–73
13 Sherrill, *Bismarck e Mussolini*, 207–8
14 *Popolo d'Italia*, 24 Oct. 1923; OO 21/28–9, 94
15 OO 18/466; *Corriere della Sera*, 31 Oct. 1922; *ibid.*, 1 Nov. 1922; Rossini, 970–1 (Rossi)
16 *Popolo d'Italia*, 30 Oct. 1923
17 Soffici, *Battaglia*, xxiv (Malaparte); Pugliese, 92, 102
18 OO 24/154; *Camera: discussioni* (17 Nov. 1922), 8420
19 OO 19/26; OO 23/51; Vaina, *La monarchia*, 250–1; C. Rossi, *Mussolini com'era*, 115, 122, 129
20 *New York Times*, 29–31 Oct. 1922; Ciccotti, *Il fascismo*, 401–3
21 OO 19/1 (1 Nov. 1922)
22 *Settimana Incom*, 31 Dec. 1955 (Giuriati); De Begnac, *Palazzo Venezia*, 235
23 Orano, *Mussolini da vicino*, 60–1
24 Sheridan, *In Many Places*, 257–62, 268–9; Sheridan, *My Crowded Sanctuary*, 209–11
25 Rocca, *Come il fascismo*, 115; *Corriere della Sera*, 13 Dec. 1922 (Mussolini)
26 OO 19/35 (21 Nov. 1922), 46; Orano, *Mussolini da vicino*, 64
27 OO 19/47–8 (27 Nov. 1922), 57 (6 Dec. 1922)
28 Terzaghi, *Fascismo e massoneria*, 52
29 OO 19/17–23; OO 21/368
30 *Camera: discussioni* (17 Nov. 1922), 8437–9 (Conti)
31 Salandra, *Memorie*, 32
32 F. Turati and Kuliscioff, *Carteggio*, 5/600 (24 Nov. 1922); Salandra, *Memorie*, 32; *Corriere della Sera*, 17 Nov. 1922; Ansaldo, *Il ministro*, 495
33 *The Times*, 12 Jan. 1923; Pernot, *L'expérience*, 232–4
34 OO 19/45 (27 Nov. 1922)
35 *Senato: discussioni* (28 Nov. 1922), 4279
36 *Senato: discussioni* (28 Nov. 1922), 4280
37 *Senato: discussioni* (26 Nov. 1922), 4213–14; Albertini, *In difesa della libertà*, 39–47
38 *Senato: discussioni* (27–28 Nov. 1922), 4259, 4279 (13 Nov. 1923), 5370–1
39 Sheridan, *In Many Places*, 265
40 OO 17/13 (27 June 1921); OO 21/169 (15 Nov. 1924), 221
41 BD 1a/3/153 (Graham); OO 19/58, 146 (16 Feb. 1923)
42 OO 19/48 (27 Nov. 1922)
43 OO 14/206 (18 Dec. 1919), 358 (7 Mar. 1920)
44 OO 18/437; OO 19/145 (16 Feb. 1923); De Begnac, *Palazzo Venezia*, 352–3
45 OO 21/164; *Camera; discussioni* (10 Feb. 1923), 8976
46 Grazzi, *Il principio della fine*, 8–10; Rumi, *Alle origini della politica estera*, 281
47 Cassels, *Mussolini's Early Diplomacy*, 388–9

48 OO 19/420; Rumi, 270

49 Gorgolini, *La rivoluzione*, 55–6

50 Sheridan, *To the Four Winds*, 194; Steffens, *The Autobiography*, 2/808; Ward Price, *Extra-Special Correspondent*, 199

51 Hemingway, *By-Line*, 85 (27 Jan. 1923)

52 *Basler Presse*, 23 Nov. 1922 (cit. by R. Moscati in *Studi Politici*, Sept. 1953, 412)

53 Grew, *Turbulent Era*, 1/487

54 Nicolson, *Curzon*, 289–90

55 DDI 7/1/92 (22 Nov. 1922)

56 BL Add.MS 60753 F (Keyes, 7 Dec. 1922); Varè, *The Two Impostors*, 249; Lees-Milne, *Harold Nicolson*, 184; Borsa, *Memorie*, 422; Mussolini, *My Autobiography*, 13 (Child); Grew, 1/495–6; Rumi, 278, 280

57 DDI 7/1/113 (30 Nov. 1922)

58 Saint-Aulaire, *Confession*, 642–3

59 *Morning Post*, 13 Dec. 1922; *Daily Herald*, 9 Dec. 1922; Ward Price, *Extra-Special Correspondent*, 138; OO 19/426

60 Albertini, *Epistolario*, 4/1662–5 (12 Dec. 1922, Rizzini)

61 OO 19/428–9; St A. 331/10; *Corriere della Sera*, 13 Dec. 1922; *Studi Politici*, Sept. 1953, 419 (Moscati)

62 *Daily Herald*, 13 Dec. 1922

63 Tamaro, *Due anni*, 1/36; Luciolli, *Palazzo Chigi*, 52–3; Albertini, *Epistolario*, 4/1664

64 De Begnac, *Palazzo Venezia*, 351

65 OO 19/9, 39, 146; *Revue des Deux Mondes*, 1 Mar. 1926, 199–200; Di Nolfo, *Mussolini e la politica estera*, 71

66 DDI 7/1/219; *Studi Politici*, Sept. 1953 (Moscati), 424–5

67 OO 35/283 (14 Jan. 1923)

68 OO 20/103; OO 35/287

69 Boncour, *Entre deux guerres*, 2/338; BD 1/21/30–1; Amery, *My Political Life*, 2/247; Guedalla, *The Hundred Years*, 327; Nitti, *Rivelazioni*, 198; Lees-Milne, 217

70 Farinacci, *Un periodo aureo*, 161; Bertoldi, *La guerra*, 80 (Pisenti); OO 38/170–1

71 Lumbroso, *La crisi del fascismo*, 69; Vinciguerra, *Il fascismo*, 78

72 Ojetti, *I taccuini*, 154 (18 Oct. 1924); Camilleri, *Polizia in azione*, 161–5; Rocca, *Come il fascismo*, 147–9

73 Marongiù, *Nel decennale*, 64–7

74 St A. 1/10 (Dumini)

75 OO 19/138; Mussolini, *My Autobiography*, 122–3

76 OO 19/47; OO 38/151, 212

77 OO 19/129 (10 Feb. 1923)

78 *Camera: discussioni* (30 Nov. 1923), 11101; OO 19/274 (18 June 1923); OO 20/63 (28 Oct. 1923), 171, 175; Gobetti, *Le riviste*, 289

79 Marvasi, *Echi del terrore*, 26; *Popolo d'Italia*, 27 Dec. 1922; Rossini, *Il delitto Matteotti*, 933–4, 971–2, 978–9, 983–4, 988–9

80 Jemolo, *Anni di prova*, 131; Giglio, *The Triumph of Barabbas*, 186; Salvemini, *Scritti*, 1/109; Lussu, *Enter Mussolini*, 118; Conti, *Nella battaglia*, 108–9

81 *Manchester Guardian*, 19 Nov. 1924

82 Staderini, 'Una fonte', 796; De Begnac, *Palazzo Venezia*, 235

83 *Critica Politica*, 25 Dec. 1924, 499 (Mantica); Gasparotto, *Diario*, 247; Tamaro, *Venti anni*, 1/471; Chiesa, *La mano nel sacco*, 111–12, 124; Prezzolini, *Fascism*, 61; Lumbroso, 10; *Nineteenth Century*, Feb. 1943, 58 (Fasciolo)

84 St A. 227/059054 (Pisenti); Tamaro, *Venti anni*, 1/328 (Giuriati); *Settimana Incom*, 31 Dec. 1955 (Giuriati)

85 Heineman, *Hitler's First Foreign Minister*, 25 (von Neurath)

86 Rocca, *Le fascisme*, 85, 89; C. Senise, *Quando ero capo*, 16–17

87 De Begnac, *Palazzo Venezia*, 207 (Feb. 1940)

88 Dinale, *Quarant'anni di colloqui con lui*, 327

89 OO 37/191; Salvatorelli, *Nazionalfascismo*, 66, 104; *Corriere della Sera*, 1 Sept. 1927 (Volpe); *Critica Fascista*, 1 Nov. 1926, 403 (Bottai); Rocca, *Le fascisme*, 108

90 Mussolini, *My Autobiography*, 42; OO 19/33, 74 (26 Dec. 1922), 274; OO 20/92, 293; *Critica Fascista*, 15 July 1923, 51

91 Beyens, *Quatre ans à Rome*, 136–8

92 OO 19/139–40, 196 (Mar. 1923), 209 (Apr. 1923)

93 OO 19/66, 316; Albertini, *Vita*, 219

94 OO 19/48, 116, 253

95 Dinale, 96–7; C. Rossi, *Trentatre vicende*, 175

96 OO 19/100 (13 Jan. 1923), 314 (15 July 1923); OO 20/62, 72–3

97 Lyttleton, *The Seizure*, 111; OO 38/323; Alessio, *La crisi dello stato parlamentare*, 1; Tasca, *Nascita e avvento del fascismo*, 512

98 Guspini, *L'orecchio*, 26; OO 38/211

99 *Risorgimento* (Milan), Oct. 1959, 179 (Gifuni); OO 19/360

100 Roberts, *Black Magic*, 136

101 OO 20/53 (24 Oct. 1923)

102 OO 13/211; OO 14/12, 54 (9 Oct. 1919), 207 (20 Dec. 1919)

103 Giunta, *Un po' di fascismo*, 63; *Rivista . . . 'Popolo d'Italia'*, Nov. 1942, 17 (Amicucci)

104 OO 20/60 (27 Oct. 1923), 147; Bertoldi, *Mussolini*, 166 (Giuriati); Pedrazza, *Giornalismo di Mussolini*, 177

Chapter 6 The Matteotti crisis

1 *The Times*, 23 May 1924; Ciccotti, *Il fascismo*, 435–6

2 Benelli, *Schiavitù*, 60–1

3 OO 19/319 (15 July 1923)

4 Lussu, *Enter Mussolini*, 172; Terzaghi, *Fascismo e massoneria*, 85; Misuri, *Rivolta*, 186; Riboldi, *Vicende socialiste*, 112

5 *The Times*, 19 May 1924; Federzoni, *Italia di ieri*, 92

6 OO 20/137, 171 (28 Jan. 1924), 191, 348; Rocca, *Come il fascismo*, 185

7 OO 19/301 (10 July 1923); OO 38/464, 505 (27 Sept. 1923); De Begnac, *Palazzo Venezia*, 355; Rossini, *Il delitto Matteotti*, 988

8 C. Senise, *Quando ero capo*, 119; Nitti, *Rivelazioni*, 581–2; Rossini, 984

9 *Popolo d'Italia*, 23 Aug. 1923; Amendola, *Una scelta*, 78–82; Rossini, 261, 502–3, 785, 933; Seldes, *The Truth*, 50

10 C. Rossi, *Il delitto Matteotti*, 221–3; Silvestri, *Matteotti*, 127, 200; Terzaghi, 85; Rossini, 990–1

11 OO 20/161, 175–6 (1 Feb. 1924), 215, 371–2; C. Rossi, *Trentatre vicende*, 197

12 Sarfatti, *Dux*, 291; Albertini, *In difesa della libertà*, 65; Rossini, 989

13 Mack Smith, *Storia . . . 'Corriere della Sera'*, 274–5 (14 July 1923)

14 *Camera: discussioni* (22 Nov. 1924), 704 (Federzoni)

15 OO 19/204, 230 (1 June 1923), 234; *Popolo d'Italia*, 4 Apr. 1923; Gobetti, *Le riviste*, 288; Pennino, *La politica*, 86–7

16 OO 14/213–14 (22 Dec. 1919); OO 16/159 (6 Feb. 1921); Morandi, *La critica a Versailles*, 9; Historicus, *Il problema*, 55

17 OO 18/453 (24 Oct. 1922); OO 20/73 (30 Oct. 1923)

18 OO 19/13; OO 35/374 (21 Dec. 1923)

19 DDI 7/1/173 (21 Dec. 1922); Cassels, *Mussolini's Early Diplomacy*, 86–7

20 DDI 7/1/187 (29 Dec. 1922), 299, 393, 503; St A. 41/022403, 022436

21 Tur, *Plancia*, 3/35–6; DDI 7/2/271 (30 Sept. 1923); Foschini, 'A trent'anni', 401–2; Cassels, 98

22 Sforza, *L'Italia*, 151

23 Rumi, *Alle origini della politica estera fascista*, 314–15

24 Barros, *The Corfu Incident*, 204–5

25 Bernotti, *Cinquant' anni*, 132–3; DDI 7/2/229 (13 Sept. 1923)

26 OO 35/343, 360 (13 Sept. 1923)

27 *Popolo d'Italia*, 1 Nov. 1923; OO 20/63, 108

28 Ciano (2), 299; Wagnière, *Dix-huit ans à Rome*, 117; Percy, *Some Memories*, 166

29 Landmans, *Catologo dei francobolli*, 63; *Popolo d'Italia*, 1 Nov. 1923; Guariglia, *Ricordi*, 29; *Politica estera Italiana*, 84 (Moscati)

30 *Labour Magazine*, Oct. 1923, 253 (Toynbee); FO 371/8616 (Kennard, 6 Sept. 1923)

31 OO 39/88 (5 Mar. 1924), 101, 122; DDI 7/3/43–4 (8 Mar. 1924)

32 OO 39/66–7, 119, 128; Lumbroso, *La crisi del fascismo*, 143; *Camera: discussioni* (2 Dec. 1924), 1035 (Starace)

33 *New Statesman*, 1 Mar. 1924, 596–7; *ibid.*, 12 Apr. 1924, 5

34 Silvestri, *Matteotti*, 172; *Corriere della Sera*, 20 Mar. 1924; Amendola, *Una scelta*, 85

35 *Daily Herald*, 3 Mar. 1924

36 Corner, *Fascism in Ferrara*, 263–4; *Lavoro*, 29 Nov. 1924; Sforza, *L'Italia*, 128; De Rosa, *Giolitti e il fascismo*, 22, 91; *Civiltà Cattolica*, 1924, 2/183–7

37 OO 20/192, 204, Rocca, *Come il fascismo*, 244; Misuri, *Rivolta*, 190; *Ricostruzione fascista*, 66, 161; Conti, *Dal taccuino*, 320; *Corriere della Sera*, 29 Nov. 1924; Lyttleton, *The Seizure of Power*, 141–8; Zavoli, *Nascita di una dittatura*, 160 (Fasciolo)

38 *Daily Herald*, 8 Mar. 1924

39 *Idea Nazionale*, 8 Apr. 1924

40 Zachariae, *Mussolini si confessa*, 65

41 *Critica Politica*, 25 Apr. 1924, 183–5; *ibid.*, 25 July 1924, 330; *Nineteenth Century*, Feb. 1943, 57 (Murphy); *Manchester Guardian*, 23 Apr. 1924; *Daily Herald*, 7 Apr. 1924; *New Leader*, 25 Apr. 1924; Ferrero, *Four Years*, 125–6; Nitti, *Bolshevism*, 82; Misuri, *Rivolta*, 191; De Begnac, *Palazzo Venezia*, 226

42 Rossini, *Il delitto Matteotti*, 258, 977; Margiotta Broglio, *Italia e Santa Sede*, 152–4; De Felice (2), 587; *Manchester Guardian*, 23 Apr. 1924; *The Times*, 10 Apr. 1924

43 Rocca, *Come il fascismo*, 169–71; OO 20/253 (Apr. 1924)

44 Rossini, 450–1; Dumini, *17 Colpi*, 70

45 LSE 1/184–9; LSE 3/10/29 (Thierschwald)

46 *Avanti!*, 17 June 1924; St A. 1/1, 12 (Dumini's memorandum of 1926)

47 Schiavi, *La vita*, 132

48 *Popolo d'Italia*, 3 May 1923

49 *New Leader*, 28 Mar. 1924; *Daily Herald*, 16 June 1924; *English Life*, July 1924, 87

50 OO 20/303–4 (1 June 1924), 356 (2 June 1924)

51 Riboldi, *Vicende socialiste*, 119

52 Rocca, *Come il fascismo*, 243
53 Silvestri, *Matteotti*, 116, 130–1, 201
54 De Begnac, *Palazzo Venezia*, 282
55 *Camera: discussioni* (4 June 1924), 143; *ibid.* (6 June 1924), 204, 206
56 *Corriere della Sera*, 9 June 1924
57 Silvestri, *Matteotti*, 117–18; Rossini, 989
58 Maurano, *Ricordi*, 31
59 LSE 2/592 (Quilici)
60 *Daily Herald*, 12 Mar. 1926 (Rossi); C. Rossi, *Il delitto Matteotti*, 55–6, 102
61 Orano, *Mussolini da vicino*, 73
62 Rossini, 929 (Filippelli)
63 Silvestri, *Matteotti*, 61
64 *Corriere della Sera*, 15 Feb. 1947 (Fasciolo)
65 Pirelli, *Dopoguerra*, 133; Navarra, *Memorie*, 31; Rocca, *Come il fascismo*, 199
66 Dinale, *Quarant'anni di colloqui con lui*, 115; Silvestri, *Turati*, 111–12; Lussu, *Enter Mussolini*, 185; Riboldi, 126
67 Spriano, *Storia*, 1/390
68 Mack Smith, 'Mussolini e il "caso Matteotti"', 72–3
69 St A. 222/057009–73 (Mussolini's personal file on Dumini)
70 *Stampa*, 17 June 1924; *Rivoluzione Liberale*, 1 July 1924; *Lavoro*, 24 July 1924
71 De Felice (2), 778 (Mussolini, 7 Aug. 1924)
72 Federzoni, *Italia di ieri*, 90
73 OO 21/19 (19 July 1924)
74 De Begnac, *Palazzo Venezia*, 291, 357
75 FO 371/9939/10823 (28 June 1924, Odo Russell); FO 371/10783/27 (7 Jan. 1925, Russell); Beyens, *Quatre ans à Rome*, 237; De Rosa, *Storia*, 2/492–3
76 Levi della Vida, *Fantasmi*, 195; Croce, *Pagine sparse*, 2/377–9
77 Ojetti, *I taccuini*, 150 (6 July 1924); Salandra, *Memorie*, 49–50; *Corriere della Sera*, 2 Apr. 1949
78 Valeri, *D'Annunzio*, 117
79 Farinacci, *Un periodo*, 27; Tamaro, *Due anni*, 1/307; Dinale, 113; Soleri, *Memorie*, 183; De Begnac, *Palazzo Venezia*, 245
80 FO 371/9939/255 (Graham, 26 June 1924); *ibid.* 273 (27 June 1924); *ibid.* 361 (4 July 1924)
81 Rocca, *Come il fascismo*, 206; *Impero*, 28 July 1924; *The Times*, 24 June 1924; Santini, *Mussolini*, 150–2
82 OO 21/23 (22 July 1924)
83 De Felice (2), 780–2 (7 Aug. 1924); OO 21/38, 40, 57, 94 (4 Oct. 1924)
84 FO 371/9940/182 (19 Sept. 1924, Kennard)
85 OO 21/139–40 (11 Nov. 1924)
86 *Chicago Daily Tribune*, 11 Nov. 1924 (Larry Rue)
87 *Camera: discussioni* (15 Nov. 1924), 521–2
88 OO 21/181 (22 Nov. 1924)
89 *Ricostruzione fascista*, 48–52, 56–7 (22 Nov. 1924)
90 *Manchester Guardian*, 19 Nov. 1924
91 OO 21/514–15 (1 Dec. 1924); OO 39/164 (15 May 1924); Carli, *Fascismo*, 248, 255
92 Dinale, 116; Tamaro, *Venti anni*, 2/56–7
93 OO 21/196, 201, 203 (5 Dec. 1924)
94 *Corriere della Sera*, 27 Dec. 1924; *Camera: discussioni* (17 Dec. 1924), 1663–4; *Camera: discussioni* (19 Dec. 1924), 1829

95 St A. 266/076691 (report by General Agostino on Tamburini); *Impero*, 30 Dec. 1924; *Cremona Nuova*, 23–4 Dec. 1924; Carli, *Fascismo*, 248

96 *Camera: discussioni* (22 Nov. 1924), 734

97 Paolucci, *Il mio piccolo mondo*, 257–60; De Grand, *The Italian Nationalist Association*, 167–70; St A. 250/068207 (Acerbo, 29 Dec. 1924); Zavoli, *Nascita di una dittatura*, 192 (D'Andrea)

98 FO 371/9940/180–2 (19 Sept. 1924); FO 371/9941/353 (27 Nov. 1924); *Lavoro*, 23 Dec. 1924; *Critica Politica*, 25 Jan. 1925, 3; Croce, *Nuove pagine*, 1/65

99 Scorza, *La notte del Gran Consiglio*, 156

100 Salandra, *Diario*, 311 (30 Dec. 1924); Sarrocchi, *Ricordi*, 27

101 *Idea Nazionale*, 31 Dec. 1924; Rachele Mussolini, *La mia vita*, 82; St A. 166/048980 (report on Federzoni *c*. July 1924)

102 Galbiati, *Il 25 luglio*, 35–45; Montagna, *Mussolini*, 24–8; Tamaro, *Venti anni*, 2/62; Settimelli, *Edda contro Benito*, 94

103 *Caffè*, 268–9 (11 Jan. 1925); *Critica Politica*, 25 Jan. 1925, 1; *Corriere della Sera*, 13 May 1925; Lussu, 192

104 FO 371/10783/12 (Graham, quoting McClure, 2 Jan. 1925)

105 OO 21/236–40; *Gerarchia*, Jan. 1926, 63

Chapter 7 Fascist government at work

1 Salandra, *Diario*, 321 (3 Jan. 1925)

2 Sarrocchi, *Ricordi*, 63; Salandra, *Memorie*, 68; St A. 274/079833–5 (Sarrocchi, 4 Jan. 1925)

3 Aquarone, *L'organizzazione*, 50–1 (5 Jan. 1925)

4 *Daily News*, 26 Jan. 1925; *Manchester Guardian*, 6 Feb. 1925

5 Spriano, *Storia del partito comunista*, 1/425

6 *Fortnightly Review*, Feb. 1925, 164–5, 174; FO 371/10783/52

7 FO 371/9939/361 (Graham, 4 July 1924)

8 *Camera: discussioni* (3 Jan. 1925), 2047–8

9 St A. 274/079838 (4 Jan. 1925); *Educazione Politica*, June 1925, 145

10 *Camera: discussioni* (16 Jan. 1925), 2248–53, Orlando, *Discorsi*, 4/1579 (16 Jan. 1925)

11 Salvemini, *Scritti*, 1/240

12 *Camera: discussioni* (11 Mar. 1925), 2451; ibid. (16 Mar. 1925), 3663; ibid. (20 June 1925), 4400; Spriano, 1/430–1

13 *Camera: discussioni* (14 Jan. 1925), 2014–15; *Critica Politica*, 25 Apr. 1925, 183; OO 21/262–3

14 Farinacci, *Un periodo aureo*, 15–19, 56, 70, 76, 107, 194, 236, 404

15 Silvestri, *Turati l'ha detto*, 39; Balabanoff, *Il traditore*, 131; *Camera: discussioni* (11 Mar. 1925), 2424

16 Castellani, *Tra microbi e re*, 14–15

17 OO 1/213 (3 Sept. 1902)

18 *Manchester Guardian*, 20 Nov. 1924; De Begnac, *Palazzo Venezia*, 295; Rachele Mussolini, *La mia vita*, 82

19 *Giornale del Mattino*, 4 Apr. 1946 (Boratto); Aniante, *Mussolini*, 77–8; OO 34/397

20 Wagnière, *Dix-huit ans*, 139; Federzoni, *Italia di ieri*, 193; F. Turati and Kuliscioff, *Carteggio*, 6/378 (24 Feb. 1925)

21 *Lavoro*, 27 Mar. 1925

22 Castellani, 10
23 OO 21/358–9 (22 June 1925), 393 (27 Sept. 1925)
24 Aniante, 71; Nitti, *Meditazioni dell'esilio*, 16; OO 20/384 (1 June 1924)
25 OO 39/528 (13 Oct. 1925); OO 40/353 (23 May 1927); St A. 53/026546 (13 Oct. 1925)
26 *The Times*, 5 Nov. 1925
27 Mack Smith, *Storia … 'Corriere della Sera'*, 283–90
28 Seldes, *Sawdust Caesar*, 173; *Daily Express*, 26 Jan. 1927; Salvemini, *Scritti*, 2/251–2; St A. 273/079490–2 (Suardo, 10 Sept. 1926); GEC, *Il cesare di cartapesta*, 3; King, *Il fascismo*, 66
29 OO 21/253 (Jan. 1925); *Manchester Guardian*, 2 Feb. 1925; *Camera: discussioni* (16 May 1925), 3660
30 *The Times*, 26 June 1925
31 *The Times*, 24 Feb. 1925; *ibid.*, 22 July 1925; L.W., *Fascism*, 7; Giglio, *The Triumph of Barabbas*, 288; *Harper's*, Nov. 1927, 734–6; Seldes, *Sawdust Caesar*, 310–11, 325–6
32 Winner, 'Fascism', 6–8; Zurcher, 'State propaganda', 50; Page, *L'Americano di Roma*, 295; Seldes, *The Truth*, 42; Diggins *Mussolini and Fascism*, 42–5
33 Morgan, *Spurs on the Boot*, 122; Darrah, *Hail Caesar*, 42; Seldes, *Sawdust Caesar*, 164–7
34 *New York World*, 29 July 1929
35 DDI 7/4/138–9, 151, 156–7; Santini, *Mussolini*, 239; OO 22/262 (Nov. 1926)
36 Darrah, 48; Vaina, *La granda tragedia*, 52; *Gerarchia*, Jan. 1926, 40; OO 19/234 (3 June 1923); OO 20/27–8 (21 Sept. 1923), 170; OO 23/87 (1 Jan. 1928); Settimelli, *Mussolini visto da Settimelli*, 89–90
37 OO 40/12 (27 Jan. 1926)
38 OO 19/1
39 OO 19/283; OO 20/19 (10 Sept. 1923), 260, 266 (10 May 1924); OO 21/97; Policastro, *Mussolini e la Sicilia*, 19
40 Ferretti, *Esempi e idee*, 254; Zingali, *Liberalismo e fascismo*, 2/340; *Bibliografia Fascista*, July 1936, 469; OO 28/229–30; Guerri, *Rapporto al Duce*, 55
41 OO 41/452 (27 July 1931); *Popolo d'Italia*, 24 Oct. 1923; Barzini, *The Italians*, 144
42 *Politica Sociale*, Aug. 1939, 288 (Maggiore); Lyttleton, *The Seizure of Power*, 199; De Felice (2), 409; Mack Smith, *Modern Sicily*, 514–15
43 *Carteggio D'Annunzio*, 36–8 (Jan. 1923)
44 St A. 135/037992; *ibid.*, 136/038349–50; *ibid.*, 273/079561
45 St A. 30/014439–42 (Pellizzi, 24 Oct. 1923)
46 *Camera: discussioni* (30 Nov. 1923), 11103; Grasso, *Il fascismo*, 3–4; Volt, *Programma della destra*, 74–5; Fanelli, *Dall'insurrezione*, 183–4, 188–93
47 OO 21/293 (29 Apr. 1925); *Gerarchia*, Nov. 1925, 697; *Bibliografia Fascista*, 31 Aug. 1926, 7; *ibid.*, 31 Oct. 1926, 8
48 Amery, *Diaries*, 1/348–9
49 Guariglia, *Ricordi*, 39; Donosti, *Mussolini e l'Europa*, 9–10
50 OO 20/216 (23 Mar. 1924), 295 (27 May 1924), 305; OO 21/122 (25 Oct. 1924); OO 22/37 (11 Dec. 1925); Dinale, *Quarant'anni di colloqui con lui*, 116
51 OO 16/158 (6 Feb. 1921); OO 17/336
52 *Popolo d'Italia*, 24 Oct. 1923; OO 20/33 (4 Oct. 1923), 107–8
53 OO 20/293 (24 May 1924)
54 Coppola, *La pace coatta*, 18, 34–6; *The Times*, 27 Feb. 1925; OO 20/323 (7 June 1924); Salter, *Personality in Politics*, 234
55 OO 19/37 (21 Nov. 1922)
56 DDI 7/3/364 (Di Giorgio, Dec. 1924)
57 OO 21/350–1 (19 June 1925)

334

58 OO 39/116 (19 Mar. 1924), 300 (10 Dec. 1924)
59 Lessona, *Memorie*, 102; OO 39/331, 363 (22 Feb. 1925); OO 41/152 (24 July 1928)
60 DDI 7/3/464 (24 Feb. 1925); OO 39/464 (9 July 1925); Tiltman, *The Terror*, 209
61 OO 19/195, 310; OO 20/110, 127, 205; Attico, *Politica della verità*, 13; Nitti, *La libertà*, 41; Litvinov, *Notes for a Journal*, 110; Carocci, *Amendola*, 157
62 Pesce, *Da Lenin a Mussolini*, 133; Navarra, *Memorie*, 49; *Corriere della Sera*, 27 Apr. 1924
63 Barmine, *One Who Survived*, 155; Krassin, *Leonid Krassin*, 244; De Begnac, *Palazzo Venezia*, 359; OO 20/122
64 OO 35/388–9 (6 Feb. 1924); OO 39/44–5; DDI 7/2/434 (6 Feb. 1924)
65 DDI 7/2/330; DDI 7/3/27, 30 (4 Mar. 1924), 57; Cassels, *Mussolini's Early Diplomacy*, 161
66 OO 12/306 (17 Mar. 1919); OO 13/135; OO 16/165
67 DDI 7/4/18 (8 June 1925); OO 21/319–20; OO 39/385 (28 Mar. 1925)
68 OO 13/360–1 (11 Sept. 1919); OO 16/435 (21 June 1921)
69 OO 16/291 (30 Apr. 1921)
70 OO 22/73 (6 Feb. 1926); OO 39/541–3 (1 Nov. 1925); OO 41/280 (23 Apr. 1929), 396, 478; Reut-Nicolussi, *Tyrol*, 206–8, 222–3, 246
71 Marks, 'Mussolini and Locarno', 424; Carocci, *La politica*, 43
72 OO 39/385, 498
73 Guariglia, *Ricordi*, 39–40; DDI 7/5/632 (Grandi, 21 Dec. 1927)
74 Kelen, *Peace in their Time*, 155
75 *Daily Herald*, 17 Oct. 1925; Slocombe, *The Tumult*, 245–6
76 OO 21/411–12, 533
77 OO 11/258–61 (8 Aug. 1918); OO 13/76 (23 Apr. 1919), 109, 126
78 Gorgolini, *Il fascismo*, 245; Fiori, *Il grande nocchiero*, 55
79 DDI 7/3/554 (7 May 1925); OO 22/262; *Daily Express*, 24 Jan. 1927; *Politica*, Feb. 1926, 29–31 (Coppola); Bottai, *Mussolini costruttore d'impero*, 34
80 DDI 7/5/273 (Grandi, June 1927); DDI 7/6/427 (Guariglia, 17 July 1928)
81 *Almanacco 'Popolo d'Italia'* (1923), 148
82 *Corriere della Sera*, 28 Sept. 1924; De Vecchi, *Orizzonti d'impero*, 37, 131, 246; Del Boca, *Gli Italiani in Africa*, 54; De Begnac, *Palazzo Venezia*, 209
83 *Gerarchia*, Mar. 1925, 143
84 DDI 7/1/149; Hess, *Italian Colonialism*, 171; Del Boca, 128; OO 35/311 (31 Mar. 1923)
85 OO 35/237–8 (28 Aug. 1923), 334–5; DDI 7/2/256 (21 Sept. 1923); Harmsworth, *Abyssinian Adventure*, 142–3
86 OO 39/465 (11 July 1925); Del Boca, 38; Cora, 'Un diplomatico', 92
87 Del Boca, 41–2; OO 23/77 (15 Dec. 1927)
88 DDI 7/2/4 (29 Apr. 1923); *Nuova Italia d'Oltremare*, 1/125
89 Graziani, *Ho difeso la patria*, 38–9; Canevari, *La guerra*, 1/302; De Leone, *La colonizzazione*, 2/532; *Gerarchia*, Apr. 1926, 212
90 *Atti del primo congresso di studi coloniali* (1931), 6/270–1
91 *Popolo d'Italia*, 17 Apr. 1926; Maurano, *Mentalità fascista*, 129
92 Guariglia, *Ricordi*, 51
93 DDI 7/4/319 (10 Sept. 1926); DDI 7/7/61–2 (Nov. 1928), 135; Pomba, *La civiltà fascista*, 261; Macro, *Yemen*, 64
94 OO 41/218 (28 Nov. 1928), 327 (6 Aug. 1929); DDI 7/9/479–80 (De Bono, 29 Oct. 1930)
95 DDI 7/5/232, 237 (May 1927), 454–5 (Oct. 1927)
96 DDI 7/3/528 (21 Apr. 1925); DDI 7/4/157; DDI 7/5/350 (Bastianini, 18 Aug. 1927), 372 (2 Sept. 1927); St A. 329/112744 (Balbo, 25 Sept. 1931)
97 OO 23/161 (5 June 1928); Mattioli, *Mussolini aviatore*, 114

98 *Camera: discussioni* (18 June 1925), 4302 (Grandi); DDI 7/4/76 (18 Aug. 1925)

99 OO 21/344, 363 (22 June 1925)

100 *Rivista 'Popolo d'Italia'*, July 1925, 5

101 OO 21/271 (2 Apr. 1925), 324, 342, 388, 426, 444 (4 Nov. 1925); OO 22/12, 37 (11 Dec. 1925)

102 Dinale, 135; Pennino, *La politica mondiale*, 85; *Vita Italiana*, 15 Mar. 1927, 147–8; *Daily Mail*, 1 Sept. 1925; OO 21/96, 437; OO 22/10, 14; Mascarel, *Mussolini, son programme*, 31 (30 Jan. 1926)

103 OO 21/348 (19 June 1925)

104 St A. 263/074467

105 OO 21/288, 348–9 (19 June 1925); OO 40/99 (21 July 1926)

106 De' Stefani, *Una riforma*, 11–13; *Critica Politica*, 25 May 1924, 199, 202; *ibid.*, 25 Oct. 1924, 403; *ibid.*, 25 Apr. 1925, 156; *ibid.*, 25 May 1925, 230; Sarti, *Fascism and the Industrial Leadership*, 46

107 *The Times*, 23 May 1924; OO 20/209; OO 39/15, 140; Pisenti, *Una repubblica necessaria*, 64

108 OO 21/349 (19 June 1925); OO 29/325; OO 39/328; OO 40/246, 452; *Gazzetta Ufficiale*, 4 Jan. 1926

109 Leto, *Ovra*, 58; OO 40/186, 526 (30 Nov. 1927); OO 41/147, 283 (7 May 1929); Schreiber, *Rome après Moscou*, 108–9

110 Mussolini, *Corrispondenza*, 59–60 (14 May 1925); *Critica Fascista*, 15 Feb. 1925, 64–5 (Volt); *Imperium*, Dec. 1926, 1 (Maurano)

111 *Gerarchia*, July 1925, 411 (Maraviglia)

112 Farinacci *Un periodo aureo*, 154–5, 169

113 OO 21/359–63, 437; OO 22/66

114 *Gerarchia*, Aug. 1925, 486 (Volpe)

115 OO 7/341 (21 Apr. 1915); OO 17/220 (8 Nov. 1921)

116 OO 21/418, 425

117 OO 22/287 (Dec. 1926, to Shaw Desmond)

118 Forges Davanzati, *Fascismo e cultura*, 40

119 Dinale, *Quarant'anni di colloqui con lui*, 128

120 Fried, *The Italian Prefects*, 180, 209; Dolfin, *Con Mussolini*, 121–2; R. Rossi, *Mussolini nudo alla meta*, 68; OO 19/254; OO 20/40 (12 Oct. 1923)

121 OO 6/180 (3 May 1914); OO 7/456 (1 Dec. 1914); OO 17/74 (27 July 1921); Mussolini, *Giovanni Huss*, 7; *Popolo d'Italia*, 22 Mar. 1919

122 *Daily Herald*, 13 Dec. 1922; OO 20/1 (22 Aug. 1923), 36

123 OO 21/264 (Feb. 1924); Gatti, *Ancoraggi alle rive*, 283

124 *Popolo d'Italia*, 10 May 1923 (Farinacci); *ibid.*, 1 Nov. 1923 (Binda); *Critica Fascista*, 15 Sept. 1923, 138; Monelli, *Mussolini*, 157; *Senato: discussioni* (11 June 1923), 5057 (Rolandi Ricci)

125 Sheridan, *In Many Places*, 258; OO 19/168 (11 Mar. 1923); OO 20/163–4, 173 (29 Jan. 1924); C. Rossi, *Trentatre vicende*, 553

126 St A. 166/048983–5 (Federzoni, 26 May 1925)

127 OO 20/269 (12 May 1924); OO 39/420; D'Agata, *Mussolini*, 173–5

128 *Corriere della Sera*, 21 Nov. 1923

129 Tamaro, *Venti anni*, 2/126; *Dottrina Fascista*, Oct. 1939, 399; Aquarone, *L'organizzazione*, 75–7

130 *Daily Express*, 24 Jan. 1927

131 OO 40/7 (16 Jan. 1926), 129

132 St A. 111/030623 (Farinacci, 4 July 1925); Farinacci, *Un periodo aureo*, 276; *Critica Fascista*, 1 Oct. 1930, 360; Maurano, *Ricordi*, 38

133 St A. 263/074278–85; De Begnac, *Palazzo Venezia*, 283, 298–9, 349, 353
134 OO 40/26, 39–40 (15 Mar. 1926)
135 St A. 112/030788 (Farinacci, 13 Jan. 1926)
136 OO 40/87 (10 July 1926)

Chapter 8 Mussolini as leader

1 Theodoli, *A cavallo di due secoli*, 117–18; Prezzolini, *Fascism*, 59; Raimondi, *Mezzo secolo*, 419; Gorla, *L'Italia*, 224; Ojetti, *I taccuini*, 418
2 C. Rossi, *Mussolini com'era*, 190, 246; OO 38/314; Luciolli, *Palazzo Chigi*, 113
3 D'Aroma, *Mussolini*, 374
4 *Revue des Deux Mondes*, 15 Mar. 1928, 422; *Meridiano*, 10 Aug. 1951, 1; Kelen, *Peace in their Time*, 289, 292; Carboni, *Memorie*, 57; *The Listener*, 1 Feb. 1940, 204
5 Cora, 'Un diplomatico', 90
6 De Begnac, *Palazzo Venezia*, 134 (Mar. 1935)
7 BD 2/6/21; Rachele Mussolini, *La mia vita*, 93; Castellani, *Tra microbi e re*, 15
8 *Daily News*, 8 Jan. 1927
9 *Domenica dell'Agricoltore*, 29 Sept. 1929, 3
10 OO 39/377 (18 Mar. 1925), 450; OO 40/438; Farinacci, *Andante mosso*, 229
11 OO 37/ll; Rachele Mussolini, 147
12 St A. 104/028393, 028398, 028401; Dollmann, *Roma*, 364; Staderini, 'Una fonte', 769–70; C. Senise, *Quando ero capo*, 95
13 Pini–Susmel, *Mussolini*, 3/434; De Ambris, 'Mussolini', 71–3
14 OO 26/244
15 St A. 242/065165–6; D'Aroma, *Vent'anni*, 151; Rachele Mussolini, 131; Flora, *Ritratto di un ventennio*, 88–9; *Carteggio Arnaldo*, 28–31
16 Morgan, *Spurs on the Boot*, 107; *Harper's*, Feb. 1936, 301–2 (Gunther); OO 23/308
17 St A. 270/078585–8, 078599–605; D'Agostini, *Colloqui*, 92
18 *Giornale del Mattino*, 3 Apr. 1946 (Boratto); Bertoldi, *Mussolini*, 63
19 Navarra, *Memorie*, 65, 70–1, 81–3; D'Aroma, *Mussolini*, 352; Bastianini, *Uomini, cose, fatti*, 41; Gravelli, *Mussolini aneddotico*, 203–4
20 *Rivista 'Popolo d'Italia'*, Dec. 1926, 18–23
21 OO 37/xliii (c. 1938)
22 Vittorio Mussolini, *Vita con mio padre*, 18, 29–30
23 Sheridan, *In Many Places*, 260; OO 34/211; De Begnac, *Palazzo Venezia*, 122; Zangrandi, *Il lungo viaggio*, 20–1
24 OO 37/lii; OO 42/13; *Rivista 'Popolo d'Italia'*, Dec. 1926, 23; Castellani, 20
25 De Begnac, *Palazzo Venezia*, 462
26 OO 32/178; Megaro, *Mussolini in the Making*, 322
27 OO 20/252–3 (Apr. 1924); OO 44/210 (15 May 1937); Pini, *Benito Mussolini* (1940), 234–5; D'Aroma, *Mussolini*, 17
28 Sarfatti, *Dux*, 306–13; Ludwig, *Colloqui con Mussolini* (1932), 107; OO 18/428; OO 19/354
29 Bottai, *Vent'anni*, 93, 188–9; Daquanno, *Vecchia guardia*, 219; D'Aroma, *Mussolini*, 208; OO 19/35
30 Vittorio Mussolini, *Vita*, 19; Ludwig, *Colloqui con Mussolini* (1932), 112; Lagardelle, *Mission à Rome*, 169–70; D'Aroma, *Mussolini*, 125
31 Béraud, *Dictateurs d'aujourd'hui*, 35–6

32 C. Senise, *Quando ero capo*, 110; De Begnac, *Palazzo Venezia*, 42, 116

33 OO 24/133 (14 Sept. 1929); Ludwig, *Colloqui con Mussolini* (1932), 216; Castellani, 11

34 Mussolini, *My Autobiography*, 282; OO 21/389; Pini, *Benito Mussolini* (1926), 119

35 *Grandi racconta*, 7; C. Rossi, *Mussolini*, 244; Navarra, 42

36 De Begnac, *Palazzo Venezia*, 110 (Apr. 1938)

37 Morgan, 77–8

38 D'Agata, *Mussolini*, 304; *The Listener*, 14 June 1933, 936; OO 24/356; Navarra, 19, 141; Ojetti, *I taccuini*, 303; GEC, *Il cesare di cartapesta*, 8, 10; Bottai, *Vent'anni*, 209; Sarfatti, *Dux*, 52; *Harper's*, Feb. 1936, 303 (Gunther)

39 Balbo, *Diario*, 18–19; Acerbo, *Fra due plotoni*, 558; Guariglia, *Ricordi*, 425; Vailati, *Badoglio risponde*, 236; Moellhausen, *La carta perdente*, 325 (Buffarini); Lessona, *Un ministro*, 176; Conti, *Dal taccuino*, 455; *Settimana Incom,*, 14 Jan. 1956 (Giuriati); Bastianini, 5–6; Bottai, *Vent'anni*, 25–6

40 Dinale, *Quarant'anni di colloqui con lui*, 107, 301

41 *Daily Express*, 5 Nov. 1922; OO 22/170 (June 1926, to *Daily Mail*); OO 44/21; Sarfatti, *Dux*, 299

42 OO 20/65 (28 Oct. 1923); Morgan, 75–6; Sarfatti, *Dux*, 258; *Corriere della Sera*, 17 Sept. 1929

43 Navarra, 59, 129; Leto, *Ovra*, 111; Frassati, *Il destino passa per Varsavia*, 40; Nicolson, *Diaries*, 1/106 (6 Jan. 1932); Rachele Mussolini, *La mia vita*, 93

44 OO 21/356; OO 22/488; Marga, *Aneddoti*, 92; Munro, *Through Fascism*, 409; Pini, *Benito Mussolini* (1939), 122–3

45 OO 24/14 (10 Mar. 1929); De Begnac, *Palazzo Venezia*, 651 (Mar. 1940)

46 Sherrill, *Bismarck e Mussolini*, 322

47 BD 1a/2/136 (Graham, 2 July 1926); BD 1a /5/73 (May 1928)

48 Beltramelli, *L'uomo nuovo*, 130; Settimelli, *Benito Mussolini*, 46–7; Sarfatti, *Dux*, 282

49 Bottai, *Vent'anni*, 28; Bertoldi, *Mussolini*, 270 (Grandi); Borghi, *Mussolini*, 109; Rocca, *Come il fascismo*, 284; Bojano, *In the Wake*, 34, 37; *Giornale del Mattino*, 30 Mar. 1946 (Boratto); Pan, *Il fascismo*, 27; *Le Figaro*, 25 Mar. 1959, 5 (Haile Selassie)

50 De Ambris, 'Mussolini', 79

51 Settimelli, *Edda contro Benito*, 73

52 Vergani, *Ciano*, 40

53 *Daily Herald*, 12 Mar. 1926; Rossini, *Il delitto Matteotti*, 968; C. Rossi, *Trentatre vicende*, 20

54 Fanelli, *Cento pagine su Mussolini*, 75, 93; Sarfatti, *The Life*, 329; Sarfatti, *Dux*, 149, 263; Marroni, *Mussolini*, 9–10; OO 19/208 (25 Apr. 1923)

55 Bordeux, *Benito Mussolini*, 287; Pini, *Mussolini* (1939), 211; Ciano (1), 59

56 FO 371/7659 (Graham, 2 Nov. 1922); Amery, *My Political Life*, 2/325; Asquith, *Places*, 252; Mosley, *A Life*, 151; Macartney, *One Man Alone*, 69; Hindle, *Foreign Correspondent*, 31 (Munro)

57 Mariano, *Forty Years*, 157 (Berenson); Eden, *Facing the Dictators*, 225; Salter, *Personality*, 229–30; Noël, *Les illusions de Stresa*, 63; Ludwig, *Three Portraits*, 70

58 Bordeaux, *La claire Italie*, 108; Navarra, *Memorie*, 22, 29

59 Aloisi, *Journal*, 152 (11 Oct. 1933)

60 *Raccolta delle circolari*, 2/517 (26 Apr. 1933)

61 Navarra, *Memorie*, 60–1; Belisha, *The Private Papers*, 117

62 OO 29/150–1 (20 Sept. 1938); Rintelen, *Mussolini als Bundesgenosse*, 104; Bottai, *Vent'anni*, 182

63 *Mussolini e lo sport*, 20–2; Cannistraro, *La fabbrica del consenso*, 82; Seldes, *The Truth*, 77

64 Collier, *Duce*, 57

338

65 Béraud, *Men of the Aftermath*, 75; Hoffman, *Hitler*, 90; Hindle, *Foreign Correspondent*, 38 (Munro); Massock, *Italy from within*, 206–9

66 *Lo Stato*, Jan. 1931, 5 (quoting Mussolini on 24 Dec. 1924); *Gerarchia*, Sept. 1928, 677; *ibid.*, Apr. 1939, 253

67 Bastianini, *Uomini, cose, fatti*, 42; De Begnac, *Palazzo Venezia*, 110

68 C. Senise, *Quando ero capo*, 72

69 Arpinati, *Arpinati mio padre*, 256–7

70 *Grandi racconta*, 8; C. Senise, 119; Bianchi, *Rivelazioni sul conflitto*, 122 (De Bono); Bottai, *Vent'anni*, 46; Rocca, *Come il fascismo*, 161

71 Ludwig, *Colloqui con Mussolini* (1932), 204

72 Dinale, *Quarant'anni di colloqui con lui*, 287; Sarfatti, *Dux*, 254–5

73 Sarfatti, *The Life*, 345; Sarfatti, *Dux*, 314; OO 5/351

74 Alvaro, *Quasi una vita*, 111; Edda Ciano, *My Truth*, 34; Nanni, *Bolscevismo*, 201; Aniante, *Mussolini*, 41; Lumbroso, *La crisi*, 20

75 OO 14/193 (12 Dec. 1919); OO 44/74; *Daily News*, 7 Jan. 1927; Morgan, 76; Finer, *Mussolini's Italy*, 402–3; Navarra, 157

76 OO 24/155 (27 Oct. 1929); Seldes, *The Truth*, 77

77 Pini, *Filo diretto*, 180; Gorla, *L'Italia*, 44; Galbiati, *Il 25 luglio*, 43; Dolfin, *Con Mussolini nella tragedia*, 88; Leto, *Ovra*, 169–70; Arpinati, 257; Castellani, 21; Puntoni, 139 (Victor Emanuel); *Giorno*, 16 June 1972 (Balella); D'Aroma, *Mussolini*, 450; Navarra, 147; Zavoli, *Nascita di una dittatura*, 156 (Spirito)

78 Dollmann, *The Interpreter*, 136; Carboni, *Memorie*, xiv–xv

79 D'Agostini, *Colloqui*, 16

80 Seldes, *The Truth*, 81

81 Hemingway, *By-Line*, 84; Mussolini, *My Autobiography*, 191; *New York Times*, 29 Jan. 1931; *Manchester Guardian*, 17 Feb. 1931; Daffinà, *Mussolini e il fascismo*, 47 (Ferretti); Ludwig, *Leaders of Europe*, 340; *Giornale del Mattino*, 28 Mar. 1946; Schuschnigg, *Austrian Requiem*, 98

82 OO 21/40 (2 Aug. 1924); OO 22/381–2 (26 May 1927)

83 BD 1a/1/702 (Graham, 30 Apr. 1926); *Nation*, 5 Mar. 1927, 750 (Hackett)

84 OO 21/433; OO 23/80; OO 41/174; OO 43/34

85 De Begnac, *Palazzo Venezia*, 377; C. Senise, 108

86 Ciano (1), 53; Ludwig, *Three Portraits*, 81; De Begnac, *Palazzo Venezia*, 108; Navarra, 221–7; Sermoneta, *Sparkle Distant Worlds*, 15; Morgan, *Spurs on the Boot*, 108; Giudice, *Pirandello*, 460

87 St A., 326/111337–9 (Massarenti, 26 Mar. 1933); Mecheri, *Chi ha tradito?*, 112; Gasparotto, *Diario*, 300; Soleri, *Memorie*, 248, 252; Rocca, *Come il fascismo*, 185, 190; Navarra, 221; Camilleri, *Polizia in azioni*, 201

88 Aniante, 193; Rygier, *Mussolini*, 9–10; Misuri, *'Ad bestias'*, 43; *Grandi racconta*, 8; De Begnac, *Palazzo Venezia*, 240; C. Rossi, *Mussolini*, 48, 240, 243–4; *Forum and Century*, Oct. 1937, 173

89 Tamaro, *Venti anni*, 2/371

90 De Felice, *Mussolini*, 2/475 (Colonna di Cesarò); Mosconi, *La mia linea*, 26; Salandra, *Memorie*, 31; Mecheri, 201; Bertoldi, *Mussolini*, 142 (De' Stefani); OO 18/434 (4 Oct. 1922)

91 C. Rossi, *Trentatre vicende*, 40–2, 277–80; Salandra, *Diario*, 310

92 OO 21/100

93 DDI 7/4/294 (8 Aug. 1926)

94 Guarneri, *Battaglie economiche*, 1/435; *ibid.*, 2/46–7; De' Stefani, *Baraonda*, 520; Acerbo, *Fra due plotoni*, 559; De Begnac, *Palazzo Venezia*, 544 (Scialoja); Conti, *Dal taccuino*, 493,

549; Iraci, *Arpinati*, 101; Armellini, *Diario*, 151; *Giorno*, 16 June 1972 (Balella); FO R6/9/22 (Perth, 27 Dec. 1938)

95 *Domenica dell 'Agricoltore*, 28 Nov. 1926, 2; Amery, *Diaries*, 1/311; Gorgolini, *Il fascismo*, 51–2; *Critica Fascista*, 1 Dec. 1926, 441; OO 19/181; OO 44/17 (Nov. 1926)

96 OO 19/26, 115; Soffici, *Battaglia*, 113; Gorgolini, *Il fascismo*, 123–30

97 St A., 286/087260 (police report, 3 Oct. 1927); *Camera: discussioni* (16 May 1925), 3661 (Mussolini); Melograni, *Gli industriali*, 57, 111; De Felice (2), 399–400, 554–5

98 OO 21/19; FO 371/9940/185 (Mitchell, 12 Sept. 1924); Gasparotto, 245–7; Einaudi, *Cronache economiche*, 7/765; Sarti, *Fascism and the Industrial Leadership*, 51, 64

99 Mussolini, *Vita ... di Arnaldo*, 178; OO 20/126 (5 Dec. 1923), 184, 287–8 (24 May 1924, to *Chicago Daily News*)

100 Gorla, *L'Italia*, 213; Guarneri, *Battaglie economiche*, 1/55

101 FO 371/22436/6 (Perth, 13 Jan. 1938)

102 *Labour Magazine*, Mar. 1928, 498–9 (Labriola)

103 OO 19/12, 86, 181 (18 Mar. 1923)

104 Cassese, 'Aspetti', 2/186; *Rivista d'Italia*, 15 June, 1923, 179–80

105 Sforza, *European Dictatorships*, 62; Seldes, *Can These Things Be*, 37; *Italy Today*, July 1932, 17–18 (Vandervelde); Wiskemann, *The Europe I Saw*, 174; Ludwig, *Three Portraits*, 85

106 *Critica Politica*, Sept. 1925, 311; BD 1a/5/232; Maurano, *Ricordi*, 40; Clough, *The Economic History of Modern Italy*, 226–7; De Begnac, *Palazzo Venezia*, 262, 356; Lyttleton, *The Seizure of Power*, 335–9

107 OO 14/380; OO 19/10, 12 (12 Nov. 1922)

108 OO 22/92–3; OO 24/145 (14 Sept. 1929); BD 1a/2/190 (Graham, 28 July 1926)

109 OO 22/287 (Dec. 1926)

110 OO 24/8, 241 (20 May 1930)

111 OO 22/388; OO 24/214, 258 (1 Oct. 1930)

112 Rosenstock-Franck, *L'économie*, 392–4; Rosenstock-Franck, *Les étapes*, 14; Meenan, *The Italian Corporative System*, 339–41; Lyttleton, *The Seizure of Power*, 319–21; Sarti, 80; *Critica Fascista*, 1 Aug. 1943 (qv. *ABC*, 16 July 1956, 16)

113 *Camera: discussioni* (15 May 1930), 2689 (Paoloni)

114 De' Stefani, *Una riforma*, 12

115 *Diritto del Lavoro* (1939), 13/1/395

116 Turati and Bottai, *La carta del lavoro*, 43

117 OO 22/310 (28 Jan. 1927), 334; OO 24/8 (20 June 1929), 124; OO 28/93–4; OO 32/179 (20 Mar. 1945)

118 Capoferri, *Venti anni*, 58–9; OO 24/241–2 (21 May 1930); Ebenstein, *Fascist Italy*, 166, 173–4; Schmidt, *The Corporate State*, 119, 125; Finer, *Mussolini's Italy*, 530–4

119 Benjamin, *Mussolini*, 246; *English Review*, Apr. 1929, 423; OO 22/310 (28 Jan. 1928)

120 Béraud, *Ce que j'ai vu*, 139; Ebenstein, 126; Rosenstock-Franck, *L'économie*, 155

121 Mussolini, *Scritti e discorsi*, 4/321 (25 Oct. 1924)

122 *Senato: discussioni* (22 June 1929), 1158; OO 24/324; OO 26/258

123 *New York Times*, 17 Dec. 1933; Barzini, *The Italians*, 144; Naudeau, *L'Italie fasciste*, 155; OO 41/387 (20 Aug. 1930)

124 *Le Professioni e le Arti*, Oct. 1932, 2 (Mussolini)

125 OO 22/384 (26 May 1927); OO 39/373 (8 Mar. 1925); Mussolini, *Corrispondenza*, 95 (2 July 1928)

126 OO 19/104 (18 Jan. 1923); *Popolo d'Italia*, 25 Aug. 1923; *ibid.*, 23 Feb. 1926

127 OO 20/183; OO 21/38 (2 Aug. 1924); OO 22/235 (10 Oct. 1926); OO 24/7

128 Gorla, 20, 25; OO 23/95; OO 40/296, 298 (24 Mar. 1927); OO 41/160

129 OO 22/318; OO 23/256–7, 263 (Nov.–Dec. 1928); OO 26/125 (20 Dec. 1933); Melograni, *Gli industriali*, 203–4; *Rivista di Politica Economica*, July 1941, 570–4

130 OO 20/184 (21 Feb. 1924)

131 *Senato: discussioni* (20 May 1930), 2464–5 (Ciccotti); McGuire, *Italy's International Economic Position*, 115 (1927); *Critica Politica*, June 1925, 245

132 Tassinari, *L'économie*, 127–8

133 Schmidt, *The Corporate State*, 58, 70–2; Ebenstein, 202

134 OO 21/84 (24 Sept. 1924); De Begnac, *Palazzo Venezia*, 463 (Sept. 1941)

135 OO 22/67

136 *Senato: discussioni* (28 Nov. 1922), 4277 (Mussolini); OO 19/93 (6 Jan. 1923); OO 39/6 (6 Jan. 1924)

137 DDI 7/4/294–5; Griziotti, *La politica finanziaria*, 77–8

138 OO 23/201 (23 July 1928); *Senato: discussioni* (24 June 1930), 2856 (Mussolini)

139 *Senato: discussioni* (24 June 1930), 2870–2 (Ciccotti): Naudeau, *L'Italie fasciste*, 179–80; Béraud, *Ce que j'ai vu*, 148, 175; *The Times*, 2 Jan. 1931; Ebenstein, 210–11; Zoppi, *Il senato*, 33; Mortara, *Prospettive economiche* (1930), 522–3; *Riforma Sociale*, Sept. 1928, 500

140 OO 22/464 (30 Dec. 1924); *Nuova Antologia*, Jan. 1980, 169 (Lenti)

141 Daffinà, vii–viii

142 Bottai, *Mussolini*, 5; *Critica Fascista*, 1 June 1927, 203

143 A. Mussolini, *Polemiche*, 298, 324–5 (9 Apr. and 5 Nov. 1926); Ojetti, 340; Lessona, *Ministro*, 151

144 Ludwig, *Talks with Mussolini*, 116; Ludwig, *Colloqui con Mussolini* (1932), 116; Gorgolini, *Il fascismo*, 19; *Domenica dell'Agricoltore*, 14 Nov. 1926, 6; Longanesi, *Vade-mecum*, 53; De Begnac, *Palazzo Venezia*, 652; C. Senise, *Quando ero capo*, 118.

145 OO 21/437 (Oct. 1925); OO 22/137, 141 (24 May 1926); OO 40/23; Dinale, *Quarant'anni di colloqui con lui*, 65

146 Pomba, *La civiltà fascista*, 488–9 (Renda)

147 St A. 267/077254 (11 Sep. 1926); Naudeau, 23; *Nation*, 5 Mar. 1927, 750; De Begnac, *Palazzo Venezia*, 349

148 Scorza, *Brevi note*, 263, 265, 325; Fanelli, *Cento pagine*, 92

149 Prezzolini, *L'Italiano inutile*, 273

150 Salvemini, *Scritti*, 3/388

151 Pini, *Benito Mussolini* (1926), 131

152 Berneri, *Mussolini* 40; Tuzet, 'The education', 8

153 St A. 1/000030–1 (contract, dated 11 Jan. 1924); St A. 290/089161 (19 Oct. 1929, letter from Arnaldo); *Carteggio Arnaldo*, 134, 159 (and information from Hughes Massie)

154 De Begnac, *Palazzo Venezia*, 463; OO 4/171; Bastianini, *Uomini, cose, fatti*, 48

155 Salvemini, *G. B. Shaw*, 58–9; Béraud, *Ce que j'ai vu*, i–iii; St A. 288/088407 (10 Oct. 1927); *The Times*, 18 Aug. 1927

156 Sheridan, *In Many Places*, 252–3; De Begnac, *Palazzo Venezia*, 295; OO 14/352; OO 18/410 (17 Sept. 1922), 414 (20 Sept. 1922); OO 21/381 (Aug. 1925, to *Daily Express*)

157 Ludwig, *Three Portraits*, 76–7; Phayre, 'Mussolini', 81; Sheridan, *My Crowded Sanctuary*, 209–11

158 Mussolini, *My Autobiography*, 162; Sarfatti, *Dux*, 219; OO 21/358 (22 June 1925)

159 De Begnac, *Palazzo Venezia*, 295, 651 (Aug. 1939); OO 22/91 (11 Mar. 1926); OO 39/565 (9 Dec. 1925); Roya, *Histoire de Mussolini*, 32

160 Caviglia, *Diario*, 213

161 D'Aroma, *Mussolini*, 125; Dinale, 287, 306

162 OO 22/156

Mussolini as leader

163 Yeats-Brown, *European Jungle*, 85
164 Galbiati, *Il 25 luglio*, 67; Bastianini, 115
165 Nitti, *Bolshevism*, 98
166 St A., 166/048974 (Federzoni, 22 July 1923); Lessona, *Memorie*, 283, 288; OO 21/404
167 Bottai, *Vent'anni*, 95; Bastianini, 29, 56; OO 37/310 (5 Feb. 1926)
168 De Begnac, *Palazzo Venezia*, 456
169 Bertoldi, *Mussolini*, 142 (De' Stefani), 259 (Grandi); Conti, *Dal taccuino*, 494 (10 Oct. 1932); Germino, *The Italian Fascist Party*, 48; Tamaro, *Venti anni*, 3/230 (Ciarlantini); Sarfatti, *Dux*, 309–10
170 Leto, *Ovra*, 156; C.Senise, 113; Arpinati, *Arpinati mio padre*, 257; Giolli, *Come fummo condotti*, 59; Mecheri, *Chi ha tradito?* 126; Navarra, *Memorie*, 42; Bastianini, 55
171 C. Senise, 21; Bottai, *Vent'anni*, 96; Navarra, 152; C. Rossi, *Trentatre vicende*, 422–3
172 C. Rossi, *Mussolini*, 135, 258–61; Luciano, *Rapporto al Duce*, 14; Navarra, 67–8; Senise, 117; Ludwig, *Colloqui con Mussolini* (1932), 185
173 OO 22/209 (Sept. 1926), 469; OO 24/121, 124 (June–July 1929)
174 Mecheri, 109–11, 122; Dinale, 140; C. Senise, 41, 112–13
175 OO 24/133 (14 Sept. 1929); OO 40/425 (5 Aug. 1927); Guarneri, *Battaglie economiche*, 1/29; Monelli, *Mussolini*, 158; Tur, *Plancia ammiraglio*, 3/139
176 Bastianini, 235; Carboni, *Memorie*, 65; De Begnac, *Palazzo Venezia*, 165; Rochat, 'Mussolini et les forces armées', 51
177 Lessona, *Memorie*, 161; Leto, *Ovra*, 22, 70; Galbiati, *Il 25 luglio*, 130; Soffici and Prezzolini, *Diari*, 179; Guariglia, *Ricordi*, 177
178 OO 23/126–31, 149–54 (meetings of 28 Mar. and 28 May 1928)
179 Guarneri, *Battaglie economiche*, 1/435; Leto, *Ovra*, 145–6; Terzaghi, *Fascismo e massoneria*, 89–90; C. Senise, *Quando ero capo*, 94
180 Castellani, *Tra microbi e re*, 11; C. Senise, 113; Mussolini, *Corrispondenza*, 114; OO 24/200; OO 41/407; Bottai, *Vent'anni*, 78
181 De Begnac, *Palazzo Venezia*, 13
182 OO 22/169 (June 1926, to *Daily Mail*); *Daily Express*, 24 Jan. 1927
183 Leto, *Ovra*, 23, 146; C. Senise, 122–3; Carboni, *Memorie*, 15; D'Aroma, *Mussolini*, 450
184 Tamaro, *Venti anni*, 1/378 (Pantalcone)
185 Ojetti, *I'taccuini*, 215 (Volpi, Mar 1926); Conti, *Dal taccuino*, 455 (Jan. 1931); C. Senise, 93; Leto, *Ovra*, 146; Donosti, *Mussolini e l'Europa*, 178–9; D'Aroma, *Vent'anni*, 152; Settimelli, *Edda*, 97
186 Guariglia, *Ricordi*, 30, 64; Gorla, 25; Navarra, 114; De Begnac, *Palazzo Venezia*, 11, 105; Grandi racconta, 8
187 Dinale, *Quarant'anni di colloqui con lui*, 97; Navarra, 234
188 Anfuso, *Roma*, 154; C. Senise, 96; Bastianini, *Uomini, cose, fatti*, 39; Orlando, *Memorie*, 566; Federzoni, *Italia di ieri*, 83–4
189 Benjamin, *Mussolini et son peuple*, 240
190 OO 20/291
191 Navarra, 190
192 Ludwig, *Leaders of Europe*, 336
193 OO 41/4 (8 Jan. 1928); Daffinà, 5–6 (Rocco), 32–6 (Bodrero)
194 Zachariae, *Mussolini si confessa*, 145; Ludwig, *Mussolinis Gespräche*, 34; Ludwig, *Colloqui con Mussolini* (1932), 34
195 *Gerarchia*, Apr. 1939, 250; D'Aroma, *Vent'anni*, 149
196 Puntoni, 101 (Vittorio Emanuele)
197 OO 29/15 (26 Oct. 1937); Navarra, 156, 159

342

198 *Critica Fascista*, 15 Jan. 1927, 23 (Aniante, Settimelli); *ibid.*, 15 Feb. 1927, 62; *Regime Fascista*, 11 July 1939 (Capasso); *Gli Oratori del Giorno*, June 1939, 15 (Piovene); Gentizon, *Souvenirs*, 98; Volpicelli, *Motivi*, 62–4; Gustarelli, *Mussolini scrittore*, 17; Ardau, *L'eloquenza mussoliniana*, 85; Il Dramma, 15 Nov. 1935, 28 (Pirandello); Bianchi, *Mussolini Scrittore*, 11–12, 77; Signoretti, *La stampa*, 39

199 e.g. Trabalza and Allòdoli, *La grammatica* (5th ed. 1938); also *Vocabolario della lingua* (ed. Accademia Reale, 1941), *passim*

200 *Antilei*, 34 (Ada Negri), 36 (Quasimodo), 81 (Vittorini), 85 (Praz), 92 (Pratolini); Pini, *Filo diretto*, 198, 201; OO 38/36

201 Pini–Susmel, *Mussolini*, 3/209; *Augustea*, 31 Mar. 1932, 177; *New York Times*, 25 Apr. 1939, 22; Forzano, *Mussolini autore*, xxix, xxxiv

202 St A. 299/088093 (Forzano, 22 Nov. 1932); Ciano (2), 87; *Fascismo e antifascismo*, 1/342 (Grassi)

203 Freddi, *Il cinema*, 1/345–6; *ibid.*, 2/78

204 Mussolini, *My Autobiography*, 34

205 D'Aroma, *Mussolini*, 83; Zachariae, 41–2, 45; Orano, *Mussolini da vicino*, 100; Mussolini, *My Autobiography*, 192; Ludwig, *Colloqui con Mussolini* (1932), 130; Pini, *Benito Mussolini* (1939), 231; OO 23/291; OO 32/160; OO 38/356 (8 Nov. 1923)

206 D'Aroma, *Mussolini*, 260; Navarra, *Memorie*, 44, 92; Bottai, *Vent'anni*, 107; *Critica Fascista*, 1 Aug. 1931, 292–3

207 OO 28/138 (9 Mar. 1937)

208 OO 32/161; Rafanelli, *Una donna e Mussolini*, 28–9; Anfuso, 411–12

209 OO 15/218; OO 17/269; OO 31/188; *Le Professioni*, Oct. 1932, 3; Sarfatti, *The Life*, 10

210 OO 22/41; OO 24/329; OO 44/16; De Begnac, *Palazzo Venezia*, 108; *Critica Fascista*, 1 Dec. 1926, 441

211 *Gerarchia*, July 1930, 586–7 (Dinale); *Ordine Fascista*, Nov. 1933, 699–700 (Orestano); Orestano, *Idee e concetti*, 98

212 Orano, *Il fascismo*, 2/441

213 OO 22/213–27; Ferri, *Mussolini*, 33; *Critica Fascista*, 15 Oct. 1926, 394; Nitti, *La democrazia*, 1/322 (Prof. Ettore Pais)

214 Carlini, *Saggio sul pensiero*, 52; Quaroni, *Valigia diplomatica*, 191–7; OO 20/251, 258; OO 25/90–1; OO 38/536

215 OO 21/365; OO 25/261, 294; OO 26/26–7; De Vecchi, *Bonifica fascista della cultura*, 96, 102

216 De Fiori, *Mussolini*, 52–3; Navarra, 62–4

217 Ward Price, *I Know These Dictators*, 172; Sapori, *L'arte e il Duce*, 133; De Begnac, *Palazzo Venezia*, 650; De Rensis, *Mussolini musicista*, 21–3; Castellani, *Tra microbi e re*, 11

218 OO 41/425 (12 Mar. 1931)

219 Vittorio Mussolini, *Vita*, 43; Rachele Mussolini, *La mia vita*, 103; D'Aroma, *Mussolini*, 354–5

220 D'Aroma, *Mussolini*, 304

221 *Corriere della Sera*, 9 Dec. 1922; *Daily Herald*, 9 Dec. 1922

222 *Corriere della Sera*, 24–7 Apr. 1926; Sachs, *Toscanini*, 179; OO 22/123

223 St A. 166/049273 (1 Feb. 1932)

224 *Critica Fascista*, 15 Apr. 1932, 150; St A. 166/049296 (Federzoni)

225 OO 26/291 (31 July 1934); Cione, *Storia della repubblica*, 188

226 OO 22/250; OO 23/287, 302 (1 Jan. 1928); Marconi, *Per la ricerca*, 29; Farinacci, *Un periodo aureo*, 160–1; *Nuova Antologia*, July 1936, 4–5 (Parravano); *Augustea*, 31 Oct. 1942, 611

227 OO 29/334 (5 Dec. 1939)

228 Zachariae, *Mussolini si confessa*, 46–7

Mussolini as leader

229 De Vecchi, *Bonifica*, 47; Pini, *Benito Mussolini* (1926), 98

230 Ojetti, *I taccuini*, 437 (19 June 1934)

231 Magistrati, *L'Italia*, 124; Bottai, *Vent'anni*, 171, 207; Federzoni, 231; Ciano (2), 231

232 Sarfatti, *The Life*, 158

233 Sarfatti, *Dux*, 262; OO 19/13; Naudeau, *L'Italie fasciste*, 72; Béraud, *Ce que j'ai vu*, 13; D'Aroma, *Mussolini*, 188

234 Soffici, *Ricordi*, 174; *Imperium*, Dec. 1926, 8; OO 20/275; *Stirpe*, Aug. 1927, 449 (Signoretti)

235 OO 22/230; Alloway, *The Venice Biennale*, 96; *Rapporti* (Convegno Volta), 15, 42

236 OO 22/83; Ojetti, 414, 437

237 OO 24/184, 331; A. Mussolini, *Orientamenti*, 125-6; *Atti primo congresso giuridico*, 32 (5 Oct. 1932); *Senato: discussioni* (12 Apr. 1930), 2404

238 *Le Professioni e le Arti*, Oct. 1932, 2; *Scuola e Cultura*, 10 Sept. 1932, 292

239 Bottai, *Politica fascista delle arti*, 59, 65, 76, 114, 118, 148

240 *Gerarchia*, Oct. 1939, 705-6; *Popolo d'Italia*, 18 May 1940; Tempesti, *Arte*, 230; Keene, *Neither Liberty nor Bread*, 148 (L. Venturi)

241 OO 31/130-1 (30 Nov. 1942); Ciano (2), 231 (3 Mar. 1940); Bottai, *Vent'anni*, 207 (22 July 1941)

242 Navarra, 186

243 *Corriere della Sera*, 20 Oct. 1938; Ojetti, 499-500; OO 7/116; *Diritti della Scuola*, 24 May 1931, 107

244 OO 20/361 (26 Oct. 1923); OO 22/48 (31 Dec. 1925), 98; OO 25/84-6; OO 26/187 (Mar. 1934); Belisha, *The Private Papers*, 116

245 OO 26/367; Cederna, *Mussolini urbanista*, x; Insolera, *Roma moderna*, 138-42

246 OO 27/25; *Gerarchia*, Mar. 1935, 272; *Camera: discussioni* (26 May 1934), 335-6

247 OO 37/348 (Aug. 1929); Sapori, *L'arte*, 130; *Obelisco Mussolini* (plates 1-23)

248 *Foro Mussolini*, (plates 264-6); Navarra, 145-7

Chapter 9 Consolidation and achievement

1 Labriola, *Le due politiche*, 204; Lumbroso, *La crisi del fascismo*, 81; Panunzio, *Che cos'è il fascismo?*,76-9; Dorso, *La rivoluzione*, 89; Guariglia, *Ricordi*, 10; Tasca, *Nascita del fascismo*, 529; *Critica fascista*, 1 Oct. 1923, 149

2 Grandi, *Le origini del fascismo*, 61

3 Mussolini, *Messaggi*, 39

4 OO 19/208; OO 20/214; *Rinascita Liberale*, June 1925, 12; Spampanato, *Contromemoriale*, 2/56

5 OO 20/279

6 OO 20/65, 283; OO 21/362; Sarfatti, *Dux*, 294

7 OO 19/208, 289; OO 21/27; OO 22/42; Filareti, *In margine del fascismo*, 397-8

8 OO 19/162; OO 20/213, 285; OO 39/507

9 Pini, *Benito Mussolini* (1926), 116; *Gerarchia*, July 1930, 582

10 *Critica Fascista*, 1 June 1925, 210; Bottai, *Pagine*, 414; Volt, *Programma della destra*, 68; Volpe, *Scritti*, 2/218; L. W., *Fascism*, 22

11 Gutkind, *Mussolini*, 117 (Balbino Giuliano); *Gerarchia*, Nov. 1922, 601; OO 19/260; OO 20/207

12 OO 19/317; OO 21/194; Dauli, *Mussolini*, 56; Ciccotti, *Il fascismo*, 434

13 OO 22/23

14 OO 22/449; *Camera: discussioni* (16 May 1925), 3660; Rocco, *Scritti*, 3/828
15 OO 24/126, 354
16 Ludwig, *Colloqui con Mussolini* (1932), 108; OO 26/78
17 OO 25/135; Ardemagni, *Supremazia di Mussolini*, 54
18 OO 11/197, 204; *Utopia*, 309 (15 Aug. 1914)
19 OO 22/109; *Tribuna*, 17 Mar. 1927 (A. Turati)
20 OO 22/191–2; Sheridan, *In Many Places*, 252–3
21 OO 22/229; OO 28/70; OO 35/98; *The Listener*, 14 June 1933, 936 (Vernon Bartlett); Ercole, *Dal nazionalismo*, 151; *Civiltà Fascista*, June 1936, 334 (Gentile)
22 *English Life*, Aug. 1924, 155; *Daily Express*, 18 Aug. 1925; Gorla, *L'Italia*, 26; OO 19/196; OO 24/145
23 *Nation*, 5 Mar. 1927, 750
24 *Corriere della Sera*, 31 Mar. 1925; OO 21/479
25 *Polemica*, Apr. 1925, 129; *Senato: discussioni* (12 Jan. 1934), 7076
26 *Rivista 'Popolo d'Italia'*, Apr. 1925, 5 (Parini); Pellizzi, *Fascismo*, 45–6; Papa, *Storia di due manifesti*, 49
27 *Corriere della Sera*, 31 Mar. 1926; *Harvard Educational Review*, 1937, 526 (Salvemini); Garin, *Cronache di filosofia*, 487
28 *Critica Fascista*, 15 Apr. 1926, 150; Forges Davanzati, *Fascismo*, 8; OO 22/184; OO 40/45
29 OO 24/108–9
30 Ludwig, *Leaders of Europe*, 343
31 Castellani, *Tra microbi e re*, 21; Maurano, *Ricordi*, 57
32 OO 21/359; *Gerarchia*, Dec. 1922, 602; *ibid.*, Aug. 1925, 487; *Daily News*, 26 Jan. 1925; Mussolini, *Corrispondenza*, 95; Malaparte, *L'Italia barbara*, 192–3; A. Mussolini, *Orientamenti*, 122; *Giovinezza Fascista*, 26 July 1927
33 OO 22/172; OO 25/15, 58
34 Gentile, *Che cosa è il fascismo*, 139–40; *Educazione Politica*, Jan. 1926, 3; *Educazione Fascista*, Dec. 1930, 681; *Politica Sociale*, Mar. 1931, 168
35 *Vita Nova*, May 1930, 433; Gentile, *Fascismo e cultura*, 106; *Civiltà Fascista*, June 1936, 322
36 *Senato: discussioni* (12 Apr. 1930), 2401; *Civiltà Fascista*, Jan. 1934, 3; *Educazione Fascista*, Oct. 1933, 836
37 *Nuova Politica Liberale*, Apr. 1924, 89; *Foreign Affairs*, Jan. 1928, 290; *Gerarchia*, Mar. 1929, 175; Gentile, *Che cosa è il fascismo*, 54–5; Gentile, *Epistolario*, 9/329
38 *Gran Consiglio ... nei primi cinque anni*, x; OO 22/287; *Bibliografia Fascista*, 31 Dec. 1926, 1
39 *Imperium*, Dec. 1926, 10 (Carli); Barnes, *The Universal Aspects of Fascism*, xvii
40 Daffinà, *Mussolini e il fascismo*, vii (A. Turati); *Critica Fascista*, 15 Oct. 1929, 390; Ercole, *La rivoluzione fascista*, 126–7
41 OO 24/145, 348; OO 26/78; De Begnac, *Palazzo Venezia*, 164
42 Tamaro, *Venti anni*, 2/480; *Tempo*, 1 Mar. 1960, 9 (De Vecchi); Lazzari, *L'enciclopedia*, 83–4; St A. 261/072888; Iraci, *Arpinati*, 177
43 *Civiltà fascista*, Jan. 1937, 68; Spinetti, *Difesa di una generazione*, 40–1; *Economia Italiana*, Mar. 1940, 217; *Lo Stato*, Mar. 1940, 138; *Critica Fascista*, 15 Mar. 1943, 117
44 OO 40/143; C. Rossi, *Il tribunale speciale*, 55–7; C. Rossi, *Trentatre vicende*, 273; Seldes, *Sawdust Caesar*, 218
45 Navarra, *Memorie*, 33; Leto, *Ovra*, 36–8; Candido, *Mussolini in pantofole*, 62–3
46 Federzoni, *Italia di ieri*, 113; Tamaro, *Venti anni*, 2/208; De Begnac, *Palazzo Venezia*, 111, 372; Jemolo, *Anni di prova*, 148–50; Seldes, *Sawdust Caesar*, 222
47 De Felice (3), 205–6; Rossi, *Il tribunale*, 233; Artieri, *Tre ritratti*, 191–201; Leto, *Ovra*, 38; Guspini, *L'orecchio del regime*, 86

48 OO 22/272–3, 375; OO 40/195, 206
49 DDI 7/4/379
50 De Begnac, *Palazzo Venezia*, 366; OO 6/81; De Felice (2), 762
51 Farinacci, *Un periodo aureo*, 81; *Critica Fascista*, 15 Sept. 1926, 341 (Bottai)
52 Federzoni, *Italia* 157–8; Gasparotto, *Diario*, 221; Balabanoff, *My Life*, 80
53 *Corriere della Sera*, 6 Sept. 1930; Trentin, *Le fascisme*, 145; Ebenstein, *Fascist Italy*, 84; Baskerville, *What Next O Duce?* 141; Massock, *Italy from Within*, 28
54 OO 23/253; OO 34/343; Soleri, *Memorie*, 208
55 Leto, *Ovra*, 55; C. Rossi, *Trentatre vicende*, 457
56 Leto, *Ovra*, 147–8; C. Senise, *Quando ero capo*, 87; Iraci, 121; Navarra, *Memorie*, 134–5; Ojetti, *I taccuini*, 233
57 *The Times*, 8 Jan. 1925
58 BD la/1/293 (Graham, 1 Jan. 1926); BD la/2/192 (28 July 1926)
59 Lyon, *The Fruits of Folly*, 37
60 OO 22/384
61 *Daily Express*, 26 Jan. 1927
62 OO 22/384; OO 41/74, 388
63 Capoferri, *Venti anni*, 58
64 *Daily Herald*, 2, 8, 15, and 16 July 1927; Darrah, *Hail Caesar* 177–8, 193; OO 41/183, 452
65 Federzoni, 17–19; Tamaro, *Venti anni*, 2/223; Ojetti, 312; *Senato: discussioni* (14 Mar. 1930), 1969 (Ciccotti)
66 *The Times*, 2 Jan. 1931; Melograni, *Gli industriali*, 250–2; De Sanctis, *Ricordi*, 143; BD la/6/469–70 (Graham, 1 Aug. 1929)
67 *Senato: discussioni* (24 June 1930), 2885–6
68 OO 40/226, 248, 277–8, 466; OO 41/88, 155
69 Dinale, *Quarant'anni di colloqui con lui*, 312; OO 3/119; OO 22/378
70 OO 40/187; OO 41/405
71 Camilleri, *Polizia in azione*, 198–9; *Diritto Fascista*, 28 Jan. 1933, 16 (Sen. Silvio Longhi)
72 Aquarone, *L'organizzazione*, 105–6; Herfort, *Chez les romains*, 187
73 *Manchester Guardian*, 15 Apr. 1933 (Rosselli); Gavagnin, *Una lettera*, 69; Trentin, *Le fascisme*, 170–2; Elwin, *Fascism*, 114–17; Colombi, *Nelle mani del nemico*, 92–4; *Fascist war on Women*, 5–9
74 St A. 268/077487
75 *The Times*, 17 Aug. 1927; Canevari, *Graziani*, 153; Camilleri, 207
76 Bertoldi, *Mussolini*, 47
77 Navarra, 86
78 Riboldi, *Vicende socialiste*, 42
79 OO 19/275
80 OO 22/192; Camilleri, 190–3; Leto, *Ovra*, 40; Navarra, 25, 90–1; *Fortune*, July 1934, 104–5
81 Leto, *Ovra*, 52; *Gerarchia*, Dec. 1930, 1051
82 St A. 112/030848; *ibid.*, 132/036690
83 Fossani, *Marinelli*, 57, 67
84 OO 22/286–7, 379; OO 37/53–4; A. Mussolini, *Polemiche*, 286
85 *Critica Fascista*, 15 Sept. 1926, 341–3; *ibid.*, 15 Oct. 1926, 381–2; *ibid.*, 15 Nov. 1927, 421–2; *ibid.*, 1 Dec. 1927, 445; *ibid.*, 15 June 1929, 233–4; *ABC*, 16 July 1956, 17; *Imperium*, Feb. 1927, 58
86 *Foglio d'Ordine*, 12 Nov. 1926
87 Mussolini, *Vita di ... Arnaldo*, 180–1; OO 23/58; *Popolo d'Italia*, 28 Aug. 1927; A. Mussolini, *Commenti*, 342

88 OO 22/107; OO 23/86; A. Turati, *Una rivoluzione*, 124–5, 130–3, 145; *Foglio d'Ordine*, 23 June 1928; *Tribuna*, 9 Feb. 1927

89 Sarfatti, *Dux*, 293; Pellizzi, *Fascism*, 128

90 OO 22/385

91 *Critica Fascista*, 15 Apr. 1929, 146; *ibid.*, 15 Aug. 1929, 313

92 *Atlantic Monthly*, July 1928, 113

93 OO 24/145; OO 31/167

94 Romano, *Corso di diritto costituzionale*, 119; *Daily Express*, 26 Jan. 1927; Naudeau, *L'Italie fasciste*, 257, 268

95 Iraci, *Arpinati*, 103; Dinale, 128, 132

96 OO 21/362–3; OO 22/246; Pomba, *La civiltà fascista*, v (Mussolini); Gentile, *Fascismo e cultura*, 86

97 *Bibliografia Fascista*, 30 Dec. 1927, 13; OO 23/59; OO 25/61

98 OO 24/90; OO 37/lvii; *Antieuropa*, 1929, 5/400–1

99 OO 21/424; OO 22/23, 25, 450; OO 23/78; De Begnac, *Palazzo Venezia*, 292

100 Sulis, *Imitazione di Mussolini*, 11, 58

101 Sheridan, *In Many Places*, 260

102 OO 37/340; Ojetti, *I taccuini*, 231–2

103 OO 22/190; OO 24/380; *Rivista 'Popolo d'Italia'*, July 1929, 5; *Popolo d'Italia*, 20 Aug. 1929

104 OO 24/143, 145; OO 37/339–40; A. Mussolini, *Orientamenti*, 69; A. Mussolini, *Azione fascista*, 70

105 *Evening Standard*, 13 Dec. 1927; Mussolini, *My Autobiography*, 280; Farinacci, *Un periodo aureo*, 271, 311; *Critica Fascista*, 1 Dec. 1925, 443; OO 22/118, 145

106 DDI 7/4/158 (De Bosdari, 4 Feb. 1926)

107 DDI 7/4/429; *Bibliografia Fascista*, 31 May 1926, 3; Grandi, *Memoriale*, 18; Settimelli, *Mussolini*, 222

108 OO 22/287; *Critica Fascista*, 1 July 1928, 241–2

109 OO 24/283

110 OO 23/122; *Politica*, June 1933, 33–4 (Roberto Ducci)

111 BD la/1/293 (Graham, 1 Jan. 1926); BD la/2/136 (2 July 1926); BD la/4/11 (Grandi); DDI 7/5/240 (4 June 1927)

112 DDI 7/4/413; Soleri, *Memorie*, 222

113 OO 22/37, 147 (25 May 1926)

114 OO 22/248, 385–6; OO 40/436 (15 Aug. 1927)

115 Carli, *Fascismo intransigente*, 95, 215–16; Pomba, *La civiltà fascista*, 181–2 (Marinetti)

116 *Tribuna*, 15 Jan. 1927; Maurano, *Mentalità fascista*, 123, Interlandi, *Pane bigio*, 38

117 *Camera: discussioni* (31 Mar. 1927), 7425; DDI 7/5/254–5; OO 23/189–90

118 *Legionario*, 14 Jan. 1926, 6; *Senato: discussioni* (3 June 1931), 4137; Donosti, *Mussolini e l'Europa*, 15; Luciolli, *Palazzo Chigi*, 22; De Begnac, *Palazzo Venezia*, 139, 415; Cantalupo, *Fula Spagna*, 31–2

119 Barnes, *The Universal Aspects of Fascism*, 24–5

120 DDI 7/5/586, 590; BD la/4/139; BD la/5/49–50; Carocci, *La politica estera*, 94–100

121 DDI 7/6/452; DDI 7/7/118, 151, 476; Carocci, *La politica*, 204

122 BD la/1/65; Cassels, *Mussolini's Early Diplomacy*, 397

123 OO 24/38; Balfour, *Atatürk*, 459

124 DDI 7/4/238 (4 June 1926)

125 OO 39/391, 427

126 Booth, *Italy's Aegean Possessions*, 209–10, 237, 249

127 *Dodecanesian*, Mar. 1936, 4

128 *Gerarchia*, June 1927, 451; *Rivista Coloniale*, May 1927, 229; *Rassegna Italiana*, May 1927, 491; Sertoli Salis, *Le isole*, 313; Carocci, *La politica*, 255; Booth, 264–5

129 OO 37/24; OO 40/164; DDI 7/5/601 (7 May 1927); St A. 329/112735 (Mussolini, 5 Nov. 1929); *Critica Fascista*, 1 Feb. 1924, 316 (Tamaro)

130 Guariglia, *Ricordi*, 99; OO 41/194

131 DDI 7/4/346–7 (2 Oct. 1926)

132 Gerbore, *Il vero diplomatico*, 151; DDI 7/5/280, 317 (14 July 1927), 414; DDI 7/7/44, 180; DDI 7/8/68, 146 (Oct. 1929)

133 DDI 7/5/391, 419, 436; OO 40/462–3

134 DDI 7/5/515, 518

135 DDI 7/5/450–1; BD 1a/4/281; OO 41/79, 156

136 *Foreign Relations of the U.S.* (1931), 1/545 (Grandi); DDI 7/4/281; DDI 7/5/483, 495; DDI 7/6/451; DDI 7/7/236; DDI 7/8/398 (18 Apr. 1930, Grandi)

137 DDI 7/4/199; DDI 7/5/433–5, 633; Ishii, *Diplomatic Commentaries*, 223–4

138 OO 22/327; Wertheimer, *The International Secretariat*, 250–1; De Madariaga, *Morning Without Noon*, 101, 279; DDI 7/5/46, 138–9, 435; DDIi 7/9/351, 355, 690

139 OO 22/78 (10 Feb. 1926)

140 DDI 7/4/260–1; DDI 7/5/412, 632; *Documents Diplomatiques Suisses*, 9/295 (10 Mar. 1926); Sarfatti, *Tunisiaca*, xxiv–xxv; Santini, *Mussolini*, 168–75; OO 42/27

141 Guariglia, *Ricordi*, 82; De Felice (4), 848–9 (Vitetti, 10 July 1932); De Begnac, *Palazzo Venezia*, 709

142 Rumi, *Alle origini della politica estera*, 240; DDI 7/5/166, 326; DDI 7/7/299–300, 401; Aloisi, *Journal*, 16

143 DDI 7/6/14–5, 17, 72, 126, 291, 532; BD 1a/4/238; Seldes, *Sawdust Caesar*, 264–6

144 OO 40/412; DDI 7/7/429, 490; DDI 7/9/319, 673–4; Guariglia, *Ricordi*, 76

145 DDI 7/6/4–5, 430; De Begnac, *Palazzo Venezia*, 653

146 OO 23/186, 271 (8 Dec. 1928)

147 OO 22/385–6 (26 May 1927); Tamaro, *Venti anni*, 2/308; *Christian Science Monitor*, 27 Jan. 1928 (to Willis Abbot); Béraud, *Ce que j'ai vu*, 61

148 St A. 263/074466–7; OO 24/138 (14 Sept. 1929); Daffinà, 257–8 (Cavallero); *Gerarchia*, Mar. 1926, 199

149 *Gerarchia*, Dec. 1922, 602; Argiolas, *Corfu*, 137

150 DDI 7/8/158 (5 Nov. 1929), 334 (8 Jan. 1930); St A. 54/026840–8 (4 Aug. 1932); De Felice (4), 380; De Felice, *L'Italia fra tedeschi*, 65 (Grandi); *Gerarchia*, Feb. 1929, 113

151 OO 41/351 (10 Jan. 1930)

152 Aloisi, *Journal*, 12, 115; Tamaro, *Venti anni*, 2/460; Ciano (1), 275–6

153 OO 24/125 (11 July 1929), 228 (13 May 1930), 235 (17 May 1930)

154 DDI 7/9/71; OO 24/245; BD 2/1/368, 379–81

155 Ludwig, *Colloqui con Mussolini* (1950), xlvii; Carocci, *La politica estera*, 53

156 Ludwig, *Colloqui con Mussolini* (1932), 200

157 OO 24/282–4 (27 Oct. 1930)

158 *Grandi racconta*, 12; Guariglia, *Ricordi*, 71, 425

159 Carocci, *La politica*, 365 (Chamberlain, 6 Sept. 1926)

160 Orano, *Il fascismo*, 2/441

161 BD 1a/4/238 (Graham, 3 Feb. 1928); BD 1a/7/522 (Graham, 14 Mar. 1930)

162 *Foreign Affairs of the U.S.*, Jan. 1928, 201–2 (Hamilton Fish Armstrong)

163 Navarra, *Memorie*, 50; Barzini, *From Caesar*, 140

164 *Critica Fascista*, 15 June 1927, 228; *ibid.*, 15 Dec 1927, 464; Ricci, *Avvisi*, 69

165 OO 25/155; Gorla, 34; De Begnac, *Palazzo Venezia*, 39; Pini–Susmel, *Mussolini*, 3/318

166 OO 26/399 (2 Dec. 1934)

167 Sarfatti, *The Life of Benito Mussolini*, 332

168 Mussolini, *My Autobiography*, 42; Munro, *Through Fascism*, 280; Pini, *Benito Mussolini* (1950), 251

169 OO 21/80; *Rivista 'Popolo d'Italia'*, Nov. 1925, 17; Barnes, *Universal Aspects*, 30; Carlini, *Saggi sul pensiero del fascismo*, 55; Delcroix, *Un uomo e un popolo*, 412

170 Bastianini, *Uomini, cose, fatti*, 26; Hachey, *Anglo-Vatican Relations*, 63; St A. 105/028704; OO 21/515; OO 37/3; Binchy, *Church and State*, 368

171 DDI 7/5/419–20; DDI 7/6/412; DDI 7/7/151

172 DDI 7/7/178 (Sola, 8 Jan. 1929), 269; Quaroni, *Valigia diplomatica*, 97–8

173 DDI 7/2/452; Casavis, *The Religion of the Dodecanesians*, 13–8; *Dodecanesian*, Nov. 1934; *ibid.*, Nov. 1937

174 *Camera: discussioni* (15 May 1925), 3627; OO 22/376 (26 May 1927); OO 44/211 (15 May 1937)

175 OO 35/25 (June 1913); Rafanelli, *Una donna e Mussolini*, 137

176 OO 21/221; OO 22/295; *Codice penale* (1930), art. 553

177 OO 22/364 (26 May 1927); OO 23/216 (Sept. 1928); OO 44/258; *Senato: discussioni* (8 Apr. 1930), 2249

178 OO 21/303

179 *Panorami di realizzazioni*, 1/109–9 (Madia); *Gerarchia*, July 1929, 522 (Pende); Meldini, *Sposa e madre esemplare*, 121–7; *Codice penale*, arts 546, 551, 554, 559, 566, 571–2

180 OO 20/290; OO 24/82 (13 May 1929); Bedel, *Fascisme*, 16; De Begnac, *Palazzo Venezia*, 376

181 *Camera* (11 June 1924), 273–4; *Codice penale*, art. 724

182 *Evening Standard*, 13 Dec. 1927

183 *Tribuna*, 14 Jan. 1927 (Forges Davanzati); Wagnière, *Dix-huit ans à Rome*, 151–3; Edda Ciano, *My Truth*, 63; St A. 105/028717–9

184 OO 22/363; OO 23/297; OO 25/35; OO 38/500

185 *The Times*, 18 Aug. 1927; Bedel, 17; Munro, 325; De Begnac, *Palazzo Venezia*, 622

186 *Vita Nova*, July 1925, 3; Navarra, 142

187 Naudeau, *L'Italie fasciste*, 262; A. Turati, *Il partito*, 204–5; *Critica Fascista*, 15 Mar. 1930, 106–7

188 Washington, 527/29/865/4063/11 (11 May 1928); Hachey, 141–2 (Odo Russell, 9 May 1929)

189 *Gerarchia*, July 1929, 521–3; *ibid.*, Nov. 1930, 952–3; OO 41/296

190 Hachey, 63 (Russell, 28 Feb. 1925), 80–1 (Russell, 21 Apr. 1926)

191 Conti, *Dal taccuino*, 668; Nitti, *Meditazioni*, 462; *Daily Chronicle*, 4 Mar. 1929; Margiotta Broglio, *Italia e Santa Sede*, 50, 68, 249–50

192 OO 23/317; OO 24/79; Guspini, *L'orecchio*, 92–3

193 BD 1a/6/468, 477; Salvemini, *Mussolini*, 384–5; Silvestri, *I responsabili*, 170; Aquarone, *L'organizzazione*, 295–7; Guspini, 95–6

194 Ojetti, *I taccuni*, 325 (Cantalupo)

195 OO 24/44–5 (13 May 1929)

196 OO 24/89; C. Senise, *Quando ero capo*, 105

197 OO 24/75, 101; OO 41/441; Ciano (4), 80

198 Hachey, 253–4 (Clive, 1 Jan. 1934); *Tempo*, 1 Mar. 1960 (De Vecchi)

199 OO 37/129

200 Hachey, 254

201 DDI 7/7/409; Mussolini, *Corrispondenza*, 123

202 Scoppola, 'Il fascismo', 353, 359; Jemolo, *Chiesa e stato*, 676; Seldes, *The Vatican*, 309; Bracco, *Persecuzione*, 11

Consolidation and achievement

203 *Popolo d'Italia*, 2 May 1931; Suner, *Entre Hendaya*, 103; *Harper's,* Feb. 1936, 302 (Gunther)
204 Gorla, 34; C. Senise, 105–7; Jemolo, *Chiesa e stato*, 594
205 Farinacci, *Un periodo aureo*, 106; Turati, *Una rivoluzione*, 34–5; Forges Davanzati, *Fascismo*, 23; Gorgolini, *La rivoluzione*, 33; Zangara, *Rivoluzione sindicale*, 152; Pesce, *Da Lenin a Mussolini*, 76
206 Carli, *Colloqui coi vivi*, 123
207 Ardali, *San Francesco e Mussolini*, 37; Scorza, *Brevi note sul fascismo*, vii
208 Settimelli, *Mussolini*, 303; Ferretti, *Esempi e idee*, 274–5
209 *Popolo d'Italia*, 29 Apr. 1926
210 *The Times*, 18 Oct. 1927, 15; *Vita Italiana*, Jan. 1930, 100
211 *Popolo d'Italia*, 8 Feb. 1927; *ibid.*, 11 Sept. 1927; *ibid.*, 25 Aug. 1928
212 *Annuario della Stampa* (1929–30), 136
213 *Carteggio Arnaldo*, 288; A. Mussolini, *Fascismo e civiltà*, 128–9, 150–1
214 Pomba, 510 (Amicucci)
215 *Carteggio Arnaldo*, 30–1; Licata, *Storia*, 247; Navarra, *Memorie*, 164–5
216 *Carteggio Arnaldo*, 83, 204
217 Page, *L'Americano di Roma*, 582; Cannistraro, *La fabbrica del consenso*, 79; St A. 273/079627 (Agnelli)
218 Ludwig, *Colloqui con Mussolini* (1950), 50; OO 23/231; Cannistraro, 193–6; Sperco, *Tel fut Mussolini*, 119
219 *Annuario della stampa* (1931–2), 483–6
220 Amicucci, *La stampa*, 80
221 OO 20/61 (26 Oct. 1923)
222 Iraci, *Arpinati*, 151; De Felice (3), 414 (De Bono, 16 Feb. 1929)
223 *Corriere della Sera*, 17 Nov., 25 Nov., 10 Dec. 1930
224 Tamaro, *Venti anni*, 2/428
225 St A. 109/029737A; Lessona, *Un ministro di Mussolini*, 181–2; De Begnac, *Palazzo Venezia*, 557; Aniante, *Mussolini*, 189–90
226 *The Times*, 17 Aug. 1927; BD 1a/6/470–1 (Graham, 1 Aug. 1929); OO 24/143
227 St A. 111/030732; St A. 236/062821–7; Tamaro, *Venti anni*, 2/170
228 Mosconi, *La mia linea*, 24; Mecheri, *Chi ha tradito?*, 111; *Daily Herald*, 3 Aug. 1927; Rocca, *Come il fascismo*, 222
229 OO 39/280; *ABC*, 16 Nov. 1953, 15 (Rocca)
230 A. Mussolini, *Azione fascista*, 109; A. Mussolini, *Orientamenti*, 61; *Gioventù Fascista*, 4 Oct. 1931, 18
231 St A. 294/090732–5; Tamaro, *Venti anni*, 2/377
232 OO 37/329; *Critica Fascista*, 15 Mar. 1929, 105–6; *Senato: discussioni* (8 Apr. 1930), 2245
233 Giolitti, *Discorsi parlamentari*, 4/1886; Darrah, *Hail Caesar*, 81
234 OO 23/272; *Popolo d'Italia*, 24 Apr. 1929
235 St A. 105/028715–16
236 *The Review of Reviews*, Apr. 1929, 302; *Contemporary Review*, Apr. 1930, 487; *Manchester Guardian*, 15 Apr. 1929; Haider, *Capital and Labour*, 258–9; BD 1a/6/469 (Graham, 1 Aug. 1929); Caviglia, *Diario*, 73; Calamandrei, 'La funzione parlamentare', 81; Schuschnigg, *Austrian Requiem*, 100
237 Rignani, *Lugo*, 61
238 Zoppi, *Il Senato*, 35, 38; Darrah, 104; Seldes, *The Truth*, 79; Paolucci, *Il mio piccolo mondo*, 290; OO 25/164; Monghini, *Dal decennale alla catastrofe*, 39; Ojetti, 325
239 OO 22/383
240 Schreiber, *Rome après Moscou*, 115

241 *Corriere della Sera*, 17 Sept. 1929

242 *Contemporary Review*, Apr. 1930, 487; Heller, *Europa und der Fascismus*, 74, 90–5

243 Béraud, *Ce que j'ai vu*, 37–41

244 OO 24/2

245 *Critica Fascista*, 15 Sept. 1929, 349–50; Maurano, *Mentalità*, 35, 46

246 Daffinà, vii (Turati), 5–6 (Rocco), 47 (Ferretti)

247 Conti, *Dal taccuino*, 518; Ojetti, *I taccuini*, 421

248 *Gerarchia*, July 1930, 584–7

249 *Gerarchia*, Aug. 1937, 526–7; Petrone, 'Mussolini giurista', 327, 336; Pini–Susmel, *Mussolini*, 3/206; *Critica Fascista*, 1 Oct. 1929, 382; *Diritto Fascista*, 28 Jan. 1933, 3

250 Pini, *Filo diretto*, 95 (19 Apr. 1937)

251 Navarra, *Memorie*, 18, 25, 96; Mecheri, 199; Ojetti, 324, 382; Luciolli, *Palazzo Chigi*, 118; Tamaro, *Venti anni*, 2/369–70

252 Hindle, *Foreign Correspondent*, 30, 34 (Munro)

253 DDI 7/6/282; DDI 7/8/154; C. Conti, *Servizio segreto*, 20–1 (Aloisi); Starhemberg, *Between Hitler and Mussolini*, 189; Bojano, *In the Wake*, 38; Tamaro, *Venti anni*, 3/88

254 BD 1a/6/120–1 (Graham, 7 Feb. 1929); Ojetti, 325 (Cantalupo, 7 July 1929)

255 *Daily Express*, 24 Jan. 1927 (Ashmead-Bartlett)

256 Federzoni, *Italia di ieri*, 226; St A. 53/026364–5; Ciano (2), 129; Lessona, *Un ministro di Mussolini*, 178

257 OO 23/223; Tamaro, *Venti anni*, 2/216–18

258 OO 21/416 (23 Oct. 1925); OO 22/385 (26 May 1927); Rocca, *Come il fascismo*, 295; Farinacci, *Un periodo aureo*, 234; Rocco, *Scritti*, 3/980 (10 Dec. 1925)

259 Ludwig, *Colloqui con Mussolini* (1932), 133; Ludwig, *Mussolinis Gespräche*, 133

260 D'Aroma, *Mussolini*, 152 (Apr. 1938)

261 De Begnac, *Palazzo Venezia*, 455–6

Chapter 10 In search of strife

1 DDI 7/4/281 (18 July 1926)

2 DDI 7/6/177–9 (30 Mar. 1928); DDI 7/8/172; *Foglio d'ordine*, 12 Jan. 1930; Canevari, *La guerra*, 1/211; D'Aroma, *Mussolini*, 72–3; Ferretti, *Esempi e idee*, 243

3 St A. 256/070538 (Federzoni, 24 Nov. 1926); BD 2/14/189–90 (Simon, 11 May 1935)

4 OO 40/304, 479–80, 504

5 St A. 329/112801–5, 112809

6 *Oriente Moderno*, Oct. 1929, 451–2

7 Giglio, *La confraternità senussita*, 133; Pieri and Rochat, *Badoglio*, 609–14; Rochat, 'La repressione della resistenza araba', 9–11

8 *Rivista delle Colonie*, June 1932, 437–8 (Valenzi)

9 Biani, *Ali italiane*, 38; Holmboe, *Desert Encounter*, 239, 261; DF 2/11/442; DGFP D/5/1114; Salerno, *Genocidio in Libia*, 50–62

10 Graziani, *Cirenaica*, 262–3; DDI 7/10/327 (Grandi); Santarelli, *Omar*, 308 (Tuninetti)

11 OO 24/283 (21 Oct. 1930); OO 26/10, 45, 60, 302; OO 37/405–6; *Critica Fascista*, 15 June 1930, 222

12 OO 21/317 (20 May 1925); DGFP C/1/894 (Hassell, 6 Oct. 1933); Dinale, *Quarant'anni di colloqui con lui*, 331; *Educazione Fascista*, June 1932, 470 (Berto Ricci); Edvige Mussolini, 142; Carocci, *La politica estera*, 358

In search of strife

13 Guarneri, *Battaglie economiche*, 1/10; Mussolini, *Corrispondenza*, 70; OO 40/473; Carocci, *La politica*, 63

14 D'Aroma, *Mussolini*, 64; OO 25/135 (16 Oct. 1932)

15 OO 26/58, 84 (4 Nov. 1933); *Critica Fascista*, 15 Oct. 1931, 385

16 *Gerarchia*, Jan. 1930, 27; *ibid.*, Feb. 1931, 105; *Universalità Fascista*, Feb. 1932, 69–70; *ibid.*, Feb. 1933, 68; *Augustea*, 30 Apr. 1933, 226; Ciarlantini, *Mussolini*, 44–5; Galbiati, *Il 25 luglio*, 65; *Ottobre*, 30 Nov. 1932, 10 (Pascazio)

17 Gilbert, *Churchill*, 5/13; *Corriere della Sera*, 21 Jan. 1927

18 Yeats-Brown, *European Jungle*, 90–1

19 Croce, *Quaderni della Critica*, Mar. 1947, 83; Theodoli, *A cavallo*, 116; Federzoni, *Italia*, 287; Bastianini, *Uomini, cose, fatti*, 33; De Felice (4), 554–7

20 St A. 267/077152–3 (Appelius); *Fascismo e antifascismo*, 1/332 (Sacchi)

21 BD 1a/7/409, 839–40; DDI 7/9/516; Guariglia, *Ricordi*, 147; Coppola, *La pace coatta*, 90; *Critica Fascista*, 15 Oct. 1929, 390; *ibid.*, 15 May 1930, 182; *ibid.*, 15 Aug. 1930, 301–2

22 DDI 7/8/311, 471; Montgomery, *Hungary*, 248

23 Faldella, *L'Italia* (1960), 16

24 DDI 7/9/528 (12 Nov. 1930, Grandi); *Akten*, B/14/425 (Neurath, 27 Mar. 1930)

25 Aloisi, *Journal*, 49–50 (14 Jan. 1933); De Felice (4), 398–400 (July 1931)

26 Cassels, *Mussolini's Early Diplomacy*, 162; Trentin, *Le fascisme*, 166; Petersen, *Hitler e Mussolini*, 21, 24

27 Ludwig, *Three Portraits*, 83

28 DDI 7/1/79–80 (17 Nov. 1922); DDI 7/2/238, 285; Hoepke, *Die deutsche Rechte*, 304; Ludecke, *I knew Hitler*, 72–4

29 Cora, 'Un diplomatico', 90; Michaelis, *Mussolini and the Jews*, 45; Cassels, 354; Guariglia, *Ricordi*, 76; Seldes, *Iron, Blood, and Profits*, 262–3; DDI 7/5/174–5; DDI 7/7/618; De Begnac, *Palazzo Venezia*, 585

30 Starhemberg, *Between Hitler and Mussolini*, 21, 94

31 Aloisi, *Journal*, 96 (17 Mar. 1933); Bullock, *Hitler*, 116; Starhemberg, 92; Pini–Susmel, *Mussolini*, 3/299

32 St A. 287/087721 (Gravelli, 2 Oct. 1930)

33 DDI 7/8/608; *Gerarchia*, Sept. 1930, 709

34 St A. 170/050264 (Renzetti, 21 June 1932); DDI 7/8/418 (14 Feb. 1930); DDI 7/9/405

35 Fest, *Hitler*, 265; Ciarlantini, *Hitler*, 19

36 De Begnac, *Palazzo Venezia*, 112

37 Guariglia, *Ricordi*, 85; Aloisi, *Journal*, 12; Galland, *The First and the Last*, 12–13; DGFP C/3/731, 766–7

38 Favagrossa, *Perchè perdemmo*, 11

39 OO 25/104 (23 May 1932); OO 34/124; *Gioventù Fascista*, 18 Oct. 1931, 1

40 Cantalupo, *Fu la Spagna*, 41–3; Ojetti, *I taccuini*, 395–6; Guariglia, *Ricordi*, 80–2, 177; Tamaro, *Venti anni*, 2/466

41 St A. 54/026888; *The Times*, 21 July 1932

42 BD 1a/6/120 (Graham, 22 Feb. 1929); *Foreign Relations* (1931), 1/544 (9 July 1931), 546 (Stimson); Stimson and Bundy, *On Active Service*, 269

43 OO 25/147 (25 Oct. 1932); *Popolo d'Italia*, 27 July 1932 (De Vecchi); Cantalupo, 43–4

44 Aloisi, *Journal*, 13 (5 Oct. 1932); Pedrazzi, *Roma alla testa*, 3; A. Mussolini, *La conciliazione*, 186–7; *Gerarchia*, Oct. 1932, 878 (Sarfatti)

45 *Convegno Volta*, 1/358 (Bodrero); *Vita Italiana*, Nov. 1933, 523 (De' Stefani); *Critica Fascista*, 1 Nov. 1933, 401–2 (Casini)

46 OO 37/384

47 *Gerarchia*, Jan. 1932, 40–1 (Sarfatti); *ibid.*, Oct. 1932, 801

48 DDI 7/6/228 (20 Apr. 1928); DDI 7/7/241 (25 Jan. 1929), 405–6, 422–3 (15 May 1929); DDI 7/8/169; DDI 7/10/241–2, 271–2 (27 Mar. 1931), 329 (11 June 1931), 645; St A. 256/070678

49 Guariglia, *Ricordi*, 170

50 Graziani, *Ho difeso*, 76–7; Rochat, *Militari e politici*, 27, 371; Mussolini, *My Autobiography* (1939), 337

51 De Felice (4), 417–8

52 Aloisi, *Journal*, 45

53 Dinale, *Quarant'anni di colloqui con lui*, 322

54 C. Senise, *Quando ero capo*, 42; Tamaro, *Venti anni*, 2/327, 456; Maurano, *Ricordi*, 128; Mecheri, *Chi ha tradito?*, 113–14

55 Savino, *La nazione operante* (1934), 55; St A. 130/035997–8, 036133; St A. 131/036241, 036262–4; St A. 255/069995

56 Zangrandi, *Il lungo viaggio*, 127

57 OO 32/170 (20 Mar. 1945)

58 Tamaro, *Venti anni*, 2/457

59 Finer, *Mussolini's Italy*, 545; FO R/5362/16/22 (Jan. 1934); *Rivista 'Popolo d'Italia'*, Sept. 1933, 5–6 (Morgagni); Pini, *Filo diretto*, 47, 65; *Vademecum dello stile fascista*, 28, 216–17

60 *The Times*, 25 Aug. 1933

61 De Begnac, *Palazzo Venezia*, 577–9; *Critica Fascista*, 15 July 1939, 289

62 Ludwig, *Colloqui con Mussolini* (1932), 112; Matteini, *Ordini alla stampa*, 33

63 St A. 131/036424 (7 Aug. 1937)

64 OO 32/170; Navarra, *Memorie*, 48–55; Bertoldi, *Mussolini*, 86; Monelli, *Roma*, 32

65 Barzini, *The Italians*, 137

66 Guarneri, *Battaglie economiche*, 2/382; Simoni, *Berlino ambasciata*, 101

67 *Gioventù Fascista*, 15 Nov. 1933, 13

68 *Gerarchia*, May 1939, 356; Alfieri, *Due dittatori di fronte*, 57

69 Paolucci, *Il mio piccolo mondo*, 299–300; *Corriere della Sera*, 24 Dec. 1931; *Critica Fascista*, 1 Jan. 1932, 4 (Pavolini); *Universalità Fascista*, Jan. 1937, 165 (Spinetti)

70 OO 26/372

71 Andrew, *Through Fascist Italy*, 147–50; Dalton, *The Fateful Years*, 32

72 Aloisi, *Journal*, 212; Ciano (2), 12 (1 Jan. 1939)

73 Bottai, *Vent'anni*, 233

74 Phillips, *Ventures in Diplomacy*, 159; OO 41/112; *Settimana Incom*, 14 Jan. 1956 (Giuriati)

75 Luciano, *Rapporto al Duce* 12–13; Caviglia, *Diario*, 190–1; Ciano (2), 308

76 OO 29/335; Parkinson, *Peace for Our Time*, 91; C. Senise, 107

77 Blondel, *Au fil de la carrière*, 360–1; C. Senise, 45–6, 93

78 St A. 131/036441; Bastianini, *Uomini, cose, fatti*, 114

79 St A. 263/074884 (Starace, 15 Feb. 1935); Renda, *Lo statuto*, 51

80 *Vita Italiana*, Apr. 1930, 436; *ibid.*, Nov. 1934, 651; *Critica Fascista*, 1 Mar. 1932, 96

81 *Gerarchia*, July 1935, 623

82 OO 29/205, 243, 370; OO 30/11

83 OO 31/70 (18 May 1942)

84 *Critica Fascista*, 15 Oct. 1933, 382; *ibid.*, 15 May 1934, 190

85 OO 26/401 (2 Dec. 1934)

86 Maurano, *Ricordi*, 261

87 Federzoni, *Italia di ieri*, 286–8

88 C. Senise, *Quando ero capo*, 128–9; Tamaro, *Venti anni*, 3/228; Germino, *The Fascist Party*, 48; De Begnac, *Palazzo Venezia*, 449, 486, 638

89 OO 37/389 (7 July 1933); *Assalto*, 4 Feb. 1933

90 OO 22/301, 383; OO 25/136; OO 37/358; *Christian Science Monitor*, 27 Jan. 1928

91 *Vita Nova*, Jan. 1928, 59; *Primato*, 1 Nov. 1930; *Critica Fascista*, 1 Oct. 1934, 363–4

92 OO 25/26, 136 (16 Oct. 1932)

93 St A. 326/111313; Mosconi, *La mia linea*, 23

94 Zurlo, *Memorie inutili*, 29, 73, 130, 186, 342; Freddi, *Il cinema*, 388–91

95 Zurlo, 148, 178, 182–4

96 Darrah, *Hail Caesar*, 95

97 C.Senise, 47; Bastianini, 228

98 *Le Professioni*, Sept. 1932, 3; *ibid.*, Oct. 1932, 1–3; Cannistraro, *La fabbrica del consenso*, 31–6

99 De Sanctis, *Ricordi*, 145

100 Operti, *Lettera aperta a Croce*, 11

101 Mussolini, *Corrispondenza*, 129 (6 Dec. 1931)

102 Borgese, *Goliath*, 303–5, 314–15; *Manchester Guardian*, 7 Mar. 1933

103 OO 25/150 (16 Oct. 1932); OO 32/177; Leto, *Ovra*, 135

104 OO 26/82; OO 31/24–5; Dinale, *Quarant'anni di colloqui con lui*, 100; Bottai, *Vent'anni*, 225; *Gerarchia*, July 1939, 499; Sermoneta, *Sparkle Distant Worlds*, 94–5

105 OO 26/248 (24 May 1934); OO 29/153; OO 32/178; Ciano (1), 191 (18 June 1938), 207, 211; Ciano (2), 221 (7 Feb. 1939); Ciano (3), 146; Luciano, *Rapporto al Duce*, 13; Bottai, *Vent'anni*, 191; OO 44/91 (29 Oct. 1934); Sulis, *Imitazione di Mussolini*, 111

106 OO 26/192 (18 Mar. 1934); OO 29/188 (25 Oct. 1938)

107 Ciano (1), 50 (13 Nov. 1937), 183 (31 May 1938)

108 Ciano (1), 207 (10 July 1938)

109 Crocikia, *Mussolini homme de gauche*, 244; DF 2/13/257–8 (Poncet, 14 Dec. 1938); BD 3/3/497–8 (Perth, 27 Dec. 1938); FO 371/22436/91 (Perth, 13 Jan. 1938); Ciano (1), 34

110 Ciano (2), 300, 332

111 Iraci, *Arpinati*, 145; *Rivista 'Popolo d'Italia'*, Feb. 1933, 14; OO 25/200; *Goebbels Diaries*, 390

112 St A. 170/050275 (Spengler, 31 Jan. 1933); Spengler, *Jahre der Entscheidung*, 23, 55–6, 135

113 Aloisi, *Journal*, 50 (14 Jan. 1933); DGFP C/1/29–30 (Neurath, 7 Feb. 1933); DGFP C/4/103

114 DGFP C/1/552 (10 June 1933), 894 (6 Oct. 1933); Aloisi, *Journal*, 46

115 OO 42/36; Aloisi, *Journal*, 109 (17 Apr. 1933); De Felice, *Storia degli ebrei*, 128–9

116 *Gerarchia*, July 1931, 607; OO 26/43 (20 Aug. 1933), 232–3, 298, 309, 319, 327

117 Graziani, *Cirenaica*, 117; OO 37/407

118 Starhemberg, 26–7, 91; *Documents diplomatiques Belges*, 3/54–5 (18 Jan. 1933)

119 Sweet, 'Mussolini and Dollfuss', 165–6, 184, 197–8; Aloisi, *Journal*, 109, 121

120 Guariglia, *Ricordi*, 99; Bastianini, *Uomini, cose, fatti*, 31–2; Aloisi, *Journal*, 96

121 OO 26/62

122 OO 26/57 (19 Sept. 1933), 84 (4 Nov. 1933); OO 29/63–4 (1 Mar. 1938); Massis, *Entretien*, 13; Ciocca, *Giudizio*, 33–4, 268–73; Bertoni, *Russia: trionfo del fascismo*, 6, 9; *Civiltà Fascista*, Feb. 1934, 187; *ibid.*, 15 Nov. 1935, 1018; *Gerarchia*, July 1934, 571–3; Souvarine, *Stalin*, 673; Matthews, *I frutti del fascismo*, 296; *Critica Fascista*, 15 Oct. 1931, 385; *ibid.*, 1 Jan. 1932, 18; *ibid.*, 15 July 1937, 306, 319.

123 OO 26/44, (22 Aug. 1933) 48, 82, 110 (5 Dec. 1933); Massis, *Entretien*, 24; *Rivista 'Popolo d'Italia'*, Aug. 1933, 15

124 OO 26/27–8; Mussolini, *Corrispondenza*, 138 (25 July 1933)

125 OO 26/42–3 (20 Aug. 1933)

126 DF 1/4/197 (15 Aug. 1933); DGFP C/1/895 (6 Oct. 1933); BD 2/5/702 (21 Oct. 1933)

127 Bojano, *In the Wake*, 41; DF 1/4/540 (11 Oct. 1933); DF 1/8/597 (7 Jan. 1935)
128 BD 2/5/312 (2 June 1933), 646 (28 Sept. 1933)
129 OO 26/36–7, 110 (5 Dec. 1933); Aloisi, *Journal*, 164 (3 Dec. 1933); BD 2/6/117, 255 (4 Jan. 1934)
130 Aloisi, *Journal*, 152
131 Aloisi, *Journal*, 167 (11 Dec. 1933)
132 BD 2/5/354–5, 395–6, 430–1 (18 July 1933); Aloisi, *Journal*, 159
133 BD 2/5/674
134 DGFP C/2/142–3 (20 Nov. 1933); Taylor, *Munich*, 155–6; Aloisi, *Journal*, 160
135 BD 2/6/299 (1 Jan. 1934), 342; OO 26/188 (18 Mar. 1934); OO 44/77 (7 Feb. 1934)
136 Gehl, *Austria, Germany and the Anschluss*, 82–3; Zingarelli, *Questo è il giornalismo*, 144
137 BD 2/6/403, 414 (12–13 Feb. 1934)
138 OO 26/191 (17 Mar. 1934); *Oriente Moderno*, Jan. 1934, 18–19
139 Darrah, *Hail Caesar*, 275; *Augustea*, 30 Apr. 1934, 231–2
140 OO 26/192, 258–9 (26 May 1934); DGFP C/2/855
141 DGFP C/2/704–5; OO 26/188–9
142 De Felice (4), 491 (Renzetti, 13 June 1934)
143 Petersen, *Hitler e Mussolini*, 311; Cerruti, *Ambassador's Wife*, 147; Ojetti, *I taccuini*, 437; Signoretti, *La stampa*, 178
144 Wiedemann, *Der Mann*, 64; Bojano, *In the Wake*, 42; Bartlett, *This is My Life*, 269–70; Aloisi, *Journal*, 198; *Illustrazione Italiana*, 24 June 1934, 960
145 Rintelen, *Mussolini als Bundesgenosse*, 11; Bojano, 41; Papen, *Memoirs*, 332
146 Vergani, *Ciano*, 36; Petersen, 314; Starhemberg, *Between Hitler and Mussolini*, 150
147 Heineman, *Neurath*, 103; Rosenberg, *Das politische Tagebuch*, 28–9; DGFP C/3/10 (15 June 1934); DF 1/6/726, 762–3
148 Tamaro, *Venti anni*, 3/99–100
149 DGFP C/4/109; Meissner, *Staatsekretär*, 454; Tamaro, *Venti anni*, 3/95; Rosenberg, 28
150 Cerruti, 150; Theodoli, *A cavallo*, 145–6, 189
151 Badoglio, *L'Italia*, 23; François-Poncet, *Les lettres*, 13; Massock, *Italy from Within*, 36; Dollmann, *Roma*, 99; *Grandi racconta*, 15; Starhemberg, 150
152 OO 42/81 (15 July 1934); Edvige Mussolini, *Mio fratello Benito*, 147, DGFP C/4/110
153 Starhemberg, 170; OO 26/422 (25 July 1934)
154 Wiedemann, *Der Mann*, 64; Rintelen, 11; DGFP C/3/456 (Hassell, 4 Oct. 1934)
155 Schuschnigg, *Austrian Requiem*, 98
156 Aloisi, *Journal*, 214
157 DF 1/7/459; Petersen, 336
158 DF 1/8/131; *Processo Roatta*, 30–1
159 BD 2/12/25–6; Aloisi, *Journal*, 213
160 Grazzi, *Il principio della fine*, 13; *Peace and War*, 279 (13 Sept. 1935)
161 OO 26/306–8 (24 Aug. 1934), 317, 330 (14 Sept. 1934); OO 42/88; Aloisi, *Journal*, 212 (29 Aug. 1934)
162 OO 26/333, 336–8; OO 27/24, 88, 162 (7 Oct. 1934)
163 Armellini, *La crisi*, 64; Roatta, *Otto milioni di baionetti*, 41; Caracciolo, *E poi?*, 123; Canevari, *La guerra*, 1/597
164 OO 26/315, 319 (Sept. 1934); Acerbo, *Fra due plotoni*, 420; Starhemberg, 170
165 Ledeen, *Universal Fascism*, 118–23; *Gerarchia*, Jan. 1935, 77–9
166 *Processo Roatta*, 41, 63, 106
167 DDI 7/7/273–5 (13 Feb. 1929)
168 *Vita Italiana*, Dec. 1940, 671; Villari, *Italian Foreign Policy*, 119

169 Aloisi, *Journal*, 225–6 (10 Oct. 1934)
170 *Processo Roatta*, 49; Aloisi, *Journal*, 340 (7 Jan. 1936)

Chapter 11 War policy

 1 Ciarlantini, *Il capo e la folla*, 25
 2 De Begnac, *Palazzo Venezia*, 652 (Dec. 1934)
 3 Ciarlantini, *Mussolini immaginario*, 143; Alcino, *La dittatura di Mussolini*, 255, 279–80; Tamaro, *Venti anni*, 2/459
 4 Luciano, *Rapporto al Duce*, 10
 5 Lessona, *Memorie*, 333–4; Ciano (2), 171
 6 *New York Times*, 17 Dec. 1933; Cantalupo, *Fu la Spagna*, 246, 271
 7 Sulis, *Imitazione di Mussolini*, 58; Corbino, *Conferenze*, 222–3 (13 Jan. 1934)
 8 BD 2/12/64; Bartlett, 267–8; De Begnac, *Palazzo Venezia*, 623; Lipski, *Diplomat in Berlin*, 61
 9 Canevari, *Graziani*, 146; Tamaro, *Venti anni*, 2/459
10 OO 24/146, 174, 377; Gentizon, *Il mito di Mussolini*, 49; Phayre, 'Mussolini', 79
11 Dinale, *Quarant'anni di colloqui con lui*, 304; D'Aroma, *Mussolini*, 104; Tempera, *Benito: emulo di Cesare*, 17, 27; Lombardo, *Cesare e Mussolini*, 9; Viganoni, *Mussolini e i Cesari*, 39; OO 44/210 (15 May 1937)
12 Ludwig, *Three Portraits*, 72–4; Ludwig, *Colloqui con Mussolini* (1932), 62–3; OO 24/146; *Senato: discussioni* (24 June 1930), 2962
13 Ferri, *Mussolini*, 41; *Legionario*, 16 July 1927, 12 (Torre); Pomba, 128–9 (Cian); Scorza, *Il segreto*, 328–31; D'Andrea, *Mussolini motore del secolo*, 197, 264–5; *Vita Italiana*, June 1936, 587; Gravelli, *Uno e molti*, 28; Pini, *Benito Mussolini* (1939), 240
14 St A. 131/036345–6 (Starace)
15 *News Chronicle*, 12 Jan. 1933; Butler, *Across the Busy Years*, 2/165
16 Cantalupo, *Fu la Spagna*, 45; Guarneri, *Battaglie economiche*, 2/46; OO 44/74 (26 Oct. 1933)
17 Lessona, *Memorie*, 269
18 Schreiber, *Rome après Moscou*, 108, 112; *News Chronicle*, 12 Jan. 1933
19 Melograni, *Gli industriali*, 312; OO 24/191; OO 25/64; OO 41/345, 361; Conti, *Dal taccuino*, 493
20 OO 26/67, 87, 90, 135–6; Aloisi, *Journal*, 138
21 *Senato: discussioni* (11 May 1932), 4940 (Ciccotti); Schreiber, 211; OO 26/256; *Camicia Rossa*, Sept. 1932, 175
22 OO 26/172 (24 Feb. 1934), 266 (19 June 1934), 378
23 *Gran consiglio ... quindici*, 34
24 OO 28/112, 179 (15 May 1937); Meenan, *The Italian Corporative System*, 148–9, 305, 339–41; *The Times*, 18 Dec. 1937; Attico, *Politica*, 24; *ABC*, 16 Oct. 1953, 9–11 (Pacces)
25 Conti, *Dal taccuino*, 645–6 (25 Aug. 1939); Federzoni, *Italia di ieri*, 21; Ebenstein, *Fascist Italy*, 187; Sarti, *Fascism and the Industrial Leadership*, 106; Leto, *Ovra*, 152; De Begnac, *Palazzo Venezia*, 394–5, 467–8, 522; *Compendio Statistico* (1934), 172
26 St A. 120/032701–4 (13 Feb. 1935)
27 OO 30/155 (3 Jan. 1942)
28 Guarneri, *Battaglie economiche*, 2/46; FO 371/21166/103 (Drummond, 28 May 1937)
29 *Impero, A.O.I.*, ix (Badoglio); Cipriani, *Un assurdo etnico*, 327; *Rubicone*, July 1935, 4–5
30 Guariglia, *Ricordi*, 173–4, 315–16, 763
31 *Atti del primo congresso di studi coloniali*, 3/365–6, 369 (Franchetti); *Processo Roatta*, 43; Livius, *Africa orientale*, 13; *Lettura*, Nov. 1935, 970–1 (Molinari)

32 Guariglia, *Ricordi*, 171–2; Aloisi, *Journal*, 382
33 Schuschnigg, *Austrian Requiem*, 95; FO 371/18032 (Murray, 21 Sept. 1934, cit. Rotunda, *The Rome Embassy*, 155–6); Dall'Ora, *Intendenza*, 10–12; Mori, 'Delle cause', 664–5; DF 1/7/523, 539, 554, 579
34 DF 1/7/687
35 BD 2/14/32–3; Baer, *The Coming of the Ethiopian War*, 45–6, 51–6
36 Funke, *Sanktionen*, 31–2; Aloisi, *Journal*, 224
37 OO 37/141–3
38 De Felice (4), 645 (Suvich); *Killearn Diaries*, 51 (Lessona)
39 DF 1/7/930–1; Laval, *Diary*, 34; Duroselle, *La décadence*, 507
40 OO 27/287 (19 Feb. 1936)
41 Aloisi, *Journal*, 255 (6 Feb. 1935); St A. 120/032671, 032692–3 (10–12 Feb. 1935) (18 Oct. 1934)
42 OO 42/89 (18 Oct. 1934); Serra, 'La questione italo–etiopica', 315 (Vitetti)
43 BD 2/14/136–7, 148–9; Mori, *Mussolini e la conquista*, 11–12, 16, 305–6; Kirkpatrick, *Mussolini*, 289
44 BD 2/14/169–70, 176 (26 Feb. 1935), 184–6 (7 Mar. 1935); Aloisi, *Journal*, 255–6 (Feb. 1935); Guariglia, *Ricordi*, 216–17
45 St A. 54/026874–5, 026928 (20 Feb. 1935); Bianchi, *Perchè e come cadde il fascismo*, 680; Puntoni, *Parla Vittorio Emanuele*, 119
46 OO 27/53–4 (11 Apr. 1935)
47 Zurlo, *Memorie*, 265
48 Federzoni, 132; St A. 120/032738, 032741–2; OO 27/26–7 (20 Feb. 1935); *Roma Fascista*, 28 Feb. 1935, 1
49 Bianchi, *Rivelazioni sul conflitto*, 59, 153–4
50 Caracciolo, *E poi?*, 30–1
51 Cora, 'Un diplomatico', 94
52 Dall'Ora, *Intendenza*, 16–17; Tur, *Plancia ammiraglio*, 3/156–7; Bernotti, *Cinquant'anni nella marina* 232–3; Lessona, *Memorie*, 159–61
53 DGFP C/3/802, 1039; DGFP C/4/102
54 *Gerarchia*, Apr. 1935, 308, 317–19
55 BD 2/12/532–3; BD 2/14/206
56 BD 2/12/679–80 (20 Mar. 1935)
57 Serra, 322–5; BD 2/14/208, 216
58 Thompson, *Front-Line Diplomat*, 99; Templewood, *Nine Troubled Years*, 156; Gladwyn, *Memoirs*, 48–9; Harvey, *Diplomatic Diaries*, 137; *Spectator*, 28 May 1943, 500 (Drummond); Jones, *A Diary*, 190; Darrah, *Hail Caesar*, 290
59 Serra, 332–4; BD 2/14/220–2 (Thompson, 12 Apr. 1935)
60 BD 2/12/914; BD 2/14/x; Noël, *Les illusions de Stresa*, 81, 85
61 Berio, 'L'affare etiopico', 188
62 BD 2/14/234–41
63 BD 2/14/279–81; Guariglia, *Ricordi*, 237
64 Aloisi, *Journal*, 276 (28 May 1935)
65 BD 2/14/303–4
66 *Grandi racconta*, 18
67 Aloisi, *Journal*, 269 (4 May 1935); *Gerarchia*, July 1935, 579–80
68 Reynaud, *La France a sauvé l'Europe*, 1/176; Roatta, *Otto milioni di baionetti*, 353; Bandini, *Gli Italiani in Africa*, 522; Noël, 94–6
69 DGFP C/4/113, 209, 337, 417; OO 42/102

War policy

70 Aloisi, *Journal*, 66, 99, 224, 317; Guariglia, *Ricordi*, 248, 269; Amè, *Guerra Segreta*, 203; Guspini, *L'orecchio*, 241

71 Bottai, *Vent'anni*, 87; Castellani, *Tra microbi e re*, 12; Danzi, *Europa senza europei*, 44; Ojetti, *I taccuini*, 464 (26 Sept. 1935); Guariglia, *Ricordi*, 343

72 Guariglia, *Ricordi*, 234

73 Federzoni, 133; Wiedemann, *Der Mann*, 151–2; Giglio, *Inghilterra d'oggi*, 158; Pascazio, *La crisi*, 168; Castellani, 13; *Secolo Fascista*, 15 Mar. 1933, 97; Sammarco, *Fronte interno*, 22

74 *Gerarchia*, Feb. 1936, 98; Lessona, *Verso l'impero*, 34–5, 73; BD 2/14/448

75 Guariglia, *Ricordi*, 272; Aloisi, *Journal*, 294 (11 Aug. 1935); *Foreign Affairs*, Jan. 1936, 258 (Salvemini); *Daily Express*, 20 Apr. 1935 (Pemberton)

76 De Felice (4), 554

77 OO 42/108 (26 June 1935), 117 (21 Aug. 1935); Bianchi, *Rivelazioni*, 64, 184

78 Salvemini, *Prelude to World War*, 237; Bernotti, *Storia della guerra*, 18

79 OO 42/104 (18 May 1935); Aloisi, *Journal*, 292 (5 Aug. 1935); Chambrun, *Traditions*, 218–19; Rochat, *Militari*, 225–6; Bianchi, *Rivelazioni*, 164–5

80 Ciano (1), 71; Tur, *Plancia ammiraglio*, 3/150; Pricolo, *Ispezione*, 10–11

81 BD 2/15/197 (30 Oct. 1935); OO 27/138–9 (15 Sept. 1935); Aloisi, *Journal*, 293 (9 Aug. 1935)

82 OO 27/297 (19 Sept. 1935); Ojetti, *I taccuini*, (26 Sept. 1935); Lagardelle, *Mission à Rome*, 160

83 Darrah, *Hail Caesar*, 302

84 BD 2/14/688 (23 Sept. 1935)

85 OO 32/137; Aloisi, *Journal*, 346, 369; St A. 129/035493 (Balbo); *Camera: discussioni* (15 Mar. 1938), 4687 (Ferretti); Ciano (1), 71

86 F. Rossi, *Mussolini e lo stato maggiore*, 25; Tur, *Plancia*, 3/154; Faldella *L'Italia* (1960), 127–8; Aloisi, *Journal*, 349

87 BD 2/14/410–12 (Montgomery, 23 July 1935), 631

88 Harris, *The U.S. and the Ethiopian Crisis*, 159 (Long); BD 2/14/691–2 (Drummond, 23 Sept. 1935)

89 Rochat, *Militari e politici*, 400–4; Pricolo, 'La difesa', 4; Pricolo, 'L'aeronautica', 9–10

90 De Bono, *Anno XIII*, 46, 54; Aloisi, *Journal*, 374; L. Mosley, *Haile Selassie*, 199

91 Mussolini, *Il tempo*, 18; Scorza, *La notte*, 35; Gorla, *L'Italia*, 41; DGFP C/4/691; Funke, *Sanktionen*, 51 (12 Oct. 1935)

92 OO 27/203 (18 Dec. 1935), 225 (1 Feb. 1936); *Storia e Politica*, Mar. 1977, 139 (Mori)

93 BD 2/15/132, 196 (Drummond, 30 Oct. 1935)

94 Schmidt, *Hitler's Interpreter*, 60, 112; Harvey, *Diplomatic Diaries*, 137 (Ingram); Marder, *From the Dardanelles*, 77

95 BD 2/15/413; Guariglia, *Ricordi*, 290, 303; Peterson, *Both Sides of the Curtain*, 122; Farinacci, *Realtà storiche*, 29

96 Bianchi, *Rivelazioni*, 110, 184, 193, 197–9

97 Lessona, *Memorie*, 182

98 Petrie, *Chapters of Life*, 180; BD 2/15/125, 541; Aloisi, *Journal*, 347

99 Guariglia, *Ricordi*, 287

100 Cora, 'Un diplomatico', 95–6

101 *Processo Roatta*, 57, 258–60; C. Conti, *Servizio segreto*, 70–4; Bandini, *Gli Italiani*, 353, 532–3; Bandini, *Vita e morte*, 346–7; Del Boca, *Gli Italiani in Africa*, 498–9

102 OO 42/131–4 (15 Dec. 1935)

103 DGFP C/4/1075 (27 Jan. 1936); Romains, *Seven Mysteries*, 216; Mori, *Mussolini e la conquista*, 242–3; Aloisi, *Journal*, 334 (26 Dec. 1935)

104 OO 27/306 (28 Dec. 1935); Mori, *Mussolini*, 164

105 OO 23/77 (15 Dec. 1927)
106 Sbacchi, 'Legacy of bitterness', 36–9; Del Boca, 489; St A. 129/035709; Balbo, *La politica aeronautica*, 24; *Esercito e Nazione*, July 1934, 513
107 Mussolini, *My Autobiography* (1939), 337; Dall'Ora, 220; *Nuova Antologia*, Nov. 1935, 91 (Bollati)
108 Villari, *Storia diplomatica*, 88; Mancini, *La donna fascista*, 21
109 Vailati, *Badoglio risponde*, 240; Lessona, *Un ministro di Mussolini*, 112; Lessona, *Memorie*, 292
110 Fuller, *The First of the League Wars*, 39; Macfie, *An Ethiopian Diary*, xi–xii; BD 2/16/314; *Espresso*, 26 Sept. 1965, 6–7 (Haile Selassie, cit. Gambino); Steer, *Caesar in Abyssinia*, 9; *Survey of International Affairs* (1935), 2/479
111 *Patriot*, 7 May 1936, 392; *Spectator*, 10 Apr. 1936; *Daily Mail*, 28 Apr. 1936; Waley, *British Public Opinion*, 73–6
112 Mori, *Mussolini*, 270–3; Guariglia, *Ricordi*, 308–9, 314
113 OO 42/144 (12 Mar. 1936), 149, 151, 156 (25 Apr. 1936)
114 OO 27/320 (3 May 1936); OO 28/265–6
115 BD 2/16/462–4. 524; OO 28/25, 148; Scoppa, *La pace impossibile*, 174; Ward Price, *I Know These Dictators*, 239
116 Bottai, *Vent'anni*, 125
117 Bottai, *Vent'anni*, 105, Benelli, *Schiavitù*, 128, *Chi è?* (1940), 651, Luciano, *Rapporto al Duce*, 8, 14; Navarra, *Memorie*, 192; Lessona, *Memorie*, 185–6
118 OO 28/190 (4 June 1937); OO 29/193; Badoglio, *La via che conduce*, 29; *Annali dell'Africa* (1938), 3/1261
119 Farago, *Abyssinian Stop Press*, 16 (Fuller); Bandini, *Tecnica della sconfitta*, 346; Barker, *The Civilizing Mission*, 318
120 Maugeri, *Mussolini mi ha detto*, 41–2; Federzoni, *Italia di ieri*, 278
121 *Camera: discussioni* (18 May 1938), 5014–16 (Di Revel); *Compendio Statistico* (1937), 185; Maione, *L'imperialismo*, 131
122 Pariani, *Chiacchiere e realtà*, 24; Spigo, *Premesse tecniche*, 43
123 OO 28/32; *Società Italiana per il progresso delle scienze* (1938), 2/326 (Cabiati); Caracciolo, 31
124 OO 28/59 (24 Oct. 1936); Dinale, 159
125 Guarneri, *Battaglie economiche*, 1/437; Catalano, 'L'économie de guerre', 102–3; Mori, *Mussolini*, 310; *Spectator*, 15 May 1936
126 Baer, *Test Case*, 83; Roskill, *Hankey*, 3/189 (26 Nov. 1935); Jones, *A Diary*, 191; Harris, *The United States*, 145; Diggins, *Mussolini and Fascism*, 291–2, 323–5; Blondel, *Au fil de la carrière*, 335
127 Dinale, *Quarant'anni di colloqui con lui*, 153; Aloisi, *Journal*, 382; Benelli, *Schiavitù*, 132; Gravelli, *Mussolini*, 273
128 OO 27/242–5 (23 Mar. 1936)
129 Mosconi, *La mia linea politica*, 27–8; Aloisi, *La mia attività*, 4–5, 14; Spigo, *Premesse tecniche*, 44–5; Pricolo, *Ignavia contro eroismo*, 135
130 Darrah, *Hail Caesar*, 109; Navarra, 174; Pini, *Benito Mussolini* (1939), 249
131 Luciolli, *Palazzo Chigi*, 119–20; Bastianini, *Uomini, cose, fatti*, 39, 50; C. Senise, *Quando ero capo*, 97; Tur, *Con i marinai*, 39; Carboni, *Memorie*, 36; Zanussi, *Guerra e catastrofe*, 1/133
132 Gravelli, *Uno e molti*, 29–30, 42, 55, 91; D'Andrea, *Mussolini motore del secolo*, 253; Ardemagni, *Supremazia di Mussolini*, 98–9; Coppola, *Vittoria*, 65, 81
133 OO 29/331; *Gli Oratori del Giorno*, Oct. 1936, 50; *Popolo d'Italia*, 8 Apr. 1940; Pini, *Benito Mussolini* (1940), 266; *Centro di preparazione*, 56

War policy

134 Pini, *Benito Mussolini* (1939), 238–9
135 Ludwig, *Colloqui* (1932), 63
136 *Berliner Tageblatt*, 20 June 1936
137 Caviglia, *Diario*, 142, 247–8; De Begnac, *Palazzo Venezia*, 12–13; Vergani, *Ciano*, 81, 181–4; Tamaro, *Venti anni*, 2/230
138 Dinale, 153–4, 304
139 Cantalupo, *Fu la Spagna*, 55–6, 267
140 Bottai, *Vent'anni*, 28, 85–6, 95–6; *Critica Fascista*, 1 Nov. 1936, 2
141 Bastianini, 38–40, 48–52
142 Ojetti, *I taccuini*, 436 (1 May 1934); De Begnac, *Palazzo Venezia*, 185 (Feb. 1935)
143 Aloisi, *Journal*, 364 (25 Mar. 1936)
144 Dinale, 254
145 OO 28/33 (30 Aug. 1936)
146 OO 27/244 (23 Mar. 1936); Lessona, *Memorie*, 276; Bottai, *Vent'anni*, 105; OO 44/188 (20 Aug. 1936)
147 *Peace and War*, 279 (Long, 13 Sept. 1935); FO R/6020/23/22 (Perth, 5 July 1938); Caviglia, 141 (2 Apr. 1936)
148 OO 42/149 (6 Apr. 1936), 164; C.M.R., *Histoire du fascisme*, 275
149 DGFP C/4/113 (2 May 1935), 209 (26 May 1935)
150 Wiedemann, *Der Mann*, 151; Speer, *Inside the Third Reich*, 117
151 Farago, *The Game of the Foxes*, 12–13; Robertson, *Mussolini as Empire-Builder*, 182
152 Starhemberg, *Between Hitler and Mussolini*, 192; DGFP C/2/576
153 Whealey, 'Mussolini's ideological diplomacy', 435 (Roland Strunk, 31 Jan. 1936); DGFP D/1/376 (Hassell, 16 Jan. 1937)
154 DF 2/1/700–1 (De Chambrun, 29 Mar. 1936); Michaelis, *Mussolini and the Jews*, 97; Aloisi, *Journal*, 364
155 DGFP C/4/1015 (Hassell, 20 Jan. 1936); Guarneri, *Battaglie economiche*, 2/72; Funke, *Sanktionen*, 43–5, 80
156 Petersen, *Hitler e Mussolini*, 422–3; DF 2/2/494; Aloisi, *Journal*, 365; Tamaro, *Venti anni*, 3/191
157 BD 2/16/462 (Grandi, 28th May 1936); DF 2/2/148–9 (18 Apr. 1936); Aloisi, *Journal*, 361, 364
158 DGFP C/5/576 (23 May 1936)
159 Starhemberg, 222; *The Daily Telegraph*, 28 May 1936; Bastianini, 318
160 Funke, 171–2, 176; Aloisi, *Journal*, 385 (13 May 1936); *Rassegna Italiana*, July 1936, 489; Schuschnigg, *Austrian Requiem*, 97
161 Ciano (1), 13 (6 Sept, 1937); Anfuso, *Roma*, 43; Donosti, *Mussolini e l'Europa*, 47; Vergani, 62; Guerri, *Galeazzo Ciano*, 275–7; De Felice (4), 729 (Giunta, Dec. 1934)
162 Dinale, 325–6; Ciano (1), 73
163 DF 2/6/70 (10 June 1937); Aloisi, *Journal*, 167
164 *Journal of Modern History*, June 1952, 181–3 (Askew); Guariglia, *Ricordi*, 189–90; Coverdale, *Italian Intervention*, 57–9
165 DGFP D/11/214; Guarneri, *Battaglie*, 2/132; Acerbo, *Fra due plotoni*, 384; Caviglia, 319
166 BD 2/17/74–5, 259; Ciano (4), 52
167 Guariglia, *Ricordi*, 342 (Balbo); Canevari, *La guerra*, 1/419 (Baistrocchi); D'Aroma, *Vent'anni*, 242 (Vittorio Emanuele)
168 OO 37/xlv (10 Dec. 1936)
169 Caracciolo, 36; *Processo Roatta*, 33; Guariglia, *Ricordi*, 325; BD 2/18/118; *The Times*, 18 Mar. 1937, 16

170 DGFP D/1/37 (Hitler, 10 Nov. 1937); DGFP D/3/172 (Hassell, 18 Dec. 1936)
171 OO 35/118 (6 Nov. 1937)
172 Bernanos, *A Diary*, 102–7; St A. 268/077733 (Balbo, 11 Feb. 1937); Guerri, *Galeazzo Ciano*, 240; BD 2/17/679
173 OO 28/133 (2 Mar. 1937); Rochat, *Il colonialismo*, 200; Mack Smith, *Mussolini's Roman Empire*, 79–80
174 DGFP C/5/1002
175 OO 35/95; Schuster, *Gli ultimi tempi di un regime*, 168
176 Ciano (4), 75 (23 Sept. 1936)
177 Ciano (4), 77–9; DGFP C/5/1000–2
178 OO 28/69 (1 Nov. 1936)
179 BD 2/16/505 (12 June 1936); Ciano (4), 98; *Rivista 'Popolo d'Italia'*, Sept. 1936, 5
180 Ciano (4), 93, 95 (24 Oct. 1936)
181 Susmel, *Vita sbagliata*, 66
182 OO 28/60, 67; Bottai, *Vent'anni*, 105–6; *Critica Fascista*, 1 Nov. 1936, 2 (Bottai)
183 Lessona, *Memorie*, 276
184 *Gerarchia*, Dec. 1935, 1029; *Bibliografia Fascista*, Jan. 1936, 42
185 Villa, *L'ultima Inghilterra*, 7–8, 98; *Foreign Affairs*, Apr. 1936, 395–6 (Federzoni)
186 OO 31/112; *Dizionario di politica*, 3/50 (Valori)
187 D'Aroma, *Mussolini*, 108; De Begnac, *Palazzo Venezia*, 351; OO 42/173 (13 Nov. 1936)
188 *Gerarchia*, Dec. 1937, 851–2; ibid., Jan. 1938, 48–9
189 OO 28/103 (14 Jan. 1937); DGFP D/1/5; Baskerville, *What Next O Duce?*, 291
190 OO 35/102–3 (23 Jan. 1937)
191 DGFP C/5/1002 (23 Sept. 1936); Aloisi, *Journal*, 372 (14 Apr. 1936); *Vita Italiana*, June 1936, 549, 552 (Canevari); *Azione Coloniale*, 27 Mar. 1936
192 OO 29/195 (25 Oct. 1938); Aloisi, *Journal*, 386 (23 May 1936)
193 OO 28/79 (18 Nov. 1936); OO 29/117
194 Bastianini, *Uomini, cose, fatti*, 49; Guarneri, *Battaglie economiche*, 2/498; OO 26/281–3; OO 28/107 (17 Jan. 1937); DGFP D/1/3; Ciano (1), 251 (29 Sept. 1938)
195 OO 42/33–4 (25 Jan. 1933)
196 Dinale, *Quarant'anni di colloqui con lui*, 226; Bottai, *Vent'anni*, 107
197 *Gerarchia*, May 1939, 332; ibid., May 1941, 264–5
198 OO 28/95; OO 29/37, 221, 340; *Raccolta delle leggi … d'interesse demografico*, 31
199 OO 28/79, 117; Pini, *Filo diretto*, 169 (20 Oct. 1938)
200 OO 28/124 (17 Feb. 1937)
201 OO 28/111 (30 Jan. 1937)
202 *Gerarchia*, Apr. 1940, 226
203 St A. 263/074956; OO 26/64–5 (1 Oct. 1933)
204 BD 2/17/529, 667; BD 2/18/70, 104, 118, 267–8; DGFP D/11/708; Eden, *Facing the Dictators*, 432–3, 451
205 OO 42/176 (10 Feb. 1937); Mussolini, *Corrispondenza*, 234; Cantalupo, *Fu la Spagna*, 102, 148–50, 159
206 OO 42/178–9
207 Coverdale, 'The battle', 67; Tamaro, *Venti anni*, 3/247–8; Canevari, *La guerra*, 1/470–1
208 DGFP D/3/376, 410; Ciano (1), 36; *Foreign Relations*, 1937, 1/268 (30 Mar. 1937)
209 Mussolini, *Corrispondenza*, 162 (26 Mar. 1937)
210 St A. 165/048762–3 (17 Mar. 1937)
211 OO 42/184–5 (25 Mar. 1937)
212 OO 28/201 (17 June 1937); OO 37/463; Incisa, *Spagna*, 54

War policy

213 BD 2/18/758
214 OO 42/180
215 Hansard, 23 Dec. 1937, 2262; Ebenstein, *Fascist Italy*, 67; *Corriere della Sera*, 13 May 1937;
    The Times, 14 May 1937; OO 44/200, 204
216 FO 371/22436/23 (Perth, 13 Jan. 1938); OO 28/152 (23 Mar. 1937)
217 Garosci, *Vita di Rosselli*, 2/147–8; Algardi, *Processi ai fascisti*, 54
218 Conti, *Servizio segreto*, 262; *Processo Roatta*, 77; Carboni, *Memorie*, 17, 62; Susmel, *Vita
    sbagliata*, 74–4; Ciano (1), 189; Guerri, *Galeazzo Ciano*, 249
219 Ciano (1), 132 (12 Mar. 1938); *Annali del Fascismo*, Oct. 1937, 11–12
220 *The Times*, 3–4 Sept. 1937; Tamaro, *Venti anni*, 3/263
221 Rintelen, *Mussolini als Bundesgenosse*, 16
222 DGFP D/3/443; *Sommergibili*, 111–50; Tur, *Plancia ammiraglio*, 3/227

Chapter 12 The axis with Germany

 1 Maravigna, *Come abbiamo perduto*, 4–5; Zanussi, *Guerra e catastrofe*, 1/71–4; Bruttini and
   Puglisi, *L'impero tradito*, 15
 2 DGFP D/3/327–8 (12 June 1937); OO 28/227 (24 July 1937)
 3 BD 2/18/892 (15 June 1937); *Difesa Nazionale*, 9–11; OO 28/187; Ciano (1), 53 (17 Nov.
   1937)
 4 Bottai, *Vent'anni*, 110 (12 Apr. 1937); Pini, *Filo diretto*, 73 (20 Jan. 1937); *Problemi
   Mediterranei*, Feb. 1937, 4; OO 44/215–16 (18 Aug. 1937)
 5 Bottai, *Vent'anni*, 113 (26 Oct. 1937)
 6 OO 7/146; OO 17/213 (8 Nov. 1921); Sarfatti, *The Life of Mussolini*, 17
 7 Roatta, *Otto milioni di baionetti*, 17
 8 OO 29/82 (30 Mar. 1938); *Das Heer des fascistischen Italien*, 3; *Impero Fascista*, Aug. 1935,
   9–10 (Settimelli)
 9 OO 21/341 (5 June 1925); Spigo, *Premesse tecniche*, 47; Valle, *Pace e guerra*, 147
10 Canevari, *La guerra*, 1/548–9; *Settimana Incom*, 14 Jan. 1956 (Giuriati); St A.
   168/049417–19 (Giuriati, 22 Feb. 1931)
11 Bruttini, 10–11 (Baistrocchi); OO 29/76 (30 Mar. 1938)
12 OO 28/32 (30 Aug. 1936), 59; *Gerarchia*, Mar. 1937, 190
13 *Forze armate dell'Italia fascista*, xv; *Corriere della Sera*, 26 June 1938 (Pariani); Pini, *Filo
   diretto*, 155
14 *The Economist*, 12 Sept. 1936, 479; *Le Matin*, 9 Feb. 1937; Baskerville, *What Next O Duce?*,
   219–20
15 *Forze armate dell'Italia fascista*, 123–8 (Pariani); Ciano (1), 112–13 (14 Feb. 1938)
16 DGFP D/6/1114; DF 2/2/442; Ciano (1), 246; *Esercito Anno XVII*, 155–6
17 Giamberardino, *La marina*, 39; De Begnac, *Palazzo Venezia*, 317; OO 22/90 (9 Mar. 1926)
18 Favagrossa, *Perchè perdemmo*, 6–7; Dollmann, *The Interpreter*, 71
19 Ciano (4), 171; Bottai, *Vent'anni*, 112 (7 Sept. 1937); Lessona, *Un ministro di Mussolini*, 187;
   Corriere della Sera, 1 Feb. 1953 (Lessona, cit. Montanelli)
20 Badoglio, *La via*, 13; Algardi, *Processi ai fascisti, 38;* Dollmann, *Roma*, 105–10
21 Magistrati, *L'Italia a Berlino*, 44–6; *Rivista 'Popolo d'Italia'*, July 1937, 9; Rintelen,
   Mussolini als Bundesgenosse, 20–4; Tamaro, *Venti anni*, 3/344
22 OO 28/239 (18 Aug. 1937); *Omnibus*, 11 Sept. 1937, 1; Canevari, *La guerra*, 1/562–4
23 OO 28/249–53 (28 Sept. 1937)

24 Anfuso, *Roma*, 56–7; OO 42/195 (4 Oct. 1937)
25 Lipski, *Diplomat in Berlin*, 331–2; Ciano (4), 224
26 Ciano (4), 220
27 Speer, *Spandau*, 125–6
28 *Libro e Moschetto*, 30 Sept. 1937, i; *Stirpe*, Oct. 1937, 290
29 Bottai, *Vent'anni*, 113 (31 Oct. 1937)
30 Magistrati, *L'Italia a Berlino*, 66–7
31 OO 29/27–9
32 Ciano (1), 34 (14 Oct. 1937), 69 (19 Dec. 1937)
33 Dinale, *Quarant'anni di colloqui*, 154; Ciano (1), 50 (13 Nov. 1937), 71
34 DGFP D/1/1152 (18 July 1938); Ciano (1), 112; Ciano (4), 222; Magistrati, *L'Italia a Berlino*, 123–4
35 BD 2/18/795 (Lampson, 22 May 1937); Ciano (1), 63
36 DGFP D/3/533; FO 371/22436/6 (Perth, 13 Jan. 1938); Ciano (1), 122
37 Bottai, *Vent'anni*, 113
38 Ciano (1), 7 (28 Aug. 1937), 79 (31 Dec. 1937), 103 (2 Feb. 1938), 137 (20 Mar. 1938); Mackenzie, *Propaganda Boom*, 181; *Difesa Nazionale*, 12; *Leggi*, no. 1415 (8 July 1938), 2482
39 Ciano (2), 44–5; *Processo Roatta*, 25; Conti, *Servizio segreto*, 215–16, 230, 252, 271; Algardi, *Processi ai fascisti*, 29; DGFP D/3/626
40 Giolli, *Come fummo condotti alla catastrofe*, 15–19
41 Ciano (1), 46 (6 Nov. 1937)
42 Ciano (1), 76, 88–9; Guarneri, *Battaglie economiche*, 2/157
43 Cora, 'Un diplomatico', 97; Cogni, *I valori della stirpe*, 84; Pini, *Filo diretto*, 127; D'Aroma, *Mussolini*, 167
44 Magistrati, *L'Italia*, 124; Ciano (1), 104–5 (3 Feb. 1938), 109; Szembek, *Journal*, 273
45 Ciano (1), 110 (11 Feb. 1938), 115; Beck, *Dernier rapport*, 146
46 Magistrati, *L'Italia*, 124
47 *The Times*, 28 Jan. 1938, 14
48 Ciano (1), 102 (31 Jan. 1938)
49 OO 29/189 (25 Oct. 1938); OO 34/402; *Illustrazione Italiana*, 6 Feb. 1938, 163; Tamaro, *Venti anni*, 3/293–4
50 OO 26/188, 358, 422
51 OO 29/69 (16 Mar. 1938); Schuschnigg, *Austrian Requiem*, 36
52 *Camera: discussioni* (16 Mar. 1938), 4733
53 DGFP D/1/37–9 (Hossbach, 10 Nov. 1937)
54 St A. 121/033766 (Mussolini, 10 Feb. 1940); *The Economist*, 22 July 1939, 165; Acerbo, *Fra due plotoni*, 386; Gangemi, *Conseguenze economiche*, 90; Ciano (1), 162
55 Ciano (1), 164 (24 Apr. 1938), 171; *New York Times*, 1 May 1939, 11; DF 2/10/442
56 OO 29/77 (30 Mar. 1938), 458–9; *Tempo*, 8 Mar. 1960, 33 (De Vecchi)
57 *Camera: discussioni* (30 Mar. 1938), 3817–18; Federzoni, *Italia di ieri*, 168–9; Zoppi, *Il senato*, 32
58 Spampanato, *Contromemoriale*, 1/10
59 Bandinelli, *Dal diario*, 174–5, 188–9; Pini, *Filo diretto*, 150; Navarra, *Memorie*, 124, 132
60 *Processo Graziani*, 1/108; Graziani, *Ho difeso la patria*, 167
61 Rintelen, *Mussolini als Bundesgenosse*, 46–8
62 Irving, *The War Path*, 93–6; Taylor, *Munich*, 382–3
63 Kordt, *Wahn und Wirklichkeit*, 106–7; Schmidt, *Hitler's Interpreter*, 83; Donosti, *Mussolini*, 104
64 Ciano (1), 173, 180; Susmel, *Vita sbagliata*, 99

65 Magistrati, *L'Italia*, 206; OO 29/117, 159; Mondini, *Prologo del conflitto*, 12; *Ala d'Italia*, June 1938, 66; Ciano (1), 178 (23 May 1938), 182, 227; *Dal Regno all'Impero*, 34 (Federzoni)

66 Pratt, *East of Malta*, 64, 97, 111–13, 116

67 Toscano, *Origins of the Pact of Steel*, 79 (Pariani, 18 Nov. 1938); *Harper's*, Apr. 1938, 511–12

68 BD 3/2/356; Westphal, *Heer in Fesseln*, 158–9; Murray, 'The role of Italy', 44–5

69 OO 16/439; OO 24/82; OO 37/333 (29 Nov. 1929); OO 40/435; Starhemberg, *Between Hitler and Mussolini*, 93

70 OO 23/73–4; OO 26/298 (14 Aug. 1934); *Vita Italiana*, May 1934, 629 (Preziosi); *Critica Fascista*, 1 Sept. 1934, 325–6 (Contri)

71 Theodoli, *A cavallo*, 170–1; DDI 7/9/722; *Gerarchia*, May 1936, 329–30; Carpi, 'Il problema ebraico', 46–56

72 OO 26/319 (6 Sept. 1934)

73 OO 8/21 (15 June 1915), 28, 179; OO 16/239 (3 Apr. 1921); OO 23/117

74 OO 24/46 (13 May 1929); OO 31/165; Ciano (1), 161 (20 Apr. 1938)

75 OO 13/169–70 (4 June 1919); OO 15/269; DDI 7/5/345–6 (14 Aug. 1927); Guariglia, *Ricordi*, 182; D'Aroma, *Mussolini*, 86; DGFP C/1/552

76 De Felice, *Storia degli ebrei*, 150; Michaelis, *Mussolini and the Jews*, 59, 415

77 OO 27/110 (31 July 1935), 321 (5 May 1936); *Gerarchia*, Dec. 1936, 859–60; Aloisi, *Journal*, 185 (2 Apr. 1934); *Antieuropa*, Mar. 1933, 137; Vittorelli, *Dal fascismo*, 54; Farinacci, *Realtà storiche*, 86; *Foreign Relations* (1938), 2/587 (Ciano, 29 July 1938)

78 OO 29/190–1; Ciano (1), 216 (30 July 1938); *Leggi*, n.880 (19 Apr. 1937), 2/1447; *Difesa della Razza*, 5 Sept. 1942, 4 (Landra)

79 DGFP D/1/2 (2 Oct. 1937)

80 Zurlo, *Memorie*, 235; Aloisi, *Journal*, 332 (20 Dec. 1935); Michaelis, 101, 115

81 Pini, *Filo diretto*, 58 (23 Dec. 1936), 73 (20 Jan. 1937)

82 D'Aroma, *Mussolini*, 167; Ciano (1), 13; Pini, *Filo diretto*, 90 (23 Mar. 1937)

83 Kallay, *Hungarian Premier*, 159; Spampanato, *Contromemoriale*, 2/131–2

84 Ciano (1), 107 (6 Feb. 1938); Guarneri, *Battaglie economiche*, 2/372

85 St A. 300/095297–326 (29 anti-Jewish press articles from 28 Jan. 1938 onwards); *Regime Fascista*, 12 Jan. 1938

86 Pini, *Filo diretto*, 158; Ciano (1), 209; *Difesa della Razza*, 5 May 1942, 4

87 OO 29/126, 146 (18 Sept. 1938), 497

88 *Lo Stato*, Aug. 1941, 337

89 OO 29/191 (25 Oct. 1938); *Gerarchia*, Sept. 1938, 596; Maurano, *Ricordi*, 224; DF 2/12/241 (15 Oct. 1938, Rivière quoting Mons. Tardini)

90 Ciano (1), 211 (17 July 1938)

91 Ciano (1), 291 (12 Nov. 1938); DGFP D/4/548 (4 Jan. 1939)

92 OO 29/168, 190 (25 Oct, 1938); Phillips, *Ventures in Diplomacy*, 120–1; Ciano (1), 264 (6 Oct. 1938), 287

93 Cadogan, *Diaries*, 137; De Begnac, *Palazzo Venezia*, 642 (Sept. 1940)

94 OO 24/280 (27 Oct 1930); OO 25/135 (16 Oct. 1932); OO 29/250 (26 Mar. 1939); Ciano (1), 74 (24 Dec. 1937)

95 Ciano (2), 45 (22 Feb. 1939)

96 Maugeri, *Mussolini mi ha detto*, 28, 41–2; Federzoni, *Italia di ieri*, 278

97 Vergani, *Ciano*, 151

98 Ciano (1), 216–17 (8 Aug. 1938), 223, 231, 307 (14 Dec. 1938)

99 Ciano (1), 217 (8 Aug. 1938); Ciano (2), 202

100 Gorla, *L'Italia nella seconda guerra*, 394 (23 Jan. 1943)

101 *Actes et documents du Saint Siège*, 7/335; *Hitler's Table Talk*, 607; Agricola, *Mussolini in prigionia*, 11; Ciano (2), 263 (12 May 1940)

102 *Actes et documents du Saint Siège*, 5/443; Guariglia, *Ricordi*, 499; Ciano (3), 130, 213

103 Ciano (1), 132 (13 Mar. 1938); OO 29/142, 499; Amery, *My Political Life*, 3/240; BD 2/18/652; Beck, *Dernier rapport*, 146

104 DGFP D/2/357 (29 May 1938), 533; Ciano (1), 180; Ciano (4), 353

105 Ciano (1), 236 (12 Sept. 1938), 240, 246

106 BD 3/3/347; *Camera: discussioni* (30 Nov. 1938), 5228 (Ciano)

107 Ciano (1), 238, 250 (28 Sept. 1938)

108 BD 3/2/587

109 Celovsky, *Das Munchener Abkommen*, 461–3; Bruegel, *Czechoslovakia*, 292–3; Taylor, *Munich*, 21; Schmidt, *Hitler's Interpreter*, 111

110 OO 29/192; Dinale, *Quarant'anni di colloqui con lui*, 161; Dollmann, *Roma nazista*, 381; Gravelli, *Mussolini*, 208; Anfuso, *Roma, Berlino, Salò*, 100–1

111 BD 3/3/319 (3 Oct. 1938)

112 OO 34/439; C. Senise, *Quando ero capo*, 46; Giolli, *Come fummo condotti*, 69

113 Ciano (1), 276, 280; Ciano (4), 375–8 (28 Oct. 1938)

114 Ciano (1), 264 (7 Oct. 1938)

115 OO 29/192–5 (25 Oct. 1938); Ciano (1), 172; Ciano (4), 378; Ardemagni, *La Francia*, 38

116 DF 2/12/59–60, 613; DF 2/13/49, 258

117 Guariglia, *Ricordi*, 357, 381–2; Ojetti, *I taccuini*, 503; Ciano (1), 282

118 Donosti, *Mussolini e L'Europa*, 137–40; Ciano (4), 384–5

119 St A. 300/095219 (Cavallero, 13 Jan. 1939)

120 *Corriere della Sera*, 22 and 25 Jan. 1939 (Monelli); St A. 1/000044 (Mussolini, 5 Feb. 1939); Ciano (1), 315

121 BD 3/3/469

122 DF 2/12/409; DF 2/13/12, 51; Washington, T. 120/101 (1 Dec. 1938)

123 Cianfarra, *The War and the Vatican*, 139–40; Matthews, *I frutti del fascismo*, 287; Massock, *Italy from Within*, 93; *The Economist*, 17 Dec. 1938, 582

124 BD 3/3/466–7 (Perth, 2 Dec. 1938)

125 Guariglia, *Ricordi*, 369–72; Milza, *L'Italie fasciste*, 219–22; Donosti, 146; Massis, *Maurras*, 308

126 *Camera: discussioni* (14 Dec. 1938), 5621, 5626

127 BD 3/3/459–60 (16 Nov. 1938); *Rivista 'Popolo d'Italia'*, Feb. 1939, 5; D'Aroma, *Venti anni*, 276

128 Ciano (2), 19

129 Harvey, *The Diaries*, 239–42; BD 3/3/532; DF 2/13/677

130 Aster, *The Making of the Second World War*, 48–9

131 *Gerarchia*, Jan. 1939, 32; Navarra, *Memorie*, 48–9

132 OO 37/153–6 (4 Feb. 1939); *In Africa settentrionale*, 50; Giolli, 119

133 *Relazioni Internazionali*, 11 Feb. 1939, 93; Maurano, *Ricordi*, 234; Maurano, *Francia la sorellastra*, 266

134 Ciano (2), 20, 22, 40, 42 (19 Feb. 1939)

Chapter 13 Alliance with Germany

1 Ciano (1), 313 (23 Dec. 1938); Ciano (2), 12

2 Ciano (2), 18–19 (8 Jan. 1939); Ciano (4), 392–4

3 Bastianini, *Uomini, cose, fatti*, 266–7

4 OO 29/193; Ciano (2), 56

5 OO 29/246–9 (18 Mar. 1939); Bottai, *Vent'anni*, 125; DGFP D/6/175; Ciano (2), 57–8

6 Alfieri, *Due dittatori di fronte*, 226; Vergani, *Ciano*, 76; Ciano (2), 60–2

7 DGFP D/6/104–5 (22 Mar. 1939); Ciano (2), 14–15

8 Ciano (2), 56 (15 Mar. 1939)

9 OO 29/252–3 (26 Mar. 1939), 257 (31 Mar. 1939); DGFP D/6/1109

10 D'Aroma, *Mussolini*, 188–9

11 Cantalupo, *Fu la Spagna*, 262; Irving, *The War Path*, 54

12 Zangrandi, *Il lungo viaggio*, 101–2; Paolucci, *Il mio piccolo mondo*, 354; Matthews, *I frutti del fascismo*, 2, 287–90; Cantalupo, 279; Montanelli and Cervi, *L'Italia littoria*, 350–3

13 Dinale, *Quarant'anni di colloqui*, 164; Agricola, *Mussolini in prigionia*, 28; DDI 9/4/620; OO 35/253

14 DGFP D/2/972; DGFP D/3/865

15 Guarneri, *Battaglie economiche*, 2/109, 132–5, 276–9

16 OO 30/51; OO 31/70–1; DGFP D/9/541; Spigo, *Premesse tecniche*, 45; Zanussi, *Guerra e catastrofe*, 1/54

17 DGFP D/3/566, 719, 729–32; Donosti, *Mussolini e l'Europa*, 52–3; Cantalupo, 179; Magistrati, *Il prologo del dramma*, 190–1

18 Ciano (1), 165, 170, 175

19 DGFP D/4/578–9; Villari, *Italian Foreign Policy*, 220; Bottai, *Vent'anni*, 107; Freddi, *Il cinema*, 1/380; Ciano (1), 267

20 Guarneri, *Battaglie economiche*, 2/347; Ciano (4), 305–8

21 Ciano (1), 189, 278, 304–5; Ciano (5), 220–1; Susmel, *Vita sbagliata*, 116–17

22 FO *Lisbon Papers*, 32 (Jacomoni, 9 Feb. 1939); Cianfarra, *The War and the Vatican*, 160; Guspini, *L'orecchio del regime*, 160–1

23 Valle, *Pace e guerra*, 147; Pricolo, *La regia aeronautica*, 39; Baudino, *Una guerra assurda*, 32, 54; Bastianini, *Uomini, cose, fatti*, 232

24 Ciano (5), 277 (4 Apr. 1939); Pini, *Filo diretto*, 190 (23 Mar. 1939); Susmel, *Vita sbagliata*, 136

25 BD 3/5/120, 128

26 Valle, 149–53; Guerri, *Galeazzo Ciano*, 380–1; De Begnac, *Palazzo Venezia*, 617; *Critica Fascista*, 1 May 1939, 208 (Canevari)

27 Ciano (2), 85 (21 Apr. 1939), 99, 106–7; OO 44/231 (14 May 1939)

28 DGFP D/6/57–8 (20 Mar. 1939), 1110–11 (4 Apr. 1939); Stehlin, *Témoignage*, 378; Halder, *Kriegstagebuch*, 1/15

29 DGFP D/6/57; Ciano (2), 56; Giolli, *Come fummo condotti*, 118–19; Kordt, *Wahn und Wirklichkeit*, 168; Toscano, *Origins of the Pact of Steel*, 214, 226

30 Faldella (1960), 88; DGFP D/6/1113 (24 Apr. 1939); Toscano, *Origins*, 289; Ciano (2), 92

31 St A., 131/036447–8 (Starace, 6 May 1939); Ciano (2), 93; Magistrati, *L'Italia a Berlino*, 341; Dollmann, *The Interpreter*, 155; *Relazioni Internazionali*, 13 May 1939, 375

32 DGFP D/6/260 (18 Apr. 1939)

33 Ciano (2), 80–3, 101; DGFP D/6/445 (4 May 1939); Anfuso, *Roma, Berlino, Salò*, 117

34 *Corriere della Sera*, 9 May 1939

35 DGFP D/6/580 (23 May 1939)

36 Bastianini, *Uomini, cose, fatti*, 253

37 Gafencu, *Ultimi giorni*, 131–2; Ciano (2), 92, 99, 107; Ciano (4), 431; *Organizzazione della marina*, 1/350

38 OO 35/136 (30 May 1939)

39 *Actes et documents du Saint Siège*, 1/171 (7 June 1939); DGFP D/6/619 (30 May 1939); Ciano (2), 101

40 OO 35/135; Alfieri, *Due dittatori*, 156; *Grandi racconta*, 25; Signoretti, *La stampa*, 187

41 DDI 8/12/382 (7 July 1939), 497–8 (24 July 1939); Ciano (4), 436 (2 July 1939)

42 Frassati, *Il destino*, 38; *Forze armate dell'Italia fascista*, vii (Badoglio), 114 (Soddu); *Nazione Militare*, July 1939, 539, 561, 566; *Espansione Imperiale*, July 1939, 312; D'Aroma, *Mussolini*, 193

43 Ciano (2), 106, 117; François-Poncet, *Au palais*, 110

44 Aloisi, *Journal*, 340; Jacomoni, *La politica*, 224; BD 2/14/468, 726

45 Grazzi, *Il principio della fine*, 226; Cantalupo, 157; Scoppa, *Colloqui*, 33, 37; Ojetti, *I taccuini*, 564; *Foreign Relations* (1938), 2/585–6 (Suvich, 28 July 1938); Susmel, 118–19, 233–4

46 DDI 9/2/164; Simoni, *Berlino ambasciata*, 203–4, 207

47 Alfieri, 225–6, 229–30, 343

48 Phillips, *Ventures in Diplomacy*, 197; Varè, *The Two Impostors*, 184; D'Aroma, *Mussolini*, 195

49 DDI 8/12/374 (Attolico, 7 July 1939), 378–9, 400–1, 487, 561 (1 Aug. 1939)

50 Pini, *Filo diretto*, 193

51 DGFP D/6/971 (24 July 1939); Magistrati, *L'Italia a Berlino*, 380, 382–4; OO 43/15 (29 July 1936)

52 DDI 8/12/497–8 (24 July 1939); Cadogan, *Diaries*, 197

53 Ciano (2), 138–9 (6–9 Aug. 1939); Guerri, *Galeazzo Ciano*, 417 (M. del Drago)

54 Magistrati, *L'Italia*, 395; Ciano (2), 139; Tamaro, *Venti anni*, 3/379

55 Halder, *Kriegstagebuch*, 1/15 (14 Aug. 1939); *Nazi Conspiracy*, 4/511 (12 Aug. 1939); Ciano (2), 140; Ciano (4), 457; Dollmann, *The Interpreter*, 166

56 DDI 8/13/26; DGFP D/7/53; Magistrati, *L'Italia*, 401–2

57 Rintelen, *Mussolini als Bundesgenosse*, 72; Ciano (2), 144

58 Donosti, *Mussolini e l'Europa*, 8, 189; Ciano (2), 142; Cantalupo, 47

59 Faldella, *L'Italia* (1960), 133

60 OO 35/138

61 OO 29/415 (25 Aug. 1939); Ciano (2), 147; Vitetti, 'Diario', 495 (22–5 Aug. 1939)

62 DGFP D/7/201–5; BD 3/7/258

63 Ciano (2), 149 (25 Aug. 1939)

64 DDI 8/13/46 (Canaris, 16 Aug. 1939), 205; Höhne, *Canaris*, 343; Ciano (1), 149; Dollmann, *Roma nazista*, 325

65 Halder, 1/15; Ciano (2), 148–9

66 *Hitler Directs his War*, 32; Siebert, *Italiens Weg*, 303–4; Halder, 1/34; Weizsäcker, *Memoirs*; 206–7; *Trial of the Major German War Criminals*, 9/300; *ibid.*, 10/183

67 BD 3/6/658–9 (Loraine, 11 Aug. 1939); BD 3/7/139, 147–8 (Loraine, 22–3 Aug. 1939); Susmel, *Vita sbagliata*, 86–7

68 Favagrossa, *Perchè perdemmo* 105–7; Donosti, 214; *Grandi racconta*, 28; Vitetti, 496 (26 Aug. 1939)

69 DGFP D/7/204 (22 Aug. 1939)

70 Halder, 1/39 (26 Aug. 1939); DGFP D/7/352, 392, 410 (29 Aug. 1939)

71 D'Aroma, *Mussolini*, 197–8; Ciano (2), 151–2

72 DDI 8/13/221–2

73 Ciano (2), 155 (31 Aug. 1939)

74 Federzoni, 290; Varè, *The Two Impostors*, 253–4

75 Guarneri, *Battaglie economiche*, 2/429; Bottai, *Vent'anni*, 135–7 (1 Sept. 1939); Ciano (2), 156–7

76 Pini, *Filo diretto*, 196–7; Matteini, *Ordini alla stampa*, 77

77 *Relazioni Internazionali*, 9 Sept. 1939, 661–2; Zanussi, 1/40; *Critica Fascista*, 1 Aug. 1939, 311–12; *ibid.*, 1 Sept. 1939, 335–6

78 Canevari, *La guerra*, 2/74 (Soddu); Ciano (2), 167–8 (Guzzoni, 18 Sept. 1939)

79 Santoro, *L'aeronautica*, 1/17–19; Higham, *Air Power*, 95; C. Senise, *Quando ero capo*, 115; Maurano, *Ricordi*, 238 (Balbo); Ciano (2), 168

80 Graziani, *Ho difeso la patria*, 182; Carboni, *Memorie*, 6; Pariani, *Chiacchiere e realtà*, 17; Faldella (1960), 87–8; Favagrossa, 110

81 *Forze armate*, 119 (Soddu), 275 (Valle); Bastico, *Guerra totalitaria*, 20; *Rivista Aeronautica*, Sept. 1939, 426

82 Fioravanzo, *Il soldato*, 11–12, 20; Faldella (1960) 711–12; Roatta, *Otto milioni di baionetti*, 29–32; Carboni, *Memorie*, 381; Caracciolo, *E poi? 105–6;* Prasca, *Io ho aggredito la Grecia*, 25–6

83 Guarneri, *Battaglie economiche*, 1/391; Pricolo, *Ignavia contro eroismo*, 65–6; Bastianini, *Uomini, cose, fatti*, 63

84 St A. 53/026447 (Pariani, June 1937); Federzoni, *Italia di ieri*, 167–8

85 Maurano, *Ricordi*, 271 (Leto)

86 Pariani, 17; Raimondi, *Mezzo secolo*, 323; Guarneri, *Battaglie*, 2/40–1; Maugeri, *From the Ashes*, 105–6; Armellini, *Diario*, 101 (3 Oct. 1940)

87 *Regime Corporativo*, May 1937, 283 (Dupuis)

88 Pini, *Benito Mussolini* (1939), 147; Bastianini, *Uomini, cose, fatti*, 30; *Dottrina Fascista*, Sept. 1939, 385

89 Pini, *Filo diretto*, 84 (24 Feb. 1937); C. Senise, *Quando ero capo*, 115–16

90 Badoglio, *L'Italia*, 38; Caviglia, *Diario*, 303–4; Giamberardino, *La politica bellica*, 79, 82; Dollmann, *Roma nazista*, 127 (Rommel); Armellini, *La crisi*, 155; Messe, *La guerra al fronte Russo*, 16; Carboni, *Memorie*, 63–4

91 BD 3/2/356; BD 3/5/421; Dollmann, *Roma*, 124; Phillips, *Ventures in Diplomacy*, 126–7; Werner, *The Military Strength of the Powers*, 261

92 Ciano (2), 92 (2 May 1939), 171 (24 Sept. 1939)

93 Pini, *Filo diretto*, 154 (17 June 1938)

94 Pini, *Filo diretto*, 192–4; Leto, *Ovra*, 133; Dal Pont, *Giornali fuori legge*, 24; Ebenstein, *Fascist Italy*, 68

95 Zangrandi, *Il lungo viaggio*, 207; Leto, *Ovra*, 185, 203; Melograni, *Rapporti segreti*, 36, 42

96 Giannini, *Io spia dell'ovra*, 2/37–9; Ojetti, *I taccuini*, 537

97 Conti, *Dal taccuino*, 673 (2 Jan. 1940)

98 FO 434/7/7006/149 (Charles, 11 Apr. 1940)

99 Graziani, *Ho difeso*, 167–8, 178–9

100 Vitetti, 'Diario', 498 (15 Sept. 1939); Ciano (2), 209 (2 Jan. 1940), 211

101 DDI 9/2/624; Ciano (2), 205 (31 Dec. 1939)

102 Guarneri, *Battaglie economiche*, 2/499

103 DGFP D/8/36 (9 Sept. 1939), 190–1; DDI 9/1/84–5 (10 Sept. 1939)

104 Ciano (2), 159

105 Bottai, *Vent'anni*, 144 (30 Sept. 1939)

106 François-Poncet, *Ricordi*, 260; Amicucci, *I 600 giorni*, 82–3; Ciano (2), 165

107 Ciano (2), 161–2, 176 (3 Oct. 1939); Alfieri, 40

108 Frassati, *Il destino*, 119–20 (8 Jan. 1940)

109 Dollmann, *Roma*, 376 (Bocchini); Bellotti, *La repubblica*, 212; *Politica estera Italiana*, 219 (Toscano)

110 Mosley, *A Life*, 151; François-Poncet, *Ricordi*, 247; Hitler, *The Testament*, 103

111 Dietrich, *The Hitler I Knew*, 248; Speer, *Spandau*, 125; DGFP D/1/33; *Goebbels Diaries*, 390; *Hitler's Table Talk*, 9, 267; Bottai, *Vent'anni*, 187, 211

112 DGFP D/8/442 (23 Nov. 1939); Halder, *Kriegstagebuch*, 1/102–3 (10 Oct. 1939); *Führer Conferences*, 47 (25 Nov. 1939)

113 DGFP D/4/530–1 (26 Nov. 1938)

114 Ciano (2), 176 (4 Oct. 1939); Giolli, *Come fummo condotti*, 182–3; Guarneri, *Battaglie economiche*, 2/430; Bottai, *Vent'anni*, 151

115 DDI 9/1/84; Ciano (2), 158, 169

116 Orano, *Il fascismo*, 2/454

117 Acerbo, *Fra due plotoni*, 422; Federzoni, *Italia di ieri*, 164, 192, 282

118 Ciano (2), 187, 189 (20 Nov. 1939), 201–2 (26 Dec. 1939); Santoro, *L'aeronautica*, 1/75–6

119 Halder, 1/142 (14 Dec. 1939), 150; *Documents diplomatiques Belges*, 5/447–8 (3 Jan. 1940); *Trial of the Major German War Criminals*, 15/340 (Jodl); Weizsäcker, *Memoirs*, 222; Ciano (2), 204, 209

120 St A. 121/933841 (Mussolini, 14 Feb. 1940); St A. 267/077159–66 (Appelius, Oct. 1939); Acerbo, 423–4; Caviglia, *Diario*, 219; Bottai, *Vent'anni*, 157, 159

121 Gorla, *L'Italia nella seconda guerra*, 77; Roatta, *Otto milioni di baionetti*, 89–90; Dollmann, *Roma*, 120, 123; Minniti, 'Il problema degli armamenti', 19; U. Cavallero, *Comando supremo*, 307

122 Toscano, *Storia ... Alto Adige*, 187–91; De Felice, *Il problema*, 53; Rusinow, *Italy's Austrian Heritage*, 260; Alcock, *History of the South Tyrol*, 57–8

123 Ciano (2), 180 (16 Oct. 1939); *Critica Fascista*, 15 Oct. 1939, 382 (Berto Ricci); *ibid.*, 1 Dec. 1939, 44 (Napolitano); Bottai, *Vent'anni*, 138

124 DGFP D/8/611

125 *Hitler e Mussolini*, 37–8

126 *Actes et documents du Saint Siège*, 1/417 (4 Apr. 1940); Ciano (2), 204; Pini, *Filo diretto*, 197–9 (from 22 Sept. to 11 Nov. 1939); Pini–Susmel, *Mussolini*, 4/57

127 Bottai, *Vent'anni*, 89, 146, 153–4; Ciano (2), 202–3; Carboni, *Memorie*, 15; Hassell, *Diaries*, 122

128 *Führer conferences*, 9 (26 Jan. 1940); DGFP D/8/613 (3 Jan. 1940)

129 Ciano, 2/219–21 (30 Jan., 7 Feb. 1940)

130 St A. 121/033842

131 St A. 121/033775, 033786–7, 033831

132 St A. 121/033754, 033769, 033775; Ciano (2), 225; *Bibliografia Fascista*, Aug. 1940, 598; *Politica Estera*, Aug. 1945, 21–6

133 OO 30/217 (6 Nov. 1941); U. Cavallero 109; Ciocca and Toniolo, *L'economia Italiana*, 188 (Covino, Gallo, Mantovani)

134 Medlicott, *Economic Blockade*, 1/283; *Harper's*, Apr. 1938, 513 (G.F. Eliot)

135 St A. 121/033781; U. Cavallero, 194, 217, 253

136 St A. 121/033841; Guarneri, *Battaglie economiche*, 2/409–11, 475–6; Ciano (2), 111

137 St A. 121/033840; DDI 9/3/99, 172; Favagrossa, 29; Santoro, 1/14, 39; *Processo Graziani*, 2/244; Guarneri, *Battaglie economiche*, 2/157, 442–4

138 St A. 53/026445 (18 Mar. 1943); Guarneri, *Battaglie economiche*, 1/395

139 *Italia d'oggi*, 246–7 (Ansaldo)

140 St A. 120/032929 (Mussolini, Feb. 1940)

141 Favagrossa, *Perchè perdemmo la guerra*, 72; Canevari, *La guerra*, 1/537/8

142 OO 30/156 (3 Jan. 1940)

143 Leto, *Ovra*, 154

144 *Economia Italiana*, May 1939, 401 (Volpi); *Problemi e Informazioni*, Jan. 1940, 3–5 (Volpi)

Alliance with Germany

145 St A. 120/032902 (Mussolini, 9 Feb. 1940); St A. 121/033274 (Feb. 1940)
146 OO 28/240 (20 Aug. 1937)
147 Guarneri, *Autarchia*, 23; *Rivista Italiana di Scienze Economiche*, Jan. 1940, 22 (De' Stefani);
   Economia Fascista, Feb. 1940, 10 (Tassinari); *Critica Fascista*, 1 Sept. 1939, 330
148 St A. 121/033260, 033766–7 (10 Feb. 1940); Spigo, 94
149 St A. 121/033759, 033762 (Mussolini and Tassinari, 10 Feb. 1940); *Camera: commissioni
   (bilancio)*, 288 (12 Apr. 1940); Toniolo, *L'economia del Italia fascista*, 311

Chapter 14 The Second World War

1 Ciano (2), 217, 227, 229, 233; Dinale, *Quarant' anni di colloqui con lui*, 160–1; Frassati, *Il
   destino passa per Varsavia*, 125–6
2 Anfuso, *Roma, Berlino, Salò*, 135; Carboni, *Memorie*, 57
3 OO 35/156, 162 (11 Mar. 1940)
4 DGFP D/9/5–16; Warlimont, *Im Hauptquartier der Wehrmacht*, 79; Irving, *Hitler's War*, 90;
   Schmidt, *Hitler's Interpreter*, 172; Simoni, *Berlino ambasciata*, 87; Ciano, 4/549
5 Ciano (2), 240
6 Ciano (2), 236–7, 245–6; Bottai, *Vent'anni*, 163 (29 Mar. 1940)
7 Faldella, *L'Italia* (1960), 147; Quartararo, 'Inghilterra e Italia', 706–9; Ciano (2), 246–8
8 St A. 1/000328
9 De Begnac, *Pagine nella tormenta*, 365, 395; *Almanacco 'Popolo d'Italia'* (1940), 35; OO
   35/139; Guariglia, *Ricordi*, 452
10 St A. 128/035329 (De Bono, 17 Nov. 1939); Faldella, *L'Italia* (1960), 730 (Badoglio, 9 Apr.
   1940)
11 Roatta, *Otto milioni di baionetti*, 91; Iachino, *Tramonto di una marina*, 29–31; Graziani, *Ho
   difeso la patria*, 188; OO 21/341
12 OO 29/366 (31 Mar. 1940); Tur, *Plancia ammiraglio*, 3/306–7; *Organizzazione della marina*,
   1/351–2; Canevari, *La guerra*, 1/211; *ibid.*, 2/37
13 Messe, *La mia armata in Tunisia*, 16; Ciano (4), 222
14 St A. 120/032887; Favagrossa, *Perchè perdemmo*, 232; Roatta, 54, 65, 108–9; Graziani,
   Africa settentrionale, 114; Westphal, *Heer in Fesseln*, 170
15 Canevari, *La guerra*, 2/76–9
16 Spampanato, *Contromemoriale*, 1/164–5
17 *In Africa settentrionale*, 161–2; Faldella (1960), 729–30; Canevari, *La guerra*, 2/53
18 Halder, *Kriegstagebuch*, 1/237-8, 241-2, 302, 307–8 (25 May 1940); Westphal, 123–4;
   Rintelen, *Mussolini als Bundesgenosse*, 81–2; Graziani, *Ho difeso*, 200–4; Messe, *La mia
   armata in Tunisia* 23
19 D'Aroma, *Mussolini*, 388; Ciano (2), 251
20 Faldella (1960), 73; Faldella (1967), 17, 28; Dinale, *Quarant' anni de colloqui con lui*, 164
21 Susmel, *Vita sbagliata*, 201; Phillips, *Ventures in Diplomacy*, 138; Melograni, *Rapporti
   segreti*, 64
22 Ciano (2), 252, 254 (25 Apr. 1940); Bottai, *Vent'anni*, 170; OO 29/375
23 Ciano (11 Apr. 1940) 251; Bertoldi, *Mussolini*, 53; Bottai *Vent'anni*, 171
24 Appelius, *La tragedia della Francia*, 72; Borsa, *Gli inglesi*, 73; Matteini, *Ordini alla stampa*,
   98; *Bibliografia Fascista*, June 1940, 476–7; *Lavoro Fascista*, 20 Mar. 1940; *Popolo d'Italia*, 6,
   7, 14, 22 May 1940
25 St A. 54/026895–6 (Grandi, 9 Aug. 1940); *Bollettino parlamentare*, 63 (27 Apr. 1940,
   Grandi); Federzoni, *Italia di ieri*, 207–8; *Africa Italiana*, June 1940, 1–2 (Federzoni)

26 Federzoni, 166; Bottai, *Vent'anni*, 174; Ciano (2), 271 (29 May 1940); OO 29/77

27 Lessona, *Memorie*, 426; D'Aroma, *Mussolini*, 388; Tamaro, *Venti anni*, 3/412; Mariano, *Forty Years*, 243; Maurano, *Ricordi*, 213-14

28 Armellini, *La crisi*, 98; *Bibliografia Fascista*, June 1940, 476-9 (Pavolini); *Gerarchia*, Jan. 1940, 17, 21

29 Federzoni, 192, 283

30 OO 29/400-1 (4 June 1940)

31 DDI 9/4/373, 439-40, 463, 498-99; OO 35/398; Ciano (2), 242

32 Ciano (2), 270 (27 May 1940); De Begnac, *Palazzo Venezia*, 396 (Jan. 1942); Harvey, *Diaries*, 373; François-Poncet, *Au palais Farnèse*, 173; OO 44/244 (26 Apr. 1940)

33 OO 29/398

34 OO 31/128 (2 Dec. 1942)

35 OO 32/173 (20 Mar. 1945); Pricolo, *La regia aeronautica*, 212; Ciano (2). 264 (13 May 1940); Faldella (1967) 29; Hitler, *The Testament*, 70; Alfieri, *Due dittatori*, 279

36 Anfuso, *Roma*, 156; Ciano (2), 227

37 Badoglio, *L'Italia*, 37; Guarneri, *Battaglie economiche*, 2/498; Carboni, *Memorie*, 92; Vailati, *Badoglio risponde*, 70; Guspini, *L'orecchio del regime*, 173; Lessona, *Memorie*, 398-9; *Memoriale Grandi*, 26

38 Anfuso, 151-2

39 Dollmann, *Roma nazista*, 125; Donosti, *Mussolini e l'Europa*, 234; Bojano, *In the Wake*, 158; Keitel, *Memoirs*, 111-12

40 Graziani, *Ho difeso*, 189; DDI 9/4/192; Washington T. 821/127/IT A1141 (6 June 1940); Santoro, *L'aeronautica*, 1/77-8

41 Ciano (2), 271 (29 May 1940); *Hitler e Mussolini*, 48 (30 May 1940); DGFP D/9/503 (2 June 1940)

42 Armellini, *Diario*, 23-4, 33 (21 June 1940); Faldella, *L'Italia* (1960) 166, 743-4 (5 June 1940)

43 OO 29/451-2 (2 June 1940); OO 30/161 (12 June 1940); DGFP D/9/541

44 F. Rossi, *Mussolini e lo stato maggiore*, 8-10; Messe, *La mia armata*, 25; Anfuso, 151; Roatta, *Otto milioni di baionetti*, 26-7

45 OO 31/161 (12 June 1940)

46 Boelcke, *Kriegspropaganda*, 392; Rintelen, *Mussolini als Bundesgenosse*, 88-90; Westphal, *Heer in Fesseln*, 152; Irving, *Hitler's war*, 129

47 Ciano (2), 280; Zanussi, *Guerra e catastrofe*, 1/23; Canevari, *La guerra*, 2/40

48 DDI 9/5/60; Ciano (2), 281

49 Roatta, 101-2; Faldella (1960), 197; Ciano (4), 563

50 Halder, *Kriegstagebuch*, 1/367, 370 (24 June 1940); *Battaglia delle Alpi*, 47-9, 117-22

51 *Popolo d'Italia*, 21 June 1940; Guerri, *Rapporto al Duce*, 331; Mayneri, *Parla un comandante*, 38; Ciano (2), 289

52 Bottai, *Vent'anni*, 181 (1 July 1940), 184, 189-91; Ciano (2), 281, 297-8, 300; De Begnac, *Palazzo Venezia*, 295 (Sept. 1940)

53 Bastianini, *Uomini, cose, fatti*, 149, 257; Armellini, *Diario*, 56 (15 August. 1940)

54 OO 13/124-5; OO 21/365 (June 1925)

55 *Popolo d'Italia*, 20 June 1940; *ibid.*, 19 July 1940; DDI 9/5/720-1, 757; DGFP D/10/539; OO 35/176; *Critica Fascista*, 1 Aug. 1940, 306

56 Ciano (2), 294 (22 July 1940)

57 Zachariae, *Mussolini si confessa*, 87; OO 32/174; Iurato and Antonelli, *Con Mussolini a Campo Imperatore*, 8

58 Ciano (4), 571-2 (7 July 1940)

59 Page, *L'Americano di Roma*, 607 (Paresce); *Storia e Politica Internazionale*, Dec. 1940, 584

(Bastianini); Phillips, *Ventures in Diplomacy*, 172 (Bastianini); Armellini, *Diario di guerra*, 33 (Grandi)

60 Ciano (4), 590; Dinale, *Quarant' anni di colloqui con lui*, 323–4; Maugeri, *Mussolini mi ha detto*, 24–5; Pini, *Filo diretto*, 206; OO 31/138; *Cronache della Guerra*, 21 Sept. 1940, 383, 386; *Critica Fascista*, 15 July 1940, 299 (Paresce)

61 DDI 9/5/100 (26 June 1940), 187–8 (7 July 1940)

62 OO 32/174–5 (20 Mar. 1945); Zachariae, 86–8

63 Graziani, *Africa*, 42–3; Ciano (2), 189; Armellini, *Diario*, 49; *Cronache*, 16 July 1940, 19; *ibid.*, 20 Aug. 1940, 160; *Rassegna di Cultura*, Sept. 1940, 252 (Rinaldi)

64 Armellini, *Diario*, 47–8, 53, 82, 103, 235; Roatta, 144; Faldeila (1960), 210, 313; *Politica estera Italiana*, 265 (André)

65 DGFP D/10/152; *Hitler e Mussolini*, 55

66 Bandini, *Tecnica della sconfitta*, 882–96; Da Zara, *Pelle d'ammiraglio*, 333–4

67 *Bollettini della guerra*, 31; *Popolo d'Italia*, 17 July 1940; OO 30/166; Da Zara, 336; Roskill, *The Navy at War*, 298; Ciano (2), 292–3

68 Bragadin, *Il dramma della marina*, 107; Weichold, *War in the Mediterranean*, 11, 18; DGFP D/11/257

69 Maugeri, *Mussolini*, 23; Zachariae, 93; Cucco, *Non volevamo perdere*, 84; *Rivista Aeronautica*, Dec. 1940, 504 (Mecozzi)

70 *Führer Conferences* (1940), 93, 104; Weichold, *War in the Mediterranean*, 15

71 Halder, 2/45 (30 July 1940); Van Creveld, *Hitler's Strategy*, 53–5; Weichold, 10; DGFP D/11/984

72 Canevari, *La guerra*, 2/187; Faldella (1960), 249

73 Warlimont, *Im Hauptquartier*, 124; Halder, 2/88, 100, 102; Westphal, 155; *Kriegstagebuch des Oberkommandos*, 1/73 (11 Sept. 1940); Rintelen, *Mussolini als Bundesgenosse*, 93; Spampanato, *Contromemoriale*, 1/164–5

74 *Kriegstagebuch des Oberkommandos*, 1/81 (18 Sept. 1940); *Rommel Papers*, 91; Fuller, *Machine Warfare*, 154–5

75 Graziani, *Africa settentrionale*, 15, 20, 228; St A. 2/000792–3 (19 Aug. 1940)

76 *Rivista Aeronautica*, Feb. 1940, 185–8 (Pricolo); *ibid.*, Dec. 1940, 497; Pricolo, *La regia aeronautica*, 150; *Ala d'Italia*, 30 Dec. 1940, 3

77 Cambria, *Maria José*, 73; Armellini, *Diario*, 91 (23 Sept. 1940); Ciano (2), 304–5, 311; Ciano (4), 589

78 Washington T. 821/126/IT.A.1139 (11 Sept. 1940)

79 Santoro, 1/116–22; Armellini, *Diario*, 88; *Kriegstagebuch des Oberkommandos*, 1/118–19 (Von Pohl, 10 Oct. 1940), 171

80 Puntoni, *Parla Vittorio Emanuele*, 39; Armellini, *Diario*, 48

81 Grazzi, *Il principio della fine*, 100; Guariglia, *Ricordi*, 478

82 OO 35/176 (19 Sept. 1940); Armellini, *Diario*, 152; Faldella *L'Italia* (1960), 762; Reisoli, *Fuoko*, 44–5; *Esercito Italiano*, 124, 196

83 DGFP D/10/538

84 DGFP D/11/256; DDI 9/5/658; Rintelen, 101–2; Faldella (1960), 247–8

85 DGFP D/11/256

86 Washington T. 821/127/It.A.1143 (1 and 3 Oct. 1940); Faldella (1960), 246; F. Rossi *Mussolini e lo stato maggiore*, 76–8

87 Ciano (2), 313–14 (5 Oct. and 12 Oct. 1940)

88 *Processo Graziani*, 1/133; *ibid.*, 2/246

89 *Hitler Directs his War*, 38; Greiner, 'Support', 22; Mueller-Hillebrand, 'Germany and her Allies', 2/71

90 Compare the same document in Mussolini, *Il tempo*, 45–7, with OO 34/430–4; and with F. Rossi, *Mussolini*, 176–83

91 Ciano (3), 17 (18 Jan. 1941)

92 Roatta, *Otto milioni di baionetti*, 127; Armellini, *Diario*, 113, 122

93 F. Rossi, *Mussolini*, 111, 176, 181; DDI 9/5/712, 716

94 Mondini, *Prologo del conflitto*, 220–1; Grazzi, *Il principio della fine*, 125, 218–20; *Processo Roatta*, 63; Amè, *Guerra segreta*, 26–7; Spigo, *Premesse tecniche*, 132; DDI 9/5/644, 701; DGFP D/11/818

95 DDI 9/5/746–7; Bastianini, *Uomini, cose, fatti*, 257–8; Mondini, 229; Packard, *Balcony Empire*, 115; Massock, *Italy from Within*, 224–5; OO 43/43; OO 44/248

96 DDI 9/5/726, 738; Grazzi, 236–8; Pricolo, *Ignavia contro eroismo*, 9

97 Armellini, *Diario*, 145 (9 Nov. 1940); Ciano (2), 317 (24 Oct. 1940)

98 Kordt, *Wahn und Wirklichkeit*, 259–60; DGFP D/11/427, 496; *Greek White Book*, 113; *Kriegstagebuch des Oberkommandos*, 1/125–6 (24–5 Oct. 1940)

99 *Kriegstagebuch des Oberkommandos*, 1/130; Armellini, *Diario*, 128–9

100 DGFP D/11/607, 821–2, 912; Halder, *Kriegstagebuch*, 2/158–9; Keitel, *Memoirs*, 248–9; Greiner, 'Operation Felix', 6; *Hitler's Table Talk*, 175

101 *Bollettini della guerra*, 119–20; OO 30/33; *Popolo d'Italia*, 12 Nov. 1940; *Cronache*, 23 Nov. 1940, 731–3; Gorla, *L'Italia*, 99–100; Melograni, *Rapporti segreti*, 121–3

102 St A. 1/000882 (10 Nov. 1940); Pricolo, *Ignavia*, 108; Grazzi, 257

103 DGFP D/11/818–9; Ciano (2), 320, 327; OO 44/254

104 Waterfield, *Professional Diplomat*, 259

105 Keitel, 120; Irving, *The Trail of the Fox*, 60; Liddell Hart, *The Other Side*, 234–6; Rintelen, *Mussolini als Bundesgenosse*, 101–2

106 Ciano (2), 214; Dinale, *Quarant'anni di colloqui con lui*, 250; Badoglio, *L'Italia*, 30; Lessona, *Memorie*, 367; Volpe, *Storia del movimento fascista*, 224

107 Rintelen, 47; Westphal, *Heer in Fesseln*, 211–12; Dollmann, *The Interpreter*, 182; Zachariae, *Mussolini si confessa*, 50; Ludwig, *Three Portraits*, 79; *New York Times*, 5 June 1938, 31 (H. G. Wells); Kirkpatrick, *Mussolini*, 18; Bastianini, 144

108 Starhemberg, *Between Hitler and Mussolini*, 170; Vittorio Mussolini, *Vita con mio padre*, 167; Ciano (1), 169

109 Bottai, *Vent'anni*, 166; Ciano (2), 236; *Memoriale Grandi*, 18; Lessona, *Un ministro di Mussolini*, 204–5; Vittorio Mussolini, *Vita*, 21; François-Poncet, *Les lettres*, 11

110 Alfieri, 154–5

Chapter 15 Defeat, 1940–3

1 OO 30/173 (26 Oct. 1940)

2 Pricolo, *Ignavia contro eroismo*, 75; Brown, *Bodyguard of Lies*, 49–50; Messe, *La mia armata in Tunisia*, 41; Ceva, 'La guerre', 134; De Risio, *Generali, servizi segreti e fascismo*, 35–6; Barclay, *Against Great Odds*, 13–14, 29

3 Weygand, *Rappelé au service*, 3/28, 39; *Minerva*, 15 June 1940, 261

4 Ciano (2), 336

5 Bottai, *Vent'anni*, 189, 194 (15 Nov. 1940); Gorla, *L'Italia*, 167–8; C. Senise, *Quando ero capo*, 97

6 *Prima offensiva*, 1/119 (12 Dec. 1940); St A. 20/009426 (Reichert, 26 Dec. 1940)

7 Ciano (2), 330 (4 Dec. 1940)

8 DGFP D/11/917, 998; U. Cavallero, *Comando supremo*, 32; Ciano (2), 336

9 Washington T. 821/127/IT.A.1141 (31 Dec. 1940); DGFP D/11/802; OO 35/189; Gorla, *L'Italia nella seconda guerra*, 105; Ciano (2), 335; Armellini, *Diario*, 158

10 Caracciolo, *E poi?*, 115; Santoro, *L'aeronautica*, 1/66, 167; U. Cavallero, 101–3; Canevari, *La guerra*, 1/210–11

11 Armellini, *Diario*, 177, 179, 243

12 Ciano (3), 14, 17

13 Ciano (2), 329, 335, 339; Ciano (3), 13–14

14 DGFP D/11/986; Simoni, *Berlino ambasciata*, 190, 192 (30 Dec. 1940); Melograni, *Rapporti segreti*, 126; Armellini, *Diario*, 183

15 DGFP D/11/821 (8 Dec. 1940); *Führer Conferences*, 136 (27 Dec. 1940)

16 DGFP D/11/1006–9, 1016 (4 Jan. 1941)

17 DGFP D/11/45, 76, 229, 269, 826–7; DGFP D/12/13; Sadat, *Revolt on the Nile*, 34–6; Hitler, *The Testament*, 70–1; Weichold, *War in the Mediterranean*, 48

18 DGFP D/11/986; Rintelen, *Mussolini als Bundesgenosse*, 128, 134; *Führer Conferences*, 8 (8 Jan. 1941)

19 DGFP D/11/845, 987; DGFP D/12/28, 45, 62–3; Belot, *The Struggle*, 95; Simoni, 194; Langer and Gleason, *The Undeclared War*, 392 (Phillips)

20 DGFP D/11/999; Ciano (3), 13

21 Alfieri, *Due dittatori*, 115–21; *Daily Telegraph*, 22 Apr. 1941 (John Whitaker)

22 Gorla, 139; Phillips, *Ventures in Diplomacy*, 179; Soffici and Prezzolini, *Diari*, 96; Bottai, *Vent'anni*, 201

23 DGFP D/12/199; Simoni, 212; Roatta, *Otto milioni di baionetti*, 135

24 Pricolo, *Ignavia*, 141; Puntoni, *Parla Vittorio Emanuele*, 45

25 OO 30/246 (14 May 1941); Soffici and Prezzolini, *Diari*, 101; *Bollettini della guerra*, 216–21; *Cronache della Guerra*, 24 May 1941, 645; *Battaglia risolutiva*, 17–19

26 OO 30/93; DGFP D/12/358

27 *Bollettini della guerra*, 223–4; *Popolo d'Italia*, 30 Mar. 1941; Maugeri, *From the Ashes*, 25–8; Lewin, *Ultra Goes to War*, 196; Brown, 51

28 *Azioni navali*, 505 (31 Mar. 1941); U. Cavallero, 119; (25 July 1941); Pricolo, *La regia aeronautica*, 360

29 DGFP D/12/360

30 OO 30/71–2

31 Grazzi, *Il principio della fine*, 257

32 *Actes et documents du Saint Siège*, 4/421

33 Washington T. 821/127/IT.A.1146 (31 Mar. 1941); OO 30/244; Rintelen, 139–40; U. Cavallero, 82

34 OO 30/195–6; Halder, *Kriegstagebuch*, 2/335–7; Irving, *Hitler's War*, 260

35 U. Cavallero, 86

36 DGFP D/12/647 (Rintelen, 23 Apr. 1941)

37 Halder, 2/374–5 (21–2 Apr. 1941); Keitel, *Memoirs*, 142; DGFP D/12/646; Rintelen, 140

38 OO 30/71, 93; OO 44/262–4; OO 34/434; Anfuso, *Roma, Berlino, Salò*, 219–20; Gorla, 178 (8 May 1941); Pettinato, *Tutto da rifare*, 79; Araldi, *Il giuoco*, 224, 238

39 Puntoni, 19; Gorla, 191; Ciano (3), 24

40 Ciano (3), 60 (17 July 1941)

41 St A. 25/012255 (July 1942), 012266 (31 Aug. 1941); Roatta, *Otto milioni di baionetti*, 166; *Senato: Commissioni*, 1477 (Bottai, 23 May 1942)

42 Kitsikis, 'La famine',17; *Rassegna d'Oltremare*, Jan. 1941, 33; DGFP D/13/218–19, 513, 677; OO 31/18

43 *Senato: commissioni*, 1382 (Zupelli, 18 May 1942); Gorla, 362, 418–19; Ciano (3), 133

44 Ciano (3), 85 (11 Nov. 1941); OO 31/97 (31 July 1942); Apih, *Italia*, 423–6; Rusinow, *Italy's Austrian Heritage*, 280; Maurano, *Ricordi*, 287, 293, 315; Zanussi, *Guerra e catastrofe*, 1/241; Duroselle, *Le conflit*, 109

45 Ciano (3), 27 (6 May 1941)

46 OO 30/55–7, 113

47 *Due anni di guerra*, 39

48 *Rommel Papers*, 111; Messe, *La mia armata in Tunisia*, 52; Westphal, *Heer in Fesseln*, 160–1; *Prima offensiva*, 1/371–2

49 *Processo Graziani*, 2/307, 338; Gorla, *L'Italia nella seconda guerra*, 218, 262, 294

50 Gorla, 217; (5 July 1941); Bottai, *Vent'anni*, 207; *Rommel Papers*, 139

51 DGFP D/13/191–2 (Hitler, 20 July 1941); Caviglia, *Diario*, 324; Rintelen, *Mussolini als Bundesgenosse*, 156–9

52 *Leggi* (1941), 3/2302–3 (27 June 1941); U. Cavallero, *Comando supremo*, 102–3

53 Ciano (3), 38

54 OO 30/98; Gorla, 173–4

55 Gorla, 219; U. Cavallero, 127; Ciano (1), 132

56 Maugeri, *Mussolini*, 28; Gorla, 173, 175, 378–9 (21 Nov. 1942); Ciano (3), 60 (15 July 1941), 95

57 Ciano (3), 29, 51 (30 June 1941)

58 Roatta, 155

59 Bottai, *Vent'anni*, 199; Gorla, 201

60 De Lorenzis, *Dal primo all'ultimo giorno*, 94

61 OO 30/147; U. Cavallero, 394, 400

62 *Akten zur deutschen Politik*, E/4/172 (26 Oct. 1942)

63 Alfieri, *Due dittatori di fronte*, 158; Ciano (3), 38–9

64 D'Aroma, *Mussolini*, 293; Agricola, *Mussolini in prigionia*, 28

65 Ciano (2), 180, 297, 320; DDI 9/5/26; DGFP D/11/1032; *Critica Fascista*, 15 Nov. 1940, 30; *Cronache*, 19 Apr. 1941, 501; Rossi, *The Russo-German Alliance*, 146–7; Alfieri, 206, 230

66 OO 30/84, 103; Keitel, 159; Alfieri, 290

67 *Rassegna di Politica Internazionale*, Sept. 1938, 501–2; Gorla, 216; Ciano (3), 47; Wagnière, *Dix-huit ans à Rome*, 204; DGFP D/6/735

68 Ciano (3), 60 (15 July 1941)

69 OO 30/211–12 (24 July 1941)

70 OO 30/104, 211–12; Ciano (3), 56; Anfuso, 239

71 Ciano (3), 63; *Hitler e Mussolini*, 105; Irving, *Hitler's War*, 308

72 Ciano (3), 51 (15 July 1941)

73 Acerbo, *Fra due plotoni*, 457; OO 30/112; DGFP D/13/313–14; Ciano (3), 49

74 Halder, *Kriegstagebuch*, 3/219

75 Alfieri, 220

76 Anfuso, *Roma, Berlino, Salò*, 249–50

77 Bullock, *Hitler*, 658; OO 30/117; Alfieri, 223

78 Messe, *La guerra al fronte Russo*, 53

79 OO 35/201

80 DGFP D/13/695; Ciano (3), 71

81 *BBC Monitoring Service*, 13 Oct. 1941; *Cronache*, 18 Oct. 1941, 435; *Critica Fascista*, 15 Nov. 1941, 27

82 DGFP D/13/660; Messe, *La guerra*, 50, 178

83 *Hitler Directs his War*, 33 (20 May 1943); DGFP D/12/648; Rintelen, *Mussolini als Bundesgenosse*, 146

84 Ciano (3), 30, 38, 41–3, 55–6, 61; Anfuso, 241

85 Alfieri, 227–8; Ciano (4), 677; Bottai, *Vent'anni*, 226; C. Senise, *Quando ero capo*, 102; U. Cavallero, *Comando supremo*, 110; Bianchi, *Perchè e come cadde il fascismo*, 792 (De Bono)

86 Anfuso, 505; Alfieri, 164–5; Donosti, *Mussolini e l'Europa*, 92–4; DGFP D/12/128; DGFP D/13/454, 562; Gorla, *L'Italia nella seconda guerra*, 200–1; Bottai, *Vent'anni*, 204; OO 32/199

87 Weichold, *War in the Mediterranean*, 66; DGFP D/13/ 938–9

88 U. Cavallero, 155; OO 30/220; *Rommel Papers*, 369; *Seconda offensiva*, 82–3; Weichold, 67; C. Cavallero, *Il dramma*, 127

89 OO 31/24 (9 Mar. 1942)

90 *Popolo d'Italia*, 22 Jan. 1941; *Come si mangia in Europa*, 4, 32

91 OO 31/236 (1 Nov. 1942); DGFP D/12/110 (16 Feb. 1941)

92 Gorla, 242 (27 Sept. 1941); Bottai, *Vent'anni*, 299; Ciano (3), 66; Soffici and Prezzolini, *Diari*, 140

93 Ciano (2), 216 (20 Jan. 1940)

94 OO 31/28 (26 Mar. 1942)

95 *Popolo d'Italia*, 10 Mar. 1942; OO 31/72

96 *Popolo d'Italia*, 26 Apr. 1942

97 OO 31/85 (24 June 1943), 292; OO 32/69; OO 44/277

98 Bottai, *Vent'anni*, 225–6 (27 May 1942)

99 OO 31/191 (26 May 1942); Vittorio Mussolini, *Mussolini*, 52–3; Caviglia, 366

100 OO 31/76 (26 May 1942); Cortesi, *Mussolini*, (24 June 1943)

101 OO 31/72

102 OO 31/286–7; *Gerarchia*, Sept. 1942, 374; *ibid.*, July 1943, 253–5

103 Gorla, 213 (5 July 1941), 222, 243–4; Longanesi, *Parliamo dell'elefante*, 69; Ciano (3), 66, 138; Tamaro, *Venti anni* 3/455

104 *Critica Fascista*, 15 Mar. 1943, 117; Marroni, *Mussolini se stesso*, 9–10

105 *Storia e Politica Internazionale*, June 1942, 159, 163; Ceva, *La condotta*, 194–5 (Perrone); *Augustea*, 1 Oct. 1942, 602

106 OO 31/72–5 (26 May 1942)

107 Gorla, 348 (11 Aug. 1942); Sperco, *L'écroulement*, 76; Kesselring, 'Italy as a Military Ally', 7; Kesselring, 'The War', 1/10

108 St A. 234/062202–3 (Mussolini, 17 April 1943)

109 D'Aroma, *Mussolini*, 195, 200 (Aug. 1939), 214; OO 30/57; OO 43/39; Ciano (1), 13 (6 Sept. 1937)

110 Ciano (2), 81; Ciano (3), 36–7; Pozzi, *Come li ho visti io*, 162–3 (3 July 1943); Rachele Mussolini, *La mia vita*, 168; Packard, *Balcony Empire*, 227

111 Dinale, *Quarant'anni di colloqui con lui*, 254–7; OO 35/163; *Popolo d'Italia*, 2 June 1940 (Barzini)

112 Guariglia, *Ricordi*, 443; Guarneri, *Battaglie economiche*, 2/498; Vergani, *Ciano*, 82

113 Grazzi, *Il principio della fine*, 219; Gorla, 217 (5 July 1941); OO 30/100 (10 June 1941); OO 44/264

114 DGFP D/11/152 (22 Sept. 1940)

115 OO 31/121; DGFP D/13/941–2 (3 Dec. 1941)

116 OO 30/155 (3 Jan. 1942); OO 31/21; Gorla, 266, 275 (27 Dec. 1941); Ciano (3), 93–4, 104

117 C. Senise, *Quando ero capo*, 99; Galbiati, *Il 25 luglio*, 127; Bottai, *Vent'anni*, 215

118 Ciano (3), 115

119 *Rommel Papers*, 181; Westphal, *Heer in Fesseln*, 173–4; Trizzino, *Gli amici dei nemici*, 145, 169–80

120 Mellenthin, *Panzer Battles*, 87–8; *Rommel Papers*, 183

121 Gorla, *L'Italia nella seconda guerra*, 284

122 OO 31/25, 34, 47, 69; De Begnac, *Palazzo Venezia*, 112; Gorla, 321; Guerri, *Rapporto al Duce*, 195 (27 Jan. 1942)

123 OO 37/228 (28 Sept. 1942); Dinale, 172–3

124 OO 31/51–2 (25 Apr. 1942)

125 Ciano (3), 140 (24 Mar. 1942)

126 Tamaro, *Due anni*, 3/552; Bianchi, *Perchè e come cadde*, 792 (De Bono, 24 Jan. 1942)

127 Ciano (3), 129, 134

128 Ciano (3), 129; (20 Feb. 1942); Rintelen, 218

129 Roatta, 148

130 Rintelen, *Mussolini als Bundesgenosse*, 257; Navarra, *Memorie*, 180; Donosti, *Mussolini e l'Europa*, 86

131 Fest, *Hitler*, 611; Dollmann, *Roma*, 79; Roatta, *Otto milioni di baionetti*, 155

132 *Akten zur deutschen Politik*, E/4/41–4 (8 Oct. 1942)

133 C. Senise, *Quando ero capo*, 50; Guariglia, *Ricordi*, 616; Donosti, 82–3

134 Moellhausen, *La carta perdente*, 291; Schmidt, *Hitler's Interpreter*, 64; Rintelen, 193; Anfuso, *Roma, Berlino, Salò*, 59–60; Donosti, 84; Navarra, *Memorie*, 180; Dollmann, *Roma*, 79–80; Bertoldi, *I tedeschi*, 131–2

135 Ciano (3), 164, (26 May 1942), 174; Bianchi, *Perchè e come cadde il fascismo*, 795; U. Cavallero, *Comando supremo*, 281

136 Pedoja, *La disfatta nel deserto*, 24; Dinale, 171; Puntoni, *Parla Vittorio Emanuele*, 91; Monelli, *Roma*, 11; Navarra, 181; Ciano (3), 167 (2 June 1942)

137 Westphal, *Heer in Fesseln*, 212; Rintelen, 173; Navarra, 183; Ciano (3), 184

138 Pedoja, 84–5; Bottai, *Vent'anni*, 227–8; Puntoni, 92; Gorla, 362

139 *Annali dell'Africa* (1942), 2/289; Pedoja, 92–3, 98; Ciano (3), 185

140 *Seconda controffensiva*, 388 (19 July 1942)

141 Bottai, *Vent'anni*, 90; Ciano (2), 13, 84–5 (12 Nov. 1941); Rintelen, 208

142 OO 31/134; Bragadin, *Vampe sul mare*, 42, 48–53; Trizzino, *sopra di noi*, 194–6, 202–10; Morison, *The Battle of the Atlantic*, 380; *Sette Giorni*, 30 May 1942, 7; *Tempo*, 9 July 1942, 30

143 U. Cavallero, 292/3; Roatta, 188; Messe, *La guerra*, 169–70, 174–9; Faldella, *L'Italia* (1960), 468

144 Bottai, *Vent'anni*, 239; U. Cavallero, 417–18 (18 Dec. 1942); *Hitler e Mussolini*, 145, 152 (25 Mar. 1943)

145 OO 31/120 (2 Dec. 1942)

146 OO 31/138 (3 Jan. 1943)

147 OO 31/120–1; *Almanacco del 'Popolo d'Italia'* (1942), 110

148 OO 32/173–4; Bottai, *Vent'anni*, 239 (15 Dec. 1942); Dolfin, *Con Mussolini nella tragedia*, 74–6; Pini, *Itinerario tragico*, 252

149 Anfuso, 561

150 Winterbotham, *Ultra Secret*, 79–80

151 Ciano (3), 190 (11 Aug. 1942); D'Aroma, *Mussolini*, 257

152 *Akten zur deutschen Politik*, E/4/174, 176 (23 Oct. 1942); St A. 1/000123–4, 000138 (1 Oct. 1942); *Augustea*, 1 Oct. 1942, 643 (Appelius)

153 *Akten zur deutschen Politik*, E/4/148–9 (11 Oct. 1942)

154 OO 31/236 (1 Nov. 1942)

155 OO 34/306; Bottai, *Vent'anni*, 297

156 Maravigna, *Come abbiamo perduto*, 341; Messe, *La mia armata*, 79–80; Ruge, *Sea Warfare*, 196; U. Cavallero, 367; Rintelen, 175; *Seconda controffensiva*, 393 (22 July 1942)

157 Kesselring, 'The War', 1/76; Messe, *La mia armata*, 91; *Rommel Papers*, 395; Winterbotham, 77; Macintyre, *The Battle for the Mediterranean*, 201; U. Cavallero, 364; Rintelen, 177

158 OO 31/122; *Actes et documents du Saint Siège*, 7/80–1 (10 Nov. 1942)

159 Guerri, *Rapporto al Duce*, 405 (28 Nov. 1942)

160 *Kersten Memoirs*, 159; Vergani, *Ciano*, 192

161 OO 31/117; Ciano (3), 214; Westphal, 170

162 Gorla, *L'Italia nella seconda guerra*, 290; Dolfin, 225; Brocchi, *'L'Universale'*, 14 (Montanelli)

163 Guariglia, *Ricordi*, 452; Zachariae, *Mussolini si confessa*, 23

164 Bottai, *Vent'anni*, 30–1; Pariani, *Chiacchiere e realtà*, 17

165 OO 29/194; De Begnac, *Palazzo Venezia*, 650; Mellini, *Guerra diplomatica*, 127; Roatta, *Otto milioni di baionetti*, 21; Bastianini, *Uomini, cose, fatti*, 28–9

166 *Rassegna di Cultura*, Sept 1940, 250; Dolfin, 88, 136; Bottai, *Vent'anni*, 95; Cione, *Storia della repubblica*, 189; OO 32/157; *Camera: commissioni*, 1244 (14 Apr. 1943)

167 A. Sapori, *Mondo finito*, 269; Packard, *Balcony Empire*, 176; Caviglia, 322

168 OO 32/170, 177; Gorla, 25–6; Soffici and Prezzolini, *Diari*, 190; St A. 234/062208 (17 Apr. 1943)

169 OO 31/42 (18 Apr. 1942); Massola, *Gli scioperi*, 180 (Mussolini to party directorate on 17 Apr. 1943); Dinale, *Quarant'anni di colloqui con lui*, 173; Bottai, *Vent'anni*, 222 (28 Mar. 1942)

170 *Dottrina Fascista*, June 1940, 775; Mezzetti, *Mussolini*, 201–4

171 St A. 117/031966 (10 May 1941)

172 St A. 116/031768 (5 Mar. 1943); *Popolo d'Italia*, 17 June 1941; *Critica Fascista*, 15 Dec. 1938, 49

173 St A. 43/022950–6 (26 Apr. 1943)

174 Luciolli, *Palazzo Chigi*, 120–1; Carboni, *Memorie*, 143; Castellano, *Come firmai l'armistizio*, 34

175 *Settimana Incom*, 14 Jan. 1956 (Giuriati)

176 Bottai, *Vent'anni*, 78; C. Senise, *Quando ero capo*, 113

177 OO 31/24; Giolli, 56; *Relazioni Internazionali*, 22 May 1943, 458; C. Senise, 113; St A. 231/061189, 061259–60 (7 July 1943)

178 Bastianini, *Uomini, cose, fatti*, 244; Phillips, *Ventures in Diplomacy*, 114; Alfieri, *Due dittatori*, 113; Guarneri, *Battaglie economiche*, 2/244; Anfuso, *Roma, Berlino, Salò*, 107

179 OO 32/177 (20 Mar. 1945); De Begnac, *Palazzo Venezia*, 109 (Sept. 1939); Bastianini, 41

180 Scorza, *La notte del Gran Consiglio*, 169, 189–90 (July 1943); D'Aroma, *Mussolini*, 217 (February. 1940): Leto, *Polizia segreta*, 76; Galbiati, *Il 25 luglio*, 225, 306; Lessona, *Memorie*, 333; Spampanato, *Contromemoriale*, 1/32

181 Westphal, *Heer in Fesseln*, 211

182 C. Senise, 152; Bottai, *Vent'anni*, 266; Gorla, 365

183 Caracciolo, 105; Gorla, 408; Vergani, *Ciano*, 177; Alfieri, 322; Bastianini, 52

184 Soffici and Prezzolini, *Diari*, 179–80 (Bottai, 22 Jan. 1943); Gorla, 173, 182, (8 May 1941), 221

185 Scorza, *La notte*, 154–5, 185; Jacomoni, *La politica dell' Italia*, 259; Moellhausen, *La carta perdente*, 320; Bastianini, 56; Ceva, *La condotta*, 25

186 C. Senise, 115–16; Zachariae, 53

187 C. Senise, 120; Giannini, *Io spia dell'ovra*, 2/30; Bottai, *Vent'anni*, 230; Galbiati, 88

188 Scorza, *La notte, 143–4 (25 July 1943); St A. 159/046289–90; Conti, Dal taccuino*, 681–3; (12 May 1940); C. Senise, 97; *Politica Nuova*, 1 May 1942, 50 (Spampanato)

189 Zingali, *L'invasione della Sicilia*, 71–2; OO 43/54 (5 Aug. 1941)

190 De Begnac, *Palazzo Venezia*, 294 (Aug. 1939); Ciano (2), 335 (14 Dec. 1940); Cucco, *Non volevamo perdere*, 42–3; *Bibliografia Fascista*, Oct. 1940, 760 (Evola); Benelli, *Schiavitù*, 54; Frassati, *Il destino*, 39 (10 June 1939); C. Senise, 118

191 Gorla, 250; Federzoni, *Italia di ieri*, 276; Guerri, *Rapporto*, 70–1

192 D'Aroma, *Mussolini*, 265; Bianchi, *Perchè e come cadde il fascismo*, 727 (26 Jan. 1943)

193 *Akten zur deutschen Politik*, E/5/299; Anfuso, 407

194 St A. 1/000194–5 (29 Jan. 1943); Favagrossa, *Perchè perdemmo*, 289

195 Favagrossa, 282; U. Cavallero, *Comando Supremo*, 227; Puntoni, *Parla Vittorio Emanuele*, 95

196 Washington T. 821/125. IT. 122 (8 Mar. 1943; 2 Apr. 1943); St A. 1/000151 (Scuero, 1 Oct. 1942)

197 Washington T. 821/144. IT.1223–6 (8 Mar. 1943); Roatta, *Otto milioni di baionetti*, 246; *Critica Fascista*, 1 Feb. 1943, 83

198 *Rivista Aeronautica*, May 1942, 14–19 (Mecozzi)

199 Favagrossa, 283; Washington T. 821/125 (11 Feb. 1943); Federzoni, *Italia di ieri*, 179; Rintelen, 198

200 Bastianini, 93; Favagrossa, 293; Washington T. 821/125 (10 Mar. 1943)

201 OO 32/325 (28 Feb. 1944); OO 34/367; Cucco, *Non volevamo perdere*, 84; Zachariae, *Mussolini si confessa*, 70–1; *Politica Nuova*, 1 May 1942, 50

202 OO 32/174–5 (20 Mar. 1945); D'Aroma, *Mussolini*, 273 (May 1943); Bastianini, 98

203 St A. 292/089626

204 Cortesi, *Mussolini*, 32–3 (24 June 1943); Ciano (3), 58 (11 July 1941)

205 OO 30/155 (3 Jan. 1942); OO 31/33–4, 119 (2 Dec. 1942), 144

206 DGFP D/12/102 (15 Feb. 1941); Kesselring, *Memoirs*, 108; Packard, *Balcony Empire*, 175–6; Massock, *Italy from Within*, 331; Sperco, *L'écroulement*, 65–6; Bottai, *Vent'anni*, 231; Pettinato, *Gli intellettuali*, 12, 31; *Daily Telegraph*, 22 Apr. 1941

207 C. Senise, *Quando ero capo*, 135–8; Leto, *Ovra*, 240–3; Galbiati, 129–32; Puntoni, 77; Ciano (3), 58; Soffici and Prezzolini, *Diari*, 99

208 Caviglia, *Diario*, 326 (14 Apr. 1941)

209 OO 31/74–6 (26 May 1942)

210 Guerri, *Rapporto*, 100 (24 Jan. 1942)

211 Bottai, *Vent'anni*, 234 (21 Nov. 1942)

212 Dolfin, *Con Mussolini*, 218; *Testamento politico di Mussolini*, 31; Maugeri, *Mussolini*, 26; Tamaro, *Due anni*, 1/77; Ciano (3), 56–7; Bastianini, *Uomini, cose, fatti*, 34; OO 32/178

213 OO31/163–5 (11 Mar. 1942); Benedetti *Benedetto Croce*, 96; Canevari, *Graziani*, 149; Dinale, *Quarant'anni*, 181, 184; Tamaro, *Due anni*, 2/371; Guerri, *Rapporto*, 84

214 Bertoldi, *Mussolini*, 47; OO 32/159

215 OO 31/50–1 (25 Apr. 1942); Dollmann, *Roma nazista*, 81; Bastianini, 37

216 OO 31/25 (9 Mar. 1942); OO 44/284 (27 May 1942); Zachariae, 67–8; Gorla. *L'Italia nella seconda guerra*, 393–4 (23 Jan. 1943); Ciano (2), 219, 221 (7 Feb. 1940), 281, 297 (5 Aug. 1940)

217 Ciano (2), 214 (15 Jan. 1940); Zachariae, 207; Welles, *Time for Decision*, 69–70

218 Ciano (2), 296; Rachele Mussolini, *La mia vita*, 184

219 Lessona, *Memorie*, 426; Maurano, *Ricordi*, 213–14; Giannini, 2/70; Ciano (3), 76 (21 Oct. 1941)

220 *New York Times*, 28 July 1940; Massock, 206–8; Matthews, *I frutti del fascismo*, 333–4

221 *New York Times*, 11 Aug. 1939

222 Simoni, *Berlino*, 368

Defeat, 1940–3

223 Matteini, *Ordini alla stampa*, 87, 184, 233; *Corriere della Sera*, 20 Apr. 1941
224 OO 31/68 (14 May 1942)
225 St A. 141/040053 (Mussolini, 24 Dec. 1943); Bottai, *Vent'anni*, 207 (23 July 1941)
226 Ciano (3), 76 (Bottai, 21 Oct. 1941), 242 (16 Jan. 1943); Pozzi, *Come li ho visti io*, 121; Rintelen, 186
227 Truelove, 'The irritable colon syndrome', 307–12; Burnett, 'A syndrome following prolonged intake of milk', 787–94
228 Pozzi, 114; Bottai, *Vent'anni*, 227–8, 239–40; Gorla, 367–70, 373, 375, 378, 386; *Augustea*, 1 Oct. 1942, 646 (Pascazio)
229 Gorla, 370–1 (23 Oct. 1942); Puntoni, 98 (Hazon, 27 Oct. 1942)
230 *Akten*, E/5/138 (27 Jan. 1943); Rachele Mussolini, 173; Pozzi, 213–15 (19–20 Nov. 1942)
231 FO 4924/E/257792 (Mackensen, 16 Jan. 1943); Ciano (3), 239
232 Malaparte, *Kàputt*, 595; Page, *L'Americano di Roma*, 646; Alfieri, *Due dittatori*, 263
233 Susmel, *Vita sbagliata*, 267; Leto, *Ovra*, 175–6; Giannini, 2/79; De Begnac, *Palazzo Venezia*, 664
234 Maurano, *Ricordi*, 260; Page, 623–4, 822
235 Leto, *Ovra*, 198–9; Spampanato, *Contromemoriale*, 1/226; Pini–Susmel, *Mussolini*, 4/66
236 Ciano (3), 207; Monelli, *Mussolini*, 223
237 Ciano (3), 143, 166/8, 174–7, 239; Freddi, *Il cinema*, 1/354, 374–5; *Corriere della Sera*, 29 Aug. 1943; Luciano, *Rapporto al Duce*, 6–7; Cantelmo, *Mussolini*, 188–9; Edda Ciano, *My Truth*, 182–5; C. Senise, 154
238 Gorla, 362; Puntoni, 148; Biondi, *La fabbrica del Duce*, 112; Bandini, *Vita e morte*, 181; Maugeri, *From the Ashes*, 105
239 C. Senise, *Quando ero capo*, 40–2; Leto, *Polizia*, 163; FO 4924/E/257596 (Mackensen, 29 May 1942)

Chapter 16 The fall from power

1 Federzoni, *Italia di ieri*, 275; Goebbels, *Diaries*, 274, 292; Dollmann, *Roma, nazista*, 127; U. Cavallero, *Comando supremo*, 433
2 Anfuso, *Roma, Berlino, Salò*, 337; Von Plehwe, *The End of an Alliance*, 17; Silva, *Io difendo la monarchia*, 141; Kallay, *Hungarian Premier*, 165; Giudice, *Benito Mussolini*, 580; T. Senise, *Mussolini ... dal punto di vista psichiatrico*, 26, 37; Bertoldi, *Mussolini*, 182–3 (Pozzi); Veneziani, *Vent'anni di beffe*, 345 (Mingazzini); Settimelli, *Edda contro Benito* 83–6; Canevari, *La guerra*, 2/755, 758; Gorla, *L'Italia nella seconda guerra*, 352, 358, 420; Bandini, *Vita e morte segreta*, 180–1
3 Kallay, 167, 176
4 Fanelli, *Agonia di un regime*, 38; Paolucci, *Il mio piccolo mondo*, 414; Leto, *Ovra*, 250; Rintelen, *Mussolini als Bundesgenosse*, 196, 198
5 Zangrandi, *Il lungo viaggio*, 506; Deakin, *The Brutal Friendship*, 220 (Feb. 1943)
6 St A. 234/062201 (17 Apr. 1943); OO 31/162–3 (11 Mar. 1943)
7 OO 31/142 (3 Jan. 1943); Ciano (3), 245; Bottai, *Vent'anni*, 248
8 OO 31/144; Gorla, 242–3
9 Bottai, *Vent'anni*, 237 (2 Dec. 1942); Washington T. 821/125 (5 Feb. 1943 and 9 Mar. 1943); Irving, *The Trail of the Fox*, 258–9
10 Vergani, *Ciano*, 228–9; Gorla, 389, 395
11 Gorla, 393; *Akten zur deutschen Politik*, E/5/139 (27 Jan. 1943); Bianchi, *Perchè e come cadde il fascismo*, 729 (26 Jan. 1943)

12 Gorla, 394 (23 Jan. 1943)

13 De Begnac, *Palazzo Venezia*, 643 (Oct. 1941); U. Cavallero, 357 (28 Oct. 1942)

14 *Akten zur deutschen Politik*, E/4/150 (11 Oct. 1942); *ibid.* E/5/296–7 (25 Feb. 1943); *Hitler e Mussolini*, 145 (8 Mar. 1943)

15 Washington T. 321/126 (22 Apr. 1944)

16 Washington T. 821/125 (5 Feb. 1943); *Akten zur deutschen Politik*, E/4/522–3 (16 Dec. 1942)

17 Pozzi, *Come li vistiio*, 131 (20 Feb. 1943)

18 OO 31/51, 70, 137; *Popolo d'Italia*, 2 Oct. 1942; Bottai, *Vent'anni*, 257 (14 Apr. 1943)

19 OO 34/287

20 St A. 266/076859–77; Gorla, 370, 407; Acerbo, *Fra due plotoni*, 485; Dollmann, *The Interpreter*, 207

21 OO 31/202 (19 July 1943)

22 *Akten zur deutschen Politik*, E/4/257 (7 Nov. 1942)

23 *Akten zur deutschen Politik*, E/5/399 (13 Mar. 1943); *Journal de Genève*, 26 July 1945

24 Cucco, *Non volevamo perdere*, 119, 251; Spampanato, *Contromemoriale*, 3/11–13; Tamaro, *Due anni*, 1/176

25 Kallay, 147–8, 154–8, 161

26 St A. 53/026570 (Bismarck, 25 Mar. 1943); Alfieri, *Due dittatori*, 292; Bastianini, *Uomini, cose, fatti*, 96; Dollmann, *Roma nazista*, 80, 147; Simoni, *Berlino*, 331; Deakin, 264

27 Dollmann, *The Interpreter*, 208; Alfieri, 294; Von Plehwe, 9; Bastianini, 95–7; Monelli, *Roma*, 58–9; Irving, *Hitler's War*, 504

28 OO 31/240; Pozzi, 143–5 (8–9 Apr. 1943)

29 Bastianini, 95–6; Ambrosio, 'Questionnaire', 3–4

30 Bastianini, 159; Simoni, 331; Dollmann, *Roma nazista*, 147; Alfieri, 155; Zachariae, *Mussolini si confessa*, 91–2

31 *Hitler Directs his War*, 37 (20 May 1943)

32 Irving, *Hitler's War*, 519–21

33 *Führer Conferences* (1943), 14, 30, 32; Westphal, *Heer in Fesseln*, 218

34 OO 34/308–9, 319

35 *Actes et documents du Saint Siège*, 7/318, 331 (10 and 12 May 1943)

36 Bastianini, 117–18; Guariglia, *Ricordi*, 574

37 Spampanato, 1/343 (14 June 1943)

38 Bastianini, 111–12

39 Gorla, 421 (4 June 1943); Washington T. 621/144 (Ambrosio's diary, 17, 26–7 May, 7–14 June); Rachele Mussolini, *La mia vita*, 182; Pozzi, 157–8; Tamaro, *Due anni*, 1/76 (Santillo)

40 *Actes et documents du Saint Siège*, 7/331–2 (12 May 1943)

41 OO 31/249; Bottai, *Vent'anni*, 261–2; Washington T. 821/125 (4 May 1943); *Führer Conferences* (1943), 30–2

42 OO 31/196; Gorla, *L'Italia nella seconda guerra*, 424; Leonardi, *Luglio 1943*, 49; Zingali, *L'invasione della Sicilia*, 91–2

43 *Actes et documents du Saint Siège*, 7/335 (13 May 1943)

44 OO 31/141; Pozzi, *Come li ho visti io*, 157 (25 June 1943); Washington T. 821/125 (25 June 1943)

45 Bottai, *Vent'anni*, 265 (2 July 1943)

46 *Akten zur deutschen Politik*, E/5/306 (25 Feb. 1943)

47 OO 31/197 (3 Jan. 1943); Dinale, *Quarant'anni di colloqui con lui*, 208; Cortesi, *Mussolini e il fascismo*, 24, 40 (24 June 1943)

48 *Actes et documents du Saint Siège*, 7/92 (15 Nov. 1942)

49 *Actes et documents du Saint Siège*, 8/362 (1 Dec. 1941); Ciano (3), 92

The fall from power

50 OO 31/107 (1 Oct. 1942), 124–5, 159 (11 Mar. 1943); OO 31/190; *Führer Conferences*, 32 (13 May 1943); Pedoja, *La disfatta*, 38, 83–4; Cortesi, 31–2; Monelli, *Roma*, 1943, 11

51 OO 30/31 (18 Nov. 1940); Dinale, 163; *Relazioni Internazionali*, 8 May 1943, 405; *Due anni di guerra*, 57 (Gayda)

52 OO 31/126 (2 Dec. 1942), 140; *Akten zur deutschen*, (25 Feb. 1943); Gorla, 122

53 Dinale, 320; Zachariae, 76–7

54 OO 31/128 (2 Dec. 1942); D'Aroma, *Mussolini*, 253 (July 1942), 291; Pozzi, 162 (3 July 1943)

55 *Popolo d'Italia*, 25 July 1943; OO 31/133, 139, 195 (24 June 1943); *Antieuropa*, 1942, 8/354–5; *Politica*, Apr. 1943, 167; Pozzi, 165; *Giornale d'Italia*, 17 Feb. 1943; Matteini, *Ordini alla stampa*, 254; Casini, *Una volontà*, 68

56 OO 34/324

57 Faldella, *L'Italia* (1960), 597–602; Cucco, *Non volevamo perdere*, 81; Washington T.821/126 (3 May 1943)

58 Tur, *Plancia ammiraglio*, 3/464; Federzoni, *Italia di ieri*, 275; Gorla, 276, 350

59 Zuckerman, *From Apes to Warlords*, 186–94

60 OO 32/325 (28 Feb. 1944); OO 34/322; Westphal, 219

61 *Processo Roatta*, 235–6; Bianchi, *Perchè e come cadde il fascismo*, 754–5 (Cini, 19 June 1943)

62 St A. 161/046634–38 (Cini, 24 June 1943)

63 Scoppa, *Colloqui*, 110, 114; Bastianini, *Uomini, cose, fatti*, 113–14

64 Bottai, *Vent'anni*, 265 (2 July 1943)

65 Pozzi, 164 (13 July 1943)

66 St A. 1/000393 (14 July 1943); Federzoni, 276; Maugeri, *Mussolini mi ha detto*, 27; Dolfin, *Con Mussolini*, 183; OO 32/239; *Relazioni Internazionali*, 24 July 1943, 611 (Scorza)

67 Bastianini, 115; Alfieri, *Due dittatori*, 305 (Bastianini, 19 July 1943); Guerri, *Galeazzo Ciano*, 564 (7 Feb. 1943); Monelli, *Roma*, 110

68 Tarchi, *Teste dure*, 14 (21 July 1943); Bottai, *Vent'anni*, 273, 277, 279; Bianchi, *Perchè e come cadde il fascismo*, 805 (De Bono, 19 July 1943)

69 *Führer Conferences*, 40 (17 July 1943)

70 *Kriegstagebuch des Oberkommandos*, 3/2/789–90 (15 July 1943); Rintelen, *Mussolini als Bundesgenosse*, 212; Alfieri, 318

71 Alfieri, 311–12, 319

72 Schmidt, *Hitler's Interpreter*, 263; Dinale, 245–8; Bastianini, 164

73 Alfieri, 308, 313; Bastianini, 121, 165; Deakin, *The Brutal Friendship*, 407

74 OO 34/297–8

75 Alfieri, 315

76 *Akten zur deutschen Politik*, E/6/295 (24 July 1943); Bastianini, 124

77 OO 37/xx; Signoretti, *La stampa*, 252–3; Longanesi, *In piedi e seduti*, 206; Vittorio Mussolini, *Vita*, 169; Hoettl, *Hitler's Paper Weapon*, 64–5

78 Puntoni, *Parla Vittorio Emanuele*, 141 (22 July 1943)

79 Pini–Susmel, *Mussolini*, 4/253–4 (Marinetti); Pascal, *Mussolini alla vigilia*, 16

80 Leto, *Polizia*, 53, 73–4; Dinale, 179–80, 183–6, 193, 248

81 Scorza, *La notte del Gran Consiglio*, 26

82 Leto, *Polizia segreta in Italia*, 76–7

83 Kallay, *Hungarian Premier*, 160

84 Ludwig, *Three Portraits*, 74

85 Scorza, *La notte del Gran Consiglio*, 177

86 Acerbo, *Fra due plotoni*, 499

87 Federzoni, 309, 311; Bertoldi, *Mussolini*, 216–17 (Grandi); Scorza, *La notte del Gran Consiglio*, 43–5, 47, 126, 139–40

88 Acerbo, 512; Scorza, *La notte del Gran Consiglio*, 73

89 Scorza, *La notte del Gran Consiglio*, 38–9 (De Bono), 48 (Grandi); Federzoni, 197, 283; Bottai, *Vent'anni,* 305–6

90 Scorza, *La notte*, 45–6

91 Scorza, *La notte*, 50–1, 135; Alfieri, 331–2; Federzoni, 291

92 Scorza, *La notte*, 79, 92

93 Scorza, *La notte*, 85, 98–9, 104–5, 181

94 Alfieri, 337–8

95 Bottai, *Vent'anni*, 314; Alfieri, 340; Scorza, *La notte*, 111, 118–19

96 Federzoni, *Italia di ieri*, 306; Acerbo, 514; Alfieri, 338; Bottai, *Vent'anni*, 314

97 Scorza, *La notte*, 130–1

98 Scorza, *La notte*, 125, 157; Tamaro, *Due anni*, 1/15 (Marinelli)

99 *Actes et documents du Saint Siège*, 7/521 (De' Stefani); Bertoldi, *Mussolini*, 216–17 (De' Stefani); Mayer, *La verità*, 44 (Marinelli), 65 (Farinacci), 67 (Bastianini), 75 (Alfieri), 84 (Bignardi); F. Orlando, *Mussolini volle il 25 luglio*, 36 (Gottardi)

100 Dinale, *Quarant'anni di colloqui con lui*, 247

101 Spampanto, *Contromemoriale*, 2/31

102 Scorza, *La notte del Gran Consiglio*, 160

103 *Ibid,* 164, 171, 179

104 *Ibid*, 191; Bastianini *Uomini, cose, fatti*, 131; Alfieri, 342

105 Bastianini, *Uomini, cose, fatti*, 132; Tamaro, *Due anni*, 1/72

106 Scorza, 191–3

107 OO 34/274; Scorza, 185; Rachele Mussolini, *La mia vita*, 190; *Oggi*, 20 June 1963, 17 (Montagna)

108 OO 37/164: St A. 222/057210 (Melchiori, 24 July 1943); *Processo Graziani*, 1/160; Federzoni, 204; Guspini, *L'orecchio del regime*, 230

109 OO 31/211; Castellano, *Come firmai l'armistizio*, 49–50

110 OO 31/213; Bastianini, 131

111 Puntoni, *Parla Vittorio Emanuele*, 144–5, 148; Benigno, *Occasioni mancate*, 78–81; *Due anni*, 1/26–33, 72–3

112 *Popolo d'Italia*, 26 July 1943

113 C. Senise, *Quando ero capo*, 206–7

114 St A. 3/001260–99

115 De Marsanich, *Lo stato*, 148–9; Dollmann, *Roma nazista*, 171–2, 366; Tamaro, *Due anni*, 1/16; Spampanato, 1/353

116 OO 34/358 (26 July 1943)

117 Carboni, *L'Italia tradita*, 89

118 Muratore and Persia, *La verità*, 13; Agricola, *Mussolini in prigionia*, 13–14; Gravelli, *Mussolini*, 233

119 Agricola, *Mussolini in prigionia*, 24; Pozzi, 140

120 OO 31/265; OO 34/290; Agricola, 20, 27; Schuster, *Gli ultimi tempi di un regime*, 163

121 OO 34/277; Monelli, *Mussolini*, 313

122 OO 34/285

123 OO 34/294

124 OO 34/277–8, 287

125 Maugeri, *Mussolini*, 38–9; Edvige Mussolini, *Mio fratello*, 198

126 Maugeri, *Mussolini*, 25–6, 37; Agricola, 19

127 Hoettl, *Hitler's Paper Weapon*, 67–74; Schellenberg, *Memoirs*, 386; Speer, *Inside the Third Reich*, 308

128 Iurato and Antonelli, *Con Mussolini a Campo Imperatore*, 7–10

129 OO 32/2 (18 Sept. 1943); Iurato and Antonelli, 12; Agricola, 31; Giudice, *Benito Mussolini*, 643–4

130 *Akten zur deutschen Politik*, E/7/674; Dolfin, *Con Mussolini nella tragedia*, 234, 247, 250; C. Senise, 258–9; St A. 103/027709–11 (Senise, 8 Sept. 1943); Washington T. 821/126 (Miranda, 5 Aug. 1943)

131 Skorzeny, *Special Missions*, 79–80; Rachele Mussolini, 217; Foley, *Commando Extraordinary*, 60

132 OO 324, 231–2 (15 Sept. 1943)

133 Zachariae, *Mussolini si confessa*, 11–12; Dolfin, 24, 27, 34, 45

134 St A. 261/072802–3 (3 Nov. 1943)

135 Dolfin, vii, 84–5, 88 (9 and 12 Nov. 1943)

136 St A. 300/095328; D'Aroma, *Mussolini*, 278–9; Dolfin, 26

137 OO32/92–3 (30 May 1944); OO 34/387; Spampanato, 2/128; Dinale, 191

138 OO 32/180, 190 (18 Apr. 1945); Rahn, *Ambasciatore di Hitler*, 275; Dolfin, 107, 145; Anfuso, *Roma, Berlino, Salò*, 443

139 Dolfin, 78–80, 89–90, 107

140 Manunta, *La caduta degli angeli*, 70; Tamaro, *Due anni*, 2/5

141 Bellotti, *La repubblica*, 63

142 Dolfin, 55, 136, 151

143 Spampanato, 2/33, 73

144 OO 32/272–3 (23 Nov. 1943); Tamaro, *Due anni*, 2/249–51; Dinale, 272

145 OO 32/8 (27 Nov. 1943), 28 (16 Dec. 1943)

146 Amicucci, *I 600 giorni*, 110, 112

147 St A. 261/072851–2 (Mezzasoma, 12 Dec. 1944)

148 OO 32/209 (11 June 1944)

149 OO 34/288; Dolfin, 115, 140 (7 Dec. 1943), 197 (10 Jan. 1944); Edda Ciano, 26, 202; Silvestri, *Albergo agli scalzi*, 77; *Oggi*, 4 July 1963, 14 (Montagna)

150 OO 32/4 (18 Sept. 1943); Amicucci, *I 600 giorni*, 86; Skorzeny, 89

151 OO 32/11 (27 Oct. 1943); Dolfin, 180–1, 189; Bocca, *La repubblica di Mussolini*, 117–18

152 *Akten zur deutschen Politik*, E/7/122 (27 Oct. 1943), 283 (Pavolini, 28 Dec. 1943); OO 32/12 (27 Oct. 1943)

153 Tamaro, *Due anni*, 2/351; Susmel, *Vita sbagliata*, 343

154 St A. 103/027856 (Suardo, 7 Dec. 1943); Edda Ciano, 234–6 (Zarca); Bocca, 116; Amicucci, *I 600 giorni*, 81 (Giobbe)

155 Montagna, *Mussolini e il processo di Verona*, 172; St A. 229/060035 (24 Nov. 1943); Bertoldi, *Salò*, 156

156 *Per l'Onore Decima Flottiglia Mas*, 25 Dec. 1943

157 Amicucci, *I 600 giorni*, 81; Edda Ciano, 213; Dolfin, 43; Silvestri, *Albergo*, 84

158 OO 32/179 (20 Mar. 1945); Montagna, 226

159 Dolfin, 188–9 (7 Jan. 1944); Pisenti, *Una repubblica necessaria*, 96

160 Moellhausen, *La carta perdente*, 304; Dolfin, 114; Tamaro, *Due anni*, 2/369 (Mazzolini); OO 32/209 (11 June 1943)

161 Montagna, 83, 172–3

162 Montagna, 205; Saporiti, *Empty Balcony*, 85–6

163 Benini, *Vigilia a Verona*, 111; Tamaro, *Due anni*, 2/352

164 Benini, 122 (De Bono)

165 Montagna, 226–8; Dolfin, 197; Silvestri, *Albergo*, 134; Deakin, *The Brutal Friendship*, 647 (Rahn)

166 Pisenti, 95; Bertoldi, *Salò*, 165–9; Bertoldi, *I tedeschi*, 99–100 (Harster); Acerbo, 553; Saporiti, 86; Susmel, 355
167 *Akten zur deutschen*, E/7/333 (Rahn, 14 Jan. 1944); Amicucci, *I 600 giorni*, 89
168 Montagna, 229
169 Tarchi, *Teste dure*, 72; *Akten zur deutschen Politik*, E/7/334 (14 Jan. 1944); Tamaro, *Due anni*, 2/361; Dolfin, 204 (11 Jan. 1944)
170 Dolfin, 284; Cortesi, *Mussolini*, 35; Bocca, 124
171 *Processo Graziani*, 2/22; OO 32/456; Amicucci, *I 600 giorni*, 102–3
172 Amicucci, *I 600 giorni*, 101; OO 35/435; Pisenti, 96–7; Tamaro, *Due anni*, 3/51

Chapter 17 The republic of Salò

1 Dinale, *Quarant'anni di colloqui con lui*, 273–4; Amicucci, *I 600 giorni*, 121–2; *Due anni*, 2/224–8; Dolfin, *Con Mussolini nella tragedia*, 95–9, 121–2, 138–9
2 Mellini, *Guerra diplomatica*, 84–5, 111–12; Schuster, *Gli ultimi tempi*, 30; Dollmann, *Roma*, 375; Spampanato, *Contromemoriale*, 2/220
3 Tamaro, *Due anni*, 3/289, 524; Bertoldi, *Salò*, 193, 220; OO 35/451 (3 Oct. 1944); Moellhausen, *La carta perdente*, 292–3
4 St A. 231/061120–2 (Buffarini, Oct. 1944); Lanfranchi, *L'inquisizione nera*, 79–82
5 St A. 270/078642–56 (Bettini, 10 Oct. 1944)
6 Pestalozza, *Il processo alla Muti*, xxi
7 Moellhausen, 214, 288; Zachariae, *Mussolini si confessa*, 95; St A. 16/007072–4 (10 May 1944); Dolfin, 50, 107, 178, 245; Cione, *Storia della repubblica*, 242; *Goebbels Diaries*, 378
8 *Actes et documents du Saint Siège*, 10/49 (Andreotti, 27 Jan. 1944)
9 Collotti, *L'amministrazione tedesca*, 139; Moellhausen, 279, 287
10 Tamaro, *Due anni*, 3/270
11 Bertoldi, *Salò*, 53; A. 154/045326 (24 Dec. 1944)
12 Bertoldi, *I tedeschi*, 136 (Dollmann)
13 *Akten zur deutschen Politik*, E/7/671–2 (23 Apr. 1944); Anfuso, *Roma, Berlino, Salò*, 387, 389, 476; *Processo Graziani*, 1/256; Dollmann, *Roma nazista*, 368
14 Moellhausen, 275
15 Tamaro, *Due anni*, 3/266–7; *Processo Graziani*, 1/113–14; Rahn, *Ambasciatore*, 295–6
16 *Storia Illustrata*, Oct. 1980, 48 (Don Pacino)
17 St A. 16/006997–7004 (Alfieri, 1 Dec. 1944)
18 *Processo Graziani*, 2/675; *Trial of the Major German War Criminals*, 2/312; *Akten zur deutschen Politik*, E/7/657 (22 Apr. 1944), 655; Moellhausen, 142, 146–8; Bertoldi, *Salò*, 90
19 *Processo Graziani*, 1/227, 322–3; *Corriere della Sera*, 5 Apr. 1944
20 St A. 223/057480–3 (Prefect of Aosta, 22 Dec. 1943); *Processo Graziani*, 2/192, 371, 460, 464; OO 43/137, 142, 151
21 Dolfin, 173–4; Tamaro, *Due anni*, 3/285; Bertoldi, *Salò*, 93
22 Tamaro, *Due anni*, 2/362; Dolfin, 150, 220; *Processo Graziani*, 1/305–7; *ibid.*, 2/227
23 Bellotti, *La repubblica*, 94–5
24 *Akten zur deutschen Politik*, E/7/664 (23 Apr. 1944); *ibid.*, E/8/235 (21 July 1944); Castelli, *Storia segreta di Roma*, 221–2
25 Moellhausen, 201–2, 245–6; Anfuso, 469; Dollmann, *Roma nazista*, 249–51; *Processo Graziani*, 1/344
26 Moellhausen, 427

The republic of Salò

27 OO 32/114 (14 Oct. 1944)

28 St A. 166/049222, 049228 (14 Nov. 1944); Tamaro, *Due anni*, 3/399, 510

29 OO 32/232 (21 June 1944); OO 35/441 (30 June 1944)

30 Graziani, *Ho difeso la patria*, 427; *Processo Graziani*, 1/373; Pansa, *L'esercito*, 180

31 Moellhausen, 341–3; Bertoldi, *Salò*, 236–9

32 OO 32/82 (18 Apr. 1944); Tamaro, *Due anni*, 2/434–5; St A. 229/059866–7 (21 Mar. 1944); Bocca, *La repubblica di Mussolini*, 268

33 OO 37/167; St A. 239/063865 (29 July 1944); *Processo Graziani*, 1/374, 386; *ibid.*, 244, 752

34 Zachariae, 13–19; Rachele Mussolini, *La mia vita*, 247–8; Vittorio Mussolini, *Vita*, 210

35 St A. 165/048516 (Mussolini to Dr Morell, 22 Sept. 1944)

36 Pini–Susmel, *Mussolini*, 4/427, 481

37 Zachariae, 26

38 Dolfin, 18–20, 61–3, 124–5; Anfuso, *Roma, Berlino, Salò*, 453–4

39 Dolfin, 70–1; Querel, *Il paese di Benito*, 99; Petacco, *Riservato per il Duce*, 116–23; Ruinas, *Pioggia sulla repubblica*, 113–117; Deakin, *The Brutal Friendship*, 609 (Jandl)

40 Zachariae, 28; Dolfin, 144, 159–60, 184; Pini–Susmel, 4/446

41 Moellhausen, *La carta perdente*, 300–1

42 Moellhausen, 296

43 Tarchi, *Teste dure*, 137–9; *Oggi*, 16 May 1963, 63–5

44 Dolfin, 102, 110–12; St A. 108/029730–4 (31 Mar. 1944)

45 Rahn, 296; Anfuso, 411; Zachariae, *Mussolini si confessa*, 23, 40–5; Dolfin, *Con Mussolini nella tragedia*, 35, 73, 159

46 Tarchi, 53; Amicucci, *I 600 giorni*, 167; *Oggi*, 20 June 1963 (Montagna)

47 Manunta, *La caduta degli angeli*, 203, 206; Rahn, *Ambasciatore di Hitler*, 274; Silvestri, *Mussolini*, 49, 547; Zachariae, 60; Tamaro, *Due anni*, 3/528–9

48 Edvige Mussolini, *Mio fratello*, 202, 227; Schuster, *Gli ultimi tempi*, 163

49 Zachariae, 47–9, 164; Pini–Susmel, 4/407, 427, 491; OO 44/330–2

50 Schuster, 163; Bertoldi, *Salò*, 297–9

51 D'Aroma, *Mussolini*, 308–9; Zachariae, 69–70, 176–7

52 OO 32/177; OO 34/287; Dinale, *Quarant'anni de colloqui con lui*, 287

53 Manunta, 204; Dinale, 268; Cione, *Storia della repubblica*, 12

54 Dinale, 269; Gentizon, *Mito di Mussolini*, 49; Maugeri, *Mussolini*, 15; Dolfin, 24, 187; Tamaro, *Due anni*, 2/343

55 OO 34/296, 437; Dinale, 257, 283, 288; Maugeri, *Mussolini*, 33; Tamaro, *Due anni*, 2/202

56 OO 32/171; Anfuso, *Roma, Berlino, Salò*, 450–1; Spampanato, 2/265

57 OO 32/20 (24 Nov. 1943), 267

58 OO 32/129 (16 Dec. 1944), 149, 171, 178–9, 318; Zachariae, 139

59 *Corriere della Sera*, 9 Apr. 1944; Silvestri, *Mussolini*, 339

60 *Corriere della Sera*, 21 Mar. 1944

61 OO 32/183 (21 Mar. 1945)

62 Pini, *Itinerario tragico*, 164–5; Amicucci, *I 600 giorni*, 151; Edvige Mussolini, 223; Spampanato, *Contromemoriale*, 2/338, 370

63 *Verità*, 28 Feb. 1942, 71 (Bombacci); Dolfin, 236

64 OO 32/57 (3 Mar. 1944)

65 Manunta, *La caduta degli angeli*, 35; *ABC*, 16 June 1953, 8–9 (Pellizzi)

66 Rahn, 325–6; Amicucci, *I 600 giorni*, 152

67 Zachariae, 169; De Begnac, *Palazzo Venezia*, 642–3; Spampanato, 2/131–2

68 OO 31/5 (12 Jan. 1942); Guerri, *Rapporto al Duce*, 134, (25 Jan. 1942), 274; *Gerarchia*, May 1942, 206; DGFP D/12/951 (3 June 1941)

69 St A. 160/046363–4 (Vidusioni, 24 Oct. 1942); *Akten zur deutschen Politik*, E/4/150 (Himmler, 11 Oct. 1942); Donosti, *Mussolini*, 98; Simoni, *Berlino*, 203; Anfuso, 504; *Ponte*, Nov. 1978, 1431–2; Mayda, *Ebrei sotto Salò*, 21–3

70 Zanussi, *Guerra e catastrofe*, 1/274; De Felice, *Storia degli ebrei*, 447–8, 453; Michaelis, *Mussolini and the Jews*, 390–2

71 Fölkel, *La risiera*, 23–4, 150; Momigliano, *Storia tragica*, 117–18

72 Bellotti, *La repubblica di Mussolini*, 137; Dolfin, 44, 114–15, 142

73 Moellhausen, *La carta perdente*, 288–91, 320

74 Bocca, *La repubblica di Mussolini*, 335 (Almirante); Silvestri, *Contro la vendetta*, 341; Ruinas, *Pioggia sulla repubblica*, 40–1; Moellhausen, 319

75 St A. 234/062223 (23 June 1943)

76 Carboni, *Memorie*, 143, 153; Federzoni, *Italia di ieri*, 260

77 *Testamento politico di Mussolini*, 34–5, 46–7 (20 Apr. 1945); OO 32/161, 344 (17 Apr. 1944), 423; Dolfin, 295; Zachariae, *Mussolini si confessa*, 56; Dinale, 268; Spampanato, 2/376 (24 Apr. 1945)

78 Moellhausen, 290

79 OO 32/170–1, 175–6, 179 (20 Mar. 1945), 195; OO 34/391; Zachariae, 58, 173–4; Maugeri, *Mussolini*, 39

80 Zachariae, 146–8

81 OO 32/131 (16 Dec. 1944); OO 35/467 (14 Feb. 1945); OO 37/169 (26 Nov. 1944); Pini, *Itinerario tragico*, 188–90, 273–4

82 Cione, 405, 416

83 Silvestri, *Mussolini*, 9, 24, 81; Silvestri, *Contro la vendetta*, 153

84 Amicucci, *I 600 giorni*, 170–1; *Nuova Antologia*, Jan. 1945, 44; OO 34/305–444 (24 June–18 July 1944)

85 OO 32/159–60 (Mar. 1945)

86 *Testamento politico*, 27–9; Anfuso, 406

87 OO 32/93 (30 May 1944), 185 (23 Mar. 1945)

88 OO 32/163, 175–6; *Civiltà Fascista*, June 1944, 34, 42 (Pareti)

89 St A. 13/006990 (18 Nov. 1944), 007007 (14 Dec. 1944)

90 Turchi, *Prefetto con Mussolini*, 196; Zachariae, 195–6

91 Dinale, 207, 284; Dolfin, 28 (5 Oct. 1943)

92 Dolfin, 152, 183 (1 Jan. 1944), 191, 218, 246, 275 (6 Mar. 1944)

93 *Testamento politico*, 31

94 Anfuso; *Roma, Berlino, Salò*, 407; Tamaro, *Due anni*, 2/371 (Mazzolini); OO 32/196, 400; Tarchi, *Teste dure*, 73

95 D'Aroma, *Mussolini*, 321; Zachariae, 57

96 OO 32/187 (18 Apr. 1945)

97 Maugeri, *Mussolini*, 23

98 Zachariae, 93

99 Mellini, 101 (28 Feb. 1945)

100 OO 32/173–5 (20 Mar. 1945); Gravelli, *Mussolini*, 288

101 Mellini, *Guerra diplomatica*, 106 (5 Mar. 1945); Dolfin, 116 (28 Nov. 1943)

102 OO 32/160; Dinale, 250–1; Zachariae, 90–2

103 OO 32/180 (20 Mar. 1945)

104 Dolfin, 235–7 (5 Feb. 1944); Amicucci, *I 600 giorni*, 312; Bellotti, *La repubblica di Mussolini*, 204; Spampanato, 2/265 (31 Oct. 1944)

105 OO 32/188–9; Dinale, 265; Zachariae, 82–3

106 Dinale, 328; Dolfin, 109, 136–7 (6 Dec. 1943), 214; Amicucci, *I 600 giorni*, 112

107 Anfuso, 554; Ruinas, *Pioggia sulla repubblica*, 219–20
108 OO 32/179 (20 Mar. 1945)
109 Edvige Mussolini, *Mio fratello*, 222
110 Zachariae, 76–7; Edvige Mussolini, 225
111 Cucco, *Non volevamo perdere*, 250–1; Amicucci, *I 600 giorni*, 162; Tamaro, *Due anni*, 1/166; Pini–Susmel, *Mussolini*, 4/488
112 Dinale, 208; Amicucci, *I 600 giorni*, 309, 312
113 *Akten zur deutschen Politik*, E/7/665 (23 Apr. 1944)
114 Silvestri, *Mussolini*, 227–8
115 Vittorio Mussolini, *Vita*, 25; Zachariae, *Mussolini si confessa*, 183
116 OO 32/425–6 (28 Oct. 1944), 460; Pini, *Itinerario tragico*, 295
117 OO 32/138, 140 (16–17 Dec. 1944); Manunta, 206–7
118 Silvestri, *Mussolini*, 81; Dolfin, 144
119 OO 32/175–6 (20 Mar. 1945); Hoettl, *Hitler's Paper Weapon*, 115–17
120 *Processo Graziani*, 1/313–14; St A. 16/006968–76 (Anfuso, 20 Sept. 1944); Graziani, *Ho difeso*, 426; Anfuso, 533; Amicucci, *I 600 giorni*, 306
121 OO 32/134–5 (16 Dec. 1944), 320 (26 Feb. 1944); Zachariae, 173; Rahn, 276
122 *Actes et documents du Saint Siège*, 7/335 (13 May 1943)
123 OO 32/114 (14 Oct. 1944), 137, 165 (6 Mar. 1945)
124 Graziani, *Ho difeso*, 490; Spampanato, *Contromemoriale*, 2/284–6, 337, 372; *Akten zur deutschen Politik*, E/7/664 (23 Apr. 1944); Moellhausen, *La carta perdente*, 300
125 OO 35/457 (16 Dec. 1944); St A. 2/000891, 000948–9, 000957; OO 35/457 (Sept. 1944)
126 Moellhausen, 420–1
127 Bandini, *Le ultime 95 ore*, 23; Bocca, *La repubblica di Mussolini*, 292–3
128 Zachariae, 19
129 OO 32/188 (18 Apr. 1945); Dinale; *Quarant'anni di colloqui con lui*, 289
130 Dinale, 250, 268, 286
131 OO 32/158–9, 161 (Mar. 1945)
132 Rahn, *Ambasciatore di Hitler*, 328–9; Schuster, *Gli ultimi tempi*, 35, 102–6; Tarchi, *Teste dure*, 152; OO 32/193
133 Zachariae, 199; Mellini, 106 (5 Mar. 1945); Anfuso, 561–3; Silvestri, *Mussolini*, 229; *Processo Graziani*, 2/662
134 OO 32/212 (24 Apr. 1945); Pini–Susmel, *Mussolini*, 4/488; Valiani, *Tutte le strade*, 327, 334; Hoettl, *The Secret Front*, 284–5
135 OO 32/188, 202 (23 Apr. 1945)
136 Gravelli, *Mussolini aneddotico*, 304, 313; Re, *Storia di un archivio*, 21
137 Amicucci, *I 600 giorni*, 230–1; Bertoldi, *La guerra*, 58–62; Pini–Susmel, *Mussolini*, 4/487
138 Mellini, 139 (16 Apr. 1945); Anfuso, 574–5
139 Tutaev, *The Consul of Florence*, 241–51; Schuster, 162–4; Zachariae, 19; Bellotti, 210
140 Gravelli, *Mussolini*, 320; *Mussolini giudicato dal mondo*, 215 (Sprigge)
141 Valiani, *Tutte le strade*, 344; *Ponte*, Dec. 1946, 1061 (Lombardi); Schuster, 167
142 Silvestri, *Turati l'ha detto*, 103–4; OO 32/181, 213; D'Agostini, *Colloqui*, 96; Valiani, 346
143 Cadorna, *La riscossa*, 252–3; Bertoldi, *La guerra*, 46; Valiani, 352
144 Gravelli, *Mussolini*, 308; Bellotti, *La repubblica di Mussolini*, 221
145 Tarchi, 171; Bertoldi, *La guerra*, 35–7 (Tarchi); *Processo Graziani*, 2/24; Bandini, *Le ultime 95 ore*, 7, 63, 103–4, 151, 154–5; Amicucci, *I 600 giorni*, 271–3; Lanfranchi, *La resa*, 295
146 Spampanato, 3/128–39; Lada-Mocarski, 'The last three days of Mussolini', 44–5; Pini–Susmel, *Mussolini*, 4/518, 526

List of works cited in the notes

ABC: quindicinale di critica politica, Rome 1953–

Acerbo, G., *Fra due plotoni di esecuzione: avvenimenti e problemi dell' epoca fascista*, Rocca S. Casciano 1968

Actes et documents du Saint Siège relatifs à la seconde guerre mondiale, ed. P. Blet, R.A. Graham, A. Martini and B. Schneider, Rome 1967–

Adami, E., *La lingua di Mussolini*, Modena 1939

Adamthwaite, A., *France and the Coming of the Second World War*, London 1977

Affari Esteri, Rome 1969–

Africa Italiana, Rome 1938–

Agonia e morte di Mussolini e del fascismo nel racconto di chi prese parte alla cattura, Rome 1945

Agricola, M., and Da Limbara, M., *Mussolini in prigionia*, Rome 1944

Akten zur deutschen Auswärtigen Politik 1918–1945, ed. I. Krüger-Bulcke, M. Mantzke, C. Stamm, Göttingen 1969–

Ala (L') d'Italia, Rome 1919–

Albertini, A., *Vita di Luigi Albertini*, Milan 1945

Albertini, L., *Epistolario 1911–1926*, ed. O. Barié, Milan 1968

Albertini, L., *In difesa della libertà; discorsi e scritti*, Milan 1947

Alcino, M., *La dittatura di Mussolini*, Milan 1934

Alcock, A.E., *The History of the South Tyrol Question*, London 1970

Alessi, R., *Il giovane Mussolini rievocato da un suo compagno di scuola*, Milan 1969

Alessio, G., *La crisi dello stato parlamentare e l'avvento del fascismo: memorie di un ex-ministro*, Padua 1946

Alfieri, D., *Due dittatori di fronte*, Milan 1948

Algardi, Z., *Processi ai fascisti*, Florence 1958

Alloway, L., *The Venice Biennale 1895–1968*, London 1969

Almanacco enciclopedico del 'Popolo d'Italia', Milan, 1922–

Aloisi, P., *Journal: 25 Juillet 1932–14 Juin 1936*, Paris 1957

Aloisi, P., *La mia attività a servizio della pace*, Rome 1946

Alvaro, C., *Quasi una vita*, Milan 1974

Ambrosio, General Vittorio, 'Questionnaire', in *World War II German Military Studies*, vol. XIV, New York 1979

Amè, C., *Guerra segreta in Italia 1940–1943*, Rome 1954

Amendola, G., *Una battaglia liberale: discorsi politici 1919–1923*, Turin 1924

Amendola, G., *Una scelta di vita*, Milan 1976

Amery, L.S., *My Political Life*, London 1953–5

Amery, L.S., *The Leo Amery Diaries*, ed. J. Barnes and D. Nicholson, London 1980

Amicucci, E., *I 600 giorni di Mussolini: dal Gran Sasso a Dongo*, Rome 1948

Amicucci, E., *La stampa della rivoluzione e del regime*, Milan 1938

Andrew, R.G, *Through Fascist Italy*, London 1935

Anfuso, F., *Roma, Berlino, Salò: 1936–1945*, Milan 1950

Aniante, A., *Mussolini*, Paris 1932

Mussolini

Annali del Fascismo, Naples 1931–

Annali dell'Africa Italiana, Rome 1938–

Annuario della stampa, ed. E. Amicucci, Milan 1926–

Ansaldo, G., *Il ministro della buona vita*, Milan 1950

Antieuropa, Rome 1929–

Antilei: Special issue in 1939 of *Antieuropa*

Apih, E., *Italia: fascismo e antifascismo nella Venezia Giulia (1918–1943)*, Bari 1966

Appelius, M., *La tragedia della Francia: dalla superbia di ieri agli armistizi di oggi*, Milan 1940

Appelius, M., *Parole dure e chiare*, Milan 1942

Aquarone, A., *L'organizzazione dello stato totalitario*, Turin 1965

Aquarone, A., and Vernassa, M., *Il regime fascista*, Bologna 1974

Araldi, V., *Il giuoco delle garanzie*, Bologna 1942

Ardali P., *San Francesco e Mussolini*, Mantua (*c.* 1926)

Ardau, G., *L'eloquenza Mussoliniana*, Milan 1929

Ardemagni, M., *La Francia sarà fascista?*, Milan 1937

Ardemagni, M., *Supremazia di Mussolini*, Milan 1936

Ardito d'Italia, L', Rome 1932–

Argiolas, T., *Corfu 1923*, Rome 1973

Armellini, Q., *Diario di guerra: nove mesi al comando supremo*, Cernusco 1946

Armellini, Q., *La crisi dell'esercito*, Rome 1945

Arpinati, G.C., *Arpinati mio padre*, Rome 1968

Artieri, G., *Tre ritratti politici e quattro attentati*, Rome 1953

Asquith, M., *Places and Persons*, London 1925

Assalto, L, Bologna 1922–

Aster, S., *The Making of the Second World War*, London 1963

Atlantic Monthly, Boston

Atti del primo congresso di studi coloniali, Florence 1931

Atti del primo congresso giuridico italiano: le discussioni, Rome 1933

Attico (A. Lanzillo), *Politica della verità*, Milan 1947

Augustea, Rome 1925–

Avanti!, Milan

Azione Coloniale, Rome 1936–

Azioni navali in Mediterraneo dal 10 giugno 1940 al 31 Marzo 1941, ed. G.Fioravanzo, Rome 1970

Badoglio, P., *La via che conduce agli alleati*, Venice 1944

Badoglio, P., *L'Italia nella seconda guerra mondiale*, Milan 1946

Baer, G.W., *Test Case: Italy, Ethiopia and the League of Nations*, Stanford 1976

Baer, G.W., *The Coming of the Italian-Ethiopian War*, Cambridge 1967

Balabanoff, A., *Il traditore: Mussolini e la conquista del potere*, Rome 1973

Balabanoff, A., *My Life as a Rebel*, London 1938

Balbo, I., *Diario 1922*, Milan 1932

Balbo, I., *La politica aeronautica dell'Italia fascista*, Rome 1927

Balbo, I., *Sette anni di politica aeronautica (1927–1933)*, Milan 1936

Balfour, J.P.D., *Atatürk: the rebirth of a nation*, London 1964

Bandinelli, R. Bianchi, *Dal diario di un borghese e altri scritti*, Milan 1948

Bandini, F., *Gli Italiani in Africa: storia delle guerre coloniali, 1882–1934*, Milan 1971

Bandini, F., *Le ultime 95 ore di Mussolini*, Milan 1968

Bandini, F., *Tecnica della sconfitta: storia dei quaranta giorni che precedettero e seguirono l'entrata in guerra dell'Italia*, Milan 1963

Bandini, F., *Vita e morte segreta di Mussolini*, Milan 1978

Barclay, C.N., *Against Great Odds: the first offensive in Libya in 1940–41*, London 1955

Barker, A.J., *The Civilizing Mission: A History of the Italo-Ethiopian War*, London 1968

Barmine, A., *One Who Survived*, New York 1945

Barnes, J.S., *The Universal Aspects of Fascism*, London 1928 (2nd ed.)

Barros, J., *The Corfu Incident of 1923*, Princeton 1965

Bartlett, V.O., *This Is My Life*, London 1937

Barzini, L., *From Caesar to the Mafia: Sketches of Italian Life*, London 1971

Barzini, L., *The Italians*, New York 1964

Baskerville, B., *What Next O Duce?*, London 1937

Basler Presse, Basle

Bastianini, G., *Uomini, cose, fatti: memorie di un ambasciatore*, Milan 1959

Bastico, E. *Guerra totalitaria*, Padua 1939

Battaglia delle Alpi occidentali, Giugno 1940, ed. U.Marchini, Rome 1947

Battaglia risolutiva, La, ed. Ministero di Cultura Popolare, Rome 1941

Baudino, C., *Una guerra assurda: la campagna di Grecia*, Milan 1965

BBC Monitoring Service, London

BD: *Documents on British Foreign Policy, 1919–1939*, ed. E.L. Woodward, R. Butler *et al.*

Beck, I., *Dernier rapport: politique polonaise 1926–1939*, Paris 1951

Bedel, M., *Fascisme an vii*, Paris 1929

Bedeschi, E., *La giovinezza del Duce*, Turin 1940 (2nd ed.)

Bedeschi, L. (ed), *Studi e ricerche su Giacomo Matteotti*, Urbino 1979

Bedeschi, S., and Alessi, R., *Anni giovanili di Mussolini*, Milan 1939

Belisha: *The Private Papers of Hore-Belisha*, ed. R.J. Minney, London 1960

Bellotti, F., *La repubblica di Mussolini, 26 luglio 1943–25 aprile 1945*, Milan 1947

Belot, R. de, *The Struggle for the Mediterranean 1939–1945*, Oxford 1952

Beltramelli, A., *L'uomo nuovo (Benito Mussolini)*, Milan 1940 (5th ed.)

Benedetti, U., *Benedetto Croce e il fascismo*, Rome 1967

Benelli, S., *Schiavitù*, Milan 1945

Benigno, Jo di, *Occasioni mancate: Roma in un diario segreto 1943–1944*, Rome 1945

Benini, Z., *Vigilia a Verona*, Cernusco 1949

Benjamin, R., *Mussolini et son peuple*, Paris 1937

Béraud, H., *Ce que j'ai vu à Rome*, Paris 1929

Béraud, H., *Dictateurs d'aujourd'hui*, Paris 1933

Béraud, H., *Men of the Aftermath*, London 1929

Bergamo, M., *Novissimo annuncio di Mussolini*, Milan 1962

Berio, A., 'L'affare etiopico', in *Rivista di Studi Politici Internazionali*, April 1958

Berliner Tageblatt

Bernanos, G., *A Diary of my Times*, London 1938

Berneri, C., *Mussolini: psicologia di un dittatore*, ed. P.C. Masini, Milan 1966

Bernotti, R., *Cinquant'anni nella marina militare*, Milan 1971

Bernotti, R., *Storia della guerra nel Mediterraneo: 1940–43*, Rome 1960

Berselli, A., *L'opinione pubblica inglese e l'avvento del fascismo*, Milan 1971

Bertoldi, S., *I tedeschi in Italia*, Milan 1964

Bertoldi, S., *La guerra parallela*, Milan 1966

Bertoldi, S., *Mussolini tale e quale*, Milan 1965

Bertoldi, S., *Salò: vita e morte della repubblica sociale italiana*, Milan 1976

Bertoni, R., *Russia: trionfo del fascismo*, Milan 1937

Beyens, H., *Quatre ans à Rome 1921–1926*, Paris 1934

Mussolini

Bezençon, M., *La vie âpre et aventureuse de Mussolini en Suisse*, Paris (*c.* 1938)
Bianchi, G., *Perchè e come cadde il fascismo*, Milan 1970
Bianchi, G., *Rivelazioni sul conflitto italo-etiopico*, Milan 1967
Bianchi, L., *Mussolini scrittore e oratore*, Bologna 1937
Biani, V., *Ali italiane sul deserto*, Florence 1936
Bibliografia Fascista, Rome 1926–
Binchy, D.A., *Church and State in Fascist Italy*, Oxford 1941
Biondi, D., *La fabbrica del Duce*, Florence 1967
BL: British Library mss
Blondel, J.F., *Au fil de la carrière: recit d'un diplomate 1911–1938*, Paris 1960
Bocca, G., *La repubblica di Mussolini*, Bari 1977
Boelcke, W.A., *Kriegspropaganda 1939–1941*, Stuttgart 1966
Bojano, F., *In the Wake of the Goose-Step*, London 1944
Bolla, N., *Il segreto di due re*, Milan 1951
Bollettini della guerra (Stato Maggiore Esercito), Rome 1941
Bollettino Parlamentare, Rome 1927–
Bonavita, F., *Mussolini svelato*, Milan 1924
Boncour. P.-P., *Entre deux guerres: souvenirs sur la IIIe république*, Paris 1945
Bonomi, I., *Dal socialismo al fascismo*, Rome 1942
Booth, C.D., and Booth, I.B., *Italy's Aegean Possessions*, London 1928
Boothe, C., *European Spring*, London 1941
Bordeaux, H., *La claire Italie*, Paris 1929
Bordeux, V.J., *Benito Mussolini the Man*, London 1927
Borgese, G.A., *Goliath: The March of Fascism*, London 1938
Borghi, A., *Mezzo secolo di anarchia (1898–1945)*, Naples 1954
Borghi, A., *Mussolini in camicia*, Naples 1961
Borsa, M., *Gli inglesi e noi*, Milan 1945
Borsa, M., *Memorie di un redivivo*, Rome 1945
Bortolotto, G., *Storia del fascismo*, Milan 1938
Bottai, G., *Mussolini costruttore d'impero*, Mantua 1927
Bottai, G., *Pagine di 'Critica Fascista'*, ed. F.M.Pacces, Florence 1941
Bottai, G., *Politica fascista delle arti*, Rome 1940
Bottai, G., *Vent'anni e un giorno*, Cernusco 1949
Bracco, R., *Persecuzione in Italia*, Rome n.d.
Bragadin, M'A., *Il dramma della marina Italiana 1940–1945*, Milan 1968
Bragadin, M'A., *Vampe sul mare (1940–1943)*, Rome 1954
Brighenti, A., *Uomini ed episodi del tempo di Mussolini*, Milan 1938
Brocchi, D. (ed.), *'L'Universale'*, Milan 1969
Brown, A.C., *Bodyguard of Lies*, New York 1975
Bruegel, J.W., *Czechoslovakia before Munich*, Cambridge 1973
Bruttini, A., and Puglisi, G., *L'impero tradito*, Florence 1957
Bullock, A., *Hitler: a study in tyranny*, London 1964
Burnett, H. *et al.*, 'A syndrome following prolonged intake of milk', in *The New England Journal of Medicine*, Boston, 1949
Butler, N.M., *Across the Busy Years: Recollections and Reflections*, New York 1939

Cadogan, A., *The Diaries of Sir Alexander Cadogan*, ed. D.Dilks, London 1971
Cadorna, R., *La riscossa: dal 25 luglio alla liberazione*, Milan 1948
Caffè: Antologia del 'Caffè', ed. B.Ceva, Milan 1961

Calamandrei, P., 'La funzione parlamentare sotto il fascismo', in Aquarone, *Il regime fascista*

Cambria, A., *Maria José*, Milan 1966

Camera dei deputati: commissioni legislative riunite, Rome 1943

Camera dei deputati: discussioni

Camicia Rossa, Rome 1924–

Camilleri, C., *Polizia in azione*, Rome n.d.

Campagna 1935–36 in Africa orientale, La (Ministero della guerra), Rome 1939

Candido, *Mussolini in pantofole*, Rome 1944

Canevari, E., *Graziani mi ha detto*, Rome 1947

Canevari, E., *La guerra italiana: retroscena della disfatta*, Rome 1948

Cannistraro, P.V., *La fabbrica del consenso: fascismo e mass media*, Bari 1975

Cantalupo, R., *Fu la Spagna: ambasciata presso Franco, Febbraio–Aprile 1937*, Milan 1948

Cantelmo, L.M., *Mussolini: i suoi uomini, le loro donne*, Rome 1945

Capoferri, P., *Venti anni col fascismo e con i sindacati*, Milan 1957

Caracciolo di Feroleto, M., *'E poi?: la tragedia dell'esercito italiano*, Rome 1946

Carboni, G., *L'Italia tradita dall'armistizio alla pace*, Rome 1947

Carboni, G., *Memorie segrete 1935–1948*, Florence 1955

Carli, M., *Colloqui coi vivi*, Rome 1928

Carli, M., *Fascismo intransigente*, Florence 1926

Carlini, A., *Filosofia e religione nel pensiero di Mussolini*, Rome 1934

Carlini, A., *Saggio sul pensiero filosofico e religioso del fascismo*, Rome 1942

Carocci, G., *Giovanni Amendola nella crisi dello stato italiano 1911–1925*, Milan 1956

Carocci, G., *La politica estera dell'Italia fascista (1925–1928)*, Bari 1969

Carpi, D., 'Il problema ebraico nella politica italiana fra de due guerre mondiali', in *Rivista di Studi Politici Internazionali*, 1961

Carteggio Arnaldo–Benito Mussolini, ed. D. Susmel, Florence 1954

Carteggio D'Annunzio–Mussolini (1919–1938), ed. R. De Felice and E. Mariano, Milan 1971

Casavis, J.N., *The Religion of the Dodecanesians and its Persecution by Italy*, New York 1937

Casini, G., *Una volontà, una fede*, Milan 1942

Cassels, A., *Mussolini's Early Diplomacy*, Princeton 1970

Cassese, S., 'Aspetti della storia delle istituzioni', in *Lo sviluppo economico in Italia*, ed. G.Fuà, Milan 1969

Castellani, A., *Tra microbi e re*, Milan 1961

Castellano, G., *Come firmai l'armistizio di Cassibile*, Milan 1945

Castelli, G., *Storia segrata di Roma città aperta*, Rome 1959

Castronovo, V. *La stampa italiana dall'unità al fascismo*, Bari 1970

Catalano, F., 'L'économie de guerre italienne', in *La guerre en Méditerranée 1939–1945*, Paris 1971

Cavallero, C., *Il dramma del Maresciallo Cavallero*, Milan 1952

Cavallero, U., *Comando supremo; diario 1940–43*, Rocca S. Casciano 1948

Caviglia, E., *Diario (aprile 1925–marzo 1945)*, Rome 1952

Cederna, A., *Mussolini urbanista: lo sventramento di Roma negli anni del consenso*, Bari 1979

Celovsky, B., *Das Munchener Abkommen 1938*, Stuttgart 1958

Centro di preparazione politica per i giovani (ed. Partito Nazionale Fascista), Rome 1939

Cerruti, E., *Ambassador's Wife*, London 1952

Ceva, L., *La condotta italiana della guerra: Cavallero e il comando supremo 1941–1943*, Milan 1975

Ceva, L., 'La guerre italienne en Afrique du Nord (1940–1943),' in *Revue Internationale d'Histoire Militaire*, Rome 1978

Mussolini

Ceva, L., 'Quelques aspects de l'activité du Haut Commandement italien dans la guerre en Méditerranée', in *La guerre en Méditerranée 1939–1945*, Paris 1971

Chambrun, L.C. Pineton, Comte de, *Traditions et souvenirs*, Paris 1952

Charles-Roux, F., *Huit ans au Vatican 1932–1940*, Paris 1947

Chi è? Dizionario degli Italiani d'oggi, Rome 1928, 1936, 1940

Chicago Daily Tribune

Chiesa, E., *La mano nel sacco*, Rome 1925

Childs, H.L. (ed.), *Propaganda and Dictatorship*, Princeton 1936

Chiurco, G.A., *Storia della rivoluzione fascista*, Florence 1929

Christian Science Monitor, Boston

Christo, Homem, *Mussolini bâtisseur d'avenir*, Paris 1923

Cianfarra, C.M., *The War and the Vatican*, London 1945

Ciano, Edda Mussolini, *My Truth*, ed. A.Zarca, London 1976

Ciano (1): Ciano, G., *1937–1938 Diario*, Bologna 1948

Ciano (2): Ciano, G., *Diario, volume primo 1939–1940*, Milan 1946

Ciano (3): Ciano, G., *Diario, volume secondo 1941–1943*, Milan 1946

Ciano (4): Ciano, G., *L'europa verso la catastrofe*, Milan 1947

Ciano (5): Ciano, G., *Diario 1937–1943*, ed. R. De Felice, Milan 1980

Ciarlantini, F., *Hitler e il fascismo*, Florence 1933

Ciarlantini, F., *Il capo e la folla*, Milan 1935

Ciarlantini, F., *Mussolini immaginario*, Milan 1933

Ciccotti, E., *Il fascismo e le sue fasi*, Milan 1925

Ciocca, G., *Giudizio sul bolscevismo*, Milan 1941 (7th ed.)

Ciocca, P., and Toniolo, G. (eds), *L'economia italiana nel periodo fascista*, Bologna 1976

Cione, E., *Storia della repubblica sociale italiana*, Caserta 1948

Cipriani, L., *Un assurdo etnico: l'impero etiopico*, Florence 1935

Civiltà Cattolica, Rome

Civiltà Fascista, Rome 1934–

Clough, S.B., *The Economic History of Modern Italy*, New York 1964

C.M.R., *Histoire du fascisme italien (1919–1937)*, Paris 1938

Codice della stampa, Milan 1942

Codice penale, ed. R.Mangini etc., Rome 1930

Cogni, G., *I valori della stirpe italiana*, Milan 1937

Colarizi, S., *Dopoguerra e fascismo in Puglia (1919–1926)*, Bari 1971

Collier, R.H., *Duce!: The Rise and Fall of Benito Mussolini*, London 1971

Collotti, E., *L'amministrazione tedesca dell'Italia occupata, 1943–1945*, Milan 1963

Colombi, A., *Nelle mani del nemico*, Rome 1950

Come si mangia in Europa, Milan 1941

Compendio statistico Italiano, Rome 1927–

Contemporary Review, London

Conti, C., *Servizio segreto: cronache e documenti dei delitti di stato*, Rome 1945

Conti, E., *Dal taccuino di un borghese*, Cremona 1946

Conti, G., *Nella battaglia contro la dittatura*, Rome c. 1946

Convegno Volta: convegno di scienze morali e storiche: 'L'Europa', Rome 1933

Coppola, F., *La pace coatta*, Milan 1929

Coppold, F., *La vittoria bifronte*, Milan 1936

Cora, G., 'Un diplomatico durante l'era fascista', in *Storia e Politica*, Rome 1966

Corbino, O.M., *Conferenze e discorsi*, Rome (c. 1938)

Corner, P., *Fascism in Ferrara 1915–1925*, Oxford 1975

Corriere della Sera, Milan

Cortesi, L., *Mussolini e il fascismo alla vigilia del crollo*, Rome 1975

Coverdale, J.F., *Italian Intervention in the Spanish Civil War*, Princeton 1975

Coverdale, N., 'The battle of Guadalajara', in *Journal of Contemporary History*, Jan. 1974

Cremona Nuova, Cremona 1922–

Critica Fascista, Rome 1923–

Critica Politica, Rome 1920–

Croce, B., *Pagine sparse*, Naples 1943

Croce, B., *Nuove pagine sparse*, Naples 1948

Croce, B., *Quaderni della Critica*, Bari 1945–

Croce, B., *Scritti e discorsi politici (1943–1947)*, Bari 1963

Cronache della Guerra, Rome 1939–

Cross, J.A., *Sir Samuel Hoare: a political biography*, London 1977

Cucco, A., *Non volevamo perdere*, Rocca S. Casciano 1950

Current History, New York

Da Zara, A., *Pelle d'ammiraglio*, Milan 1949

Daffinà O. (ed.), *Mussolini e il fascismo*, Rome 1929

D'Agata, R., *Mussolini: l'uomo, l'idea, l'opera*, Palermo 1927

D'Agostini, B., *Colloqui con Rachele Mussolini*, Rome 1946

Daily Chronicle, London

Daily Express, London

Daily Herald, London

Daily Mail, London

Daily News, London

Daily Telegraph, The, London

Dal Pont, A., Leonetti, A., and Massara, M., *Giornali fuori legge*, Rome 1964

Dal regno all'impero, ed. R.Accademia dei Lincei, Rome 1937

Dall'Ora, F., *Intendenza in A.O.*, Rome 1937

Dalton, H., *The Fateful Years, 1931–1945*, London 1957

D'Andrea, U., *Mussolini motore del secolo*, Milan 1937

Danese, O., *Mussolini*, Mantua 1922

Danzi, G., *Europa senza europei?*, Rome 1934

Daquanno, E., *Vecchia guardia*, Rome 1934

D'Aroma, N., *Mussolini segreto*, Rocca S. Casciano 1958

D'Aroma, N., *Vent 'anni insieme: Vittorio Emanuele e Mussolini*, Rocca S. Casciano 1957

Darrah, D., *Hail Caesar*, Boston 1936

Das Heer des fascistischen Italien, Rome 1934

Dauli, G., *Mussolini: l'uomo, l'avventuriero, il criminale*, Milan 1946

DDI: *Documenti diplomatici italiani*, ed. R.Moscati, M.Toscano and G.Carocci, Rome

De Ambris, R., 'Mussolini, la leggenda e l'uomo', in De Felice, R. (ed.), *Benito Mussolini: quattro testimonianze*, Florence 1976

De Begnac, I., *Pagine nella tormenta*, Milan 1941

De Begnac, I., *Palazzo Venezia: storia di un regime*, Rome 1950

De Begnac, I., *Trent'anni di Mussolini, 1883–1915*, Rome 1934

De Begnac, I., *Vita di Benito Mussolini*, Milan 1936–40

De Bono, E., *Anno XIII: The Conquest of an Empire*, London 1937

De Falco, G., *Il fascismo milizia di classe*, Bologna 1921

Mussolini

De Felice, R., *Il problema dell'Alto Adige nei rapporti italo-tedeschi*, Bologna 1973

De Felice, R. (ed.), *L'Italia fra tedeschi e alleati: la politica estera fascista e la seconda guerra mondiale*, Bologna 1973

De Felice, R., (1) *Mussolini il rivoluzionario 1883–1920*, Turin 1965

De Felice, R., (2) *Mussolini il fascista: la conquista del potere*, Turin 1967

De Felice, R., (3) *Mussolini il fascista: l'organizzazione dello stato fascista*, Turin 1968

De Felice, R., (4) *Mussolini il duce: gli anni del consenso*, Turin 1974

De Felice, R., *Storia degli ebrei italiani sotto il fascismo*, Turin 1952

De Fiori, V.E., *Mussolini the man of destiny*, London 1928

De Grand, A.J., *The Italian Nationalist Association and the Rise of Fascism in Italy*, Lincoln 1978

De Leone, E., *La colonizzazione dell'Africa del nord*, Padua 1960

De Lorenzis, U., *Dal primo all'ultimo giorno*, Milan 1971

De Magistris, L.F., *I sansepolcristi nella storia della rivoluzione fascista*, Milan 1939

De Marsanich, A., *Lo stato nel ventennio fascista*, Rome (c. 1950)

De Rensis, R., *Mussolini musicista*, Mantua 1927

De Risio, C., *Generali, servizi segreti e fascismo*, Milan 1978

De Rosa, G., *Giolitti e il fascismo*, Rome 1957

De Rosa, G., *Storia del movimento cattolico in Italia*, Bari 1966

De Sanctis, G., *Ricordi della mia vita*, Florence 1970

De' Stefani, A., *Baraonda bancaria*, Milan 1960

De' Stefani, A., *La restaurazione finanziaria 1922–1925*, Bologna 1926

De' Stefani, A., *Sopravvivenze e programmi nell'ordine economico*, Rome 1942

De' Stefani, A., *Una riforma al rogo*, Rome 1963

De Vecchi di Val Cismon, C.M., *Bonifica fascista della cultura*, Milan 1937

De Vecchi di Val Cismon, C.M., *Orizzonti d'impero: cinque anni in Somalia*, Milan 1935

Deakin, F.W., *The Brutal Friendship: Mussolini, Hitler and the Fall of Italian Fascism*, London 1962

Del Boca, A., *Gli italiani in Africa orientale: la conquista dell'impero*, Bari 1979

Delcroix, C., *Un uomo e un popolo*, Florence 1928

Delzell, C.F., *Mussolini's Enemies: The Anti-Fascist Resistance*, Oxford 1961

DF: *Documents Diplomatiques Français*, ed. M.Baumont, P.Renouvin etc., Paris

DGFP: *Documents on German Foreign Policy, 1918–1945*, ed. R.J. Sontag, M. Lambert, M. Baumont, *etc.* London

Di Giorgio, A., *Scritti e discorsi vari, 1899–1927*, Milan 1938

Di Nolfo, E., *Mussolini e la politica estera italiana, 1919–1933*, Padua 1960

Dietrich, O., *The Hitler I Knew*, London 1957

Difesa della Razza, Rome 1938–

Difesa nazionale, le direttive del Duce, ed. P.Orano, Rome 1937

Diggins, J.P., *Mussolini and Fascism: The View from America*, Princeton 1972

Dinale, O., *Quarant'anni di colloqui con lui*, Milan 1953

Diritti della Scuola, Rome

Diritto del Lavoro, Il, Rome 1927–

Diritto Fascista, Il, Rome 1932–

Dizionario di politica, ed. Partito Nazionale Fascista, Rome 1940

Documents diplomatiques Belges, ed. C.deVisscher and F.Vanlangenhove, Brussels 1964–

Documents diplomatiques Suisses, ed. W. Hofer and B. Mesmer, Berne 1980–

Dodecanesian, The, New York 1934–

Dolfin, G., *Con Mussolini nella tragedia: diario del capo della segreteria particolare del Duce 1943–1944*, Cernusco 1949

396

Dollmann, E., *Roma nazista*, Milan 1951
Dollmann, E., *The Interpreter*, London 1967
Domenica dell'Agricoltore: settimanale illustrato de 'Il Popolo d'Italia', Milan 1926–
Donosti, M., *Mussolini e l'Europa: la politica estera fascista*, Rome 1945
Dorso, G., *La rivoluzione meridionale*, Turin 1945 (2nd ed.)
Dorso, G., *Mussolini alla conquista del potere*, Turin 1949
Dottrina Fascista, Milan 1937–
Dramma (Il), Turin 1924–
Due anni di guerra, 10 giugno 1940–1942, (Ministero della Cultura), Rome 1942
Dumini, A., *17 colpi*, Milan 1958
Duroselle, J-B., *La décadence 1932–1939*, Paris 1979
Duroselle, J-B., *Le conflit de Trieste 1943–1954*, Brussels 1966

Ebenstein, W., *Fascist Italy*, New York 1939
Echi e Commenti, Rome 1920–
Economia Fascista, Rome 1940–
Economia Italiana dal 1961 al 1961, Milan 1961
Economia Italiana, L', Rome 1909–
Economist, The, London
Eden. A., *Facing the Dictators*, London 1962
Educazione Fascista, Rome 1927–
Educazione Politica, Rome 1923–
Einaudi, L., *Cronache economiche e politiche di un trentennio (1893–1925)*, Turin 1950–1965
Elwin, W., *Fascism at Work*, London 1934
English Life and The Illustrated Review, London 1924–
Ercole, F., *Dal nazionalismo al fascismo*, Rome 1928
Ercole, F., *La rivoluzione fascista*, Palermo 1936
Esercito Anno XVII, ed. Ministero della guerra, Rome 1939
Esercito e Nazione: rivista per l'ufficiale italiano, Rome 1926–
Esercito (L') Italiano tra la prima e la seconda guerra mondiale, Rome 1954
Espansione Imperiale, Rome 1937–
Espresso, Rome 1954–
Evening Standard, London

Fabbri, L., *La contro-rivoluzione preventiva*, Bologna 1922
Faldella, E., *L'Italia e la seconda guerra mondiale*, Rocca S. Casciano 1960 (and new edition, 1967)
Fanelli, G.A., *Agonia di un regime (Gennaio–Luglio 1943)*, Rome 1971
Fanelli, G.A., *Cento pagine su Mussolini*, Rome 1931
Fanelli, G.A., *Dall'insurrezione alla monarchia integrale*, Rome 1925
Fanizza, R., *De Vecchi, Bastico, Campioni: ultimi governatori dell'Egeo*, Forlì 1947
Farago, L., ed. *Abyssinian Stop Press*, London 1936
Farago, L., *The Game of the Foxes*, London 1971
Farinacci, R., *Andante mosso 1924–25*, Milan 1929
Farinacci, R., *Realtà storiche*, Cremona 1939
Farinacci, R., *Squadrismo: dal mio diario della vigilia*, 1919–1922, Rome 1933
Farinacci, R., *Un periodo aureo del partito nazionale fascista*, Foligno 1927
Fascismo e antifascismo (1918–1936): lezioni e testimonianze, Milan 1971
Fascist War on Women, London 1934

Mussolini

Favagrossa, C., *Perchè perdemmo la guerra: Mussolini e la produzione bellica*, Milan 1946

Federzoni, L., *Italia di ieri per la storia di domani*, Milan 1967

Ferraris, E., *La marcia su Roma veduta dal Viminale*, Rome 1946

Ferrarotto, M., *L'accademia d'Italia: intellettuali e potere durante il fascismo*, Naples 1977

Ferrero, G., *Four Years of Fascism*, London 1924

Ferretti, L., *Esempi e idee per l'Italiano nuovo*, Rome 1930

Ferri, E., *Mussolini uomo di stato*, Mantua 1927

Fest, J.C., *Hitler*, London 1974

Figaro, Le, Paris

Filareti, Generale, *In margine del fascismo*, Milan 1925

Finer, H., *Mussolini's Italy*, London 1935

Fioravanzo, G., *Il soldato di domani*, Rome 1946

Fiori, L., *Il grande nocchiero*, Florence 1927

Flora, F., *Ritratto di un ventennio*, Naples 1944

Flora, F., *Stampa dell'era fascista: le note di servizio*, Rome 1945

Flores, E., *Eredità di guerra*, Rome 1947

FO: Foreign Office, London

Foglio d'ordine (occasional publication by the fascist party), 1927–

Foley, C., *Commando Extraordinary*, London 1954

Fölkel, F., *La risiera di San Sabba*, Milan 1979

Foreign Affairs, New York

Foreign Relations of the United States: Diplomatic Papers, Washington

Forges Davanzati, R., *Cronache del regime, Anno* XIII, Milan 1936

Forges Davanzati, R., *Fascismo e cultura*, Florence 1926

Foro Mussolini, Il, Milan 1937

Fortnightly Review, London

Fortune, New York

Forum and Century, New York

Forzano, G., *Mussolini autore drammatico*, Florence 1954

Forze (Le) armate dell'Italia fascista, ed. T. Sillani, Rome 1939

Foschini, A., 'A trent'anni dell'occupazione di Corfu', *Nuova Antologia*, Dec. 1953

Fossani, I., *Giovanni Marinelli*, Rome 1932

François-Poncet, A., *Au palais Farnèse: souvenirs d'une ambassade à Rome 1938–1940*, Paris 1961

François-Poncet, A., (introduction to) *Les lettres secrètes échangées par Hitler et Mussolini*, Paris 1946

François-Poncet, A., *Ricordi di un ambasciatore a Berlino*, Milan 1947

Frassati, L., *Il destino passa per Varsavia*, Rocca S. Casciano 1949

Freddi, L., *Il cinema*, Rome 1949

Fried, R.C., *The Italian Prefects*, New Haven 1963

Führer Conferences on Naval Affairs 1939–1945, Admiralty, London 1947

Fuller, J.F.C., *Machine Warfare*, London 1942

Fuller, J.F.C., *The First of the League Wars*, London 1936

Funke, M., *Sanktionen und Kanonen: Hitler, Mussolini und der internationale Abessinienkonflikt 1934–36*, Düsseldorf 1970

Gafencu, G., *Ultimi giorni dell'Europa: viaggio diplomatico nel 1939*, Milan 1947

Galbiati, E., *Il 25 luglio e la M.V.S.N.*, Milan 1950

Galland, A., *The First and the Last: The German Fighter Force in World War* II, London 1955

Gamelin, M.G., *Servir*, Paris 1946–7

Gangemi, L., *Conseguenze economiche delle mutazioni territoriali nell'Europa centrale*, Naples 1939

Garin, E., *Cronache di filosofia italiana (1900–1943)*, Bari 1955

Garosci, A., *La vita di Carlo Rosselli*, Florence 1946

Gasparotto, L., *Diario di un deputato*, Milan 1945

Gatti, A., *Ancoraggi alle rive del tempo*, Milan 1938

Gavagnin, A., *Una lettera al re*, Florence 1951

Gazzetta Ufficiale, Rome

GEC, *Il cesare di cartapesta: Mussolini nella caricatura*, Turin 1945

Gehl, J., *Austria, Germany, and the Anschluss 1931–1938*, London 1963

Gentile, G., *Che cosa è il fascismo: discorsi e polemiche*, Florence 1924

Gentile, G., *Epistolario*, Florence 1974–

Gentile, G., *Fascismo e cultura*, Milan 1928

Gentizon, P., *Il mito di Mussolini*, Milan 1958

Gentizon, P., *Souvenirs sur Mussolini*, Rome 1958

Gerarchia, Milan 1922–

Gerbore, P., *Il vero diplomatico*, Milan 1956

Germino, A.L., *The Italian Fascist Party in Power*, Minneapolis 1959

Ghignoni, A., *Universalità di Mussolini*, Milan 1941

Giamberardino, O. di, *La marina nella tragedia nazionale*, Rome 1945

Giamberardino, O. di, *La politica bellica nella tragedia nazionale*, Rome 1945

Giannini, A., *Io spia dell'ovra*, Rome n.d.

Giglio, C., *Inghilterra d'oggi*, Padua 1934

Giglio, C., *La confraternità senussita, dalle sue origini ad oggi*, Padua 1932

Giglio, G., *The Triumph of Barabbas*, London 1937

Gilbert, M., *Winston S. Churchill*, London 1979

Giolitti, G., *Discorsi parlamentari di Giovanni Giolitti*, Rome 1956

Giolli, P., *Come fummo condotti alla catastrofe*, Rome 1950

Giornale d'Italia, Rome

Giornale del Mattino, Naples

Giorno, Il, Milan

Gioventù Fascista, Rome 1931–

Giovinezza Fascista, Rome 1927–

Giudice, G., *Benito Mussolini*, Turin 1971

Giudice, G., *Luigi Pirandello*, Turin 1963

Giunta, F., *Un po' di fascismo*, Milan 1935

Gladwyn: *The Memoirs of Lord Gladwyn*, London 1972

Gli Oratori del Giorno, Rome 1926–

Gobetti, P., *La rivoluzione liberale*, Turin 1948

Gobetti, P., *Le riviste di Piero Gobetti*, ed. L.Basso and L.Anderlini, Milan 1961

Goebbels Diaries, The, London 1948

Gorgolini, P., *Il fascismo nella vita italiana*, Turin 1922

Gorgolini, P., *La rivoluzione fascista*, Turin 1928

Gorla, G., *L'Italia nella seconda guerra mondiale: memorie di un milanese, ministro del re nel governo di Mussolini*, Milan 1959

Gramsci, A., *Sul fascismo*, ed. E.Santarelli, Rome 1974

Gran (Il) consiglio del fascismo nei primi cinque anni dell'era fascista, Rome 1927

Gran (Il) consiglio del fascismo nei primi quindici anni dell'era fascista, Bologna 1938

Grandi, D., *Dino Grandi racconta*, Venice 1945

Mussolini

Grandi, D., *Le origini e la missione del fascismo*, Bologna 1922

Grandi, D., *Memoriale Grandi: l'idra fascista non è ancora morta*, Bari 1945

Grasso, V., *Il fascismo e l'on Mussolini*, Palermo 1922

Gravelli, A., *Hitler, Mussolini und die Revision*, Leipzig n.d.

Gravelli, A., *Mussolini aneddotico*, Rome n.d.

Gravelli, A., *Razza in agonia*, Rome 1942

Gravelli, A., *Uno e molti: interpretazioni spirituali di Mussolini*, Rome 1938

Graziani, R., *Africa settentrionale (1940–1941)*, Rome 1948

Graziani, R., *Cirenaica pacificata*, Milan 1932

Graziani, R., *Ho difeso la patria*, Cernusco 1947

Grazzi, E., *Il principio della fine: 'l'impresa di Grecia'*, Rome 1945

Greek White Book, The: diplomatic documents relating to Italy's aggression against Greece (Greek Ministry for Foreign Affairs), London 1942

Greiner, H., 'Operation Felix', in *World War II German Military Studies*, vol. VII, New York 1979

Greiner, H., 'Support of Italy in Fall and Winter 1940–1941', in *World War II German Military Studies*, Vol. VII, New York 1979

Grew, J.C., *Turbulent Era: a Diplomatic Record of Forty Years*, London 1953

Griziotti, B., *La politica finanziaria italiana*, Milan 1926

Guariglia, R., *Primi passi in diplomazia e rapporti dall' ambasciata di Madrid, 1932–1934*, ed. R. Moscati, Naples 1972

Guariglia, R., *Ricordi, 1922–1946*, Naples 1950

Guarneri, F., *Autarchia e scambi internazionali*, Rome 1941

Guarneri, F., *Battaglie economiche tra le due grandi guerre*, Milan 1953

Guedalla, P., *The Hundred Years*, London 1936

Guerri, G.B., *Galeazzo Ciano: una vita, 1903–1944*, Milan 1979

Guerri, G.B. (ed.), *Rapporto al Duce*, Milan 1978

Gunther, J., *Inside Europe*, London 1936

Guspini, U., *L'orecchio del regime: le intercettazioni telefoniche al tempo del fascismo*, Milan 1973

Gustarelli, A., *Mussolini scrittore ed oratore*, Milan 1937

Gutkind, C., (ed.), *Mussolini e il suo fascismo*, Florence 1927

Hachey, T.E. (ed.), *Anglo-Vatican Relations, 1914–1939, confidential annual reports of the British Ministers to the Holy See*, Boston 1972

Hackett, F., 'A talk with Mussolini', in *The Nation and Athenaeum*, Mar. 1927

Haider, C., *Capital and Labor under Fascism*, New York 1930

Haile Selassie, *My Life and Ethiopia's Progress, 1892–1937*, Oxford 1976

Halder, F., *Kriegstagebuch*, ed. H.A. Jacobsen, Stuttgart 1962–6

Hansard, *Parliamentary Debates*, London

Harmsworth, G., *Abyssinian Adventure*, London 1935

Harper's Magazine, New York

Harris, B., *The United States and the Italo-Ethiopian Crisis*, Stanford 1964

Harvard Educational Review, Cambridge, Mass.

Harvey, J. (ed.), *The Diplomatic Diaries of Oliver Harvey, 1937–1940*, London 1970

Hassell, U.von, *The Von Hassell Diaries 1938–1944*, London 1948

Heineman, J.L., *Hitler's First Foreign Minister: Constantin Freiherr von Neurath*, Berkeley 1979

Heller, H., *Europa und der Fascismus*, Berlin 1939

Hemingway, E., *By-line: selected articles and dispatches of four decades*, ed. W.White, London 1968

Herfort, P., *Chez les romains fascistes*, Paris 1934

Hess, R.L., *Italian Colonialism in Somalia*, London 1966
Higham, R.D.S., *Air Power: a concise history*, London 1972
Hindle, W. (ed.), *Foreign Correspondent*, London 1939
Historicus, *Dalla prima alla seconda guerra mondiale* (Istituto Nazionale di Cultura Fascista), Rome (*c*. 1941)
Historicus, *Il problema dell'Europa centrale*, Rome 1938
Hitler, A., *The Testament of Adolf Hitler: The Hitler–Bormann documents Feb.–Apr. 1945*, ed. F.Genoud, London 1959
Hitler Directs his War, ed. F.Gilbert, New York 1950
Hitler e Mussolini: lettere e documenti, Milan 1946
Hitler's Table Talk 1941–1944, ed. N.Cameron and R.H.Stevens, London 1953
Hitler's War Directives 1939–1945, ed. H.R.Trevor-Roper, London 1964
Hoepke, K-P., *Die deutsche Rechte und der italienische Faschismus*, Düsseldorf, 1968
Hoettl, W., *Hitler's Paper Weapon*, London 1955
Hoettl, W., *The Secret Front: the story of nazi political espionage*, London 1954
Hoffmann, H., *Hitler was my Friend*, London 1955
Höhne, H., *Canaris*, London 1978
Holmboe, K., *Desert Encounter*, London 1936

I 535 deputati al parlamento per la XXVI legislatura, Milan 1922
Iachino, A., *Tramonto di una grande marina*, Milan 1966 (4th ed.)
Idea Nazionale, Rome
Illustrazione Italiana, Milan
Imperium, Rome and Como, 1926–
Impero (L'), Rome 1922–
Impero (L') A.O.I., Rome 1937
Impero Fascista, Rome 1934–
In Africa settentrionale: la preparazione al conflitto, Ottobre 1935–Settembre 1940, Rome 1955
Incisa, L., *Spagna nazional–sindacalista*, Bologna 1941
Insolera, I., *Roma moderna*, Turin 1971
Interlandi, T., *Contra Judaeos*, Milan 1938
Interlandi, T., *Pane bigio: scritti politici*, Bologna 1927
Iraci, A., *Arpinati l'oppositore di Mussolini*, Rome 1970
Irving, D., *Hitler's War*, London 1977
Irving, D., *The Trail of the Fox: the Life of Field Marshal Erwin Rommel*, London 1977
Irving, D., *The War Path: Hitler's Germany*, London 1978
Ishii, K., *Diplomatic Commentaries*, ed. A.R. Langdon, Baltimore 1936
Italia d'oggi, Rome 1941
Italia Imperiale (special number of *Rivista Illustrata del 'Popolo d'Italia'*), Milan 1937
Italy Today, London 1929–31
Italy's War Crimes in Ethiopia: evidence for the war crimes commission, ed. S.Pankhurst, London 1945
Iurato, F., and Antonelli, D., *Con Mussolini a Campo Imperatore* (*c*. 1946)
Iuvenalis, *Mussolini alla luce infrarossa*, Rome 1944

Jackson, G., *The Spanish Republic and the Civil War, 1931–1939*, Princeton 1965
Jacomoni di San Savino, F., *La politica dell'Italia in Albania*, Rocca San Casciano 1965
Jemolo, A.C., *Anni di prova*, Vicenza 1969
Jemolo, A.C., *Chiesa e stato in Italia negli ultimi cento anni*, Turin 1948

Mussolini

Jones, Thomas, *A Diary with Letters 1931–1950*, Cambridge 1954
Journal de Genève
Journal of Contemporary History, London
Journal of Modern History, Chicago

Kallay, M., *Hungarian Premier: a personal account of a nation's struggle in the second world war*, London 1954
Keene, F. (ed.), *Neither Liberty nor Bread: the meaning and tragedy of fascism*, London 1940
Keitel: *The Memoirs of Field Marshal Keitel*, London 1945
Kelen, E., *Peace in their Time*, London 1964
Kersten, F., *The Kersten Memoirs 1940–1945*, London 1956
Kesselring, A., 'The War in the Mediterranean Area', in *World War II German Military Studies*, vol. XIV, New York 1979
Kesselring, A, *The Memoirs of Field Marshal Kesselring*, London 1954
Killearn (The) Diaries 1934–46, ed. T.E. Evans, London 1972
King, Bolton, *Il Fascismo in Italia*, Bologna 1973
Kirkpatrick, I., *Mussolini: a study of a demagogue*, London 1964
Kitsikis, D., 'La famine en Grèce (1941–1942)', in *Revue d'Histoire de la Deuxième Guerre Mondiale*, Apr. 1969
Kordt, E., *Wahn und Wirklichkeit*, Stuttgart 1948
Krassin, L., *Leonid Krassin: His Life and Work*, London 1929
Kriegstagebuch des Oberkommandos der Wehrmacht, ed. W. Hubatsch, H.-A.Jacobsen and P.E.Schramm, Frankfurt 1961–5

Labour Magazine, The, London 1922–
Labriola, A., *Le due politiche: fascismo e riformismo*, Naples 1923
Labriola, A., *Polemica antifascista*, Naples 1925
Labriola, A., *Spiegazioni a me stesso: note personali e colturali*, Naples 1945
Lada-Mocarski, V., 'The last three days of Mussolini', in *The Atlantic Monthly*, Boston Dec. 1945
Lagarde, H.de, *Procès de l'Italie*, Paris 1939
Lagardelle, H., *Mission à Rome: Mussolini*, Paris 1955
Landmans: *Catalogo Landmans dei francobolli dell'impero italiano e d'Europa*, Milan 1941
Lanfranchi, F., *La resa degli ottocentomila*, Milan 1948
Lanfranchi, F., *L'inquisizione nera (banditismo fascista)*, Milan 1945
Langer, W.L., and Gleason, S.E., *The Undeclared War 1940–41*, London 1953
Lanzillo, A., *Le rivoluzioni del dopoguerra: critiche e diagnosi*, Città di Castello 1922
Laurens, F.D., *France and the Italo-Ethiopian Crisis 1935–1936*, Hague 1967
Laval: *The Unpublished Diary of Pierre Laval*, London 1948
Lavoro, Il, Genoa
Lavoro Fascista, Il, Rome 1928–
Lazzari, G., *L'enciclopedia Treccani: intellettuali e potere durante il fascismo*, Naples 1977
Ledeen, M.A., *Universal Fascism: the story and practice of the fascist international 1928–1936*, New York 1972
Lees-Milne, J., *Harold Nicolson: a biography*, London 1980
Leggi (le) e i decreti reali secondo l'ordine della inserzione nella Gazzetta Ufficiale, Rome
Legionario, Il, organo dei fasci italiani all'estero, Rome 1923–
Leonardi, D.U., *Luglio 1943 in Sicilia*, Modena 1947
Lessona, A., *Memorie*, Rome 1963

Lessona, A., *Un ministro di Mussolini racconta*, Milan 1973

Lessona, A., *Verso l'impero: memorie per la storia politica del conflitto italo-etiopico*, Florence 1939

Leto, G., *Ovra, fascismo, antifascismo*, Rocca S. Casciano 1952

Leto, G., *Polizia segreta in Italia*, Rome 1961

Lettura, La, Milan

Levi della Vida, G., *Fantasmi ritrovati*, Vicenza 1966

Lewin, R., *Ultra goes to War; the secret story*, London 1978

Libro e Moschetto, Milan 1926–

Licata, G., *Storia del 'Corriere della Sera'*, Milan 1976

Licitra, C., *Dal liberalismo al fascismo*, Rome 1925

Liddell Hart, B.H., *The Other Side of the Hill*, London 1951

Lipski, J., *Diplomat in Berlin 1933–1939*, ed. W.Jedrzejewicz, New York 1968

Listener, The, London

Litvinov, M.M., *Notes for a Journal*, London 1955

Livius, *Africa orientale: le ricchezze del sottosuolo*, Rome 1936

Stato, Lo, Rome 1930–

Lombardo, N., *Cesare e Mussolini*, Brescia 1941

Lombroso, C., *Il momento attuale*, Milan 1923

Longanesi, L., *In piedi e seduti (1919–1943)*, Milan 1948

Longanesi, L., *Parliamo dell'elefante. frammenti di un diario*, Milan 1947

Longanesi, L., *Vade-mecum del perfetto fascista*, Florence 1926

Lotti, L., *La settimana rossa*, Florence 1972

LSE: London School of Economics Library (documents on the Matteotti affair deposited by G. Salvemini)

Luciano, C., *Rapporto al Duce: nel racconto dell'ex capo-gabinetto alla stampa*, Rome 1948

Luciolli, M., *Palazzo Chigi: anni roventi. Ricordi di vita diplomatica italiana dal 1933 al 1948*, Milan 1976

Ludecke, K.G.W., *I knew Hitler*, London 1939

Ludwig, E., *Colloqui con Mussolini*, Milan 1932

Ludwig, E., *Colloqui con Mussolini: riproduzione delle bozze della prima edizione con le osservazioni autografe del Duce*, Milan 1950

Ludwig, E., *Leaders of Europe*, London 1934

Ludwig, E., *Mussolinis Gespräche mit Emil Ludwig*, Berlin 1932

Ludwig, E., *Talks with Mussolini*, London 1932

Ludwig, E., *Three Portraits: Hitler, Mussolini, Stalin*, New York 1940

Lumbroso, G., *La crisi del fascismo*, Florence 1925

Lussu, E., *Enter Mussolini: Observations and Adventures of an Anti-Fascist*, London 1936

L.W., *Fascism: Its History and Significance*, London 1924

Lyon, L., *The Fruits of Folly*, London 1929

Lyttleton, A., *The Seizure of Power: Fascism in Italy 1919–1929*, London 1973

Macartney, M.H.H., *One Man Alone*, London 1944

Macfie, J.W.S., *An Ethiopian Diary: a Record of the British Ambulance Service in Ethiopia*, Liverpool 1936

McGuire, C.E., *Italy's International Economic Position*, New York 1927

Macintyre, D., *The Battle for the Mediterranean*, London 1964

Mack Smith, D., 'Anti-British propaganda in fascist Italy', in *Inghilterra e Italia nel '900*, Florence 1973

Mussolini

Mack Smith, D., *Modern Sicily*, London 1968

Mack Smith, D., 'Mussolini e il "caso Matteotti"', in Bedeschi, *Studi*

Mack Smith, D., *Mussolini's Roman Empire*, London 1976

Mack Smith, D., *Storia di cento anni di vita italiana visti attraverso il 'Corriere della Sera'*, Milan 1978

Mackenzie, A.J., *Propaganda Boom*, London 1938

Macro, E., *Yemen and the Western World*, London 1968

Madariaga, S.de, *Morning without Noon: Memoirs*, London 1973

Magistrati, M., *Il prologo del dramma: Berlino 1934–1937*, Milan 1971

Magistrati, M., *L'Italia a Berlino (1937–1939)*, Milan 1956

Maione, G., *L'imperialismo straccione*, Bologna 1979

Malagodi, O., *Conversazioni della guerra, 1914–1919*, ed. B. Vigezzi, Milan 1960

Malaparte, C., *L'Italia barbara*, Bologna 1928

Malaparte, C., *Kaputt*, Naples 1944

Malaparte, C., *Technique du coup d'état*, Paris 1931

Manacorda, G., *Il bolscevismo*, Florence 1942 (4th ed.)

Manchester Guardian

Mancini, A., *La donna fascista nell'irrobustimento della razza*, Rome 1937

Manunta, U., *La caduta degli angeli: storia intima della repubblica sociale italiana*, Rome 1947

Maravigna, P., *Come abbiamo perduto la guerra in Africa*, Rome 1949

Marconcini, F., *Culle vuote*, Como 1935

Marconi, G., *Per la ricerca scientifica*, Rome 1935

Marder, A.J., *From the Dardanelles to Oran*, London 1974

Marga, *Aneddoti e giudizi su Mussolini*, Florence 1925

Margiotta Broglio, F., *Italia e Santa Sede dalla grande guerra alla conciliazione*, Bari 1966

Mariano, N., *Forty Years with Berenson*, London 1966

Marinetti, F.T., *Futurismo e fascismo*, Foligno 1924

Marks, S., 'Mussolini and Locarno: fascist foreign policy in microcosm', in *Journal of Contemporary History*, July 1979

Marongiù, A., *Nel decennale della marcia su Roma: la magistratura italiana prima e dopo la rivoluzione*, Rome 1932

Marpicati, A., *Arnaldo Mussolini*, Milan 1938

Marroni, C., *Mussolini se stesso*, Rome 1941

Marvasi, R., *Echi del terrore*, Rome 1946

Mascarel, A., *Mussolini: son programme, sa doctrine*, Paris 1931

Massis, H., *Chefs*, Paris 1939

Massis, H., *Entretien avec Mussolini*, Abbeville 1937

Massis, H., *Maurras et notre temps*, Paris 1961

Massock, R.G., *Italy from Within*, London 1943

Massola, E., *Gli scioperi del '43*, Rome 1973

Matin, Le, Paris

Matteini, C., *Ordini alla Stampa*, Rome 1945

Matteotti, G., *Il fascismo della prima ora*, Rome 1924

Matteotti, G., *La difesa della libertà*, Vicenza 1943

Matthews, H.L., *I frutti del fascismo*, Bari 1945

Mattioli, G., *Mussolini aviatore*, Rome 1937

Maugeri, F., *From the Ashes of Disgrace*, New York 1948

Maugeri, F., *Mussolini mi ha detto: confessioni di Mussolini durante il confino a Ponza e alla Maddalena*, Rome 1944

List of works cited in the notes

Maurano, S., *Francia la Sorellastra*, Milan 1939
Maurano, S., *Mentalità fascista*, Rome n.d.
Maurano, S., *Ricordi di un giornalista fascista*, Milan 1973
Mayda, G., *Ebrei sotto Salò*, Milan 1978
Mayer, D., *La verità sul processo di Verona*, Milan 1945
Mayneri, C.C., *Parla un comandante di truppe*, Naples 1947
Mecheri, E., *Chi ha tradito? Rivelazioni e documentazioni inedite di un vecchio fascista*, Milan 1947
Medlicott, W.N., *The Economic Blockade*, London 1952
Meenan, J., *The Italian Corporative System*, Cork 1944
Megaro, G., *Mussolini in the Making*, London 1938
Meissner, O., *Staatsekretär unter Ebert, Hindenburg, Hitler*, Hamburg 1950
Meldini, P., *Sposa e madre esemplare: ideologia e politica della donna e della famiglia durante il fascismo*, Florence 1975
Mellenthin, F.W. von, *Panzer Battles 1939–1945*, London 1955
Mellini Ponce De Leon, A., *Guerra diplomatica a Salò*, Bologna 1950
Melograni, P., *Gli industriali e Mussolini: rapporti tra confindustria e fascismo dal 1919 al 1929*, Milan 1972
Melograni, P., *Rapporti segreti della politica fascista 1938–1940*, Bari 1979
Meridiano d'Italia Illustrato, Milan 1957–
Messe, G., *La guerra al fronte Russo*, Milan 1947
Messe, G., *La mia armata in Tunisia*, Milan 1960
Mezzetti, N., *Mussolini per il suo popolo*, Rome 1942
Michaelis, M., *Mussolini and the Jews*, Oxford 1978
Milza, P., *L'Italie fasciste devant l'opinion française 1920–1940*, Paris 1967
Minergi, S., *Dal manganello alla feluca*, Rome 1944
Minerva, Turin
Minniti, F., 'Il problema degli armamenti nella preparazione militare italiana dal 1935 al 1943', in *Storia Contemporanea*, Feb. 1978
Missiroli, M., *Il fascismo e il colpo di stato dell'Ottobre 1922*, Rocca S. Casciano 1969
Missiroli, M., *L'Italia d'oggi*, Bologna 1932
Missiroli, M., *Studi sul fascismo*, Bologna 1934
Misuri, A., *'Ad bestias!': memorie d'un perseguitato*, Rome 1944
Misuri, A., *Rivolta morale: confessioni, esperienze e documenti di un quinquennio di vita pubblica*, Milan 1924
Moellhausen, E.F., *La carta perdente: memorie diplomatiche (25 Luglio 1943–2 Maggio 1945)*, ed. V. Rusca, Rome 1948
Momigliano, E., *Storia tragica e grottesca del razzismo fascista*, Milan 1946
Mondini, L., *Prologo del conflitto Italo-Greco*, Rome 1945
Monelli, P., *Mussolini piccolo borghese*, Cernusco 1950
Monelli, P., *Roma 1943*, Rome 1946 (4th ed.)
Monghini, A.S., *Dal decennale alla catastrofe*, Milan 1954
Montagna, R., *Mussolini e il processo di Verona*, Milan n.d.
Montanelli, I., and Cervi, N., *L'Italia littoria (1925–1936)*, Milan 1979
Montgomery, J.F., *Hungary the Unwilling Satellite*, New York 1947
Morandi, C., (ed.), *La critica a Versailles*, Milan 1940
Morgan, T.B., *Spurs on the Boot: Italy under her Masters*, London 1942
Mori, R., 'Delle cause dell'impresa etiopica Mussoliniana', in *Storia e Politica*, Dec. 1978
Mori, R., *Mussolini e la conquista dell'Etiopia*, Florence 1978
Morison, S.E., *The Battle of the Atlantic*, Boston 1950

Mussolini

Morning Post, London

Mortara, G., *Prospettive economiche*, Milan 1922–

Mosconi, A., *La mia linea politica*, Rome 1952

Mosley, D., *A Life of Contrasts*, London 1977

Mosley, L., *Haile Selassie, The Conquering Lion*, London 1964

Movimento (Il) di Liberazione in Italia, Milan 1949–

Mueller-Hillebrand, B., 'Germany and her Allies in World War II', in *World War II German Military Studies*, vol. xx, New York 1979

Munro, I.S., *Through Fascism to World Power*, London 1933

Muratore, G., and Persia, C., *La verità su i dodici giorni di Mussolini a Ponza*, Bologna 1944

Murray, W., 'The role of Italy in British Strategy 1938–1939', in *Journal of The Royal United Services Institute*, London 1978–9

Mussolini, A., *Azione fascista*, Milan 1930

Mussolini, A., *Commenti all'azione*, Milan 1929

Mussolini, A., *Fascismo e civiltà*, Milan 1937

Mussolini, A., *La conciliazione*, Milan 1935

Mussolini, A., *Orientamenti e battaglie*, Milan 1929

Mussolini, A., *Polemiche e programmi*, Milan 1928

Mussolini, B., *Corrispondenza inedita*, ed. D. Susmel, Milan 1972

Mussolini, B., *Giovanni Huss il veridico*, Rome 1948 (1st ed. 1913)

Mussolini, B., *Il mio diario di guerra*, Rome 1933

Mussolini, B., *Il tempo del bastone e della carota: storia di un anno*, Milan 1944

Mussolini, B., *La dottrina del fascismo*, Rome 1941 (revised ed.)

Mussolini, B., *La mia vita*, Rome 1947

Mussolini, B., *Messaggi e proclami*, Milan 1929

Mussolini, B., *My Autobiography*, London 1928 (and revised edition 1939)

Mussolini, B., *Opera omnia*, ed. E. and D. Susmel, Florence 1951–

Mussolini, B., *Scritti e discorsi di Benito Mussolini*, Milan 1934–9

Mussolini, B., *Vita di Sandro e di Arnaldo*, Milan 1934

Mussolini, Edvige, *Mio fratello Benito*, Florence 1957

Mussolini, Rachele, *La mia vita con Benito*, Milan 1948

Mussolini, Vittorio, *Mussolini: the tragic women in his life*, London 1973

Mussolini, Vittorio, *Vita con mio padre*, Milan 1957

Mussolini e lo sport, Mantua (*c.* 1926)

Mussolini giudicato dal mondo, Milan 1946

Mussolini giurista, ed. E. d'Avila (offprint from *Il Diritto Fascista*, 1938)

Nanni, T., *Bolscevismo e fascismo al lume della critica marxista: Benito Mussolini*, Bologna 1924

Nation and Athenaeum, London 1921–

Naudeau, L., *L'Italie fasciste où l'autre danger*, Paris 1926

Navarra, Q., *Memorie del cameriere di Mussolini*, Milan 1946

Nazi Conspiracy and Aggression, Washington 1946–8

Nazione Militare, Rome 1926–

Nenni, P., *Sei anni di guerra civile*, Milan 1945

Nenni, P., *Storia di quattro anni*, Turin 1946

New Leader, London

New Statesman, London

New York Times

New York World

News Chronicle, London

Nicolson, H., *Curzon: the Last Phase 1919–1925*, London 1934

Nicolson, H., *Diaries and Letters 1930–45*, London 1966–7

Niekisch, E., *Gewagtes Leben: Begegnungen und Begebnisse*, Cologne 1958

Nineteenth Century and After, London

Nitti, F.S., *Bolshevism, Fascism and Democracy*, London 1927

Nitti, F.S., *La democrazia*, Paris 1933

Nitti, F.S., *La libertà*, Turin 1926

Nitti, F.S., *Meditazioni dell'esilio*, Naples 1947 (2nd ed.)

Nitti, F.S., *Rivelazioni: dramatis personae*, Naples 1948

Nitti, F.S., *Scritti Politici*, Bari 1962 (Vol. IV. ed. G.Negri)

Noël, L., *Les illusions de Stresa: L'Italie abandonnée à Hitler*, Paris 1975

Nuova (La) Antologia, Rome

Nuova (La) Italia D'Oltremare: l'opera del fascismo nelle colonie italiane, ed. A.Piccioli, Milan 1933

Nuova Politica Liberale, Rome 1923–

Nuova Rivista Storica

Obelisco (L') Mussolini, ed. A.Furiga, Rome 1934

Oggi, Milan 1938–

Oggi Illustrato, Milan 1947–

Ojetti, U., *I taccuini 1914–1943*, Florence 1954

Omnibus, Rome 1937–

OO: *Opera omnia di Benito Mussolini*, ed. E. and D.Susmel, Florence 1951–

Operti, P., *Lettera aperta a Benedetto Croce*, Turin 1946

Orano, P., *Il fascismo*, Rome 1939–40

Orano, P., *Mussolini al fronte della storia*, Rome 1941

Orano, P., *Mussolini da vicino*, Rome 1932 (2nd ed.)

Ordine Fascista, L', Rome 1932–3

Orestano, F., *Idee e concetti*, Milan 1939

Organizzazione (L') della marina durante il conflitto, G.Fioravanzo, Rome 1972

Oriente Moderno, Rome 1921–

Orlando, F., *Mussolini volle il 25 luglio*, Milan 1946

Orlando, V.E., *Discorsi parlamentari*, Rome 1965

Orlando, V.E., *Memorie (1915–1919)*, Milan 1960

Ottobre, Rome 1932–

Packard, R., and Packard, E., *Balcony Empire: fascist Italy at war*, London 1943

Page, G.Nelson, *L'Americano di Roma*, Rome 1950

Pagine sulla guerra alla radio, Florence 1942

Pan, *Il fascismo*, Rome 1922

Panorami di realizzazioni del fascismo, ed. L. Pinti, Rome 1942

Pansa, G., *L'esercito di Salò*, Milan 1969

Panunzio, S., *Che cos'è il fascismo?*, Milan 1924

Panunzio, S., *Lo stato fascista*, Bologna 1925

Paoloni, F., *I nostri 'Boches': il giolittismo, partito tedesco in Italia*, Milan 1916

Paolucci, R., *Il mio piccolo mondo perduto*, Bologna 1947

Papa, E.R., *Storia di due manifesti*, Milan 1958

Papen, F. von, *Memoirs*, London 1952

Mussolini

Parenti, M., *Bibliografia Mussoliniana*, Florence 1940

Pariani, A., *Chiacchiere e realtà: lettera agli amici*, Milan 1949

Parkinson, R., *Peace for our time: Munich to Dunkirk*, London 1971

Pascal, P., *Mussolini alla vigilia della sua morte e l'Europa: colloquio con il poeta francese Pierre Pascal*, Rome 1948

Pascazio, N., *La crisi sociale dell'impero britannico*, Milan 1941

Patriot, The, London 1922–

Peace and War: United States Foreign Policy 1931–1941, Washington 1943

Pedoja, G., *La disfatta nel deserto*, Rome 1946

Pedrazza, P., *Giornalismo di Mussolini*, Milan 1936

Pedrazzi, O., *Roma alla testa del secolo*, Santiago 1933

Pellizzi, C., *Fascismo-aristocrazia*, Milan 1925

Pellizzi, C., *Fascism*, London 1924

Pellizzi, C., *Una rivoluzione mancata*, Milan 1949

Pennino, V.G., *La politica mondiale della nuova Italia*, Turin 1923

Per l'Onore Decima Flottiglia Mas, Milan 1943–4

Percy, E.S.C., *Some Memories*, London 1958

Pernot, M., *L'expérience italienne*, Paris 1924

Pesce, G., *Da Lenin a Mussolini*, Rome 1928

Pesenti, G., *Le guerre coloniali*, Bologna 1947

Pestalozza, L. (ed), *Il processo alla Muti*, Milan 1956

Petacco, A., *Riservato per il Duce: i segreti del regime conservati nell'archivio personale di Mussolini*, Milan 1979

Petersen, J., *Hitler e Mussolini: la difficile alleanza*, Bari 1975

Peterson, M., *Both Sides of the Curtain*, London 1950

Petrie, C.A., *Chapters of Life*, London 1950

Petrone, C., 'Mussolini giurista' (offprint from *Il Diritto Fascista*, 1939)

Petrone, I., *Il problema delle aristocrazie e il popolo nel novecento*, Florence 1939

Pettinato, C., *Gli intellettuali e la guerra*, Turin 1944

Pettinato, C., *Tutto da rifare*, Milan 1966

Phayre, I. (W.V. Fitz-Gerald), 'Mussolini', in *Current History*, New York Jan. 1937

Phillips, W., *Ventures in Diplomacy*, London 1955

Pieri, P., and Rochat, G., *Pietro Badoglio*, Turin 1974

Pini, G., *Benito Mussolini: la sua vita fino ad oggi dalla strada al potere*, Bologna 1926 (revised with various titles until the 15th edition in 1940)

Pini, G., *Filo diretto con Palazzo Venezia*, Bologna 1950

Pini, G., *Itinerario tragico (1943–1945)*, Milan 1950

Pini, G., Bresadola, F., and Giacchero, G., *Storia del fascismo*, Rome 1940 (3rd ed.)

Pini–Susmel; Pini, G., and Susmel, D., *Mussolini: l'uomo e l'opera*, Florence 1953–5

Pirelli, A., *Dopoguerra 1919–1922: note ed esperienze*, Milan 1961

Pisenti, P., *Una repubblica necessaria (R.S.I.)*, Rome 1977

Plehwe, F.-K.von, *The End of an Alliance: Rome's Defection from the Axis in 1943*, London 1971

Podrecca, G., *La nuova coscienza: dal socialismo al fascismo*, Milan 1930

Polemica, Naples 1922–

Policastro, G., *Mussolini e la Sicilia*, Mantua 1929

Politica, Rome 1918–

Politica estera, Salerno 1944–

Politica estera anno XIII, ed. C.E. Ferri and R.Mosca, Milan 1936

Politica (La) estera Italiana dal 1914 al 1943 (Radio-Audizioni Italia), Turin 1963

List of works cited in the notes

Politica Nuova, Naples 1932–

Politica Sociale, Rome 1929–

Pomba, G.L. (ed.), *La civiltà fascista, illustrata nella dottrina e nelle opere*, Turin 1928

Ponte (Il), Florence 1946–

Popolo (Il) d'Italia, Milan 1914–

Popolo (Un) nell'abisso: note di un uomo qualunque, Milan 1945

Pozzi, A., *Come li ho visti io: dal diario di un medico*, Milan 1947

Prasca, S. Visconti, *Io ho aggredito la Grecia*, Milan 1946

Pratt, L.R., *East of Malta, West of Suez, Britain's Mediterranean Crisis 1936–1939*, Cambridge 1975

Preti, L., *Gli inglesi a Malta*, Milan 1938

Prezzolini, G., *Fascism*, London 1926

Prezzolini, G., *L'Italiano inutile*, Florence 1964

Pricolo, F., *Ignavia contro eroismo: l'avventura Italo-Greca*, Rome 1946

Pricolo, F., *Ispezione ai reparti della 5 squadra aerea in A.O.I.*, Rome 1941

Pricolo, F., 'L'aeronautica e le altre forze armate', in *Echi e Commenti*, Feb. 1932

Pricolo, F., 'La difesa aerea di una grande città', in *Revista Aeronautica*, Nov. 1932

Pricolo, F., *La regia aeronautica nella seconda guerra mondiale*, Milan 1971

Prima (La) offensiva Britannica in Africa settentrionale (Ottobre 1940–Febbraio 1941), Rome n.d.

Primato, Il, Rome

Primo convegno nazionale di politica estera, Milan 1937

Problemi e Informazioni Sociali, Rome 1939–

Problemi Mediterranei, Palermo 1936–

Processo Graziani, Città di Castello 1948–50

Processo Roatta, Rome 1945

Professioni (Le) e le Arti, Rome 1931–

Prospettive, Rome 1937–

Pugliese, E., *Io difendo l'esercito*, Naples 1946

Puntoni, P., *Parla Vittorio Emanuele III*, Milan 1958

Quaroni, P., *Valigia diplomatica*, Milan 1956

Quartararo, R., 'Inghilterra e Italia dal patto di pasqua a Monaco', in *Storia Contemporanea*, December 1976

Querel, V., *Il paese di Benito*, Rome 1954

Raccolta delle circolari e istruzioni ministeriali riservate, ed. A.Toscani, Rome 1934

Raccolta delle leggi, dei decreti e regolamenti recanti norme d'interesse demografico, Rome 1940

Raccolta delle leggi e dei decreti del Regno d'Italia, Rome–

Rafanelli, L., *Una donna e Mussolini*, Milan 1946

Rahn, R., *Ambasciatore di Hitler a Vichy e a Salò*, Milan 1950

Raimondi, A., *Mezzo secolo di magistratura*, Bergamo 1951

Rapporti dell'architettura con le arti figurative (Convegno Volta), Rome 1937

Rassegna di Cultura, Milan (Istituto Nazionale di Cultura Fascista) 1939–

Rassegna di Politica Internazionale, Milan 1933–

Rassegna Italiana, Rome 1918–

Rauschning, H., *Hitler Speaks*, London 1939

Re, E., *Storia di un archivio: le carte di Mussolini*, Milan 1946

Regime Corporativo, Rome 1934–

Regime Fascista, Cremona 1925–

409

Mussolini

Reisoli, G., *Fuoko su Adolfo, fuoko su Benito*, Naples 1948
Relazioni Internazionali, Milan 1936–
Renda, U., *Lo statuto del partito nazionale fascista: testo e commento*, Turin 1938
Renda, U., *Realizzazioni del fascismo*, Turin 1937
Répaci, A., *La marcia su Roma: mito e realtà*, Rome 1963
Reut-Nicolussi, E., *Tyrol: Under the Axe of Italian Fascism*, London 1930
Review of Reviews, The, London
Revue des Deux Mondes, Paris
Revue d'Histoire de la Deuxième Guerre Mondiale, Paris 1950–
Reynaud, P., *La France a sauvé l'Europe*, Paris 1947
Riboldi, E., *Vicende socialiste: trent'anni di storia italiana nei ricordi di un deputato massimalista*, Milan 1964
Ricci, B., *Avvisi*, Florence 1943
Ricostruzione (La) fascista: novembre 1924–gennaio 1925, Milan 1925
Ridomi, C., *La fine dell'ambasciata a Berlino, 1940–43*, Milan 1972
Riforma Sociale, Turin 1900–
Rignani, R., *Lugo durante il periodo delle guerre fasciste*, Lugo 1973
Rintelen, E. von, *Mussolini als Bundesgenosse: Erinnerungen des deutschen Militärattachés in Rom 1936–1943*, Tübingen 1951
Risorgimento, Brussels 1980–
Risorgimento, Milan 1948–
Rivista Aeronautica, Rome 1925–
Rivista Coloniale, Rome 1919–
Rivista delle Colonie, Rome 1927–
Rivista di Politica Economica, Rome 1911–
Rivista di Studi Politici Internazionali, Florence 1934–
Rivista d'Italia, Milan
Rivista Illustrata del 'Popolo d'Italia', Milan 1923–
Rivista Italiana di Scienze Economiche, Rome 1929–
Rivoluzione Liberale, La, Turin 1922–
Roatta, M., *Otto milioni di baionetti: l'esercito italiano in guerra dal 1940 al 1944*, Milan 1946
Roberts, K.L., *Black Magic*, Indianapolis 1923
Robertson, E.M., *Mussolini as Empire-Builder: Europe and Africa 1932–36*, London 1977
Rocca, M., *Come il fascismo divenne una dittatura*, Milan 1952
Rocca, M., *Idee sul fascismo*, Florence 1924
Rocca, M., *Le fascisme et l'antifascisme en Italie*, Paris 1930
Rocco, A., *Scritti e discorsi politici*, Milan 1938
Rochat, G., *Il colonialismo italiano: documenti*, Turin 1973
Rochat, G., 'La repressione della resistenza araba in Cirenaica nel 1930–31', in *Movimento di Liberazione*, Jan. 1973
Rochat, G., *L'esercito italiano da Vittorio Veneto a Mussolini (1919–1925)*, Bari 1967
Rochat, G., *Militari e politici nella preparazione della campagna d'Etiopia: studio e documenti 1932–1936*, Milan 1971
Rochat, G., 'Mussolini et les forces armées', in *La Guerre en Méditerranée*, ed. H. Michel, Paris 1971
Roma Fascista, Rome 1923–
Romains, J., *Seven Mysteries of Europe*, London 1941
Romano, Santi, *Corso di diritto costituzionale*, Padua 1943 (8th ed.)
Romano, S.F., *Antonio Gramsci*, Turin 1965
Rommel Papers, The, ed. B.H. Liddell Hart, London 1953

Rosenberg, A., *Das politische Tagebuch Alfred Rosenbergs*, ed. H-G. Seraphim, Göttingen 1956
Rosengarten, F., *The Italian Anti-Fascist Press (1919–1945)*, Cleveland 1968
Rosenstock-Franck, L., *L'économie corporative fasciste en doctrine et en fait*, Paris 1934
Rosenstock-Franck, L., *Les étapes de l'économie fasciste italienne*, Paris 1939
Roskill, S.W., *Hankey: Man of Secrets*, London 1974
Roskill, S.W., *The Navy at War 1939–1945*, London 1960
Rossato, A., *Mussolini, colloquio intimo*, Milan 1922 (4th ed.)
Rossi, A., *The Russo-German Alliance August 1939–June 1941*, London 1950
Rossi, C., *Il delitto Matteotti*, Milan 1965
Rossi, C., *Il tribunale speciale*, Milan 1952
Rossi, C., *Mussolini com'era*, Rome 1947
Rossi, C., *Trentatre vicende Mussoliniane*, Milan 1958
Rossi, F., *Mussolini e lo stato maggiore: avvenimenti del 1940*, Rome 1951
Rossi, R., *Mussolini nudo alla meta*, Rome 1944
Rossini, G. (ed.), *Il delitto Matteotti tra il Viminale e l'Aventino*, Bologna 1966
Rotunda, D.T., *The Rome Embassy of Sir Eric Drummond, 1933–1939*, London 1972 (PhD thesis)
Roya, L., *Histoire de Mussolini*, Paris 1926
Rubicone, Il, Rimini 1931–
Ruge, F., *Sea Warfare 1939–1945*, London 1958
Ruinas, S., *Pioggia sulla repubblica*, Rome 1946
Rumi, G., *Alle origini della politica estera fascista (1918–1923)*, Bari 1968
Rusinow, D.I., *Italy's Austrian Heritage 1919–1946*, Oxford 1969
Rygier, M., *Mussolini, indicateur de la police française*, Brussels 1928

Sachs, H., *Toscanini*, New York 1978
Sadat, Anwar El, *Revolt on the Nile*, London 1957
St A: photographed documents in Saint Antony's College, Oxford (mainly Segreteria del Duce and Ministero della Cultura)
Saint-Aulaire, A.F., Comte de, *Confession d'un vieux diplomate*, Paris 1954
Salandra, A., *Il diario di Salandra*, ed. G.B. Gifuni, Milan 1969
Salerno, E., *Genocidio in Libia*, Milan 1979
Salter, J.A., *Personality in Politics*, London 1947
Salvatorelli, L., *Nazionalfascismo*, Turin 1923
Salvemini, G., *G.B.Shaw e il fascismo*, Parma 1955
Salvemini, G., *Mussolini diplomatico*, Rome 1945
Salvemini, G., *Prelude to World War II*, London 1953
Salvemini, G., *Preludio alla seconda guerra mondiale*, ed. A. Torre, Milan 1967
Salvemini, G., *Scritti sul fascismo*, ed. A.Valeri, A.Merola and R.Vivarelli, Milan 1966
Sammarco,P., *Fronte interno*, Milan 1942
Santarelli, E., Rochat, G., Rainero, R., Goglia, L., *Omar al-Mukhtar e la riconquista fascista della Libia*, Milan, 1981
Santini, L., *Mussolini, Garibaldi et cie*, Paris (c. 1927)
Santoro, G., *L'aeronautica italiana nella seconda guerra mondiale*, Milan 1957
Sapori, A., *Mondo finito*, Milan 1971
Sapori, F., *L'arte e il Duce*, Milan 1932
Saporiti, P., *Empty Balcony*, London 1947
Sarfatti, M., *Dux*, Milan 1926
Sarfatti, M., *The Life of Benito Mussolini*, London 1925
Sarfatti, M., *Tunisiaca*, Rome 1924

Mussolini

Sarrocchi, G., *Ricordi politici di un esule da Palazzo Madama*, Florence 1946

Sarti, R., *Fascism and the Industrial Leadership in Italy 1919–1940*, Berkeley 1971

Savino, E., *La nazione operante; profili e figure*, Milan (1928, 1934, 1937)

Sbacchi, A., 'Legacy of bitterness: poison gas and atrocities in the Italo-Ethiopian war 1935–1936', in *Genève-Afrique*, Geneva 1974

Scaroni, S., *Con Vittorio Emanuele III*, Milan 1954

Schellenberg: *The Schellenberg Memoirs*, ed. L. Hagen, London 1956

Schiavi, A., *La vita e l'opera di Giacomo Matteotti*, Rome 1957

Schmidt, C.T., *The Corporate State in Action*, London 1939

Schmidt, P., *Hitler's Interpreter*, London 1951

Schreiber, E., *Rome après Moscou*, Paris 1932

Schuschnigg, K.von, *Austrian Requiem*, London 1947

Schuster, Cardinal I., *Gli ultimi tempi di un regime*, Milan 1946

Scoppa, R. Bova, *Colloqui con due dittatori*, Rome 1949

Scoppa, R. Bova, *La pace impossibile*, Turin 1961

Scoppola, P., 'Il fascismo e le minoranze evangeliche', in *Il Fascismo e le autonomie locali*, ed. S. Fontana, Bologna 1973

Scorza, C., *Brevi note sul fascismo, sui capi, sui gregari*, Florence 1930

Scorza, C., *Il segreto di Mussolini*, Lanciano 1933

Scorza, C., *La notte del Gran Consiglio*, Milan 1968

Seconda controffensiva italo-tedesca in Africa settentrionale, Rome 1971

Scuola e Cultura, Florence 1924–

Secolo Fascista (Il), Rome 1930–

Seconda offensiva britannica in Africa settentrionale (18 Nov. 1941–17 Genn. 1942), Rome 1949

Seldes, G., *Can These Things Be?*, New York 1931

Seldes, G., *Iron, Blood and Profits*, New York 1934

Seldes, G., *Sawdust Caesar: the Untold History of Mussolini and Fascism*, London 1936

Seldes, G., *The Truth Behind the News*, London 1929

Seldes, G., *The Vatican: Yesterday, Today, Tomorrow*, London 1934

Senato: Atti del parlamento italiano, discussioni

Senato: commissioni riunite

Senise, C., *Quando ero capo della polizia 1940–1943*, Rome 1946

Senise, T., *Mussolini e Hitler dal punto di vista psichiatrico*, Naples 1947

Serge, V., *Memoirs of a revolutionary*, ed. P.Sedgwick, London 1963

Sermoneta, Duchess of, *Sparkle Distant Worlds*, London 1947

Serra, E., 'La questione italo-etiopica alla conferenza di Stresa', in *Affari Esteri*, April 1977

Sertoli Salis, R., *Le isole italiane dell'Egeo dall' occupazione alla sovranità*, Rome 1939

Servizi civili, I., ed. P.Orano, Rome 1937

Sette Giorni, Milan 1934–

Settimana Incom Illustrata, Rome 1948–

Settimelli, E., *Benito Mussolini*, Piacenza 1922

Settimelli, E., *Edda contro Benito, indagine sulla personalità del Duce attraverso un memoriale autografo di Edda Ciano Mussolini*, Rome 1952

Settimelli, E., *Mussolini visto da Settimelli*, Rome 1929

Sforza, C., *Contemporary Italy, its intellectual and moral origins*, London 1946

Sforza, C., *European Dictatorships*, London 1932

Sforza, C., *L'Italia dal 1914 al 1944 quale io la vidi*, Rome 1944

Sheridan, C., *In Many Places*, London 1923

Sheridan, C., *My Crowded Sanctuary*, London 1945

Sheridan, C., *To the Four Winds*, London 1957
Sherrill, C.H., *Bismarck e Mussolini*, Bologna 1932
Siebert, F., *Italiens Weg in den Zweiten Weltkrieg*, Frankfurt 1962
Sigillino, N., *Mussolini visto da me*, Rome 1935
Signoretti, A., *La stampa in camicia nera, 1932–1943*, Rome 1968
Silva, P., *Io difendo la monarchia*, Rome 1946
Silvestri, C., *Albergo agli scalzi*, Milan 1946
Silvestri, C., *Contro la vendetta*, Milan 1948
Silvestri, C., *I responsabili della catastrofe italiana*, Milan 1946
Silvestri, C., *Matteotti, Mussolini, e il dramma italiano*, Rome 1947
Silvestri, C., *Mussolini, Graziani, e l'antifascismo (1943–45)*, Milan 1949
Silvestri, C., *Turati l'ha detto: socialisti e democrazia cristiana*, Milan 1946
Simoni, L., *Berlino ambasciata d'Italia 1939–1943*, Rome 1946
Skorzeny, O., *Skorzeny's Special Missions*, London 1957
Slocombe, E.G., *The Tumult and the Shouting*, London 1936
Società Italiana per il progresso delle scienze: Atti, Rome
Soffici, A., *Battaglia fra due vittorie*, Florence 1923
Soffici, A., *Ricordi di vita artistica e letteraria*, Florence 1942
Soffici, A., and Prezzolini, G., *Diari 1939–1945*, Milan 1962
Soleri, M., *Memorie*, Turin 1949
Sommergibili (I) Italiani, 1895–1962, ed. P.M. Pollina (Ufficio Storio della Marina Militare), Rome 1963
Souvarine, B., *Stalin*, London 1938
Spampanato, B., *Contromemoriale*, Rome 1951–3
Spectator, London
Speer, A., *Inside the Third Reich*, London 1970
Speer, A., *Spandau*, London 1976
Spengler, O., *Jahre der Entscheidung*, Munich 1933
Sperco, W., *L'écroulement d'une dictature, 1940–45*, Paris 1946
Sperco, W., *Tel fut Mussolini*, Paris 1955
Spigo, U., *Premesse tecniche della disfatta*, Rome 1946
Spinetti, G.S., *Difesa di una generazione*, Rome 1948
Spriano, P., *Storia del partito comunista italiano: da Bordiga a Gramsci*, Turin 1967
Staderini, A., 'Una fonte per lo studio della utilizzazione dei "fondi segretii": la contabilità di Aldo Finzi', in *Storia Contemporanea*, Oct. 1979
Stampa, La, Turin
Starhemberg, E.R., *Between Hitler and Mussolini*, London 1942
Steer, G.L., *Caesar in Abyssinia*, London 1936
Steffens, L., *The Autobiography of Lincoln Steffens*, London 1931
Stehlin, P., *Témoignage pour l'histoire*, Paris 1968
Stimson, H.L., and Bundy, McGeorge, *On Active Service in Peace and War*, New York 1948
Stirpe, La, Rome 1923–
Storia Contemporanea, Bologna 1970–
Storia e Politica, Milan 1962–
Storia e Politica Internazionale, Milan 1939–
Storia Illustrata, Milan 1958–
Studi Politici, Florence 1952–
Sulis, E., *Imitazione di Mussolini*, Milan 1934
Suner, R. Serrano, *Entre Hendaya y Gibraltar*, Madrid 1947

Mussolini

Survey of International Affairs, London 1920–

Susmel, D., *Vita sbagliata di Galeazzo Ciano*, Milan 1962

Sweet, P.R., 'Mussolini and Dollfuss', in Braunthal, J., *The Tragedy of Austria*, London 1948

Szembek, J., *Journal 1933–1939*, Paris 1952

Tamaro, A., *Due anni di storia 1942–45*, Rome 1948–50

Tamaro, A., *Venti anni di storia 1922–1943*, Rome 1953–4

Tarchi, A., *Teste dure*, Milan 1967

Tasca, A., *Nascita e avvento del fascismo*, Florence 1950

Tassinari, G., *L'économie fasciste*, Rome 1937

Taylor, Telford, *Munich, The Price of Peace*, London 1979

Tempera, F., *Benito: emulo-superatore di Cesare e di Napoleone*, Rome 1927

Tempesti, F., *Arte dell'Italia fascista*, Milan 1976

Templewood, Viscount, *Nine Troubled Years*, London 1954

Tempo, Il, Rome

Terzaghi, M., *Fascismo e massoneria*, Milan 1950

Testamento politico di Mussolini: dettato corretto sigilato da lui il 22 Aprile 1945, Rome 1948

Theodoli, A., *A cavallo di due secoli*, Rome 1950

Thomas, H., *The Spanish Civil War*, London 1961 (and enlarged edition, 1977)

Thompson, G.H., *Front-Line Diplomat*, London 1959

Tiltman, H.H., *The Terror in Europe*, London 1931

Times, The, London

Todisco, A., *Organizzazione: potenza dei popoli*, Rome 1942

Toniolo, G., *L'economia dell'Italia fascista*, Bari 1980

Toscano, M., *Designs in Diplomacy*, Baltimore 1970

Toscano, M., 'Il fronte unico', in *Politica Estera Anno XIII*

Toscano, M., *Storia diplomatica della questione dell'Alto Adige*, Bari 1967

Toscano, M., *The Origins of the Pact of Steel*, Baltimore 1967

Trabalza, C. and Allòdoli, E., *La grammatica degli italiani*, Florence 1938 (5th ed.)

Trentin, S., *Dieci anni di fascismo, 1926–1936*, Rome 1975

Trentin, S., *Le fascisme à Genève*, Paris 1932

Trial of the Major German War Criminals before the International Military Tribunal, Nuremberg 1947–9

Tribuna, La, Rome

Trizzino, A., *Gli amici dei nemici*, Milan 1959

Trizzino, A., *Sopra di noi l'oceano*, Milan 1963

Truelove, S.C., and Chaudhary, N.A., 'The irritable colon syndrome', in *Quarterly Journal of Medicine*, Oxford, July 1962

Tuninetti, D.M., *Squadrismo, squadristi piemontesi*, Rome 1942

Tur, V., *Con i marinai d'Italia da Bastia a Tolone*, Rome 1948

Tur, V., *Plancia ammiraglio*, Rome 1963

Turati, A., *Il partito e i suoi compiti*, Rome 1928

Turati, A., *Ragioni ideali di vita fascista*, Rome 1926

Turati, A., *Una rivoluzione e un capo*, Milan (c. 1927)

Turati, A., and Bottai, G., *La carta del lavoro illustrata e commentata*, Rome 1929

Turati, F., and Kuliscioff, A., *Carteggio*, Turin 1953–9

Turchi, F., *Prefetto con Mussolini*, Rome 1950

Tutaev, D., *The Consul of Florence* (Dr Gerhard Wolf), London 1966

Tuzet, H., 'The education of the Italian people', in *Italy Today*, Oct. 1931

Uhlig, K., *Mussolinis Deutsche Studien*, Jena 1941
Università Fascista, Rome 1929–
Utopia (ed. B. Mussolini), Milan 1913–14

Vademecum dello stile fascista, ed. A.Gravelli, Rome 1940
Vailati, V., *Badoglio racconta*, Turin 1955
Vailati, V., *Badoglio risponde*, Milan 1958
Vaina, M., *La grande tragedia italiana: il crollo di un regime nefasto*, Milan 1946
Vaina, M., *La monarchia e il fascismo*, Rome 1951
Valeri, N., *D'Annunzio davanti al fascismo: con documenti inediti*, Florence 1963
Valiani, L., *Tutte le strade conducono a Roma*, Florence 1947
Valle, G., *Pace e guerra nei cieli*, Rome 1966
Valori, A., *Parole di fede*, Milan 1942
Van Creveld, M.L., *Hitler's Strategy 1940–41: The Balkan Case*, Cambridge 1973
Varè, D., *The Two Impostors*, London 1949
Vecchi, F., *L'arditismo civile*, Milan 1920
Veneziani, C., *Vent'anni di beffe: questo era il fascismo*, Milan 1945
Vergani, O., *Ciano, una lunga confessione*, Milan 1974
Verità, La, Rome 1936–
Viganoni, G., *Mussolini e i Cesari*, Milan 1933
Vigezzi, B. (ed.), *Dopoguerra e fascismo: politica e stampa in Italia*, Bari 1965
igeezh, fi,, 'Le radiose giornate del maggio 1915', in *Nuova Rivista Storica*, Sept. 1959
Villa, C., *L'ultima Inghilterra*, Milan 1936
Villari, L., *Italian Foreign Policy under Mussolini*, New York 1956
Villari, L., *Storia diplomatica del conflitto Italo-Etiopico*, Bologna 1943
Vinciguerra, M., *Il fascismo visto da un solitario*, Florence 1963
Vita Italiana, La, Rome 1913–
Vita Nova, Bologna 1925–
Vitetti, L., 'Diario', in *Nuova Antologia*, Dec. 1973 (ed. E. Serra)
Vittorelli, P., *Dal fascismo alla rivoluzione*, Cairo 1945
Vivarelli, R., *Il dopoguerra in Italia e l'avvento del fascismo (1918–1922)*, Naples 1967
Vocabolario della lingua Italiana, Milan 1941 (Reale Accademia)
Volpe, G., *Scritti sul fascismo*, Rome 1976
Volpe, G., *Storia del movimento fascista*, Milan 1943
Volpicelli, L., *Motivi su Mussolini*, Rome 1935
Volt (V. Fani Ciotti), *Programma della destra fascista*, Florence 1924

Wagnière, G., *Dix-huit ans à Rome 1918–1936*, Geneva 1944
Waley, D., *British Public Opinion and the Abyssinian War 1935–6*, London 1975
Ward Price, G., *Extra-Special Correspondent*, London 1957
Ward Price, G., *I Know These Dictators*, London 1937
Warlimont, W., *Im Hauptquartier der deutschen Wehrmacht 1939–1945*, Frankfurt 1962
Washington: microfilm held by the National Archives of the United States
Waterfield, G., *Professional Diplomat, Sir Percy Loraine*, London 1973
Weichold, E., 'War in the Mediterranean' (Mss. Admiralty Library, London)
Weizsäcker, E., *Memoirs of Ernst von Weizsäcker*, London 1951
Welles, Sumner, *The Time for Decision*, London 1944
Werner, M., *The Military Strength of the Powers*, London 1939

Mussolini

Wertheimer, E.F.Ranshofen, *The International Secretariat*, Washington 1945

Westphal, S., *Heer in Fesseln: aus den Papieren des Stabschefs von Rommel, Kesselring und Rundstedt*, Bonn 1950

Weygand, General, *Rappelé au service*, Paris 1950

Whealey, R.H., 'Mussolini's ideological diplomacy: an unpublished document', in *Journal of Modern History*, December 1967

Wiedemann, F., *Der Mann der Feldherr werden wollte*, Dortmund 1964

Winner, P., 'Fascism: Year VIII', in *Italy Today*, Feb. 1931

Winterbotham, F.W., *Ultra Secret*, London 1974

Wiskemann, E., *The Europe I Saw*, London 1968

World War II German Military Studies, ed. D.S.Detwiller, C.B.Burdick and J.Rohwer, New York 1979

Yeats-Brown, F.C.C., *European Jungle*, London 1939

Zachariae, G., *Mussolini si confessa; rivelazioni del medico tedesco inviato da Hitler al Duce*, Cernusco 1948

Zangara, V., *Rivoluzione sindacale: lo stato corporation*, Rome 1927

Zangrandi, R., *Il lungo viaggio attraverso il fascismo: contributo alla storia di una generazione*, Milan 1963

Zanussi, G., *Guerra e catastrofe d'Italia, giugno 1940–giugno 1943*, Rome 1943

Zavoli, S., *Nascita di una dittatura*, Turin 1973.

Zerboglio, A., *Il fascismo; dati, impressioni, appunti*, Bologna 1922

Zibordi, G., *Critica socialista del fascismo*, Bologna 1922

Zingali, G., *Liberalismo e fascismo nel mazzogiorno d'Italia*, Milan 1933

Zingali, G., *L'invasione della Sicilia (1943)*, Catania 1962

Zingarelli, I., *Questo è il giornalismo*, Rome 1946

Zoppi, O., *Il senato e l'esercito nel 'ventennio'*, Milan 1948

Zuckerman, S., *From Apes to Warlords*, London 1978

Zurcher, A.J., 'State propaganda in Italy', in Childs (ed.), *Propaganda and Dictatorship*, Princeton 1936

Zurlo, L., *Memorie inutili: la censura teatrale nel ventennio*, Rome 1952

Index

Index

Index

Index

Index

Index

A NOTE ON THE TYPE

The text of this book was set in a film version of a face called Times Roman, designed by Stanley Morison for *The Times* (London), and first introduced by that newspaper in 1932.

Among typographers and designers of the twentieth century, Stanley Morison has been a strong forming influence, as typographical adviser to the English Mono-type Corporation, as a director of two distinguished English publishing houses, and as a writer of sensibility, erudition, and keen practical sense.

Printed and bound by
Haddon Craftsmen, Scranton, Pennsylvania.

Display typography and binding design
by Albert Chiang.